Turbo C/C++:
The Complete Reference,
Second Edition

Herbert Schildt

Osborne **McGraw-Hill**

Berkeley New York St. Louis San Francisco
Auckland Bogotá Hamburg London Madrid
Mexico City Milan Montreal New Delhi Panama City
Paris São Paulo Singapore Sydney
Tokyo Toronto

Osborne **McGraw-Hill**
2600 Tenth Street
Berkeley, California 94710
U.S.A.

For information on translations or book distributors outside of the U.S.A., please write to Osborne **McGraw-Hill** at the above address.

Turbo C/C++:   The Complete Reference, Second Edition

4567890 DOC 9987654

ISBN 0-07-881776-5

This book is printed on acid-free paper.

Publisher ——————————
Kenna S. Wood

Acquisitions Editor ——————
Jeffrey M. Pepper

Associate Editor ——————
Emily R. Rader

Project Editor ——————
Madhu Prasher

Technical Editor ——————
Robert Goosey

Copy Editors ——————
Dusty Bernard
Margaret Flynn

Proofreaders ——————
Louise Sellers
Mick Arellano

Indexer ——————
Valerie Robbins

Computer Designer ——————
Lance Ravella

Cover Design ——————
Bay Graphics Design, Inc.
Mason Fong

CONTENTS

18

Mathematical Functions   453

19

Time-, Date-, and System-Related Functions   473

20

Dynamic Allocation 543

21

Directory Functions 563

22

Process Control Functions   **581**

23

**Text and Graphics
Functions**   **591**

24

Miscellaneous Functions   673

Part IV
Turbo/Borland C++

Part V
The Turbo/Borland C++
Environment

32

The Integrated
Development Environment 921

33

Using the Editor 939

34

Using the Command-Line
Compiler, VROOMM, and
Multiple-File Projects 957

Part VI
Windows Programming Using
Borland C++

35

Windows Programming
Overview 973

Introduction

This book is about Turbo/Borland C and C++.

Turbo C was first introduced by Borland in the mid-1980s and it has become one of the world's most widely used (and liked) C compilers. It is known for its speed of compilation and the efficiency of the code that it produces. In fact, Turbo C has been used to produce some of the best known software products. Another important feature of Turbo C is that it complies with the ANSI C standard. This means that programs you write using Turbo C will be portable and easily maintained. At the time of this writing, both C in general and Turbo C in particular are widely used. In fact, it will most likely be a very long time before C is deemed obsolete as a programming language.

Borland C is the professional version of Turbo C. Although it contains essentially the same compiler as Turbo C, it comes with more programming support tools.

As the popularity of C continued to increase during the 1980s, a new way to program was beginning to emerge. This programming method is called object-oriented programming (OOP for short) and the C version of this approach is called C++. Because of the importance of object-oriented programming, C++ is expected to grow in popularity. Some predict that it will become the dominant language of the 1990s. To address the demand for a high quality C++ compiler, Borland began secret work on Turbo C++ in 1988. They started with their extremely powerful Turbo C and added to it the C++ OOP extensions. It was not an easy task. C++, although easy for the programmer to use, is a rigorous exercise in compiler construction. To create Turbo C++, Borland assembled a group of some of the best compiler programmers available. Their efforts paid off because Turbo C++ retains the speed and efficiency of Turbo C but adds support for object-oriented programming. Turbo C++ is truly a language for the 1990s.

Borland C++ is the professional version of Turbo C++. It contains the same compiler as Turbo C++ but comes with additional programming tools.

Whether you use Turbo C, Turbo C++, Borland C, or Borland C++ the purpose of this guide is to help you unleash the power of these impressive compilers.

About This Book

This book covers the Turbo/Borland C/C++ programming languages and their environments. It provides you with a comprehensive source of information about these important compilers. It includes numerous example programs which help illustrate the elements that form each language. It is designed for programmers at all skill levels. If you are just learning to program in Turbo/Borland C/C++, this guide makes an excellent companion to any tutorial, providing answers to your specific questions. If you are an experienced C or C++ programmer, this book serves as a handy desk reference.

How This Book Is Organized

This book is organized in such a way that it can be effectively utilized by programmers using Turbo/Borland C, C++, or both. Towards this goal, the book has seven parts. They are:

Part 1   The C Language

Part 2   The Turbo C Environment

Part 3   The Library

Part 4   Turbo/Borland C++

Part 5   The Turbo/Borland C++ Environment

Part 6   Windows Programming Using Borland C++

Part 7   Appendixes

Part One details the C language. The material in Part One is also fully applicable to Turbo/Borland C++ because C is the base language for C++. Part Two describes the Turbo C environment, including the Integrated Development Environment (IDE) and the editor. Part Three describes all of Turbo/Borland C/C++'s library functions. Part Four discusses in depth the Turbo/Borland C++ object-oriented extensions to the C language. Part Four assumes that you are a proficient C programmer, so if you aren't you will want to read Part One first. Part Five discusses the Turbo/Borland C++ environment. The Turbo/Borland C++ environment differs from Turbo C's environments discussed in Part Two. For example, Turbo/Borland C++ allows the use of a mouse, Turbo C does not. Part Six examines Windows Programming using Turbo/Borland C++. Finally, Part Seven provides several useful appendixes.

The organization of this book allows the Turbo/Borland C user to quickly find material related to that language and environment while at the same time letting the Turbo/Borland C++ programmer find the material appropriate to that environment. Further, if you are currently a C programmer and want to become proficient at C++, the organization of this book prevents you from "wading through" reams of information that you already know. You can simply concentrate on the C++ sections of the book.

Conventions Used in This Book

In this book, keywords, operators, function names, and variable names are shown in bold when referenced in text. General forms are shown in italics. Also, when referencing a function name in text, the name is followed by parentheses. In this way, you can easily distinguish a variable name from a function name.

Diskette Offer

There are many useful and interesting functions and programs contained in this book. If you're like me, you probably would like to use them, but hate typing them into the computer. When I key in routines from a book it always seems that I type something wrong and spend hours trying to get the program to work. For this reason, I am offering the source code on diskette for all the functions and programs contained in this book for $24.95. Just fill in the order blank on the next page and mail it, along with your payment, to the address shown. Or, if you're in a hurry, just call (217) 586-4021 (the number of my consulting office) and place your order by telephone. (VISA and MasterCard accepted.)

Please send me _____ copies, at $24.95 each, of the programs in *Turbo C/C++: The Complete Reference,* Second Edition, on IBM compatible diskette.

Foreign orders only: Checks must be drawn on a U.S. bank, and please add $5 for shipping and handling.

_____

Name

_____

Address

_____   _____   _____

City   State   ZIP

_____

Telephone

Diskette size (check one): 5 1/4" _____   3 1/2" _____

Method of payment: check _____   VISA _____   MC _____

Credit card number: _____

Expiration date: _____

Signature: _____

Send to:

Herbert Schildt
398 County Road 2500 N
Mahomet, Il 61853

or phone: (217) 586-4021
or FAX: (217) 586-4997

This offer is subject to change or cancellation at any time.

Please allow 3 to 6 weeks for delivery. Osborne/McGraw-Hill assumes NO responsibility for this offer. This is solely an offer of the author, Herbert Schildt, and not of Osborne/McGraw-Hill.

Part *I*

The C Language

Part One of this guide presents a discussion of the Turbo C programming language. Because Turbo/Borland C++ is a superset of Turbo C, virtually everything presented in this section is applicable to the C++ environment. If you are new to C and C++, you will need to learn to program in C before you learn to program in C++.

Since Turbo C closely conforms to the ANSI C standard, most of the information presented in Part One is also valid for any ANSI C standard environment.

Chapter *1*

An Overview of C

This chapter presents an overview of the origins, uses, and philosophy of the C programming language.

The Origins of the C Language

Dennis Ritchie invented and first implemented the C programming language on a DEC PDP-11 that used the UNIX operating system. The language is the result of a development process that started with an older language called BCPL. Martin Richards developed BCPL, which influenced Ken Thompson's invention of a language called B, which led to the development of C in the 1970s.

For many years the de facto standard for C was the version supplied with the UNIX System V operating system. It is described in *The C Programming Language* by Brian Kernighan and Dennis Ritchie (Prentice-Hall, 1978). The growing popularity of microcomputers led to the creation of a large number of C implementations. In what could almost be called a miracle, the source code accepted by most of these implementations is highly compatible. However, because no standard existed, there are discrepancies. To rectify this situation, ANSI established a committee in the beginning of the summer of 1983 to create an ANSI standard for the C language. The standard was finally adopted in 1990, and Turbo C fully implements the resulting ANSI standard for C. Turbo C is a fast, efficient compiler, and provides both an integrated programming environment and the more traditional command-line version to satisfy the needs and desires of a wide variety of programmers.

A Middle-Level Language

C is often called a *middle-level computer language*. This does not mean that C is less powerful, harder to use, or less developed than a high-level language such as BASIC or Pascal; nor does it imply that C is similar to, or presents the problems associated with, assembly language. The definition of C as a middle-level language means that it combines elements of high-level languages with the functionalism of assembly language. Table 1-1 shows how C fits into the spectrum of languages.

As a middle-level language, C allows the manipulation of bits, bytes, and addresses—the basic elements with which the computer functions. C code is very portable. (*Portability* means that it is possible to adapt software written for one type of computer to another.) For example, if a program written for an Apple II+ can be moved easily to an IBM PC, that program is portable.

All high-level programming languages support the concept of data types. A *data type* defines a set of values that a variable can store along with a set of operations that can be performed on that variable. Common data types are integer, character, and real. Although C has five basic built-in data types, it is not a strongly typed language like Pascal or Ada. In fact C will allow almost all type conversions. For example, character and integer types may be freely intermixed in most expressions. Traditionally C performs no run-time error checking such as array-boundary checking or argument-type compatibility checking. These checks are the responsibility of the programmer.

A special feature of C is that it allows the direct manipulation of bits, bytes, words, and pointers. This suits it to system-level programming, where these operations are common. Another important aspect of C is that it has only 32 keywords (27 from the Kernighan and Ritchie standard and 5 added by the ANSI standardization commit-

Highest level	Ada
	Modula-2
	Pascal
	COBOL
	FORTRAN
	BASIC
Middle level	C
	FORTH
	Macro-assembly language
Lowest level	Assembly language

Table 1-1.   *C's Place in the World of Languages*

tee), which are the commands that make up the C language. (Turbo C contains 11 more keywords to support various enhancements and extensions.) As a comparison, consider that BASIC for the IBM PC contains 159 keywords!

A Structured Language

Although the term *block-structured language* does not strictly apply to C, C is commonly called a structured language because of structural similarities to ALGOL, Pascal, and Modula-2. (Technically, a block-structured language permits procedures or functions to be declared inside other procedures or functions. In this way the concepts of "global" and "local" are expanded through the use of *scope rules,* which govern the "visibility" of a variable or procedure. Since C does not allow the creation of functions within functions, it is not really block structured.)

The distinguishing feature of a structured language is *compartmentalization* of code and data. Compartmentalization is the language's ability to section off and hide from the rest of the program all information and instructions necessary to perform a specific task. One way of achieving compartmentalization is to use subroutines that employ local (temporary) variables. By using local variables, the programmer can write subroutines so that the events that occur within them cause no side effects in other parts of the program. This capability makes it very easy for C programs to share sections of code. If you develop compartmentalized functions, you only need to know what a function does, not how it does it. Remember that excessive use of global variables (variables known throughout the entire program) may allow bugs to creep into a program by allowing unwanted side effects. (Anyone who has programmed in BASIC is well aware of this problem!)

A structured language allows you a variety of programming possibilities. It directly supports several loop constructs, such as **while, do-while,** and **for**. In a structured language the use of **goto** is either prohibited or discouraged and is not the common form of program control as it is in BASIC and FORTRAN. A structured language allows you to indent statements and does not require a strict field concept.

Here are some examples of structured and nonstructured languages:

Structured	**Nonstructured**
Pascal	FORTRAN
Ada	BASIC
C	COBOL
Modula-2	

Structured languages tend to be newer; nonstructured languages are older. Today it is widely maintained that the clarity of structured languages makes programming and maintenance easier than with nonstructured languages.

The main structural component of C is the function—C's stand alone subroutine. In C, functions are the building blocks in which all program activity occurs. They allow the separate tasks in a program to be defined and coded separately, thus allowing your programs to be modular. After a function has been created, you can rely on it to work properly in various situations, without creating side effects in other parts of the program. The fact that you can create stand alone functions is extremely critical in larger projects where one programmer's code must not accidentally affect another's.

Another way to structure and compartmentalize code in C is to use code blocks. A *code block* is a logically connected group of program statements that is treated as a unit. In C a code block is created by placing a sequence of statements between opening and closing curly braces. In this example,

```
if(x<10) {
  printf("too low, try again");
  reset_counter(-1);
}
```

the two statements after the **if** and between the curly braces are both executed if **x** is less than 10. These two statements together with the braces are a code block. They are a logical unit: One of the statements cannot execute without the other. Code blocks not only allow many algorithms to be implemented with clarity, elegance, and efficiency, but also help the programmer conceptualize the true nature of the routine.

A Programmer's Language

One might respond to the statement, "C is a programmer's language," with the question, "Aren't all programming languages for programmers?" The answer is an unqualified "No!" Consider the classic examples of nonprogrammer's languages, COBOL and BASIC. COBOL was designed to enable nonprogrammers to read and, presumably, understand the program. BASIC was created essentially to allow nonprogrammers to program a computer to solve relatively simple problems.

In contrast, C stands almost alone in that it was created, influenced, and field-tested by real working programmers. The end result is that C gives the programmer what the programmer wants: few restrictions, few complaints, block structures, stand alone functions, and a compact set of keywords. It is truly amazing that by using C, a programmer can achieve nearly the efficiency of assembly code, combined with the structure of ALGOL or Modula-2. It is no wonder that C is easily the most popular language among topflight professional programmers.

The fact that C can often be used in place of assembly language contributes greatly to its popularity among programmers. Assembly language uses a symbolic representation of the actual binary code that the computer executes. Each assembly language operation maps into a single task for the computer to perform. Although assembly language gives programmers the potential for accomplishing tasks with maximum flexibility and efficiency, it is notoriously difficult to use when developing and debugging a program. Furthermore, since assembly language is unstructured, the final program tends to be spaghetti code—a tangled mess of jumps, calls, and indexes. This lack of structure makes assembly language programs difficult to read, enhance, and maintain. Perhaps more important, assembly language routines are not portable between machines with different central processing units (CPUs).

Initially, C was used for systems programming. A *systems program* is part of a large class of programs that forms a portion of the operating system of the computer or its support utilities. For example, the following are usually called systems programs:

- Operating systems

- Interpreters

- Editors

- Assembly programs

- Compilers

- Database managers

As C grew in popularity, many programmers began to use it to program all tasks because of its portability and efficiency. Because there are C compilers for almost all computers, it is possible to take code written for one machine and compile and run it on another with few or no changes. This portability saves both time and money. In addition, C compilers tend to produce tighter and faster object code than most other types of compilers.

Perhaps the most significant reason that C is used in all types of programming tasks is that programmers like it! It has the speed of assembly language and the extensibility of FORTH but few of the restrictions of Pascal or Modula-2. Each C programmer can create and maintain a unique library of functions that have been tailored to his or her personality and can be used in many different programs. Because it allows—indeed, encourages—separate compilation, C allows programmers to manage large projects easily and minimize duplication of effort.

Compilers Versus Interpreters

The terms *compiler* and *interpreter* refer to the way in which a program is executed. In theory, any programming language can be either compiled or interpreted, but some languages are usually executed one way or the other. For example, BASIC is usually interpreted and C is usually compiled. (C interpreters have some value as debugging aids.) The way a program is executed is not defined by the language in which it is written. Interpreters and compilers are simply sophisticated programs that operate on your program source code.

An interpreter reads the source code of your program one line at a time and performs the specific instructions contained in that line. A compiler reads the entire program and converts it into *object code*, which is a translation of the program source code into a form that can be directly executed by the computer. Object code is also called binary code and machine code. Once a program is compiled, a line of source code is no longer meaningful in the execution of the program.

When you use an interpreter, it must be present each time you wish to run your program. For example, in BASIC you have to execute the BASIC interpreter first and then load your program and type RUN each time you want to use it. The BASIC interpreter then examines your program one line at a time for correctness and then executes it. This slow process occurs every time the program runs. By contrast, a compiler converts your program into object code that can be directly executed by your computer. Because the compiler translates your program only once, all you need to do is execute your program directly, usually by the simple process of typing its name. Thus, compilation is a one-time cost, while interpreted code incurs an overhead cost each time a program runs.

Two terms that you will often see in this book and in your C compiler manual are *compile time,* which refers to the events that occur during the compilation process, and *run time,* which refers to the events that occur while the program is actually executing. You usually see these terms in discussions of errors, as in the phrases "compile-time errors" and "run-time errors."

The Form of a C Program

Table 1-2 lists the 43 keywords that, combined with the formal C syntax, form the Turbo C programming language.

All C keywords are lowercase. In C uppercase and lowercase are different: **else** is a keyword; ELSE is not. A keyword may not be used for any other purpose in a C program—that is, it may not serve as a variable or function name.

All C programs consist of one or more functions. The only function that absolutely must be present is called **main( )**, and it is the first function called when program execution begins. In well-written C code, **main( )** outlines what the program does. The outline is composed of function calls. Although **main( )** is technically not part of the C language, treat it as if it were. Don't try to use **main** as the name of a variable, for example.

The general form of a C program is illustrated in Figure 1-1, where **f1( )** through **fN( )** represent user-defined functions.

The 32 keywords as defined by the ANSI standard

auto	double	int	struct
break	else	long	switch
case	enum	register	typedef
char	extern	return	union
const	float	short	unsigned
continue	for	signed	void
default	goto	sizeof	volatile
do	if	static	while

The Turbo C extended keywords

asm	_cs	_ds	_es
_ss	cdecl	far	huge
interrupt	near	pascal	

Table 1-2.   *A List of Turbo C Keywords*

The Library and Linking

Technically speaking, it is possible to create a useful, functional C program that consists solely of the statements actually created by the programmer. However, this is rarely done because C does not, within the actual definition of the language, provide any method of performing I/O operations. As a result, most programs include calls to various functions contained in C's standard library.

Turbo C comes with a standard library that provides functions that perform most commonly needed tasks. When you call a function that is not part of the program you wrote, Turbo C "remembers" its name. Later the *linker* combines the code you wrote with the object code already found in the standard library. This process is called *linking*.

The functions that are kept in the library are in *relocatable* format. This means that the memory addresses for the various machine-code instructions have not been absolutely defined; only offset information has been kept. When your program links with the functions in the standard library, these memory offsets are used to create the actual addresses used. There are several technical manuals and books that explain this process in more detail. However, you do not need any further explanation of the actual relocation process to program in Turbo C.

```
global declarations
main( )
{
   local variables
   statement sequence
}
f1( )
{
   local variables
   statement sequence
}
f2( )
{
   local variables
   statement sequence
}
   .
   .
   .
fN( )
{
   local variables
   statement sequence
}
```

Figure 1-1.   *The general form of a C program*

Separate Compilation

Most short C programs are completely contained within one source file. However, as a program gets longer, so does its compile time, and long compile times make for short tempers! Hence, Turbo C allows a program to be broken into pieces and contained in many files, and for each file to be compiled separately. Once all files have been compiled, they are linked together, along with any library routines, to form the complete object code. The advantage of separate compilation is that a change in the code of one file does not necessitate the recompilation of the entire program. On all but the simplest projects, the time saving is substantial.

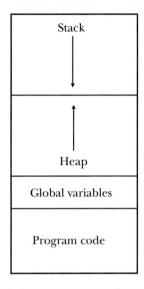

Figure 1-2. *A conceptual memory map of a C program*

Turbo C's Memory Map

A compiled Turbo C program creates and uses four logically distinct regions of memory that serve specific functions. The first region is the memory that actually holds the code of your program. The next region is the memory where global variables are stored. The remaining two regions are the stack and the heap. The *stack* is used for a great many things while your program executes. It holds the return address of function calls, arguments to functions, and local variables. It is also used to save the current state of the CPU. The *heap* is a region of free memory, which your program can use via Turbo C's dynamic allocation functions, for things like linked lists and trees.

Although the exact physical layout of each of the four regions of memory differs, based on the way you tell Turbo C to compile your program, the diagram in Figure 1-2 shows conceptually how your C programs appear in memory.

A Review of Terms

The terms that follow will be used frequently throughout the remainder of this book. You should be completely familiar with their meaning.

Source code	The text of a program that a user can read; commonly thought of as the program. The source code is input into the C compiler.
Object code	Translation of the source code of a program into machine code, which the computer can read and execute directly. Object code is the input to the linker.
Linker	A program that links separately compiled functions together into one program. It combines the functions in the standard C library with the code that you wrote. The output of the linker is an executable program.
Library	The file containing the standard functions that can be used by your program. These functions include all I/O operations as well as other useful routines.
Compile time	The events that occur while your program is being compiled. A common occurrence during compile time is a syntax error.
Run time	The events that occur while your program is executing.

Chapter *2*

Variables, Constants, Operators, and Expressions

Variables and constants are manipulated by operators to form expressions. These are the atomic elements of the Turbo C and C++ language. This chapter will examine each element closely.

Identifier Names

The names that are used to reference variables, functions, labels, and various other user-defined objects are called *identifiers*. An identifier in Turbo C can vary from 1 to 32 characters. The first character must be a letter or an underscore with subsequent characters being either letters, numbers, or the underscore. Turbo C also allows the $ to be used in an identifier name, but this is nonstandard and its use is not recommended. Here are some examples of correct and incorrect identifier names:

Correct	Incorrect
count	1count
test23	hi!there
high_balance	high..balance

In C, upper- and lowercase are treated differently. Hence, **count**, **Count**, and **COUNT** are three separate identifiers. An identifier cannot be the same as a Turbo C keyword, and it should not have the same name as functions that you wrote or that are in the Turbo C library.

Data Types

There are five atomic data types in C: character, integer, floating point, double floating point, and valueless. The sizes of these types are shown in Table 2-1.

Values of type **char** are used to hold ASCII characters or any 8-bit quantity. Variables of type **int** are used to hold integer quantities. Variables of type **float** and **double** are used to hold real numbers. (Real numbers have both an integer and a fractional component.)

The **void** type has three uses. The first is to declare explicitly a function as returning no value; the second is to declare explicitly a function as having no parameters; the third is to create generic pointers. Each of these uses is discussed in subsequent chapters.

Turbo C supports several *aggregate* types, including structures, unions, bit fields, enumerations, and user-defined types. These complex types are discussed in Chapter 7.

Type Modifiers

Excepting type **void**, the basic data types may have various *modifiers* preceding them. A modifier is used to alter the meaning of the base type to fit the needs of various situations more precisely. The list of modifiers is shown here:

    signed
    unsigned
    long
    short

Type	Bit Width	Range
char	8	0 to 255
int	16	–32768 to 32767
float	32	3.4E–38 to 3.4E+38
double	64	1.7E–308 to 1.7E+308
void	0	valueless

Table 2-1.   *Size and Range of Turbo C's Basic Data Types*

The modifiers **signed**, **unsigned**, **long**, and **short** may be applied to character and integer base types. However, **long** may also be applied to **double**. Table 2-2 shows all allowed combinations that adhere to the ANSI C standard, along with their bit widths and range assuming a 16-bit word.

The use of **signed** on integers is redundant (but allowed) because the default integer declaration assumes a signed number.

The difference between signed and unsigned integers is in the way the high-order bit of the integer is interpreted. If a signed integer is specified, then the compiler will generate code that assumes the high-order bit of an integer is to be used as a *sign flag*. If the sign flag is 0, then the number is positive; if it is 1, then the number is negative. For example:

127 in binary is 0 0 0 0 0 0 0 0 0 1 1 1 1 1 1 1
– 127 in binary is 1 0 0 0 0 0 0 0 0 1 1 1 1 1 1 1

sign bit

The reader is cautioned that most computers (including those based on the 8086 family of processors) will use *two's complement* arithmetic, which will cause the

Type	Bit Width	Range
char	8	–128 to 127
unsigned char	8	0 to 255
signed char	8	–128 to 127
int	16	–32768 to 32767
unsigned int	16	0 to 65535
signed int	16	–32768 to 32767
short int	16	–32768 to 32767
unsigned short int	16	0 to 65535
signed short int	16	–32768 to 32767
long int	32	–2147483648 to 2147483647
unsigned long int	32	0 to 4294967295
signed long int	32	–2147483648 to 2147483647
float	32	3.4E–38 to 3.4E+38
double	64	1.7E–308 to 1.7E+308
long double	64	1/7E–308 to 1.7E+308

Table 2-2.   *All Possible Combinations of Turbo C's Basic Types and Modifiers*

representation of –127 to appear different. However, the use of the sign bit is the same. A negative number in two's complement form has all bits reversed and one is added to the number. For example, –127 in two's complement appears like this:

1 1 1 1 1 1 1 1   1 0 0 0 0 0 0 1

Signed integers are important for a great many algorithms, but they only have half the absolute magnitude of their unsigned brothers. For example, here is 32,767:

0 1 1 1 1 1 1 1   1 1 1 1 1 1 1 1

If the high-order bit were set to 1, the number would then be interpreted as –1. However, if you had declared this to be an **unsigned int**, then when the high-order bit is set to 1, the number becomes 65,535.

Access Modifiers

C has two type modifiers that are used to control the ways in which variables may be accessed or modified. These modifiers are called **const** and **volatile**.

Variables of type **const** may not be changed during execution by your program. For example,

```
const int a;
```

will create an integer variable called **a** that cannot be modified by your program. It can, however, be used in other types of expressions. A **const** variable will receive its value either from an explicit initialization or by some hardware-dependent means. For example, this gives **count** the value of 100:

```
const int count = 100;
```

Aside from initialization, no **const** variable can be modified by your program.

The modifier **volatile** is used to tell the compiler that a variable's value can be changed in ways not explicitly specified by the program. For example, a global variable's address can be passed to the clock routine of the operating system and used to hold the real-time of the system. In this situation the contents of the variable are altered without any explicit assignment statements in the program. This is important because Turbo C automatically optimizes certain expressions by making the assumption that the content of a variable is unchanging inside that expression. Also, some optimizations may change the order of evaluation of an expression during the compilation process. The **volatile** modifier prevents these changes from occurring.

It is possible to use **const** and **volatile** together. For example, if **0x30** is assumed to be the address of a port that is changed by external conditions only, then the following declaration is precisely what you would want to prevent any possibility of accidental side effects:

```
const volatile unsigned char *port=0x30;
```

Declaration of Variables

All variables must be declared before they are used. The general form of a declaration is shown here:

type variable_list;

Here, *type* must be a valid C data type and *variable_list* may consist of one or more identifier names with comma separators. Some declarations are shown here:

```
int i, j, 1;
```

```
short int si;
```

```
unsigned int ui;
```

```
double balance, profit, loss;
```

Remember, in C, the name of a variable has nothing to do with its type.

There are three basic places where variables will be declared: inside functions, in the definition of function parameters, or outside all functions. These variables are called local variables, formal parameters, and global variables.

Local Variables

Variables that are declared inside a function are called *local variables*. In some C literature, these variables may be referred to as *automatic variables* in keeping with C's use of the (optional) keyword **auto** that can be used to declare them. Since the term *local variable* is more commonly used, this guide will continue to use it. Local variables can be referenced only by statements that are inside the block in which the variables are declared. Stated another way, local variables are not known outside their own code block. You should remember that a block of code is begun when an opening curly brace is encountered and terminated when a closing curly brace is found.

One of the most important things to understand about local variables is that they exist only while the block of code in which they are declared is executing. That is, a local variable is created upon entry into its block and destroyed upon exit.

The most common code block in which local variables are declared is the function. For example, consider these two functions:

```
void func1(void)
{
  int x;

  x = 10;
}

void func2(void)
{
  int x;

  x = -199;
}
```

The integer variable **x** was declared twice, once in **func1( )** and once in **func2( )**. The **x** in **func1( )** has no bearing on, or relationship to, the **x** in **func2( )** because each **x** is only known to the code within the same block as the variable's declaration.

The language contains the keyword **auto**, which can be used to declare local variables. However, since all nonglobal variables are assumed to be **auto** by default, it is virtually never used.

It is common practice to declare all variables needed within a function at the start of that function's code block. This is done mostly to make it easy for anyone reading the code to know what variables are used. However, it is not necessary to do this because local variables can be declared within any code block. To understand how this works, consider the following function.

```
void f(void)
{
  int t;

  scanf("%d", &t);

  if(t==1) {
    char s[80];  /* this is existent only
                    inside this block */
    printf("enter name:");
    gets(s);
    process(s);
```

```
  }
  /* s is not known here */
}
```

Here, the local variable **s** is known only within the **if** code block. Since **s** is known only within the **if** block, it may not be referenced elsewhere—not even in other parts of the function that contains it.

One reason you might want to declare a variable within its own block instead of at the top of a function is to prevent its accidental misuse elsewhere in the function. In essence, declaring variables inside the blocks of code that actually use them allows you to compartmentalize your code and data into more easily managed units.

Because local variables are destroyed upon exit from the function in which they are declared, they cannot retain their values between function calls. (As you will see shortly, however, it is possible to direct the compiler to retain their values through the use of the **static** modifier.)

Unless otherwise specified, storage for local variables is on the stack. The fact that the stack is a dynamic and changing region of memory explains why local variables cannot, in general, hold their values between function calls.

Formal Parameters

If a function is to use arguments, then it must declare variables that will accept the values of the arguments. These variables are called the *formal parameters* of the function. They behave like any other local variables inside the function. As shown in the following program fragment, their declaration occurs inside the parentheses that follow the function name.

```
/* return 1 if c is part of string s; 0 otherwise */
is_in(char *s, char c)
{
  while(*s)
    if(*s==c) return 1;
    else s++;

  return 0;
}
```

The function **is_in( )** has two parameters: **s** and **c**. You must tell C what type of variable these are by declaring them as shown above. Once this has been done, they may be used inside the function as normal local variables. Keep in mind that, as local variables, they are also dynamic and are destroyed upon exit from the function.

You must make sure that the formal parameters you declare are the same type as the arguments you will use to call the function. If there is a type mismatch, unexpected results can occur. Unlike many other languages, C is very robust and generally will do something, even if it is not what you want. There are few run-time errors and no bounds checking. As the programmer, you have to make sure that errors do not occur.

As with local variables, you may make assignments to a function's formal parameters or use them in any allowable C expression. Even though these variables perform the special task of receiving the value of the arguments passed to the function, they can be used like any other local variable.

Global Variables

Unlike local variables, *global variables* are known throughout the entire program and may be used by any piece of code. Also, they will hold their values during the entire execution of the program. Global variables are created by declaring them outside of any function. They may be accessed by any expression regardless of what function that expression is in.

In the following program, you can see that the variable **count** has been declared outside of all functions. Its declaration comes before the **main( )** function. However, it could have been placed anywhere prior to its first use, as long as it was not in a function. Common practice is to declare global variables at the top of the program.

```
#include <stdio.h>

void func1(void), func2(void);

int count;  /* count is global  */

main(void)
{
  count = 100;
  func1();
  return 0; /* return success to the system */
}

void func1(void)
{
  int temp;

  temp = count;
  func2();
  printf("count is %d", count); /* will print 100 */
}

void func2(void)
```

```
{
  int count;

  for(count=1; count<10; count++)
    putchar('.');
}
```

Looking closely at this program fragment, it should be clear that although neither **main( )** nor **func1( )** has declared the variable **count**, both may use it. However, **func2( )** has declared a local variable called **count**. When **func2( )** references **count**, it will be referencing only its local variable, not the global one. Remember that if a global variable and a local variable have the same name, all references to that name inside the function where the local variable is declared refer to the local variable and have no reference to the global variable. This is a convenient benefit. However, forgetting this can cause your program to act very strangely, even though it "looks" correct.

Storage for global variables is in a fixed region of memory set aside for this purpose by the compiler. Global variables are very helpful when the same data is used in many functions in your program. You should avoid using unnecessary global variables, however, for three reasons:

1. They take up memory the entire time your program is executing, not just when they are needed.

2. Using a global variable where a local variable will do makes a function less general because it relies on something that must be defined outside itself.

3. Using a large number of global variables can lead to program errors because of unknown, and unwanted, side effects.

One of the principal points of a structured language is the compartmentalization of code and data. In C, compartmentalization is achieved through the use of local variables and functions. For example, here are two ways to write **mul( )**—a simple function that computes the product of two integers.

```
        Two Ways to Write mul()

  General                  Specific

  -------                  -------
                           int x, y;
  mul(int x, int y)        mul(void)
  {                        {
      return(x*y);             return(x*y);
  }                        }
```

Both functions will return the product of the variables **x** and **y**. However, the generalized, or *parameterized,* version can be used to return the product of *any* two numbers, whereas the specific version can be used to find only the product of the global variables **x** and **y**.

Storage Class Specifiers

There are four storage class specifiers supported by C. They are

extern
static
register
auto

These tell the compiler how the variable that follows should be stored. The storage specifier precedes the rest of the variable declaration. Its general form is

storage_specifier type var_name;

Each specifier will be examined in turn.

extern

Because C allows separately compiled modules of a large program to be linked together to speed up compilation and aid in the management of large projects, there must be some way of telling all the files about the global variables required by the program. The solution is to declare all of your globals in one file and use **extern** declarations in the other, as shown in Table 2-3.

In File 2, the global variable list was copied from File 1 and the **extern** specifier was added to the declarations. The **extern** specifier tells the compiler that the following variable types and names have been declared elsewhere. In other words, **extern** lets the compiler know what the types and names are for these global variables without actually creating storage for them again. When the two modules are linked, all references to the external variables are resolved.

When a declaration creates storage for a variable, it is called a *definition.* **extern** statements are declarations, but not definitions. They simply tell the compiler that a definition exists elsewhere in the program.

When you use a global variable inside a function that is in the same file as the declaration for the global variable you may elect to use **extern**, although you don't have to and it is rarely done. The following program fragment shows the use of this option:

```
int first, last;  /* global definition of first
                      and last */

main(void)
{
  extern int first;  /* optional use of the
                         extern declaration */
  /* ... */
}
```

Although **extern** variable declarations can occur inside the same file as the global declaration, they are not necessary. If the C compiler encounters a variable that has not been declared, the compiler checks whether it matches any of the global variables. If it does, the compiler assumes that the global variable is the one being referenced.

static Variables

static variables are permanent variables within their own function or file. They differ from global variables because they are not known outside their function or file but

File 1	File 2
int x, y;	extern int x, y;
char ch;	extern char ch;
main(void)	void func22(void)
{	{
.	x = y/10;
.	}
.	
}	void func23(void)
	{
void func1(void)	y = 10;
{	}
x = 123;	
}	

Table 2-3.   Using Global Variables in Separately Compiled Files

they maintain their values between calls. This feature makes them very useful when you write generalized functions and function libraries, which may be used by other programmers. Because the effect of **static** on local variables is different from its effect on global ones, they will be examined separately.

static Local Variables

When **static** is applied to a local variable it causes the compiler to create permanent storage for it in much the same way that it does for a global variable. The key difference between a **static** local variable and a global variable is that the **static** local variable remains known only to the block in which it is declared. In simple terms, a **static** local variable is a local variable that retains its value between function calls.

It is very important to the creation of stand-alone functions that **static** local variables are available in C because there are several types of routines that must preserve a value between calls. If **static** variables were not allowed then globals would have to be used—opening the door to possible side effects. A simple example of how a **static** local variable can be used is illustrated by the **count( )** function in this short program:

```
#include <stdio.h>
#include <conio.h>

int count(int i);

main(void)
{
  do {
    count(0);
  } while(!kbhit());
  printf("count called %d times", count(1));
  return 0;
}

count(int i)
{
  static int c=0;

  if(i) return c;
  else c++;
  return 0;
}
```

Sometimes it is useful to know how many times a function has been executed during a program run. While it is certainly possible to use a global variable for this purpose, a better way is to have the function in question keep track of this information itself, as is done by the **count( )** function. In this example, if **count( )** is called with a value of 0 then the counter variable **c** is incremented. (Presumably in a real application, the function would also perform some other useful processing.) If **count( )** is called with any other value, it returns the number of times it has been called. Counting the number of times a function is called can be useful during the development of a program so that those functions called most frequently can receive the most attention.

Another good example of a function that would require a **static** local variable is a number series generator that produces a new number based on the last one. It is possible for you to declare a global variable for this value. However, each time the function is used in a program, you would have to remember to declare that global variable and make sure that it did not conflict with any other global variables already declared—a major drawback. Also, using a global variable would make this function difficult to place in a function library. The better solution is to declare the variable that holds the generated number to be **static**, as in this program fragment:

```
series(void)
{
  static int series_num;

  series_num = series_num+23;
  return(series_num);
}
```

In this example, the variable **series_num** stays in existence between function calls, instead of coming and going the way a normal local variable would. This means that each call to **series( )** can produce a new member of the series based on the last number without declaring that variable globally.

You may have noticed something that is unusual about the function **series( )** as it stands in the example. The static variable **series_num** is never explicitly initialized. This means that the first time the function is called, **series_num** will have the value zero, by default. While this is acceptable for some applications, most series generators will need a flexible starting point. To do this requires that **series_num** be initialized prior to the first call to **series( )**, which can be done easily only if **series_num** is a global variable. However, avoiding having to make **series_num** global was the entire point of making it **static** to begin with. This leads to the second use of **static**.

static Global Variables

When the specifier **static** is applied to a global variable it instructs the compiler to create a global variable that is known only to the *file* in which the **static** global variable is declared. This means that even though the variable is global, other routines in other files may have no knowledge of it or alter its contents directly; thus it is not subject to side effects. For the few situations where a local **static** cannot do the job, you can create a small file that contains only the functions that need the **static** global variable, separately compile that file, and use it without fear of side effects.

To see how a **static** global variable can be used, the series generator example from the previous section is recoded so that a starting "seed" value can be used to initialize the series through a call to a second function called **series_start( )**. The entire file containing **series( )**, **series_start( )**, and **series_num** follows:

```
/* This must all be in one file - preferably by itself */

static int series_num;

int series(void);
void series_start(int seed);

series(void)
{
  series_num = series_num + 23;
  return(series_num);
}

/* initialize series_num */
void series_start(int seed)
{
  series_num = seed;
}
```

Calling **series_start( )** with some known integer value initializes the series generator. After that, calls to **series( )** will generate the next element in the series.

The names of **static** local variables are known only to the function or block of code in which they are declared, and the names of **static** global variables are known only to the file in which they reside. This means that if you place the **series( )** and **series_start( )** functions in a separate file, you can use the functions, but you cannot reference the variable **series_num**. It is hidden from the rest of the code in your program. In fact, you may even declare and use another variable called **series_num** in your program (in another file, of course) and not confuse anything. In essence, the **static** modifier allows variables to exist within the functions that need them, without confusing other functions.

static variables enable you to hide portions of your program from other portions. This can be a tremendous advantage when trying to manage a very large and complex program. The **static** storage specifier lets you create very general functions that can go into libraries for later use.

Register Variables

C has one last storage specifier that originally applied only to variables of type **int** and **char**. However, the ANSI C standard has broadened its scope. The **register** specifier requests Turbo C to store a variable declared with this modifier in a manner that allows the fastest access time possible. For integers and characters, this typically means in the register of the CPU rather than in memory, where normal variables are stored. For other types of variables, Turbo C may use any other means to decrease their access time. In fact, it can also simply ignore the request altogether.

The **register** specifier may be applied to local variables and to the formal parameters in a function. You cannot apply **register** to global variables.

In general, operations on **register** variables occur much faster than on variables stored in memory. In fact, when the value of a variable is actually held in the CPU no memory access is required to determine or modify its value. This makes **register** variables ideal for loop control. Here is an example of how to declare a **register** variable of type **int** and use it to control a loop. This function computes the result of M^e for integers.

```
int_pwr(int m, register int e)
{
  register int temp;

  temp = 1;

  for(; e; e--) temp *= m;
   return temp;
}
```

In this example, both **e** and **temp** are declared to be **register** variables because both are used within the loop. In general practice, **register** variables are used where they will do the most good, that is, in places where many references will be made to the same variable. This is important because not all variables can be optimized for access time.

Turbo C allows two variables to be held in CPU registers at any one time. In effect, this means that you can have two per function. You don't have to worry about declaring too many **register** variables, though, because Turbo C will automatically do its best to reduce access time of any variable declared using **register**. Throughout this book most loop control variables will be **register**.

Assignment Statements

The general form of the *assignment statement* is

variable_name = expression;

where an expression may be as simple as a single constant or as complex as a combination of variables, operators, and constants. Like BASIC and FORTRAN, C uses a single equal sign to indicate assignment (unlike Pascal or Modula-2, which use the := construct). The target, or left part, of the assignment must be a variable, not a function or a constant.

Type Conversion in Assignments

Type conversion refers to the situation in which variables of one type are mixed with variables of another type. When this occurs in an assignment statement, the *type conversion rule* is very easy: The value of the right (expression) side of the assignment is converted to the type of the left side (target variable), as illustrated by this example:

```
int x;
char ch;
float   f;
void func(void)
{
  ch = x;      /* 1 */
  x = f;       /* 2 */
  f = ch;      /* 3 */
  f = x;       /* 4 */
}
```

In line 1, the left, high-order bits of the integer variable **x** are lopped off leaving **ch** with the lower 8 bits. If **x** was between 256 and 0 to begin with, then **ch** and **x** would have identical values. Otherwise, the value of **ch** would reflect only the lower order bits of **x**. In line 2, **x** receives the nonfractional part of **f**. In line 3, **f** converts the 8-bit integer value stored in **ch** to the same value except in the floating-point format. This also happens in line 4, except that **f** will convert an integer value into floating-point format.

When converting from integers to characters, long integers to integers, and integers to short integers, the basic rule is that the appropriate amount of high-order bits will be removed. This means 8 bits will be lost when going from an integer to a character, and 16 bits will be lost when going from a long integer to an integer.

Table 2-4 synopsizes these assignment type conversions. You must remember two important points that can affect the portability of the code you write:

1. The conversion of an **int** to a **float**, or a type **float** to **double** and so on, will not add any precision or accuracy. These kinds of conversions will only change the form in which the value is represented.

2. Some C compilers (and processors) will always treat a **char** variable as positive, no matter what value it has when converting it to an integer or **float** (as does Turbo C). Other compilers may treat **char** variable values greater than 127 as negative numbers when converting. Generally speaking, you should use **char** variables for characters, and use **int**, **short int**, or **signed char** when needed to avoid a possible portability problem in this area.

To use Table 2-4 to make a conversion not directly shown, simply convert one type at a time until you finish. For example, to convert from a **double** to an **int**, first convert from a **double** to a **float** and then from a **float** to an **int**.

If you have used a computer language like Pascal, which prohibits this automatic type conversion, you may think that C is very loose and sloppy. However, keep in mind that C was designed to make the life of the programmer easier by allowing work to be done in C rather than assembler. To do this, C has to allow such type conversions.

Variable Initializations

You can give variables in C a value at the time they are declared by placing an equal sign and a constant after the variable name. This is called an *initialization* and its general form is

type variable_name = constant;

Target Type	Expression Type	Possible Info Loss
signed char	char	If value > 127, the targets will be negative
char	short int	High-order 8 bits
char	int	High-order 8 bits
char	long int	High-order 24 bits
short int	int	None
short int	long int	High-order 16 bits
int	long int	High-order 16 bits
int	float	Fractional part and possibly more
float	double	Precision, result rounded
double	long double	Precision, result rounded

Table 2-4. *The Outcome of Common Type Conversions Assuming a 16-Bit Word*

Some examples are

```
char ch = 'a';

int first = 0;

float balance = 123.23;
```

Global and **static** global variables are initialized only at the start of the program. Local variables are initialized each time the block in which they are declared is entered. However, **static** local variables are only initialized once—not each time the block is entered. All global variables are initialized to zero if no other initializer is specified. Local and **register** variables that are not initialized will be initialized to zero.

Constants

Constants in C refer to fixed values that may not be altered by the program. They can be of any data type, as shown in Table 2-5.

C supports one other type of constant in addition to those of the predefined data types. This is a string. All string constants are enclosed between double quotes, such as **"this is a test"**. You must not confuse strings with characters. A single character constant is enclosed by single quotes, such as **'a'**. Because strings are simply arrays of characters, they will be discussed in Chapter 5.

Data Type	Constant Examples
char	'a' '\n' '9'
int	1 123 21000 −234
long int	35000 −34
short int	10 −12 90
unsigned int	10000 987 40000
float	123.23 4.34e −3
double	123.23 12312333 −0.9876324

Table 2-5.   *Constant Examples for Data Types*

Backslash Character Constants

Enclosing all character constants in single quotes works for most printing characters, but a few, such as the carriage return, are impossible to enter from the keyboard. For this reason, C uses the special backslash character constants, shown in Table 2-6.

You use a backslash code exactly the same way you would any other character. For example,

```
ch = '\t';

printf("this is a test\n");
```

first assigns a tab to **ch** and then prints "this is a test" on the screen followed by a newline.

Operators

C is very rich in built-in operators. An *operator* is a symbol that tells the compiler to perform specific mathematical or logical manipulations. There are three general

Code	Meaning
\b	Backspace
\f	Form feed
\n	Newline
\r	Carriage return
\t	Horizontal tab
\"	Double quote
\'	Single quote character
\0	Null
\\	Backslash
\v	Vertical tab
\a	Alert
\o	Octal constant
\x	Hexadecimal constant

Table 2-6.   Backslash Codes

classes of operators in C: arithmetic, relational and logical, and bitwise. In addition, C has some special operators for particular tasks.

Arithmetic Operators

Table 2-7 lists the *arithmetic operators* allowed in C. The operators +, –, *, and / all work the same way in C as they do in most other computer languages. They can be applied to almost any built-in data type allowed by C. When / is applied to an integer or character, any remainder is truncated; for example, **10/3** equals 3 in integer division.

The modulus division operator % also works in C the way it does in other languages. Remember that the modulus division operation yields the remainder of an integer division. However, as such, % cannot be used on type **float** or **double**. The following code fragment illustrates its use:

```
int x, y;

x = 10;
y = 3;

printf("%d", x/y);   /* will display 3 */
printf("%d", x%y);   /* will display 1, the remainder of
                        the integer division */

x = 1;
y = 2;

printf("%d %d", x/y, x%y); /*  will display 0 1 */
```

The reason the last line prints a 0 and 1 is because **1/2** in integer division is 0 with a remainder of 1. **1%2** yields the remainder 1.

Operator	Action
–	Subtraction, also unary minus
+	Addition
*	Multiplication
/	Division
%	Modulus division
– –	Decrement
++	Increment

Table 2-7.   *Arithmetic Operators*

The unary minus, in effect, multiplies its single operand by –1. That is, any number preceded by a minus sign switches its sign.

Increment and Decrement

C allows two very useful operators not generally found in other computer languages. These are the increment and decrement operators, ++ and ––. The operation ++ adds 1 to its operand, and –– subtracts 1. Therefore, the following are equivalent operations:

```
x = x+1;
```

is the same as

```
++x;
```

Also,

```
x = x-1;
```

is the same as

```
--x;
```

Both the increment and decrement operators may either precede or follow the operand. For example,

```
x = x+1;
```

can be written

```
++x;
```

or

```
x++;
```

However, there is a difference when they are used in an expression. When an increment or decrement operator precedes its operand, C performs the increment or decrement operation prior to using the operand's value. If the operator follows its operand, C uses the operand's value before incrementing or decrementing it. Consider the following:

```
x = 10;
y = ++x;
```

In this case, **y** is set to 11. However, if the code had been written as

```
x = 10;
y = x++;
```

y would have been set to 10. In both cases, **x** is set to 11; the difference is when it happens. There are significant advantages in being able to control when the increment or decrement operation takes place.

The precedence of the arithmetic operators is as follows:

highest	++ --
	-- (unary minus)
	* / %
lowest	+ --

Operators on the same precedence level are evaluated by the compiler from left to right. Of course, parentheses may be used to alter the order of evaluation. Parentheses are treated by C in the same way they are by virtually all other computer languages: They give an operation, or set of operations, a higher precedence level.

Relational and Logical Operators

In the term *relational operator* the word *relational* refers to the relationships values can have with one another. In the term *logical operator* the word *logical* refers to the ways these relationships can be connected together using the rules of formal logic. Because the relational and logical operators often work together, they will be discussed together here.

The key to the concepts of relational and logical operators is the idea of *true* and *false*. In C, *true* is any value other than 0. *False* is 0. Expressions that use relational or logical operators will return 0 for false and 1 for true.

Table 2-8 shows the relational and logical operators. The truth table for the logical operators is shown here using 1s and 0s:

p	q	p && q	p || q	!p
0	0	0	0	1
0	1	0	1	1
1	1	1	1	0
1	0	0	1	0

Relational Operators	
Operator	**Action**
>	Greater than
>=	Greater than or equal
<	Less than
<=	Less than or equal
==	Equal
!=	Not equal

Logical Operators	
Operator	**Action**
&&	AND
||	OR
!	NOT

Table 2-8.   *Relational and Logical Operators*

Both the relational and logical operators are lower in precedence than the arithmetic operators. This means that an expression like **10 > 1+12** is evaluated as if it were written **10 > (1+12)**. The result is, of course, false.

Several operations can be combined in one expression, as shown here:

10>5 && !(10<9) || 3<=4

which will evaluate true.

The following shows the relative precedence of the relational and logical operators:

highest	!
	> >= < <=
	== !=
	&&
lowest	||

As with arithmetic expressions, it is possible to use parentheses to alter the natural order of evaluation in a relational or logical expression. For example,

!1 && 0

will be false because the **!** is evaluated first, then the **&&** is evaluated. However, when the same expression is parenthesized as shown here, the result is true.

```
!(1 && 0)
```

Remember, all relational and logical expressions produce a result of either 0 or 1. Therefore the following program fragment is not only correct, but also prints the number 1 on the display:

```
int x;

x = 100;
printf("%d", x>10);
```

Bitwise Operators

Unlike many other languages, C supports a complete complement of *bitwise operators*. Since C was designed to take the place of assembly language for most programming tasks, it needed the ablilty to support all (or at least many) operations that can be done in assembler. Bitwise operations are the testing, setting, or shifting of the actual bits in a byte or word, which correspond to C's standard **char** and **int** data types and variants. Bitwise operators cannot be used on type **float**, **double**, **long double**, **void**, or other more complex types. Table 2-9 lists these operators.

The bitwise AND, OR, and NOT (one's complement) are governed by the same truth table as were their logical equivalents except that they work on a bit-by-bit level. The exclusive OR ^ has the truth table shown here:

p	q	p^q
0	0	0
0	1	1
1	0	1
1	1	0

Operator	Action
&	AND
|	OR
^	Exclusive OR (XOR)
~	One's complement
>>	Shift right
<<	Shift left

Table 2-9.   The Bitwise Operators

As the table indicates, the outcome of an XOR is true only if exactly one of the operands is true; it is false otherwise.

Bitwise operations most often find application in device drivers, such as modem programs, disk file routines, and printer routines, because the bitwise operations can be used to mask off certain bits, such as parity. (The parity bit is used to confirm that the rest of the bits in the byte are unchanged. It is usually the high-order bit in each byte.)

The bitwise AND is most commonly used to turn bits off. That is, any bit that is 0 in either operand causes the corresponding bit in the outcome to be set to 0. For example, the following function reads a character from the modem port using the function **read_modem( )** and resets the parity bit to 0.

```c
char get_char_from_modem(void)
{
  char ch;

  ch = read_modem(); /* get a character from the
                        modem port */
  return(ch & 127);
}
```

Parity is indicated by the eighth bit, which is set to 0 by ANDing it with a byte that has bits 1 through 7 set to 1 and bit 8 set to 0. The expression **ch & 127** means to AND together the bits in **ch** with the bits that make up the number 127. The net result is that the eighth bit of **ch** will be set to 0. In the following example, assume that **ch** had received the character **'A'** and had the parity bit set:

```
      parity bit
      |
      ↓
      1 1 0 0 0 0 0 1        ch containing an 'A'
                            with parity set
      0 1 1 1 1 1 1 1        127 in binary
  &   - - - - - - - -        do bitwise AND
      0 1 0 0 0 0 0 1        'A' without parity
```

The bitwise OR, as the reverse of AND, can be used to turn bits on. Any bit that is set to 1 in either operand causes the corresponding bit in the outcome to be set to 1. For example, **128 | 3** is

```
      1 0 0 0 0 0 0 0        128 in binary
      0 0 0 0 0 0 1 1        3 in binary
  |   - - - - - - - -        bitwise OR
      1 0 0 0 0 0 1 1        result
```

An exclusive OR, usually abbreviated XOR, will turn a bit on only if the bits being compared are different. For example, **127 ^ 120** is

	0 1 1 1 1 1 1 1	127 in binary
	0 1 1 1 1 0 0 0	120 in binary
^	– – – – – – – –	bitwise XOR
	0 0 0 0 0 1 1 1	result

In general, bitwise ANDs, ORs, and XORs apply their operations directly to each bit in the variable individually. For this reason, among others, bitwise operators are not usually used in conditional statements the way the relational and logical operators are. For example if **x=7**, then **x && 8** evaluates to true (1), whereas **x & 8** evaluates to false (0).

Relational and logical operators always produce a result that is either 0 or 1, whereas the similar bitwise operations may produce any arbitrary value in accordance with the specific operation. In other words, bitwise operations may create values other than 0 or 1, while the logical operators will always evaluate to 0 or 1.

The shift operators, **>>** and **<<**, move all bits in a variable to the right or left as specified. The general form of the shift right statement is

variable >> number of bit positions

and the shift left statement is

variable << number of bit positions

As bits are shifted off one end, bits are brought in the other end. Remember, a shift is *not* a rotate. That is, the bits shifted off one end *do not* come back around to the other. The bits shifted off are lost, and 0s are brought in. However, a right shift of a negative number shifts in ones.

Bit shift operations can be very useful when decoding external device input, like D/A converters, and reading status information. The bitwise shift operators can also be used to perform very fast multiplication and division of integers. A shift left will effectively multiply a number by 2 and a shift right will divide it by 2, as shown in Table 2-10.

The one's complement operator, **~**, will reverse the state of each bit in the specified variable. That is, all 1s are set to 0, and all 0s are set to 1.

The bitwise operators are used often in cipher routines. If you wished to make a disk file appear unreadable, you could perform some bitwise manipulations on it.

One of the simplest methods would be to complement each byte by using the one's complement to reverse each bit in the byte as shown here:

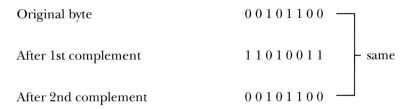

Original byte	0 0 1 0 1 1 0 0	
After 1st complement	1 1 0 1 0 0 1 1	same
After 2nd complement	0 0 1 0 1 1 0 0	

Notice that a sequence of two complements in a row always produces the original number. Hence, the first complement would represent the coded version of that byte. The second complement would decode it to its original value.

You could use the **encode( )** function shown here to encode a character:

```
/* A simple cipher function. */
char encode(char ch)
{
  return(~ch); /* complement it */
}
```

	x as Each Statement Executes	Value of x
char x;		
x=7;	0 0 0 0 0 1 1 1	7
x=x << 1;	0 0 0 0 1 1 1 0	14
x=x << 3;	0 1 1 1 0 0 0 0	112
x=x << 2;	1 1 0 0 0 0 0 0	192
x=x >> 1;	0 1 1 0 0 0 0 0	96
x=x >> 2;	0 0 0 1 1 0 0 0	24

Each left shift multiplies by 2. You should notice that information has been lost after x < < 2 because a bit was shifted off the end.

Each right shift divides by 2. Notice that subsquent division will not bring back any lost bits.

Table 2-10.   *Multiplication and Division with Shift Operators*

The ? Operator

C has a very powerful and convenient operator that can be used to replace certain statements of the if-then-else form. The ternary operator ? takes the general form

Exp1 ? Exp2 : Exp3

where *Exp1, Exp2,* and *Exp3* are expressions. Notice the use and placement of the colon.

The ? operator works like this. *Exp1* is evaluated. If it is true, then *Exp2* is evaluated and becomes the value of the expression. If *Exp1* is false, then *Exp3* is evaluated and its value becomes the value of the expression. For example:

```
x = 10;

y = x>9 ? 100 : 200;
```

In this example, **y** will be assigned the value **100**. If **x** had been less than or equal to 9, **y** would have received the value **200**. The same code written using the **if/else** statement would be:

```
x = 10;

if(x>9) y = 100;
else y = 200;
```

The ? operator will be discussed more fully in Chapter 3 in relationship to C's other conditional statements.

The & and * Pointer Operators

A *pointer* is the memory address of a variable. A pointer variable is a variable that is specifically declared to hold a pointer to a value of its specified type. Knowing a variable's address can be of great help in certain types of routines. Pointers have two main functions in C:

1. They can provide a very fast means of referencing array elements.

2. They allow C functions to modify their calling parameters.

These topics and uses will be dealt with in Chapter 6, which is devoted exclusively to pointers. However, the two operators that are used to manipulate pointers will be presented here.

The first pointer operator is **&**. It is a unary operator that returns the memory address of its operand. Remember that a unary operator only requires one operand. For example,

```
m = &count;
```

places into **m** the memory address of the variable **count**. This address is the computer's internal location of the variable. It has nothing to do with the *value* of **count**. The operation of the **&** can be remembered as returning the "the address of." Therefore, the above assignment statement could be read as "m receives the address of count."

To better understand the above assignment, assume the variable **count** resides at memory location 2000. Also assume that **count** has a value of 100. After the above assignment, **m** will have the value 2000.

The second operator, *, is the complement of the **&**. It is a unary operator that returns the *value of the variable located at the address that follows*. For example, if **m** contains the memory address of the variable **count**, then

```
q = *m;
```

places the value of **count** into **q**. Following the above example, **q** will have the value 100 because 100 is stored at location 2000, which is the memory address that was stored in **m**. The operation of the * can be remembered as "at address." In this case, the statement could be read as "q receives the value at address m."

Unfortunately the multiplication sign and the "at address" sign are the same and the bitwise AND and the "address of" sign are the same. These operators have no relationship to each other. Both **&** and * have a higher precedence than all other arithmetic operators except the unary minus, with which they are equal.

Variables that will hold memory addresses, or pointers as they are called in C, must be declared by putting a * in front of the variable name to indicate to the compiler that it will hold a pointer to that type of variable. For example, to declare a pointer type variable for a **char ch** you would write

```
char *ch;
```

Here, **ch** is not a character, but rather a pointer to a character—there is a big difference. The type of data that a pointer will be pointing to, in this case **char**, is called the *base type* of the pointer. However, the pointer variable itself is a variable that will be used to hold the address to an object of the base type. Hence, a character pointer (or any pointer for that matter) will be of sufficient size to hold an address as defined by the architecture of the computer on which it is running. The key point to remember is that a pointer should only be used to point to data that is of that pointer's base type.

You can mix both pointer and nonpointer directives in the same declaration statement. For example,

```
int x, *y, count;
```

declares **x** and **count** to be integer types, and **y** to be a pointer to an integer type.

Here, the * and **&** operators are used to put the value 10 into a variable called **target**:

```
/* Assignment with * and &. */
main(void)
{
  int target, source;
  int *m;

  source = 10;
  m = &source;
  target = *m;

  return 0;
}
```

The sizeof Compile-Time Operator

sizeof is a unary compile-time operator that returns the length, in bytes, of the variable or parenthesized type-specifier it precedes. For example,

```
float f;

printf("%f ", sizeof f);
printf("%d", sizeof(int));
```

displays **4 2**.

Remember that to compute the size of a type you must enclose the type name in parentheses (like a cast, which is explained later in this chapter). This is not necessary for variable names.

The principal use of **sizeof** is to help generate portable code when that code depends upon the size of the C built-in data types. For example, imagine a database program that needs to store six integer values per record. To make the database program portable to the widest variety of computers, you must not assume that an integer is 2 bytes; you must determine its actual length using **sizeof**. This being the case, the following routine could be used to write a record to a disk file:

```
/* write a record to a disk file */
put_rec(FILE *fp, int rec[6])
{
  int size, num;

  size = sizeof(rec);
  num = fwrite(rec, size, 1, fp);
  if(num<>1) printf("write error");
}
```

The key point of this example is that, coded as shown, **put_rec( )** will compile and run correctly on any computer—including those with 4-byte integers. Correctly using **sizeof** means that you can use Turbo C to develop code that will ultimately run in a different environment.

The Comma Operator

The comma operator is used to string together several expressions. The left side of the comma operator will always be evaluated as **void**. This means that the expression on the right side will become the value of the total comma-separated expression. For example,

```
x = (y=3, y+1);
```

first assigns **y** the value 3 and then assigns **x** the value of 4. The parentheses are necessary because the comma operator has a lower precedence than the assignment operator.

Essentially, the comma causes a sequence of operations to be performed. When it is used on the right side of an assignment statement, the value assigned is the value of the last expression of the comma separated list. For example:

```
y = 10;

x = (y=y-5, 25/y);
```

After execution, **x** will have the value 5 because **y**'s original value of 10 is reduced by 5, and then that value is divided into 25, yielding 5 as the result.

You might think of the comma operator as having the same meaning the word *and* has in normal English when it is used in the phrase "do this and this and this."

The . and --> Operators

The **.** (dot) operator and the **-->** (arrow) operator are used to reference individual elements of structures and unions. Structures and unions are compound data types that can be referenced under a single name. Unions and structures will be thoroughly covered in Chapter 7, but a short discussion of the operators used with them is given here.

The dot operator is used when operating on the actual structure or union. The arrow operator is used when a pointer to a structure or union is used. Suppose you were given the structure

```
struct employee {
  char name[80];
  int age;
  float wage;
} emp;

struct tom *p = &emp; /* address of emp into p */
```

To assign the value 123.23 to element **wage** of structure **emp**, you would write

```
emp.wage = 123.23;
```

However, the same assignment using a pointer to structure **emp** would be

```
p->wage = 123.23;
```

There is a very important difference between older versions of C and Turbo C in regard to the way they pass structures and unions to functions. It is important to understand this difference if you will be porting your code to a great many environments. In the older approach, only a pointer to a structure or union is actually passed to a function. (Notice that this is an exception to C's call-by-value method of parameter passing.) However, as specified by the ANSI standard, the entire structure or union is actually passed, making it consistent with the way other types of arguments are passed to functions. Since Turbo C follows the ANSI standard, it uses the latter approach.

[ ] and ( )

In C, parentheses do the expected job of increasing the precedence of the operations inside of them.

Square brackets perform array indexing, and will be discussed fully in Chapter 5. Simply, given an array, the expression within the square brackets provides an index into that array. For example,

```
#include <stdio.h>

char s[80];

main(void)
{
    s[3]='X';
    printf("%c", s[3]);

    return 0;
}
```

first assigns the value **'X'** to the fourth element (remember, all arrays in C begin at 0) of array **s**, and then prints that element.

Precedence Summary

Table 2-11 lists the precedence of all C operators. Note that all operators, except the unary operators and **?**, associate from left to right. The unary operators, *****, **&**, **−**, and **?** associate from right to left.

Expressions

Operators, constants, and variables are the constituents of *expressions*. An expression in C is any valid combination of those pieces. Because most expressions tend to follow the general rules of algebra, they are often taken for granted. However, there are a few aspects of expressions that relate to C specifically and will be discussed here.

Type Conversion in Expressions

When constants and variables of different types are mixed in an expression, they are converted to the same type. The compiler will convert all operands "up" to the type

Highest	() [] –> .
	! ~ ++ –– – (type) * & sizeof
	* / %
	+ –
	<< >>
	< <= > >=
	== !=
	&
	^
	|
	&&
	||
	?
	= += –= *= /=
Lowest	,

Table 2-11. *Precedence of C Operators*

of the largest operand. This is done on an operation-by-operation basis as described in the following type conversion rules:

1. All **char**s and **short int**s are converted to **int**s. All **float**s are converted to **double**s.

2. For all operand pairs, if one of the operands is a **long double**, the other operand is converted to **long double**.

   Otherwise, if one of the operands is **double**, the other operand is converted to **double**.

   Otherwise, if one of the operands is **long**, the other operand is converted to **long**.

   Otherwise, if one of the operands is **unsigned**, the other operand is converted to **unsigned**.

Once these conversion rules have been applied, each pair of operands will be of the same type and the result of each operation will be the same as the type of both operands. Please note that the second rule has several conditions that must be applied in sequence.

For example, consider the type conversions that occur in Figure 2-1.

First, the character **ch** is converted to an integer and **float f** is converted to **double**. Then the outcome of **ch/i** is converted to a **double** because **f*d** is **double**. The final result is **double** because, by this time, both operands are **double**.

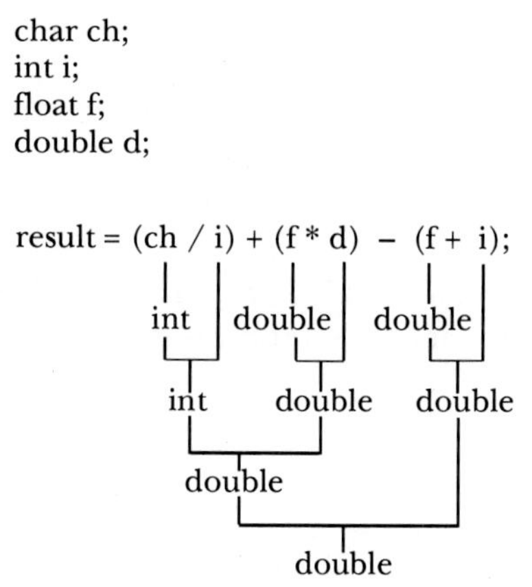
char ch;
int i;
float f;
double d;
result = (ch / i) + (f * d) – (f + i);
int
double
double
int
double
double
double
double

Figure 2-1. *An example of type conversion*

Casts

It is possible to force an expression to be of a specific type by using a construct called a *cast.* The general form of a cast is:

(type) expression

where *type* is one of the standard C data types or a user-defined type. For example, if you wished to make the expression **x/2** be evaluated to type **float** you could write it:

```
(float) x/2
```

Casts are often considered operators. As an operator, a cast is unary and has the same precedence as any other unary operator.

Although casts are not usually used a great deal in programming, there are times when they can be very useful. For example, suppose you wish to use an integer for loop control, yet perform computation on it requiring a fractional part, as in the following program:

```
#include <stdio.h>

/* Print i and i/2 with fractions. */
main(void)
{
```

```
    int i;

    for(i=1; i<=100; ++i )
      printf("%d / 2 is: %f", i, (float) i/2);
    return 0;
}
```

Without the cast (**float**), only an integer division would have been performed; but the cast ensures that the fractional part of the answer will be displayed on the screen.

Spacing and Parentheses

To aid readability, an expression in Turbo C may have tabs and spaces in it at your discretion. For example, the following two expressions are the same.

```
x=10/y~(127/x);
```

```
x = 10 / y ~(127/x);
```

Use of redundant or additional parentheses does not cause errors or slow down the execution of the expression. You are encouraged to use parentheses to clarify the exact order of evaluation, both for yourself and for others who may have to read your program later. For example, which of the following two expressions is easier to read?

```
x=y/3-34*temp&127;
```

```
x=(y/3) - (34*(temp & 127));
```

C Shorthand

C has a special shorthand that simplifies the coding of a certain type of assignment statement. For example

```
x = x+10;
```

can be written, in C shorthand, as

```
x += 10;
```

The operator pair **+=** tells the compiler to assign to **x** the value of **x** plus 10.

This shorthand works for all the binary operators in C (those that require two operands). The general form of the shorthand

var = var operator expression;

is the same as

var operator = expression;

For another example,

```
x = x-100;
```

is the same as

```
x -= 100;
```

You will see shorthand notation used widely in professionally written C programs and you should become familiar with it.

Chapter *3*

Program Control Statements

This chapter discusses C's rich and varied program control statements. These include the loop constructs **while**, **for**, and **do/while**; the **if** and **switch** conditional statements; and the **break**, **continue**, and **goto** statements. (Although the **return** statement technically affects program control, its discussion is deferred until the following chapter on functions.) The **exit( )** function is discussed here because it also can affect the flow of a program.

True and False in C

Most program control statements in any computer language, including C, rely on a conditional test that determines what course of action is to be taken. The conditional test produces either a true or false value. Unlike many other computer languages that specify special values for true and false, a true value in C is any nonzero value, including negative numbers. A false value is zero. This approach to true and false is implemented in C primarily because it allows a wide range of routines to be coded very efficiently.

C Statements

According to the C syntax, a statement can consist of one of the following: a single statement, a block of statements, or nothing (in the case of empty statements). In the descriptions presented here, the term *statement* is used to mean all three of these possibilities.

Conditional Statements

C supports two types of conditional statements: **if** and **switch**. In addition, the **?** operator is an alternative to the **if** in certain circumstances.

if

The general form of the **if** statement is

```
if(expression) statement;
else statement;
```

where *statement* may be either a single statement or a block of statements. (Remember that in C a *block* is a group of statements surrounded by braces.) The **else** clause is optional.

The general form of the **if** with blocks of statements is

```
if(expression) {
 statement sequence
}
else {
 statement sequence
}
```

If the expression is true (anything other than 0), the statement or block that forms the target of the **if** is executed; otherwise, the statement or block that is the target of the **else** is executed. Remember, only the code associated with the **if** or the code that is associated with the **else** executes, never both.

For example, consider the following program, which plays a very simple version of "guess the magic number" game. It prints the message "** Right **" when the player guesses the magic number.

```
#include <stdio.h>

/* Magic number program. */
main(void)
{
  int magic = 123;   /* magic number */
  int guess;

  printf("Enter your guess: ");
  scanf("%d", &guess);

  if(guess == magic) printf("** Right **");

  return 0;
}
```

This program uses the equality operator to determine whether the player's guess matches the magic number. If it does, the message is printed on the screen.

Taking the magic number program further, the next version illustrates the use of the **else** statement to print a message when the wrong number is tried.

```
#include <stdio.h>

/* Magic number program - improvement 1. */
main(void)
{
  int magic = 123;   /* magic number */
  int guess;

  printf("Enter your guess: ");
  scanf("%d",&guess);

  if(guess == magic) printf("** Right **");
  else printf(".. Wrong ..");

  return 0;
}
```

Nested ifs

One of the most confusing aspects of **if** statements in any programming language is nested ifs. A *nested if* is an **if** statement that is the object of either an **if** or **else**. The reason that nested **ifs** are so troublesome is that it can be difficult to know what **else** associates with what **if**. For example:

```
if(x)
  if(y) printf("1");
  else printf("2");
```

To which **if** does the **else** refer?

Fortunately, C provides a very simple rule for resolving this type of situation. In C, the **else** is linked to the closest preceding **if** that does not already have an **else** statement associated with it. In this case, the **else** is associated with the **if(y)** statement. To make the **else** associate with the **if(x)** you must use braces to override its normal association, as shown here:

```
if(x) {
  if(y) printf("1");
}
else printf("2");
```

The **else** is now associated with the **if(x)** because it is no longer part of the **if(y)** object block. Because of C's scope rules, the **else** now has no knowledge of the **if(y)** statement because they are no longer in the same block of code.

A further improvement to the magic number program provides the player with feedback on how close each guess is. This is accomplished by the use of a nested **if**.

```
#include <stdio.h>

/* Magic number program - improvement 2. */
main(void)
{
  int magic = 123;  /* magic number */
  int guess;

  printf("Enter your guess: ");
  scanf("%d", &guess);

  if(guess == magic) {
    printf("** Right ** ");
    printf("%d is the magic number", magic);
  }
  else {
    printf(".. Wrong .. ");
    if(guess > magic) printf("Too high");
    else printf("Too low");
  }
  return 0;
}
```

The if-else-if Ladder

A common programming construct is the *if-else-if ladder.* It looks like this:

if (*expression*)
  statement;
else if (*expression*)
  statement;
else if (*expression*)
  statement;
  .
  .
  .
else
  statement;

The conditions are evaluated from the top downward. As soon as a true condition is found, the statement associated with it is executed, and the rest of the ladder is bypassed. If none of the conditions are true, the final **else** is executed. The final **else** often acts as a *default condition;* that is, if all other conditional tests fail, the last **else** statement is performed. If the final **else** is not present, then no action takes place if all other conditions are false.

Using an if-else-if ladder, the magic number program becomes

```
#include <stdio.h>

/* Magic number program - improvement 3. */
main(void)
{
  int magic = 123;  /* magic number */
  int guess;

  printf("Enter your guess: ");
  scanf("%d", &guess);

  if(guess == magic) {
    printf("** Right ** ");
    printf("%d is the magic number", magic);
  }
  else if(guess > magic)
    printf(".. Wrong .. Too High");
  else printf(".. Wrong .. Too low");

  return 0;
}
```

The ? Alternative

The **?** operator can be used to replace **if/else** statements of the general form:

if(*condition*)
  expression
else
  expression

The key restriction is that the target of both the **if** and the **else** must be a single expression—not another C statement.

The **?** is called a *ternary operator* because it requires three operands and takes the general form

Exp1 ? *Exp2* : *Exp3*

where *Exp1*, *Exp2*, and *Exp3* are expressions. Notice the use and placement of the colon.

The value of an **?** expression is determined as follows. *Exp1* is evaluated. If it is true, then *Exp2* is evaluated and becomes the value of the entire **?** expression. If *Exp1* is false, then *Exp3* is evaluated and its value becomes the value of the expression. For example:

```
x = 10;

y = x>9 ? 100 : 200;
```

In this example, **y** is assigned the value 100. If **x** had been less than or equal to 9, **y** would have received the value 200. The same code written using the **if/else** statement would be

```
 x = 10;

if(x>9) y = 100;
else y = 200;
```

The use of the **?** operator to replace **if/else** statements is not restricted to assignments. Remember that all functions (except those declared as **void**) can return a value. Hence, it is permissible to use one or more function calls in a C expression. When the function's name is encountered, the function is, of course, executed so that its return value can be determined. Therefore, it is possible to execute one or more function calls using the **?** operator by placing them in the expressions that form the operands.

For example:

```
#include <stdio.h>

int f1(int n), f2(void);

main(void)
{
  int t;

  printf(": ");
  scanf("%d", &t);
  /* print proper message */
  t ? f1(t)+f2() : printf("zero entered");

}

f1(int n)
{
  printf("%d ",n);
  return 0;
}

f2(void)
{
  printf("entered");
  return 0;
}
```

In this simple example, if you enter a 0, the **printf( )** function is called and the "zero entered" message appears. If you enter any other number, then both **f1( )** and **f2( )** are executed. It is important to note that the value of the **?** expression is discarded in this example; it is not necessary to assign it to anything. Even though neither **f1( )** nor **f2( )** returns a meaningful value, they cannot be defined as returning **void** because doing so prevents their use in an expression. Therefore, the functions default to returning a 0.

Using the **?** operator, it is possible to rewrite the magic number program again as shown here:

```
#include <stdio.h>

/* Magic number program - improvement 4. */
main(void)
{
```

```
int magic = 123;  /* magic number */
int guess;

printf("Enter your guess: ");
scanf("%d", &guess);
if(guess == magic) {
  printf("** Right ** ");
  printf("%d is the magic number", magic);
}
else
  guess > magic ? printf("High") : printf("Low");

return 0;
}
```

Here, the **?** operator causes the proper message to be displayed based on the outcome of the test guess>magic.

switch

Although the if-else-if ladder can perform multiway tests, it is hardly elegant. The code can be very hard to follow and can confuse even its author at a later date. For these reasons, C has a built-in multiple-branch decision statement called **switch**. A variable is successively tested against a list of integer or character constants. When a match is found, a statement or block of statements is executed. The general form of the **switch** statement is

switch(*variable*) {
   case *constant1:*
   statement sequence
    break;
   case *constant2:*
   statement sequence
    break;
   case *constant3:*
   statement sequence
    break;
   .
   .
   .
   default:
   statement sequence
}

where the **default** statement is executed if no matches are found. The **default** is optional and, if not present, no action takes place if all matches fail. When a match is found, the statement associated with that **case** is executed until the **break** statement is reached or, in the case of the **default** (or last **case** if no **default** is present), the end of the **switch** statement is encountered.

There are three important things to know about the **switch** statement:

1. The **switch** differs from the **if** in that **switch** can only test for equality whereas the **if** can evaluate a relational or logical expression.

2. No two **case** constants in the same **switch** can have identical values. Of course, a **switch** statement enclosed by an outer **switch** may have **case** constants that are the same.

3. If character constants are used in the **switch**, they are automatically converted to their integer values.

The **switch** statement is often used to process keyboard commands, such as menu selection. As shown here, the function **menu( )** displays a menu for a spelling checker program and calls the proper procedures:

```
void menu(void)
{
  char ch;

  printf("1. Check Spelling\n");
  printf("2. Correct Spelling Errors\n");
  printf("3. Display Spelling Errors\n");
  printf("Strike Any Other Key to Skip\n");
  printf("     Enter your choice: ");

  ch = getche();  /* read the selection from
                     the keyboard */

  switch(ch) {
    case '1':
      check_spelling();
      break;
    case '2':
      correct_errors();
      break;
    case '3':
      display_errors();
      break;
    default :
```

```
        printf("No option selected");
    }
}
```

Technically, the **break** statements are optional inside the **switch** statement. They are used to terminate the statement sequence associated with each constant. If the **break** statement is omitted, execution continues into the next **case**'s statements until either a **break** or the end of the **switch** is reached. You can think of the **case**s as labels. Execution starts at the label that matches and continues until a **break** statement is found, or the **switch** ends. For example, the function shown here makes use of the "drop through" nature of the **case**s to simplify the code for a device driver input handler:

```
void inp_handler(void)
{
  int ch, flag;

  ch = read_device(); /* read some sort of device */
  flag = -1;

  switch(ch) {
    case 1:  /* these cases have common statement */
    case 2:  /* sequences */
    case 3:
      flag = 0;
      break;
    case 4:
      flag = 1;
    case 5:
      error(flag);
      break;
    default:
      process(ch);
  }
}
```

This routine illustrates two facets of the **switch** statement. First, you can have empty conditions. In this case, the first three constants all execute the same statements:

```
flag = 0;
break;
```

Second, execution continues into the next **case** if no **break** statement is present. If **ch** matches 4, **flag** is set to 1 and, because there is no **break** statement, execution continues and the statement **error(flag)** is executed. In this case, **flag** has the value 1. If **ch** had matched 5, **error(flag)** would have been called with a **flag** value of −1. The ability to run **cases** together when no **break** is present enables you to create very efficient code because it prevents the unwarranted duplication of code.

It is important to understand that the statements associated with each label are not code blocks but rather *statement sequences*. (Of course, the entire **switch** statement defines a block.) This technical distinction is important only in certain special situations. For example, the following code fragment is in error and will not even compile because it is not possible to declare a variable in a statement sequence:

```
/* This is incorrect. */
switch(c) {
  case 1:
    int t;
    .
    .
    .
```

However, a variable could be added as shown here:

```
/* This is correct. */
switch(c) {
  int t;
  case 1:
    .
    .
    .
```

Of course, it is possible to create a block of code as one of the statements in a sequence and declare a variable within it as shown here:

```
/* This is also correct. */
switch(c) {
  case 1:
    if(1) { /* always true, used to create block */
      int t;
      .
      .
      .
    }
    .
    .
    .
```

Nested switch Statements

It is possible to have a **switch** as part of the statement sequence of an outer **switch**. Even if the **case** constants of the inner and outer **switch** contain common values, no conflicts will arise. For example, the following code fragment is perfectly acceptable:

```
switch(x) {
  case 1:
    switch(y) {
      case 0: printf("divide by zero error");
              break;
      case 1: process(x,y);
    }
    break;
  case 2:
    .
    .
    .
```

Loops

In C, and all other modern programming languages, loops allow a set of instructions to be performed until a certain condition is reached. This condition may be predefined as in the **for** loop, or open-ended as in the **while** and **do** loops.

for

The general format of C's **for** loop is probably familiar to you because it is found in one form or another in all procedural programming languages. However, in C it has unexpected flexibility and power.

The general form of the **for** statement is

for(*initialization; condition; increment*) *statement;*

The **for** statement allows many variants, but there are three main parts:

1. The *initialization* is usually an assignment statement that is used to set the loop control variable.

2. The *condition* is a relational expression that determines when the loop will exit.

3. The *increment* defines how the loop control variable will change each time the loop is repeated.

These three major sections must be separated by semicolons. The **for** loop continues to execute as long as the condition is true. Once the condition becomes false, program execution resumes on the statement following the **for** loop.

For a simple example, the following program prints the numbers 1 through 100 on the terminal:

```
#include <stdio.h>

main(void)
{
  int x;

  for(x=1; x<=100; x++) printf("%d ", x);

  return 0;
}
```

In the program, **x** is initially set to 1. Since **x** is less than 100, **printf( )** is called, **x** is increased by 1, and **x** is tested to see if it is still less than or equal to 100. This process repeats until **x** is greater than 100, at which point the loop terminates. In this example, **x** is the loop *control variable,* which is changed and checked each time the loop repeats.

Here is an example of a **for** loop that contains multiple statements:

```
for(x=100; x!=65; x-=5) {
  z = sqrt(x);
  printf("The square root of %d, %f", x, z);
}
```

Both the **sqrt( )** and **printf( )** calls are executed until **x** equals 65. Note that the loop is *negative running*: **x** was initialized to 100, and 5 is subtracted from it each time the loop repeats.

An important point about **for** loops is that the conditional test is always performed at the top of the loop. This means that the code inside the loop may not be executed at all if the condition is false to begin with. For example:

```
x = 10;

for(y=10; y!=x; ++y) printf("%d", y);

printf("%d", y);
```

This loop never executes because **x** and **y** are in fact equal when the loop is entered. Because the conditional expression is false, neither the body of the loop nor the increment portion of the loop is executed. Hence, **y** still has the value 10 assigned to it, and the output is only the number 10 printed once on the screen.

for Loop Variations

The preceding discussion described the most common form of the **for** loop. However, several variations are allowed that increase its power, flexibility, and applicability to certain programming situations.

One of the most common variations is achieved by using the comma operator to allow two or more variables to control the loop. (You should recall that the comma operator is used to string together a number of expressions in a sort of "do this and this" fashion. It is described in Chapter 2.) For example, this loop uses the variables **x** and **y** to control the loop, with both variables being initialized inside the **for** statement.

```
for(x=0, y=0; x+y<10; ++x) {
  scanf("%d", &y);
    .
    .
    .
}
```

Here, commas separate the two initialization statements. Each time **x** is incremented the loop repeats, and **y**'s value is set by keyboard input. Both **x** and **y** must be at the correct value for the loop to terminate. It is necessary to initialize **y** to 0 so that its value is defined prior to the first evaluation of the conditional expression. If **y** were not defined it might, by chance or earlier program usage, contain a 10, thereby making the conditional test false and preventing the loop from executing.

Another example of using multiple loop-control variables is found in the **reverse( )** function shown here. The purpose of **reverse( )** is to copy the contents of the first string argument back-to-front into the second string argument. For example, if it is called with "hello" in **s**, upon completion, **r** contains "olleh."

```
/* Copy s into r backwards. */
void reverse(char *s, char *r)
{
  int i, j;

  for(i=strlen(s)-1, j=0; i>=0; j++,i--) r[i] = s[j];
  r[j] = '\0'; /* append null terminator */
}
```

The conditional expression does not necessarily involve simply testing the loop control variable against some target value. In fact, the condition may be any relational or logical statement. This means that you can test for several possible terminating conditions. For example, this function could be used to log a user onto a remote system. The user is given three tries to enter the password. The loop terminates when either the three tries are used up or the correct password is entered.

```c
void sign_on(void)
{
  char str[20];
  int x;

  for(x=0; x<3 && strcmp(str,"password"); ++x) {
    printf("enter password please:");
    gets(str);
  }
  if(x==3) hang_up();
}
```

Remember, **strcmp( )** is a standard library function that compares two strings and returns 0 if they match.

Another interesting variation of the **for** loop is created by remembering that each of the three sections of the **for** may consist of any valid C expression. They need not actually have anything to do with what the sections are usually used for. With this in mind, consider the following example:

```c
#include <stdio.h>

int readnum(void), prompt(void);
int sqrnum(int num);

main(void)
{
  int t;

  for(prompt(); t=readnum(); prompt()) sqrnum(t);
  return 0;
}

prompt(void)
{
  printf(": ");
  return 0;
}
```

```
readnum(void)
{
  int t;

  scanf("%d", &t);
  return t;
}

sqrnum(int num)
{
  printf("%d\n", num*num);
  return 0;
}
```

If you look closely at the **for** loop in **main( )**, you will see that each part of the **for** comprises function calls that prompt the user and read a number entered from the keyboard. If the number entered is 0, the loop terminates because the conditional expression is false; otherwise the number is squared. Thus, in this **for** loop the initialization and increment portions are used in a nontraditional, but completely valid sense.

Another interesting trait of the **for** loop is that pieces of the loop definition need not be there. In fact, there need not be an expression present for any of the sections; they are optional. For example, this loop runs until 123 is entered:

```
for(x=0; x!=123; ) scanf("%d", &x);
```

Notice that the increment portion of the **for** definition is blank. This means that each time the loop repeats, **x** is tested to see if it equals 123, but no further action takes place. If, however, you type 123 at the keyboard, the loop condition becomes false and the loop terminates.

It is not uncommon to see the initialization occur outside the **for** statement. This most frequently happens when the initial condition of the loop control variable must be computed by some complex means. For example:

```
gets(s);  /* read a string into s */
if(*s) x = strlen(s); /* get the string's length */

for( ;x<10; ) {
  printf("%d", x);
  ++x;
}
```

Here, the initialization section has been left blank and **x** is initialized before the loop is entered.

The Infinite Loop

One of the most interesting uses of the **for** loop is the creation of the infinite loop. Since none of the three expressions that form the **for** loop are required, it is possible to make an endless loop by leaving the conditional expression empty. For example:

```
for(;;) printf(" this loop will run forever.\n");
```

Although you may have an initialization and increment expression it is more common among C programmers to use the **for(;;)** with no expressions to signify an infinite loop.[1]

Actually, the **for(;;)** construct does not necessarily create an infinite loop because C's **break** statement, when encountered anywhere inside the body of a loop, causes immediate termination of the loop. (The **break** statement is discussed later in this chapter.) Program control then picks up at the code following the loop, as shown here:

```
ch = '\0';

for(;;) {
  ch = getchar();  /* get a character */
  if(ch=='A') break;  /* exit the loop */
}

printf("you typed an A");
```

This loop will run until A is typed at the keyboard.

for Loops with No Bodies

A statement, as defined by the C syntax, may be empty. This means that the body of the **for** (or any other loop) may also be empty. This fact can be used to improve the efficiency of certain algorithms as well as to create time delay loops.

One of the most common tasks to occur in programming is the removal of spaces from an input stream. For example, a database may allow a query such as "show all balances less than 400." The database needs to have each word of the query fed to it

---

[1] There is a small, but persistent, group of C programmers who use the **while(1)** method of creating an infinite loop. They both work equally well. The **for(;;)** method is recommended only because it is the more common form.

separately, without spaces. That is, the database input processor recognizes "show" but not " show" as a command. The following loop removes any leading spaces from the stream pointed to by **str**:

```
for( ; *str==' '; str++) ;
```

As you can see, there is no body to this loop—and no need for one either.

Time delay loops are often used in programs. The following shows how to create one using **for**:

```
for(t=0; t<SOME_VALUE; t++) ;
```

while

The second loop available in C is the **while**. The general form is

while(*condition*) *statement;*

where *statement,* as stated earlier, is either an empty statement, a single statement, or a block of statements that is to be repeated. The *condition* may be any expression, with true being any nonzero value. The loop iterates while the condition is true. When the condition becomes false, program control passes to the line after the loop code.

The following example shows a keyboard input routine that simply loops until A is pressed:

```
void wait_for_char(void)
{
  char ch;

  ch = '\0';  /* initialize ch */
  while(ch!='A')  ch = getchar();
}
```

First, **ch** is initialized to null. The **while** loop then begins by checking to see if **ch** is not equal to 'A'. Because **ch** was initialized to null beforehand, the test is true and the loop begins. Each time a key is pressed on the keyboard, the test is tried again. Once an 'A' is input, the condition becomes false because **ch** equals 'A', and the loop terminates.

As with the **for** loop, **while** loops check the test condition at the top of the loop, which means that the loop code may not execute at all. This eliminates having to perform a separate conditional test before the loop. A good illustration of this is the function **pad( )**, which adds spaces to the end of a string up to a predefined length. If the string is already at the desired length, no spaces will be added.

```
/* Add spaces to the end of a string. */
void pad(char *s, int length)
{
  int l;
  l = strlen(s);  /* find out how long it is */

  while(l<length) {
    s[l] = ' ';    /* insert a space */
    l++;
  }

  s[l] = '\0';  /* strings need to be
                    terminated in a null */
}
```

The two arguments to **pad( )** are **s**, a pointer to the string to lengthen, and **length**, the number of characters that **s** will be lengthened to. If the string **s** is already equal to or greater than **length**, the code inside the **while** loop never executes. If **s** is less than **length**, **pad( )** adds the required number of spaces to the string. The **strlen( )** function, which is part of the standard library, returns the length of the string.

Where several separate conditions may be needed to terminate a **while** loop, it is common to have only a single variable forming the conditional expression with the value of this variable being set at various points throughout the loop. For example:

```
void func1(void)
{
  int working;

  working = 1;   /* i.e., true */

  while(working) {
    working=process1();
    if(working)
      working=process2();
    if(working)
      working=process3();
  }
}
```

Here, any of the three routines may return false and cause the loop to exit.

There need not be any statements at all in the body of the **while** loop. For example,

```
while((ch=getchar()) != 'A') ;
```

simply loops until A is typed at the keyboard. If you feel uncomfortable with the assignment inside the **while** conditional expression, remember that the equal sign is really just an operator that evaluates to the value of the right-hand operand.

do/while

Unlike the **for** and **while** loops that test the loop condition at the top of the loop, the **do/while** loop checks its condition at the bottom of the loop. This means that a **do/while** loop always executes at least once. The general form of the **do/while** loop is

```
do {
  statement sequence;
} while(condition);
```

Although the braces are not necessary when only one statement is present, they are usually used to improve readability and avoid confusion (to the reader, not the compiler) with the **while**.

This **do/while** reads numbers from the keyboard until one is less than or equal to 100.

```
do {
  scanf("%d", &num);
} while(num>100);
```

Perhaps the most common use of the **do/while** is in a menu selection routine. When a valid response is typed it is returned as the value of the function. Invalid responses cause a reprompt. The following shows an improved version of the spelling checker menu that was developed earlier in this chapter:

```
void menu(void)
{
  char ch;

  printf("1. Check Spelling\n");
  printf("2. Correct Spelling Errors\n");
  printf("3. Display Spelling Errors\n");
  printf("    Enter your choice: ");

  do {
    ch = getche();  /* read the selection from
                       the keyboard */
```

```
     switch(ch) {
       case '1':
         check_spelling();
         break;
       case '2':
         correct_errors();
         break;
       case '3':
         display_errors();
         break;
     }
   } while(ch!='1' && ch!='2' && ch!='3');
 }
```

In the case of a menu function, you always want it to execute at least once. After the options have been displayed, the program loops until a valid option is selected.

break

The **break** statement has two uses. The first is to terminate a **case** in the **switch** statement, and is covered earlier in this chapter in the section on the **switch**. The second use is to force immediate termination of a loop, bypassing the normal loop conditional test. This use is examined here.

When the **break** statement is encountered inside a loop, the loop is immediately terminated and program control resumes at the next statement following the loop. For example:

```
#include <stdio.h>

main(void)
{
  int t;

  for(t=0; t<100; t++) {
    printf("%d ", t);
    if(t==10) break;
  }
  return 0;
}
```

This prints the numbers 0 through 10 on the screen and then terminates because the **break** causes immediate exit from the loop, overriding the conditional test **t<100** built into the loop.

The **break** statement is commonly used in loops in which a special condition can cause immediate termination. For example, here a keypress can stop the execution of the **look_up( )** routine:

```
look_up(char *name)
{
  char tname[40];
  int loc;

  loc = -1;
  do {
    loc = read_next_name(tname);
    if(kbhit()) break;
  } while(!strcmp(tname, name));
  return loc;
}
```

You might use a function like this to find a name in a database file. If the file is very long and you are tired of waiting, you could strike a key and return from the function early. The **kbhit( )** function returns 0 if no key has been hit; non-0 otherwise.

A **break** will cause an exit from only the innermost loop. For example,

```
for(t=0; t<100; +=t) {
  count = 1;
  for(;;) {
    printf("%d ", count);
    count++;
    if(count==10) break;
  }
}
```

prints the numbers 1 through 10 on the screen 100 times. Each time the **break** is encountered, control is passed back to the outer **for** loop.

A **break** used in a **switch** statement affects only that **switch** and not any loop the **switch** happens to be in.

exit( )

The function **exit( )**, which is found in the standard library, causes immediate termination of the entire program. Because the **exit( )** function stops program execution and forces a return to the operating system, its use is somewhat specific as a program control device, yet a great many C programs rely on it. The **exit( )** function has this general form:

```
void exit(int status);
```

It uses the **stdlib.h** header file. The value of *status* is returned to the operating system.

   exit( ) is traditionally called with an argument of 0 to indicate that termination is normal. Other arguments are used to indicate some sort of error that a higher-level process will be able to access.

   A common use of **exit( )** occurs when a mandatory condition for the program's execution is not satisfied. For example, imagine a computer game in which a color graphics card must be present in the system. The **main( )** function of this game might look like this:

```c
#include <stdlib.h>

main(void)
{
  if(!color_card()) exit(1);
  play();
  return 0;
}
```

where **color_card( )** is a user-defined function that returns true if the color card is present. If the card is not in the system, **color_card( )** returns false and the program terminates.

   As another example, **exit( )** is used by this version of **menu( )** to quit the program and return to the operating system:

```c
void menu(void)
{
  char ch;

  printf("1. Check Spelling\n");
  printf("2. Correct Spelling Errors\n");
  printf("3. Display Spelling Errors\n");
  printf("4. Quit\n");
  printf("    Enter your choice: ");

  do {
    ch = getchar();  /* read the selection from
                        the keyboard */
    switch(ch) {
      case '1':
        check_spelling();
        break;
```

```
      case '2':
        correct_errors();
        break;
      case '3':
        display_errors();
        break;
      case '4':
        exit(0);   /* return to OS */
    }
  } while(ch!='1' && ch!='2' && ch!='3');
}
```

continue

The **continue** statement works somewhat like the **break** statement. But, instead of forcing termination, **continue** forces the next iteration of the loop to take place, skipping any code in between. For example, the following routine displays only positive numbers:

```
do {
  scanf("%d", &num);
  if(x<0) continue;
  printf("%d ", x);
} while(x!=100);
```

In **while** and **do/while** loops, a **continue** statement causes control to go directly to the conditional test and then continue the looping process. In the case of the **for**, first the increment part of the loop is performed, next the conditional test is executed, and finally the loop continues. The previous example could be changed to allow only 100 numbers to be printed, as shown here:

```
for(t=0; t<100; ++t) {
  scanf("%d", &num);
  if(x<0) continue;
  printf("%d ", x);
}
```

In the following example, **continue** is used to expedite the exit from a loop by forcing the conditional test to be performed sooner:

```
void code(void)
{
  char done, ch;
```

```
    done = 0;
    while(!done) {
      ch = getchar();
      if(ch=='$') {
        done = 1;
        continue;
      }
      putchar(ch+1);   /* shift the alphabet one
                          position */
    }
  }
```

You could use this function to code a message by shifting all characters one letter higher; for example, 'a' would become 'b'. The function terminates when a '$' is read, and no further output occurs because the conditional test, brought into effect by **continue**, finds **done** to be true and causes the loop to exit.

Labels and goto

Although **goto** fell out of favor some years ago, it has managed to polish its tarnished image a bit. This book will not judge its validity as a form of program control. It should be stated, however, that there are no programming situations that require its use; it is a convenience which, if used wisely, can be beneficial in certain programming situations. As such, **goto** is not used extensively in this book outside of this section. (In a language like C, which has a rich set of control structures and allows additional control using **break** and **continue**, there is little need for it.) The chief concern most programmers have about the **goto** is its tendency to confuse a program and render it nearly unreadable. However, there are times when the use of the **goto** actually clarifies program flow rather than confuses it.

The **goto** requires a label for operation. A *label* is a valid C identifier followed by a colon. The label must be in the same function as the **goto** that uses it. For example, a loop from 1 to 100 could be written using a **goto** and a label as shown here:

```
x = 1;

loop1:
  x++;
  if(x<100) goto loop1;
```

One good use for the **goto** is to exit from several layers of nesting. For example:

```
for(...) {
  for(...) {
    while(...) {
      if(...) goto stop;
         .

         .

         .

    }
  }
}
stop:
  printf("error in program\n");
```

Eliminating the **goto** would force a number of additional tests to be performed. A simple **break** statement would not work here because it would only exit from the innermost loop. If you substituted checks at each loop, the code would then look like this:

```
done = 0;
for(...) {
  for(...) {
    while(...) {
      if(...) {
        done = 1;
        break;
      }
         .

         .

         .

    }
    if(done) break;
  }
  if(done) break;
}
```

You should use the **goto** sparingly, if at all. But if the code would be much more difficult to read or if execution speed of the code is critical, by all means use the **goto**.

Chapter **4**

Functions

Functions are the building blocks of C in which all program activity occurs. The general form of a function is

type-specifier function_name(parameter list)
{
    body of the function
}

The *type-specifier* specifies the type of value that the function returns using the **return** statement. It can be any valid type. If no type is specified, the function is assumed to return an integer result. The parameter list is a comma-separated list of variables that receive the values of the arguments when the function is called. A function may be without parameters, in which case the parameter list contains only the keyword **void**.

The return Statement

The **return** statement has two important uses. First, it causes an immediate exit from the function it is in. That is, it causes program execution to return to the calling code. Second, it can be used to return a value. Both of these uses are examined here.

Returning from a Function

There are two ways that a function terminates execution and returns to the caller. One way is when the last statement in the function has executed and, conceptually, the function's ending } is encountered. (Of course, the curly brace isn't actually present in the object code, but you can think of it in this way.) For example, this function simply prints a string backward on the screen:

```
void pr_reverse(char *s)
{
  register int t;

  for(t=strlen(s)-1; t>-1; t--) printf("%c", s[t]);
}
```

Once the string has been displayed, there is nothing left for the function to do, so it returns to the place it was called from.

However, not many functions use this default method of terminating their execution. Most functions rely on the **return** statement to stop execution either because a value must be returned or to simplify a function's code and make it more efficient by allowing multiple exit points. It is important to remember that a function may have several **return** statements in it. For example, the function shown here returns either the index of the first occurrence of the substring pointed to by **s1** within the string pointed to by **s2** or −1 if no match is found:

```
find_substr(char *s1, char *s2)
{
  register int t;
  char *p, *p2;

  for(t=0; s1[t]; t++) {
    p = &s1[t];
    p2 = s2;
    while(*p2 && *p2==*p) {
      p++;
      p2++;
    }
    if(!*p2) return t;
  }
  return -1;
}
```

Notice how the two **return** statements help simplify this function.

Return Values

All functions, except those of type **void**, return a value. This value is explicitly specified by the **return** statement. If a function is not specified as **void** and if no return value is specified, then an unknown garbage value is returned. As long as a function is not declared as **void** it can be used as an operand in any valid C expression. Therefore, each of the following expressions is valid in Turbo C:

```
x = power(y);

if(max(x, y) > 100) printf("greater");

for(ch=getchar(); isdigit(ch); ) ... ;
```

However, a function cannot be the target of an assignment. A statement such as

```
swap(x, y) = 100;    /* incorrect statement */
```

is wrong. Turbo C will flag it as an error and not compile a program that contains a statement like this.

Keep in mind that if a function is declared as **void** it cannot be used in any expression. For example, assume that **f( )** is declared as **void**. The following statements will not compile:

```
int t;

t = f();  /* no value to assign to t */

f()+f();  /* no value to add */
```

Although all functions not of type **void** have return values, when you write programs you generally use three types of functions. The first is simply computational. It is designed specifically to perform operations on its arguments and return a value based on that operation—it is essentially a "pure" function. Examples of this sort of function are the standard library functions **sqr( )** and **sin( )**.

The second type of function manipulates information and returns a value that simply indicates the success or failure of that manipulation. An example is **fwrite( )**, which is used to write information to a disk file. If the write operation is successful, **fwrite( )** returns the number of items successfully written. If an error occurs, the number returned is not equal to the number of items it was requested to write.

The last type of function has no explicit return value. In essence, the function is strictly procedural and produces no value. An example is **srand( )**, which is used to initialize the random-number-generating function **rand( )**. Sometimes, functions that don't produce an interesting result often return something anyway. For example,

printf( ) returns the number of characters written. It would be very unusual to find a program that actually checked this. Therefore, although all functions, except those of type **void**, return values, you don't necessarily have to use them for anything. A very common question concerning function return values is, "Don't I have to assign this value to some variable since a value is being returned?" The answer is no. If there is no assignment specified, then the return value is simply discarded. Consider the following program, which uses **mul( )**:

```
#include <stdio.h>

mul(int a, int b);

main(void)
{
  int x, y, z;

  x = 10;   y = 20;
  z = mul(x, y);             /* 1 */
  printf("%d", mul(x, y));   /* 2 */
  mul(x, y);                 /* 3 */

  return 0;
}

mul(int a, int b)
{
  return a*b;
}
```

Line 1 assigns the return value of **mul( )** to **z**. In line 2, the return value is not actually assigned, but it is used by the **printf( )** function. Finally, in line 3, the return value is lost because it is neither assigned to another variable nor used as part of an expression.

Returning Values from main( )

When you use a **return** statement in **main( )**, your program returns a termination code to the calling process (usually to the operating system). The returned value must be an integer. For many operating systems, including DOS and OS/2, a return value of 0 indicates that the program terminated normally. All other values indicate that some error occurred.

All the programs in this book return values from **main( )**, although technically this is optional. If you don't specify a **return** value, then Turbo C returns an unknown value to the operating system. For this reason, it is a good idea to use an explicit **return** statement.

Scope Rules of Functions

The *scope rules* of a language are the rules that govern whether a piece of code knows about, or has access to, another piece of code or data.

Each function in C is a discrete block of code. A function's code is private to that function and cannot be accessed by any statement in any other function except through a call to that function. (It is not possible, for instance, to use the **goto** to jump into the middle of another function.) The code that makes up the body of a function is hidden from the rest of the program and, unless it uses global variables or data, it can neither affect nor be affected by other parts of the program. In other words, the code and data that are defined within one function cannot interact with the code and data defined in another function because the two functions have a different scope.

Variables that are defined within a function are called *local variables*. A local variable comes into existence when the function is entered and is destroyed upon exit. Therefore, local variables cannot hold their value between function calls. The only exception to this rule is when the variable is declared with the **static** storage-class specifier. This causes the compiler to treat it like a global variable for storage purposes, but still limit its scope to within the function. (Chapter 2 contains a complete discussion of global and local variables.)

All functions in C are at the same scope level. That is, it is not possible to define a function within a function.

Function Arguments

If a function is to use arguments, it must declare variables that accept the values of the arguments. These variables are called the *formal parameters* of the function. They behave like other local variables inside the function and are created upon entry into the function and destroyed upon exit. As shown in the following example, the parameter declaration occurs after the function name and before the function's opening brace:

```
/* return 1 if c is part of string s; 0 otherwise */
is_in(char *s, char c)
{
  while(*s)
    if(*s==c) return 1;
```

```
      else s++;

   return 0;
}
```

The function **is_in( )** has two parameters: **s** and **c**. This function returns 1 if the character **c** is part of the string **s** and 0 otherwise.

As with local variables, you can make assignments to a function's formal parameters or use them in any allowable C expression. Even though these variables perform the special task of receiving the value of the arguments passed to the function, they can be used like any other local variable.

Call by Value, Call by Reference

In general, subroutines can be passed arguments in one of two ways. The first is called *call by value.* This method copies the value of an argument into the formal parameter of the subroutine. Changes made to the parameters of the subroutine have no effect on the variables used to call it.

Call by reference is the second way a subroutine can have arguments passed to it. In this method, the *address* of an argument is copied into the parameter. Inside the subroutine, the address is used to access the actual argument used in the call. This means that changes made to the parameter affect the variable used to call the routine.

With a few exceptions, C uses call by value to pass arguments. This means that you generally cannot alter the variables used to call the function. (You will find out later in this chapter how to generate a call by reference by using a pointer to allow changes to the calling variables.) Consider the following function:

```
#include <stdio.h>

int sqr(int x);

main(void)
{
  int t=10;

  printf("%d %d", sqr(t), t);
  return 0;
}

sqr(int x)
{
  x = x*x;
  return(x);
}
```

In this example, the value of the argument to **sqr( )**, 10, is copied into the parameter **x**. When the assignment **x=x*x** takes place, the only thing modified is the local variable **x**. The variable **t**, used to call **sqr( )**, still has the value 10. Hence, the output will be "100 10".

Remember that only a copy of the value of the argument is passed to that function. What occurs inside the function has no effect on the variable used in the call.

Creating a Call by Reference

Even though C's parameter-passing convention is call by value, it is possible to cause a call by reference by passing a pointer to the argument. Since this passes the address of the argument to the function, it is then possible to change the value of the argument outside the function.

Pointers are passed to functions just like any other value. Of course, it is necessary to declare the parameters as pointer types. For example, the function **swap( )**, which exchanges the value of its two integer arguments, is shown here:

```
void swap(int *x, int *y)
{
  int temp;

  temp = *x;   /* save the value at address x */
  *x = *y;     /* put y into x */
  *y = temp;   /* put x into y */
}
```

The * operator is used to access the variable pointed to by its operand. (A complete discussion of the * is found in Chapter 2. Also, Chapter 6 deals exclusively with pointers.) Hence, the contents of the variables used to call the function are swapped.

It is important to remember that **swap( )** (or any other function that uses pointer parameters) must be called with the *addresses of the arguments*. The following program shows the correct way to call **swap( )**:

```
#include <stdio.h>

void swap(int *x, int *y);

main(void)
{
  int x, y;

  x = 10;
  y = 20;
```

```
    swap(&x, &y);
    printf("%d %d", x, y);
    return 0;
}
```

In this example, the variable **x** is assigned the value 10, and **y** is assigned the value 20. Then **swap( )** is called with the addresses of **x** and **y**. The unary operator **&** is used to produce the addresses of the variables. Therefore, the addresses of **x** and **y**, not their values, are passed to the function **swap( )**.

Calling Functions with Arrays

Arrays will be covered in detail in Chapter 5. However, the operation of passing arrays as arguments to functions is dealt with here because it is an exception to the standard call by value parameter-passing convention.

When an array is used as an argument to a function, only the address of the array is passed, not a copy of the entire array. When you call a function with an array name, a pointer to the first element in the array is passed to the function. (Remember that in C an array name without any index is a pointer to the first element in the array.) The parameter declaration must be of a compatible pointer type. There are three ways to declare a parameter that is to receive an array pointer. First, it can be declared as an array, as shown here:

```
#include <stdio.h>

void display(int num[10]);

main(void)   /* print some numbers */
{
  int t[10], i;

  for(i=0; i<10; ++i) t[i]=i;
  display(t);
  return 0;
}

void display(int num[10])
{
  int i;

  for(i=0; i<10; i++) printf("%d ", num[i]);
}
```

Even though the parameter **num** is declared to be an integer array of 10 elements, Turbo C automatically converts it to an integer pointer because no parameter can actually receive an entire array. Only a pointer to an array is passed, so a pointer parameter must be there to receive it.

A second way to declare an array parameter is to specify it as an unsized array, as shown here,

```
void display(int num[])
{
  int i;

  for(i=0; i<10; i++) printf("%d ", num[i]);
}
```

where **num** is declared to be an integer array of unknown size. Since C provides no array boundary checks, the actual size of the array is irrelevant to the parameter (but not to the program, of course). This method of declaration also actually defines **num** as an integer pointer.

The final way that **num** can be declared—and the most common form in professionally written C programs—is as a pointer, as shown here:

```
void display(int *num)
{
  int i;

  for(i=0; i<10; i++) printf("%d ", num[i]);
}
```

This is allowed because any pointer can be indexed using [] as if it were an array. (Actually, arrays and pointers are very closely linked.)

All three methods of declaring an array parameter yield the same result: a pointer.

On the other hand, an array *element* used as an argument is treated like any other simple variable. For example, the program just examined could have been written without passing the entire array, as shown here:

```
#include <stdio.h>

void display(int num);

main(void) /* print some numbers */
{
  int t[10], i;
```

```
for(i=0; i<10; ++i) t[i]=i;
for(i=0; i<10; i++) display(t[i]);
return 0;
}

void display(int num)
{
  printf("%d ", num);
}
```

As you can see, the parameter to **display( )** is of type **int**. It is not relevant that **display( )** is called by using an array element, because only that one value of the array is passed.

It is important to understand that when an array is used as a function argument, its address is passed to a function. This is an exception to C's call by value parameter-passing convention. This means that the code inside the function operates on and potentially alters the actual contents of the array used to call the function. For example, consider the function **print_upper( )** which prints its string argument in uppercase:

```
#include <stdio.h>
#include <ctype.h>

void print_upper(char *string);

main(void)   /* print string as uppercase */
{
  char s[80];

  gets(s);
  print_upper(s);

  return 0;
}

void print_upper(char *string)
{
  register int t;

  for(t=0; string[t]; ++t)  {
    string[t] = toupper(string[t]);
    printf("%c", string[t]);
  }
}
```

After the call to **print_upper( )**, the contents of array **s** in **main( )** are changed to uppercase. If this is not what you want to happen, you could write the program like this:

```
#include <stdio.h>
#include <ctype.h>

void print_upper(char *string);

main(void)  /* print string as uppercase */
{
  char s[80];
  gets(s);
  print_upper(s);
  return 0;
}

void print_upper(char *string)
{
  register int t;

  for(t=0; string[t]; ++t)
    printf("%c", toupper(string[t]));
}
```

In this version, the contents of array **s** remain unchanged because its values are not altered.

A classic example of passing arrays to functions is found in the standard library function **gets( )**. Although the **gets( )** in Turbo C's library is more sophisticated and complex, the function shown in the following example will give you an idea of how it works. To avoid confusion with the standard function, this one is called **xgets( )**.

```
/* A  simplified version of the standard
   gets() library function. */

void xgets(char *s)
{
  register char ch;
  register int t;

  for(t=0; t<79; ) {
    ch = getche();
    switch(ch) {
```

```
    case '\r':
      s[t] = '\0'; /* null terminate the string */
      return;
    case '\b':
      if(t>0) t--;
      break;
    default:
      s[t] = ch;
      t++;
    }
  }
  s[79] = '\0';
}
```

The **xgets( )** function must be called with a character pointer, which can be either a variable that you declare to be a character pointer or the name of a character array, which by definition is a character pointer. Upon entry, **xgets( )** establishes a **for** loop from 0 to 79. This prevents larger strings from being entered at the keyboard. If more than 80 characters are typed, the function returns. Because C has no built-in bounds checking, you should make sure that any variable used to call **xgets( )** can accept at least 80 characters. As you type characters on the keyboard, they are entered in the string. If you type a backspace, the counter **t** is reduced by 1. When you enter a carriage return, a null is placed at the end of the string, signaling its termination. Because the actual array used to call **xgets( )** is modified, upon return it will contain the characters typed.

Arguments to main( )

Turbo C supports three arguments to **main( )**. The first two are the traditional arguments: **argc** and **argv**. These are also the only arguments to **main( )** defined by the ANSI standard. They allow you to pass command-line arguments to your C program. A *command-line argument* is the information that follows the program's name on the command line of the operating system. For example, when you compile programs using Turbo C's command-line version, you type something like

   tcc *program_name*

where *program_name* is the program you wish compiled. The name of the program is passed to Turbo C as an argument.

The **argc** parameter holds the number of arguments on the command line and is an integer. It will always be at least 1 because the name of the program qualifies as the first argument. The **argv** parameter is a pointer to an array of character pointers.

Each element in this array points to a command-line argument. All command-line arguments are strings; any numbers have to be converted by the program into the proper internal format. The following short program prints "Hello", then your name if you type it directly after the program name:

```
#include <stdio.h>

main(int argc, char *argv[])
{
  if(argc!=2) {
    printf("You forgot to type your name\n");
    return 1;
  }
  printf("Hello %s", argv[1]);

  return 0;
}
```

If you title this program **name** and your name is Chris, to run the program you would type "name Chris". The output from the program would be "Hello Chris". For example, if you were logged into drive A, you would see

```
A>name Chris
Hello Chris
A>
```

after running **name**.

Command-line arguments must be separated by a space or a tab. Commas, semicolons, and the like are not considered separators. For example,

```
run Spot run
```

is composed of three strings, while

```
Herb,Rick,Fred
```

is one string—commas are not legal separators.

If you want to pass a string that contains spaces or tabs as a single argument, you must enclose that string within double quotes. For example, to Turbo C, this is a single argument:

```
"this is a test"
```

It is important that you delcare **argv** properly. One common method is

```
char *argv[];
```

The empty brackets indicate that it is an array of undetermined length. You can now access the individual arguments by indexing **argv**. For example, **argv[0]** points to the first string, which is always the program's name; **argv[1]** points to the next string, and so on.

A short example using command-line arguments is the following program called **countdown**. It counts down from a value specified on the command line and beeps when it reaches 0. Notice that the first argument containing the number is converted into an integer using the standard function **atoi( )**. If the string "display" is present as the second command-line argument, the count will also be displayed on the screen.

```
/* Countdown program. */

#include <stdio.h>

main(int argc, char *argv[])
{
  int disp, count;

  if(argc<2) {
    printf("You must enter the length of the count\n");
    printf("on the command line. Try again.\n");
    return 1;
  }

  if(argc==3 && !strcmp(argv[2],"display")) disp = 1;
  else disp = 0;

  for(count=atoi(argv[1]); count; --count)
    if(disp) printf("%d ", count);

  printf("%c", 7);   /* this will ring the bell on most
                        computers */
  return 0;
}
```

Notice that if no arguments are specified, an error message is printed. It is common for a program that uses command-line arguments to issue instructions if an attempt has been made to run it without the proper information being present.

To access an individual character in one of the command strings, you add a second index to **argv**. For example, the following program displays all the arguments with which it was called, one character at a time.

```
#include <stdio.h>

main(int argc, char *argv[])
{
  int t, i;

  for(t=0; t<argc; ++t) {
    i = 0;
    while(argv[t][i]) {
      printf("%c", argv[t][i]);
      ++i;
    }
    printf(" ");
  }
  return 0;
}
```

Remember that the first index accesses the string and the second index accesses that character of the string.

You generally use **argc** and **argv** to get initial commands into your program. In theory, you can have up to 32,767 arguments, but most operating systems do not allow more than a few. You normally use these arguments to indicate a file name or an option. Using command-line arguments gives your program a very professional appearance and facilitates the program's use in batch files.

If you link the file WILDARGS.OBJ, provided with Turbo C, with your program, command-line arguments like *.EXE automatically expand into any matching file names. (Turbo C automatically processes the wildcard file name characters and increases the value of **argc** appropriately.) For example, if you link the following program with WILDARGS.OBJ, it tells you how many files match the file name specified on the command line:

```
/* Link this program with WILDARGS.OBJ. */

#include <stdio.h>

main(int argc, char *argv[])
{
  register int i;

  printf("%d files match specified name\n", argc-1);

  printf("They are: ");

  for(i=1; i<argc; i++)
```

```
      printf("%s ", argv[i]);

   return 0;
}
```

If you call this program **WA**, then executing it in the following manner tells you the number of files that have the .EXE extension, and lists their names:

```
C>WA *.EXE
```

In addition to **argc** and **argv**, Turbo C also allows a third command-line argument called **env**. The **env** parameter tells your program to access the environmental information associated with the operating system. The **env** parameter must follow **argc** and **argv** and is declared like this:

```
char *env[]
```

As you can see, **env** is declared like **argv**. Like **argv** it is a pointer to an array of strings. Each string is an environmental string defined by the operating system. The **env** parameter does not have a corresponding **argc**-like parameter that tells your program how many environmental strings there are. Instead, the last environmental string is null. The following program displays all the environmental strings currently defined by the operating system:

```
/* This program prints all the environmental
   strings.
*/

#include <stdio.h>

main(int argc, char *argv[], char *env[])
{
   int t;

   for(t=0; env[t]; t++)
     printf("%s\n", env[t]);

   return 0;
}
```

Notice that even though **argc** and **argv** are not used by this program, they must be present in the parameter list. Turbo C does not actually know the names of the parameters. Instead, their usage is determined by the order in which the parameters are declared. In fact, you can call the parameters anything you like. Since **argc**, **argv**, and **env** are traditional names, it is best to use them so anyone reading your program will instantly know that they are arguments to **main( )**.

It is quite common for a program to need to find the value of one specific environmental string. For example, under DOS, knowing the value of the PATH string allows your program to utilize the currently defined search paths. The following program shows how to find the string that defines the default search paths. It uses the standard library function **strstr( )**, which has this prototype:

char *strstr(const char *str1, const char *str2);

The **strstr( )** function searches the string pointed to by *str1* for the first occurrence of the string pointed to by *str2*. If it is found, a pointer to the first occurrence is returned. If no match exists, then **strstr( )** returns null.

```
/* This program searches the environmental
   strings for the one that contains the
   current PATH.
*/
#include <stdio.h>
#include <string.h>

main(int argc, char *argv[], char *env[])
{
  int t;

  for(t=0; env[t]; t++) {
    if(strstr(env[t], "PATH"))
      printf("%s\n", env[t]);
  }

  return 0;
}
```

Functions Returning Noninteger Values

When the return type of a function is not explicitly declared, it automatically defaults to **int**. For many functions this default is acceptable. However, when it is necessary to return a different data type you must use this two-step process:

1. The function must be given an explicit type specifier.

2. The compiler must be told the type of the function before the first call is made to it.

Only in this way can Turbo C generate correct code for functions returning noninteger values.

Functions can be declared to return any valid C data type. The method of declaration is similar to that of variables: The type specifier precedes the function name. The type specifier tells the compiler what type of data the function is to return. This information is critical if the program is going to run correctly, because different data types have different sizes and internal representations.

Before you can use a function that returns a noninteger type, its type must be made known to the rest of the program. Unless directed to the contrary, Turbo C assumes that a function is going to return an integer value. If the function actually returns some other type, then Turbo C will have generated the wrong code for the return value. In general, the way to inform Turbo C about the return type of a function involves using a *forward reference*. A forward reference declares the return type of a function but does not actually define what the function does. The function definition occurs elsewhere in the program.

There are two ways to create a forward reference. The first is the old-style method used by pre-ANSI-standard versions of C. The second is to use a function prototype (which is the method used in this book). The old-style forward reference method is explained here because much old C code is still in existence. The function prototype method is examined later in this chapter.

The old-style method of informing Turbo C about the return type of a function simply declares the return type and name of the function near the top of the program. For example, to tell Turbo C that a function called **myfunc( )** returns a **double** value, you would put this declaration near the top of your program:

```
double myfunc();
```

Even if **myfunc( )** has parameters, in this method none are shown within the parentheses. When Turbo C reads this line, it knows that **myfunc( )** returns a **double** and generates the correct return code. For example, the following is a correct (although old-style) program:

```
#include <stdio.h>
#include <math.h>

double myfunc(); /* forward declaration of myfunc() */

main(void)
{
  printf("%lf", myfunc(10.0));
  return 0;
}

double myfunc(double x)
```

```
{
  return sqrt(x) * 2.0; /* return sqr root of x * 2 */
}
```

As you can see, even though **myfunc( )** has one parameter, the traditional forward declaration says nothing about it.

Frankly, while both Turbo C and the ANSI C standard still allow the preceding function declaration method as a means to telling Turbo C about the return type of a function, it cannot be recommended. The reason for this is that the function prototype, which was added by the ANSI committee, provides a much better alternative.

Using Function Prototypes

The ANSI C standard expands on the traditional forward function declaration. This expanded declaration is called a *function prototype*. Except for the example in the preceding section, every program in this book includes a function prototype for all functions used in the program.

A function prototype performs two special tasks. First, it identifies the return type of the function so that Turbo C can generate the correct code for the return data. Second, it specifies the type and number of arguments used by the function. The prototype takes this general form:

   type function_name(parameter list);

The prototype normally goes near the top of the program and must appear before any call is made to the function.

In addition to telling the compiler about the return type of the function, function prototypes enable C to provide strong type-checking somewhat similar to that provided by languages such as Turbo Pascal. The prototypes allow Turbo C to find and report any illegal type conversions between the type of arguments used to call a function and the type definition of its parameters. They also allow Turbo C to report when a function is called with too few or too many arguments.

When possible, Turbo C automatically converts the type of an argument into the type of the parameter that is receiving it. However, some type conversions are simply illegal. When a function is prototyped, any illegal type conversion will be found and an error message will be issued. As an example, the following program causes an error message to be issued because there is an attempt to call **func( )** with a pointer instead of the **float** required. (It is illegal to transform a pointer into a **float**.)

```
/* This program uses function prototypes to
   enforce strong type checking in the calls
```

```
   to func().

   The program will not compile because of the
   mismatch between the type of the arguments
   specified in the function's prototype and
   the type of arguments used to call the function.

*/

#include <stdio.h>

float func(int x, float y); /* prototype */

main(void)
{
  int x, *y;

  x = 10;  y = &x;
  func(x, y);  /* type mismatch */
  return 0;
}

float func(int x, float y)
{
  printf("%f", y/(float)x);
  return y/(float) x;
}
```

Using a prototype also allows Turbo C to report when the number of arguments used to call a function disagrees with the number of parameters defined by the function. For example, this program will not compile because **func( )** is called with the wrong number of arguments:

```
/*
   The program will not compile because of the
   mismatch between the number of parameters
   specified in the function's prototype and
   the number of arguments used to call the function.

*/

#include <stdio.h>

float func(int x, float y); /* prototype */
```

```
main(void)
{
  func(2, 2.0, 4);  /* wrong number of args */
  return 0;
}

float func(int x, float y)
{
  printf("%f", y/(float)x);
  return y/(float) x;
}
```

Technically, when you prototype a function, you do not need to include the actual parameter names. For example, both of these are valid prototypes:

```
char func(char *, int);

char func(char *str, int count);
```

However, if you include each parameter name, Turbo C uses the names to report any type mismatch errors.

Some functions, such as **printf( )**, can take a variable number of arguments. A variable number of arguments are specified in a prototype using three periods. For example, the prototype to **printf( )** is

int printf(const char *fmt, . . .);

To create functions with a variable number of arguments, refer to the description of the standard library function **va_arg( )** in Part Four of this book.

Aside from telling the compiler about a function's return data type, use of function prototypes helps you trap bugs before they occur by preventing a function from being called with invalid arguments. They also help verify that your program is working correctly by not allowing functions to be called with the wrong number of arguments.

Standard Library Function Prototypes

Any standard library functions used by your program should be prototyped. To accomplish this, you must include the appropriate *header file* for each library function. Header files use the .H extension and are provided along with Turbo C. Turbo C's header files contain two main elements: the definitions used by the functions and the prototypes for the standard functions related to the header file. For example, **stdio.h** is included in almost all programs in this book because it contains the prototype for the **printf( )** function. If you include the appropriate header file for each library function used in a program, it is possible for Turbo C to catch any accidental errors you may make when using them.

Turbo C's header files and the category of functions for which each is used are shown in Table 4-1. In Part Four of this book, the header file required by each library function is shown along with its description.

File Name	Related Functions
alloc.h	Dynamic memory allocation
assert.h	Defines assert( )
bios.h	BIOS interface functions
conio.h	Direct console I/O functions
ctype.h	Character-related functions
dir.h	Directory-related functions
dos.h	DOS interface functions
errno.h	Defines various error codes
fcntl.h	Defines various constants used by the UNIX-like file system
float.h	Defines floating point limits
graphics.h	Graphics-related functions
io.h	Low-level I/O functions
limits.h	Defines various integer limits
locale.h	Country-specific functions
math.h	Mathematical functions
mem.h	Memory manipulation functions
process.h	Process control functions
setjmp.h	Required by setjmp( ) and longjmp( )
share.h	Support for file-sharing
signal.h	Support for signal( ) and raise( )
stdargs.h	Support for variable-length arguments
stddef.h	Defines standard types and macros
stdio.h	Standard I/O functions
stdlib.h	Miscellaneous functions
string.h	String-related functions
sys\stat.h	File-related constants
sys\timeb.h	Supports the ftime( ) function
sys\types.h	Defines time_t, which is used by the time functions
time.h	Time- and date-related functions
values.h	Various implementation-dependent constants

Table 4-1.   *Turbo C's Header Files*

Although we will look more closely at Turbo C's compiler options later in this book, you should be aware that you can let Turbo C warn you when a function prototype has not been included for any function in your program. To do this in the integrated environment, select **Options**. Under **Options** select **Compiler** followed by **Messages**. From this menu select **Frequent errors**. Finally, activate the **Call to function without prototype** option. If you are using the command-line compiler, use the **–wpro** option.

Prototyping Functions that Have No Parameters

As you know, a function prototype tells Turbo C about the type of data returned by a function as well as the type and number of parameters used by the function. However, since prototypes were not part of the original version of C, a special case is created when you need to prototype a function that takes no parameters. The reason for this is that the ANSI C standard stipulates that when no parameters are included in a function's prototype, no information whatsoever is specified about the type or number of the function's parameters. This is necessary to ensure that older C programs can be compiled by modern compilers, such as Turbo C. When you specifically want to tell Turbo C that a function actually takes no parameters you must use the keyword **void** inside the parameter list. For example, examine this short program:

```
#include <stdio.h>

void display10(void);

main(void)
{
  display10();

  return 0;
}

void display10(void)
{
  int i;

  for(i=0; i<10; i++)
    printf("%d ", i);
}
```

In this program, the prototype to **display10( )** explicitly tells the compiler that **display10( )** takes no arguments. Since the parameter list of the function must agree with its prototype, the **void** must also be included in the declaration of **display10( )**

as well as in its definition later in the program. Assuming the foregoing prototype, Turbo C will not compile a call to **display10( )** that looks like the following example:

```
display10(100);
```

However, if the **void** had been left out of the parameter list specification, no error would have been reported and the argument would simply have been ignored.

Returning Pointers

Although functions that return pointers are handled in exactly the same way as any other type of function, a few important concepts need to be discussed.

Pointers to variables are *neither* integers, *nor* unsigned integers. They are the memory addresses of a certain type of data. The reason for this distinction lies in the fact that when pointer arithmetic is performed it is relative to the base type—that is, if an integer pointer is incremented it will contain a value that is 2 greater than its previous value (assuming 2-byte words). More generally, each time a pointer is incremented, it points to the next data item of its type. Since each data type may be of a different length, the compiler must know what type of data the pointer is pointing to in order to make it point to the next data item. (The subject of pointer arithmetic is covered in detail in Chapter 6.)

For example, the following is a function that returns a pointer to a string at the place where a character match was found:

```
char *match(char c, char *s)
{
  register int count;

  count = 0;
  while(c!=s[count] && s[count]) count++;
  return(&s[count]);
}
```

The function **match( )** attempts to return a pointer to the place in a string where the first match with **c** is found. If no match is found, a pointer to the null terminator is returned.

A short program that uses **match( )** is shown here:

```
#include <stdio.h>
#include <conio.h>
```

```
char *match(char c, char *s);

main(void)
{
  char s[80], *p, ch;

  gets(s);
  ch = getche();
  p = match(ch, s);
  if(p)  /* there is a match */
    printf("%s ", p);
  else
    printf("no match found");

  return 0;
}
```

This program reads a string and then a character. If the character is in the string, it prints the string from the point of the match. Otherwise, it prints "no match found".

Classic Versus Modern Parameter Declarations

The original version of C uses its own method to declare function parameters, which sometimes is called the traditional or classic form. The declaration approach used in this book is called the modern form. Turbo C adheres closely to the ANSI standard for C, which supports both forms but strongly *recommends* the modern form. (In fact, it is rare to see new C code that is written using the classic function declarations.) However, it is important for you to know the classic form because there are literally millions of lines of C code in existence that use it. Also, many programs published in books and magazines that are more than a couple of years old use this form.

The classic function parameter declaration consists of two parts: a parameter list, which goes inside the parentheses that follow the function name, and the actual parameter declarations, which go between the closing parentheses and the function's opening curly brace. The general form of the classic parameter definition is shown here:

> *type function_name(parm1, parm2,. . .parmN)*
> *type parm1;*
> *type parm2;*
>   .
>   .
>   .

```
type parmN;
{
function code
}
```

For example, this modern declaration:

```
char *f(const char *str1, int count, int index)
{
   .
   .
   .
}
```

will look like this in its classic form:

```
char *f(str1, count, index)
char *str1;
int count, index;
{
   .
   .
   .
}
```

Notice that in the classic form more than one parameter can be listed after the type name.

There is one slight distinction that Turbo C makes between the classic and modern declaration methods. If you declare a **float** parameter using the classic declaration method, Turbo C automatically elevates it to a **double** at the time of the call. Using the modern declaration approach prevents this automatic type promotion, and the parameter and its argument remain **float**s.

Remember that even though the classic declaration form is outdated, Turbo C can still correctly compile programs that use this approach. Therefore, you need not worry if you want to compile a program that uses classic function declarations.

Recursion

In C, functions can call themselves. A function is *recursive* if a statement in the body of the function calls the function that contains it. Sometimes called *circular definition*, recursion is the process of defining something in terms of itself.

Examples of recursion abound. A recursive way to define an integer number is as the digits 0, 1, 2, 3, 4, 5, 6, 7, 8, 9, plus or minus an integer number. For example, the number 15 is the number 7 plus the number 8; 21 is 9 plus 12; and 12 is 9 plus 3.

For a computer language to allow recursion, a function must be able to call itself. A simple example is the function **factr( )**, which computes the factorial of an integer. The factorial of a number N is the product of all the whole numbers from 1 to N. For example, 3 factorial is $1 \times 2 \times 3$, or 6. Both **factr( )** and its iterative equivalent are shown here.

```
/* Compute the factorial of a number. */
factr(int n)   /* recursive */
{
  int answer;

  if(n==1) return(1);
  answer = factr(n-1)*n;
  return(answer);
}

/* Compute the factorial of a number. */
fact(int n)     /* non-recursive */
{
  int t, answer;

  answer = 1;
  for(t=1; t<=n; t++)
    answer=answer*(t);
  return(answer);
}
```

The operation of the nonrecursive version of **fact( )** should be clear. It uses a loop starting at 1 and ending at the number, and progressively multiplies each number by the moving product.

The operation of the recursive **factr( )** is a little more complex. When **factr( )** is called with an argument of 1, the function returns 1; otherwise it returns the product of **factr(n–1) *n**. To evaluate this expression, **factr( )** is called with **n–1**. This happens until **n** equals 1 and the calls to the function begin returning.

Computing the factorial of 2, the first call to **factr( )** causes a second call to be made with the argument of **1**. This call returns 1, which is then multiplied by 2 (the original **n** value). The answer is then 2. You might find it interesting to insert **printf( )** statements into **factr( )** to show the level and the intermediate answers of each call.

When a function calls itself, new local variables and parameters are allocated storage on the stack, and the function code is executed with these new variables from the beginning. A recursive call does not make a new copy of the function. Only the arguments are new. As each recursive call returns, the old local variables and parameters are removed from the stack and execution resumes at the point of the function call inside the function. Recursive functions could be said to "telescope" out and back.

Most recursive routines do not significantly save code size or memory. The recursive versions of most routines may execute a bit more slowly than the iterative equivalent because of the added function calls; but this is not significant in most cases. Many recursive calls to a function could cause a stack overrun. Because storage for function parameters and local variables is on the stack and each new call creates a new copy of these variables, the stack space could become exhausted. If this happens, a *stack overflow* occurs. You can have Turbo C watch for stack overflow by turning off the **No Stack Warning** menu entry inside the **Linker** entry under the **Options** menu of the integrated environment or by specifying the **–N** option when using the command-line version of Turbo C.

The main advantage to recursive functions is that they can be used to create versions of several algorithms that are clearer and simpler than their iterative equivalents. For example, the QuickSort sorting algorithm is quite difficult to implement in an iterative way. Some problems, especially AI-related ones, also seem to lend themselves to recursive solutions. Finally, some people seem to think recursively more easily than iteratively.

When writing recursive functions, you must have an **if** statement somewhere to force the function to return without the recursive call being executed. If you don't do this, once you call the function, it never returns. This is a very common error when writing recursive functions. Use **printf( )** and **getchar( )** liberally during development so that you can watch what is going on and abort execution if you see that you have made a mistake.

Pointers to Functions

A particularly confusing yet powerful feature of C is the *function pointer*. Even though a function is not a variable, it still has a physical location in memory that can be assigned to a pointer. The address assigned to the pointer is the entry point of the function. This pointer can then be used in place of the function's name. It also allows functions to be passed as arguments to other functions.

To understand how function pointers work, you must understand a little about how a function is compiled and called in Turbo C. As each function is compiled, source code is transformed into object code and an entry point is established. When a call is made to a function while your program is running, a machine language "call" is made to this entry point. Therefore, a pointer to a function actually contains the memory address of the entry point of the function.

The address of a function is obtained by using the function's name without any parentheses or arguments. (This is similar to the way an array's address is obtained by using only the array name without indexes.) For example, consider the following program, paying very close attention to the declarations:

```
#include <stdio.h>
#include <string.h>

void check(char *a, char *b, int (*cmp) (char *, char *));

main(void)
{
  char s1[80], s2[80];
  int   (*p)();

  p = strcmp;   /* get address of strcmp() */

  gets(s1);
  gets(s2);

  check(s1, s2, p);
  return 0;
}

void check(char *a, char *b, int (*cmp) (char *, char *))
{
  printf("testing for equality\n");
  if(!(*cmp) (a, b)) printf("equal");
  else printf("not equal");
}
```

When the function **check( )** is called, two character pointers and one function pointer are passed as parameters. Inside the function **check( )**, the arguments are declared as character pointers and a function pointer. Notice how the function pointer is declared. You must use exactly the same method when declaring other function pointers, except that the return type or parameters of the function can be different. The parentheses around the ***cmp** are necessary for the compiler to interpret this statement correctly. Without the parentheses around ***cmp** Turbo C would be confused.

When you declare a function pointer, you can still provide a prototype to it as the preceding program illustrates. However, in many cases you won't know the names of the actual parameters so you can leave them blank, or you can use any names you like.

Once inside **check( )**, you can see how the **strcmp( )** function is called. The statement

```
(*cmp) (a, b)
```

performs the call to the function, in this case **strcmp( )**, which is pointed to by **cmp** with the arguments **a** and **b**. This statement also represents the general form of using a function pointer to call the function it points to.

It is possible to call **check( )** using **strcmp** directly, as shown here:

```
check(s1, s2, strcmp);
```

This statement would eliminate the need for an additional pointer variable.

You may be asking yourself why anyone would want to write a program this way. In this example, nothing is gained and significant confusion is introduced. However, there are times when it is advantageous to pass arbitrary functions to procedures or to keep an array of functions. The following helps illustrate a use of function pointers. When an interpreter is written, it is common for it to perform function calls to various support routines, for example, the sine, cosine, and tangent functions. Instead of having a large **switch** statement listing all of these functions, you can use an array of function pointers with the proper function called determined by some index. You can get the flavor of this type of use by studying the expanded version of the previous example. In this program, **check( )** can be made to check for either alphabetical equality or numeric equality by simply calling it with a different comparison function:

```
#include <stdio.h>
#include <ctype.h>
#include <string.h>
#include <stdlib.h>

void check(char *a, char *b, int (*cmp) (char *, char *));
int numcmp(char *a, char *b);

main(void)
{
  char s1[80], s2[80];
  gets(s1);
  gets(s2);

  if(isalpha(*s1))
     check(s1, s2, strcmp);
  else
     check(s1, s2, numcmp);
   return 0;
}

void check(char *a, char *b, int (*cmp) (char *, char *))
{
```

```
  printf("testing for equality\n");
  if(!(*cmp) (a, b)) printf("equal");
  else printf("not equal");
}

numcmp(char *a, char *b)
{
  if(atoi(a)==atoi(b)) return 0;
  else return 1;
}
```

Implementation Issues

When you create C functions you should remember a few important things that affect their efficiency and usability. These issues are the subject of this section.

Parameters and General-Purpose Functions

A general-purpose function is one that is used in a variety of situations, perhaps by many different programmers. Typically, you should not base general-purpose functions on global data. All the information a function needs should be passed to it by its parameters. In the few cases in which this is not possible, you should use **static** variables.

Besides making your functions general-purpose, parameters keep your code readable and less susceptible to bugs caused by side effects.

Efficiency

Functions are the building blocks of C and crucial to the creation of all but the most trivial programs. Nothing said in this section should be construed otherwise. In certain specialized applications, however, you may need to eliminate a function and replace it with *in-line code*. In-line code is the equivalent of a function's statements used without a call to that function. In-line code is used instead of function calls only when execution time is critical.

There are two reasons in-line code is faster than a function call. First, a "call" instruction takes time to execute. Second, arguments to be passed have to be placed on the stack, which also takes time. For almost all applications, this very slight increase in execution time is of no significance. But if it is, remember that each function call uses time that would be saved if the code in the function were placed in line. For example, below are two versions of a program that prints the square of the numbers from 1 to 10. The in-line version runs faster than the other because the function call takes time.

```
in line                    function call

main(void)                 main(void)
{                          {
  int x;                     int x;

  for(x=1; x<11; ++x)        for(x=1; x<11; ++x)
  printf("%d", x*x);         printf("%d", sqr(x));
  return 0;                  return 0;
}                          }

                           sqr(int a)
                           {
                             return a*a;
                           }
```

As you create programs, you must always weigh the cost of functions in terms of execution time against the benefits of increased readability and modifiability.

Chapter 5

Arrays

An *array* is a collection of variables of the same type that are referenced by a common name. A specific element in an array is accessed by an index. In C all arrays consist of contiguous memory locations. The lowest address corresponds to the first element; the highest address corresponds to the last element. Arrays may have from one to several dimensions.

Single-Dimension Arrays

The general form of a single-dimension array declaration is

   type var_name[*size*];

In C arrays must be explicitly declared so that the compiler can allocate space for them in memory. Here, *type* declares the base type of the array, which is the type of each element in the array. *Size* defines how many elements the array will hold. For a single-dimension array, the total size of an array in bytes is computed as shown here:

   *total bytes = sizeof(base type) * number of elements*

All arrays have 0 as the index of their first element. Therefore, when you write

```
char p[10];
```

you are declaring a character array that has 10 elements, p[0] through p[9]. For example, the following program loads an integer array with the numbers 0 through 9 and displays them:

```
#include <stdio.h>

main(void)
{
  int x[10];  /* this reserves 10 integer elements */
  int t;

  for(t=0; t<10; ++t) x[t]=t;

  for(t=0; t<10; ++t) printf("%d ", x[t]);
  return 0;
}
```

In C there is no bounds checking on arrays. You could overwrite either end of an array and write into some other variable's data, or even into a piece of the program's code. It is the programmer's job to provide bounds checking when it is needed. For example, make certain that the character arrays that accept character input using **gets( )** are long enough to accept the longest input.

Single-dimension arrays are essentially lists of information of the same type. For example, Figure 5-1 shows how array **a** appears in memory if it is declared as shown here and starts at memory location 1000:

```
char a[7];
```

Passing Single-Dimension Arrays to Functions

When passing single-dimension arrays to functions, call the function with the array name without any index. This passes the address of the first element of the array to

a[0]	a[1]	a[2]	a[3]	a[4]	a[5]	a[6]
1000	1001	1002	1003	1004	1005	1006

Figure 5-1.   *A seven-element character array beginning at location 1000*

the function. In C it is not possible to pass the entire array as an argument; a pointer is automatically passed instead. For example, the following fragment passes the address of **i** to **func1( )**:

```
main(void)
{
  int i[10];

  func1(i);
  .
  .
  .
}
```

If a function is to receive a single-dimension array, you may declare the formal parameter as a pointer, as a sized array, or as an unsized array. For example, to receive **i** into a function called **func1( )**, you could declare **func1( )** as either

```
func1(int *a)  /* pointer */
{
  .
  .
  .
}
```

or

```
func1(int a[10]) /* sized array */
{
  .
  .
  .
}
```

or

```
func1(int a[]) /* unsized array */
{
  .
  .
  .
}
```

All three methods of declaration tell the compiler that an integer pointer is going to be received. In the first declaration a pointer is used; in the second the standard array declaration is employed. In the third declaration, a modified version of an array declaration simply specifies that an array of type **int** of some length is to be received. As far as the function is concerned, it doesn't matter what the length of the array actually is because C performs no bounds checking, anyway. In fact, as far as the compiler is concerned,

```
func1(int a[32])
{
    .
    .
    .
}
```

also works because Turbo C generates code that instructs **func1( )** to receive a pointer—it does not actually create a 32-element array.

Strings

By far the most common use of single-dimension arrays is for character strings. Although C defines no string type, it supports some of the most powerful string manipulation functions found in any language. In C a string is defined to consist of a character array of any length that is terminated by a null. A null is specified as **'\0'** and is 0. For this reason it is necessary to declare character arrays to be one character longer than the largest string that they are to hold. For example, if you wished to declare an array **s** that holds a 10-character string, you would write

```
char s[11];
```

This makes room for the null at the end of the string.

Although C does not have a string data type, it still allows string constants. A string constant is a list of characters enclosed between double quotes. For example, here are two string constants:

```
"hello there" "this is a test"
```

It is not necessary to add the null to the end of string constants manually; the C compiler does this for you automatically.

Turbo C supports a wide range of string manipulation functions. Some of the most common are **strcpy( )**, **strcat( )**, **strlen( )**, and **strcmp( )**, whose prototypes are shown here:

```
char *strcpy(char *s1, const char *s2);
```

char *strcat(char *s1, const char *s2);

int strlen(const char *s1);

int strcmp(const char *s1, const char *s2);

All of the functions use the **string.h** header file. The **strcpy( )** function copies the string pointed to by s2 into the one pointed to by s1. It returns s1. The **strcat( )** function concatenates the string pointed to by s2 to the one pointed to by s1. It also returns s1. The **strlen( )** function returns the length of the string pointed to by s1. The **strcmp( )** function compares s1 and s2. It returns 0 if the two strings are equal, greater than 0 if the string pointed to by s1 is greater than the one pointed to by s2, and less than zero if the string pointed to by s1 is less than the string pointed to by s2. All comparisons are done lexicographically (according to dictionary order). (These and other string functions are discussed in detail in Part Four of this book.)

The following program illustrates the use of these string functions:

```c
#include <string.h>
#include <stdio.h>

main(void)
{
  char s1[80], s2[80];

  gets(s1); gets(s2);

  printf("lengths: %d %d\n", strlen(s1), strlen(s2));

  if(!strcmp(s1, s2)) printf("The strings are equal\n");

  strcat(s1, s2);
  printf("%s\n", s1);

  return 0;
}
```

If this program is run and the strings "hello" and "hello" are entered, the output is

```
lengths: 5 5
The strings are equal
hellohello
```

It is important to remember that **strcmp( )** returns false if the strings are equal, so be sure to use the **!** to reverse the condition, as shown in this example, if you are testing for equality.

Two-Dimensional Arrays

Turbo C allows multidimensional arrays. The simplest form of the multidimensional array is the two-dimensional array. A two-dimensional array is, in essence, an array of one-dimensional arrays. Two-dimensional arrays are declared using this general form:

type array_name[2nd dimension size] [1st dimension size];

Hence, to declare a two-dimensional integer array **d** of size 10,20, you would write

```
int d[10][20];
```

Pay careful attention to the declaration. Unlike some computer languages, which use commas to separate the array dimensions, C places each dimension in its own set of brackets.

Similarly, to access point 3,5 of array **d**, use

```
d[3][5]
```

In the following example, a two-dimensional array is loaded with the numbers 1 through 12, which it then displays on the screen:

```
#include <stdio.h>

main(void)
{
  int t,i, num[3][4];

  for(t=0;t<3;++t)
    for(i=0;i<4;++i)
      num[t][i]=(t*4)+i+1;

  /* display them */
  for(t=0;t<3;++t) {
    for(i=0;i<4;++i)
      printf("%d ", num[t][i]);
    printf("\n");
  }

  return 0;
}
```

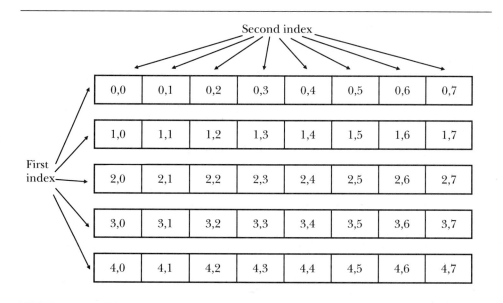

Figure 5-2. A two-dimensional array in memory

In this example, **num[0][0]** has the value 1; **num[0][1]**, the value 2, **num[0][2]** the value 3; and so on. The value of **num[2][3]** is 12.

Two-dimensional arrays are stored in a row-column matrix, where the first index indicates the row and the second indicates the column. This means that the rightmost index changes faster than the leftmost when accessing the elements in the array in the order they are actually stored in memory. See Figure 5-2 for a graphic representation of a two-dimensional array in memory. In essence, the leftmost index can be thought of as a "pointer" to the correct row.

The number of bytes of memory required by a two-dimensional array is computed using the following formula:

*bytes = 2nd dimension * 1st dimension * sizeof (base type)*

Therefore, assuming 2-byte integers, an integer array with dimensions 10,5 would have $10 \times 5 \times 2$ or 100 bytes allocated.

When a two-dimensional array is used as an argument to a function, only a pointer is passed to the first element. However, a function receiving a two-dimensional array as a parameter must minimally define the length of the first dimension, because the compiler needs to know the length of each row if it is to index the array correctly. For example, a function that will receive a two-dimensional integer array with dimensions 5,10 would be declared like this:

```
func1(int x[][10])
{
  .
  .
  .
}
```

You can specify the second dimension as well, but it is not necessary. The compiler needs to know the first dimension in order to work on statements such as

```
x[2][4]
```

inside the function. If the length of the rows is not known, it is impossible to know where the next row begins.

The short program shown here uses a two-dimensional array to store the numeric grade for each student in a teacher's classes. The program assumes that the teacher has three classes and a maximum of 30 students per class. Notice how the array **grade** is accessed by each of the functions.

```c
#include <conio.h>
#include <ctype.h>
#include <stdio.h>
#include <stdlib.h>

#define CLASSES  3
#define GRADES   30
int grade[CLASSES][GRADES];

void disp_grades(int g[][GRADES]), enter_grades(void);
int get_grade(int num);

main(void)  /* class grades program */
{
  char ch;

  for(;;) {
    do {
      printf("(E)nter grades\n");
      printf("(R)eport grades\n");
      printf("(Q)uit\n");
      ch = toupper(getche());
    } while(ch!='E' && ch!='R' && ch!='Q');

    switch(ch) {
```

```
      case 'E':
        enter_grades();
        break;
      case 'R':
        disp_grades(grade);
        break;
      case 'Q':
        return 0;
    }
  }
}

/* Enter each student's grade. */
void enter_grades(void)
{
  int t, i;

  for(t=0; t<CLASSES; t++) {
    printf("Class # %d:\n", t+1);
    for(i=0; i<GRADES; ++i)
      grade[t][i] = get_grade(i);
  }
}

/* Actually input the grade. */
get_grade(int num)
{
  char s[80];

  printf("enter grade for student # %d:\n", num+1);
  gets(s);
  return(atoi(s));
}

/* Display the class grades. */
void disp_grades(int g[][GRADES])
{
  int t, i;

  for(t=0; t<CLASSES; ++t) {
    printf("Class # %d:\n", t+1);
    for(i=0; i<GRADES; ++i)
      printf("grade for student #%d is %d\n",i+1, g[t][i]);
  }
}
```

Arrays of Strings

It is not uncommon in programming to use an array of strings. For example, the input processor to a database may verify user commands against a string array of valid commands. A two-dimensional character array is used to create an array of strings with the size of the left index determining the number of strings and the size of the right index specifying the maximum length of each string. This code fragment declares an array of 30 strings, each having a maximum length of 79 characters:

```
char str_array[30][80];
```

To access an individual string is quite easy: You simply specify only the left index. For example, this statement calls **gets( )** with the third string in **str_array**.

```
gets(str_array[2]);
```

This is functionally equivalent to

```
gets(&str_array[2][0]);
```

but the previous form is much more common in professionally written C code.

To improve your understanding of how string arrays work, study the following short program that uses one as the basis for a very simple text editor:

```
#include <stdio.h>

#define MAX 100
#define LEN 80

char text[MAX][LEN];

/* A very simple text editor. */
main(void)
{
  register int t, i, j;

  for(t=0; t<MAX; t++) {
    printf("%d: ", t);
    gets(text[t]);
    if(!*text[t]) break; /* quit on blank line */
  }
```

```
/* this displays the text one character at a time */
for(i=0; i<t; i++) {
    for(j=0; *text[i][j]; j++) printf("%c", text[i][j]);
    printf("%c", '\n');
}

    return 0;
}
```

This program inputs lines of text until a blank line is entered. Then it redisplays each line. For purposes of illustration, it displays the text one character at a time by indexing the first dimension. However, because each string in the array is null-terminated, the routine that displays the text could be simplified like this:

```
for(i=0; i<t; i++)
    printf("%s\n", text[i]);
```

Multidimensional Arrays

C allows arrays of greater than two dimensions. The general form of a multidimensional array declaration is

type name[*sizeN*]...[*size2*] [*size1*];

Arrays of more than three dimensions are rarely used because of the amount of memory required to hold them. For example, a four-dimensional character array with dimensions 10,6,9,4 would require $10 \times 6 \times 9 \times 4$ or 2,160 bytes. If the array were 2-byte integers, 4,320 bytes would be needed. If the array were **double** (assuming 8 bytes per **double**), then 34,560 bytes would be required. The storage required increases exponentially with the number of dimensions.

A point to remember about multidimensional arrays is that it takes the computer time to compute each index. This means that accessing an element in a multidimensional array will be slower than accessing an element in a single-dimensional array. For these and other reasons, when large multidimensional arrays are needed, often they are dynamically allocated a portion at a time using C's dynamic allocation functions.

When passing multidimensional arrays into functions, you must declare all but the leftmost dimension. For example, if you declare array **m** as

```
int m[4][3][6][5];
```

then a function, **func1( )**, receiving **m**, could look like

```
func1(int d[][3][6][5])
{
    .
    .
    .
}
```

Of course, you are free to include the leftmost dimension if you like.

Arrays and Pointers

Pointers and arrays are closely related in C. For example, an array name without an index is a pointer to the first element in the array. In this array,

```
char p[10];
```

the following statements are identical:

```
p
```

```
&p[0]
```

Put another way,

```
p == &p[0]
```

evaluates true because the address of the first element of an array is the same as the address of the array.

Any pointer variable can be indexed as if it were declared to be an array of the base type of the pointer. For example:

```
int *p, i[10];
```

```
p = i;
```

```
p[5] = 100;  /* assign using index */
```

```
*(p+5) = 100; /* assign using pointer arithmetic */
```

Both assigment statements place the value 100 in the sixth element of **i**. The first statement indexes **p**; the second uses pointer arithmetic. Either way, the result is the same. (Pointers and pointer arithmetic are dealt with in detail in Chapter 6.)

The same holds true for arrays of two or more dimensions. For example, assuming that **a** is a 10-by-10 integer array, these two statements are equivalent:

```
a
```

```
&a[0][0]
```

Further, the 0,4 element of **a** may be referenced either by array-indexing, **a[0][4]**, or by the pointer, ***((*a)+4)**. Similarly, element 1,2 is either **a[1][2]** or ***((*a)+12)**. In general, for any two-dimensional array

$a[j][k]$ is equivalent to $*((*a)+(j*row\ length)+k)$

Pointers are sometimes used to access arrays because pointer arithmetic is often a faster process than array-indexing. The gain in speed using pointers is the greatest when an array is being accessed in purely sequential fashion. In this situation, the pointer may be incremented or decremented using C's highly efficient increment and decrement operators. On the other hand, if the array is to be accessed in random order, then the pointer approach may not be much better than array-indexing.

In a sense, a two-dimensional array is like an array of row pointers to arrays of rows. Therefore, one easy way to use pointers to access two-dimensional arrays is by using a separate pointer variable. The following function prints the contents of the specified row for the global integer array **num**.

```
int num[10][10];
  .
  .
  .
pr_row(int j)
{
  int *p, t;

  p = num[j]; /* get address of first
                    element in row j */
  for(t=0; t<10; ++t) printf("%d ", *(p+t));
}
```

This routine can be generalized by making the calling arguments be the row, the row length, and a pointer to the first array element, as shown here:

```
/* General */
pr_row(int j, int row_dimension, int *p)
{
  int t;

  p = p + (j * row_dimension);
  for(t=0; t<row_dimension; ++t)
    printf("%d ", *(p+t));
}
```

Arrays of greater than two dimensions can be thought of in the same way. For example, a three-dimensional array can be reduced to a pointer to a two-dimensional array, which can be reduced to a pointer to a one-dimensional array. Generally, an N-dimensional array can be reduced to a pointer and an N-1 dimensional array. This new array can be reduced again using the same method. The process ends when a single-dimension array is produced.

Allocated Arrays

In many programming situations it is impossible to know how large an array will be needed. In addition, many types of programs need to use as much memory as is available, yet still run on machines having only minimal memory. A text editor or a database are examples of this. In these situations, it is not possible to use a predefined array because its dimensions are established at compile time and cannot be changed during execution. The solution is to create a *dynamic array*. A dynamic array uses memory from the region of free memory called the *heap* and is accessed by indexing a pointer to that memory. (Remember that any pointer can be indexed as if it were an array variable.)

In C you can dynamically allocate and free memory by using the standard library routines **malloc( )**, which allocates memory and returns a **void *** pointer to the start of it, and **free( )**, which returns previously allocated memory to the heap for possible reuse. The prototypes for **malloc( )** and **free( )** are

```
void *malloc(size_t num_bytes);
```

```
void free(void *p);
```

Both functions use the **stdlib.h** header file. Here, *num_bytes* is the number of bytes requested. The type **size_t** is defined in **stdlib.h** as being capable of holding the largest amount of memory that may be allocated at any one time. If there is not enough free memory to fill the request, **malloc( )** returns a null. It is important that **free( )** be called only with a valid, previously allocated pointer; otherwise damage could be done to the organization of the heap and possibly cause a program crash.

The code fragment shown here allocates 1000 bytes of memory.

```
char *p;

p = malloc(1000); /* get 1000 bytes */
```

The **p** points to the first of 1000 bytes of free memory. Notice that no cast is used to convert the **void** pointer returned by **malloc( )** into the desired **char** pointer. Because **malloc( )** returns a **void** pointer, it can be assigned to any other type of pointer and is automatically converted into a pointer of the target type.

This example shows the proper way to use a dynamically allocated array to read input from the keyboard using **gets( )**.

```
/* Print a string backwards using dynamic allocation. */

#include <stdlib.h>
#include <stdio.h>
#include <string.h>

main(void)
{
  char *s;
  register int t;

  s = malloc(80);

  if(!s) {
    printf("memory request failed\n");
    return 1;
  }

  gets(s);
  for(t=strlen(s)-1; t>=0; t--) printf("%c", s[t]);
  free(s);
  return 0;
}
```

As the program shows, **s** is tested, prior to its first use, to ensure that a valid pointer is returned by **malloc( )**. This is absolutely necessary to prevent accidental use of a null pointer. (Using a null pointer will often cause a system crash.) Notice how the pointer **s** is indexed as an array to print the string backwards.

It is possible to have multidimensional dynamic arrays, but you need to use a function to access them because there must be some way to define the size of all but the leftmost dimension. To do this, a pointer is passed to a function that has its parameter declared with the proper array bounds. To see how this works, study this short example, which builds a table of the numbers 1 through 10 raised to their first, second, third, and fourth powers:

```c
#include <stdlib.h>
#include <stdio.h>

int pwr(int a, int b);
void table(int p[5][11]), show(int p[5][11]);

/* This program displays various numbers raised to
   integer powers. */
main(void)
{
  int *p;

  p = malloc(40*sizeof(int));

  if(!p) {
    printf("memory request failed\n");
    return 1;
  }

  /* here, p is simply a pointer */
  table(p);
  show(p);
  return 0;
}

/* Build a table of numbers. */
void table(int p[5][11]) /* now the compiler thinks that
                            p is an array */
{
  register int i, j;

  for(j=1; j<11; j++)
    for(i=1; i<5; i++) p[i][j] = pwr(j, i);
}

/* Display the table. */
```

```
void show(int p[5][11])
{
  register int i, j;

  printf("%10s %10s %10s %10s\n","N","N^2","N^3","N^4");
  for(j=1; j<11; j++) {
    for(i=1; i<5; i++) printf("%10d ", p[i][j]);
    printf("\n");
  }
}

/* Raise a to the b power. */
pwr(int a, int b)
{
  register int t=1;

  for(; b; b--) t = t*a;
  return t;
}
```

The output produced by this program is

N	N^2	N^3	N^4
1	1	1	1
2	4	8	16
3	9	27	81
4	16	64	256
5	25	125	625
6	36	216	1296
7	49	343	2401
8	64	512	4096
9	81	729	6561
10	100	1000	10000

As this program illustrates, by defining a function parameter to the desired array dimensions you can "trick" Turbo C into handling multidimensional dynamic arrays. Actually, as far as the compiler is concerned, you have a 4,10 integer array inside the functions **show( )** and **table( )**; the difference is that the storage for the array is allocated manually, using the **malloc( )** statement rather than automatically, by using the normal array declaration statement. Also, note the use of **sizeof** to compute the number of bytes needed for a 4,10 integer array. This guarantees the portability of this program to computers with different-sized integers.

Array Initialization

C allows the initialization of global and local arrays at the time of declaration. The general form of array initialization is similar to that of other variables, as shown here:

type-specifier array_name[sizeN]. . .[size1] = { value-list };

The *value-list* is a comma-separated list of constants that are type-compatible with *type-specifier.* The first constant is placed in the first position of the array, the second constant in the second position, and so on. The last entry in the list is not followed by a comma. Note that a semicolon follows the **}**. In the following example, a 10-element integer array is initialized with the numbers 1 through 10:

```
int i[10] = {1, 2, 3, 4, 5, 6, 7, 8, 9, 10};
```

This means that **i[0]** has the value 1 and **i[9]** has the value 10.

Character arrays that hold strings allow a shorthand initialization in the form

char *array_name[size]* = "*string*";

In this form of initialization, the null terminator is automatically appended to the string. For example, this code fragment initializes **str** to the phrase "hello".

```
char str[6] = "hello";
```

This is the same as writing

```
char str[6] = {'h', 'e', 'l', 'l', 'o', '\0'};
```

Notice that in this version you must explicitly include the null terminator. Because all strings in C end with a null, you must make sure that the array you declare is long enough to include it. This is why **str** is six characters long even though "hello" is only five characters. When the string constant is used (as in the previous approach), the compiler automatically supplies the null terminator.

Multidimensional arrays are initialized in the same fashion as single-dimensional ones. For example, the following initializes **sqrs** with the numbers 1 through 10 and their squares:

```
int sqrs[10][2] = {
   1, 1,
   2, 4,
   3, 9,
```

```
    4, 16,
    5, 25,
    6, 36,
    7, 49,
    8, 64,
    9, 81,
    10, 100
};
```

Here, **sqrs[0][0]** contains 1, **sqrs[0][1]** contains 1, **sqrs[1][0]** contains 2, **sqrs[1][1]** contains 4, and so forth.

Unsized-Array Initializations

Imagine that you are using an array initialization to build a table of error messages as shown here:

```
char e1[12] = "read error\n";
char e2[13] = "write error\n";
char e3[18] = "cannot open file\n";
```

As you might guess, it is very tedious to count the characters in each message manually to determine the correct array dimensions. It is possible to let C dimension the arrays automatically by using *unsized arrays*. If the size of the array is not specified in an array initialization statement, the C compiler automatically creates an array big enough to hold all the initializers present. Using this approach, the message table becomes

```
char e1[] = "read error\n";
char e2[] = "write error\n";
char e3[] = "cannot open file\n";
```

Given these initializations, this statement

```
printf("%s has length %d\n", e2, sizeof e2);
```

prints

```
write error
has length 13
```

Aside from being less tedious, the unsized-array initialization method allows any of the messages to be changed without fear of accidentally counting wrong.

Unsized-array initializations are not restricted to only single-dimensional arrays. For multidimensional arrays you must specify all but the leftmost dimensions in order to allow C to index the array properly. (This is similar to specifying array parameters.) In this way, you can build tables of varying lengths and the compiler automatically allocates enough storage for them. For example, the declaration of **sqrs** as an unsized array is shown here:

```
int sqrs[][2] = {
    1, 1,
    2, 4,
    3, 9,
    4, 16,
    5, 25,
    6, 36,
    7, 49,
    8, 64,
    9, 81,
    10, 100
};
```

The advantage to this declaration over the sized version is that the table may be lengthened or shortened without changing the array dimensions.

A Tic-Tac-Toe Example

This chapter concludes with a longer example that illustrates many of the ways arrays can be manipulated using C.

Two-dimensional arrays are commonly used to simulate board game matrices, as in chess and checkers. Although it is beyond the scope of this book to present a chess or checkers program, a simple tic-tac-toe program can be developed.

The tic-tac-toe matrix is represented using a 3-by-3 character array. You are always "X" and the computer is "O". When you move, an "X" is placed in the specified position of the game matrix. When it is the computer's turn to move, it scans the matrix and puts its "O" in the first empty location of the matrix. (This makes for a fairly dull game—you might find it fun to spice it up a bit!) If the computer cannot find an empty location, it reports a draw game and exits. The game matrix is initialized to contain spaces at the start of the game. The tic-tac-toe program is shown here.

```
#include <stdio.h>
#include <stdlib.h>
```

```
/* A simple game of Tic-Tac-Toe. */

#define SPACE  ' '

char matrix[3][3] = {  /* the tic-tac-toe matrix */
  SPACE,SPACE,SPACE,
  SPACE,SPACE,SPACE,
  SPACE,SPACE,SPACE
};

void get_computer_move(void), get_player_move(void);
void disp_matrix(void);
int check(void);

main()
{
  char done;

  printf("This is the game of Tic-Tac-Toe.\n");
  printf("You will be playing against the computer.\n");

  done=SPACE;
  do {
    disp_matrix();          /* display the game board */
    get_player_move();      /* get your move */
    done=check();           /* see if winner */
    if(done!=SPACE) break;  /* winner!*/
    get_computer_move();    /* get computer's move */
    done=check();           /* see if winner */
  } while(done==SPACE);
  if(done=='X') printf("You won!\n");
  else printf("I won!!!!\n");
  disp_matrix(); /* show final positions */

  return 0;
}

/* Input the player's move. */
void get_player_move(void)
{
  int x, y;

  printf("Enter coordinates for your X: ");
  scanf("%d%d",&x, &y);
  x--; y--;
```

```
  if(matrix[x][y]!=SPACE) {
    printf("Invalid move, try again.\n");
    get_player_move();
  }
  else matrix[x][y]='X';
}

/* Get the computer's move */
void get_computer_move(void)
{
  register int t;
  char *p;

  p = (char *) matrix;
  for(t=0; *p!=SPACE && t<9; ++t) p++;
  if(t==9)  {
    printf("draw\n");
    exit(0); /* game over */
  }
  else *p = 'O';
}

/* Display the game board. */
void disp_matrix(void)
{
  int t;

  for(t=0; t<3; t++) {
    printf(" %c | %c | %c ", matrix[t][0],
      matrix[t][1], matrix [t][2]);
    if(t!=2) printf("\n---|---|---\n");
  }
    printf("\n");
}

/* See if there is a winner. */
check(void)
{
  int t;
  char *p;

  for(t=0; t<3; t++) { /* check rows */
    p = &matrix[t][0];
    if(*p==*(p+1) && *(p+1)==*(p+2)) return *p;
  }
```

```
for(t=0; t<3; t++) { /* check columns */
  p = &matrix[0][t];
  if(*p==*(p+3) && *(p+3)==*(p+6)) return *p;
}

/* test diagonals */
if(matrix[0][0]==matrix[1][1] && matrix[1][1]==matrix[2][2])
  return matrix[0][0];

if(matrix[0][2]==matrix[1][1] && matrix[1][1]==matrix[2][0])
  return matrix[0][2];

return SPACE;
}
```

The array is initialized to contain spaces because a space is used to indicate to **get_player_move( )** and **get_computer_move( )** that a matrix position is vacant. The fact that spaces are used instead of nulls simplifies the matrix display function **disp_matrix( )** by allowing the contents of the array to be printed on the screen without any translations. Note that the routine **get_player_move( )** is recursive when an invalid location is entered. This is an example of how recursion can be used to simplify a routine and reduce the amount of code necessary to implement a function.

In the main loop, each time a move is entered the function **check( )** is called. This function determines if the game has been won and by whom. The **check( )** function returns an "X" if you have won, or an "O" if the computer has won. Otherwise, it returns a space. **check( )** works by scanning the rows, the columns, and then the diagonals looking for a winning configuration.

The routines in this example all access the array **matrix** differently. You should study them to make sure that you understand each array operation.

Chapter *6*

Pointers

The correct understanding and use of pointers is critical to the creation of most Turbo C programs for four reasons:

1. Pointers provide the means by which functions can modify their calling arguments.

2. Pointers are used to support Turbo C's dynamic allocation system.

3. The use of pointers can improve the efficiency of certain routines.

4. Pointers are commonly used to support certain data structures such as linked lists and binary trees.

In addition to being one of C's strongest features, pointers are also its most dangerous feature. For example, uninitialized or wild pointers can cause the system to crash. Perhaps worse, it is very easy to use pointers incorrectly, which causes bugs that are very difficult to find.

Because arrays and pointers are interrelated in C, you will want to examine Chapter 5, which covers arrays.

Pointers Are Addresses

A *pointer* contains a memory address. Most commonly, this address is the location of another variable in memory. If one variable contains the address of another variable, the first variable is said to *point* to the second. For example, if a variable at location

1004 is pointed to by a variable at location 1000, location 1000 will contain the value 1004. This situation is illustrated in Figure 6-1.

The 8086 family of processors uses a segmented memory architecture scheme, under which a memory address consists of both a segment *and an* offset *portion. There are six different ways for Turbo C to organize memory, called* memory models, *and each model affects the way pointers are represented internally. For the purposes of this chapter, the memory organization does not matter and the examples work with all memory models. Chapter 10 covers the special cases that relate specifically to each memory model.*

Pointer Variables

If a variable is going to hold a pointer, it must be declared as such. A pointer declaration consists of a base type, an *, and the variable name. The general form for declaring a pointer variable is

type * *name*;

where *type* is any valid C type (the pointer's base type), and *name* is the name of the pointer variable.

The base type of the pointer defines what type of variables the pointer can point to. Technically, any type of pointer can point anywhere in memory, but C assumes that what the pointer is pointing to is an object of its base type. Also, as you will see, all pointer arithmetic is done relative to its base type, so the base type of a pointer is very important.

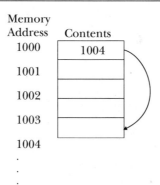

Figure 6-1.   *One variable pointing to another*

The Pointer Operators

There are two special pointer operators: * and **&**. The **&** is a unary operator that returns the memory address of its operand. (A unary operator requires only one operand.) For example,

```
m = &count;
```

places into **m** the memory address of the variable **count**. This address is the computer's internal location of the variable. It has nothing to do with the value of **count**. The operation of the **&** can be remembered as returning "the address of." Therefore, the preceding assignment statement could be read as "**m** receives the address of **count**."

For example, assume the variable **count** uses memory location 2000 to store its value. Also assume that **count** has a value of 100. Then, after the above assignment, **m** will have the value 2000.

The second operator, *, is the complement of **&**. It is a unary operator that returns the value of the variable located at the address that follows. For example, if **m** contains the memory address of the variable **count**,

```
q = *m;
```

places the value of **count** into **q**. Following through with this example, **q** has the value 100 because 100 is stored at location 2000, which is the memory address that was stored in **m**. The operation of the * can be remembered as "at address." In this case the statement could be read as "**q** receives the value at address **m**."

The following program illustrates the foregoing discussion:

```c
#include <stdio.h>

main(void)
{
  int count, q;
  int *m;

  count = 100; /* count is assigned 100 */
  m = &count;  /* m receives count's address */
  q = *m;      /* q is assigned count's value
                  indirectly through m */

  printf("%d", q); /* prints 100 */
```

```
    return 0;
}
```

The above program displays the value 100 on the screen.

Unfortunately, the multiplication sign and the "at address" sign are the same, and the bitwise AND and the "address of" sign are the same. These operators have no relationship to each other. Both **&** and * have a higher precedence than all other arithmetic operators except the unary minus, with which they are equal.

You must make sure that your pointer variables always point to the correct type of data. For example, when you declare a pointer to be of type **int**, the compiler assumes that any address it holds points to an integer value. Because C allows you to assign any address to a pointer variable, the following code fragment compiles (although Turbo C will issue a warning message) but does not produce the desired result.

```
#include <stdio.h>

main(void)
{
  float x, y;
  int   *p;

  x = 100.123;

  p = &x;
  y = *p;
  printf("%f", y);   /* this will be wrong */

  return 0;
}
```

This does not assign the value of **x** to **y**. Because **p** is declared to be an integer pointer, only 2 bytes of information will be transferred to **y**, not the 4 that normally make up a floating point number.

Pointer Expressions

In general, expressions involving pointers conform to the same rules as any other C expression. This section will examine a few special aspects of pointer expressions.

Pointer Assignments

As with any variable, a pointer may be used on the right-hand side of assignment statements to assign its value to another pointer. For example:

```
#include <stdio.h>

main(void)
{
  int x;
  int *p1, *p2;

  p1 = &x;
  p2 = p1;

  /* This will display the addresses held by
     p1 and p2. They will be the same.
  */
  printf("%p  %p", p1, p2);

  return 0;
}
```

Here, both **p1** and **p2** will contain the address of **x**.

Pointer Arithmetic

Only two arithmetic operations can be used on pointers: addition and subtraction. To understand what occurs in pointer arithmetic, let **p1** be a pointer to an integer with a current value of 2000, and assume that integers are 2 bytes long. After the expression

```
p1++;
```

the content of **p1** is 2002, not 2001! Each time **p1** is incremented, it points to the next integer. The same is true of decrements. For example,

```
p1--;
```

will cause **p1** to have the value 1998, assuming that it previously was 2000.

Each time a pointer is incremented, it points to the memory location of the next element of its base type. Each time it is decremented it points to the location of the previous element. In the case of pointers to characters this appears as "normal" arithmetic. However, all other pointers increase or decrease by the length of the data type they point to. For example, assuming 1-byte characters and 2-byte integers, when a character pointer is incremented, its value increases by 1; however, when an integer pointer is incremented its value increases by 2. This happens because all pointer arithmetic is done relative to the base type of the pointer so that the pointer is always pointing to another element of the base type. Figure 6-2 illustrates this concept.

You are not limited to increment and decrement, however. You may also add or subtract integers to or from pointers. The expression

```
p1 = p1 + 9;
```

makes **p1** point to the ninth element of **p1**'s type beyond the one it is currently pointing to.

Besides addition and subtraction of a pointer and an integer, the only other operation you can perform on a pointer is to subtract it from another pointer. For the most part, subtracting one pointer from another only makes sense when both pointers point to a common object, such as an array. The subtraction then yields the number of elements of the base type separating the two pointer values. Aside from these operations, no other arithmetic operations can be performed on pointers. You cannot multiply or divide pointers; you cannot add pointers; you cannot apply the bitwise shift and mask operators to them; and you cannot add or subtract type **float** or **double** to pointers.

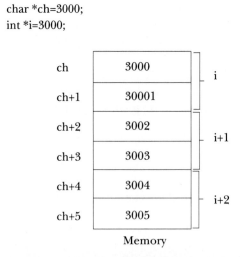

```
char *ch=3000;
int *i=3000;
```

Figure 6-2.   *All pointer arithmetic is relative to its base type*

Pointer Comparisons

It is possible to compare two pointers in a relational expression. For instance, given the pointers **p** and **q**, the following statement is perfectly valid:

```
if(p<q)printf("p points to lower memory than q\n");
```

In Turbo C, there are some special problems associated with **far** pointer comparisons. Because of this, the material presented here is applicable only to **near** or **huge** pointers. (The difficulties associated with **far** pointers are discussed in Chapter 10 when the Turbo C memory models are explained.)

Generally, pointer comparisons are used when two or more pointers are pointing to a common object. As an example, imagine that you are constructing a stack routine to hold integer values. A stack is a list that uses "first in, last out" accessing. It is often compared to a stack of plates on a table—the first one set down is the last one to be used. Stacks are used frequently in compilers, interpreters, spreadsheets, and other system-related software. To create a stack, you need two routines: **push( )** and **pop( )**. The **push( )** function puts values on the stack and **pop( )** takes them off. The stack is held in the array **stack**, which is **STCKSIZE** elements long. The variable **tos** holds the memory address of the top of the stack and is used to prevent stack underflows. Once the stack has been initialized, **push( )** and **pop( )** may be used as a stack for integers. These routines are shown here with a simple **main( )** function to drive them:

```
#include <stdio.h>
#include <stdlib.h>

#define STCKSIZE 50

void push(int i);
int pop(void);

int *p1, *tos, stack[STCKSIZE];

main(void)
{
  int value;

  p1 =  stack; /* assign p1 the start of stack */
  tos = p1;  /* let tos hold top of stack */

  do {
    printf("Enter a number (-1 to quit, 0 to pop): ");
    scanf("%d", &value);
    if(value!=0) push(value);
```

```
    else printf("this is it %d\n", pop());
  } while(value!=-1);
  return 0;
}

void push(int i)
{
  p1++;
  if(p1==(tos + STCKSIZE)) {
    printf("stack overflow");
    exit(1);
  }
  *p1 = i;
}

pop(void)
{
  if(p1==tos) {
    printf("stack underflow");
    exit(1);
  }
  p1--;
  return *(p1+1);
}
```

Both the **push( )** and **pop( )** functions perform a relational test on the pointer **p1** to detect limit errors. In **push( )**, **p1** is tested against the end of stack by adding **STCKSIZE** (the size of the stack) to **tos**. In **pop( )**, **p1** is checked against **tos** to be sure that a stack underflow has not occurred.

In **pop( )**, the parentheses are necessary in the **return** statement. Without them, the statement would look like

```
return *p1 + 1;
```

which would return the value at location **p1** plus 1, not the value of the location **p1+1**. You must be very careful to use parentheses to ensure the correct order of evaluation.

Turbo C's Dynamic Allocation Functions

Once compiled, all C programs organize the computer's memory into four regions, which hold program code, global data, the stack, and the heap. The heap is an area of free memory that is managed by C's dynamic allocation functions **malloc( )** and **free( )**.

The **malloc( )** function allocates memory and returns a pointer to the start of it, and **free( )** returns previously allocated memory to the heap for possible reuse. The general forms for **malloc( )** and **free( )** are

void ∗ malloc(size_t *num_bytes*);

void free(void ∗*p*);

Both functions use the **stdlib.h** header file. Here, *num_bytes* is the number of bytes requested. If there is not enough free memory to fill the request, **malloc( )** returns a null. The type **size_t** is defined in **stdlib.h** and specifies a type that is capable of holding the largest amount of memory that may be allocated with a single call to **malloc( )**. It is important that **free( )** be called only with a valid, previously allocated pointer; otherwise the organization of the heap could be damaged, which might cause a program crash.

The code fragment shown here allocates 25 bytes of memory:

```
char *p;

p = malloc(25);
```

After the assignment, **p** points to the first of 25 bytes of free memory. Notice that no type cast is used with **malloc( )**; the pointer type is converted automatically to the same type as the pointer variable on the left side of the assignment. As another example, this fragment allocates space for 50 integers. It uses **sizeof** to ensure portability.

```
int *p;

p = malloc(50*sizeof(int));
```

Since the heap is not infinite, whenever you allocate memory it is imperative to check the value returned by **malloc( )** to make sure that it is not null before using the pointer. Using a null pointer may crash the computer. The proper way to allocate memory and test for a valid pointer is illustrated in this code fragment:

```
if((p=malloc(100))==NULL) {
  printf("Out of memory.\n");
  exit(1);
}
```

The macro NULL is defined in **stdlib.h**. Of course, you can substitute some other sort of error handler in place of **exit( )**. The point is that you do not want the pointer **p** to be used if it is null.

You should include the header file **stdlib.h** at the top of any file that uses **malloc( )** and **free( )** because it contains their prototypes.

Pointers and Arrays

There is a close relationship between pointers and arrays. Consider this fragment:

```
char str[80], *p1;
p1 = str;
```

Here, **p1** has been set to the address of the first array element in **str**. If you wished to access the fifth element in **str** you could write

```
str[4]
```

or

```
*(p1+4)
```

Both statements return the fifth element. Remember, arrays start at 0, so a 4 is used to index **str**. You add 4 to the pointer **p1** to get the fifth element because **p1** currently points to the first element of **str**. (Remember that an array name without an index returns the starting address of the array, which is the first element.)

In essence C allows two methods of accessing array elements. This is important because pointer arithmetic can be faster than array-indexing. Since speed is often a consideration in programming, the use of pointers to access array elements is very common in C programs.

To see an example of how pointers can be used in place of array-indexing, consider these two simplified versions of the **puts( )** standard library function—one with array-indexing and one with pointers. The **puts( )** function writes a string to the standard output device.

```
/* use array */
puts(char *s)
{
  register int t;

  for(t=0; s[t]; ++t) putch(s[t]);
```

```
    return 1;
}

/* use pointer */
puts(char *s)
{
  while(*s) putch(*s++);
  return 1;
}
```

Most professional C programmers would find the second version easier to read and understand. In fact, the pointer version is the way routines of this sort are commonly written in C.

Sometimes novice C programmers make the mistake of thinking that they should never use array-indexing because pointers are much more efficient. But this is not the case. If the array is going to be accessed in strictly ascending or descending order, pointers are faster and easier to use. However, if the array is going to be accessed randomly, array-indexing may be as good as using pointer arithmetic because it will be about as fast as evaluating a complex pointer expression. Also, when you use array-indexing, you are letting the compiler do some of the work for you.

Pointers to Character Arrays

Many string operations in C are usually performed by using pointers and pointer arithmetic because strings tend to be accessed in a strictly sequential fashion.

For example, here is one version of the standard library function **strcmp( )** that uses pointers:

```
/* use pointers */
strcmp(char *s1, char *s2)
{
  while(*s1)
    if(*s1-*s2)
      return *s1-*s2;
    else {
      s1++;
      s2++;
    }
  return 0; /* equal */
}
```

Remember, all strings in C are terminated by a null, which is a false value. Therefore, a statement such as

```
while (*s1)
```

is true until the end of the string is reached. Here, **strcmp( )** returns 0 if **s1** is equal to **s2**. It returns less than 0 if **s1** is less than **s2**; otherwise it returns greater than 0.

Most string functions resemble **strcmp( )** with regard to the way it uses pointers, especially where loop control is concerned. Using pointers is faster, more efficient, and often easier to understand than using array-indexing.

One common error that sometimes creeps in when using pointers is illustrated by the following program:

```
/* This program is incorrect. */

#include <stdio.h>
#include <string.h>

main(void)
{
  char *p1, s[80];

  p1 = s;  /* assign p1 the starting address of s */
  do {
    gets(s);  /* read a string */

    /* print the decimal equivalent of each
       character */
    while(*p1) printf(" %d", *p1++);

  } while(strcmp(s, "done"));
  return 0;
}
```

Can you find the error in this program?

The problem is that **p1** is assigned the address of **s** only once—outside the loop. The first time through the loop, **p1** does point to the first character in **s**. However, in the second (and subsequent iterations), it continues from where it left off, because it is not reset to the start of the array **s**. This causes the next string input using **gets( )** to be put after the null terminator of the first string, meaning that **p1** continues to point to the null terminator of the first string. The proper way to write this program is

```
/* This program is correct. */

#include <stdio.h>
#include <string.h>
```

```
main(void)
{
  char *p1, s[80];

  do {
    p1 = s; /* assign p1 the starting address of s */
    gets(s);  /* read a string */

    /* print the decimal equivalent of each
       character */
    while(*p1) printf(" %d", *p1++);

  } while(strcmp(s, "done"));
  return 0;
}
```

Here, each time the loop iterates, **p1** is set to the start of string **s**.

Arrays of Pointers

Pointers may be arrayed like any other data type. The declaration for an **int** pointer array of size 10 is

```
int *x[10];
```

To assign the address of an integer variable called **var** to the third element of the array, you would write:

```
x[2] = &var;
```

To find the value of **var**, you would write

```
*x[2]
```

If you want to pass an array of pointers into a function, you can use the same method used for other arrays—simply call the function with the array name without any indexes. For example, a function that will receive array **x** would look like:

```
void display_array(int *q[])
{
  int t;

  for(t=0; t<10; t++)
```

```
      printf("%d ", *q[t]);
}
```

Remember, **q** is not a pointer to integers, but to an array of pointers to integers. Therefore it is necessary to declare the parameter **q** as an array of integer pointers as shown here. It may not be declared simply as an integer pointer because that is not what it is.

A common use of pointer arrays is to hold pointers to error messages. You can create a function that outputs a message given its code number, as shown here:

```
void serror(int num)
{
  static char *err[] = {
    "cannot open file\n",
    "read error\n",
    "write error\n",
    "media failure\n"
  };

  printf("%s", err[num]);
}
```

As you can see, **printf( )** inside **serror( )** is called with a character pointer that points to one of the various error messages indexed by the error number passed to the function. For example, if **num** is passed a 2, the message "write error" is displayed.

It is interesting to note that the command-line argument **argv** is an array of character pointers.

Pointers to Pointers

An array of pointers is the same as *pointers to pointers*. The concept of arrays of pointers is straightforward because the indexes keep the meaning clear. However, pointers to pointers can be very confusing.

A pointer to a pointer is a form of multiple indirection, or a chain of pointers. Consider Figure 6-3.

In the case of a normal pointer, the value of the pointer is the address of the variable that contains the value desired. In the case of a pointer to a pointer, the first pointer contains the address of the second pointer, which contains the address of the variable, which contains the value desired.

Multiple indirection can be carried on to whatever extent desired, but there are few cases where using more than a pointer to a pointer is necessary, or even wise. Excessive indirection is difficult to follow and prone to conceptual errors. (Do not

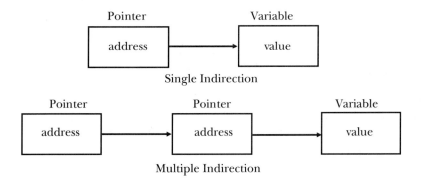

Figure 6-3. *Single and multiple indirection*

confuse multiple indirection with linked lists, which are used in databases and the like.)

A variable that is a pointer to a pointer must be declared as such. This is done by placing an additional asterisk in front of its name. For example, this declaration tells the compiler that **newbalance** is a pointer to a pointer of type **float**.

```
float **newbalance;
```

It is important to understand that **newbalance** is not a pointer to a floating point number but rather a pointer to a **float** pointer.

In order to access the target value indirectly pointed to by a pointer to a pointer, the asterisk operator must be applied twice as is shown in this short example:

```
#include <stdio.h>

main(void)
{
  int x, *p, **q;

  x = 10;
  p = &x;
  q = &p;

  printf("%d", **q); /* print the value of x */

  return 0;
}
```

Here, **p** is declared as a pointer to an integer, and **q** as a pointer to a pointer to an integer. The call to **printf( )** prints the number 10 on the screen.

Initializing Pointers

After a pointer is declared, but before it has been assigned a value, it contains an unknown value. If you try to use the pointer prior to giving it a value, you probably will crash not only your program but also the operating system of your computer—a very nasty type of error!

By convention, a pointer that is pointing nowhere should be given the value null to signify that it points to nothing. However, just because a pointer has a null value does not make it "safe." If you use a null pointer on the left side of an assignment statement you still risk crashing your program or operating system.

Because a null pointer is assumed to be unused, you can use the null pointer to make many of your pointer routines easier to code and more efficient. For example, you could use a null pointer to mark the end of a pointer array. If this is done, a routine that accesses that array knows that it has reached the end when the null value is encountered. This type of approach is illustrated by the **search( )** function shown here:

```
  /* look up a name */
search(char *p[], char *name)
{
  register int t;
  for(t=0; p[t]; ++t)
    if(!strcmp(p[t], name)) return t;

  return -1; /* not found */
}
```

The **for** loop inside **search( )** runs until either a match or a null pointer is found. Because the end of the array is marked with a null, the condition controlling the loop fails when it is reached.

It is common in professionally written C programs to initialize strings. You saw an example of this in the **serror( )** function shown earlier. Another variation on this theme is the following type of string declaration:

```
char *p = "hello world\n";
```

As you can see, the pointer **p** is not an array. The reason this sort of initialization works has to do with the way Turbo C operates. All C compilers create what is called a *string table*, which is used internally by the compiler to store the string constants used by the program. Therefore, this declaration statement places the address of "hello world," into the pointer **p**. Throughout the program **p** can be used like any other string. For example, the following program is perfectly valid:

```
#include <stdio.h>
#include <string.h>

char *p = "hello world";

main(void)
{
  register int t;

  /* print the string forward and backwards */
  printf(p);
  for(t=strlen(p)-1; t>-1; t--) printf("%c", p[t]);
  return 0;
}
```

Pointers to Functions

In Chapter 4, you were introduced to a particularly confusing yet powerful feature of C, the *function pointer*. Even though a function is not a variable, it still has a physical location in memory that can be assigned to a pointer. A function's address is the entry point of the function. Because of this a function pointer can be used to call a function. In this section, we will look at another use for the function pointer.

In certain types of programs the user can select one option from a long list of possible actions. For example, in an accounting program, you may be presented with a menu that has 20 or more selections. Once the selection has been made, the routine that routes program execution to the proper function can be handled two ways. The most common way is to use a **switch** statement. However, in applications that demand the highest performance there is a better way. An array of pointers can be created with each pointer in the array containing the address of a function. The selection made by the user is decoded and is used to index into the pointer array, causing the proper function to be executed. This method can be very fast—much faster than the **switch** method.

To see how an array of function pointers can be used as described, imagine that you are implementing a very simple inventory system that is capable of entering, deleting, and reviewing data, as well as exiting to the operating system. If the functions that perform these activities are called **enter( )**, **delete( )**, **review( )**, and **quit( )**, respectively, the following fragment correctly initializes an array of function pointers to these functions:

```
void enter(void), delete(void), review(void), quit(void);
int menu(void);

void (*options[])(void) = {
  enter,
  delete,
  review,
  quit
} ;
```

Pay special attention to the way an array of function pointers is declared. Notice the placement of the parentheses and square brackets.

Although the actual inventory routines are not developed, the following program illustrates the proper way to execute the functions by using the function pointers. Notice how the **menu( )** function automatically returns the proper index into the pointer array.

```
#include <stdlib.h>
#include <stdio.h>
#include <conio.h>
#include <string.h>

void enter(void), delete(void), review(void), quit(void);
int menu(void);

void (*options[])(void) = {
  enter,
  delete,
  review,
  quit
} ;

main(void)
{
  int i;

  i = menu(); /* get user's choice */

  (*options[i])();  /* execute it */
  return 0;

}

menu(void)
```

```
{
  char ch;

  do {

    printf("1. Enter\n");
    printf("2. Delete\n");
    printf("3. Review\n");
    printf("4. Quit\n");
    printf("Select a number: ");
    ch = getche();
    printf("\n");
  } while(!strchr("1234", ch));
  return ch-49; /* convert to an integer equivalent */
}

void enter(void)
{
  printf("in enter");
}

void delete(void)
{
  printf("in delete");
}

void review(void)
{
  printf("in review");
}

void quit(void)
{
  printf("in quit");
  exit(0);
}
```

The program works like this. The menu is displayed, and the user enters the number of the selection desired. Since the number is in ASCII, 49 (the decimal value of 0) is subtracted from it in order to convert it into a binary integer. This value is then returned to **main( )** and is used as an index to **options**, the array of function pointers. Next, the call to the proper function is executed.

Using arrays of function pointers is very common, not only in interpreters and compilers but also in database programs, because often these programs provide a large number of options and efficiency is important.

Problems with Pointers

Nothing will get you into more trouble than a "wild" pointer! Pointers are a mixed blessing. They give you tremendous power and are necessary for many programs. But when a pointer accidentally contains a wrong value, it can be the most difficult bug to track down. The pointer itself is not the problem; the problem is that each time you perform an operation using it, you are reading or writing to some unknown piece of memory. If you read from it, the worst that can happen is that you get garbage. However, if you write to it, you write over other pieces of your code or data. This may not show up until later in the execution of your program, and may lead you to look for the bug in the wrong place. There may be little or no evidence to suggest that the pointer is the problem.

Because pointer errors are such nightmares, you should do your best never to generate one. Toward this end, a few of the more common errors are discussed here.

The classic example of a pointer error is the *uninitialized pointer.* For example:

```
/* This program is wrong. */

main(void)
{
  int x, *p;

  x = 10;
  *p = x;
  return 0;
}
```

This program assigns the value 10 to some unknown memory location. The pointer **p** has never been given a value; therefore it contains a garbage value. This type of problem often goes unnoticed when your program is very small because the odds are in favor of **p** containing a "safe" address—one that is not in your code, data, stack, heap, or operating system. However, as your program grows, so does the probability of **p** pointing into something vital. Eventually your program stops working. The solution to this sort of trouble is to make sure that a pointer is always pointing at something valid before it is used.

A second common error is caused by a simple misunderstanding of how to use a pointer. For example:

```
#include <stdio.h>

/* this program is wrong */
main(void)
{
```

```
  int x, *p;

  x = 10;
  p = x;
  printf("%d", *p);
  return 0;
}
```

The call to **printf( )** does not print the value of **x**, which is 10, on the screen. It prints some unknown value because the assignment

```
p = x;
```

is wrong. That statement has assigned the value 10 to the pointer **p**, which was supposed to contain an address, not a value. To make the program correct, you should write

```
p = &x;
```

The fact that pointers can cause very tricky bugs if handled incorrectly is no reason to avoid using them. Simply be careful and make sure that you know where each pointer is pointing before using it.

Chapter 7

Structures, Unions, and User-Defined Variables

The C language gives you five ways to create custom data types:

1. The *structure* is a grouping of variables under one name and is sometimes called a *conglomerate* data type.

2. The *bit-field* is a variation of the structure and allows easy access to the individual bits within a word.

3. The *union* enables the same piece of memory to be defined as two or more different types of variables.

4. The *enumeration* is a list of symbols.

5. The *typedef* keyword simply creates a new name for an existing type.

Structures

In C, a *structure* is a collection of variables that are referenced under one name, providing a convenient means of keeping related information together. A *structure declaration* forms a template that may be used to create structure variables. The variables that make up the structure are called *structure elements*. Generally, all the elements in the structure are related to each other logically. For example, the name and address information found in a mailing list is normally represented as a structure.

To understand structures, it is best to begin with an example. The following code fragment declares a structure template that defines the name and address fields of a mailing list structure. The keyword **struct** tells the compiler that a structure is being declared.

```
struct addr {
  char name[30];
  char street[40];
  char city[20];
  char state[3];
  unsigned long int zip;
};
```

The declaration is terminated by a semicolon because a structure declaration is a statement. Also, the structure name **addr** identifies this particular data structure and is its type specifier. The structure name is often referred to as its *tag*.

At this point in the code, *no variable has actually been declared*. Only the form of the data has been defined. To declare an actual variable with this structure, you would write

```
struct addr addr_info;
```

This declares a structure variable of type **addr** called **addr_info**. When you declare a structure, you are essentially defining a complex variable type composed of the structure elements. Not until you declare a variable of that type does one actually exist.

Turbo C automatically allocates sufficient memory to accommodate all the variables that make up a structure variable. Figure 7-1 shows how **addr_info** appears in memory assuming 1-byte characters and 2-byte integers.

You may also declare one or more variables at the same time that you declare a structure. For example,

```
struct addr {
  char name[30];
  char street[40];
  char city[20];
  char state[3];
  unsigned long int zip;
} addr_info, binfo, cinfo;
```

declares a structure type called **addr** and declares variables **addr_info**, **binfo**, and **cinfo** of that type.

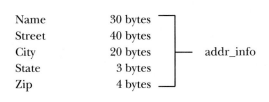

Figure 7-1. *The* **addr_info** *structure as it appears in memory*

If you need only one structure variable, the structure tag name is not needed. This means that

```
struct  {
  char name[30];
  char street[40];
  char city[20];
  char state[3];
  unsigned long int zip;
} addr_info;
```

declares one variable named **addr_info** as defined by the structure preceding it.

The general form of a structure declaration is

struct *structure_tag_name*{
 type variable_name;
 type variable_name;
 type variable_name;
 .
 .
 .
} *structure_variables;*

The *structure_tag_name* is the name of the structure—not a variable name. The *structure_variables* are a comma-separated list of variable names. Remember, either *structure_tag_name* or *structure_variables* are optional, but not both.

Referencing Structure Elements

Individual structure elements are referenced by using the . (usually called the "dot") operator. For example, the following code assigns the zip code 12345 to the **zip** field of the structure variable **addr_info** declared earlier:

```
addr_info.zip = 12345;
```

The structure variable name followed by a period and the element name references that individual structure element. All structure elements are accessed in the same way. The general form is

structure_name.element_name

Therefore, to print the zip code to the screen, you could write

```
printf("%ld", addr_info.zip);
```

This prints the zip code contained in the **zip** variable of the structure variable **addr_info**.

In the same fashion, the **addr_info.name** character array can be used with **gets( )** as shown here:

```
gets(addr_info.name);
```

This passes a character pointer to the start of the element **name**.

To access the individual elements of **addr_info.name**, you could index **name**. For example, you could print the contents of **addr_info.name** one character at a time by using this code:

```
register int t;
```

```
for(t=0; addr_info.name[t]; ++t) putch(addr_info.name[t]);
```

Arrays of Structures

Perhaps the most common use of structures is in *arrays of structures*. To declare an array of structures, you must first define a structure, and then declare an array variable of that type. For example, to declare a 100-element array of structures of type **addr**, which was declared earlier in this chapter, you would write

```
struct addr addr_info[100];
```

This creates 100 sets of variables that are organized as declared in the structure type **addr**.

To access a specific structure within the **addr_info** array, the structure variable name is indexed. For example, to print the zip code of the third structure, you would write

```
printf("%ld", addr_info[2].zip);
```

Like all array variables, arrays of structures begin their indexing at 0.

An Inventory Example

To help illustrate how structures and arrays of structures are used, consider a simple inventory program that uses an array of structures to hold the inventory information. The functions in this program interact with structures and their elements in various ways to illustrate structure usage.

In this example, the information to be stored includes

item name

cost

number on hand

You can define the basic data structure, called **inv**, to hold this information as

```
#define MAX 100

struct inv {
  char item[30];
  float cost;
  int on_hand;
} inv_info[MAX];
```

In the **inv** structure, **item** is used to hold each inventoried item's name. The element **cost** contains the item's cost, and **on_hand** represents the number of items currently available.

The first function needed for the program is **main( )**.

```
main(void)
{
  char choice;

  init_list(); /* initialize the structure array*/
  for(;;) {
    choice = menu_select();
    switch(choice) {
      case 1: enter();
        break;
```

```
      case 2: delete();
        break;
      case 3: list();
        break;
      case 4: return 0;
    }
  }
}
```

In **main( )**, the call to **init_list( )** prepares the structure array for use by putting a null character into the first byte of the **item** field. The program assumes that a structure variable is not in use if the **item** field is empty. The **init_list( )** function is defined as follows.

```
/* Initialize the structure array. */
void init_list(void)
{
  register int t;

  for(t=0; t<MAX; ++t) inv_info[t].item[0] = '\0';
}
```

The **menu_select( )** function displays the option messages and returns the user's selection:

```
/* Input the user's selection. */
menu_select(void)
{
  char s[80];
  int c;

  printf("\n");
  printf("1. Enter an item\n");
  printf("2. Delete an item\n");
  printf("3. List the inventory\n");
  printf("4. Quit\n");
  do {
    printf("\nEnter your choice: ");
    gets(s);
    c = atoi(s);
  } while(c<0 || c>4);
  return c;
}
```

The **enter( )** function prompts the user for input and places the information entered into the next free structure. If the array is full, the message "list full" is printed on the screen. The function **find_free( )** searches the structure array for an unused element.

```
/* Input the inventory information. */
void enter(void)
{
  int slot;

  slot = find_free();
  if(slot == -1) {
    printf("\nlist full");
    return;
  }

  printf("enter item: ");
  gets(inv_info[slot].item);

  printf("enter cost: ");
  scanf("%f", &inv_info[slot].cost);

  printf("enter number on hand: ");
  scanf("%d%*c",&inv_info[slot].on_hand);
}

/* Return the index of the first unused array
   location or -1 if no free locations exist.
*/
find_free(void)
{
  register int t;

  for(t=0; inv_info[t].item[0] && t<MAX; ++t) ;
  if(t == MAX) return -1; /* no slots free */
  return t;
}
```

Notice that **find_free( )** returns a −1 if every structure array variable is in use. This is a "safe" number to use because there cannot be a −1 element of the **inv_info** array.

The **delete( )** function requires the user to specify the number of the item that needs to be deleted. The function then puts a null character in the first character position of the **item** field.

```
/* Delete an item from the list. */
void delete(void)
{
  register int slot;
  char s[80];

  printf("enter record #: ");
  gets(s);
  slot = atoi(s);
  if(slot >= 0 && slot < MAX) inv_info[slot].item[0]='\0';
}
```

The final function the program needs is **list( )**. It prints the entire inventory list on the screen.

```
/* Display the list on the screen. */
void list(void)
{
  register int t;

  for(t=0; t<MAX; ++t) {
    if(inv_info[t].item[0]) {
      printf("item: %s\n", inv_info[t].item);
      printf("cost: %f\n", inv_info[t].cost);
      printf("on hand: %d\n\n", inv_info[t].on_hand);
    }
  }
  printf("\n\n");
}
```

The complete listing for the inventory program is shown here. If you have any doubts about your understanding of structures, you should enter this program into your computer and study its execution by making changes and watching their effects.

```
/* A simple inventory program using an array of structures */

#include <stdio.h>
#include <stdlib.h>

#define MAX 100

struct inv {
  char item[30];
  float cost;
```

```
    int on_hand;
} inv_info[MAX];

void init_list(void), list(void), delete(void);
void enter(void);
int menu_select(void), find_free(void);

main(void)
{
  char choice;

  init_list(); /* initialize the structure array*/
  for(;;) {
    choice = menu_select();
    switch(choice) {
      case 1: enter();
        break;
      case 2: delete();
        break;
      case 3: list();
        break;
      case 4: return 0;
    }
  }
}

/* Initialize the structure array. */
void init_list(void)
{
  register int t;

  for(t=0; t<MAX; ++t) inv_info[t].item[0] = '\0';
}

/* Input the user's selection. */
menu_select(void)
{
  char s[80];
  int c;

  printf("\n");
  printf("1. Enter an item\n");
  printf("2. Delete an item\n");
  printf("3. List the inventory\n");
  printf("4. Quit\n");
```

```
  do {
    printf("\nEnter your choice: ");
    gets(s);
    c = atoi(s);
  } while(c<0 || c>4);
  return c;
}

/* Input the inventory information. */
void enter(void)
{
  int slot;

  slot = find_free();
  if(slot == -1) {
    printf("\nlist full");
    return;
  }

  printf("enter item: ");
  gets(inv_info[slot].item);

  printf("enter cost: ");
  scanf("%f", &inv_info[slot].cost);

  printf("enter number on hand: ");
  scanf("%d%*c", &inv_info[slot].on_hand);
}

/* Return the index of the first unused array
   location or -1 if no free locations exist.
*/
find_free(void)
{
  register int t;

  for(t=0; inv_info[t].item[0] && t<MAX; ++t) ;
  if(t == MAX) return -1; /* no slots free */
  return t;
}

/* Delete an item from the list. */
void delete(void)
{
  register int slot;
```

```
  char s[80];

  printf("enter record #: ");
  gets(s);
  slot = atoi(s);
  if(slot >= 0 && slot < MAX) inv_info[slot].item[0] = '\0';
}

/* Display the list on the screen. */
void list(void)
{
  register int t;

  for(t=0; t<MAX; ++t) {
    if(inv_info[t].item[0]) {
      printf("item: %s\n", inv_info[t].item);
      printf("cost: %f\n", inv_info[t].cost);
      printf("on hand: %d\n\n", inv_info[t].on_hand);
    }
  }
  printf("\n\n");
}
```

Passing Structures to Functions

So far, all structures and arrays of structures used in the examples have been assumed to be either global or defined within the function that uses them. In this section special consideration will be given to passing structures and their elements to functions.

Passing Structure Elements to Functions

When you pass an element of a structure variable to a function, you are actually passing the value of that element to the function. Therefore, you are passing a simple variable (unless, of course, that element is an array, in which case an address is passed). For example, consider this structure:

```
struct fred {
  char x;
  int y;
  float z;
  char s[10];
} mike;
```

Here are examples of each element being passed to a function:

```
func(mike.x);   /* passes character value of x */

func2(mike.y); /* passes integer value of y */

func3(mike.z); /* passes float value of z */

func4(mike.s); /* passes address of string s */

func(mike.s[2]); /* passes character value of s[2] */
```

However, if you wished to pass the address of individual structure elements to achieve call by reference parameter passing, you would place the **&** operator before the structure name. For example, to pass the address of the elements in the structure **mike**, you would write

```
func(&mike.x);   /* passes address of character x */

func2(&mike.y); /* passes address of integer y */

func3(&mike.z); /* passes address of float z */

func4(mike.s); /* passes address of string s */

func(&mike.s[2]); /* passes address of character s[2] */
```

Notice that the **&** operator precedes the structure name, not the individual element name. Note also that the string element **s** already signifies an address, so that no **&** is required. However, when accessing a specific character in string **s**, as shown in the final example, the **&** is still needed.

Passing Entire Structures to Functions

When a structure is used as an argument to a function, the entire structure is passed using the standard call by value method. This means that any changes made to the contents of the structure inside the function to which it is passed do not affect the structure used as an argument.

When using a structure as a parameter, the most important thing to remember is that the type of the argument must match the type of the parameter. The best way to do this is to define a structure globally and then use its name to declare structure variables and parameters as needed. For example:

```
#include <stdio.h>

/* declare a structure type */
struct struct_type {
  int a, b;
  char ch;
} ;

void f1(struct struct_type parm);

main(void)
{
  struct struct_type arg;   /* declare arg */

  arg.a = 1000;

  f1(arg);

  return 0;
}

void f1(struct struct_type parm)
{
  printf("%d", parm.a);
}
```

This program prints the number 1000 on the screen. As you can see, both **arg** and **parm** are declared to be structures of type **struct_type**.

Structure Pointers

C allows pointers to structures in the same way it does to other types of variables. However, there are some special aspects to structure pointers that you must keep in mind.

Declaring a Structure Pointer

Structure pointers are declared by placing the * in front of a structure variable's name. For example, assuming the previously defined structure **addr**, the following declares **addr_pointer** to be a pointer to data of that type:

```
struct addr *addr_pointer;
```

Accessing Structure Pointers

To find the address of a structure variable, the **&** operator is placed before the structure's name. For example, given the following fragment,

```
struct bal {
  float balance;
  char name[80];
} person;

struct bal *p;  /* declare a structure pointer */
```

then

```
p = &person;
```

places the address of the structure **person** into the pointer **p**.

One of the most important things to remember about pointers to structures is that you *cannot* use the dot operator to access a structure element given a pointer to that structure. Instead, you must use the *arrow operator.* The arrow operator, –>, is formed using a minus sign and a greater-than symbol. For example, to reference the **balance** element using **p**, you would write

```
p->balance
```

To see how structure pointers can be used, examine this simple program that prints the hours, minutes, and seconds on the screen using a software timer. (The timing of the program is adjusted by varying the loop counter in **mydelay( )** to fit the speed of your computer.)

```
/* Display a software timer. */

#include <stdio.h>
#include <conio.h>

struct tm {
  int hours;
  int minutes;
  int seconds;
} ;

void update(struct tm *t), display(struct tm *t);
void mydelay(void);
```

```
main(void)
{
  struct tm time;

  time.hours = 0;
  time.minutes = 0;
  time.seconds = 0;

  for(;;) {
    update(&time);
    display(&time);
    if(kbhit()) return 0;
  }
}

void update(struct tm *t)
{
  t->seconds++;
  if(t->seconds==60) {
    t->seconds=0;
    t->minutes++;
  }
  if(t->minutes==60) {
    t->minutes=0;
    t->hours++;
  }
  if(t->hours==24) t->hours = 0;
  mydelay();
}

void display(struct tm *t)
{
  printf("%d:", t->hours);
  printf("%d:", t->minutes);
  printf("%d\n", t->seconds);
}

void mydelay(void)
{
  long int t;

  for(t=1; t<128000; ++t) ;
}
```

A global structure called **tm** is declared but no variable is declared. Inside **main( )**, the structure variable, **time**, of type **tm** is declared and initialized to 00:00:00. This means that **time** is known directly only to the **main( )** function.

The functions **update( )**, which changes the time, and **display( )**, which prints the time, are passed the address of **time**. In both functions the argument is declared to be a pointer to a structure of type **tm**.

Each structure element is actually referenced by a pointer. For example, if you wanted to set the hours back to 0 when 24:00:00 was reached, you would write

```
if(t->hours==24) t->hours = 0;
```

This line of code tells the compiler to take the address of **t** (which points to **time** in **main( )**) and assign 0 to its element called **hours**.

Use the dot operator to access structure elements when operating on the structure itself. Use the arrow operator when referencing a structure through a pointer.

As a final example of using structure pointers, the following program illustrates how a general-purpose integer input function can be designed. The function **input_xy( )** allows you to specify the **x** and **y** coordinates at which a prompting message will be displayed and then inputs an integer value. To accomplish these things it uses the structure **xyinput**.

```
/* A generalized input example using structure pointers. */

#include <stdio.h>
#include <conio.h>
#include <string.h>

struct xyinput {
  int x, y; /* screen location for prompt */
  char message[80]; /* prompting message */
  int i; /* input value */
} ;

void input_xy(struct xyinput *info);

main(void)
{
  struct xyinput mess;

  mess.x = 10; mess.y = 10;
  strcpy(mess.message, "enter an integer: ");
```

```
  clrscr();

  input_xy(&mess);

  printf("your number squared is: %d", mess.i*mess.i);
  return 0;
}

/* Display a prompting message at the specified location
   and input an integer value.
*/
void input_xy(struct xyinput *info)
{
  gotoxy(info->x, info->y);

  printf(info->message);
  scanf("%d", &info->i);
}
```

The program uses the functions **clrscr( )** and **gotoxy( )**, which are provided by Turbo C beginning with version 1.5. Both functions use the **conio.h** header file. A function like **input_xy( )** is very useful when your program must input many pieces of information. (In fact, you might want to create several functions like **input_xy( )** that input other types of data.)

Although not commonly used, there is a way to reference a structure element given a pointer to that structure that uses the dot operator instead of the arrow operator. For example, this fragment assigns the **balance** *element the value 10.10:*

```
struct bal {
  float balance;
  char name[80];
} person;

struct bal *p;  /* declare a structure pointer */

(*p).balance = 10.10;
```

*By applying the * operator to the pointer* **p***, you reference the actual structure and the dot operator can be applied. The parentheses are necessary around* **p** *because the "dot" operator has a higher priority than the ** *. Although some very old C programs may use this form, it is very rare. However, if you do encounter it, you will know that it is just another way to reference a structure element given a pointer to the structure. (This form is considered archaic and definitely not recommended for new programs. You should use the arrow operator instead.)*

Arrays and Structures Within Structures

A structure element can be either simple or complex. A simple element is any of the built-in data types, such as integer or character. You have already seen a few complex elements. The character array used in **addr_info** is an example. Other complex data types are single- and multidimensional arrays of the other data types and structures.

A structure element that is an array is treated as you might expect from the earlier examples. For example, consider this structure:

```
struct x {
  int a[10][10]; /* 10 x 10 array of ints */
  float b;
} y;
```

To reference integer 3,7 in **a** of structure **y**, you would write

```
y.a[3][7]
```

When a structure is an element of another structure, it is called a *nested structure*. For example, here the structure variable element **address** is nested inside **emp**:

```
struct emp {
  struct addr address;
  float wage;
} worker;
```

The **addr** is the structure defined earlier in this chapter. Here, a structure **emp** has been declared as having two elements. The first element is the structure of type **addr**, which contains an employee's address, and **wage**, which holds the employee's wage. The following code fragment assigns $35,000 to the **wage** element of **worker** and 98765 to the **zip** field of **address**:

```
worker.wage = 35000.00;

worker.address.zip = 98765;
```

The elements of each structure are referenced from outermost to innermost (left to right).

Structures can be nested up to any level provided there is sufficient memory.

Bit-fields

Unlike most other computer languages, C has a built-in method to access a single bit within a byte. This can be useful for three reasons:

1. If storage is limited, you can store several *Boolean* (true/false) variables in one byte.

2. Certain device interfaces transmit information encoded into bits within a single byte.

3. Certain encryption routines need to access the bits within a byte.

Although all these functions can be performed using the bitwise operators, a bit-field can add more structure and efficiency to your code.

The method C uses to access bits is based on the structure. A bit-field is really just a special type of structure element that defines how long, in bits, the element is to be. The general form of a bit-field declaration is

```
struct struc_name {
    type name1 : length;
    type name2 : length;
    .
    .
    .
    type namen : length;
}
```

A bit-field must be declared as either **int**, **unsigned**, or **signed**. Bit-fields of length 1 should be declared as **unsigned** because a single bit cannot have a sign. Bit-fields can be from 1 to 16 bits long. In Turbo C, the leftmost bit is the most significant bit.

For example, consider the structure definition below:

```
struct device {
  unsigned active : 1;
  unsigned ready : 1;
  unsigned xmt_error : 1;
} dev_code;
```

This structure defines three variables of 1 bit each. The structure variable **dev_code** might be used to decode information from the port of a tape drive, for example. The

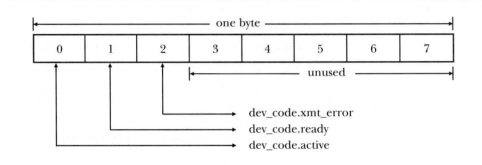

Figure 7-2.   *The bit-field variable* **dev_code** *in memory*

following code fragment writes a byte of information to the (imaginary) tape and checks for errors using **dev_code** from above:

```
wr_tape(char c)
{
  while(!dev_code.ready) rd(&dev_code); /* wait */

  wr_to_tape(c); /* write out byte */

  while(dev_code.active) rd(&dev_code); /* wait until
                                    info is written */

  if(dev_code.xmt_error) printf("write error");
}
```

Here, **rd( )** returns the status of the tape drive and **wr_to_tape( )** actually writes the data.

Figure 7-2 shows what the bit variable **dev_code** looks like in memory.

As you can see from the previous example, each bit-field is accessed using the dot operator. However, if the structure is referenced through a pointer, you must use the –> operator.

You do not have to name each bit-field. This makes it easy to reach the bit you want and pass up unused ones. For example, if the tape drive also returned an end-of-tape flag in bit 5, you could alter structure **device** to accommodate this by using

```
struct device {
  unsigned active : 1;
  unsigned ready : 1;
  unsigned xmt_error : 1;
```

```
     unsigned : 2;
     unsigned EOT : 1;
} dev_code;
```

Bit-field variables have certain restrictions. You cannot take the address of a bit-field variable. Bit-field variables cannot be arrayed. You cannot overlap integer boundaries. You cannot know, from machine to machine, whether the fields will run from right to left or from left to right; any code that uses bit-fields may have machine dependencies.

Finally, it is valid to mix other structure elements with bit-field elements. For example,

```
struct emp {
  struct addr address;
  float pay;
  unsigned lay_off:1;   /* lay off or active */
  unsigned hourly:1:    /* hourly pay or wage */
  unsigned deductions:3: /* IRS deductions */
};
```

defines an employee record that uses only 1 byte to hold three pieces of information: the employee's status, whether the employee is salaried, and the number of deductions. Without the use of the bit-field, this information would have taken 3 bytes.

Unions

In C, a **union** is a memory location that is shared by several variables that are of different types. The **union** declaration is similar to that of a structure, as shown in this example:

```
union union_type {
  int i;
  char ch;
} ;
```

As with structures, you may declare a variable either by placing its name at the end of the definition or by using a separate declaration statement. To declare a **union** variable **cnvt** of type **union_type** using the definition just given, you would write

```
union union_type cnvt;
```

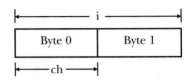

Figure 7-3. *How* **i** *and* **ch** *use the union* **cnvt**

In **union cnvt**, both integer **i** and character **ch** share the same memory location. (Of course, **i** occupies 2 bytes and **ch** uses only 1). Figure 7-3 shows how **i** and **ch** share the same address.

When a **union** is declared, the compiler automatically creates a variable large enough to hold the largest variable type in the **union**.

To access a **union** element use the same syntax that you would use for structures: the dot and arrow operators. If you are operating on the **union** directly, use the dot operator. If the **union** variable is accessed through a pointer, use the arrow operator. For example, to assign the integer 10 to element **i** of **cnvt**, you would write

```
cnvt.i = 10;
```

Using a **union** can help you produce machine-independent (portable) code. Because the compiler keeps track of the actual sizes of the variables that make up the **union**, no machine dependencies are produced. You need not worry about the size of an integer, character, **float**, or whatever.

Unions are used frequently when type conversions are needed. For example, the standard library function **putw( )** writes the binary representation of an integer to a disk file. Although there are many ways to code this function, the one shown here uses a **union**. First, a **union** composed of one integer and a 2-byte character array is created:

```
union pw {
  int i;
  char ch[2];
};
```

Now, **putw( )** is written using the **union** that follows.

```
/* putw with union */
putw(union pw word, FILE *fp)
{
```

```
    putc(word->ch[0]); /* write first half */
    putc(word->ch[1]); /* write second half */
}
```

Although called with an integer, **putw( )** uses the **union** to write both halves of the integer to the disk file.

Enumerations

An *enumeration* is a set of named integer constants that specifies all the legal values that a variable of its type can have. Enumerations are not uncommon in everyday life. For example, an enumeration of the coins used in the United States is

penny, nickel, dime, quarter, half-dollar, dollar

Enumerations are defined like structures, by using the keyword **enum** to signal the start of an enumeration type. The general form is

enum *enum_tag_name* { *enumeration list* } *variable_list*;

Both the enumeration name *enum_tag_name* and the *variable_list* are optional, but one of them must be present. As with structures, the enumeration tag name is used to declare variables of its type. The following fragment defines an enumeration called **coin** and declares **money** to be of that type:

```
enum coin { penny, nickel, dime, quarter,
            half_dollar, dollar};

enum coin money;
```

Given this definition and declaration, the following types of statements are perfectly valid:

```
money = dime;

if(money==quarter) printf("is a quarter\n");
```

The key point to understand about an enumeration is that each of the symbols stands for an integer value and can be used in any integer expression. For example,

```
printf("the value of quarter is %d ", quarter);
```

is perfectly valid.

Unless initialized otherwise, the value of the first enumeration symbol is 0, the second is 1, and so forth. Therefore,

```
printf("%d %d", penny, dime);
```

displays **0 2** on the screen.

It is possible to specify the value of one or more of the symbols by using an initializer. This is done by following the symbol with an equal sign and an integer value. Whenever an initializer is used, symbols that appear after it are assigned values greater than the previous initialization value. For example, the following assigns the value of 100 to **quarter**.

```
enum coin { penny, nickel, dime, quarter=100,
            half_dollar, dollar};
```

Now, the values of these symbols are

penny	0
nickel	1
dime	2
quarter	100
half_dollar	101
dollar	102

Using initializations, more than one element of an enumeration can have the same value.

A common misconception is that the symbols of an enumeration can be input and output directly, but this is not true. For example, the following code fragment will not perform as desired:

```
/* this will not work */

money = dollar;

printf("%s", money);
```

Remember that the symbol **dollar** is simply a name for an integer: it is not a string. Hence, it is not possible for **printf( )** to display the string "dollar." Likewise, you cannot give an enumeration variable a value using the string equivalent. That is, this code does not work:

```
/* this code will not work */

money = "penny";
```

Actually, creating code to input and output enumeration symbols is quite tedious (unless you are willing to settle for their integer values). For example, the following code is needed to display, in words, the kind of coins that **money** contains:

```
switch(money) {
  case penny: printf("penny");
     break;
  case nickel: printf("nickel");
     break;
  case dime: printf("dime");
     break;
  case quarter: printf("quarter");
     break;
  case half_dollar: printf("half_dollar");
     break;
  case dollar: printf("dollar");
}
```

Sometimes, it is possible to declare an array of strings and use the enumeration value as an index to translate an enumeration value into its corresponding string. For example, this code also outputs the proper string:

```
char name[]={
  "penny",
  "nickel",
  "dime",
  "quarter",
  "half_dollar",
  "dollar"
};
   .
   .
   .
printf("%s", name[(int)money]);
```

Of course, this works only if no symbol initializations are used, because the string array must be indexed starting at 0. The cast that precedes **money** is necessary to avoid warning errors because **money** is not technically an integer variable but an enumeration variable.

Since enumeration values must be converted manually to their human-readable string values for console I/O, they are most useful in routines that do not make such conversions. For example, an enumeration is commonly used to define a compiler's symbol table.

Using sizeof to Ensure Portability

You have seen that structures, unions, and enumerations can be used to create variables of varying sizes, and that the actual size of these variables may change from machine to machine. The **sizeof** unary operator is used to compute the size of any variable or type and can help eliminate machine-dependent code from your programs.

For example, Turbo C has the following sizes for these data types:

Type	Size in Bytes
char	1
int	2
long int	4
float	4
double	8
long double	10

Therefore, the following code will print the numbers **1**, **2**, **4**, and **10** on the screen:

```
char ch;
int i;
float f;

printf("%d", sizeof ch);

printf("%d", sizeof i);

printf("%d", sizeof f);

printf("%d", sizeof(long double));
```

The **sizeof** operator is a *compile-time* operator: All the information necessary to compute the size of any variable is known at compile time. For example, consider the following:

```
union x {
  char ch;
  int i;
  float f;
} tom;
```

The **sizeof tom** will be 4 bytes long. At run time, it does not matter what the **union tom** is *actually* holding; all that matters is the size of the largest variable it can hold because the **union** must be as large as its largest element.

Depending on what compiler options you are using, Turbo C may align data on word boundaries. This means that the size of a conglomerate data type may be slightly larger than the sum of its parts. Manually adding up the lengths of the elements of a structure, for example, may not yield its correct size. Therefore, you should always use **sizeof** to determine the size of a variable.

typedef

C allows you to define new data type names using the **typedef** keyword. You are not actually creating a new data class; you are defining a new name for an existing type. This process can help make machine-dependent programs more portable; only the **typedef** statements need to be changed. It also can help you document your code by allowing descriptive names for the standard data types. The general form of the **typedef** statement is

typedef *type name*;

where *type* is any existing data type and *name* is the new name for this type. The new name you define is an addition to, not a replacement for, the existing type name.

For example, you could create a new name for **float** by using

```
typedef float balance;
```

This statement tells the compiler to recognize **balance** as another name for **float**. Next you could create a **float** variable using **balance**:

```
balance past_due;
```

Here, **past_due** is a floating point variable of type **balance**, which is another word for **float**.

You can also use **typedef** to create names for more complex types. For example:

```
typedef struct {
  float due;
  int over_due;
  char name[40];
} client;  /* here client is the new type name */

client clist[NUM_CLIENTS]; /* define array of
                   structures of type client */
```

Using **typedef** can help make your code easier to read and more portable. But remember, you are *not* creating any new data types.

Chapter *8*

Input, Output, and Disk Files

Input and output in C are accomplished through the use of library functions; there are no C keywords that perform I/O operations. The three complete sets of I/O functions defined in Turbo C and C++ are:

1. The I/O system defined by the ANSI C standard, also called the *buffered file system* (sometimes the terms *formatted* or *high-level* are used instead).

2. The UNIX-like I/O system, sometimes referred to as the *unbuffered* file system (also called *unformatted*). The UNIX-like I/O system was created for the first C compilers, which were developed under UNIX.

3. Some low-level I/O functions that operate directly on the hardware of the computer.

This chapter discusses the ANSI and UNIX-like I/O systems. The low-level functions are covered in Part Three of this book.

The ANSI standard's failure to define the UNIX-like file system is justified by several arguments, including the fact that the two file systems are largely redundant. However, because both file systems are currently in widespread use, Turbo C supports both approaches. This chapter will cover both, but the greatest emphasis will be placed on the ANSI standard I/O system because use of the UNIX-like system is expected to decline. New code should be written using the ANSI I/O functions.

The purpose of this chapter is to present an overview of I/O in Turbo C and to illustrate the way the core functions of each file system work together. The Turbo C library contains a rich and diverse assortment of I/O routines—more than can be covered here. However, the functions presented in this chapter are sufficient for most circumstances. The remainder of the I/O functions are covered in Part Three of this book.

During this discussion, keep in mind that the prototype declarations and several predefined types and constants for the Turbo C buffered I/O library functions are found in the file **stdio.h**. The header file **io.h** is used for the UNIX-like routines.

Streams and Files

Before beginning our discussion of the ANSI C I/O system, it is important to understand the difference between the terms *streams* and *files*. The ANSI C I/O system supplies a consistent interface to the C programmer independent of the actual device being accessed. That is, the ANSI C I/O system provides a level of abstraction between the programmer and the hardware. This abstraction is called a stream; the actual device is called a file. It is important to understand how they interact.

Streams

The buffered file system is designed to work with a wide variety of devices, including terminals, disk drives, and tape drives. Even though each device is very different, the buffered file system transforms each into a logical device called a stream. All streams are similar in behavior. Because streams are largely device independent, the functions that write to a disk file can also write to the console. There are two types of streams: text and binary.

A *text stream* is a sequence of characters. In a text stream, certain character translations may occur as required by the host environment. For example, a newline may be converted to a carriage return-linefeed pair. Therefore, there may not be a one-to-one relationship between the characters that are written or read and those on the external device. Also, because of possible translations, the number of characters written or read may not be the same as those found on the external device.

A *binary stream* is a sequence of bytes that have a one-to-one correspondence to those found on the external device. That is, no character translations will occur. Also, the number of bytes written or read will be the same as the number found on the external device. The ANSI standard does specify, however, that a binary stream may have an implementation-defined number of null bytes appended to its end. These null bytes might be used to pad the information so that it fills a sector on a disk, for example.

Files

In the ANSI C I/O system, a *file* is a logical concept that can be applied to everything from disk files to terminals. A stream is associated with a specific file by performing an *open* operation. Once a file is open, information can be exchanged between it and your program.

Not all files have the same capabilities. For example, a disk file can support random access, but a modem cannot. This illustrates an important point about the ANSI C I/O system: All streams are the same but all files are not.

If the file can support random access (sometimes referred to as *position requests*), opening that file initializes the *file position indicator* to the start of the file. As each character is read from or written to the file, the position indicator is incremented, ensuring progression through the file.

The smallest accessible portion of a disk is a sector, which is usually 512 bytes long. Information is written to or read from a disk one sector at a time. Thus, even if your program only needs a single byte of data, an entire sector of data will be read. This data is put into a region of memory called a *buffer* until it can be used by your program. When data is output to a disk file, it is buffered until a full sector's worth of information has been accumulated, at which point it is actually physically written to the file.

A stream is disassociated from a specific file using a *close* operation. Closing a stream causes any contents of its associated buffer to be written to the external device (it will be padded, if necessary, to fill out a complete sector). This process is generally called *flushing* the buffer, and it guarantees that no information is accidentally left in the disk buffer. All files are closed automatically when your program terminates normally by **main( )** returning to the operating system or by calling to **exit( )**. However, it is better to actually close a file using **fclose( )** as soon as it is no longer needed because several events can prevent the buffer from being written to the disk file. For example, files are not written if a program terminates through a call to **abort( )**, if it crashes, or if the user turns the computer off before terminating the program.

At the beginning of a program's execution five predefined text streams are opened. They are **stdin**, **stdout**, **stderr**, **stdaux**, and **stdprn**, and they refer to the standard I/O devices connected to the system, as shown here:

Stream	Device
stdin	Keyboard
stdout	Screen
stderr	Screen
stdaux	First serial port
stdprn	Printer

The first three streams are defined by the ANSI C standard, and any code that uses them is fully portable. The last two are specific to Turbo C and may not be portable to other C compilers. Most operating systems, including DOS, allow I/O redirection, so routines that read or write to these streams can be redirected to other devices. (Redirection of I/O is the process whereby information that would normally go to one device is rerouted to another device by the operating system.) You should never try explicitly to open or close these files.

Each stream that is associated with a file has a file control structure of type **FILE**. This structure is defined in the header **stdio.h**. You must not make modifications to this structure.

The ANSI C I/O System: Conceptual vs. Actual

As far as the programmer is concerned, all I/O takes place through streams. All streams are the same. The file system links a stream to a file, which is any external device capable of I/O. Because different devices have differing capabilities, all files are not the same. However, these differences are minimized by the ANSI C I/O system, which converts the raw information coming from the device into a stream (and vice versa). Aside from the limitation that only certain types of files support random access, the programmer need not worry about the actual physical device and is free to concentrate on the logical device—the stream.

If this approach seems confusing or strange, look at it in the context of languages like BASIC or FORTRAN, in which each device supported by the implementation has its own completely separate I/O system. In C's approach, the programmer need think only in terms of streams and use only one file system to accomplish all I/O operations.

Console I/O

Console I/O refers to operations that occur at the keyboard and screen of your computer. Because input and output to the console is such a common affair, a subsystem of the ANSI I/O file system was created to deal exclusively with console I/O. Technically, these functions direct their operations to the standard input and standard output of the system. It is possible to redirect the console I/O to other devices. For simplicity of discussion, however, it is assumed that the console will be the device used since it is the most common.

getche( ) and putchar( )

The simplest of the console I/O functions are **getche( )**, which reads a character from the keyboard, and **putchar( )**, which prints a character to the screen at the current cursor location. The **getche( )** function waits until a key is pressed and then returns its value. The key pressed is also *echoed* to the screen automatically. The prototypes for **getche( )** and **putchar( )** are shown here:

```
int getche(void);
int putchar(int c);
```

The **getche( )** function returns the character pressed. The **putchar( )** function returns *c* if successful, or **EOF** if an error occurs. (**EOF** is a macro defined in **stdio.h** that stands for *end of file*.) Even though *c* is declared as an integer, only the low-order byte is displayed on the screen. Similarly, even though **getche( )** returns an integer, the low-order byte will contain the character entered at the keyboard.

The following program inputs characters from the keyboard and prints them in reverse case. That is, uppercase prints as lowercase, and lowercase as uppercase. The program halts when a period is typed.

```
#include <conio.h>
#include <stdio.h>
#include <ctype.h>

main(void)  /* case switcher */
{
  char ch;

  do {
    ch = getche();
    if(islower(ch)) putchar(toupper(ch));
    else putchar(tolower(ch));
  } while (ch!='.'); /* use a period to stop*/
  return 0;
}
```

The **getche( )** function is not part of the ANSI C I/O system, but is closely related. It requires the **conio.h** header file.

There are two important variations on **getche( )**. The first is **getchar( )**, which is the character input function defined by ANSI C. The trouble with **getchar( )** is that it buffers input until a carriage return is entered. The reason for this is that the original UNIX systems line-buffered terminal input—that is, you had to enter a carriage return for anything you had just typed to actually be sent to the computer. To be compatible with the UNIX implementation, many C compilers, including Turbo C, have implemented **getchar( )** so that it line-buffers input. This is quite annoying in today's interactive environments and the use of **getchar( )** is not recommended. It is supported by Turbo C only to ensure portability with UNIX-based programs. You may want to play with it a little to understand its effect better. However, no programs in this guide use **getchar( )**.

A second, more useful, variation on **getche( )** is **getch( )**, which operates like **getche( )** except that the character you type is not echoed to the screen. You can use this fact to create a rather humorous (if disconcerting) program to run on some unsuspecting user. The program, shown here, displays what appears to be a standard DOS prompt and waits for input. However, every character the user types is displayed as the next letter in the alphabet. That is, an "A" becomes "B", and so forth. To stop the program, press CTRL-A.

```c
/* This program appears to act as a DOS gone wild. It
   displays the DOS prompt but displays every character
   the user types as the next letter in the alphabet.
*/

#include <stdio.h>
#include <conio.h>

main(void)
{
  char ch;

  do {
    printf("C>");
    for(;;) {
      ch = getch(); /* read chars without echo */
      if(ch=='\r' || ch==1) {
        printf("\n");
        break;
      }
      putchar(ch+1);
    }
  } while(ch!=1) ; /* exit on control-A */
  return 0;
}
```

Use this program with caution; it has been known to cause panic in novice computer users!

gets( ) and puts( )

On the next step up, in terms of complexity and power, are the functions **gets( )** and **puts( )**. They enable you to read and write strings of characters at the console.

The **gets( )** function reads a string of characters entered at the keyboard and places them at the address pointed to by its character pointer argument. You may type characters at the keyboard until you strike a carriage return. The carriage return does not become part of the string; instead a null terminator is placed at the end, and **gets( )** returns. In fact, it is impossible to use **gets( )** to obtain a carriage return (**getchar( )** and its variants can, though). Typing mistakes can be corrected by using the backspace before pressing RETURN. The **gets( )** function has the prototype

char *gets(char *s);

where *s* is a character array. For example, the following program reads a string into the array **str** and prints its length:

```
#include <stdio.h>
#include <string.h>

main(void)
{
  char str[80];

  gets(str);
  printf("length is %d", strlen(str));
  return 0;
}
```

The **gets( )** function returns a pointer to *s*.

The **puts( )** function writes its string argument to the screen followed by a newline. Its prototype is

char *puts(const char *s);

It recognizes the same backslash codes as **printf( )**, such as \t for tab. A call to **puts( )** requires far less overhead than the same call to **printf( )** because **puts( )** outputs only a string of characters; it does not output numbers or do format conversions. It takes up less space and runs faster than **printf( )**. The **puts( )** function returns a pointer to its string argument. The following statement writes "hello" on the screen.

```
puts("hello");
```

The simplest functions that perform console I/O operations are summarized in Table 8-1.

Function	Operation
getchar()	Reads a character from the keyboard; waits for carriage return
getche()	Reads a character with echo; does not wait for carriage return
getch()	Reads a character without echo; does not wait for carriage return
putchar()	Writes a character to the screen
gets()	Reads a string from the keyboard
puts()	Writes a string to the screen

Table 8-1.   *The Basic Console I/O Functions*

Formatted Console I/O

In addition to the simple console I/O functions, the Turbo C standard library contains two functions that perform formatted input and output on the built-in data types: **printf( )** and **scanf( )**. The term *formatted* refers to the fact that these functions can read and write data in various formats that are under your control. The **printf( )** function is used to write data to the console; **scanf( )**, its complement, reads data from the keyboard. Both **printf( )** and **scanf( )** can operate on any of the built-in data types, including characters, strings, and numbers.

printf( )

The **printf( )** function has this prototype

    int printf(const char *fmt_string, . . .);

The first argument, *fmt_string*, defines the way any subsequent arguments are displayed. Often called the *format string*, it consists of two types of items: characters that will be printed on the screen, and format commands that define the way arguments that follow the format string are displayed. A format command begins with a percent sign and is followed by the format code. The format commands are shown in Table 8-2. There must be exactly the same number of arguments as there are format commands, and the format commands and arguments are matched in order. For example, this **printf( )** call

```
printf("Hi %c %d %s", 'c', 10, "there!");
```

Code	Format
%c	A single character
%d	Decimal
%i	Decimal
%e	Scientific notation
%f	Decimal floating point
%g	Uses %e or %f, whichever is shorter
%o	Octal
%s	String of characters
%u	Unsigned decimal
%x	Hexadecimal
%%	Prints a % sign
%p	Displays a pointer
%n	The associated argument shall be to an integer pointer into which is placed the number of characters written so far

Table 8-2.   **printf( )** *Format Specifiers*

displays "Hi c 10 there!". The **printf( )** function returns the number of characters output. It returns **EOF** if an error occurs.

The format commands may have modifiers that specify the field width, the number of decimal places, and a left-justification flag. An integer placed between the % sign and the format command acts as a *minimum-field-width specifier*. This pads the output with spaces to ensure that it is at least a certain minimum length. If the string or number is greater than that minimum, it is printed in full even if it overruns the minimum. If you wish to pad the output with 0s, place 0 before the field-width specifier. For example, **%05d** pads a number of less than five digits with 0s so that its total length is five.

To specify the number of decimal places printed for a floating point number, place a decimal point after the field-width specifier, followed by the number of decimal places you wish to display. For example, **%10.4f** displays a number at least ten characters wide with four decimal places. When this is applied to strings or integers the number following the period specifies the maximum field length. For example, **%5.7s** displays a string of at least five characters and not more than seven. If the string is longer than the maximum field width, the characters are truncated off the right end.

By default, all output is *right-justified:* If the field width is larger than the data printed, the data is placed on the right edge of the field. You can force the information to be left-justified by placing a minus sign directly after the %. For example, **%–10.2f** will left-justify a floating point number with two decimal places in a ten-character field. The following program illustrates the field-width specifiers and left-justification:

```
#include <stdio.h>

main(void)
{
  printf("|%10.4f|\n", 123.23);
  printf("|%-10.4f|\n", 123.23);
  printf("|%10.4s|\n", "Hello there");
  printf("|%-10.4s|\n", "Hello there");
  return 0;
}
```

There are two format command modifiers that allow **printf( )** to display **short** and **long** integers. These modifiers can be applied to the **d, i, o, u,** and **x** format specifiers. The **l** modifier tells **printf( )** that a **long** data type follows. For example, **%ld** means that a **long int** is to be displayed. The **h** modifier instructs **printf( )** to display a **short int**. Therefore, **%hu** indicates that the data is of type **short unsigned int**.

The **l** modifier may also prefix the floating point commands of **e, f,** and **g,** and indicates that a **double** follows. The **L** modifier may prefix **double** to indicate **long double**.

With **printf( )**, you can output virtually any format of data you desire. Figure 8-1 shows some examples.

scanf( )

The general-purpose console input routine is **scanf( )**. It reads all the built-in data types and automatically converts numbers into the proper internal format. It is like the reverse of **printf( )**. The general form of **scanf( )** is

int scanf(const char *fmt_string, . . .);

The control string consists of three classifications of characters:

- Format specifiers
- White-space characters
- Non-white-space characters

The **scanf( )** function returns the number of fields that are input. It returns **EOF** if a premature end of file is reached.

printf( ) statement	Output
("%-5.2 f",123.234)	123.23
("%5.2 f", 3.234)	3.23
("%10s","hello")	hello
("%−10s","hello")	hello
("%5.7s","123456789")	1234567

Figure 8-1.   *Some* **printf( )** *examples*

The input format specifiers are preceded by a **%** sign and tell **scanf( )** what type of data is to be read next. These codes are listed in Table 8-3. For example, **%s** reads a string, while **%d** reads an integer.

A white-space character in the control string causes **scanf( )** to skip over one or more white-space characters in the input stream. A white-space character is either a space, a tab, or a newline. In essence, one white-space character in the control string causes **scanf( )** to read, but not store, any number (including zero) of white-space characters up to the next non-white-space character.

A non-white-space character causes **scanf( )** to read and discard a matching character. For example, **"%d,%d"** causes **scanf( )** to read an integer, then read and discard a comma, and finally read another integer. If the specified character is not found, **scanf( )** terminates.

Code	Meaning
%c	Read a single character
%d	Read a decimal integer
%i	Read a decimal integer
%e	Read a floating point number
%f	Read a floating point number
%h	Read a short integer
%o	Read an octal number
%s	Read a string
%x	Read a hexadecimal number
%p	Read a pointer
%n	Receives an integer value equal to the number of characters read so far

Table 8-3.   **scanf( )** *Format Specifiers*

All the variables used to receive values through **scanf( )** must be passed by their addresses. This means that all arguments must be pointers to the variables used as arguments. This is C's way of creating a "call by reference," and it allows a function to alter the contents of an argument. For example, if you wish to read an integer into the variable **count**, use the following **scanf( )** call:

```
scanf("%d", &count);
```

Strings are read into character arrays, and the array name, without any index, is the address of the first element of the array. To read a string into the character array **address**, you would use

```
char address[80];

scanf("%s", address);
```

In this case, **address** is already a pointer and need not be preceded by the **&** operator.

The input data items must be separated by spaces, tabs, or newlines. Punctuation marks such as commas, semicolons, and the like do not count as separators. This means that

```
scanf("%d%d", &r, &c);
```

accepts an input of **10 20**, but fails with **10,20**. As in **printf( )**, the **scanf( )** format codes are matched in order with the variables receiving input in the argument list.

An ***** placed after the **%** and before the format code reads data of the specified type but suppresses its assignment. Thus, given the input "10/20",

```
scanf("%d%*c%d", &x, &y);
```

places the value 10 into **x**, discards the division sign, and gives **y** the value 20.

The format commands can specify a maximum-field-length modifier. This is an integer number placed between the **%** and the format command code that limits the number of characters read for any field. For example, if you wish to read no more than 20 characters into **str**, write:

```
scanf("%20s", str);
```

If the input stream is greater than 20 characters, a subsequent call to input begins where this call leaves off. If

ABCDEFGHIJKLMNOPQRSTUVWXYZ

is entered as the response to the **scanf( )** call in this example, only the first 20 characters, or up to the "T" are placed into **str** because of the maximum size specifier. The remaining characters, "UVWXYZ" have not yet been used. If another **scanf( )** call is made, such as

```
scanf("%s", str);
```

then "UVWXYZ" is placed into **str**. Input for a field may terminate before the maximum field length is reached if a white-space character is encountered. In this case, **scanf( )** moves on to the next field.

Although spaces, tabs, and newlines are used as field separators, when reading a single character, they are read like any other character. For example, with an input stream of "x y",

```
scanf("%c%c%c", &a, &b, &c);
```

returns with the character "x" in **a**, a space in **b**, and "y" in **c**.

Be careful: If you have any other characters in the control string—including spaces, tabs, and newlines—those characters will be used to match and discard characters from the input stream. For example, given the input stream "10t20",

```
scanf("%st%s", &x, &y);
```

will place 10 into **x** and 20 into **y**. The "t" is discarded because of the **t** in the control string. For another example,

```
scanf("%s ", name);
```

will *not* return until you type a character *after* you type a white-space character. This is because the space after the **%s** has instructed **scanf( )** to read and discard spaces, tabs, and newline characters.

Another feature of **scanf( )** is the *scanset*. A scanset defines a list of characters that will be matched by **scanf( )** and stored in a character array variable. The **scanf( )** function inputs characters, putting them into the corresponding character array, as long as they are members of the scanset. When a character is entered that does not match any in the scanset, **scanf( )** null-terminates the corresponding array and moves on to the next field.

A scanset is defined by putting a list of the characters you want to scan for inside square brackets. The beginning square bracket must be prefixed by a percent sign. For example, this scanset tells **scanf( )** to read only the letters "X", "Y", and "Z".

```
%[XYZ]
```

The argument corresponding to the scanset must be a pointer to a character array. Upon return from **scanf( )**, the array will contain a null-terminated string composed of the characters read. For example, this program uses a scanset to read digits into **s1**. As soon as a non-digit is entered, **s1** is null-terminated and characters are read into **s2** until the next white-space character is entered.

```
/* A simple scanset example. */
#include <stdio.h>

main(void)
{
  char s1[80], s2[80];

  printf("Enter numbers, then some letters\n");
  scanf("%[0123456789]%s", s1, s2);
  printf("%s %s", s1, s2);
  return 0;
}
```

You can specify a range inside a scanset using a hyphen. For example, this tells **scanf( )** to accept the characters "A" through "Z".

```
%[A-Z]
```

You can specify more than one range within a scanset. For example, this program reads digits and then letters:

```
/* A scanset example using ranges. */
#include <stdio.h>

main(void)
{
  char s1[80], s2[80];

  printf("Enter numbers, then some letters\n");
  scanf("%[0-9]%[a-zA-Z]", s1, s2);
  printf("%s %s", s1, s2);
  return 0;
}
```

You can specify an inverted set if the first character in the set is a caret (^). When the ^ is present, it instructs **scanf( )** to accept any character that *is not* defined by the scanset. Here, the previous program uses the ^ to invert the type of characters the scanset will read:

```
/* A scanset example using inverted ranges. */
#include <stdio.h>

main(void)
{
  char s1[80], s2[80];

  printf("Enter non-numbers, then some non-letters\n");
  scanf("%[^0-9]%[^a-zA-Z]", s1, s2);
  printf("%s %s", s1, s2);
  return 0;
}
```

One important point to remember is that the scanset is case-sensitive. Therefore, if you want scan for both uppercase and lowercase letters they must be specified individually.

The ANSI C File System

The ANSI C file system is composed of several interrelated functions. The most common are shown in Table 8-4.

The header file **stdio.h** must be included in any program in which these functions are used.

The File Pointer

The common thread that ties the buffered I/O system together is the *file pointer*. A file pointer is a pointer to information that defines various things about the file, including its name, status, and current position. In essence, the file pointer identifies a specific disk file and is used by the stream associated with it to tell each of the buffered I/O functions where to perform operations. A file pointer is a pointer variable of type **FILE**, which is defined in **stdio.h**.

fopen( )

The **fopen( )** function opens a stream for use, links a file with that stream, and then returns a **FILE** pointer to that stream. Most often (always for the purpose of this discussion) the file is a disk file. The **fopen( )** function has this prototype

FILE *fopen(const char *filename, const char *mode);

Name	Function
fopen()	Opens a stream
fclose()	Closes a stream
putc()	Writes a character to a stream
getc()	Reads a character from a stream
fseek()	Seeks to specified byte in a stream
fprintf()	Is to a stream what printf( ) is to the console
fscanf()	Is to a stream what scanf( ) is to the console
feof()	Returns true if end of file is reached
ferror()	Returns true if an error has occurred
rewind()	Resets the file position locator to the beginning of the file
remove()	Erases a file

Table 8-4.   *The Most Common Buffered File System Functions*

where *mode* points to a string containing the desired open status. The legal values for *mode* in Turbo C are shown in Table 8-5. The *filename* must be a string of characters that provides a valid file name for the operating system and may include a path specification.

The **fopen( )** function returns a pointer of type **FILE**. This pointer identifies the file and is used by most other file system functions. It should never be altered by your code. The function returns a null pointer if the file cannot be opened.

As Table 8-5 shows, a file can be opened in either text or binary mode. In text mode, carriage return-linefeed sequences are translated into newline characters on input. On output, the reverse occurs: newlines are translated to carriage return-linefeeds. No such translations occur on binary files.

If you wish to open a file for writing with the name **test**, write:

```
fp = fopen("test", "w");
```

Where **fp** is a variable of type **FILE ***. However, you usually see it written like this:

```
if((fp = fopen("test", "w"))==NULL) {
  puts("cannot open file");
  exit(1);
}
```

Mode	Meaning
"r"	Open a text file for reading
"w"	Create a text file for writing
"a"	Append to a text file
"rb"	Open a binary file for reading
"wb"	Create a binary file for writing
"ab"	Append to a binary file
"r+"	Open a text file for read/write
"w+"	Create a text file for read/write
"a+"	Open or create a text file for read/write
"r+b"	Open a binary file for read/write
"w+b"	Create a binary file for read/write
"a+b"	Open or create a binary file for read/write
"rt"	Open a text file for reading
"wt"	Create a text file for writing
"at"	Append to a text file
"r+t"	Open a text file for read/write
"w+t"	Create a text file for read/write
"a+t"	Open or create a text file for read/write

Table 8-5. *The Legal Values for Mode*

This method detects any error in opening a file, such as a write-protected or full disk, before attempting to write to it. **NULL** is a macro defined in **stdio.h**.

If you use **fopen( )** to open a file for output, then any preexisting file by that name is erased and a new file started. If no file by that name exists, then one is created. If you want to add to the end of the file, you must use mode **a**. If the file does not exist, it will be created. Opening a file for read operations requires an existing file. If no file exists, an error is returned. If a file is opened for read/write operations it is not erased if it exists; if no file exists, one is created.

putc( )

The **putc( )** function is used to write characters to a stream that was previously opened for writing using the **fopen( )** function. The prototype for **putc( )** is

```
int putc(int ch, FILE *fp);
```

where *fp* is the file pointer returned by **fopen( )** and *ch* is the character to be output. The file pointer tells **putc( )** which disk file to write to. For historical reasons, *ch* is formally called an **int**, but only the low-order byte is used.

If a **putc( )** operation is a success, it returns the character written. If **putc( )** fails, an **EOF** is returned.

getc( )

The **getc( )** function is used to read characters from a stream opened in read mode by **fopen( )**. The prototype is

```
int getc(FILE *fp);
```

where *fp* is a file pointer of type **FILE** returned by **fopen( )**. For historical reasons, **getc( )** returns an integer, but the high-order byte is 0.

The **getc( )** function returns an **EOF** when the end of the file has been reached. To read a text file to the end, you could use the following code:

```
ch = getc(fp);

while(ch!=EOF) {
  ch = getc(fp);
}
```

As stated earlier, the buffered file system can also operate on binary data. When a file is opened for binary input, an integer value equal to the **EOF** mark may be read. This would cause the routine just given to indicate an end-of-file condition even though the physical end of the file had not been reached. To solve this problem, Turbo C includes the function **feof( )**, which is used to determine the end of the file when reading binary data. It has this prototype:

```
int feof(FILE *fp);
```

where *fp* identifies the file. The **feof( )** function returns non-0 if the end of the file has been reached; otherwise 0 is returned. Therefore, the following routine reads a binary file until the end-of-file mark is encountered:

```
while(!feof(fp)) ch = getc(fp);
```

This method can be applied to text files as well as binary files.

fclose( )

The **fclose( )** function is used to close a stream that was opened by a call to **fopen( )**. It writes any data still remaining in the disk buffer to the file and does a formal operating-system-level close on the file. A call to **fclose( )** frees the file control block associated with the stream and makes it available for reuse. There is an operating system limit to the number of open files you can have at any one time, so it may be necessary to close one file before opening another.

The **fclose( )** function has the prototype

int fclose(FILE *fp*);

where *fp* is the file pointer returned by the call to **fopen( )**. A return value of 0 signifies a successful close operation; an **EOF** is returned if an error occurs. Generally, **fclose( )** will fail only when a diskette has been prematurely removed from the drive or if there is no more space on the diskette.

ferror( ) and rewind( )

The **ferror( )** function is used to determine whether a file operation has produced an error. The function **ferror( )** has this prototype

int ferror(FILE *fp*)

where *fp* is a valid file pointer. It returns true if an error has occurred during the last file operation; it returns false otherwise. Because each file operation sets the error condition, **ferror( )** should be called immediately after each file operation; otherwise an error may be lost.

The **rewind( )** function resets the file position locator to the beginning of the file specified as its argument. The prototype is

void rewind(FILE *fp*)

where *fp* is a valid file pointer.

Using fopen( ), getc( ), putc( ), and fclose( )

The functions **fopen( )**, **getc( )**, **putc( )**, and **fclose( )** comprise a minimal set of file routines. A simple example of using **putc( )**, **fopen( )**, and **fclose( )** is the following program, **ktod**. It simply reads characters from the keyboard and writes them to a disk file until a dollar sign is typed. The file name is specified from the command line. For example, if you call this program **ktod**, then typing **ktod test** allows you to enter lines of text into the file called **test**.

```
/* ktod: key to disk. */

#include <stdio.h>

main(int argc, char *argv[])
{
  FILE *fp;
  char ch;

  if(argc!=2) {
    printf("You forgot to enter the filename\n");
    return 1;
  }

  if((fp=fopen(argv[1],"w")) == NULL) {
    printf("cannot open file\n");
    return 1;
  }

  do {
    ch = getchar();
    putc(ch, fp);
  } while (ch!='$');

  fclose(fp);
  return 0;
}
```

The complementary program **dtos** will read any text file and display the contents on the screen. You must specify the name of the file on the command line.

```
/* dtos: disk to screen. */
#include <stdio.h>

main(int argc, char *argv[])
{
  FILE *fp;
  char ch;

  if(argc!=2) {
    printf("You forgot to enter the filename\n");
    return 1;
  }
```

```
  if((fp=fopen(argv[1], "r")) == NULL) {
    printf("cannot open file\n");
    return 1;
  }

  ch = getc(fp);    /* read one character */

  while (ch!=EOF) {
    putchar(ch);   /* print on screen */
    ch = getc(fp);
  }

  fclose(fp);
  return 0;
}
```

The following program copies a file of any type. Notice that the files are opened in binary mode and **feof( )** is used to check for the end of the file. (No error checking is performed on output, but in a real-world situation it would be a good idea. Try to add it as an exercise.)

```
/* This program will copy a file to another. */
#include <stdio.h>

main(int argc, char *argv[])
{
  FILE *in, *out;
  char ch;

  if(argc!=3) {
    printf("You forgot to enter a filename\n");
    return 1;
  }

  if((in=fopen(argv[1], "rb")) == NULL) {
    printf("cannot open source file\n");
    return 1;
  }
  if((out=fopen(argv[2], "wb")) == NULL) {
    printf("cannot open destination file\n");
    return 1;
  }
```

```
/* this code actually copies the file */
while(!feof(in)) {
    ch = getc(in);
    if(!feof(in)) putc(ch, out);
}

fclose(in);
fclose(out);
return 0;
}
```

getw( ) and putw( )

In addition to **getc( )** and **putc( )**, Turbo C supports two additional buffered I/O functions: **putw( )** and **getw( )**. (Although these functions are not defined by the ANSI standard, they are included with Turbo C and are commonly found in most other C compiler libraries.) They are used to read and write integers from and to a disk file. These functions work exactly the same as **putc( )** and **getc( )** except that instead of reading or writing a single character, they read or write 2 bytes. For example, the following code fragment writes an integer to the disk file pointed to by **fp**:

```
putw(100, fp);
```

fgets( ) and fputs( )

The Turbo C buffered I/O system includes two functions that can read and write strings from and to streams: **fgets( )** and **fputs( )**. Their prototypes are

> int fputs(const char *str, FILE *fp);
> char *fgets(char *str, int length, FILE *fp);

The function **fputs( )** works much like **puts( )** except that it writes the string to the specified stream. The **fgets( )** function reads a string from the specified stream until either a newline character or *length*–1 characters have been read. If a newline is read, it will be part of the string (unlike **gets( )**). However **fgets( )** is terminated, the resultant string will be null-terminated.

fread( ) and fwrite( )

The ANSI C file system provides two functions, **fread( )** and **fwrite( )**, that allow the reading and writing of blocks of data. Their prototypes are

> size_t fread(void *buffer, size_t *num_bytes*, size_t *count*, FILE *fp);
> size_t fwrite(const void *buffer, size_t *num_bytes*, size_t *count*, FILE *fp);

In the case of **fread( )**, *buffer* is a pointer to a region of memory that receives the data read from the file. For **fwrite( )**, *buffer* is a pointer to the information to be written to the file. The length of each item, in bytes, to be read or written is specified by *num_bytes*. The argument *count* determines how many items (each being *num_bytes* in length) will be read or written. Finally, *fp* is a file pointer to a previously opened stream. Both functions return the number of items actually written or read, which may be less than *count* if the end of the file is reached first or an error occurs.

As long as the file has been opened for binary data, **fread( )** and **fwrite( )** can read and write any type of information. For example, this program writes a **float** to a disk file:

```
/* Write a floating point number to a disk file. */
#include <stdio.h>

main(void)
{
  FILE *fp;
  float f=12.23;

  if((fp=fopen("test","wb"))==NULL) {
    printf("cannot open file\n");
    return 1;
  }

  fwrite(&f, sizeof(float), 1, fp);

  fclose(fp);
  return 0;
}
```

As this program illustrates, the buffer can be, and often is, simply a variable.

One of the most useful applications of **fread( )** and **fwrite( )** involves the reading and writing of arrays (or structures). For example, this fragment writes the contents of the floating point array **balance** to the file **balance** using a single **fwrite( )** statement. Next, it reads the array, using a single **fread( )** statement, and displays its contents.

```
#include <stdio.h>

main(void)
{
  register int i;
  FILE *fp;
  float balance[100];
```

```
/* open for write */
if((fp=fopen("balance","wb"))==NULL) {
  printf("cannot open file\n");
  return 1;
}

for(i=0; i<100; i++) balance[i] = (float) i;

/* this saves the entire balance array in one step */
fwrite(balance, sizeof balance, 1, fp);
fclose(fp);

/* zero array */
for(i=0; i<100; i++) balance[i] = 0.0;

/* open for read */
if((fp=fopen("balance","rb"))==NULL) {
  printf("cannot open file\n");
  return 1;
}

/* this reads the entire balance array in one step */
fread(balance, sizeof balance, 1, fp);

/* display contents of array */
for(i=0; i<100; i++) printf("%f ", balance[i]);

fclose(fp);
return 0;
}
```

Using **fread( )** and **fwrite( )** to read or write complex data is more efficient than using repeated calls to **getc( )** and **putc( )**.

fseek( ) and Random Access I/O

You can perform random read and write operations using the buffered I/O system with the help of **fseek( )**, which sets the file position locator. Its prototype is

   int fseek(FILE *fp*, long *num_bytes*, int *origin*);

where *fp* is a file pointer returned by a call to **fopen( )**; *num_bytes*, a long integer, is the number of bytes from *origin* to seek to; and *origin* is one of the following macros (defined in **stdio.h**):

Origin	Macro Name
Beginning of file	SEEK_SET
Current position	SEEK_CUR
End of file	SEEK_END

The macros are defined as integer values with **SEEK_SET** being 0, **SEEK_CUR** being 1, and **SEEK_END** being 2. Therefore, to seek *num_bytes* from the start of the file, *origin* should be **SEEK_SET**. To seek from the current position use **SEEK_CUR**, and to seek from the end of the file use **SEEK_END**.

The use of **fseek( )** on text files is not recommended because the character translations cause position errors. Use of **fseek( )** is suggested only for binary files.

For example, you could use the following code to read the 234th byte in a file called **test**:

```
func1(void)
{
  FILE *fp;

  if((fp=fopen("test", "rb")) == NULL) {
    printf("cannot open file\n");
    exit(1);
  }

  fseek(fp, 234L, 0);
  return getc(fp);    /* read one character */
                      /* at 234th position */
  }
}
```

A return value of 0 means that **fseek( )** succeeded. A non-0 value indicates failure.

Another example that uses **fseek( )** is the following **dump** program, which lets you examine the contents in both ASCII and hexadecimal of any file you choose. You can look at the file in 128-byte "sectors" as you move about the file in either direction. The output displayed is similar in style to the format used by the DEBUG command when given the **D** (dump memory) command. To exit the program, type a **–1** when prompted for the sector. Notice the use of **fread( )** to read the file. At the end-of-file mark, less than **SIZE** number of bytes are likely to be read, so the number returned by **fread( )** is passed to **display( )**. (Remember that **fread( )** returns the number of items actually read.) Enter this program into your computer and study it until you are certain how it works:

```
/* dump: A simple disk look utility using fseek. */
#include <stdio.h>
```

```c
#include <ctype.h>

#define SIZE 128

void display(int numread);

char buf[SIZE];
void display();

main(int argc, char *argv[])
{
  FILE *fp;
  int sector, numread;

  if(argc!=2) {
    printf("usage: dump filename\n");
    return 1;
  }

  if((fp=fopen(argv[1], "rb"))==NULL) {
    printf("cannot open file\n");
    return 1;
  }

  do {
    printf("enter sector: ");
    scanf("%ld", &sector);
    if(sector>=0) {
      if(fseek(fp, sector*SIZE, SEEK_SET)) {
        printf("seek error\n");
      }
      if((numread=fread(buf, 1, SIZE, fp)) != SIZE)
        printf("EOF reached\n");

      display(numread);
    }
  } while(sector>=0);
  return 0;
}

/* Display the contents of a file. */
void display(int numread)
{
  int i, j;
```

```
for(i=0; i<numread/16; i++) {
  for(j=0; j<16; j++) printf("%3X", buf[i*16+j]);
  printf("  ");
  for(j=0; j<16; j++) {
    if(isprint(buf[i*16+j])) printf("%c", buf[i*16+j]);
    else printf(".");
  }
  printf("\n");
}
}
```

Notice that the library function **isprint( )** is used to determine which characters are printing characters. The **isprint( )** function returns true if the character is printable and false otherwise, and requires the use of the header file **ctype.h**, which is included near the top of the program. A sample output with **dump** used on itself is shown in Figure 8-2.

```
enter sector: 0
 2F 2A 20 44 55 4D 50 3A 20 41 20 73 69 6D 70 6C   /* dump: A simpl
  6  5 20 64 69 73 6B 20 6C 6F 6F 6B 20 75 74 69 6C   e disk look util
 69 74 79 20 75 73 69 6E 67 20 66 73 65 65 6B 2E   ity using fseek.
 20 2A 2F  D  A 23 69 6E 63 6C 75 64 65 20 3C 73    */..#include <s
 74 64 69 6F 2E 68 3E  D  A 23 69 6E 63 6C 75 64   tdio.h>..#includ
 65 20 3C 63 74 79 70 65 2E 68 3E  D  A  D A 23   e <ctype.h>....#
 64 65 66 69 6E 65 20 53 49 5A 45 20 31 32 38  D   define SIZE 128.
  A  D  A 76 6F 69 64 20 64 69 73 70 6C 61 79 28   ...void display(

enter sector: 1
 69 6E 74 20 6E 75 6D 72 65 61 64 29 3B  D  A  D   int numread);...
  A 63 68 61 72 20 62 75 66 5B 53 49 5A 45 5D 3B   .char buf[SIZE];
  D  A 76 6F 69 64 20 64 69 73 70 6C 61 79 28 29   ..void display()
 3B  D  A  D  A 6D 61 69 6E 28 69 6E 74 20 61 72   ;....main(int ar
 67 63 2C 20 63 68 61 72 20 2A 61 72 67 76 5B 5D   gc, char *argv[]
 29  D  A 7B  D  A 20 20 46 49 4C 45 20 2A 66 70   )..{.. FILE *fp
 3B  D  A 20 20 69 6E 74 20 73 65 63 74 6F 72 2C   ;.. int sector,
 20 6E 75 6D 72 65 61 64 3B  D  A  D  A 20 20 69    numread;.... i

enter sector: -1
```

Figure 8-2.   *Sample output from the* **dump** *program*

The Standard Streams

Whenever a Turbo C program starts execution, five streams are opened automatically. They are **stdin**, **stdout**, **stderr**, **stdaux**, and **stdprn**. Because these are file pointers, they may be used by any function in the ANSI C I/O system that uses file pointers. For example, **putchar( )** could be defined as

```
putchar(int c)
{
  putc(c, stdout);
}
```

fprintf( ) and fscanf( )

In addition to the basic I/O functions, the buffered I/O system includes **fprintf( )** and **fscanf( )**. These functions behave exactly like **printf( )** and **scanf( )** except that they operate with disk files. The prototypes of **fprintf( )** and **fscanf( )** are

> int fprintf(FILE *fp, const char *fmt_string, . . .);
> int fscanf(FILE *fp, const char *fmt_string, . . .);

where *fp* is a file pointer returned by a call to **fopen( )**. Except for directing their output to the file defined by *fp*, they operate exactly like **printf( )** and **scanf( )** respectively.

To illustrate how useful these functions can be, the following program maintains a simple telephone directory in a disk file. You may enter names and numbers or look up a number given a name.

```
/* A simple telephone directory */

#include <conio.h>
#include <stdlib.h>
#include <stdio.h>
#include <ctype.h>
#include <string.h>

void add_num(void), lookup(void);
int menu(void);

main(void)  /* fscanf - fprintf example */
{
  char choice;
```

```
  do {
    choice = menu();
    switch(choice) {
      case 'a': add_num();
        break;
      case 'l': lookup();
        break;
    }
  } while (choice!='q');
  return 0;
}

/* Display menu and get request. */
menu(void)
{
  char ch;

  do {
    printf("(A)dd, (L)ookup, or (Q)uit: ");
    ch = tolower(getche());
    printf("\n");
  } while(ch != 'q' && ch != 'a' && ch != 'l');

  return ch;
}

/* Add a name and number to the directory. */
void add_num(void)
{
  FILE *fp;
  char name[80];
  int a_code, exchg, num;

  /* open it for append */
  if((fp=fopen("phone","a")) == NULL) {
    printf("cannot open directory file\n");
    exit(1);
  }

  printf("enter name and number: ");
    fscanf(stdin, "%s%d%d%d", name, &a_code, &exchg, &num);
  fscanf(stdin, "%*c"); /* remove CR from input stream */
```

```
  /* write to file */
  fprintf(fp,"%s %d %d %d\n", name, a_code, exchg, num);

  fclose(fp);
}

/* Find a number given a name. */
void lookup(void)
{
  FILE *fp;
  char name[80], name2[80];
  int a_code, exchg, num;

  /* open it for read */
  if((fp=fopen("phone","r")) == NULL) {
    printf("cannot open directory file\n");
    exit(1);
  }

  printf("name? ");
  gets(name);

  /* look for number */
  while(!feof(fp)) {
    fscanf(fp,"%s%d%d%d", name2, &a_code, &exchg, &num);
    if(!strcmp(name, name2)) {
      printf("%s: (%d) %d-%d\n",name, a_code, exchg, num);
      break;
    }
  }
  fclose(fp);
}
```

Enter this program and run it. After you have entered a couple of names and
numbers, examine the file **phone**. As you would expect, it appears just the way it
would if the information had been displayed on the screen using **printf( )**.

Although **fprintf( )** *and* **fscanf( )** *are often the easiest way to write and read assorted
data to disk files, they are not always the most efficient. Because formatted ASCII data is
being written just as it would appear on the screen (instead of in binary) you incur extra
overhead with each call. If speed or file size is a concern, you should probably use* **fread( )**
and **fwrite( )**.

Erasing Files

The **remove( )** function erases the specified file. Its prototype is

int remove(const char *filename*);

It returns 0 upon success, non-0 if it fails.

This program uses **remove( )** to erase a file specified by the user.

```
/* A remove() example. */

#include <stdio.h>

main(void)
{
  char fname[80];

  printf("name of file to remove: ");
  gets(fname);

  if(remove(fname)) {
    printf("Error removing file\n");
    return 1;
  }
  else return 0;
}
```

The UNIX-Like File Routines

Because C was originally developed under the UNIX operating system, a second disk-file I/O system was created. It uses functions that are separate from the ANSI file system functions. The low-level, UNIX-like disk I/O functions are shown in Table 8-6. These functions all require that the header file **io.h** be included near the beginning of any program that uses them. The disk I/O subsystem comprising these functions is sometimes called the *unbuffered I/O system* because the programmer must provide and maintain *all* disk buffers; the routines do not do it for you. Unlike the functions **getc( )** and **putc( )**, which read and write characters from or to a stream of data, the functions **read( )** and **write( )** will read or write one complete buffer of information with each call. (This is similar to **fread( )** and **fwrite( )**.)

As stated at the beginning of this chapter, the UNIX-like file system is not defined by the ANSI standard. This implies that programs that use it will have portability

Name	Function
read()	Reads a buffer of data
write()	Writes a buffer of data
open()	Opens a disk file
close()	Closes a disk file
lseek()	Seeks to the specified byte in a file
unlink()	Removes a file from the directory

Table 8-6. *The UNIX-Like Unbuffered I/O Functions*

problems at some point in the future. The unbuffered file system's use is expected to diminish over the next few years, but it is included in this chapter because a great many existing C programs use it, and it is supported by virtually all existing C compilers.

open( ), creat( ), and close( )

Unlike the ANSI C I/O system, the UNIX-like system does not use file pointers of type **FILE**, but rather file descriptors called *handles* of type **int**. A file is opened using the **open( )** function, which has the prototype

int open(const char *filename, int *mode*, int *access*);

The **open( )** function requires both the **fnctl.h** and the **io.h** header files. The string pointed to by *filename* is any valid file name and *mode* is one of the following macros defined in **fcntl.h**:

Mode	Effect
O_RDONLY	Read-only
O_WRONLY	Write-only
O_RDWR	Read/write

Turbo C also allows some options to be added to these basic modes, so consult your manual.

The *access* parameter only relates to UNIX environments and is included for compatibility. In the examples in this chapter, *access* will be set to 0.

Turbo C also defines a DOS-specific version of **open( )** called **_open( )** that has this prototype:

int _open(const char *filename, int mode);

This function bypasses the *access* parameter altogether.

A successful call to **open( )** returns a positive integer. A return value of –1 means that the file cannot be opened.

You usually see the call to **open( )** like this:

```
if((fd=open(filename, mode, 0)) == -1)  {
  printf("cannot open file\n");
  exit(1);
}
```

If the file specified in the **open( )** statement does not appear on the disk, the operation fails. It will not create the file.

To close a file using the UNIX-like I/O system, use **close( )**. Its prototype is

int close(int *fd*);

If **close( )** returns a –1, it was unable to close the file. This could occur if the diskette were removed from the drive, for example.

A call to **close( )** releases the file descriptor so that it can be reused for another file. There is always some limit to the number of open files that can exist simultaneously, so you should **close( )** a file when it is no longer needed. More important, a close operation forces any information in the internal disk buffers of the operating system to be written to disk. Failure to close a file can lead to loss of data.

You use **creat( )** to create a new file for write operations. The prototype of **creat( )** is

int creat(const char *filename, int access);

where *filename* is any valid file name. The *access* argument is used to specify access modes and to mark the file as being either binary or text. Because **creat( )**'s use of *access* relates to the UNIX environment, Turbo C provides a special MS-DOS version called **_creat( )**, which takes a file attribute byte for *access* instead. In DOS, each file is associated with an attribute byte that specifies various bits of information. Table 8-7 shows how this attribute byte is organized.

The values in the table are additive. That is, if you wish to create a read-only hidden file you would use the value 3 (1 + 2) for *access*. Generally, to create a standard file, *access* will be 0.

Bit	Value	Meaning
0	1	Read-only file
1	2	Hidden file
2	4	System file
3	8	Volume label name
4	16	Subdirectory name
5	32	Archive
6	64	Unused
7	128	Unused

Table 8-7.   *The Organization of the DOS Attribute Byte*

write( ) and read( )

Once a file has been opened for writing it can be accessed by **write( )**. The prototype for **write( )** is

    int write(int *fd*, void **buf*, unsigned *size*);

Each time a call to **write( )** is executed, *size* characters are written to the disk file specified by *fd* from the buffer pointed to by *buf*. The prototype for **write( )** is in **io.h**. The **write( )** function returns the number of bytes written to the file. If an error occurs, **write( )** returns –1.

The **read( )** function is the complement of **write( )**. Its prototype is

    int read(int *fd*, void **buf*, unsigned *size*);

where *fd, buf,* and *size* are the same as for **write( )**, except that **read( )** places the data read into the buffer pointed to by *buf*. If **read( )** is successful, it returns the number of characters actually read. It returns 0 upon the physical end of the file, and –1 if errors occur. The prototype for **read( )** is in **io.h**.

The program shown here illustrates some aspects of the unbuffered I/O system. It reads lines of text from the keyboard, and writes them to a disk file, then reads them back.

```
#include <stdio.h>
#include <fcntl.h>
```

```
#include <io.h>
#include <string.h>
#include <stdlib.h>

#define BUF_SIZE   128

void display(char *buf, int fd2);
void input(char *buf, int fd1);

main(void)  /* read and write using UNIX-like I/O */
{
  char buf[BUF_SIZE];
  int fd1, fd2;

  if((fd1=_creat("oscar", O_WRONLY ))==-1) { /* open for write */
    printf("cannot open file\n");
    return 1;
  }

  input(buf, fd1);

  /* now close file and read back */
  close(fd1);

  if((fd2=open("oscar", 0, O_RDONLY))==-1) { /* open for write */
    printf("cannot open file\n");
    return 1;
  }

  display(buf,fd2);
  close(fd2);
  return 0;
}

void input(char *buf, int fd1)
{
  register int t;

  printf("Enter test (quit to stop): ");
  do {
    for(t=0; t<BUF_SIZE; t++) buf[t]='\0';
    gets(buf); /* input chars from keyboard */
    if(write(fd1, buf, BUF_SIZE)!=BUF_SIZE) {
      printf("error on write\n");
      exit(1);
```

```
    }
  } while (strcmp(buf, "quit"));
}

void display(char *buf, int fd2)
{
  for(;;) {
    if(read(fd2, buf, BUF_SIZE)==0) return;
    printf("%s\n",buf);
  }
}
```

unlink( )

If you wish to remove a file from the directory, use **unlink( )**. Although **unlink( )** is considered part of the UNIX-like I/O system, it removes any file from the directory. The standard form of the call is

  int unlink(const char *filename);

where *filename* is a character pointer to any valid file name. The **unlink( )** function returns an error (−1) if it is unable to erase the file. This could happen if the file is not present on the diskette to begin with, or if the diskette is write-protected. The prototype for **unlink( )** is in **io.h**.

Random Access Files and lseek( )

Turbo C supports random access file I/O under the unbuffered I/O system via calls to **lseek( )**. Its prototype is

  long lseek(int *fd*, long *numbytes*, int *origin*);

where *fd* is a file descriptor returned by a **creat( )** or **open( )** call. Here, *numbytes* specifies the number of bytes to move from *origin*. *origin* must be one the following macros:

Origin	Name
Beginning of file	SEEK_SET
Current position	SEEK_CUR
End of file	SEEK_END

To seek *numbytes* from the start of the file, *origin* must be **SEEK_SET**. To seek from the current position, use **SEEK_CUR**; to seek from the end of the file, use **SEEK_END**.

The **lseek( )** function returns *numbytes* on success. Upon failure, a –1 is returned. The prototype for **lseek( )** is in **io.h**.

A simple example using **lseek( )** is the **dump** program developed earlier in this chapter, which is recoded for the UNIX-like I/O system. It not only shows the operation of **lseek( )** but also illustrates many of the UNIX-like I/O functions.

```
/* dump using the UNIX-like file system. */

#include <fcntl.h>
#include <io.h>
#include <ctype.h>
#include <stdio.h>
#include <stdlib.h>

#define SIZE  128

char buf[SIZE];
void display(int numread);

main(int argc, char *argv[])
{
  char s[10];
  int fd, sector, numread;
  long pos;

  if(argc!=2) {
    printf("You forgot to enter the file name.");
    return 1;
  }

  if((fd=open(argv[1], O_RDONLY, 0))==-1) { /* open for read */
    printf("cannot open file\n");
    return 1;
  }

  do {
    printf("\n\nbuffer: ");
    gets(s);

    sector = atoi(s); /* get the sector to read */
```

```
    pos = (long) (sector*SIZE);
    if(lseek(fd, pos, SEEK_SET)!=pos)
      printf("seek error\n");

    numread = read(fd, buf, SIZE);

    display(numread);
  } while(sector>=0);
  close(fd);
  return 0;
}

void display(int numread)
{
  int i, j;

  for(i=0; i<numread/16; i++) {
    for(j=0; j<16; j++) printf("%3X", buf[i*16+j]);
    printf("  ");
    for(j=0; j<16; j++) {
      if(isprint(buf[i*16+j])) printf("%c", buf[i*16+j]);
      else printf(".");
    }
    printf("\n");
  }
}
```

Choosing an Approach

The buffered I/O system defined by the ANSI C standard is recommended for new projects. Because the ANSI standard committee has elected not to standardize the UNIX-like unbuffered I/O system, it cannot be recommended for future projects. However, existing code should be maintainable for a number of years. There is probably no reason to rush into a rewrite at this time.

Within the buffered I/O system, you should use text mode and **getc( )** and **putc( )** when you are working with character files, such as the text files created by a word processor. However, when it is necessary to store binary data or complex data types, you should use binary files and **fread( )** and **fwrite( )**.

A final word of warning: never try to mix the I/O systems inside the same program. Because the way they approach files is different, they could accidentally interfere with each other.

Chapter **9**

The Preprocessor

The source code for a C (and C++) program can include various instructions to the compiler. Although not actually part of the Turbo C language, these *preprocessor directives* expand the scope of its programming environment. This chapter also examines Turbo C's built-in macros.

This chapter also discusses some additions to the preprocessor made by Turbo and/or Borland C++.

The C preprocessor as defined by the ANSI standard contains the following directives:

#if
#ifdef
#ifndef
#else
#elif
#endif
#include
#define
#undef
#line
#error
#pragma

All preprocessor directives begin with a # sign. Turbo C supports all of these directives, and each is examined in turn.

#define

The **#define** directive is used to define an identifier and a character sequence that will be substituted for the identifier each time it is encountered in the source file. The identifier is called a *macro-name* and the replacement process is called *macro-substitution*. The general form of the directive is

>#define *macro-name character-sequence*

Notice that there is no semicolon in this statement. There may be any number of spaces between the identifier and the character sequence, but once it begins, it is terminated only by a new line.

For example, if you wish to use **TRUE** for the value 1 and **FALSE** for the value 0, then you would declare two macro **#define**s:

```
#define TRUE 1
#define FALSE 0
```

This causes the compiler to substitute a 1 or a 0 each time the name **TRUE** or **FALSE** is encountered in your source file. For example, the following prints "0 1 2" on the screen:

```
printf("%d %d %d", FALSE, TRUE, TRUE+1);
```

Once a macro-name has been defined, it can be used as part of the definition of other macro-names. For example, this code defines the names **ONE**, **TWO**, and **THREE** to their respective values:

```
#define ONE    1
#define TWO    ONE+ONE
#define THREE ONE+TWO
```

It is important to understand that the macro-substitution is simply replacing an identifier with its associated string. Therefore, if you wished to define a standard error message, you might write something like this:

```
#define E_MS "standard error on input\n"
```

```
.
.
.
printf(E_MS);
```

Turbo C substitutes the string "standard error on input\n" when the identifier **E_MS** is encountered. To the compiler, the **printf( )** statement actually appears to be

```
printf("standard error on input\n");
```

No text substitutions occur if the identifier occurs within a string. For example,

```
#define XYZ this is a test
.
.
.
printf("XYZ");
```

does not print "this is a test" but "XYZ".

If the string is longer than one line, you can continue it on the next line by placing a backslash at the end of the line, as shown in this example:

```
#define LONG_STRING "this is a very long \
string that is used as an example"
```

It is common practice among C programmers to use capital letters for defined identifiers. This convention helps anyone reading the program know at a glance that a macro-substitution will take place. Also, it is best to put all **#define**s at the start of the file or, perhaps, in a separate include file rather than sprinkling them throughout the program.

The most common use of macro-substitutions is to define "magic numbers" that occur in a program. For example, you may have a program that defines an array and has several routines that access that array. Instead of "hard-coding" the array's size with a constant, it is better to define a name that represents the size and use that name whenever the size of the array is needed. Therefore, if the size of the array changes, you have to change it in only one place in the file and recompile. For example:

```
#define MAX_SIZE 100

float balance[MAX_SIZE];
```

The **#define** directive has another powerful feature: the macro-name can have arguments. Each time the macro-name is encountered, the arguments associated with it are replaced by the actual arguments found in the program. For example:

```
#include <stdio.h>

#define MIN(a,b)   ((a)<(b)) ? a : b

main(void)
{
  int x, y;

  x = 10;
  y = 20;
  printf("the minimum is: %d", MIN(x, y));
  return 0;
}
```

When this program is compiled, the expression defined by **MIN(a,b)** is substituted, except that **x** and **y** are used as the operands. That is, the **printf( )** statement is substituted to look like this:

```
printf("the minimum is: %d",((x)<(y)) ? x : y);
```

Be very careful how you define macros that take arguments; otherwise, there can be some surprising results. For example, examine this short program, which uses a macro to determine whether a value is even or odd:

```
/* This program will give the wrong answer. */

#include <stdio.h>

#define EVEN(a) a%2==0 ? 1 : 0

main(void)
{
  if(EVEN(9+1)) printf("is even");
  else printf("is odd");
  return 0;
}
```

This program will not work correctly because of the way the macro-substitution is made. When Turbo C compiles this program, the **EVEN(9+1)** is expanded to

```
9+1%2==0 ? 1 : 0
```

As you may recall, the **%** (modulus) operator has higher precedence than the plus operator. This means that the **%** operation is first performed on the 1 and that result is added to 9, which (of course) does not equal 0. To fix the trouble, there must be parentheses around **a** in the macro definition of **EVEN**, as shown in this corrected version of the program:

```
#include <stdio.h>

#define EVEN(a) (a)%2==0 ? 1 : 0

main(void)
{
  if(EVEN(9+1)) printf("is even");
  else printf("is odd");
  return 0;
}
```

Now, the **9+1** is evaluated prior to the modulus operation. In general, it is a good idea to surround macro parameters with parentheses to avoid troubles like the one just described.

The use of macro-substitutions in place of real functions has one major benefit: it increases the speed of the code because no overhead for a function call is incurred. However, this increased speed might be paid for with an increase in the size of the program because of duplicated code.

#error

The **#error** directive forces Turbo C to stop compilation when it is encountered. It is used primarily for debugging. The general form of the directive is

#error *error-message*

The *error-message* is not between double quotes. When the compiler encounters this directive, it displays the following information and terminates compilation:

```
Fatal: filename linenum Error directive: error-message
```

#include

The **#include** preprocessor directive instructs the compiler to include another source file with the one that has the **#include** directive in it. The source file to be read in must be enclosed between double quotes or angle brackets. For example, these two directives both instruct Turbo C to read and compile the header for the disk file library routines:

```
#include "stdio.h"
#include <stdio.h>
```

It is valid for included files to have **#include** directives in them. This is referred to as *nested includes*. For example, this program, shown with its include files, includes a file that includes another file:

```
/* The program file: */
#include <stdio.h>

main(void)
{
  #include "one"
}




/* Include file ONE: */

printf("This is from the first include file.\n");
#include "two"




/* Include file TWO: */

printf("This is from the second include file.\n");
```

If explicit path names are specified as part of the file name identifier, only those directories are searched for the included file. Otherwise, if the file name is enclosed in quotes, first the current working directory is searched. If the file is not found, any directories specified on the command line are searched. Finally, if the file has still not been found, the standard directories are searched.

If no explicit path names are specified and the file name is enclosed by angle brackets, the file is searched for in the standard directories. At no time is the current working directory searched.

Conditional Compilation Directives

There are several directives that allow you to selectively compile portions of your program's source code. This process is called *conditional compilation* and is used widely by commerical software houses that provide and maintain many customized versions of one program.

#if, #else, #elif, and #endif

The general idea behind the **#if** is that if the constant expression following the **#if** is true, the code that is between it and an **#endif** is compiled; otherwise, the code is skipped. The **#endif** is used to mark the end of an **#if** block.

The general form of **#if** is

```
#if constant-expression
    statement sequence
#endif
```

If the constant expression is true, the block of code is compiled; otherwise, it is skipped. For example:

```
/* A simple #if example */
#include <stdio.h>

#define MAX 100
main(void)
{
#if MAX>99
  printf("compiled for array greater than 99\n");
#endif
  return 0;
}
```

This program displays the message on the screen because, as defined in the program, **MAX** is greater than 99. This example illustrates an important point. The expression that follows the **#if** is *evaluated at compile time*. Therefore, it must contain only identifiers that have been previously defined and constants; no variables can be used.

The **#else** works in much the same way as the **else** that forms part of the C language: it establishes an alternative if the **#if** fails. The previous example can be expanded as shown here:

```
/* A simple #if/#else example */
#include <stdio.h>

#define MAX 10
main(void)
{
#if MAX>99
  printf("compiled for array greater than 99\n");
#else
  printf("compiled for small array\n");
#endif
  return 0;
}
```

In this case, **MAX** is defined to be less than 99, so the **#if** portion of the code is not compiled, but the **#else** alternative is. Therefore, the message "compiled for small array" is displayed.

Notice that the **#else** is used to mark both the end of the **#if** block and the beginning of the **#else** block. This is necessary because there can be only one **#endif** associated with any **#if**.

The **#elif** means "else if" and is used to establish an if-else-if ladder for multiple compilation options. The **#elif** is followed by a constant expression. If the expression is true, that block of code is compiled and no other **#elif** expressions are tested or compiled. Otherwise, the next in the series is checked. The general form is

> #if *expression*
>   *statement sequence*
> #elif *expression 1*
>   *statement sequence*
> #elif *expression 2*
>   *statement sequence*
> #elif *expression 3*
>   *statement sequence*
> #elif *expression 4*
>   .
>
>   .
>
>   .
>
> #elif *expression N*

statement sequence
#endif

For example, this fragment uses the value of **ACTIVE_COUNTRY** to define the currency sign:

```
#define US 0
#define ENGLAND 1
#define FRANCE 2

#define ACTIVE_COUNTRY US

#if ACTIVE_COUNTRY==US
  char currency[] = "dollar";
#elif ACTIVE_COUNTRY==ENGLAND
  char currency[] = "pound";
#else
  char currency[] = "franc";
#endif
```

#ifs and **#elif**s can be nested with the **#endif**, **#else**, or **#elif** associated with the nearest **#if** or **#elif**. For example, the following is perfectly valid:

```
#if MAX>100
   #if SERIAL_VERSION
      int port = 198;
   #elif
      int port = 200;
   #endif
#else
   char out_buffer[100];
#endif
```

In Turbo C, but not ANSI C, you can use the **sizeof** compile-time operator in an **#if** statement. For example, the next fragment determines whether a program is being compiled for a small or large data model (memory models are discussed in Chapter 10).

```
#if (sizeof(char *) == 2)
  printf("Program compiled for small model.");
#else
  printf("Program compiled for large model.");
#endif
```

#ifdef and #ifndef

Another method of conditional compilation uses the directives **#ifdef** and **#ifndef**, which mean "if defined" and "if not defined," respectively, and which refer to macro names. The general form of **#ifdef** is

> #ifdef *macro-name*
>   *statement sequence*
> #endif

If the *macro-name* has been previously defined in a **#define** statement, the statement sequence between the **#ifdef** and **#endif** is compiled.

The general form of **#ifndef** is

> #ifndef *macro-name*
>   *statement sequence*
> #endif

If *macro-name* is currently undefined by a **#define** statement, the block of code is compiled.

Both the **#ifdef** and **#ifndef** can use an **#else** statement but not the **#elif**. For example,

```
#include <stdio.h>

#define TED 10

main(void)
{
#ifdef TED
  printf("Hi Ted\n");
#else
  printf("Hi anyone\n");
#endif
#ifndef RALPH
  printf("RALPH not defined\n");
#endif
  return 0;
}
```

prints "Hi Ted" and "RALPH not defined". However, if **TED** were not defined, "Hi anyone" would be displayed, followed by "RALPH not defined".

You can nest **#ifdef**s and **#ifndef**s in the same way as **#if**s. You can also use the **#if** directive to see if a macro is defined using the general form

```
#if defined macro-name
   .
   .
   .
#endif
```

Here, *macro-name* is the name of the macro that is checked. You can precede **defined** with an **!** to cause code to be compiled only when a macro-name is not defined.

#undef

The **#undef** directive is used to remove a previously defined definition of the macro-name that follows it. The general form is

```
#undef macro-name
```

For example:

```
#define LEN 100
#define WIDTH 100

char array[LEN][WIDTH];

#undef LEN
#undef WIDTH
/* at this point both LEN and WIDTH are undefined */
```

Both **LEN** and **WIDTH** are defined until the **#undef** statements are encountered.

The principal use of **#undef** is to allow macro-names to be localized to only those sections of code that need them.

#line

The **#line** directive is used to change the contents of _ _**LINE**_ _ and _ _**FILE**_ _, which are predefined macro-names in Turbo C. _ _**LINE**_ _ contains the line number of the line currently being compiled and _ _**FILE**_ _ contains the name of the file being compiled. The basic form of the **#line** command is

```
#line number "filename"
```

where *number* is any positive integer and the optional *filename* is any valid file identifier. The line number is the number of the current source line and the file name is the name of the source file. **#line** is primarily used for debugging purposes and special applications.

For example, the following specifies that the line count will begin with 100. The **printf( )** statement displays the number 102 because it is the third line in the program after the **#line 100** statement.

```
#include <stdio.h>

#line 100    /* reset the line counter */
main(void)      /* line 100 */
{ /* line 101 */
  printf("%d\n", __LINE__);  /* line 102 */
  return 0;
}
```

#pragma

The **#pragma** directive is defined by the ANSI standard to be an implementation-defined directive that allows various instructions, defined by the compiler's creator, to be given to the compiler. The general form of the **#pragma** directive is

#pragma *name*

where *name* is the name of the **#pragma** you want. Turbo C defines these three **#pragma** statements:

inline
saveregs
warn

Turbo/Borland C++ adds these six **#pragma**s:

argsused
exit
option
startup
hdrfile
hdrstop

Borland C++ adds this additional **#pragma**:

intrinsic

The **argsused** directive must precede a function. It is used to prevent a warning message if an argument to the function that the **#pragma** precedes is not used in the body of the function.

The **exit** directive specifies one or more functions that will be called when the program terminates. The **startup** directive specifies one or more functions that will be called when the program starts running. They have these general forms:

```
#pragma exit function-name priority
#pragma startup function-name priority
```

The *priority* is a value between 64 and 255 (the values 0 through 63 are reserved). The priority determines the order in which the functions are called. If no priority is given, it defaults to 100. All startup and exit functions must be declared as shown here:

```
void func(void);
```

The following example defines a startup function called **start( )**.

```
#include <stdio.h>

void start(void);

#pragma startup start 65

main(void)
{
  printf("in main");
  return 0;
}

void start(void)
{
  printf("in start");
}
```

As this example shows, you must provide a function prototype for all exit and startup functions prior to the **#pragma** statement.

Another **#pragma** directive is **inline**. It has the general form

```
#pragma inline
```

This tells the compiler that in-line assembly code is contained in the program. For the fastest compile times, Turbo C needs to know in advance that in-line assembly code is contained in a program.

The **option** directive allows you to specify command-line options within your program instead of actually specifying them on the command line. It has the general form

#pragma option *option-list*

For example, this causes the program that contains it to be compiled for the large memory model:

```
#pragma option -ml
```

The following options *cannot* be used by the **option** directive:

–B	–c	–d	–D	–e	–E	–F
–H	–I	–L	–l	–M	–o	–P
–Q	–S	–T	–U	–V	–X	–Y

For some options, the **option** directive must precede all declarations, including function prototypes. For this reason, it is a good idea to make it one of the first statements in your program.

The **saveregs** directive prevents a function declared as **huge** from altering the value of any registers. This directive must immediately precede the function and affects only the function that it precedes.

The **warn** directive causes the compiler to override warning message options. It takes the form

#pragma warn *setting*

where *setting* is one of the various warning error options. These options are discussed later in this book.

The **hdrfile** directive names the file that will be used to hold precompiled headers. Its general form is

#pragma hdrfile "*fname*.sym"

where *fname* is the name of the file (the extension must be **.SYM**). By default, the file **TCDEF.SYM** is used. This **#pragma** directive applies only to Turbo/Borland C++.

The **hdrstop** directive tells Turbo/Borland C++ to stop precompiling header files.

Using Borland C++, it is possible to tell the compiler to generate in-line code instead of an actual function call for the following functions using the **intrinsic** directive. It has the general form

#pragma intrinsic *func-name*

where *func-name* is the name of the function that you want to in-line.

If you set an option in the IDE or use the –Oi command-line switch, Borland C++ automatically in-lines the following functions:

memchr	memcmp	memcpy	stpcpy	strcat
strchr	strcmp	strcpy	strlen	strncat
strncmp	strncpy	strnset	strrchr	rotl
rotr	fabs	alloca		

You can override the automatic in-lining by using this form of the **intrinsic** directive:

#pragma intrinsic –*func-name*

The # and ## Preprocessor Operators

Turbo C provides two preprocessor operators: **#** and **##**. These operators are used in conjunction with **#define**.

The **#** operator causes the argument it precedes to be turned into a quoted string. For example, consider this program:

```
#include "stdio.h"

#define mkstr(s)  # s

main()
{
  printf(mkstr(I like C));

  return 0;
}
```

The C preprocessor turns the line

```
printf(mkstr(I like C));
```

into

```
printf("I like C");
```

The **##** operator is used to concatenate two tokens. For example:

```
#include "stdio.h"

#define concat(a, b)   a ## b

main()
{
  int xy = 10;

  printf("%d", concat(x, y));

  return 0;
}
```

The preprocessor transforms

```
printf("%d", concat(x, y));
```

into

```
printf("%d", xy);
```

If these operators seem strange to you, keep in mind that they are not needed or used in most programs. They exist primarily to allow some special cases to be handled by the preprocessor.

Predefined Macro Names

The ANSI standard specifies five built-in predefined macro names. They are

```
_ _LINE_ _
_ _FILE_ _
_ _DATE_ _
```

_ _TIME_ _
_ _STDC_ _

Turbo C defines these additional built-in macros:

_ _CDECL_ _
_ _COMPACT_ _
_ _HUGE_ _
_ _LARGE_ _
_ _MEDIUM_ _
_ _MSDOS_ _
_ _PASCAL_ _
_ _SMALL_ _
_ _TINY_ _
_ _TURBOC_ _

Turbo C++ includes all of the preceding macros and adds these predefined macros:

_ _cplusplus
_ _OVERLAY_ _
_ _TCPLUSPLUS_ _
_ _TEMPLATES_ _

Borland C++ includes all macros defined by Turbo C and Turbo C++ and adds these predefined macros:

_ _BCPLUSPLUS_ _
_ _BORLANDC_ _
_ _DLL_ _
_Windows

The _ _**LINE**_ _ and _ _**FILE**_ _ macros were dicussed in the **#line** discussion earlier in this chapter. The others are examined here.

The _ _**DATE**_ _ macro contains a string in the form *month/day/year* that is the date of the translation of the source file into object code.

The length of time since the beginning of the compilation of the source code into object code up to the point at which the _ _**TIME**_ _ macro is encountered is contained as a string in _ _**TIME**_ _. The form of the string is *hour:minute:second*.

If the macro _ _**STDC**_ _ is defined, the program was compiled with ANSI C standard compliance checking turned on. If this is not the case, _ _**STDC**_ _ is undefined (if defined, its value is 1).

When a program is compiled using overlays, _ _**OVERLAY**_ _ is defined as 1. Otherwise, _ _**OVERLAY**_ _ is undefined.

The _ _**CDECL**_ _ macro is defined if the standard C calling convention is used—that is, if the Pascal option is not in use. If this is not the case, the macro is undefined (if defined, its value is 1).

Only one of the following macros is defined, based upon the memory model used during compilation: _ _**TINY**_ _, _ _**SMALL**_ _, _ _**COMPACT**_ _, _ _**MEDIUM**_ _, _ _**LARGE**_ _, and _ _**HUGE**_ _.

The _ _**MSDOS**_ _ macro is defined with the value 1 in all situations when using the MS-DOS version of Turbo/Borland C/C++.

The _ _**PASCAL**_ _ macro is defined as 1 only if the Pascal calling conventions are used to compile a program. Otherwise, it is undefined.

_ _**TURBOC**_ _ contains the version number of Turbo C. It is represented as a hexadecimal constant. The two rightmost digits represent the minor revision numbers and the leftmost digit represents the major revision. For example, the number 202 represents version 2.02. For Turbo/Borland C++, this value no longer represents the version number. Instead, it represents a hexadecimal value that is increased with each new release.

When using Turbo/Borland C++, if your program is compiled as a C++ program, _ _**cplusplus** is defined as 1. Otherwise, it is not defined.

If you are using Turbo/Borland C++, the macro _ _**TCPLUSPLUS**_ _ is defined if you have compiled your program as a C++ program. It is undefined otherwise. If using Borland C++, compiling a C++ program also causes _ _**BCPLUSPLUS**_ _ to be defined. Both these macros contain hexadecimal values that will increase with each new release of the compiler.

For Turbo/Borland C++, _ _**TEMPLATES**_ _ is defined as 1 for all versions of these compilers that support templates. It is undefined otherwise.

If you compile your program using Borland C/C++, _ _**BORLANDC**_ _ is defined as a hexadecimal value. This value will increase with each new release of the compiler.

For Borland C++, _ _**DLL**_ _ is defined as 1 when creating a Windows DLL object file. Otherwise, it is undefined.

Finally, for Borland C++, _**Windows** is defined if your program is compiled for use under Windows. Otherwise, it is undefined.

The following program illustrates the use of some of these macros:

```
#include <stdio.h>

main(void)
{
  printf("%s %d %s %s\n", __FILE__, __LINE__, __DATE__,
         __TIME__);

  printf("Program being compiled using the ");
#ifdef __TINY__
```

```
    printf("tiny model");
#endif
#ifdef __SMALL__
  printf("small model");
#endif
#ifdef __COMPACT__
  printf("compact model");
#endif
#ifdef __MEDIUM__
  printf("medium model");
#endif
#ifdef __LARGE__
  printf("large model");
#endif
#ifdef __HUGE__
  printf("huge model");
#endif
  printf("\n");

  return 0;
}
```

The output from this program is shown here:

```
example.c 5 Jan 23 1992 15:43:36
Program being compiled using the small model
```

For the most part, these built-in macros are used in fairly complex programming environments when several different versions of a program are developed or maintained.

Chapter **10**

Understanding Memory Models

For reasons that will become clear, you can compile a Turbo/Borland C/C++ program using any of the six different *memory models* defined by the 8086 family of processors. Each model organizes the memory of the computer differently and governs the size of a program's code, data, or both. It also determines how quickly your program will execute. Because the model used has a profound effect on your program's speed of execution and the way a program accesses the system resources, this chapter discusses in detail the various memory models and concludes with a program that lets you inspect and change any part of the RAM in your system.

The 8086 Family of Processors

Before you can understand the way the various memory models work you need to understand how the 8086 family of processors addresses memory. (For the rest of this chapter, the CPU will be called the 8086, but the information applies to all processors in this family, including the 8088, 80186, 80286, 80386, and 80486. For the 80286, 80386, and 80486, the following information is applicable only when the processor is running in 8086 emulation mode.)

The 8086 contains 14 registers into which information is placed for processing or program control. The registers fall into the following categories:

- General-purpose registers

- Base-pointer and index registers

- Segment registers

- Special-purpose registers

All the registers in the 8086 CPU are 16 bits (2 bytes) wide.

The *general-purpose registers* are the "workhorse" registers of the CPU. Values are placed in these registers for processing, including arithmetic operations, such as adding or multiplying; comparisons, including equality, less than, greater than, and the like; and branch (jump) instructions. Each of the general-purpose registers can be accessed, either as a 16-bit register or as two 8-bit registers.

The *base-pointer* and *index registers* provide support for such things as relative addressing, the stack pointer, and block move instructions.

The *segment registers* help implement the 8086's segmented memory scheme. The CS register holds the current code segment, the DS holds the current data segment, the ES holds the extra segment, and the SS holds the stack segment.

Finally, the *special-purpose registers* are the flag register, which holds the state of the CPU, and the instruction pointer, which points to the next instruction for the CPU to execute.

Figure 10-1 shows the layout of the 8086 registers.

Address Calculation

The 8086 has a total address space of 1 megabyte (the more powerful CPUs in the family can address more memory, but not when used in 8086 emulation mode). To access a megabyte of RAM requires a 20-bit address. However, on the 8086 no register is larger than 16 bits. This means that the 20-bit address must be divided between two registers. Unfortunately, the way the 20 bits are divided is a little more complex than one might assume.

For the 8086, all addresses consist of a segment and an offset. In fact, the addressing method used by the 8086 is generally called the *segment:offset method*. A *segment* is a 64K region of RAM that must start on an even multiple of 16 bytes. In 8086 jargon, 16 bytes is called a *paragraph*; hence the term *paragraph boundary* is sometimes used to reference these even multiples of 16 bytes. The 8086 has four segments: one for code, one for data, one for stack, and one extra. (These segments may overlap each other or be separate.) The location of any byte within a segment is determined by the *offset*. The value of the segment register determines which 64K segment is referred to and the value of the offset determines which byte, within that segment, is actually being addressed. Thus, the physical 20-bit address of any specific byte within the computer is the combination of the segment and the offset.

To calculate the actual byte referred to by the combination of the segment and offset you first shift the value in the segment register to the left by 4 bits and then add this value to the offset. This makes a 20-bit address. For example, if the segment

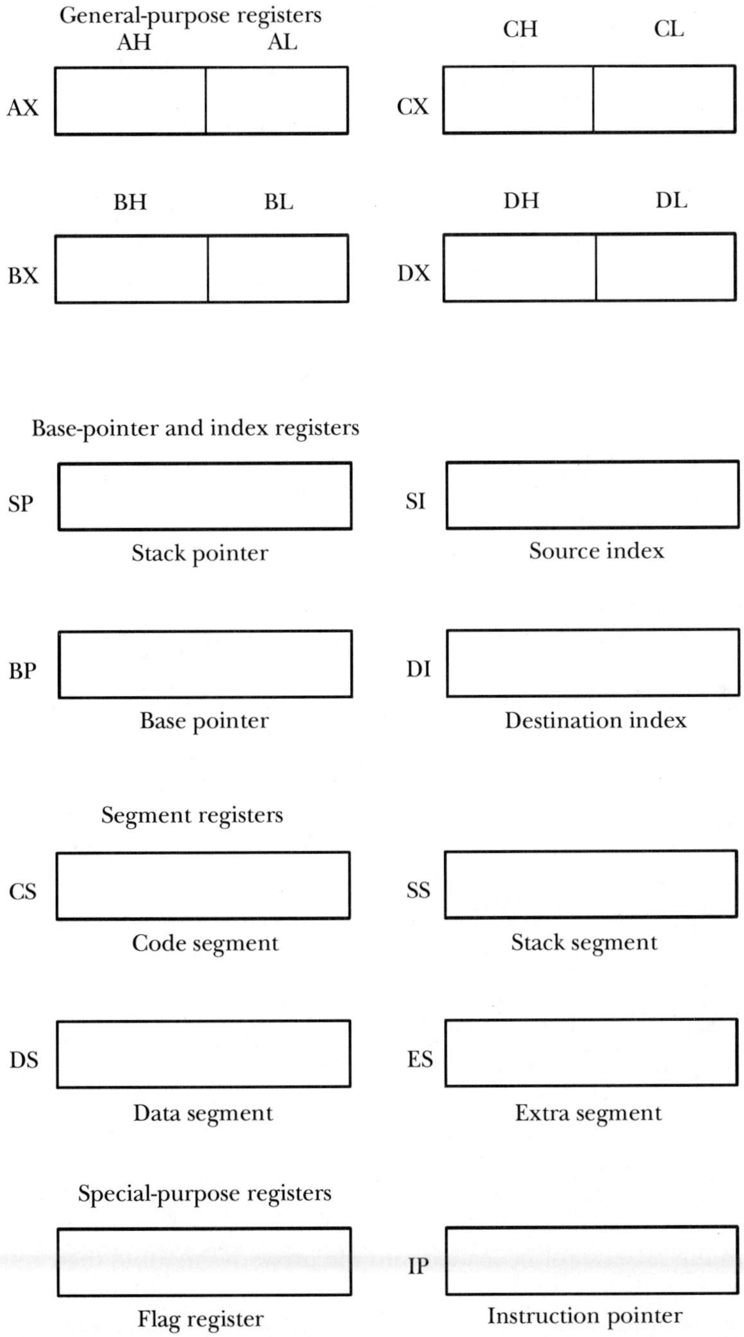

General-purpose registers

AH   AL

AX [|]

CH   CL

CX [|]

BH   BL

BX [|]

DH   DL

DX [|]

Base-pointer and index registers

SP [   ]

Stack pointer

SI [   ]

Source index

BP [   ]

Base pointer

DI [   ]

Destination index

Segment registers

CS [   ]

Code segment

SS [   ]

Stack segment

DS [   ]

Data segment

ES [   ]

Extra segment

Special-purpose registers

[   ]

Flag register

IP [   ]

Instruction pointer

Figure 10-1.   *The 8086 CPU registers*

register holds the value 0x20 and the offset 0x100, the following sequence shows how the actual address is derived. The absolute 20-bit address is 0x300.

```
segment register:          0000  0000  0010  0000
segment shifted: 0000      0000  0010  0000
offset:                    0000  0001  0000  0000
-----------------------------------------------
segment+offset:  0000      0000  0011  0000  0000
```

Here is another example:

```
segment:                   1111  0000  0000  0000
shifted segment: 1111      0000  0000  0000
offset:                    0000  0000  0000  0001
-----------------------------------------------
segment+offset:  1111      0000  0000  0000  0001
```

In this case, a segment value of 0xF000 is shifted by 4 bits to become 0xF0000 and is added to the offset value of 1. The resulting 20-bit address is 0xF0001.

In the 8086, addresses are most commonly referred to in segment:offset form. In this form the outcome of the first example is usually notated as 0020:0100 rather than 300.

Note that by convention, addresses are shown using the hexadecimal number system. Many segment:offsets can describe the same byte because the segments overlap each other. For example, 0000:0010 is the same as 0001:0000.

Near Versus Far Pointers

To access addresses within the segment currently loaded in a segment register, only the offset of the address needs to be loaded into a register. This means that any object referenced using only a 16-bit address must be within the currently loaded segment. This is referred to as a *near* address or a *near pointer.*

To access an address not in the current segment, both the segment and the offset of the desired address must be loaded. This is called a *far* address or a *far pointer.* A far pointer can access any address within the 1 megabyte address space.

As stated, to access memory within the current segment you need only load the 16-bit offset. However, if you wish to access memory outside that segment, both the segment and the offset must be loaded with the proper values into their respective registers. Since it takes twice as long to load two 16-bit registers as it does to load one, it takes longer to load a far pointer than a near pointer. Hence, when using far pointers your programs run much slower, but they allow you to have larger programs or data. The exact way these things are affected is the subject of the next section.

Memory Models

Turbo/Borland C/C++ for the 8086 family of processors can compile your program six different ways; each way organizes the memory in the computer differently and affects different aspects of your program's performance. The six models are called tiny, small, medium, compact, large, and huge. Let's look at how these differ.

Tiny Model

The tiny model compiles a program so that all the segment registers are set to the same value and all addressing is done using 16 bits (near pointers). This means that the code, data, and stack must all be within the same 64K segment. This method of compilation produces the smallest, fastest code. (Programs compiled using this memory model can be converted to .COM files using the /t option to the Turbo C++ linker.) The tiny model produces the fastest run-times.

Small Model

The small model is the default mode of compilation and is useful for a wide variety of tasks. Although all addressing is done using only the 16-bit offset, the code segment is separate from the data, stack, and extra segments, which are in their own segment. The total size of a program compiled this way is 128K split between code and data. Since the small model uses only near pointers, the execution speed is as good as it is for the tiny model, but the program can be approximately twice as big.

Medium Model

The medium model is for large programs where the code exceeds the one-segment restriction of the small model. The code may use multiple segments and requires 20-bit (far) pointers, but the data and extra segments are in their own segment and use 16-bit (near) addressing. This is good for large programs that use little data. Your programs will run slower as far as function calls are concerned, but references to data will be as fast as the small model.

Compact Model

The complement of the medium model is the compact model. In this version, program code is restricted to one segment, but data may occupy several segments. This means that all accesses to data require 20-bit (far) addressing but the code uses 16-bit (near) addressing. This is good for programs that require large amounts of data but little code. Your program will run as fast as the small model except when referencing data.

Large Model

The large model allows both code and data to use multiple segments. However, the largest single item of data, such as an array, is limited to 64K. This model is used when you have large code and data requirements. It also runs much slower than any of the previous versions.

Huge Model

The huge model is the same as the large model with the exception that individual data items may exceed 64K. This makes run-time speed even slower than in the large model.

Selecting a Model

Generally, you should use the small model unless there is a reason to do otherwise. Select the medium model if you have a lot of program but not much data. Use the compact model if you have a lot of data but not much program. If you have a large amount of both code and data, use the large model unless you need single data items to be larger than 64K, in which case you will need to use the huge model. Remember, both the large and huge models have substantially slower run times than the others.

There is another consideration that may affect how you compile your program. If you are compiling your program for either the compact or large memory models, all pointer references to data will be through far pointers. This creates two problems. First, most pointer comparisons will not generate correct results because more than one segment:offset pair can map to the same physical address. When far pointers are compared, only the offset is checked. This means that two pointers may actually point to the same physical address, but compare as unequal, or point to different addresses and compare as equal. The only comparison that is guaranteed to be valid for far pointers is equality with 0 (the null pointer).

The second problem with far pointers is that when a far pointer is incremented or decremented, only the offset is altered, making the pointer "wrap" past a segment boundary.

Pointers generated when compiling from the huge model are called *huge pointers*. They are similar to far pointers in that they use a full 20-bit address, but they do not suffer from the limitations of far pointers. First, huge pointers can be correctly compared because they are *normalized*. The normalization process ensures that there is only one segment:offset address for each physical address. Thus, all comparisons are valid. However, the normalization process takes time, thus slowing execution speed. Second, when a pointer is incremented or decremented past a segment boundary, the segment is adjusted accordingly and the "wraparound" problem experienced with far pointers is eliminated, thus allowing access to a single data object that is larger than 64K.

The Memory Model Compiler Options

Turbo/Borland C/C++ compiles your program using the small model by default. To use a different model you must give the compiler the proper instructions. In the integrated environment version, you select the memory model by using the Options/Compiler menu. For the command-line version, you use one of the following command-line options:

Option	Memory Model
–mc	Compact
–mh	Huge
–ml	Large
–mm	Medium
–ms	Small (default)
–mt	Tiny

Overriding a Memory Model

It is unfortunate that even a single reference to data in another segment would require you to use the compact rather than the small model, for example, causing the execution speed of the entire program to degrade even though only an isolated part of it actually needs a far pointer. In general, this sort of situation arises in a variety of ways. For example, even though the rest of a program might only need near pointers, it is necessary to use 20-bit addressing to access the video RAM of a PC. The solution to this and other related problems is the *segment override* type modifiers, **far**, **near**, and **huge**, which are enhancements provided by Turbo/Borland C/C++. When these modifiers are applied to pointers they affect the way data is accessed. It is also possible to apply the **near** and **far** modifiers to functions, in which case they affect the way you call or return from the function.

These modifiers follow the base type and precede the variable name. For example, the following declares a **far** pointer called **f_pointer**:

```
char far *f_pointer;
```

In this example, the function **myfarfunc( )** is declared as **far**:

```
void far myfarfunc(int *p);
```

The following sections look at these modifiers.

far

It is very common to want to access some region of memory that is (or may be) outside the data segment. However, if the entire program is compiled for one of the large data models, all access to data becomes very slow. The solution to this problem is to declare explicitly the pointers to data outside the current data segment as **far** and compile using the small memory model. In this way, only references to objects actually outside the default data segment incur the additional overhead.

The use of **far** functions is less common and is generally restricted to specialized programming situations in which a function lies outside the current code segment, such as a ROM-based routine. In these cases, the use of **far** ensures the proper calling and returning sequences are used.

Explicitly declared **far** pointers suffer from the same trouble as those implicitly generated when compiling for one of the large data models. First, pointer arithmetic affects only the offset and can cause "wraparound." This means that when a **far** pointer with the value 0000:FFFF is incremented, its new value will be 0000:0000, not 1000:0000. The value of the segment is never changed. Second, two **far** pointers should not be used in a relational expression because only their offsets will be checked. It is possible to have two different pointers actually contain the same physical address but have different segments and offsets. If you need to compare 20-bit pointers, you must use **huge** pointers. However, you can compare a **far** pointer against the null pointer.

near

A **near** pointer is a 16-bit offset that uses the value of the appropriate segment to determine the actual memory location. The **near** modifier forces Turbo/Borland C/C++ to treat the pointer as a 16-bit offset to the segment contained in the DS register. You use a **near** pointer when you have compiled a program using either the medium, large, or huge memory model.

Using **near** on a function causes that function to be treated as if it were compiled using the small code model. (The address of the function is computed using the CS register). When a function is compiled using either the tiny, small, or compact models, all calls to the function place a 16-bit return address on the stack. Compiling with a large code model causes a 20-bit address to be pushed on the stack. Therefore, in programs that are compiled for the large code model, a highly recursive function should be declared as **near** (if possible) to conserve stack space and decrease execution time.

Whether you use **near** or **far** on a function, you must include a prototype to it in any file in which it is called so that the compiler can generate the correct calling and returning sequence.

huge

The **huge** modifier can be applied only to data, not functions. A **huge** pointer is like a pointer generated when compiling for the huge memory model. It is normalized so that comparisons between **huge** pointers are meaningful. When a **huge** pointer is incremented, both the segment and the offset may change: it does not suffer from the "wraparound" problem as do **far** pointers. Also, a **huge** pointer can access objects that are larger than 64K.

Turbo C's Segment Specifiers

In addition to **far**, **near**, and **huge**, Turbo/Borland C/C++ supports these four addressing modifiers: **_cs**, **_ds**, **_ss**, and **_es**. When these type modifiers are applied to a pointer's declaration they cause the pointer to become a 16-bit offset into the specified segment. That is, given this statement,

```
int _es *ptr;
```

ptr contains a 16-bit offset into the extra segment.

Turbo/Borland C/C++ also includes the **_seg** modifier, which creates pointers that are 16 bits long and contain only the segment address. The offset is assumed to be 0. There are several restrictions to **_seg** pointers. You cannot increment or decrement them. In an expression that adds or subtracts an integer value from a **_seg** pointer, a far pointer is generated. When dereferencing a **_seg** pointer, it is converted into a far pointer. You can add a near pointer to a **_seg** pointer and the result is a far pointer.

The use of these modifiers is generally reserved for only the most exotic of applications.

Keep in mind that **near**, **far**, **huge**, **_es**, **_cs**, **_ds**, **_ss**, and **_seg** modifiers are not defined by the ANSI standard and are not fully portable. However, most 8086-based C compilers support some, if not all, of these modifiers.

A Memory Display and Change Program

Now that you understand how the memory models work, it is time to put this knowledge to use. A simple program will be developed that allows you to examine any byte in RAM and, if desired, alter its value. The program should be compiled using a large data model. This ensures that far pointers are used, allowing all memory to be accessed.

The display_mem( ) Function

The first function needed is **display_mem( )**, which is used to display the contents of memory at the address requested by the user. It first asks for the 20-bit address to be entered in hexadecimal segment:offset form and then displays the contents of 256 bytes beginning with the specified address. The output is arranged with 16 values per line and 16 lines. The address of each line is shown on the left. The **display_mem( )** function is shown here:

```
/* Displays 256 bytes of memory starting at specified
   address.
*/
void display_mem(void)
{
  register int i;
  unsigned char ch;
  unsigned char *p;

  /* get a 20-bit address */
  printf("beginning address (in hex): ");
  scanf("%p%*c", &p);

  printf("%p: ", p); /* print address */
  for(i=1; i<=256; i++) {
    ch = *p;
    printf("%02x ", ch); /* display in hex */
    p++;
    if(!(i%16)) { /* every 16 bytes use new line */
      printf("\n");
      if(i!=256) printf("%p: ", p); /* print address */
    }
  }
}
```

The change_mem( ) Function

The second function required by the program is called **change_mem( )**. It is used to change the contents of a specified byte. It operates by requesting the 20-bit address to be changed and then prompting for the new value. The **change_mem( )** function is shown here:

```
/*  Change the contents of a byte of memory. */
void change_mem(void)
{
  unsigned char *p;
  char value;

  /* get a 20-bit address */
  printf("Enter address to change (in hex): ");
  scanf("%p%*c", &p);
  printf("Enter new value (in hex): ");
  scanf("%x", &value);

  /* change the value */
  *p = (unsigned char) value;
}
```

The Entire Memory Display and Change Program

The entire memory display and change program is shown here. It operates by prompting for input using the |< symbol. Press D to display memory, C to change it, and Q to exit the program.

```
/* Display and/or change memory program.
   Compile using a large data model.
*/
#include <ctype.h>
#include <stdlib.h>
#include <stdio.h>
#include <conio.h>
void display_mem(void), change_mem(void);

main(void)
{
  char ch;

  for(;;) {
    printf("|< "); /* display the prompt symbol */
    ch = getche(); /* read command */
    printf("\n");
    switch(tolower(ch)) {
      case 'd': display_mem();
      break;
      case 'c': change_mem();
      break;
      case 'q': exit(0);
```

```
      }
    }
  }

/* Displays 256 bytes of memory starting at specified
    address.
*/
void display_mem(void)
{
  register int i;
  unsigned char ch;
  unsigned char *p;

  /* get a 20-bit address */
  printf("beginning address (in hex): ");
  scanf("%p%*c", &p);

  printf("%p: ", p); /* print address */
  for(i=1; i<=256; i++) {
    ch =  *p;
    printf("%02x ", ch); /* display in hex */
    p++;
    if(!(i%16)) { /* every 16 bytes use new line */
      printf("\n");
      if(i!=256) printf("%p: ", p); /* print address */
    }
  }
}

/*  Change the contents of a byte of memory. */
void change_mem(void)
{
  unsigned char *p;
  char value;

  /* get a 20-bit address */
  printf("Enter address to change (in hex): ");
  scanf("%p%*c", &p);
  printf("Enter new value (in hex): ");
  scanf("%x", &value);

  /* change the value */
  *p = (unsigned char) value;
}
```

A sample of the program's output is shown here:

```
|< d
beginning address (in hex): e001a
000E:001A: 70 02 45 14 70 02 59 ec 00 f0 3d 04 00 e0 0d 21
000E:002A: 00 f0 66 52 00 e0 0d 21 00 f0 0d 21 00 f0 5d 02
000E:003A: 00 e0 0d 21 00 f0 0d 21 00 f0 0d 21 00 f0 0d 21
000E:004A: 00 f0 0d 21 00 f0 0d 21 00 f0 0d 21 00 f0 0d 21
000E:005A: 00 f0 0d 21 00 f0 0d 21 00 f0 0d 21 00 f0 0d 21
000E:006A: 00 f0 0d 21 00 f0 0d 21 00 f0 0d 21 00 f0 0d 21
000E:007A: 00 f0 0d 21 00 f0 0d 21 00 f0 0d 21 00 f0 0d 21
000E:008A: 00 f0 0d 21 00 f0 0d 21 00 f0 0d 21 00 f0 0d 21
000E:009A: 00 f0 0d 21 00 f0 00 00 00 00 00 00 00 00 00 00
000E:00AA: 00 00 00 00 00 00 00 00 00 00 00 00 00 00 00 00
000E:00BA: 00 00 00 00 00 00 0d 21 00 f0 0d 21 00 f0 0d 21
000E:00CA: 00 f0 0d 21 00 f0 0d 21 00 f0 0d 21 00 f0 0d 21
000E:00DA: 00 f0 0d 21 00 f0 a3 01 7a 0e 5c 21 00 f0 0d 21
000E:00EA: 00 f0 0d 21 00 f0 d1 05 7a 0e 65 21 00 f0 59 06
000E:00FA: 7a 0e 0d 21 00 f0 00 00 00 00 00 00 00 00 00 00
000E:010A: 00 00 00 00 00 00 00 00 00 00 00 00 00 00 00 00
|< c
Enter address to change (in hex): e001b
Enter new value (in hex): 00
|< d
beginning address (in hex): e001a
000E:001A: 70 00 45 14 70 02 59 ec 00 f0 3d 04 00 e0 0d 21
000E:002A: 00 f0 66 52 00 e0 0d 21 00 f0 0d 21 00 f0 5d 02
000E:003A: 00 e0 0d 21 00 f0 0d 21 00 f0 0d 21 00 f0 0d 21
000E:004A: 00 f0 0d 21 00 f0 0d 21 00 f0 0d 21 00 f0 0d 21
000E:005A: 00 f0 0d 21 00 f0 0d 21 00 f0 0d 21 00 f0 0d 21
000E:006A: 00 f0 0d 21 00 f0 0d 21 00 f0 0d 21 00 f0 0d 21
000E:007A: 00 f0 0d 21 00 f0 0d 21 00 f0 0d 21 00 f0 0d 21
000E:008A: 00 f0 0d 21 00 f0 0d 21 00 f0 0d 21 00 f0 0d 21
000E:009A: 00 f0 0d 21 00 f0 00 00 00 00 00 00 00 00 00 00
000E:00AA: 00 00 00 00 00 00 00 00 00 00 00 00 00 00 00 00
000E:00BA: 00 00 00 00 00 00 0d 21 00 f0 0d 21 00 f0 0d 21
000E:00CA: 00 f0 0d 21 00 f0 0d 21 00 f0 0d 21 00 f0 0d 21
000E:00DA: 00 f0 0d 21 00 f0 a3 01 7a 0e 5c 21 00 f0 0d 21
000E:00EA: 00 f0 0d 21 00 f0 d1 05 7a 0e 65 21 00 f0 59 06
000E:00FA: 7a 0e 0d 21 00 f0 00 00 00 00 00 00 00 00 00 00
000E:010A: 00 00 00 00 00 00 00 00 00 00 00 00 00 00 00 00
```

Chapter 11

Turbo C's Screen and Graphics Functions

Although the ANSI standard for C does not define screen or graphics functions, they are obviously important to most contemporary programming tasks. They are not defined by the ANSI standard because there are wide differences between the capabilities and interfaces of different types of hardware. However, since Turbo C is designed to run on the IBM line of microcomputers, it provides a comprehensive set of screen-handling and graphics functions for these machines, beginning with Turbo C Version 1.5. This chapter presents an overview of both the screen and graphics functions, along with some short sample programs that illustrate their use. The screen and graphics systems are so large that it is not possible to discuss every function in detail here. However, this chapter presents an overview of the text screen and graphics systems and gives you a taste of their capabilities. (All the text and graphics functions are discussed thoroughly later in the book.)

This chapter begins with a brief discussion of the various video modes available for the PC line of computers. It then explores the functions that control the screen in text mode before moving on to the graphics routines.

The PC Video Adapters and Modes of Operation

As you probably know, several different types of video adapters are currently available for the PC line of computers. The most common are the monochrome, the CGA (Color Graphics Adapter), the EGA (Enhanced Graphics Adapter), and the VGA (Video Graphics Array). Together, these adapters support many different modes of video operation. These video modes are synopsized in Table 11-1. As you can see by looking at the table, some modes are for text and some are for graphics. In a text mode only text can be displayed. The smallest user-addressable part of the screen in a text mode is one character. In a graphics mode both graphic images and text can be displayed. The smallest user-addressable part of the screen in a graphics mode is one pixel. (Actually, the term *pixel* originally referred to the smallest individual phosphor element on the video monitor that can be individually energized by the scan beam. However, in recent years, use of the term has been generalized to refer to the smallest addressable point on a graphics display.)

In both the text and graphics modes, individual locations on the screen are referenced by their row and column numbers. In the graphics modes the upper-left corner of the screen is location 0,0. For unknown reasons, in text modes the upper-left corner is 1,1.

Mode	Type	Dimensions	Adapters
0	text, b/w	40×25	CGA, EGA, VGA
1	text, 16 colors	40×25	CGA, EGA, VGA
2	text, b/w	80×25	CGA, EGA, VGA
3	text, 16 colors	80×25	CGA, EGA, VGA
4	graphics, 4 colors	320×200	CGA, EGA, VGA
5	graphics, 4 gray tones	320×200	CGA, EGA, VGA
6	graphics, b/w	640×200	CGA, EGA, VGA
7	text, b/w	80×25	monochrome
8	graphics, 16 colors	160×200	PCjr
9	graphics, 16 colors	320×200	PCjr
10	graphics, 4 colors	640×200	PCjr
11	reserved		
12	reserved		
13	graphics, 16 colors	320×200	EGA, VGA
14	graphics, 16 colors	640×200	EGA, VGA
15	graphics, 4 colors	640×350	EGA, VGA
16	graphics, 16 colors	640×350	VGA
17	graphics, 2 colors	640×480	VGA
18	graphics, 16 colors	640×430	VGA
19	graphics, 256 colors	640×200	VGA

Table 11-1.   *The Video Modes for the IBM Line of Microcomputers*

The text screen examples shown in this chapter use video mode 3, 80-column color mode. The graphics routines use VGA mode 16. If your hardware does not support one or both of these modes, you will have to make the appropriate changes to the examples.

The Text Screen Functions

Turbo C supports a complete set of text screen functions that fall into the following categories:

- Basic input and output
- Screen manipulation
- Attribute control
- Screen status

These functions require the header file **conio.h** to be included with any program that uses them. This file contains several variables, types, and constants used by the functions, as well as their function prototypes.

Windows

The Turbo C text functions operate through windows. Fortunately, the default window is the entire screen, so you don't need to worry about creating any special windows to use the text and graphics routines. However, it is important to understand the basic concept of windows to get the most from the Turbo C screen functions.

A window is a portal that your program uses to send messages to the user. A window can be as large as the entire screen or as small as just a few characters. In sophisticated software it is not uncommon for the screen to have several active windows at one time—one for each separate task performed by the program.

Turbo C lets you define the location and dimensions of a window. After you define a window, Turbo C's routines that manipulate text affect only the window you have defined, not the entire screen. For example, Turbo C's **clrscr( )** function clears the active window, not the entire screen. (Unless, of course, the active window is the entire screen, as it would be by default.) In addition, all position coordinates are relative to the active window instead of the screen.

One of the most important aspects of Turbo C's windows is that output is automatically prevented from spilling past the boundaries of a window.

The subject of windows will be resumed later in this chapter after the basic screen control functions have been discussed.

Function	Purpose
cprintf( )	Writes formatted output to the active window
cputs( )	Writes a string to the active window
putch( )	Outputs a character to the active window
getche( )	Inputs a character from the active window
cgets( )	Inputs a string from the active window

Table 11-2.   *The Basic Text I/O Functions for Use with Windows*

Basic Input and Output

Because the standard C output routines, such as **printf( )**, are not designed for use in a window-oriented screen environment, Turbo C contains I/O functions that recognize windows. When you are using the default window, which is the entire screen, it does not matter significantly whether you use the window-based I/O functions or the standard I/O functions. However, if you are using a smaller window, then you will want to use the window-oriented functions because they automatically prevent text from being written outside the active window. These functions are shown in Table 11-2.

The **cprintf( )** function operates like **printf( )**, and **cputs( )** is similar to **puts( )**. Both functions differ from their standard I/O counterparts in that they recognize windows and neither converts a newline character (**\n**) into a carriage return-linefeed pair. (To output a carriage return-linefeed pair, explicitly specify **\n\r**.) The **putch( )** function is similar to **putchar( )**, but does not allow a character to be written outside the current window. The **getche( )** function does not echo input outside the active window.

The **cgets( )** function works a little differently than its non-windowed relative **gets( )**. The **cgets( )** function has this prototype:

char *cgets(char *str);

When you call **cgets( )**, you must place into $str[0]$ the maximum length of the string you want to read. When **cgets( )** returns, the number of characters actually read is returned in $str[1]$ and the string begins with $str[2]$. This means that the longest string you can read using **cgets( )** is 255 characters long. The **cgets( )** function continues reading characters until a carriage return is received. The carriage return is converted into a null terminator. If you continue to enter characters past the specified maximum, they will be ignored. The **cgets( )** function returns a pointer to $str[2]$ (the start of the string). This program shows how to use **cgets( )** to read a string that is at most 20 characters long:

```
#include <conio.h>

main(void)
{
  char s[80], *p;

  s[0] = 20;
  cprintf("Enter a string (max 20 chars): ");

  /* read up to 20 characters */
  p = cgets(s); /* p will point to start of string */

  cprintf("\n\rHere is your string: %s", p);
  return 0;
}
```

One other thing to understand about these basic I/O functions is that they are not redirectable. That is, Turbo C's (and ANSI C's) standard I/O functions allow output to be redirected to or from a disk file or auxiliary device. This is not the case with the window-based text screen functions.

When text output exceeds the line length of a window, it is wrapped. How text is wrapped at the end of a window is determined by the value of **_wscroll**, which is a built-in global variable. By default **_wscroll** is 1, which causes text to be wrapped to the next line and the window to be scrolled if necessary. If **_wscroll** is 0, then text is wrapped to the same line (thus overwriting preexisting text) and no scrolling takes place.

The Screen Manipulation Functions

Turbo C's text screen manipulation functions are shown in Table 11-3.

The **clrscr( )** function clears a text window. Its prototype is

void clrscr(void);

The **clreol( )** function clears a line from the current cursor position to the right boundary of the window. Its prototype is

void clreol(void);

The companion functions **delline( )** and **insline( )** are used to delete a line or insert a blank line, respectively. Their prototypes are

```
void delline(void);
void insline(void);
```

A call to **delline( )** deletes the line the cursor is on and moves up all lines below that line. A call to **insline( )** inserts a blank line just below the line that currently holds the cursor, and moves all lines below it down one line.

One of the most useful functions is **gotoxy( )**, which is used to position the cursor within the active window. Its prototype is

```
void gotoxy(int x, int y);
```

Here, *x* and *y* specify the coordinates at which the cursor will be positioned. If either coordinate is out of range, no action is taken.

No matter how a window is sized or positioned, in text modes the upper-left corner is always 1,1. Assuming that the entire screen is being used, in 80-column text modes the valid range for *x* is 1 through 80; for *y* it is 1 through 25.

The companion functions **gettext( )** and **puttext( )** are used to copy text from the screen to a buffer and from a buffer to the screen, respectively. Their prototypes are

```
int gettext(int left, int top, int right, int bottom, void *buffer);
int puttext(int left, int top, int right, int bottom, void *buffer);
```

Function	Purpose
clrscr( )	Clears the active window
clreol( )	Clears from the cursor to the end of the current line
delline( )	Deletes the line the cursor is on
gettext( )	Copies part of the screen into a character buffer
gotoxy( )	Sends the cursor to the specified location
insline( )	Inserts a blank line below the current cursor position
movetext( )	Copies text from one part of the screen to another
puttext( )	Copies text from a buffer onto the screen
textmode( )	Sets the screen's text mode

Table 11-3. *Turbo C's Text Screen Manipulation Functions*

For **gettext( )** you specify the coordinates of the upper left corner and lower right corner of the region of the screen you want. The pointer **buffer** must point to a region of memory large enough to hold the text. The size of the buffer is computed with this formula:

size in bytes = rows × columns × 2

Each character displayed on the screen requires 2 bytes of video memory. The first byte holds the actual character, the second holds its *screen* attribute. For this reason, the number of bytes required to hold the text is twice as large as the number of characters. For example, if you called **gettext( )** with 1,1 for the first coordinate pair and 10,10 for the second, you would need 10*10*2 (200) bytes of storage. Both functions return 0 if one or more coordinates is out of range; otherwise they both return 1.

To copy text already in a buffer to the screen, you simply call **puttext( )** with the coordinates of the upper left and lower right corners of the region that will receive the text along with a pointer to the buffer that holds it.

If you want to copy text from one part of the screen to another, using the **movetext( )** function is more efficient than calling **gettext( )** and then **puttext( )**. The prototype for **movetext( )** is

int movetext(int *top*, int *left*, int *right*, int *bottom*, int *newtop*, int *newleft*);

The function **movetext( )** returns 0 if one or more coordinates is out of range; otherwise it returns 1.

The **window( )** function activates a text window of specified dimensions. Its prototype is

void window(int *left*, int *top*, int *right*, int *bottom*);

If any coordinate is invalid, **window( )** takes no action. Once a call to **window( )** has been successfully completed, all references to location coordinates are interpreted relative to the window, not the screen. For example, this fragment of code creates a window and writes a line of text at location 2,3 inside that window:

```
window(10, 10, 60, 15);
gotoxy(2, 3);
cprintf("at location 2, 3");
```

The action of this fragment is illustrated in Figure 11-1.

It is important to understand that coordinates used to call **window( )** are screen absolute—not relative to the currently active window. In this way you can use multiple windows that are not nested inside each other.

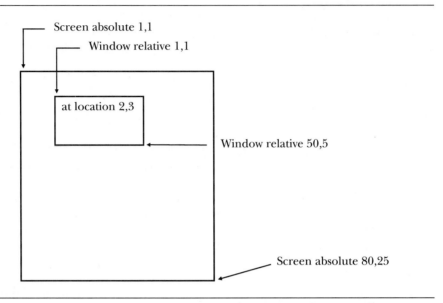

Figure 11-1. *Illustration of relative coordinates inside a window*

The following program first draws a border around the screen (for perspective), then creates two separate windows with borders. The position of the text inside each window is specified by **gotoxy( )** statements that are relative to each window.

```
/* A text window demonstration program */
#include <conio.h>

void border(int startx, int starty, int endx, int endy);

main(void)
{
  clrscr();

  /* draw a border around the screen for perspective */
  border(1, 1, 79, 25);

  /* create first window */
  window(3, 2, 40, 9);
  border(3, 2, 40, 9);
  gotoxy(3, 2);
  cprintf("first window");
```

```
  /* create a second window */
  window(30, 10, 60, 18);
  border(30, 10, 60, 18);
  gotoxy(3, 2);
  cprintf("second window");
  gotoxy(5, 4);
  cprintf("hello");

  getche();
  return 0;
}


/* Draws a border around a text window. */
void border(int startx, int starty, int endx, int endy)
{
  register int i;

  gotoxy(1, 1);
  for(i=0; i<=endx-startx; i++)
    putch('-');

  gotoxy(1, endy-starty);
  for(i=0; i<=endx-startx; i++)
    putch('-');

  for(i=2; i<endy-starty; i++) {
    gotoxy(1, i);
    putch('|');
    gotoxy(endx-startx+1, i);
    putch('|');
  }
}
```

Text Attribute Control

It is possible to change video modes, control the color of the text and background, and set the display to high or low intensity. The functions that do these things are shown in Table 11-4 and are applicable to all video adapters with the exception of the monochrome adapter, which supports only one mode and one color.

The functions **highvideo( )** and **lowvideo( )** set the display to high-intensity and low-intensity video, respectively. Their prototypes are

```
  void highvideo(void);
  void lowvideo(void);
```

Function	Purpose
highvideo( )	Displays text in high intensity
lowvideo( )	Displays text in low intensity
normvideo( )	Displays text in the original intensity
textattr( )	Sets both the color of the text and the color of the background at the same time
textbackground( )	Sets the background color
textcolor( )	Sets the color of the text
textmode( )	Sets the video mode

Table 11-4.   *The Text Attribute Functions*

The function **normvideo( )** causes characters to be displayed in the intensity that was active when the program began execution. Its prototype is

```
void normvideo(void);
```

The **textcolor( )** function determines the color of subsequent text displayed. It can also be used to cause the text to blink. The prototype of **textcolor( )** is

```
void textcolor(int color);
```

The argument *color* may have the values 0 through 15 with each corresponding to a different color. However, the macro names defined in **conio.h** for each of these colors are easier to remember. These macros and their integer equivalents are shown in Table 11-5.

It is important to understand that a change in the color of the text affects only subsequent write operations; it does not change any text currently displayed on the screen.

To make text blink you must OR the value 128 (**BLINK**) with the color you desire. For example, this fragment causes subsequent text output to be green and blinking:

```
textcolor(GREEN | BLINK);
```

Macro	Integer Equivalent
BLACK	0
BLUE	1
GREEN	2
CYAN	3
RED	4
MAGENTA	5
BROWN	6
LIGHTGRAY	7
DARKGRAY	8
LIGHTBLUE	9
LIGHTGREEN	10
LIGHTCYAN	11
LIGHTRED	12
LIGHTMAGENTA	13
YELLOW	14
WHITE	15
BLINK	128

Table 11-5.   *The Color Macros and Integer Equivalents for Text*

The function **textbackground( )** is used to set the background color of a text screen. As with **textcolor( )**, a call to **textbackground( )** affects only the background color of subsequent write operations. Its prototype is as follows:

    void textbackground(int *color*);

The value for *color* must be in the range 0 through 7. This means that only the first eight colors shown in Table 11-5 can be used for background.

The function **textattr( )** sets both the text and background colors. Its prototype is

    void textattr(int *attribute*);

The value of *attribute* represents an encoded form of the color information as shown here:

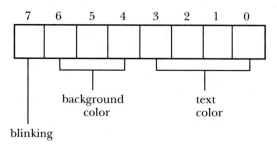

If bit 7 is set, the text will blink. Bits 6 through 4 determine the background color. Bits 3 through 0 set the color for the text. The easiest way to encode the background color into the attribute byte is to multiply the number of the color you desire by 16 and then OR that with the text color. For example, to create a green background with blue text you would use **GREEN * 16 | BLUE**. To cause the text to blink, OR the text color, background color, and **BLINK** (128) together. For example, this causes the text to be red and blinking with a blue background:

```
textattr(RED | BLINK | BLUE*16);
```

The **textmode( )** function is used to change the video mode. Its prototype is

void textmode(int *mode*);

The argument *mode* must be one of the values shown in Table 11-6. You may use either the integer value or the macro name. (The macros are defined in **conio.h**.)

Macro Name	Integer Equivalent	Description
BW40	0	40-column black and white
C40	1	40-column color
BW80	2	80-column black and white
C80	3	80-column color
MONO	7	80-column monochrome
LASTMODE	−1	Previous mode
C4350	64	EGA, 80×43; VGA, 80×50

Table 11-6.   *The Text Video Modes*

The Text Screen Status Functions

Turbo C provides three text mode functions that return the status of the screen. They are shown in Table 11-7.

The **gettextinfo( )** function returns the status of the current window in a structure of type **text_info**, which is defined in **conio.h**. The prototype of **gettextinfo( )** is

```
void gettextinfo(struct text_info *info);
```

The structure **text_info** is defined as shown here:

```
struct text_info {
  unsigned char winleft;      /* left X coordinate */
  unsigned char wintop;       /* top Y coordinate */
  unsigned char winright;     /* right X coordinate */
  unsigned char winbottom;    /* bottom Y coordinate */
  unsigned char attribute;    /* text attribute */
  unsigned char normattr;     /* normal attribute */
  unsigned char currmode;     /* current video mode */
  unsigned char screenheight;/* height of screen in lines */
  unsigned char screenwidth; /* width of screen in chars */
  unsigned char curx;         /* cursor's X coordinate */
  unsigned char cury;         /* cursor's Y coordinate */
};
```

When you use **gettextinfo( )**, remember to pass a pointer to a structure of type **text_info** so that the elements of the structure can be set by the function. Do not try to pass the structure variable itself. For example, this fragment illustrates how to call **gettextinfo( )**:

```
struct text_info screen_status;

gettextinfo(&screen_status);
```

Function	Purpose
gettextinfo( )	Returns information about the current text window
wherex( )	Returns the *x* coordinate of the cursor
wherey( )	Returns the *y* coordinate of the cursor

Table 11-7.   *The Text Screen Status Functions*

The **wherex( )** and **wherey( )** functions have the prototypes

```
int wherex(void);
int wherey(void);
```

The **wherex( )** function returns the X coordinate of the current cursor location. The **wherey( )** function returns the Y coordinate of the current cursor location. Both of the coordinates are relative to the current text window.

The directvideo Variable

For IBM PCs and 100 percent compatibles, it is possible to bypass the DOS and ROM-BIOS screen output routines and, instead, place output directly into the video RAM. Using this method produces the fastest possible output operations. However, for computers that are not hardware compatible with the PC line but are BIOS compatible, the direct video RAM output cannot be used. To allow for this possibility, Turbo C provides a built-in global variable called **directvideo**, which controls how output is performed. When **directvideo** is true, as it is by default, all screen output is performed via direct video RAM accesses. To cause the BIOS routines to be used rather than writing directly to the video RAM, set **directvideo** to 0 (false).

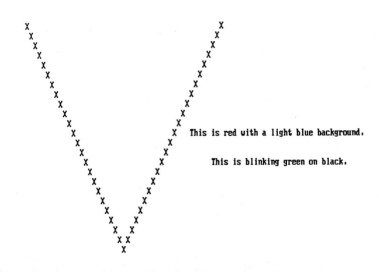

Figure 11-2.   *Sample output from the text screen control functions*

A Short Demonstration Program

The following program illustrates the use of several of the text screen functions. Its output is shown in Figure 11-2.

```c
#include <conio.h>

main(void)
{
  register int i, j;

  textmode(C80); /* 80 column text mode */

  clrscr();

  /* demonstrate the gotoxy() function */
  for(i=1, j=1; j<24; i++, j++) {
    gotoxy(i, j);
    cprintf("X");
  }
  for(; j>0; i++, j--) {
    gotoxy(i, j);
    cprintf("X");
  }

  /* examples of different foreground and background colors */
  textbackground(LIGHTBLUE);
  textcolor(RED);
  gotoxy(40, 12);
  cprintf("This is red with a light blue background.");

  gotoxy(45, 15);
  textcolor(GREEN | BLINK);
  textbackground(BLACK);
  cprintf("This is blinking green on black.");

  getch();

  /* an example of movetext() */
  /* this moves the "inverted peak" of the X's to the
     top of the screen
  */
  movetext(20, 20, 28, 24, 20, 1);
  getch();
  textmode(LASTMODE);
```

```
    return 0;
}
```

Turbo C's Graphics Functions

Turbo C's graphics functions can be grouped into the following categories:

- Video adapter mode control
- Basic graphing
- Text output
- Screen status
- Screen manipulation

The graphics functions require that the header file **graphics.h** be included in any program that uses them.

Keep in mind that the computer must be equipped with a graphics video adapter in order to use Turbo C's graphics routines. This means that systems with only a monochrome adapter will not be able to display graphics output. The examples shown here all use VGA mode 16 (640×350, 16 colors). If you do not have a VGA, you will have to make the appropriate alterations to the examples.

One other important point: All graphics functions are declared as **far**, and any parameters to them that are pointers are declared as **far** pointers. This means that it is imperative that you include **graphics.h** with any program that uses graphics functions.

Viewports

All of Turbo C's graphics functions operate through *viewports*. Viewport is really just another name for a window, and a graphics viewport has essentially the same qualities as a text window. By default the entire screen is the viewport. However, you can create viewports of other dimensions. You will see how to do this later in this chapter. As you read through the following discussions, keep in mind that all graphics output is relative to the current viewport, which is not necessarily the same as the screen.

Video Mode Control Functions

Before any of the graphics functions can be used, it is necessary to put the video adapter into one of the graphics modes. By default, the vast majority of systems that have graphics video adapters use 80-column text mode 3 for DOS communications.

Since this is not a graphics mode, Turbo C's graphics functions cannot work. To set the adapter to a graphics mode, use the **initgraph( )** function. Its prototype is

void far initgraph(int far *driver*, int far *mode*, char far *path*);

The **initgraph( )** function loads into memory a graphics driver that corresponds to the number pointed to by *driver*. Without a graphics driver loaded into memory, no graphics functions can operate. The *mode* parameter points to an integer that specifies the video mode used by the graphics functions. Finally, you can specify a path to the driver in the string pointed to by *path*. If no path is specified, the current working directory is searched.

The graphics drivers are contained in .BGI files, which must be available on the system. However, you need not worry about the actual name of the file because you only have to specify the driver by its number. The header file **graphics.h** defines several macros that you can use for this purpose. They are shown here:

Macro	Equivalent
DETECT	0
CGA	1
MCGA	2
EGA	3
EGA64	4
EGAMONO	5
IBM8514	6
HERCMONO	7
ATT400	8
VGA	9
PC3270	10

When you use **DETECT**, **initgraph( )** automatically detects the type of video hardware present in the system and selects the video mode with the greatest resolution.

The value of *mode* must be one of the graphics modes shown in Table 11-8. Notice that the value pointed to by *mode* is *not* the same as the value recognized by the BIOS routine that actually sets the mode. Instead the value used to call BIOS to initialize a video mode is created by **initgraph( )** using both the driver and the mode. For example, to cause the graphics system to be initialized to CGA 4-color, 320×200 graphics, you would use the following fragment (equivalent to BIOS video mode 4). It assumes that the graphics driver's .BGI file is in the current working directory.

Driver	Mode	Equivalent	Resolution
CGA	CGAC0	0	320×200
	CGAC1	1	320×200
	CGAC2	2	320×200
	CGAC3	3	320×200
	CGAHI	4	640×200
MCGA	MCGAC0	0	320×200
	MCGAC1	1	320×200
	MCGAC2	2	320×200
	MCGAC3	3	320×200
	MCGAMED	4	640×200
	MCGAHI	5	640×480
EGA	EGALO	0	640×200
	EGAHI	1	640×350
EGA64	EGA64LO	0	640×200
	EGA64HI	1	640×350
EGAMONO	EGAMONOHI	3	640×350
HERC	HERCMONOHI	0	720×348
ATT400	ATT400C0	0	320×200
	ATT400C1	1	320×200
	ATT400C2	2	320×200
	ATT400C3	3	320×200
	ATT400CMED	4	640×200
	ATT400CHI	5	640×400
VGA	VGALO	0	640×200
	VGAMED	1	640×350
	VGAHI	2	640×480
PC3270	PC3270HI	0	720×350
IBM8514	IBM8514HI	0	1024×768
	IBM8514LO	0	640×480

Table 11-8. *The Turbo C Graphics Drivers and Modes Macros*

```
#include <graphics.h>
        .
        .
        .
int driver, mode;

driver = CGA;
mode = CGAC0;

initgraph(&driver, &mode, "");
```

CGA 4-color graphics gives you access to four palettes to choose from and four colors per palette. The colors are numbered 0 through 3, with 0 always being the background color. The palettes are also numbered 0 through 3. To select a palette, set the *mode* parameter equal to **CGAC***x* where *x* is the palette number. The palettes and their associated colors are shown in Table 11-9.

In EGA/VGA 16-color mode, a palette consists of 16 colors selected out of a possible 64 colors.

To change the palette, use the **setpalette( )** function, whose prototype is

```
void far setpalette(int index, int color);
```

The operation of this function is a little difficult to understand at first. In essence, it associates the value of *color* with an index, specified by *index*, into a table that Turbo C uses to map the color actually shown on the screen with that being requested. The values for the color codes are shown in Table 11-10.

For CGA modes, only the background color can be changed using **setpalette()**. The background color is always index 0. So, for CGA modes, the following changes the background color to green:

```
setpalette(0, GREEN);
```

	Color Number			
Palette	**0**	**1**	**2**	**3**
0	background	green	red	yellow
1	background	cyan	magenta	white
2	background	lightgreen	lightred	yellow
3	background	lightcyan	lightmagenta	white

Table 11-9.   Palettes and Colors in Video Mode 4

CGA Codes (Background Only)

Macro	Value
BLACK	0
BLUE	1
GREEN	2
CYAN	3
RED	4
MAGENTA	5
BROWN	6
LIGHTGRAY	7
DARKGRAY	8
LIGHTBLUE	9
LIGHTGREEN	10
LIGHTCYAN	11
LIGHTRED	12
LIGHTMAGENTA	13
YELLOW	14
WHITE	15

EGA and VGA

Macro	Value
EGA_BLACK	0
EGA_BLUE	1
EGA_GREEN	2
EGA_CYAN	3
EGA_RED	4
EGA_MAGENTA	5
EGA_LIGHTGRAY	7
EGA_BROWN	20
EGA_DARKGRAY	56
EGA_LIGHTBLUE	57
EGA_LIGHTGREEN	58
EGA_LIGHTCYAN	59
EGA_LIGHTRED	60
EGA_LIGHTMAGENTA	61
EGA_YELLOW	62
EGA_WHITE	63

Table 11-10.   *The Color Codes for the* **setpalette( )** *Function*

The EGA can display 16 colors at a time with the total number of different colors being 64. You can use **setpalette( )** to map a color onto one of the 16 different indexes. For example, the following sets the value of color 5 to cyan:

```
setpalette(5, EGA_CYAN);
```

If you call **setpalette( )** with invalid arguments, a –1L is returned.

When you want to set all the colors in an EGA/VGA palette, it is easier to use the **setallpalette( )** function, which has the prototype

void far setallpalette(struct *palettetype* far *pal*);

Here, *palettetype* is defined as

```
struct palettetype {
  unsigned char size;
  signed char colors[MAXCOLORS+1];
};
```

You must set **size** to equal the number of colors in the palette and then load the color for each index into its corresponding element in the array **colors**. The **MAXCOLORS** macro is defined in **graphics.h,** and it specifies the maximum number of colors in a palette.

You can set just the background color using **setbkcolor( )**. Its prototype is

void far setbkcolor(int *color*);

The value of *color* must be one of the following:

Macro	Value
BLACK	0
BLUE	1
GREEN	2
CYAN	3
RED	4
MAGENTA	5
BROWN	6
LIGHTGRAY	7
DARKGRAY	8
LIGHTBLUE	9
LIGHTGREEN	10

Macro	Value
LIGHTCYAN	11
LIGHTRED	12
LIGHTMAGENTA	13
YELLOW	14
WHITE	15

To stop using a graphics video mode and return to a text mode, use either **closegraph( )** or **restorecrtmode( )**. Their prototypes are

```
void far closegraph(void);
void far restorecrtmode(void);
```

The **closegraph( )** function should be used when your program is going to continue executing in text mode. It frees memory used by the graphics functions and resets the video mode to what it was prior to the call to **initgraph( )**. If your program is terminating, you can use **restorecrtmode( )** because it resets the video adapter to the mode it was in prior to the first call to **initgraph( )**.

The Basic Graphing Functions

The most fundamental graphing functions are those that draw a point, a line, and a circle. In Turbo C these functions are called **putpixel( )**, **line( )**, and **circle( )**, respectively. Their prototypes are

```
void far putpixel(int x, int y, int color);
void far line(int startx, int starty, int endx, int endy);
void far circle(int x, int y, int radius);
```

The **putpixel( )** function writes the specified color to the location determined by *x* and *y*. The **line( )** function draws a line from the location specified by *startx,starty* to *endx,endy* in the current drawing color, line style, and thickness. The **circle( )** function draws a circle of radius *radius* in the current drawing color and thickness, with the center at the location specified by *x,y*. If any of the coordinates are out of range, no action is taken.

You can set the current drawing color using **setcolor( )**. Its prototype is

```
void far setcolor(int color);
```

The value of *color* must be in the range valid for the current graphics mode.

You can fill any enclosed shape using the **floodfill( )** function. Its prototype is

```
void far floodfill(int x, int y, int bordercolor);
```

To use this function to fill an enclosed shape, call it with the coordinates of a point inside the shape and the color of the lines that make up the shape (its border). You must make sure that the object that you are filling is completely enclosed. If it isn't, the area outside the shape will get filled as well. What the object is filled with is determined by the current fill pattern and fill color. The background color is used by default. However, you can change the way objects are filled using **setfillstyle( )**. Its prototype is

> void far setfillstyle(int *pattern*, int *color*);

The values for *pattern* are shown here along with their macro equivalents (defined in **graphics.h**):

Macro	Value	Meaning
EMPTY_FILL	0	Fill with background color
SOLID_FILL	1	Fill with solid color
LINE_FILL	2	File with lines
LTSLASH_FILL	3	Fill with light slashes
SLASH_FILL	4	Fill with slashes
BKSLASH_FILL	5	Fill with backslashes
LTBKSLASH_FILL	6	Fill with light backslashes
HATCH_FILL	7	Fill with light hatching
XHATCH_FILL	8	Fill with hatching
INTERLEAVE_FILL	9	Fill with interleaving
WIDE_DOT_FILL	10	Fill with widely spaced dots
CLOSE_DOT_FILL	11	Fill with closely spaced dots
USER_FILL	12	Fill with custom pattern

You can define a custom fill pattern using **setfillpattern( )**, which is described in Chapter 23.

The following program demonstrates these basic graphics functions. As you will see by looking at the program, the function **box( )** is used to draw a box in a specified color given the coordinates of the upper left and lower right corners. It is an example of how higher-level graphics functions can be easily constructed from the core of routines provided by Turbo C. The output of the program is shown in Figure 11-3.

```
/* Points, lines, circles, and fills demonstration program. */
#include <graphics.h>
#include <conio.h>

void border(void);
void box(int startx, int starty, int endx, int endy,
```

```
           int color);

main(void)
{
  int driver, mode;

  register int i;

  driver = VGA;
  mode = VGAMED;
  initgraph(&driver, &mode, "");

  border();

  setcolor(1);
  line(0, 0, 639, 349);

  box(100, 100, 300, 200, 1);

  setcolor(2);
  floodfill(110, 110, 1); /* fill part of a box */

  setcolor(1);
  line(50, 200, 400, 125);
```

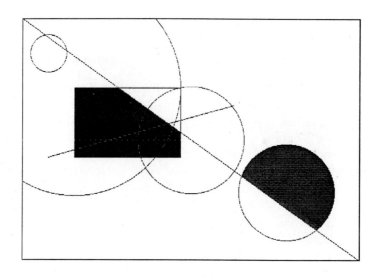

Figure 11-3.   *Output from the points, lines, and circles demonstration program*

```
/* some points */
for(i=0; i<640; i+=10) putpixel(i, 175, 5);

/* draw some circles */
circle(50, 50, 35);
circle(320, 175, 100);
circle(500, 250, 90);
circle(100, 100, 200);

setfillstyle(SOLID_FILL, GREEN);
floodfill(500, 250, 1); /* fill part of a circle */

getch(); /* wait until keypress */
restorecrtmode();

return 0;
}

/* Draw a border around the screen for perspective. */
void border(void)
{
  line(0, 0, 639, 0);
  line(0, 0, 0, 349);
  line(0, 349, 639, 349);
  line(639, 0, 639, 349);
}

/* Draw a box given the coordinates of its two corners. */
void box(int startx, int starty, int endx, int endy,
         int color)
{
  setcolor(color);

  line(startx, starty, startx, endy);
  line(startx, starty, endx, starty);
  line(endx, starty, endx, endy);
  line(endx, endy, startx, endy);
}
```

Text Output in Graphics Mode

Although you can use the standard screen output functions such as **printf( )** to display text while in a graphics mode, in many situations it is better to use the function **outtext( )**, which is designed specifically for this purpose. Its prototype is

```
void far outtext(char far *str);
```

This function outputs the string pointed to by *str* at the current position. (In graphics modes, there is no visible cursor, but the current position on the screen is maintained as if there were an invisible cursor.) In the Turbo C documentation, this position is referred to as CP. The principal advantage to using **outtext( )** is that it can output text in different fonts, sizes, or directions.

To change the style, size, or direction of the text, use **settextstyle( )**. Its prototype is

```
void far settextstyle(int font, int direction, int charsize);
```

The *font* parameter determines the type of font used. The default is the hardware-defined 8×8 bit-mapped font. You can give *font* one of these values (the macros are defined in **graphics.h**):

Macro	Value	Font Type
DEFAULT_FONT	0	8×8 bit-mapped
TRIPLEX_FONT	1	Stroked triplex
SMALL_FONT	2	Small stroked font
SANS_SERIF_FONT	3	Stroked sans serif
GOTHIC_FONT	4	Stroked gothic

The direction in which the text will be displayed, from either left to right or top to bottom, is determined by the value of *direction*, which may be either **HORIZ_DIR** (0) or **VERT_DIR** (1).

The *charsize* parameter is a multiplier that increases the character size. It may have a value of 0 through 10.

The bit-mapped font is built into Turbo C's graphics. In the bit-mapped font, each character is constructed within a pixel matrix. The bit-mapped fonts are excellent as long as they don't have to be enlarged. When enlarged too far, they take on a grainy appearance. By contrast, stroked fonts are defined by the line segments needed to construct them. Therefore, as stroked fonts are increased in size, they do not degrade in appearance. All stroked fonts are contained in files that use the extension .CHR. These files are provided with Turbo C and must be loaded when your program begins execution.

The following program illustrates the use of the **settextstyle( )** function

```
/* Demonstrate some different text fonts and sizes. */

#include <graphics.h>
#include <conio.h>
```

```
main(void)
{
  int driver, mode;

  driver = VGA;
  mode = VGAMED;
  initgraph(&driver, &mode, "");

  outtext("Normal ");

  /* Gothic font, twice normal size */
  settextstyle(GOTHIC_FONT, HORIZ_DIR, 2);
  outtext("Gothic ");

  /* Triplex font, twice normal size */
  settextstyle(TRIPLEX_FONT, HORIZ_DIR, 2);
  outtext("Triplex ");

  /* Sans serif font, 7 times normal size*/
  settextstyle(SANS_SERIF_FONT, HORIZ_DIR, 7);
  outtext("Sans serif");

  getch();
  restorecrtmode();

  return 0;
}
```

To put text at a specific viewport location, use the **outtextxy( )** function. Its prototype is

void far outtextxy(int *x*, int *y*, char far **str*);

The string is written at the specified viewport coordinates. If either *x* or *y*, or both, is out of range, no output is displayed.

Graphics Mode Status

You can use several functions to get information about the graphics screen. Three of the most important are examined in this section. The first, **getviewsettings( )**, loads a structure with assorted information about the current viewport. Its prototype is void far getviewsettings(struct viewporttype far *info*);

The structure **viewporttype** is found in **graphics.h** and is defined as shown here:

```
struct viewporttype {
  int left, top, right, bottom;
  int clip;
};
```

The fields **left, top, right,** and **bottom** hold the coordinates of the upper left and lower right corners of the viewport. When **clip** is 0, there is no clipping of output that overruns the viewport boundaries. Otherwise, clipping is performed to prevent boundary overrun.

For information about the current graphics text settings use **gettextsettings( )**. Its prototype is

void far gettextsettings(struct textsettingstype far *info*);

The structure **textsettingstype** is defined in **graphics.h** and is shown here:

```
struct textsettingstype {
  int font;      /* font type */
  int direction; /* horizontal or vertical */
  int charsize;  /* size of characters */
  int horiz;     /* horizontal justification */
  int vert;      /* vertical justification */
};
```

The **font** element contains one of the following values (as defined in **graphics.h**):

Macro	Value	Font Type
DEFAULT_FONT	0	8×8 bit-mapped
TRIPLEX_FONT	1	Stroked triplex
SMALL_FONT	2	Small stroked font
SANS_SERIF_FONT	3	Stroked sans serif
GOTHIC_FONT	4	Stroked gothic

The direction element must be set to either **HORIZ_DIR** (the default) for horizontal text or **VERT_DIR** for vertical text. The **charsize** element is a multiplier used to scale the size of the output text. The values of **horiz** and **vert** indicate how text is justified relative to the current position (CP). The values will be one of the following (the macros are defined in **graphics.h**):

Macro	Value	Meaning
LEFT_TEXT	0	CP at left
CENTER_TEXT	1	CP in the center
RIGHT_TEXT	2	CP at right
BOTTOM_TEXT	3	CP at the bottom
TOP_TEXT	4	CP at the top

Another graphics status function is **getpixel( )**, which returns the color of a specified pixel. Its prototype is

unsigned far getpixel(int x, int y);

It returns the current color at the specified x,y location.

The Graphics Screen Manipulation Functions

There are seven graphics functions that allow you to manipulate the screen and one function that allows you to create graphics windows. These functions are shown in Table 11-11.

The prototypes for these functions are

void far clearviewport(void);

void far getimage(int *left*, int *top*, int *right*, int *bottom*, void far **buf*);

Function	Purpose
clearviewport( )	Clears the active viewport
getimage( )	Copies part of a viewport to a buffer
imagesize( )	Returns the number of bytes needed to save an image
putimage( )	Copies a buffer to the viewport
setactivepage( )	Determines which page will be affected by the graphics routines
setviewport( )	Creates a graphics window
setvisualpage( )	Determines which page is displayed

Table 11-11. *The Graphics Screen Control Functions*

unsigned far imagesize(int *left*, int *top*, int *right*, int *bottom*);

void far putimage(int *left*, int *top*, void far **buf*, int *op*);

void far setactivepage(int *pagenum*);

void far setviewport(int *left*, int *top*, int *right*, int *bottom*, int *clipflag*);

void far setvisualpage(int *pagenum*);

For some video modes, there is enough memory in video adapters to have two or more complete screens' worth of information stored at the same time. The RAM that holds the information displayed on the screen is called a *page*. By default, DOS always uses page 0. However, you can use any of the video pages supported by your hardware, switching between them as desired. Although only one screen's worth of data can be displayed at one time, it is occasionally useful to build an image as a background task in a page that is not currently displayed so that it is ready without delay when needed. To activate the image, simply switch to that display page. This method is particularly useful in cases where complex images take a long time to construct.

In order to support this sort of approach, Turbo C supplies the functions **setactivepage( )** and **setvisualpage( )**. The **setactivepage( )** function determines the video page to which the output of Turbo C's graphics functions will be directed. Turbo C uses video page 0 by default. If you call **setactivepage( )** with another page, subsequent graphics output is written to the new page, not necessarily to the one currently displayed. To display pages other than 0, use the **setvisualpage( )** function. For example, to display video page 1 you would call **setvisualpage( )** with an argument of 1.

The **getimage( )** function copies a region of the graphics window into a buffer and **putimage( )** puts the contents of a buffer onto the screen. The **getimage( )** function copies the contents of a rectangular portion of the screen defined by its upper left and lower right coordinates to the buffer pointed to by *buf*. The size of the buffer in bytes for a given region is returned by the **imagesize( )** function. The **putimage( )** function displays a buffer of graphics data previously stored using **getimage( )**. You need to specify only the upper left corner coordinates of the place where you want the image displayed. The value of *op* determines exactly how the image is written to the screen. Its valid enumerated values are

Name	Value	Meaning
COPY_PUT	0	Copy as is
XOR_PUT	1	Exclusive-OR with destination
OR_PUT	2	Inclusive-OR with destination
AND_PUT	3	AND with destination
NOT_PUT	4	Invert source image

The following program demonstrates use of the **getimage( )**, **imagesize( )**, and **putimage( )** functions. Its output is shown in Figure 11-4.

```
/* This program demonstrates how a graphics image can be
   moved using getimage(), imagesize(), and putimage().
*/
#include <conio.h>
#include <graphics.h>
#include <stdlib.h>

void box(int startx, int starty, int endx, int endy,
         int color);

main(void)
{
  int driver, mode;
  unsigned size;
  void *buf;

  driver = VGA;
  mode = VGAMED;
  initgraph(&driver, &mode, "");

  box(20, 20, 200, 200, 15);

  setcolor(RED);
  line(20, 20, 200, 200);
  setcolor(GREEN);
  line(20, 200, 200, 20);
  getch();

  /* move the image */

  /* first, get the image's size */
  size = imagesize(20, 20, 200, 200);
  if(size !=-1) { /* alloc memory for the image */
    buf = malloc(size);
    if(buf) {
      getimage(20, 20, 200, 200, buf);
      putimage(100, 100, buf, COPY_PUT);
      putimage(300, 50, buf, COPY_PUT);
    }
  }
  outtext("press a key");
```

```
  getch();
  restorecrtmode();
  return 0;
}

/* Draw a box given the coordinates of its two corners. */
void box(int startx, int starty, int endx, int endy,
         int color)
{
  setcolor(color);

  line(startx, starty, startx, endy);
  line(startx, starty, endx, starty);
  line(endx, starty, endx, endy);
  line(endx, endy, startx, endy);
}
```

You can create windows in much the same way they are created in text mode. As stated earlier, all the graphics output is relative to the coordinates of the active viewport. This means the coordinate of the upper left corner of the window is 0,0 no matter where the viewport is on the screen.

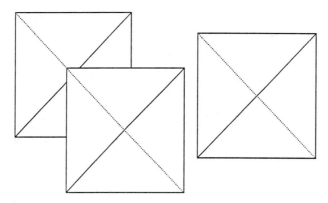

Figure 11-4.   *Output from the move image demonstration program*

The function you use to create a graphics viewport is called **setviewport( )**. To use it, you specify the coordinates of the upper left and lower right corners of the screen. If the *clipflag* parameter is non-zero, then output that would exceed the viewport's boundaries is automatically truncated. With clipping turned off, output can overrun the viewport. Keep in mind, however, that the clipping of output is not considered an error condition by Turbo C. The following program illustrates how to create a viewport and the clipping of output. The output is shown in Figure 11-5.

```
/* This program illustrates the use of setviewport(). */

#include <conio.h>
#include <graphics.h>

void box(int startx, int starty, int endx, int endy,
         int color);

main(void)
{
  int driver, mode;

  driver = VGA;
  mode = VGAMED;
  initgraph(&driver, &mode, "");
```

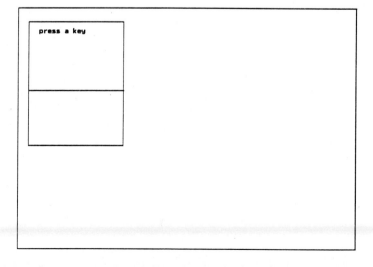

Figure 11-5. *Sample output from the graphics viewport demonstration program*

```
/* frame the screen for perspective */
box(0, 0, 639, 349, WHITE);

setviewport(20, 20, 200, 200, 1);
box(0, 0, 179, 179, RED);

/* Attempt to draw a line past the edge of the
   viewport.
*/

setcolor(WHITE);
line(0, 100, 400, 100);

outtextxy(20, 10, "press a key");
getch();
restorecrtmode();

return 0;
}

/* Draw a box given the coordinates of its two corners. */
void box(int startx, int starty, int endx, int endy,
         int color)
{
  setcolor(color);

  line(startx, starty, startx, endy);
  line(startx, starty, endx, starty);
  line(endx, starty, endx, endy);
  line(endx, endy, startx, endy);
}
```

As you can see, the line is clipped at the edge of the viewport when an attempt is
made to draw outside the active viewport boundaries.

Part II

The Turbo C Environment

Part Two of this guide explores the Turbo C programming environment, including the operation of both the integrated and command-line versions. Part Two also examines the Turbo C built-in editor and the various compiler options.

Chapter 12

The Turbo C Integrated Programming Environment

The integrated development environment, or IDE for short, makes it possible to edit, compile, link, and run a program without ever leaving the Turbo C environment. This allows extremely rapid recompilation cycles, which make the creation, testing, and debugging of software easier and faster.

Executing Turbo C

To execute the integrated version of Turbo C, simply type **TC** followed by a carriage return at the DOS prompt. When Turbo C begins execution you see the screen shown in Figure 12-1. This is called the main menu screen and consists of four parts, in order from top to bottom:

- The main menu

- The editor status line and window

- The compiler message window

- The "hot key" quick reference line

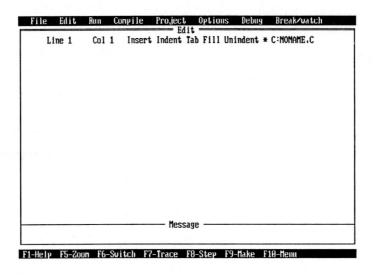

Figure 12-1.   *The Turbo C opening screen*

To exit Turbo C, press ALT-X.

This chapter examines each of these areas.

The Main Menu

The main menu is used either to tell Turbo C to do something, such as execute the editor or compile a program, or to set an environmental option. When you first execute the Turbo C IDE, the main menu is active. (If, for some reason, the main menu is not active, press F10 to reactivate it.) There are two ways to make a main menu selection.

1. You can use the arrow keys to highlight the item you want and then press ENTER.

2. You can simply type the first letter of the menu item you want. For example, to select **Edit** you type an **E**. You may enter the letters in either upper- or lowercase.

Table 12-1 summarizes what each menu selection does.

Most of the main menu options have their own submenus, which are presented as a pull-down menu beneath the main menu. For example, if you move the highlight to **File** and press ENTER, you activate the **File** pull-down menu as shown in Figure 12-2.

Item	Option
File	Loads and saves files, handles directories, invokes DOS, and exits Turbo C
Edit	Invokes the Turbo C editor
Run	Compiles, links, and runs the program currently loaded in the environment
Compile	Compiles the program currently in the environment
Project	Manages multifile projects
Options	Sets various compiler and linker options
Debug	Sets various debug options
Break/watch	Watches expressions and manages breakpoints

Table 12-1.   *Summary of the Main Menu Items*

Some of the submenus have further options of their own, in which case another pull-down menu is displayed. The number of menus and submenus presented varies according to the needs of each main option.

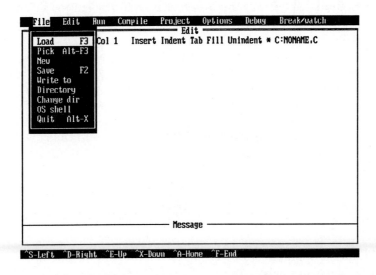

Figure 12-2.   *The File pull-down menu*

To make a selection from a pull-down submenu, either use the arrow keys to highlight the option you desire and press ENTER, or type the capitalized letter of the selection. (This is generally, but not always, the first letter of the selection.) To exit a pull-down menu, press ESC.

Each of the main options and their suboptions are examined next.

File

The **File** option has nine suboptions. They are

Load
Pick
New
Save
Write to
Directory
Change dir
OS shell
Quit

The **Load** option prompts you for a file name and then loads that file into the editor. **Pick** displays a menu that contains a list of the last nine files that you loaded into the IDE. Use the arrow keys to move the highlight until it is on the file you wish to load and press ENTER to load the file. **New** erases the current contents of the editor and lets you edit a new file. If the previous file has been changed but not yet saved to disk, the **New** option first asks if you want to save the file before erasing it. The new file is called NONAME.C. The **Save** option saves the file currently in the editor. If you have edited a new file called NONAME.C, you will be prompted to change its name if you desire. The **Write to** option lets you save a file using a different file name. The **Directory** option displays the contents of the current working directory. You may specify a mask or use the default *.* mask. The **Change dir** command displays the path name of the current working directory and allows you to change it to another if you desire. The **OS shell** option loads the DOS command processor and lets you execute DOS commands. You must type **EXIT** to return from DOS to Turbo C. The **Quit** option quits Turbo C. (Remember that you can also use the ALT-X key combination to exit Turbo C.)

Edit

Selecting the **Edit** option activates Turbo C's built-in editor. The operation of the editor is the subject of Chapter 13.

Run

The **Run** option activates a submenu containing six selections:

Run
Program reset
Go to cursor
Trace into
Step over
User screen

The **Run** option on the submenu executes the current program. If the program has not yet been compiled, **Run** compiles it.

The next four options relate to the execution of a program using the debugger. To use them you must compile your program with the debugging information option turned on, as it is by default. (A discussion of the debugger appears in Appendix B.) The **Program reset** option terminates a program being run in a debug mode and allows you to rerun your program from the beginning. **Go to cursor** executes your program until it reaches the line of code where the cursor is positioned. The **Trace into** option executes the next statement. If that statement includes a subroutine call, the subroutine will be traced into. The **Step over** option executes the next line of code, but does not trace into any subroutines that are called.

The **User screen** option lets you view the output produced by your program.

Compile

There are six options under the **Compile** main menu selection:

Compile to OBJ
Make EXE file
Link EXE file
Build all
Primary C file
Get info

The first option allows you to compile the file currently in the editor (or an alternate primary file) to an *.OBJ file,* which is a relocatable object file that is ready to be linked into an .EXE file that can be executed. The **Make EXE file** option compiles your program directly into an executable file. The **Link EXE file** option links the current .OBJ and library files. The **Build all** option recompiles and links all files in a project whether they are out of date or not. The **Primary C file** option lets you specify a primary file to be compiled instead of the one that is currently loaded into the editor. The **Get info** option displays information about the current session.

Project

The **Project** option is used to aid in the development and maintenance of large, multifile programs.

There are five options under the **Project** main menu selection:

Project name
Break make on
Auto dependencies
Clear project
Remove messages

The **Project name** option lets you specify the name of a project file that contains the names of the files that make up the project. These files are then compiled (if necessary) and linked to form the final executable program. For example, if a project file contains the file names FILE1.C, FILE2.C, and FILE3.C, all three files will be compiled and linked to form the program. A project file is essentially the IDE version of a **MAKE** file used by the standalone **MAKE** utility. In fact, the Turbo C user's guide refers to the process of building the final executable program as a *make*. All project files must have the extension .PRJ.

The **Break make on** option lets you specify what type of conditions cause a make to stop. You can specify to stop the make on warnings, errors, fatal errors, or before linking.

The **Auto dependencies** option causes Turbo C to automatically re-create files that depend on other files that have changed. Files are re-created when a file used to construct the dependent file is newer than the dependent file. For example, if a C source file is newer than a header file used by that source file, the .OBJ file is automatically re-created, and the program is relinked. If **Auto dependencies** is turned off, only the .OBJ/C dependency is checked.

The **Clear project** option removes the project file name from the system and resets the message window.

The **Remove messages** option clears the message window.

Options

The **Options** selection determines the way the integrated development environment operates. It includes the following options:

Compiler
Linker
Environment
Directories
Arguments

Save options
Retrieve options

Each of these entries produces its own pull-down menu with a list of related options. Because compiler, linker, and IDE options are so numerous and complex, much of Chapter 14 is dedicated to a discussion of them. No further explanation is given here.

Debug

The **Debug** option lets you perform various debugging operations and set various debugging options. The selections you can choose from in this menu are

Evaluate
Call stack
Find function
Refresh display
Display swapping
Source debugging

The **Evaluate** option allows you to view or alter the value of any variable or expression in your program. (However, the expression cannot include function calls or macros.)

The **Call stack** option displays the functions that have been called, but not yet returned, in stack-wise order. In other words, it displays the *call stack,* meaning that the most recently called function is on top of the stack and the least recently called function is on the bottom.

The **Find function** option displays the source code to the function that you specify. (The function source code must be available to Turbo C.)

The **Refresh display** option redisplays the Turbo C IDE screen. This option is useful if an application program overwrites the IDE screen.

The **Display swapping** option lets you determine how the screen switches between the IDE screen and the user screen.

The **Source debugging** option lets you include debugging information in the executable form of your program. You need to include debugging information in your program if you want to use Turbo C's debugger.

Break/watch

The **Break/watch** option is part of Turbo C's debugger. It lets you specify various expressions to watch while your program is executing. It also lets you manage breakpoints. A *breakpoint* is a location you define in your program at which execution stops.

The options available in the **Break/watch** menu are

Add watch
Delete watch
Edit watch
Remove all watches
Toggle breakpoint
Clear all breakpoints
View next breakpoint

The following discussion provides a brief overview of these options.

The **Add watch** option displays the value of an expression during the execution of your program. (The expression can be as simple as a single variable or as complex as any valid C expression.) The value of the expression is displayed in the *watch window*. There can be several watched expressions displayed in the watch window. There are two restrictions to watched expressions: They cannot include function calls or macro names.

The **Delete watch** option allows you to remove a watched expression.

The **Edit watch** option lets you modify the highlighted watched expression.

The **Remove all watches** option removes all watched expressions.

The **Toggle breakpoint** option lets you alternately activate (set) or deactivate (clear) a breakpoint.

The **Clear all breakpoints** option deactivates all breakpoints set previously in your program.

The **View next breakpoint** option positions the cursor over the location of the next breakpoint in your program.

The Edit and Message Windows

Immediately below the main menu are the edit and message windows. The edit window is used by Turbo C's text editor. The message window is beneath the edit window and is used to display various compiler or linker messages.

The Hot Keys

The Turbo C IDE contains several *hot keys*, which are shorthand for menu selections. Several hot keys are shown on the reference line at the bottom of the screen; these appear by default. You can see two other sets of hot keys by pressing the ALT key and the CTRL key, respectively. However, the hot keys that are displayed on the status line are not the only hot keys available for use. The hot keys are summarized in Table 12-2. Some of the most commonly used hot keys are also discussed here.

Hot Key	Meaning
F1	Activate the on-line help system
F2	Save the file currently being edited
F3	Load a file
F4	Execute program until cursor is reached
F5	Zoom the window
F6	Switch between windows
F7	Trace into function calls
F8	Trace, but skip function calls
F9	Compile and link a program
F10	Toggle between the main menu and the editor
ALT-F1	Last help screen
ALT-F3	Pick a file to load
ALT-F5	Switch between user screen and IDE
ALT-F6	Switch between watch and message windows
ALT-F7	Previous error
ALT-F8	Next error
ALT-F9	Compile file to .OBJ
ALT-C	Activate the compile menu
ALT-D	Activate the debug menu
ALT-E	Activate the editor
ALT-F	Activate the file menu
ALT-O	Activate the options menu
ALT-P	Activate the project menu
ALT-R	Activate the run menu
ALT-X	Quit Turbo C
CTRL-F1	Request help about the item that contains the cursor
CTRL-F2	Reset program
CTRL-F3	Show function call stack
CTRL-F4	Evaluate an expression
CTRL-F7	Set a watch expression (debugging)
CTRL-F8	Set or clear a breakpoint
CTRL-F9	Execute the current program

Table 12-2.   *The Turbo C Hot Keys*

Help

The on-line help system is activated by pressing F1. It is *context sensitive,* which means that Turbo C displays information related to what you are currently doing. You may also select a help topic manually by pressing F1 a second time. You are shown a list of topics from which to choose. To receive help on a Turbo C keyword or library function, position the cursor on that word and press CTRL-F1. To exit the help system, press the ESC key.

Switching Windows and Zoom

By pressing the F5 key you can enlarge either the edit or message window to encompass the full size of the screen. This feature somewhat simulates the zoom lens of a camera; hence the name. The F5 key is a toggle, so pressing it again returns the edit or message window to its regular size. The window that is enlarged is determined by using the F6 key. The F6 key is a toggle that switches between the edit and message windows. Pressing it once selects the message window; pressing it again returns control to the edit window. You may want to select the message window to examine the various messages generated by the compiler.

Make

The **MAKE** key is F9. The **MAKE** option provides a simple way to compile programs consisting of multiple source files.

The ALT-X Key Combination

You can exit Turbo C at any time by pressing the ALT-X combination.

The TCINST Program

Included with Turbo C is an installation program called TCINST that is used to set various attributes and default settings in the Turbo C integrated environment. To execute the program simply type **TCINST** from the command line. When it begins to execute you see a menu with the following items:

    Compile
    Project
    Options
    Debug
    Editor commands

Mode for display
Set colors
Resize windows
Quit/save

Each of these options is discussed in this section.

Compile

Selecting the **Compile** option allows you to define a default primary file. This option is similar to its corresponding entry in the IDE main menu.

Project

Selecting the **Project** option allows you to define a project name. It also lets you set the default state of various project-related features. This option is similar to its corresponding entry in the IDE main menu.

Options

The **Options** selection lets you set various compiler, linker, and environmental parameters. This option is similar to its corresponding entry in the IDE main menu.

Debug

The **Debug** option allows you to determine how the built-in debugger operates. This option is similar to its corresponding entry in the IDE main menu.

Editor Commands

You can customize the Turbo C editor by selecting the **Editor commands** option, which produces the screen shown in Figure 12-3.

Using this option, you can customize the Turbo C editor to imitate your favorite editor by changing the keystrokes for each command. The left keystroke column contains the primary keystrokes to activate a command. By default the primary keystrokes are WordStar-like commands. The right column contains alternate keystrokes that invoke the same command. You can change either (or both) the primary or secondary keystrokes associated with each command. Use the left and right arrow keys to move between the two columns.

To change the keystrokes that execute a command, position the highlight on the command and column that you want to change and press ENTER. To clear the old

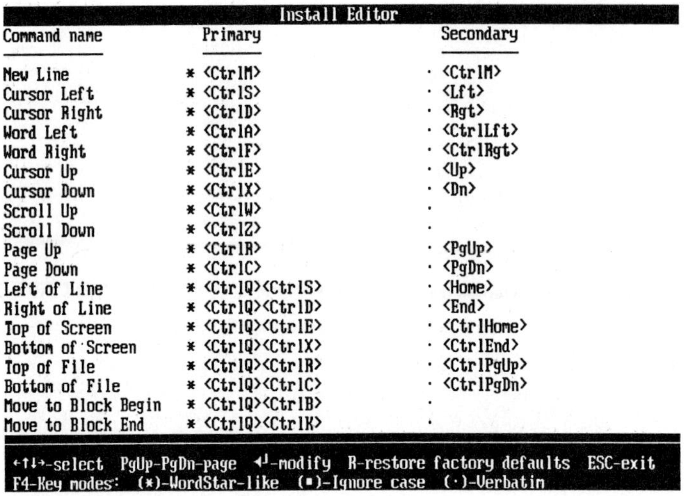

```
┌─────────────────────────── Install Editor ───────────────────────────┐
│ Command name        Primary              Secondary                    │
│                                                                       │
│ New Line          * <CtrlM>            · <CtrlM>                       │
│ Cursor Left       * <CtrlS>            · <Lft>                         │
│ Cursor Right      * <CtrlD>            · <Rgt>                         │
│ Word Left         * <CtrlA>            · <CtrlLft>                     │
│ Word Right        * <CtrlF>            · <CtrlRgt>                     │
│ Cursor Up         * <CtrlE>            · <Up>                          │
│ Cursor Down       * <CtrlX>            · <Dn>                          │
│ Scroll Up         * <CtrlW>            ·                               │
│ Scroll Down       * <CtrlZ>            ·                               │
│ Page Up           * <CtrlR>            · <PgUp>                        │
│ Page Down         * <CtrlC>            · <PgDn>                        │
│ Left of Line      * <CtrlQ><CtrlS>     · <Home>                        │
│ Right of Line     * <CtrlQ><CtrlD>     · <End>                         │
│ Top of Screen     * <CtrlQ><CtrlE>     · <CtrlHome>                    │
│ Bottom of Screen  * <CtrlQ><CtrlX>     · <CtrlEnd>                     │
│ Top of File       * <CtrlQ><CtrlR>     · <CtrlPgUp>                    │
│ Bottom of File    * <CtrlQ><CtrlC>     · <CtrlPgDn>                    │
│ Move to Block Begin * <CtrlQ><CtrlB>   ·                               │
│ Move to Block End   * <CtrlQ><CtrlK>   ·                               │
├───────────────────────────────────────────────────────────────────────┤
│ ←↑↓→-select PgUp-PgDn-page ↵-modify R-restore factory defaults ESC-exit│
│ F4-Key modes:  (*)-WordStar-like  (■)-Ignore case  (·)-Verbatim        │
└───────────────────────────────────────────────────────────────────────┘
```

Figure 12-3.   *The Editor commands screen of TCINST*

keystrokes, press F3. Next, enter the new keystrokes you want for that command. Use the BACKSPACE key if you accidentally type a wrong key. Pressing F2 restores the previous keystrokes. To cancel the modification process press ESC. Once you have entered the new keystrokes, press ENTER.

Although the editor is quite flexible, you must follow certain rules when customizing its commands:

1. No command sequence can be longer than six keystrokes. All special keys, such as ALT, the arrow keys, and the function keys count as two keystrokes.

2. The first character must be a control key or special key, not an alphanumeric key.

3. To enter an ESC, press CTRL-[; for a BACKSPACE, press CTRL-H; and for ENTER, press CTRL-M.

4. It is best not to use any of Turbo C's hot keys as editor commands.

Screen Mode

The **Mode for display** option is used to determine how Turbo C communicates with the video controller in your computer. You can let Turbo C determine what type of adapter you have or you can specify that it is either color, black and white, or monochrome. Depending on how your system is set up you may experience "snow" when using the fastest screen output method. The **Mode for display** option allows you to test for snow based on the type of video adapter you have.

Set Colors

The **Set Colors** option lets you select the color scheme used by Turbo C when running in a color environment. There are three built-in color options. In addition, you can define your own color scheme for every part of the Turbo C user interface. To do this select the **Custom Colors** option. You are then asked what area you wish to modify. For example, if you select the main menu, you are shown another menu that lets you select the part of the main menu you wish to change. Your screen will look like Figure 12-4. When you have selected what you wish to change, you are shown a table of color options. As you try each option, the partial view of the main menu changes to reflect each different color scheme.

Resize Windows

It is possible to change the size of the edit and message windows relative to each other by using the **Resize windows** option. After selecting this option you can use the arrow keys to move the line that separates the two windows.

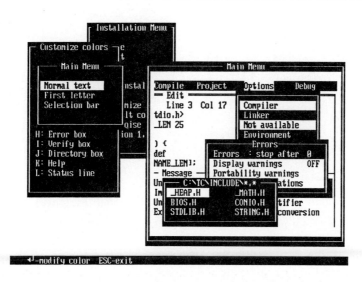

Figure 12-4.   *Selecting custom colors with TCINST*

Quit/save

The **Quit/save** option terminates the installation program. You are asked whether you want the changes you made while running the program to be written into Turbo C and become its default mode of operation. If you do, answer **Y** for "yes." If you don't, answer **N** for "no."

Chapter *13*

The Turbo C
Text Editor

This chapter discusses the text editor supplied with Turbo C's integrated programming environment. Its operation is similar to both Micropro's WordStar program and the editors provided by Turbo Pascal and SideKick. The Turbo C editor contains about 50 commands and is quite powerful.

Editor Commands

With few exceptions, all editor commands begin with a control character (CTRL). Many are then followed by another character. For example, the sequence CTRL-Q F is the command that tells the editor to find a string. This means that you type a CTRL-Q and then an F in either upper- or lowercase.

Invoking the Editor and Entering Text

When Turbo C begins, it waits at the sign-on message until you press a key. After that the main menu option **File** is highlighted. To invoke the editor you either use the cursor keys to move the highlight to **Edit** or simply type an **e**. To leave the editor, press the F10 key.

The top line of the editor window is the *editor status line,* which tells you various things about the state of the editor and the file you are editing. The first two items, **Line** and **Col**, display the line number and column of the cursor. The **Insert** message means that the editor is in insert mode. That is, as you enter text it is inserted in the middle of what (if anything) is already there. The opposite is called *overwrite* ; in this mode of operation new text overwrites existing text. You can toggle between these two modes by pressing the INS key. The **Indent** message means that autoindentation is on. You will see how this works shortly. You toggle the indentation mode by using the sequence CTRL-O I. The **Tab** message means that you can insert tabs using the TAB key. This is toggled by using the sequence CTRL-O T. The **Fill** message tells you that a series of spaces will be filled using an optimal number of spaces and tabs. If **Fill** is not on, only spaces are used. You can toggle this feature using CTRL-O F. At the end of the line the name of the file you are editing is displayed.

As soon as you invoke the editor it is ready to accept text. If you make mistakes you can use the BACKSPACE key to correct them. For example, enter the lines

This is a
test of the Turbo C
editor.

Your screen now looks like Figure 13-1. Notice the position of the cursor and the values associated with **Line** and **Col**.

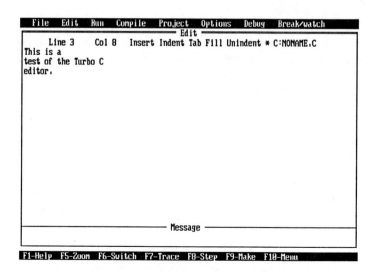

Figure 13-1. *Editor screen with text entered*

You can use the arrow keys to move the cursor around in the file. As you move the cursor, the line and column numbers are updated to reflect its current position.

If you put the cursor in the middle of a line and enter more text, the existing line is moved to the right when the editor is in insert mode. For example, if you move the cursor to the start of the second line of text entered from the previous example, and type the word "good," the screen looks like Figure 13-2. If you toggle the editor into overwrite mode, the original line is overwritten.

Deleting Characters, Words, and Lines

You can delete a single character two ways: with the BACKSPACE key or with the DEL key. The BACKSPACE key deletes the character immediately to the left of the cursor, while DEL deletes the character under the cursor.

You can delete an entire word to the right of the cursor by typing CTRL-T. A word is any set of characters delimited by one of the following characters:

space $ / − + * ' ^ [ ] ( ) . ; , < >

You can remove an entire line by typing CTRL-Y. It does not matter where the cursor is positioned in the line; the entire line is deleted.

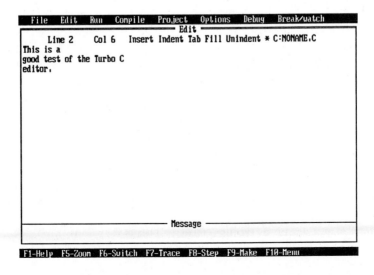

Figure 13-2.   *Editor after inserting text*

If you wish to delete from the current cursor position to the end of the line, type the sequence CTRL-Q Y.

Moving, Copying, and Deleting Blocks of Text

The Turbo C editor allows you to manipulate a block of text by moving or copying it to another location or deleting it altogether. To do any of these things you must first define a block. You do this by moving the cursor to the start of the block and typing the sequence CTRL-K B. Next, move the cursor to the end of the block and type the sequence CTRL-K K. The block that you have defined will be highlighted (or in a different color if you have a color system).

To move the block of text, place the cursor where you want the text to go and type the sequence CTRL-K V. This removes the previously defined block of text from its current position and places it at the new location. To copy a block, type the sequence CTRL-K C. To delete the currently marked block, type the sequence CTRL-K Y.

You can mark a single word as a block by positioning the cursor under the first character in the word and typing CTRL-K T.

More on Cursor Movement

The Turbo C editor has a number of special cursor commands, which are summarized in Table 13-1. The best way to learn these commands is to practice them a little each day until you have them memorized.

Find and Find with Replace

To find a specific sequence of characters, type CTRL-Q F. You are prompted at the status line for the string of characters you wish to find. Enter the string you are looking for and then press ENTER. You are then prompted for search options. The search options shown in Table 13-2 modify the way the search is conducted. For example, typing **G2** causes Turbo C to find the second occurrence of the string. No options need be specified; you can simply press ENTER. If no options are present, the search proceeds from the current cursor position forward with case sensitivity and substring matches allowed.

You can repeat a search by typing a CTRL-L. This is very convenient when you are looking for something specific in the file.

Command	Action
CTRL-A	Move to the start of the word to the left of the cursor
CTRL-S	Move left one character
CTRL-D	Move right one character
CTRL-F	Move to the start of the word to the right of the cursor
CTRL-E	Move the cursor up one line
CTRL-R	Move the cursor up one full screen
CTRL-X	Move the cursor down one line
CTRL-C	Move the cursor down one full screen
CTRL-W	Scroll screen up
CTRL-Z	Scroll screen down
PGUP	Move the cursor up one full screen
PGDN	Move the cursor down one full screen
HOME	Move the cursor to the start of the line
END	Move the cursor to the end of the line
CTRL-Q E	Move the cursor to the top of the screen
CTRL-Q X	Move the cursor to the bottom of the screen
CTRL-Q R	Move the cursor to the top of the file
CTRL-Q C	Move the cursor to the bottom of the file
CTRL-PGUP	Move the cursor to the top of the file
CTRL-PGDN	Move the cursor to the bottom of the file
CTRL-HOME	Move the cursor to the top of the screen
CTRL-END	Move the cursor to the bottom of the screen

Table 13-1.   *The Cursor Commands*

To activate the find-and-replace command, type CTRL-Q A. Its operation is identical to the find command except that it allows you to replace the string you are looking for with another. If you specify the **N** option you will not be asked whether to replace each occurrence of the search string with the replacement string. Otherwise you will be prompted for a decision each time a match occurs.

You can enter control characters into the search string by typing a CTRL-P followed by the control character you want.

Option	Effect
B	Search the file backwards starting from the current cursor position
G	Search the entire file regardless of where the cursor is located
N	Replace without asking; for find-and-replace mode only
L	Search only the current block
U	Match either upper- or lowercase
W	Match only whole words, not substrings within words
n	Where *n* is an integer, causes the *n*th occurrence of the string to be found

Table 13-2.   *The Options to the Find Command*

Setting and Finding Place Markers

You can set up to four place markers in your file by typing CTRL-K *n*, where *n* is the number of the place marker (0 to 3). After a marker has been set, the command CTRL-Q *n*, where *n* is the marker number, causes the cursor to go to that marker.

Saving and Loading Your File

There are three ways to save your file. Two of the ways save it to a file that has the same name as that shown on the status line. The third way saves the file to a disk file with a different name and then makes that name the current name of your file. Let's look at how each method works.

The first way you can save your file is to exit the editor (by pressing F10) and select the **File** main menu option. In the **File** submenu, choosing the **Save** option saves what is currently in the editor into a disk file by the name shown on the status line.

The second way to save the file does not require you to exit the editor. If you press the F2 key while you are using the editor, the file is saved under the current name.

If you want to use a different file name, select the **Write to** option. This allows you to enter the name of the file you wish to write the current contents of the editor to. It also makes this name the default file name.

To load a file you can either press F3 while inside the editor or select the **Load** option in the **File** menu. Once you have done that, you are prompted for the name of the file you wish to load. There are two ways to specify the file name.

1. If you know the name, you can type it in at this time.

2. If you are unsure of the name, do not enter anything and Turbo C will display all files with the .C extension, from which you can choose one. You use the arrow keys to highlight the file you want and then press ENTER.

Understanding Autoindentation

Good programmers use indentation to help make the programs they write clearer and easier to understand. To assist you in this practice, after you press ENTER the Turbo C editor automatically places the cursor at the same indentation level as the line previously typed, assuming that autoindentation is on. (Remember that you toggle this feature by typing CTRL-O I.) For example, enter the following few lines exactly as they are shown here and notice how the autoindentation works.

```
main()
{
  int i;

  for(i=0; i<100; i++) {
   printf("this is i: ");
   printf("%d\n", i);
  }
}
```

As you write Turbo C programs, you will find this feature quite handy.

Moving Blocks of Text to and from Disk Files

It is possible to move a block of text into a disk file for later use. This is done by first defining a block and then typing CTRL-K W. After you have done this, you are prompted for the name of the file you wish to save the block in. The original block of text is not removed from your program.

To read a block in, type the sequence CTRL-K R. You are prompted for the file name, and the contents of that file are read in at the current cursor location.

These two commands are most useful when you are moving text between two or more files, as is so often the case during program development.

Pair Matching

Several delimiters in C work in pairs, including { }, [ ], and ( ). In very long or complex programs, it is sometimes difficult to find the proper companion to a delimiter. Starting with version 1.5 of Turbo C it is possible to have the editor find the corresponding companion delimiter automatically.

The Turbo C editor finds the companion delimiter for the following delimiter pairs:

```
{ }
[ ]
( )
< >
/* */
" "
' '
```

To find the matching delimiter, place the cursor on the delimiter you wish to match and type CTRL-Q [for a forward match or CTRL-Q] for a backward match. The editor moves the cursor to the matching delimiter. Some delimiters are nestable, and some are not. The nestable delimiters are: { }, [ ], ( ), < >, and sometimes the comment symbols (when the nested comments option is enabled). The editor finds the proper matching delimiter according to C syntax. For example, in Figure 13-3 the lines indicate which curly braces match.

If for some reason the editor cannot find a proper match, the cursor is not moved.

```
main()
{
    int i, j;


    for(i=0; i<100; i++) {
        for(j=0; j<100; j++) {
            .
            .
            .
        }
    }
}
```

Figure 13-3.   *How the editor matches the curly braces*

Miscellaneous Commands

You can abort any command that requests input by typing a CTRL-U at the prompt. For example, if you execute the find command and then change your mind, simply type CTRL-U. (You can also press the ESC key to abort input.)

If you wish to enter a control character into a file you first type CTRL-P followed by the control character you want. Control characters are displayed in either low intensity or reverse intensity depending on how your system is configured.

To undo changes made to a line before you have moved the cursor off that line, type CTRL-Q L. Remember that once the cursor has been moved off the line changes cannot be undone.

If you wish to go to the start of a block, type CTRL-Q B. Typing CTRL-Q K takes you to the end of a block.

One particularly useful command is CTRL-Q P, which puts the cursor back to its previous position. This is handy if you want to search for something and then return to where you were.

Invoking Turbo C with a File Name

You can specify the name of the file you want to edit when you invoke Turbo C. To do this you simply put the name of the file after the **TC** on the command line. For example, **TC MYFILE** executes Turbo C and loads MYFILE.C into the editor. The .C extension is added automatically by Turbo C. If MYFILE does not exist, it is created.

Command Summary

Table 13-3 shows all the Turbo C editor commands.

Cursor Commands

Command	*Action*
LEFT ARROW or CTRL-S	Left one character
RIGHT ARROW or CTRL-D	Right one character
CTRL-A	Left one word
CTRL-F	Right one word

Table 13-3. *Turbo C Editor Command Summary by Category*

Command	Action
UP ARROW or CTRL-E	Up one line
DOWN ARROW or CTRL-X	Down one line
CTRL-W	Scroll up
CTRL-Z	Scroll down
PGUP or CTRL-R	Up one page
PGDN or CTRL-C	Down one page
HOME or CTRL-Q S	Go to start of line
END or CTRL-Q D	Go to end of line
CTRL-Q E	Go to top of screen
CTRL-Q X	Go to bottom of screen
CTRL-Q R	Go to top of file
CTRL-Q C	Go to bottom of file
CTRL-Q B	Go to start of block
CTRL-Q K	Go to end of block
CTRL-Q P	Go to last cursor position

Insert Commands

Command	Action
INS or CTRL-V	Toggle insert mode
ENTER or CTRL-N	Insert a blank line

Delete Commands

Command	Action
CTRL-Y	Entire line
CTRL-Q Y	To end of line
BACKSPACE	Character to left
DEL or CTRL-G	Character at cursor
CTRL-T	Word to the right

Block Commands

Command	Action
CTRL-K B	Mark beginning
CTRL-K K	Mark end
CTRL-K T	Mark a word

Table 13-3. *Turbo C Editor Command Summary by Category* (continued)

Command	*Action*
CTRL-K C	Copy a block
CTRL-K Y	Delete a block
CTRL-K H	Hide or display a block
CTRL-K V	Move a block
CTRL-K R	Read a block from disk
CTRL-K W	Write a block to disk
CTRL-K I	Indent a block
CTRL-K U	Unindent a block
CTRL-K P	Print a block

Find Commands

Command	*Action*
CTRL-Q F	Find
CTRL-Q A	Find and replace
CTRL-Q N	Find place marker
CTRL-L	Repeat find

Pair Matching

Command	*Action*
CTRL-Q [	Match pair forward
CTRL-Q]	Match pair reverse

Miscellaneous Commands

Command	*Action*
CTRL-U	Abort
CTRL-O I	Toggle autoindentation mode
CTRL-P	Control character prefix
F10	Exit editor
F3	New file
CTRL-Q W	Restore overwritten error message
F2	Save
CTRL-K N	Set place marker
CTRL-O T	Toggle tab mode
CTRL-Q L	Undo

Table 13-3.   *Turbo C Editor Command Summary by Category* (continued)

Chapter **14**

Compiler and Linker Options

Turbo C provides many options that affect the way programs are compiled and linked. Although Turbo C's default settings accommodate a wide variety of programming projects, there will almost certainly be times when you want to alter some of these settings to suit your specific application. This chapter discusses the compiler options available in both the integrated environment and the command-line version of Turbo C. With the exception of the options and settings that deal exclusively with the integrated environment, all the options available in the integrated environment are also available for use in the command-line version. However, there are a few options available in the command-line version that are not supported by the integrated environment.

The chapter ends with a look at the standalone Turbo C linker called TLINK.

Integrated Development Environment Options

These are the options available in the **Options** menu:

Compiler
Linker
Environment
Directories
Arguments

Save options
Retrieve options

Each area will be examined in turn.

Compiler Options

After selecting **Compiler** you see these compiler options:

Model
Defines
Code generation
Optimization
Source
Errors
Names

Model

The **Model** option allows you to select which memory model is used to compile your program. The default is "small," which is adequate for most applications. For a complete discussion of the available memory models, refer to Chapter 10.

Defines

The **Defines** option allows you to define temporary preprocessor symbols to be used automatically by your program. You can define one or more macros by separating them with semicolons. This feature is most useful during program development and debugging. For example, in the following fragment, testing is performed with known input even though the final program uses a number generated by the random number generator **rand( )**. If you define the macro **RAND_ON** using the **Defines** option, the random number is used; otherwise the number is input from the keyboard. Remember that you could also define **RAND_ON** in the program by using the preprocessor command **#define**.

```
main()
{
  int i;

  #ifdef RAND_ON
```

```
  i = rand();
#else
  /* for testing, read number from keyboard */
  printf("input number: ");
  scanf("%d", &i);
#endif
  .
  .
  .
}
```

Code Generation

Selecting **Code generation** presents you with a large number of switches that you can set. The options are

> Calling convention
> Instruction set
> Floating point
> Default char type
> Alignment
> Generate underbars
> Merge duplicate strings
> Standard stack frame
> Test stack overflow
> Line numbers
> OBJ debug information

You can choose between the C calling convention and the Pascal calling convention. A *calling convention* is simply the method by which functions are called and arguments are passed. Generally, you should use the C calling convention.

If you know that the object code of your program will be used on an 80186/80286 processor, you can tell Turbo C to use the 80186/80286 extended instruction set using the **Instruction set** option. It will cause your program to execute a little faster, but it will not be able to run on 8088/8086-based computers. The default is 8088/8086 instructions.

You can control the way Turbo C implements floating-point operations. The default—and most common—method is to use 8087/80287 emulation routines. The 8087 chip is the math coprocessor for the 8086 family of CPUs, while the 80287 is the math coprocessor for the 80286 CPU. When these coprocessors are in the system, they allow very rapid floating-point operations. However, if you don't have a math coprocessor or if your program will be used in a variety of computers, the 8087's operation must be emulated in software, which is much slower. The emulation mode uses the math coprocessor by default if one is in the system, or calls the emulation routines if no math coprocessor is installed. However, if you know in advance that the coprocessor is present in every system on which the program will run, you can select the 8087/80287 option, which generates in-line 8087/80287 code. This is the fastest way to implement floating-point operations. Finally, you can deselect floating point altogether when your program doesn't use it, thereby allowing the object code to be much smaller.

The **Default char type** option determines whether the type **char** is signed or unsigned. By default, **char** is signed in Turbo C.

The **Alignment** option determines whether data is aligned on byte or word boundaries. On the 8086 family of processors, memory accesses are quicker if data is word-aligned. However, there is no difference on the 8088. The default is byte-alignment.

The **Generate underbars** option, which is on by default, determines whether an underscore is added to the start of each indentifier in the link file. You should not turn this off unless you are an experienced programmer and understand the inner workings of Turbo C.

Elimination of duplicate string constants is a common compiler optimization that you can instruct Turbo C to perform. That is, all identical strings can be merged into one string, the result being smaller programs. You can control this by toggling the **Merge duplicate strings** option. It is off by default.

The **Standard stack frame** option is used to force Turbo C to generate standard calling and returning code for each function call to help in debugging. This option is on by default. You will not generally have to worry about or use this option.

You can force Turbo C to check for stack overflows by turning on the **Test stack overflow** option. This makes your program run more slowly, but it may be necessary in order to find certain bugs. If your program crashes inexplicably from time to time, you might want to compile it with this test turned on to see if stack overflows are the problem.

With the **Line numbers** option, you can force Turbo C to enter the number of each line of the source file into the object file. This is useful when using a debugger.

Finally, the **OBJ debug information** option controls whether debug information is compiled into your file. This information is necessary when you are using a debugger. This option is on by default.

Optimization

The **Optimization** option contains four toggles:

Optimize for
Use register variables
Register optimization
Jump optimization

Turbo C is very efficient, but, for various reasons, some optimizations that make the object code smaller also make it slower. Other optimizations make the object code faster but larger. Turbo C lets you decide whether you want to optimize for speed or size by using the **Optimize for** option. The default is size.

The **Use register variables** option, if turned off, suppresses use of register variables. Unless you are interfacing to non-Turbo C code, leave this option on.

When the **Register optimization** option, which is off by default, is turned on, it allows Turbo C to perform some additional optimizations that prevent redundant load and store operations. However, Turbo C cannot know if a variable has been modified through a pointer, so you must use this option with care.

By toggling **Jump optimization** on, you allow Turbo C to rearrange the code within loops and switch statements. This can cause higher performance. However, if you are using a debugger on your object code, turn this option off.

Source

The **Source** option lets you set the number of significant characters in an identifier, determine whether comments can be nested, and force Turbo C to accept only the ANSI keywords.

By default, Turbo C identifiers have 32 significant characters. However, you can set this number anywhere in the range 1 through 32. You would most commonly want to reduce the number of significant characters when you are compiling source code written for a different compiler. Years ago it was common to have compilers recognize only the first six to eight characters. Some programmers exploited this limitation by embedding "comments" into their variables to help with debugging. For example, programmers occasionally encoded the usage count into a variable's name as shown here:

```
/* Assuming 7 significant characters, the variables
   on the left side of the assignment statement all
   resolve to a single variable called counter.
*/

counter1 = 10;

counter2 = 20;

counter3 = 30;
```

This practice of encoding a "comment" in the variable's name has been discredited, but some older source code may still contain instances of it.

Turbo C supports the ANSI C standard, but it has added various enhancements to the language to support the 8086 processor better. If you want to make sure that you are writing code that uses only the ANSI keywords, toggle on the option **ANSI keywords only**. Otherwise, leave it in its default (off) position.

In its standard form, C (including Turbo C) does not allow one comment to be inside another. For example, in standard C, the following code causes a compile-time error:

```
/* In standard ANSI C this will not compile. */

/*
  if(x<10) printf("all OK"); /* signal status */
  else printf("failure in port 102");
*/
```

Here, the programmer attempted to "comment out" a section of code, but failed to notice that a nested comment was created. By selecting the **Nested comments** option, you can tell Turbo C to allow situations like the preceding example and allow the entire block to be ignored. This can be very useful when you wish to remove a section of code temporarily. Note that the standard and portable way to do this is to use an **#ifdef** preprocessor command. The use of the **Nested comments** option is best reserved for special exceptions encountered while debugging.

Errors

The **Errors** option lets you determine how errors are reported during the compilation process. There are seven options in this menu:

    Errors: stop after
    Warnings: stop after
    Display warnings
    Portability warnings
    ANSI violations
    Common errors
    Less common errors

You can set how many fatal errors can be reported before the compilation process stops by using the **Errors: stop after** option. The default is 25.

You can set how many warning errors can be reported before compilation stops by using the **Warnings: stop after** option. The default setting is 100. Turbo C is very forgiving and tries to make sense out of your source code no matter how unusual it may seem. However, if Turbo C has a suspicion that what you have written is incorrect, it displays a warning error. A warning error does not stop compilation; it simply informs you of Turbo C's concerns over a certain construct. It is for you to decide whether Turbo C is correct in its concern.

Several types of warning errors can be generated. The first are portability errors, which reflect coding methods that would render the program nonportable to another type of processor. The second type of warning error is generated by non-ANSI code practices. The third group consists of common programming errors, and the final group consists of less common programming errors. These categories are summarized in Table 14-1.

Portability Errors

Error	*Default*
Nonportable pointer conversion	On
Nonportable pointer assignment	On
Nonportable pointer comparison	On
Constant out of range in comparison	On
Constant is long	Off
Conversion may lose significant digits	Off
Mixing pointers to signed and unsigned **char**	Off

ANSI Violations

Error	*Default*
Identifier not part of structure	On
Zero length structure	On
Void functions may not return a value	On
Both return and return of a value used	On
Suspicious pointer conversion	On
Undefined structure identifier	On
Redefinition of an identifer is not identical	On
Hexadecimal or octal constant is too large	On

Common Errors

Error	*Default*
Function should return a value	Off
Unreachable code	On
Code has no effect	On

Table 14-1. *The Types of Warning Errors Issued by Turbo C*

Error	*Default*
Possible use of an identifier before definition	On
Identifier assigned a value that is never used	On
Parameter identifier is never used	On
Possibly incorrect assignment	On

Less Common Errors

Error	*Default*
Superfluous & with function or array	Off
Identifier declared but never used	Off
Ambiguous operators need parentheses	Off
Structure passed by value	Off
No declaration for function	Off
Call to function with no prototype	Off

Table 14-1.   *The Types of Warning Errors Issued by Turbo C* (continued)

Names

The **Names** option lets you change the names Turbo C uses for the various memory segments used by your program. You will need to change these only in unusual situations. Don't change the names unless you are an experienced assembly language programmer and know what you are doing.

Linker Options

If you select the **Linker** options, you see the following list of choices:

Map file	Warn duplicate symbols
Initialize segments	Stack warning
Default libraries	Case-sensitive link
Graphics library	

Let's examine each area in turn.

Map File

By default, Turbo C's linker does not create a map file of your compiled program. A map file shows the relative positions of the variables and functions that make up your program and where they reside in memory. You may need to create a map file for debugging certain programs in complex situations. You can create a map file in three ways. The first shows only the segments. The second shows the public (global) symbols. The third creates a detailed (complete) map.

Initialize Segments

By default, **Initialize segments** is off. It is turned on in highly specialized situations to force the linker to initialize segments, but this is seldom necessary.

Default Libraries

The **Default libraries** option applies only when you are linking modules compiled by other C compilers. By default this option is off. If you turn it on, the linker searches the libraries defined in the separately compiled modules before searching Turbo C's libraries. Again, this is a highly specialized situation that you will probably not need to worry about.

Graphics Library

The **Graphics library** option is on by default. This causes Turbo C to search the GRAPHICS.LIB library automatically when linking your program. This enables you to use Turbo C's graphics functions. There is little reason to turn this option off.

Warn Duplicate Symbols

By default, **Warn duplicate symbols** is on. This means that the linker warns you if you have defined duplicate global identifiers. By turning it off, you do not see this message and the linker chooses which one to use.

Stack Warning

If you are using Turbo C to create routines to link with external assembly language programs, you might receive the link-time message **No stack specified**. You can eliminate this message by turning **Stack warning** off.

Case-Sensitive Link

Case-sensitive link is on by default because C is case-sensitive. However, if you are trying to link Turbo C modules with FORTRAN modules, for example, you may need to turn this option off.

Environment Options

By selecting the **Environment** option from the **Options** menu you can change the way Turbo C's integrated environment works. The following selections are available:

> Message tracking
> Keep messages
> Config auto save
> Edit auto save
> Backup files
> Tab size
> Zoomed windows
> Screen size

By default, Turbo C *tracks* (displays) errors found only in the current source file loaded in the editor. However, you can tell it to track messages in all files related to a program or to not track errors at all by toggling the **Message tracking** option.

If the **Keep messages** option is off (its default state), error messages are cleared before each recompilation. If you turn this option on, old error messages are retained and new ones are added to the list.

When **Config auto save** is on, any changes made to the configuration file are automatically saved each time you run a program, use the OS shell command, or exit Turbo C. If it is off, the configuration is saved only on your command. This option is off by default.

When **Edit auto save** is on, the editor automatically saves your source file to disk each time you run the program or use the OS shell command. If the option is off, your file is saved only when you specifically command it. It is off by default.

When you save a file, Turbo C automatically renames the previous version of that file from a .C extension to a .BAK extension. In this way, you always have the previous version as a backup. You can turn off this option by toggling **Backup files**. About the only reason for turning this off is to save disk space if it is very limited.

The default tab size is 8; you can change it using the **Tab size** option.

If **Zoomed windows** is on, the active window occupies the entire screen. The option is off by default.

Finally, if you have an EGA or VGA video adapter you can tell Turbo C to use a 43-line display. If you have a VGA, you can use a 50-line display. These settings are specified using the **Screen size** option. A 25-line display is used by default.

The Directories Option

After selecting the **Directories** option you are presented with a menu consisting of these entries:

    Include directories
    Library directories
    Output directory
    Turbo C directory
    Pick file name

This option also reports the current pick file.

If you select the **Include directories** option, you can specify a list of directories to be searched for your include files. The list can be up to 127 characters long, and the file names must be separated by semicolons.

If you select the **Library directories** option, you can specify a list of directories to be searched for your library files. This list can also be up to 127 characters long, and the file names must be separated by semicolons.

Selecting the **Output directory** option allows you to specify the directory used for output. The file and path name must not be longer than 63 characters.

You can specify where Turbo C looks for its help files and the TCCONFIG.TC file by using the **Turbo C directory** option. The file and path name must not be longer than 63 characters.

You can specify the path for pick files using the **Pick file name** option.

Arguments

As you know, when you run a program in the interactive environment you do not type the program name as you do from the DOS system prompt. Hence, it is not possible to specify command-line arguments directly when running a program in the integrated environment. However, Turbo C allows you to run programs that use the command-line arguments in the IDE by using the **Arguments** option.

When you select **Arguments** you are prompted to enter the command-line arguments required by your program. Enter the arguments desired—but not the program name. Then, each time you run the program, the command-line arguments you specified will be used.

Saving and Loading Options

Once you have customized Turbo C by changing various options, you have two choices: You can use your chosen options during your current session only, or you can save them. The two entries **Save options** and **Retrieve options** in the **Options** menu allow you to save and load the options. Let's see how.

The TCCONFIG.TC File

The first thing that Turbo C does when it begins executing the integrated environment is to look for a file called TCCONFIG.TC. This file holds the configuration information for the system. You can change the contents of this file by using the **Save** option. In this way, the changes you make to Turbo C will still be there the next time you execute it.

Turbo C looks for the TCCONFIG.TC file first in the current working directory. If the file is not found it then looks in the TURBO directory, should one exist. If you are going to modify TCCONFIG.TC, it is best to keep a copy of the unmodified file handy in case you need to go back to the default settings for some reason.

Using Other Configuration Files

When you save the changes you have made to Turbo C, you don't have to save them into the TCCONFIG.TC file. You can specify any file you desire. When Turbo C begins executing the integrated environment it uses the default settings. To load the options you want, simply select the **Options** menu and select **Retrieve options**. Then specify the name of the file that contains the settings you want to use. The advantage of this approach is that Turbo C's default settings are always available if you need them, but you can easily customize Turbo C to your liking.

The Command-Line Version of Turbo C

If you are new to C, there is no doubt that you will find Turbo C's integrated environment the easiest way to develop programs. However, if you have been programming and using your own editor for some time, you might find the command-line version of Turbo C more to your liking. For long-time C programmers, the command-line version represents the traditional method of compilation and linking. Also, the command-line version of the compiler can do a few things that the integrated environment version can't. For example, if you wish to generate an assembly language listing of the code generated by Turbo C or if you want to use in-line assembly code, you must use the command-line version. The name of the command-line compiler is TCC.EXE.

Compiling with the Command-Line Compiler

Assume that you have a program called X.C. To compile this program using the command-line version of Turbo C, your command line will look like this:

```
C>TCC X.C
```

Assuming that there are no errors in the program, this causes X.C to be compiled and linked with the proper library files. This is the simplest form of the command line.

The general form of the command line is

TCC [*option1 option2 . . . optionN*] *fname1 fname2 . . . fnameN*

where *option* is a compiler or linker option and *fname* is either a C source file, an .OBJ file, or a library. Additional .OBJ or .LIB files on the command line are passed along to the linker for inclusion in the final program. Remember, however, that Turbo C automatically includes its standard libraries, so they need not be specified.

All compiler/linker options begin with a minus sign. Generally, following an option with a minus sign turns that option off. Table 14-2 shows the options available in the command-line version of Turbo C. Keep in mind that the options are case-sensitive.

Option	Meaning
–A	Recognize ANSI keywords only
–a	Use word alignment for data
–a–	Use byte alignment for data
–B	In-line assembly code in source file
–C	Accept nested comments
–c	Compile to .OBJ only
–D*name*	Defines a macro name
–D*name=string*	Defines and gives a value to a macro name
–d	Merge duplicate strings
–e*fname*	Specifies project name
–f	Use floating-point emulation
–f–	No floating point
–f87	Use 8087

Table 14-2.   *Turbo C's Command-Line Options*

Option	Meaning
–G	Optimize code for speed
–g*N*	Stop after *N* warning errors
–I*path*	Specifies the path to the include directory
–i*N*	Specifies identifier length
–j*N*	Stop after *N* fatal errors
–K	**char** unsigned
–K–	**char** signed
–k	Generate standard stack frame
–L*path*	Specifies library directory
–l*xxx*	Pass *xxx* option to linker
–M	Create map file
–mc	Use compact memory model
–mh	Use huge memory model
–ml	Use large memory model
–mm	Use medium memory model
–ms	Use small memory model
–mt	Use tiny memory model
–N	Check for stack overflows
–n*path*	Specifies output directory
–O	Optimize jumps
–o*fname*	Specify object file name
–p	Use Pascal calling conventions
–p–	Use C calling conventions
–r	Use register variables
–S	Generate assembly code output
–U*name*	Undefine a macro name
–u	Generate underscores
–w	Display warning errors (see Table 14-3)
–w–	Do not display warning errors
–y	Embed line numbers into object code
–Z	Register optimization on
–z	Specifies segment names (see Turbo C reference guide)
–1	Generate 80186/80286 instructions
–1–	Do not generate 80186/80286 instructions

Table 14-2.   *Turbo C's Command-Line Options* (continued)

For example, to compile X.C with the stack checked for overflow, your command line would be

```
C>TCC -N X.C
```

The **–w**, enable warning messages option, allows you to set which types of warning messages are displayed by the command-line version of the compiler. By default, the command-line compiler displays the same messages as the integrated version. The exact form of the **–w** command is shown in Table 14-3. For example, to enable the "identifier declared but not used" message, when compiling a file called TEST.C, you would use this command line:

```
TCC -wuse TEST.C
```

Portability Warnings

Error	*Command-Line Option*
Nonportable pointer assignment	–wapt
Nonportable pointer comparison	–wcpt
Constant out of range in comparison	–wrgn
Constant is long	–wcln
Conversion may lose significant digits	–wsig
Nonportable return type conversion	–wrpt
Mixing pointers to signed and unsigned **char**	–wucp

ANSI Violations

Error	*Command-Line Option*
Hexadecimal or octal constant too big	–wbig
Identifier not part of structure	–wstr
Zero length structure	–wzst
Void functions may not return a value	–wvoi
Both return and return of a value used	–wret
Suspicious pointer conversion	–wsus
Undefined structure identifier	–wstu
Redefinition of an identifier is not identical	–wdup

Table 14-3. *The Command-Line Warning Message Options*

Common Errors

Error	*Command-Line Option*
Function should return a value	–wrvl
Unreachable code found in program	–wrch
Code has no effect	–weff
Possible use of an identifier before definition	–wdef
Identifier assigned a value that is never used	–waus
Parameter never used	–wpar
Possibly incorrect assignment	–wpia

Less Common Errors

Error	*Command-Line Option*
Unnecessary & with function or array	–wamp
Identifier declared but never used	–wuse
Ambiguous operators need parentheses	–wamb
Structure passed by value	–wstv
No declaration for function	–wnod
Call to function with no prototype	–wpro

Table 14-3. *The Command-Line Warning Message Options* (continued)

On the other hand, to tell the command-line compiler not to display a suspicious pointer conversion, you would use this option:

```
-w-sus
```

The only warnings that are not on by default are

```
–wamb
–wamp
–wcln
–wnod
–wpro
–wrvl
–wsig
–wstv
–wucp
–wuse
```

What's in a File Name?

The Turbo C command-line version does not require the .C extension. For example, both of these command lines are functionally the same:

```
C>TCC X.C
C>TCC X
```

You can compile a file with an extension other than .C by specifying its extension. For example, to compile X.TMP, the command line would be

```
C>TCC X.TMP
```

You can specify additional object files to be linked with the source file you are compiling by specifying them after the source file. All included files must have been previously compiled and have a .OBJ extension. For example, if your program consists of the files P1, P2, and P3, and if P2 and P3 have already been compiled to .OBJ files, the following command line first compiles P1.C and then links it with P2.OBJ and P3.OBJ:

```
C>TCC P1 P2.OBJ P3.OBJ
```

If you have additional libraries other than those supplied with Turbo C, you can specify them by using the .LIB extension.

In the foregoing example, it was assumed that P2.OBJ and P3.OBJ existed. The way to produce these files starting from their .C source files is to compile each using the **−c** compiler option. This option causes the compiler to create .OBJ files, but no link process takes place.

The executable output file produced by the linker is generally the name of the source file being compiled with an .EXE extension. However, you can specify a different name using the **−e** option. The name that follows the **−e** is the name the compiler uses as the executable file. There can be no spaces between the **−e** and the file name. For example, this compiles the file TEST.C and creates an executable file called MYPROG.EXE.

```
C>TCC -eMYPROG test
```

TLINK: The Turbo C Standalone Linker

Unlike the integrated development environment, which has a built-in linker, the command-line version of Turbo C uses a standalone linker called TLINK. You may not be aware of TLINK because it is loaded automatically by the command-line compiler upon conclusion of a successful compilation. However, it is possible to use TLINK by itself. This section explores TLINK's use as a standalone linker.

TLINK is run completely from the command line and takes this general form:

TLINK *OBJ files, output filename, map filename, libraries*

In the first field you list all the .OBJ files you want to link, using spaces to separate the list. The second field specifies the name of the .EXE file that holds the output. If it is not specified, the name of the first .OBJ file is used. The map section holds the map file. The map file has the extension .MAP. If the map file name is not specified, the name of the .EXE file is used. Finally, the libraries field holds a space-separated list of libraries. For example, the following code links the files MYFILE1.OBJ and MYFILE2.OBJ with TEST.EXE as the output file and MYMAP as the map file name. No libraries are used.

```
TLINK MYFILE1 MYFILE2, TEST, MYMAP,
```

Notice that you need not explicitly use the .EXE or .MAP extensions for the output or map file. TLINK supplies these for you.

Although the output file name and the map file name are optional, you must be sure to include the proper number of commas; otherwise TLINK will not know which field is which.

Linking Turbo C Programs

Some special instructions apply to TLINK when you want to use it manually to link object files produced by Turbo C into an executable program. First, every time a Turbo C program is linked, the first object file on the link line must be one of Turbo C's initialization modules. There is a module for each memory model supported by Turbo C, which must agree with the type of memory model used to compile the program. The module names and their associated memory models are shown here:

Initialization Module Name	Memory Model
C0T.OBJ	Tiny
C0S.OBJ	Small
C0C.OBJ	Compact
C0M.OBJ	Medium
C0L.OBJ	Large
C0H.OBJ	Huge

You also need to ensure that the proper standard library file is linked. Like the initialization module, it must agree with the memory model used to compile the program. The library files are shown here:

Library Name	Memory Model
CT.LIB	Tiny
CS.LIB	Small
CC.LIB	Compact
CM.LIB	Medium
CL.LIB	Large
CH.LIB	Huge

If your program uses any floating point, you must include either EMU.LIB or FP87.LIB on the link line. If you have an 8087/80287, use FP87.LIB; otherwise use EMU.LIB.

The mathematics routines are contained in MATHx.LIB where x is one of the following letters and corresponds to the proper memory model: **t, s, c, m, l, h.** Remember, the memory model used to compile your program must agree with that of the library.

Given this information, to link a program file called TCTEST that uses floating-point emulation (but no math routines) using the small memory model, use the following link line:

```
TLINK \TC\LIB\C0S TCTEST, , , EMU \TC\LIB\CS
```

Option	Meaning
/c	Case is significant in PUBLIC and EXTRN symbols
/d	Display warning if duplicate symbols are found in the libraries
/e	Do not use extended keywords
/i	Initialize all segments
/l	Include source line numbers for debugging
/m	Include public symbols in map file
/n	Ignore the default libraries
/s	Include detailed segment map in map file
/t	Create a .COM rather than an .EXE file (tiny model only)
/v	Include complete debugging information
/x	Do not create a map file
/3	Use full 32-bit processing

Table 14-4.   *The TLINK Options*

TLINK Options

TLINK supports twelve options, summarized in Table 14-4. Each option consists of a slash followed by a letter. These options can be placed at any point in the TLINK command line. For example, the following link line does not produce a map file and causes source code line numbers to be included in the executable file:

```
TLINK /x /l \TC\LIB\C0s MYFILE, , , \TC\LIB\CS
```

If you have compiled your C program using the tiny memory model, you can create a .COM rather than an .EXE file if you specify the /t linker option.

Part *III*

The Library

Part Three examines the function library included with all versions of Turbo/Borland C/C++. Chapter 15 begins with a discussion of linking, libraries, and header files. Chapters 16 through 24 describe the functions found in the library, with each chapter concentrating on a specific group.

The library functions discussed in this part include all those currently defined by Turbo/Borland C++. If you have an older compiler, a small number of the functions discussed here will be unavailable in your version.

The class libraries supplied by Turbo/Borland C++ are not discussed in this part. A description of these items can be found in Part Four.

Chapter 15

Linking, Libraries, and Header Files

The creation of a C or C++ compiler involves two major efforts. The first is the construction of the compiler itself. The second is the creation of the function library. Because the Turbo/Borland library contains so many functions, it is safe to assume that it requires a substantial programming effort. (Consider that even a description of functions requires several hundred pages!) Every C or C++ program relies upon library functions to perform many of the tasks carried out by the program. Because of the fundamental role that the library plays in your program it is important to have an overview of how the library works. Specifically, you need to understand how the linker works, how libraries differ from object files, and the role of header files. These items are examined here.

The Linker

The output of the compiler is a relocatable object file and the output of the linker is an executable file. The role the linker plays is twofold. First, it physically combines the files specified in the link list into one program file. Second, it resolves external references and memory addresses. An external reference is created any time the code in one file refers to code found in another file. This may be through either a function call or a reference to a global variable. For example, when the two files shown here are linked together, file two's reference to **count** must be resolved. It is the linker that "tells" the code in file two where **count** will be found in memory.

File one:

```
int count;
extern void display(void);

main(void)
{
  count = 10;
  display();
  return 0;
}
```

File two:

```
#include <stdio.h>
extern int count;

void display(void)
{
  printf("%d", count);
}
```

In a similar fashion, the linker also "tells" file one where the function **display( )** is located so that it may be called.

When the compiler generates the object code for file two, it substitutes a place-holder for the address of **count** because it has no way of knowing where **count** would be located in memory. The same sort of thing occurs when file one is compiled. The address of **display( )** is not known so a placeholder is used. This process forms the basis for *relocatable code*. When the files are joined by the linker, the placeholders are replaced with relative addresses.

To better understand relocatable code, you must first understand *absolute code*. Although it is seldom used today, in the earlier days of computers, it was not uncommon for a program to be compiled to run at a specific memory location. When compiled in this way, all addresses are fixed at compile time. Because the addresses are fixed, the program can only be loaded into and executed in exactly one region of memory: the one for which it was compiled. *Relocatable code*, on the other hand, is compiled in such a way that the address information is not fixed. When making a relocatable object file, the linker assigns the address of each call, jump, or global variable an offset. When the file is loaded into memory for execution, the loader automatically resolves the offsets into addresses that will work for the location in memory into which it is being loaded. This means that a relocatable program can be loaded into and run from many different memory locations.

Library Files Versus Object Files

Although libraries are similar to object files they have one crucial difference: not all the code in the library is added to your program. When you link a program that consists of several object files, all the code in each object file becomes part of the finished executable program. This happens whether the code is actually used or not. In other words, all object files specified at link time are "added together" to form the program. However, this is not the case with library files.

A library is a collection of functions. Unlike an object file, a library file stores the name of each function, the function's object code, and relocation information necessary to the linking process. When your program references a function contained in a library, the linker looks up that function and adds that code to your program. In this way, only functions that you actually use in your program are added to the executable file.

Since the Turbo/Borland C/C++ functions are contained in a library, only those actually used by your program will be included in your program's executable code. (If they were in object files, every program you wrote would be several hundred thousand bytes long!)

The C/C++ Standard Library

The ANSI C standard has defined both the content and the form of the C standard library. All Turbo and Borland C and C++ compilers supply all functions defined by the ANSI standard. However, to allow the fullest possible use and control of the computer, Turbo/Borland C/C++ contains many additional functions. For example, a complete set of screen and graphics functions are included even though these functions are not defined by the ANSI standard. As long as you will not be porting the programs you write to a new environment, it is perfectly fine to use these enhanced functions. This book discusses all functions included in the Turbo/Borland C/C++ library.

Header Files

Many functions found in the library work with their own specific data types and structures to which your program must have access. These structures and types are defined in *header files* supplied with the compiler and they must be included (using **#include**) in any file that uses the specific functions to which they refer. In addition, all functions in the library have their prototypes defined in a header file. This is done for two reasons. First, in C++, all functions must be prototyped. Second, although in C, prototyping is an option, its use is suggested because it provides a means of stronger type checking. In a C program, by including the header files that correspond to the standard functions used by your program, you can catch potential type-mismatch errors. For example, including **string.h**, the string function's header, will cause the following code to produce a warning message when compiled.

```
#include <string.h>

char s1[20] = "hello ";
char s2[] = "there.";

main(void)
{
  int p;

  p = strcat(s1, s2);
  return 0;
}
```

Because **strcat( )** is declared as returning a character pointer in its header file, Turbo C can now flag as a possible error the assignment of that pointer to the integer **p**.

Remember, although the inclusion of many header files is optional (yet advisable) in C, they must be included in all C++ programs.

The header files supplied with Turbo/Borland C/C++ are shown in Table 15-1. In the remaining chapters of Part Three, the description of each function will specify which header file is associated with it.

Header File	Purpose or Use
ALLOC.H	Dynamic allocation functions
ASSERT.H	Defines the **assert( )** macro (ANSI C)
BCD.H	Defines the bcd class (C++)
BIOS.H	ROM-BIOS functions
COMPLEX.H	Defines the complex number class (C++)
CONIO.H	Screen-handling functions
CONSTREA.H	Console I/O (C++)
CTYPE.H	Character-handling functions (ANSI C)
DIR.H	Directory-handling functions

Table 15-1.   *The Standard Header Files*

Header File	Purpose or Use
DIRECT.H	Directory management (C++)
DIRENT.H	Support for POSIX (C++)
DOS.H	DOS interfacing functions
ERRNO.H	Defines error codes (ANSI C)
FCNTL.H	Defines constants used by **open( )** function
FLOAT.H	Defines implementation-dependent floating-point values (ANSI C)
FSTREAM.H	File I/O class definitions (C++)
GENERIC.H	Macros for making generic class declarations (C++)
GRAPHICS.H	Graphics functions
IO.H	UNIX-like I/O routines
IOMANIP.H	Defines I/O manipulators (C++)
IOSTREAM.H	Defines I/O stream class (C++)
LIMITS.H	Defines various implementation-dependent limits (ANSI C)
LOCALE.H	Country and language specific functions (ANSI C)
MALLOC.H	Dynamic allocation
MATH.H	Various definitions used by the math library (ANSI C)
MEM.H	Memory manipulation functions
MEMORY.H	Same as MEM.H
NEW.H	Allows alternative function to be called when NEW fails
PROCESS.H	**Spawn( )** and **exec( )** functions
SEARCH.H	Searching and sorting
SETJMP.H	Nonlocal jumps (ANSI C)
SHARE.H	File sharing
SIGNAL.H	Defines signal values (ANSI C)
STDARG.H	Variable-length argument lists (ANSI C)
STDDEF.H	Defines some commonly used constants (ANSI C)
STDIO.H	Declarations for standard I/O streams (ANSI C)
STDIOSTR.H	Stream classes that use FILE structures (C++)
STDLIB.H	Miscellaneous declarations (ANSI C)
STREAM.H	Defines old stream class (C++)

Table 15-1.   *The Standard Header Files* (continued)

Header File	Purpose or Use
STRING.H	String handling (ANSI C)
STRSTREA.H	**istrstream** and **ostrstream** class definitions (C++)
SYS\LOCKING	File locking
SYS\STAT.H	Defines constants for file opening
SYS\TIMEB.H	Declarations needed for the **ftime( )** function.
SYS\TYPES.H	Type declarations used with time functions.
TIME.H	System time functions (ANSI C)
UTIME.H	Declares the **utime( )** function
VALUES.H	Machine-dependent constants
VARARGS.H	Variable length arguments (obsolete)

Table 15-1.   *The Standard Header Files* (continued)

Macros in Header Files

Many of the library functions are not actually functions at all but rather parameterized macro definitions contained in a header file. Generally, this is of little consequence, but this distinction will be pointed out when discussing such "functions."

Chapter *16*

I/O Functions

The functions that make up the C input/output system can be grouped into three major categories: console I/O, buffered file I/O, and the UNIX-like unbuffered file I/O. Strictly speaking, console I/O is made up of functions that are special-case versions of the more general functions found in the buffered file system. However, in general usage, console I/O and file I/O have enough differences that they are often thought of as conceptually separate, especially by beginners. In the first part of this book, the console and buffered file I/O were treated as somewhat separate as a means of emphasizing their differences. In this section, however, no such distinction is made because they use a common logical interface.

The unbuffered UNIX-like I/O system is not defined by the ANSI C standard and is expected to decline in popularity. The UNIX-like I/O system functions are included in Turbo/Borland C/C++'s library to ensure compatibility with existing programs.

The I/O Functions

This chapter describes each of the I/O functions, including the UNIX-like ones. (Remember that the nonstandard UNIX-like I/O functions include **open( )**, **close( )**, **read( )**, **write( )**, **creat( )**, and **unlink( )**.)

For the ANSI C standard I/O system functions, the header **stdio.h** is required. For the UNIX-like routines the header **io.h** is required.

Many of the I/O functions set the predefined global integer variable **errno** to an appropriate error code when an error occurs. This variable is declared in **errno.h**.

int access(const char *filename, int mode)

Description

The prototype for **access( )** is found in **io.h**.

The **access( )** function belongs to the UNIX-like file system and is not defined by the ANSI C standard. It is used to see if a file exists. It can also be used to tell whether the file is write-protected and if it can be executed. The name of the file in question is pointed to by *filename*. The value of *mode* determines exactly how **access( )** functions. The legal values are

0	Check for file existence
1	Check for executable file
2	Check for write access
4	Check for read access
6	Check for read/write access

The **access( )** function returns 0 if the specified access is allowed; otherwise it returns −1. Upon failure, the predefined global variable **errno** is set to one of these values:

ENOENT	File not found
EACCES	Access denied

Example

The following program checks to see if the file **TEST.TST** is present in the current working directory:

```
#include <stdio.h>
#include <io.h>

main(void)
{
  if(!access("TEST.TST", 0))
    printf("file present");
  else
    printf("file not found");
  return 0;
}
```

Related Functions

chmod( )

int _chmod (const char *filename, int get_set, int attrib)

Description

The prototype for **_chmod( )** is found in **io.h**.

The **_chmod( )** function is not defined by the ANSI C standard. It is used to read or set the attribute byte associated with the file pointed to by *filename* as allowed by DOS. If *get_set* is 0, **_chmod( )** returns the current file attribute and *attrib* is not used. If *get_set* is 1, the file attribute is set to the value of *attrib*. The *attrib* argument can be one of these macros:

FA_RDONLY	Set file to read only
FA_HIDDEN	Make hidden file
FA_SYSTEM	Mark as a system file
FA_LABEL	Make volume label
FA_DIREC	Make directory
FA_ARCH	Mark as archive

The **_chmod( )** function returns the file attribute if successful. Upon failure, it returns a –1 and sets **errno** to either **ENOENT** if the file does not exist or **EACCES** if access to the file is denied.

Example

This line of code sets the file **TEST.TST** to read only.

```
if(_chmod("TEST.TST", 1, FA_RDONLY)==FA_RDONLY)
  printf("file set to read-only mode");
```

Related Functions

chmod( ), **access( )**

int chmod(const char *filename, int mode)

Description

The prototype for **chmod( )** is found in **io.h**.

The **chmod( )** function is not defined by the ANSI C standard. It changes the access mode of the file pointed to by *filename* to that specified by *mode*. The value of *mode* must be one or both of the macros **S_IWRITE** and **S_IREAD**, which correspond to write access and read access, respectively. To change a file's mode to read/write status, call **chmod( )** with *mode* set to **S_IWRITE | S_IREAD**.

The **chmod( )** function returns 0 if successful and –1 if unsuccessful.

Example

This call to **chmod( )** attempts to set the file **TEST.TST** to read/write access:

```
if(!chmod("TEST.TST", S_IREAD | S_IWRITE))
  printf("file set to read/write access");
```

Related Functions

access( ), **_chmod( )**

int chsize(char handle, long size)

Description

The prototype for **chsize( )** is found in **io.h**.

The **chsize( )** function is not defined by the ANSI C standard. It extends or truncates the file specified by *handle* to the value of *size*.

The **chsize( )** function returns 0 if successful. Upon failure, it returns –1 and **errno** is set to one of the following:

EACCES	Access denied
EBADF	Bad file handle

Example

This call to **chsize( )** attempts to change the size of **TEST.TST**.

```
/*
 Assume that a file associated with handle
 has been opened.
*/

if(!chsize(handle, 256))
  printf("file size is now 256 bytes.");
```

Related Functions

open( ), **close( )**, **creat( )**

void clearerr(FILE *stream)

Description

The prototype for **clearerr( )** is found in **stdio.h**.

The **clearerr( )** function is used to reset the file error flag pointed to by *stream* to 0 (off). The end-of-file indicator is also reset.

The error flags for each stream are initially set to 0 by a successful call to **fopen( )**. Once an error has occurred, the flags stay set until an explicit call to either **clearerr( )** or **rewind( )** is made.

File errors can occur for a wide variety of reasons, many of which are system dependent. The exact nature of the error can be determined by calling **perror( )**, which displays which error has occurred (see **perror( )**).

Example

This program copies one file to another. If an error is encountered, a message is printed and the error is cleared.

```
#include <stdio.h>
#include <stdlib.h>

main(int argc, char *argv[])  /* copy one file to another */
{
  FILE *in, *out;
  char ch;

  if(argc!=3) {
    printf("You forgot to enter a filename\n");
    exit(0);
  }

  if((in=fopen(argv[1],"rb")) == NULL) {
    printf("cannot open file\n");
    exit(0);
  }
  if((out=fopen(argv[2],"wb")) == NULL) {
    printf("cannot open file\n");
    exit(0);
  }

  while(!feof(in)) {
    ch = getc(in);
    if(ferror(in)) {
```

```
      printf("read error");
      clearerr(in);
    } else {
      putc(ch, out);
      if(ferror(out)) {
        printf("write error");
        clearerr(out);
      }
    }
  }
  fclose(in);
  fclose(out);
  return 0;
}
```

Related Functions

feof( ), **ferror( )**, **perror( )**

int close(int fd)
int _close(int fd)

Description

The prototypes for **close( )** and **_close( )** are found in **io.h**.

The **close( )** function belongs to the UNIX-like file system and is not defined by the ANSI C standard. When **close( )** is called with a valid file descriptor, it closes the file associated with it and flushes the write buffers if applicable. (File descriptors are created through a successful call to **open( )** or **creat( )** and do not relate to streams or file pointers.)

When successful, **close( )** returns a 0; if unsuccessful, it returns a –1. Although there are several reasons why you might not be able to close a file, the most common is the premature removal of the medium. For example, if you remove a diskette from the drive before the file is closed, an error will result.

The **_close( )** function works exactly like **close( )**.

Example

This program opens and closes a file using the UNIX-like file system:

```
#include <stdio.h>
#include <fcntl.h>
#include <sys\stat.h>
#include <io.h>
#include <stdlib.h>
```

```
main(int argc, char *argv[])
{
  int fd;

  if((fd=open(argv[1],O_RDONLY))==-1) {
    printf("cannot open file");
    exit(1);
  }

  printf("file is existent\n");

  if(close(fd))
    printf("error in closing file\n");
  return 0;
}
```

Related Functions

open( ), **creat( )**, **read( )**, **write( )**, **unlink( )**

int creat(const char *filename, int pmode)
int _creat(const char *filename, int attrib)
int creatnew(const char *filename, int attrib)
int creattemp(const char *filename, int attrib)

Description

The prototypes for these functions are found in **io.h**.

The **creat( )** function is part of the UNIX-like file system and is not defined by the ANSI C standard. Its purpose is to create a new file with the name pointed to by *filename* and to open it for writing. On success **creat( )** returns a file descriptor that is greater than or equal to 0; on failure it returns a –1. (File descriptors are integers and do not relate to streams or file pointers.)

The value of *pmode* determines the file's access setting, sometimes called its *permission mode*. The value of *pmode* is highly dependent upon the operating system. For DOS, its values can be **S_IWRITE** or **S_IREAD**. If *pmode* is set to **S_IREAD**, a read-only file is created. If it is set to **S_IWRITE**, a writable file is created. You can OR these values together to create a read/write file.

If, at the time of the call to **creat( )**, the specified file already exists, it is erased and all previous contents are lost unless the original file was write-protected.

The **_creat( )** function works like **creat( )** but uses a DOS attribute byte. The *attrib* argument may be one of these macros:

FA_RDONLY	Set file to read only
FA_HIDDEN	Make hidden file
FA_SYSTEM	Mark as a system file

The **creatnew( )** function is the same as **_creat( )** except that if the file already exists on disk, **creatnew( )** returns an error and does not erase the original file.

The **creattemp( )** function is used to create a unique temporary file. You call **creattemp( )** with *filename* pointing to the path name ending with a backslash. Upon return, *filename* contains the name of a unique file. You must make sure that *filename* is large enough to hold the file name.

In the case of an error in any of these functions, **errno** is set to one of these values:

ENOENT	Path or file does not exist
EMFILE	Too many files are open
EACCES	Access denied
EEXIST	File exists (**creatnew( )** only)

Example

The following code fragment creates a file called **test**:

```
#include <stdio.h>
#include <sys\stat.h>
#include <io.h>
#include <stdlib.h>

main(void)
{
  int fd;

  if((fd=creat("test",S_IWRITE))==-1) {
    printf("cannot open file\n");
    exit(1);
  }
  .
  .
  .
```

Related Functions

open( ), **close( )**, **read( )**, **write( )**, **unlink( )**, **eof( )**

int dup(int handle)
int dup2(int old_handle, int new_handle)

Description

The prototypes for **dup( )** and **dup2( )** are found in **io.h**.

The **dup( )** function returns a new file descriptor that fully describes (i.e., duplicates) the state of the file associated with *handle*. It returns nonnegative on success; –1 on failure.

The **dup2( )** function duplicates *old_handle* as *new_handle*. If there is a file associated with *new_handle* prior to the call to **dup2( )**, it is closed. It returns 0 if successful, –1 when an error occurs. In the case of an error, **errno** is set to one of these values:

EMFILE	Too many files are open
EBADF	Bad file handle

Example

This fragment assigns **fp2** a new file descriptor:

```
FILE *fp, *fp2;
  .
  .
  .
fp2 = dup(fp);
```

Related Functions

close( ), **creat( )**

int eof(int fd)

Description

The prototype for **eof( )** is found in **io.h**.

The **eof( )** function is part of the UNIX-like file system and is not defined by the ANSI C standard. When called with a valid file descriptor, **eof( )** returns 1 if the end of the file has been reached; otherwise it returns a 0. If an error has occurred, it returns a –1 and **errno** is set to **EBADF** (bad file number).

Example

The following program displays a text file on the console using **eof( )** to determine when the end of the file has been reached.

```
#include <stdio.h>
#include <io.h>
#include <fcntl.h>
#include <stdlib.h>

main(int argc, char *argv[])
{
  int fd;
  char ch;

  if((fd=open(argv[1],O_RDWR))==-1) {
    printf("cannot open file\n");
    exit(1);
  }

  while(!eof(fd)) {
    read(fd, &ch, 1);   /* read one char at a time */
    printf("%c", ch);
  }

  close(fd);
  return 0;
}
```

Related Functions

open( ), **close( )**, **read( )**, **write( )**, **unlink( )**

int fclose(FILE *stream)
int fcloseall(void)

Description

The prototypes for **fclose( )** and **fcloseall( )** are found in **stdio.h**.

The **fclose( )** function closes the file associated with *stream* and flushes its buffer. After an **fclose( )**, *stream* is no longer connected with the file and any automatically allocated buffers are deallocated.

If **fclose( )** is successful, a 0 is returned; otherwise a non-0 number is returned. Trying to close a file that has already been closed is an error.

The **fcloseall( )** function closes all open streams except **stdin**, **stdout**, **stdaux**, **stdprn**, and **stderr**. It is not defined by the ANSI C standard.

Example

The following code opens and closes a file:

```
#include <stdio.h>
#include <stdlib.h>

main(void)
{
  FILE *fp;

  if((fp=fopen("test","rb"))==NULL) {
    printf("cannot open file\n");
    exit(1);
  }
  .
  .
  .
  if(fclose(fp))
    printf("file close error\n");
  return 0;
}
```

Related Functions

fopen( ), freopen( ), fflush( )

FILE *fdopen(int handle, char *mode)

Description

The prototype for **fdopen( )** is found in **stdio.h**.

The **fdopen( )** function is not defined by the ANSI C standard. It returns a stream that shares the same file that is associated with *handle,* where *handle* is a valid file descriptor obtained through a call to one of the UNIX-like I/O routines. In essence, **fdopen( )** is a bridge between the ANSI stream-based file system and the UNIX-like file system. The value of *mode* must be the same as that of the mode that originally opened the file.

See **open( )** and **fopen( )** for details.

Related Functions

open( ), **fopen( )**, **creat( )**

int feof(FILE *stream)

Description

The prototype for **feof( )** is found in **stdio.h**.

The **feof( )** macro checks the file position indicator to determine if the end of the file associated with *stream* has been reached. A non-0 value is returned if the file position indicator is at the end of the file; a 0 is returned otherwise.

Once the end of the file has been reached, subsequent read operations return **EOF** until either **rewind( )** is called or the file position indicator is moved using **fseek( )**.

The **feof( )** macro is particularly useful when working with binary files because the end-of-file marker is also a valid binary integer. You must make explicit calls to **feof( )** rather than simply testing the return value of **getc( )**, for example, to determine when the end of the file has been reached.

Example

This code fragment shows the proper way to read to the end of a binary file:

```
/*
  Assume that fp has been opened as a binary file
  for read operations.
*/
while(!feof(fp)) getc(fp);
```

Related Functions

clearerr( ), **ferror( )**, **perror( )**, **putc( )**, **getc( )**

int ferror(FILE *stream)

Description

The prototype for the **ferror( )** macro is found in **stdio.h**.

The **ferror( )** function checks for a file error on the given *stream*. A return value of 0 indicates that no error has occurred while a non-0 value indicates an error.

The error flags associated with *stream* stay set until either the file is closed, or **rewind( )** or **clearerr( )** is called.

Use the **perror( )** function to determine the exact nature of the error.

Example

The following code fragment aborts program execution if a file error occurs:

```
/*
  Assume that fp points to a stream opened for write
  operations.
*/

while(!done) {
  putc(info,fp);
  if(ferror(fp)) {
    printf("file error\n");
    exit(1);
  }
  .
  .
  .
}
```

Related Functions

clearerr( ), **feof( )**, **perror( )**

int fflush(FILE *stream)

Description

The prototype for **fflush( )** is found in **stdio.h**.

If *stream* is associated with a file opened for writing, a call to **fflush( )** causes the contents of the output buffer to be physically written to the file. If *stream* points to an input file, the input buffer is cleared. In either case the file remains open.

A return value of 0 indicates success, while non-0 means a write error has occurred.

All buffers are automatically flushed upon normal termination of the program or when they are full. Closing a file flushes its buffer.

Example

The following code fragment flushes the buffer after each write operation.

```
/*
  Assume that fp is associated with an output file.
*/
```

```
      .
      .
      .
fwrite(buf,sizeof(data_type),1,fp);
fflush(fp);
      .
      .
      .
```

Related Functions

fclose( ), **fopen( )**, **flushall( )**, **fwrite( )**

int fgetc(FILE *stream)

Description

The prototype for **fgetc( )** is found in **stdio.h**.

The **fgetc( )** function returns the next character from the input *stream* from the current position and increments the file position indicator.

If the end of the file is reached, **fgetc( )** returns **EOF**. However, since **EOF** is a valid integer value, when working with binary files you must use **feof( )** to check for end-of-file. If **fgetc( )** encounters an error, **EOF** is also returned. Again, when working with binary files you must use **ferror( )** to check for file errors.

Example

This program reads and displays the contents of a binary file:

```
#include <stdio.h>
#include <stdlib.h>

main(int argc, char *argv[])
{
  FILE *fp;
  char ch;

  if((fp=fopen(argv[1],"r"))==NULL) {
    printf("cannot open file\n");
    exit(1);
}

  while((ch=fgetc(fp))!=EOF) {
    printf("%c",ch);
```

```
}
  fclose(fp);
  return 0;
}
```

Related Functions

fputc( ), **getc( )**, **putc( )**, **fopen( )**

int fgetchar(void)

Description

The prototype for **fgetchar( )** is found in **stdio.h**.

The **fgetchar( )** macro is defined as **fgetc(stdin)**. Refer to **fgetc( )** for details.

int *fgetpos(FILE *stream, fpos_t *pos)

Description

The prototype for **fgetpos( )** is found in **stdio.h**.

The **fgetpos( )** function stores the current location of the file pointer associated with *stream* in the variable pointed to by *pos*. The type **fpos_t** is defined in **stdio.h**.

If successful, **fgetpos( )** returns 0; upon failure, a value other than 0 is returned and **errno** is set to one of the following values:

EBADF	Bad file stream
EINVAL	Invalid argument

Example

This program uses **fgetpos( )** to display the current file position:

```
#include <stdio.h>
#include <stdlib.h>
main(int argc, char *argv[])
{
  FILE *fp;
  long l;
  int  i;
  fpos_t *pos;  /* fpos_t is defined in stdio.h */
  pos = &l;
```

```
if((fp=fopen(argv[1],"w+"))==NULL) {
  printf("cannot open file\n");
  exit(1);
}

for (i=0; i<10; i++)
  fputc('Z', fp);  /* write 10 Z's to the file */
fgetpos(fp, pos);

printf("We are now at position %ld in the file.", *pos);
fclose(fp);
return 0;
}
```

Related Functions

fsetpos( ), fseek( ), ftell( )

char *fgets(char *str, int num, FILE *stream)

Description

The prototype for **fgets( )** is found in **stdio.h**.

The **fgets( )** function reads up to *num–1* characters from *stream* and places them into the character array pointed to by *str*. Characters are read until either a newline or an **EOF** is received or until the specified limit is reached. After the characters have been read, a null is placed in the array immediately after the last character read. A newline character will be retained and will be part of *str*.

If successful, **fgets( )** returns *str;* a null pointer is returned upon failure. If a read error occurs, the contents of the array pointed to by *str* are indeterminate. Because a null pointer is returned when either an error occurs or the end of the file is reached, you should use **feof( )** or **ferror( )** to determine what has actually happened.

Example

This program uses **fgets( )** to display the contents of the text file specified in the first command-line argument:

```
#include <stdio.h>
#include <stdlib.h>

main(int argc, char *argv[])
{
  FILE *fp;
  char str[128];
```

```
if((fp=fopen(argv[1],"r"))==NULL) {
  printf("cannot open file\n");
  exit(1);
}

while(!feof(fp)) {
  if(fgets(str,126,fp))
    printf("%s",str);
}
fclose(fp);
return 0;
}
```

Related Functions

fputs( ), **fgetc( )**, **gets( )**, **puts( )**

long filelength(int handle)

Description

The prototype for **filelength( )** is found in **io.h**.

The **filelength( )** function is not defined by the ANSI C standard. It returns the length, in bytes, of the file associated with the file descriptor *handle*. Remember that the return value is of type **long.** If an error occurs, –1L is returned and **errno** is set to **EBADF**, which means bad file handle.

Example

This fragment prints the length of a file whose file descriptor is **fd**:

```
printf("The file is %ld bytes long.", filelength(fd));
```

Related Functions

open( )

int fileno(FILE *stream)

Description

The prototype for the **fileno( )** macro is found in **stdio.h**.

The **fileno( )** function is not defined by the ANSI C standard. It is used to return a file descriptor to the specified stream.

Example

After this fragment has executed, **fd** is associated with the file pointed to by **stream**:

```
FILE *stream;
int fd;

if(!(stream=fopen("TEST", "r"))) {
  printf("cannot open TEST file");
  exit(1);
}

fd = fileno(stream);
```

Related Functions

fdopen( )

int flushall(void)

Description

The prototype for **flushall( )** is found in **stdio.h**. It is not defined by the ANSI C standard.

A call to **flushall( )** causes the contents of all the output buffers associated with file streams to be physically written to their corresponding files and all the input buffers to be cleared. All streams remain open.

The number of open streams is returned.

All buffers are automatically flushed upon normal termination of the program or when they are full. Also, closing a file flushes its buffer.

Example

The following code fragment flushes all buffers after each write operation:

```
/*
  Assume that fp is associated with an output file.
*/
  .
  .
  .
```

```
fwrite(buf,sizeof(data_type),1,fp);
flushall();
    .
    .
    .
```

Related Functions

fclose( ), **fopen( )**, **fcloseall( )**, **fflush( )**

FILE *fopen(const char *fname, const char *mode)

Description

The prototype for **fopen( )** is found in **stdio.h**.

The **fopen( )** function opens a file whose name is pointed to by *fname* and returns the stream that is associated with it. The type of operations that are allowed on the file are defined by the value of *mode*. The legal values for *mode* are shown in Table 16-1. The parameter *fname* must be a string of characters that constitutes a valid file name and can include a path specification.

If **fopen( )** is successful in opening the specified file, a **FILE** pointer is returned. If the file cannot be opened, a null pointer is returned.

As Table 16-1 shows, a file can be opened in either text or binary mode. In text mode, carriage return, linefeed sequences are translated to newline characters on input. On output, the reverse occurs: newlines are translated to carriage return, linefeeds. No such translations occur on binary files.

If the *mode* string does not specify either a **b** (for binary) or a **t** (for text), the type of file opened is determined by the value of the built-in global variable **_fmode**. By default, **_fmode** is **O_TEXT**, which means text mode. It can be set to **O_BINARY**, which means binary mode. These macros are defined in **fcntl.h**.

One correct method of opening a file is illustrated by this code fragment:

```
FILE *fp;

if ((fp = fopen("test","w"))==NULL) {
  printf("cannot open file\n");
  exit(1);
}
```

This method detects any error in opening a file, such as a write-protected or full disk, before attempting to write to it. A null, which is 0, is used because no file pointer ever has that value. **NULL** is defined in **stdio.h**.

Mode	Meaning
"r"	Open file for reading
"w"	Create a file for writing
"a"	Append to file
"rb"	Open binary file for reading
"wb"	Create binary file for writing
"ab"	Append to a binary file
"r+"	Open file for read/write
"w+"	Create file for read/write
"a+"	Open file for read/write
"rb+"	Open binary file for read/write
"wb+"	Create binary file for read/write
"ab+"	Open binary file for read/write
"rt"	Open a text file for reading
"wt"	Create a text file for writing
"at"	Append to a text file
"r+t"	Open a text file for read/write
"w+t"	Create a text file for read/write
"a+t"	Open or create a text file for read/write

Table 16-1.   *Legal Values for Mode*

If you use **fopen( )** to open a file for write operations, any preexisting file by that name is erased, and a new file is started. If no file by that name exists, one is created. If you want to add to the end of the file, you must use mode **a**. If the file does not exist, an error is returned. Opening a file for read operations requires an existing file. If no file exists, an error is returned. Finally, if a file is opened for read/write operations, it is not erased if it exists; however, if no file exists, one is created.

Example

This fragment opens a file called **test** for binary read/write operations:

```
FILE *fp;

if(!(fp=fopen("test","rb+"))) {
  printf("cannot open file\n");
  exit(1);
}
```

Related Functions

fclose( ), **fread( )**, **fwrite( )**, **putc( )**, **getc( )**

int fprintf(FILE *stream, const char *format, arg-list)

Description

The prototype for **fprintf( )** is found in **stdio.h**.

The **fprintf( )** function outputs the values of the arguments that make up *arg-list* as specified in the *format* string to the stream pointed to by *stream*. The return value is the number of characters actually printed. If an error occurs, a negative number is returned.

The operations of the format control string and commands are identical to those in **printf( )**; see the **printf( )** function for a complete description.

Example

This program creates a file called **test** and writes the string "this is a test 10 20.01" into the file using **fprintf( )** to format the data:

```
#include <stdio.h>
#include <stdlib.h>

main(void)
{
  FILE *fp;

  if(!(fp=fopen("test","w"))) {
    printf("cannot open file\n");
    exit(1);
  }

  fprintf(fp, "this is a test %d %f", 10, 20.01);
```

```
  fclose(fp);
  return 0;
}
```

Related Functions

printf( ), fscanf( )

int fputc(int ch, FILE *stream)

Description

The prototype for **fputc( )** is found in **stdio.h**.

The **fputc( )** function writes the character *ch* to the specified stream at the current file position and then increments the file position indicator. Even though *ch* is declared to be an **int**, it is converted by **fputc( )** into an **unsigned char**. Because all character arguments are elevated to integers at the time of the call, you generally see character variables used as arguments. If an integer is used, the high-order byte is simply discarded.

The value returned by **fputc( )** is the value of the character written. If an error occurs, **EOF** is returned. For files opened for binary operations, **EOF** may be a valid character, and the function **ferror( )** must be used to determine whether an error has actually occurred.

Example

This function writes the contents of a string to the specified stream:

```
write_string(char *str, FILE *fp)
{
  while(*str) if(!ferror(fp)) fputc(*str++, fp);
}
```

Related Functions

fgetc( ), fopen( ), fprintf( ), fread( ), fwrite( )

int fputchar(int ch)

Description

The prototype for **fputchar( )** is found in **stdio.h**.

The **fputchar( )** function writes the character *ch* to **stdout**. Even though *ch* is declared to be an **int**, it is converted by **fputchar( )** into an **unsigned char**. Because all character arguments are elevated to integers at the time of the call, you generally see character variables used as arguments. If an integer is used, the high-order byte is simply discarded. A call to **fputchar( )** is the functional equivalent of a call to **fputc(ch, stdout)**.

The value returned by **fputchar( )** is the value of the character written. If an error occurs, **EOF** is returned. For files opened for binary operations, **EOF** may be a valid character and the function **ferror( )** must be used to determine whether an error has actually occurred.

Example

This function writes the contents of a string to **stdout**:

```
write_string(char *str)
{
  while(*str) if(!ferror(fp)) fputchar(*str++);
}
```

Related Functions

fgetc( ), **fopen( )**, **fprintf( )**, **fread( )**, **fwrite( )**

int fputs(const char *str, FILE *stream)

Description

The prototype for **fputs( )** is found in **stdio.h**.

The **fputs( )** function writes the contents of the string pointed to by *str* to the specified stream. The null terminator is not written.

The **fputs( )** function returns the last character written on success, **EOF** on failure.

If the stream is opened in text mode, certain character translations may take place. This means that there may not be a one-to-one mapping of the string onto the file. However, if it is opened in binary mode, no character translations occur and a one-to-one mapping exists between the string and the file.

Example

This code fragment writes the string "this is a test" to the stream pointed to by **fp**.

```
fputs("this is a test",fp);
```

Related Functions

fgets( ), **gets( )**, **puts( )**, **fprintf( )**, **fscanf( )**

size_t fread(void *buf, size_t size, size_t count, FILE *stream)

Description

The prototype for **fread( )** is found in **stdio.h**.

The **fread( )** function reads *count* number of objects—each object being *size* number of characters in length—from the stream pointed to by *stream* and places them in the character array pointed to by *buf*. The file position indicator is advanced by the number of characters read.

The **fread( )** function returns the number of items actually read. If fewer items are read than are requested in the call, either an error has occurred or the end of the file has been reached. You must use **feof( )** or **ferror( )** to determine what has taken place.

If the stream is opened for text operations, then carriage return, linefeed sequences are automatically translated into newlines.

Example

This program reads ten floating point numbers from a disk file called **test** into the array **bal**:

```
#include <stdio.h>
#include <stdlib.h>

main(void)
{
  FILE *fp;
  float bal[10];

  if(!(fp=fopen("test","rb"))) {
    printf("cannot open file\n");
    exit(1);
  }

  if(fread(bal, sizeof(float), 10, fp)!=10) {
    if(feof(fp)) printf("premature end of file");
    else printf("file read error");
  }

  fclose(fp);
  return 0;
}
```

Related Functions

fwrite( ), **fopen( )**, **fscanf( )**, **fgetc( )**, **getc( )**

FILE *freopen(const char *fname, const char *mode, FILE *stream)

Description

The prototype for **freopen( )** is found in **stdio.h**.

The **freopen( )** function is used to associate an existing stream with a different file. The new file's name is pointed to by *fname,* the access mode is pointed to by *mode,* and the stream to be reassigned is pointed to by *stream.* The string *mode* uses the same format as **fopen( )**; a complete discussion is found in the **fopen( )** description.

When called, **freopen( )** first tries to close a file that is currently associated with *stream.* However, failure to achieve a successful closing is ignored, and the attempt to reopen continues.

The **freopen( )** function returns a pointer to *stream* on success and a null pointer otherwise.

The main use of **freopen( )** is to redirect the system-defined files **stdin**, **stdout**, and **stderr** to some other file.

Example

The program shown here uses **freopen( )** to redirect the stream **stdout** to the file called **OUT**. Because **printf( )** writes to **stdout**, the first message is displayed on the screen and the second is written to the disk file.

```
#include <stdio.h>
#include <stdlib.h>

main(void)
{
  FILE *fp;

  printf("This will display on the screen\n");

  if(!(fp=freopen("OUT","w",stdout))) {
    printf("cannot open file\n");
    exit(1);
}

  printf("this will be written to the file OUT");
  fclose(fp);
```

```
    return 0;
}
```

Related Functions

fopen( ), **fclose( )**

int fscanf(FILE *stream, const char *format, arg-list)

Description

The prototype for **fscanf( )** is found in **stdio.h**.

The **fscanf( )** function works exactly like the **scanf( )** function except that it reads the information from the stream specified by *stream* instead of **stdin**. See the **scanf( )** function for details.

The **fscanf( )** function returns the number of arguments actually assigned values. This number does not include skipped fields. A return value of **EOF** means that an attempt was made to read past the end of the file.

Example

This code fragment reads a string and a **float** number from the stream **fp**:

```
char str[80];
float f;

fscanf(fp, "%s%f", str, &f);
```

Related Functions

scanf( ), **fprintf( )**

int fseek(FILE *stream, long offset, int origin)

Description

The prototype for **fseek( )** is found in **stdio.h**.

The **fseek( )** function sets the file-position indicator associated with *stream* according to the values of *offset* and *origin*. Its main purpose is to support random I/O operations. The *offset* is the number of bytes from *origin* to make the new position. The *origin* is either a 0, 1, or 2, with 0 being the start of the file, 1 the current position, and 2 the end of the file. The following macros for *origin* are defined in **stdio.h**:

Name	Origin
SEEK_SET	Beginning of file
SEEK_CUR	Current position
SEEK_END	End of file

A return value of 0 means that **fseek( )** succeeded. A non-0 value indicates failure.

As specified by the ANSI C standard, *offset* must be a **long int** in order to support files larger than 64K.

You can use **fseek( )** to move the position indicator anywhere in the file, even beyond the end. However, it is an error to attempt to set the position indicator before the beginning of the file.

The **fseek( )** function clears the end-of-file flag associated with the specified stream. Furthermore, it nullifies any prior **ungetc( )** on the same stream. (See **ungetc( )**.)

Example

The function shown here seeks to the specified structure of type **addr**. Notice the use of **sizeof** both to obtain the proper number of bytes to seek and to ensure portability.

```
struct addr {
  char name[40];
  char street[40];
  char city[40];
  char state[3];
  char zip[10];
} info;

void find(long client_num)
{
  FILE *fp;

  if(!(fp=fopen("mail","rb"))) {
    printf("cannot open file\n");
    exit(1);
  }

  /* find the proper structure */
  fseek(client_num*sizeof(struct addr), 0);

  /* read the data into memory */
  fread(&info, sizeof(struct addr), 1, fp);
  fclose(fp);
}
```

Related Functions

ftell( ), **rewind( )**, **fopen( )**

int fsetpos(FILE *stream, const fpos_t *pos)

Description

The prototype for **fsetpos( )** is found in **stdio.h**.

The **fsetpos( )** function sets the file pointer associated with *stream* to the location pointed to by *pos*. This value was set by a previous call to **fgetpos( )**. The type **fpos_t** is defined in **stdio.h.** It is capable of representing any file location.

If successful, **fsetpos( )** returns 0; upon failure, a value other than 0 is returned, and **errno** is also set to a non-0 value.

Example

This program uses **fsetpos( )** to reset the current file position to an earlier value:

```
#include <stdio.h>
#include <stdlib.h>

main(int argc, char *argv[])
{
  FILE *fp;
  long l;
  int  i;
  fpos_t *pos;  /* fpos_t is defined in stdio.h */
  pos = &l;

  if((fp=fopen(argv[1],"w+"))==NULL) {
    printf("cannot open file\n");
    exit(1);
  }

  for (i=0; i<10; i++)
    fputc('Y', fp);  /* write 10 Y's to the file */
  fgetpos(fp, pos);

  for (i=0; i<10; i++)
    fputc('Z', fp);  /* write 10 Z's to the file */
  fsetpos(fp, pos);  /* reset to the end of the Y's */
```

```
   fputc('A', fp);      /* replace first Z with an A. */
   fclose(fp);
   return 0;
}
```

Related Functions

fgetpos( ), **fseek( )**, **ftell( )**

FILE *_fsopen(const char *fname, const char *mode, int shflg)

Description

The prototype for **_fsopen( )** is found in **stdio.h**. You will also need to include **share.h**. This function is not defined by the ANSI C standard.

The **_fsopen( )** function opens a file whose name is pointed to by *fname* and returns a **FILE** pointer to the stream associated with it. The file is opened for shared-mode access using a network. It returns null if the file cannot be opened.

_fsopen( ) is similar to the standard library function **_fopen( )** except that it is designed for use with networks to manage file sharing. The string pointed to by *mode* determines the type of operations that may be performed on the file. Its legal values are the same as for **fopen( )**. (Refer to **fopen( )** for details.)

The *shflg* parameter determines how file sharing will be allowed. It will be one of the following macros (defined in **share.h**):

shflg	Meaning
SH_COMPAT	Compatibility mode
SH_DENYRW	No reading or writing
SH_DENYWR	No writing
SH_DENYRD	No reading
SH_DENYNONE	Allow reading and writing
SH_DENYNO	Allow reading and writing

Example

This call to **_fsopen( )** opens a file called **TEST.DAT** for binary output and denies network input operations:

```
fp=_fsopen("TEST.DAT", "wb", SH_DENYRD);
```

Related Functions

fopen(), **sopen()**

int fstat(int handle, struct stat *statbuf)

Description

The prototype for **fstat( )** is found in **sys\stat.h**.

The function is not defined by the ANSI C standard. The **fstat( )** function fills the structure *statbuf* with information on the file associated with the file descriptor *handle*. Information on the contents of **stat** can be found in the file **sys\stat.h**.

Upon successfully filling the **stat** structure, 0 is returned. On error, –1 is returned and **errno** is set to **EBADF**.

Example

The following example opens a file, fills the **stat** structure, and prints out one of its fields:

```
#include <stdio.h>
#include <sys\stat.h>
#include <stdlib.h>

main(void)
{
  FILE *fp;
  struct stat buff;

  if(!(fp=fopen("test","rb"))) {
    printf("cannot open file\n");
    exit(1);
  }

  /* fill the stat structure */
  fstat(fileno(fp), &buff);

  printf("size of the file is: %ld\n", buff.st_size);
  fclose(fp);
  return 0;
}
```

Related Functions

stat( ), **access( )**

long ftell(FILE *stream)

Description

The prototype for **ftell( )** is found in **stdio.h**.

The **ftell( )** function returns the current value of the file-position indicator for the specified stream. This value is the number of bytes the indicator is from the beginning of the file.

The **ftell( )** function returns –1L when an error occurs. If the stream is incapable of random seeks—if it is the console, for instance—the return value is undefined.

Example

This code fragment returns the current value of the file-position indicator for the stream pointed to by **fp**:

```
long i;
if((i=ftell(fp))==-1L) printf("A file error has occurred\n");
```

Related Functions

fseek( )

size_t fwrite(const void *buf, size_t size, size_t count, FILE *stream)

Description

The prototype for **fwrite( )** is found in **stdio.h**.

The **fwrite( )** function writes *count* number of objects—each object being *size* number of characters in length—to the stream pointed to by *stream* from the character array pointed to by *buf*. The file-position indicator is advanced by the number of characters written.

The **fwrite( )** function returns the number of items actually written, which, if the function is successful, equals the number requested. If fewer items are written than are requested, an error has occurred.

Example

This program writes a **float** to the file **test**. Notice that **sizeof** is used both to determine the number of bytes in a **float** variable and to ensure portability.

```
#include <stdio.h>
#include <stdlib.h>

main(void)
{
  FILE *fp;
  float f=12.23;

  if(!(fp=fopen("test","wb"))) {
    printf("cannot open file\n");
    exit(1);
  }

  fwrite(&f, sizeof(float), 1, fp);

  fclose(fp);
  return 0;
}
```

Related Functions

fread( ), **fscanf( )**, **getc( )**, **fgetc( )**

int getc(FILE *stream)

Description

The prototype for **getc( )** is found in **stdio.h**.

The **getc( )** macro returns the next character from the current position in the input *stream* and increments the file-position indicator. The character is read as an **unsigned char** that is converted to an integer.

If the end of the file is reached, **getc( )** returns **EOF**. However, since **EOF** is a valid integer value, when working with binary files you must use **feof( )** to check for the end of the file. If **getc( )** encounters an error, **EOF** is also returned. Remember that if you are working with binary files you must use **ferror( )** to check for file errors.

Example

This program reads and displays the contents of a text file:

```
#include <stdio.h>
#include <stdlib.h>

main(int argc, char *argv[])
{
  FILE *fp;
  char ch;

  if(!(fp=fopen(argv[1],"r"))) {
    printf("cannot open file\n");
    exit(1);
  }

  while((ch=getc(fp))!=EOF)
    printf("%c", ch);

  fclose(fp);
  return 0;
}
```

Related Functions

fputc( ), **fgetc( )**, **putc( )**, **fopen( )**

int getch(void)
int getche(void)

Description

The prototypes for **getch( )** and **getche( )** are found in **conio.h**.

The **getch( )** function returns the next character read from the console but does not echo that character to the screen.

The **getche( )** function returns the next character read from the console and echoes that character to the screen.

Neither function is defined by the ANSI C standard.

Example

This fragment uses **getch( )** to read the user's menu selection for a spelling checker program.

```
do {
  printf("1: check spelling\n");
  printf("2: correct spelling\n");
```

```
    printf("3: look up a word in the dictionary\n");
    printf("4: quit\n");

    printf("\nEnter your selection: ");
    choice = getch();
} while(!strchr("1234", choice));
```

Related Functions

getc( ), getchar( ), fgetc( )

int getchar(void)

Description

The prototype for **getchar( )** is found in **stdio.h**.

    The **getchar( )** macro returns the next character from **stdin**. The character is read as an **unsigned char** that is converted to an integer. If the end-of-file marker is read, **EOF** is returned.

    The **getchar( )** macro is functionally equivalent to **getc(stdin)**.

Example

This program reads characters from **stdin** into the array **s** until a carriage return is entered and then displays the string.

```
#include <stdio.h>

main(void)
{
  char s[256], *p;

  p = s;

  while((*p++=getchar())!='\n') ;
  *p = '\0';  /* add null terminator */
  printf(s);
  return 0;
}
```

Related Functions

fputc( ), fgetc( ), putc( ), fopen( )

char *gets(char *str)

Description

The prototype for **gets( )** is found in **stdio.h**.

The **gets( )** function reads characters from **stdin** and places them into the character array pointed to by *str*. Characters are read until a newline or an **EOF** is reached. The newline character is not made part of the string but is translated into a null to terminate the string.

If successful, **gets( )** returns *str;* if unsuccessful, it returns a null pointer. If a read error occurs, the contents of the array pointed to by *str* are indeterminate. Because a null pointer is returned when either an error has occurred or the end of the file is reached, you should use **feof( )** or **ferror( )** to determine what has actually happened.

There is no limit to the number of characters that **gets( )** will read; it is the programmer's job to make sure that the array pointed to by *str* is not overrun.

Example

This program uses **gets( )** to read a file name:

```c
#include <stdio.h>
#include <stdlib.h>

main(void)
{
  FILE *fp;
  char fname[128];

  printf("Enter filename: ");
  gets(fname);

  if(!(fp=fopen(fname,"r"))) {
    printf("cannot open file\n");
    exit(1);
  }

  .
  .
  .

  fclose(fp);
  return 0;
}
```

Related Functions

fputs( ), **fgetc( )**, **fgets( )**, **puts( )**

int getw(FILE *stream)

Description

The prototype for **getw( )** is found in **stdio.h**.

The **getw( )** function is not defined by the ANSI C standard.

The **getw( )** function returns the next integer from *stream* and advances the file-position indicator appropriately.

Because the integer read may have a value equal to **EOF**, you must use **feof( )** or **ferror( )** to determine when the end-of-file marker is reached or an error has occurred.

Example

This program reads integers from the file **inttest** and displays their sum.

```
#include <stdio.h>
#include <stdlib.h>

main(void)
{
  FILE *fp;
  int sum = 0;

  if(!(fp=fopen("inttest","rb"))) {
    printf("cannot open file\n");
    exit(1);
  }

  while(!feof(fp))
    sum = getw(fp)+sum;

  printf("the sum is %d",sum);
  fclose(fp);
  return 0;
}
```

Related Functions

putw( ), **fread( )**

int isatty(int handle)

Description

The prototype for **isatty( )** is found in **io.h**.

The function **isatty( )** is not defined by the ANSI C standard. It returns non-0 if *handle* is associated with a character device that is either a terminal, console, printer, or serial port; otherwise, it returns 0.

Example

This fragment reports whether the device associated with **fd** is a character device:

```
if(isatty(fd)) printf("is a character device");
else printf("is not a character device");
```

Related Functions

open( )

int lock(int handle, long offset, long length)

Description

The prototype for **lock( )** is found in **io.h**.

The **lock( )** function is not defined by the ANSI C standard. It is used to lock a region of a file, thus preventing another program from using it until the lock is removed. To unlock a file use **unlock( )**. These functions provide control for file sharing in network environments.

The file to be locked is associated with *handle*. The portion of the file to be locked is determined by the starting *offset* from the beginning of the file and the *length*.

If **lock( )** is successful, 0 is returned. Upon failure, –1 is returned.

Example

This fragment locks the first 128 bytes of the file associated with **fd**:

```
lock(fd, 0, 128);
```

Related Functions

unlock( ), **sopen( )**

int locking(int handle, int mode, long length)

Description

The prototype for **locking( )** is in **io.h**. You must also include **sys\locking.h**.

The **locking( )** function is not defined by the ANSI C standard. It is used to lock a region of a shared file when using a network. Locking the file prevents other users from accessing it.

The *mode* parameter must be one of these macros:

Mode	Meaning
LK_LOCK	Lock the specified region. If the locking request fails, retry 10 times, once each second
LK_RLCK	Same as LK_LOCK
LK_NBLCK	Lock the specified region. If the locking request fails, perform no retries
LK_NBRLCK	Same as LK_NBLCK
LK_UNLCK	Unlock the specified region

The handle of the file to lock is specified in *handle*. The file will be locked (or unlocked) beginning with the current position and extending *length* number of bytes.

The **locking( )** function returns 0 if successful and −1 otherwise. On failure, **errno** is set to one of these values:

EBADF	Bad file handle
EACCESS	Access denied
EDEADLOCK	File cannot be locked
EINVAL	Invalid argument

Example

This call to **locking( )** unlocks 10 bytes in the file described by **fd**:

```
if(locking(fd, LK_UNLOCK, 10)) {
  // process error
}
```

Related Functions

lock( ), sopen( )

long lseek(int handle, long offset, int origin)

Description

The prototype for **lseek( )** is found in **io.h**.

The **lseek( )** function is part of the UNIX-like I/O system and is not defined by the ANSI C standard.

The **lseek( )** function sets the file position indicator to the location specified by *offset* and *origin* for the file specified by *handle*.

How **lseek( )** works depends on the values of *origin* and *offset*. The *origin* may be either 0, 1, or 2. The following chart explains how the *offset* is interpreted for each *origin* value:

Origin	Effect of Call to lseek( )
0	Count the offset from the start of the file
1	Count the offset from the current position
2	Count the offset from the end of the file

The following macros are defined in **io.h**. They can be used for a value of *origin* in order of 0 through 2.

```
SEEK_SET
SEEK_CUR
SEEK_END
```

The **lseek( )** function returns *offset* on success. Therefore, **lseek( )** will be returning a **long** integer. Upon failure, a −1L is returned and **errno** is set to one of these values;

EBADF	Bad file number
EINVAL	Invalid argument

Example

The example shown here allows you to examine a file one sector at a time using the UNIX-like I/O system. You will want to change the buffer size to match the sector size of your system.

```c
#include <stdio.h>
#include <fcntl.h>
#include <sys\stat.h>
#include <io.h>
#include <stdlib.h>

#define BUF_SIZE   128

/* read buffers using lseek() */
main(int argc, char *argv[])
{
  char buf[BUF_SIZE+1], s[10];
  int fd, sector;

  buf[BUF_SIZE+1]='\0'; /* null terminate buffer for printf */
  if((fd=open(argv[1], O_RDONLY))==-1) { /* open for write */
    printf("cannot open file\n");
    exit(0);
  }
  do {
    printf("buffer: ");
    gets(s);

    sector = atoi(s); /* get the sector to read */

    if(lseek(fd, (long)sector*BUF_SIZE,0)==-1L)
      printf("seek error\n");

    if(read(fd, buf, BUF_SIZE)==0) {
      printf("sector out of range\n");
    }
    else
      printf(buf);
    } while(sector>0);
    close(fd);
    return 0;
}
```

Related Functions

read( ), write( ), open( ), close( )

int open(const char *filename, int access, unsigned mode)
int _open(const char *filename, int access)

Description

The prototypes for **open( )** and **_open( )** are found in **io.h**.

The **open( )** function is part of the UNIX-like I/O system and is not defined by the ANSI C standard.

Unlike the buffered I/O system, the UNIX-like system does not use file pointers of type **FILE**, but rather file descriptors of type **int**. The **open( )** function opens a file with the name *filename* and sets its access mode as specified by *access*. You can think of *access* as being constructed of a base mode of operation plus modifiers. The following base modes are allowed.

Base	Meaning
O_RDONLY	Open for read only
O_WRONLY	Open for write only
O_RDWR	Open for read/write

After selecting one of these values, you may **OR** it with one or more of the following access modifiers:

Access modifiers	Meaning
O_NDELAY	Not used; included for UNIX compatibility
O_APPEND	Causes the file pointer to be set to the end of the file prior to each write operation
O_CREAT	If the file does not exist, creates it with its attribute set to the value of *mode*
O_TRUNC	If the file exists, truncates it to length 0 but retains its file attributes
O_EXCL	When used with O_CREAT, will not create output file if a file by that name already exists
O_BINARY	Opens a binary file
O_TEXT	Opens a text file

The *mode* argument is only required if the **O_CREAT** modifier is used. In this case, *mode* may be one of three values:

Mode	Meaning
S_IWRITE	Write access
S_IREAD	Read access
S_IWRITE | S_IREAD	Read/write access

A successful call to **open( )** returns a positive integer that is the file descriptor associated with the file. A return value of –1 means that the file cannot be opened, and **errno** is set to one of these values:

ENOENT	File does not exist
EMFILE	Too many open files
EACCES	Access denied
EINVACC	Access code is invalid

The function **_open( )** accepts a larger number of modifiers for the *access* parameter if executing under DOS 3.x or greater. These additional values are

Access Modifier	Meaning
O_NOINHERIT	File not passed to child programs
O_DENYALL	Only the current file descriptor has access to the file
O_DENYWRITE	Only read access to the file allowed
O_DENYREAD	Only write access to the file allowed
O_DENYNONE	Allows shared files

Example

You will usually see the call to **open( )** like this:

```
if((fd=open(filename, mode)) == -1)  {
  printf("cannot open file\n");
  exit(1);
}
```

Related Functions

close( ), **read( )**, **write( )**

void perror(const char *str)

Description

The prototype for **perror( )** is found in **stdio.h**.

The **perror( )** function maps the value of the global **errno** onto a string and writes that string to **stderr**. If the value of *str* is not null, the string is written first, followed by a colon, and then the proper error message as determined by the value of **errno**.

Example

This program purposely generates a domain error by calling **asin( )** with an out-of-range argument. The output is "Program Error Test: Math argument".

```
#include <stdio.h>
#include <math.h>
#include <errno.h> /* contains declaration for errno */

main(void)
{
  /* this will generate a domain error */
  asin(10.0);
  if(errno==EDOM)
    perror("Program Error Test");
  return 0;
}
```

Related Functions

ferror( )

int printf(const char *format, arg-list)

Description

The prototype for **printf( )** is found in **stdio.h**.

The **printf( )** function writes to **stdout** the arguments that make up *arg-list* under the control of the string pointed to by *format*.

The string pointed to by *format* consists of two types of items. The first type is made up of characters that will be printed on the screen. The second type contains format commands that define the way the arguments are displayed. A format command begins with a percent sign and is followed by the format code. The format commands are shown in Table 16-2. There must be exactly the same number of arguments as there are format commands, and the format commands and the arguments are matched in order. For example, this **printf( )** call,

```
printf("Hi %c %d %s",'c',10,"there!");
```

displays "Hi c 10 there!".

If there are insufficient arguments to match the format commands, the output is undefined. If there are more arguments than format commands, the remaining arguments are discarded.

The **printf( )** function returns the number of characters actually printed. A negative return value indicates that an error has taken place.

The format commands can have modifiers that specify the field width, the number of decimal places, and left-justification. An integer placed between the percent sign and the format command acts as a *minimum field width specifier.* If the string or number is greater than that minimum, it will be printed in full. If it is smaller than the minimum, the output is padded with spaces or 0s to ensure that it is the specified length. The default padding is done with spaces. If you wish to pad with 0s, place a

Code	Format
%c	A single character
%d	Decimal
%i	Decimal
%e	Scientific notation
%f	Decimal floating-point
%g	Uses %e or %f, whichever is shorter
%o	Octal
%s	String of characters
%u	Unsigned decimal
%x	Hexadecimal
%%	Prints a % sign
%p	Displays a pointer
%n	The associated argument will be an integer pointer into which is placed the number of characters written so far

Table 16-2. **printf( )** *Format Commands*

0 before the field-width specifier. For example, **%05d** pads a number of fewer than five digits with 0s so that its total length is five.

To specify the number of decimal places printed for a floating-point number, place a decimal point after the field width specifier followed by the number of decimal places you wish to display. For example, **%10.4f** displays a number at least ten characters wide with four decimal places. When this kind of format is applied to strings or integers, the number following the period specifies the maximum field length. For example, **%5.7s** displays a string that is at least five characters long and no longer than seven. If the string is longer than the maximum field width, the characters will be truncated off the end.

By default, all output is right-justified: If the field width is larger than the data printed, the data will be placed on the right edge of the field. You can force the information to be left-justified by placing a minus sign directly after the %. For example, **%\–10.2f** left-justifies a floating-point number with two decimal places in a ten-character field.

There are two format-command modifiers that allow **printf( )** to display **short** and **long** integers. These modifiers can be applied to the **d**, **i**, **o**, **u**, and **x** type specifiers. The **l** modifier tells **printf( )** that a **long** data type follows. For example, **%ld** means that a **long int** is to be displayed. The **h** modifier instructs **printf( )** to display a **short int**. Therefore, **%hu** indicates that the data is of the type **short unsigned int**.

The **l** modifier can also prefix the floating-point commands of **e**, **f**, and **g** and indicates that a **double** follows.

The **%n** command causes the number of characters that have been written at the time the **%n** is encountered to be placed in an integer variable whose pointer is specified in the argument list. For example, this code fragment displays the number 14 after the line "this is a test":

```
int i;

printf("this is a test%n",&i);
printf("%d",i);
```

The pointer type specifiers (**%p**, **%s**, and **%n**) can be modified using **F** or **N** to explicitly specify **far** or **near** pointers, respectively. These modifiers override the default memory model used to compile the program.

Example

This program displays the output shown in its comments:

```
#include <stdio.h>

main(void)
```

```
{
  /* This prints "this is a test" left-justified
     in a 20-character field.
  */
  printf("%-20s", "this is a test");

  /* This prints a float with 3 decimal places in a
     10-character field. The output will be "    12.235".
  */
  printf("%10.3f", 12.234657);
  return 0;
}
```

Related Functions

scanf( ), fprintf( )

int putc(int ch, FILE *stream)

Description

The prototype for **putc( )** is found in **stdio.h**.

The **putc( )** macro writes the character contained in the least significant byte of *ch* to the output stream pointed to by *stream*. Because character arguments are elevated to integers at the time of the call, you can use character variables as arguments to **putc( )**.

If successful, **putc( )** returns the character written; it returns **EOF** if an error occurs. If the output stream has been opened in binary mode, **EOF** is a valid value for *ch*. This means that you must use **ferror( )** to determine whether an error has occurred.

Example

The following loop writes the characters in string **str** to the stream specified by **fp**. The null terminator is not written.

```
for(; *str; str++) putc(*str, fp);
```

Related Functions

fgetc( ), fputc( ), getchar( ), putchar( )

int putch(int ch)

Description

The prototype for **putch( )** is in **conio.h**. This function is not defined by the ANSI C standard.

The **putch( )** function displays the character specified in *ch* on the screen. This function writes directly to the screen and not to **stdout**. Therefore, no character translations are performed and no redirection will occur.

If successful, **putch( )** returns *ch*. On failure, **EOF** is returned.

Example

This outputs the character X to the screen:

```
putch('X');
```

Related Function

putchar( )

int putchar(int ch)

Description

The prototype for **putchar( )** is found in **stdio.h**.

The **putchar( )** macro writes the character contained in the least significant byte of *ch* to **stdout**. It is functionally equivalent to **putc(ch,stdout)**. Because character arguments are elevated to integers at the time of the call, you can use character variables as arguments to **putchar( )**.

If successful, **putchar( )** returns the character written; if an error occurs it returns **EOF**. If the output stream has been opened in binary mode, **EOF** is a valid value for *ch*. This means that you must use **ferror( )** to determine if an error has occurred.

Example

The following loop writes the characters in string **str** to **stdout**. The null terminator is not written.

```
for(; *str; str++) putchar(*str);
```

Related Functions

fputchar( ), **putc( )**

int puts(const char *str)

Description

The prototype for **puts( )** is found in **stdio.h**.

The **puts( )** function writes the string pointed to by *str* to the standard output device. The null terminator is translated to a newline.

The **puts( )** function returns a newline if successful and an **EOF** if unsuccessful.

Example

The following writes the string "this is an example" to **stdout**.

```
#include <stdio.h>
#include <string.h>

main(void)
{
  char str[80];

  strcpy(str, "this is an example");
  puts(str);
  return 0;
}
```

Related Functions

putc( ), **gets( )**, **printf( )**

int putw(int i, FILE *stream)

Description

The prototype for **putw( )** is in **stdio.h**. The **putw( )** function is not defined by the ANSI C standard and may not be fully portable.

The **putw( )** function writes the integer *i* to *stream* at the current file position and increments the file-position pointer appropriately.

The **putw( )** function returns the value written. A return value of **EOF** means an error has occurred in the stream if it is in text mode. Because **EOF** is also a valid integer value, you must use **ferror( )** to detect an error in a binary stream.

Example

This code fragment writes the value 100 to the stream pointed to by **fp**:

```
putw(100, fp);
```

Related Functions

getw( ), **printf( )**, **fwrite( )**

int read(int fd, void *buf, unsigned count)
int _read(int fd, void *buf, unsigned count)

Description

The prototypes for **read( )** and **_read( )** are found in **io.h**.

Neither the **read( )** nor the **_read( )** function is defined by the ANSI C standard. The **read( )** function is part of the UNIX-like I/O system. The **_read( )** function is specific to Turbo/Borland C/C++ and the MS-DOS operating system.

The **read( )** function reads *count* number of bytes from the file described by *fd* into the buffer pointed to by *buf*. The file-position indicator is incremented by the number of bytes read. If the file is opened in text mode, character translations may take place.

The return value is the number of bytes actually read. This number will be smaller than *count* if an end-of-file marker is encountered or an error occurs before *count* number of bytes have been read. A value of –1 is returned if an error occurs, and a value of 0 is returned if an attempt is made to read at end-of-file. If an error occurs, then **errno** is set to one of these values:

EACCES	Access denied
EBADF	Bad file number

The difference between **read( )** and **_read( )** is that **read( )** removes carriage returns and returns **EOF** when a CTRL-Z is read from a text file. The **_read( )** function does not perform these actions.

Example

This program reads the first 100 bytes from the file **TEST.TST** into the array **buffer**:

```
#include <stdio.h>
#include <io.h>
#include <fcntl.h>
#include <stdlib.h>
```

```
main(void)
{
  int fd;
  char buffer[100];

  if((fd=open("TEST.TST", O_RDONLY))==-1) {
    printf("cannot open file\n");
    exit(1);
  }

  if(read(fd, buffer, 100)!=100)
    printf("Possible read error.");
  return 0;
}
```

Related Functions

open( ), **close( )**, **write( )**, **lseek( )**

int remove(const char *fname)

Description

The prototype for **remove( )** is found in **stdio.h**.

  The **remove( )** function erases the file specified by *fname*. It returns 0 if the file was successfully deleted and –1 if an error occurred. If an error occurs, then **errno** is set to one of these values:

ENOENT	File does not exist
EACCES	Access denied

Example

This program removes the file specified on the command line:

```
#include <stdio.h>

main(int argc, char *argv[])
{
  if(remove(argv[1])==-1)
    printf("remove error");
  return 0;
}
```

Related Functions

rename( )

int rename(const char *oldfname, const char *newfname)

Description

The prototype for **rename( )** is found in **stdio.h**.

The **rename( )** function changes the name of the file specified by *oldfname* to *newfname*. The *newfname* must not match any existing directory entry.

The **rename( )** function returns 0 if successful and non-0 if an error has occurred. If an error occurs, then **errno** is set to one of these values:

ENOENT	File does not exist
EACCES	Access denied
ENOTSAM	Device not the same

Example

This program renames the file specified as the first command-line argument to that specified by the second command-line argument. Assuming the program is called **change**, a command line consisting of "change this that" will change the name of a file called **this** to **that**.

```
#include <stdio.h>

main(int argc, char *argv[])
{
  if(rename(argv[1], argv[2])!=0)
    printf("rename error");
  return 0;
}
```

Related Functions

remove( )

void rewind(FILE *stream)

Description

The prototype for **rewind( )** is found in **stdio.h**.

The **rewind( )** function moves the file-position indicator to the start of the specified stream. It also clears the end-of-file and error flags associated with *stream*. It returns 0 if successful and non-0 otherwise.

Example

This function reads the stream pointed to by **fp** twice, displaying the file each time:

```
void re_read(FILE *fp)
{
  /* read once */
  while(!feof(fp)) putchar(getc(fp));

  rewind(fp);

  /* read twice */
  while(!feof(fp)) putchar(getc(fp));
}
```

Related Functions

fseek( )

int scanf(const char *format, arg-list)

Description

The prototype for **scanf( )** is in **stdio.h**. The **scanf( )** function is a general-purpose input routine that reads the stream **stdin**. It can read all the built-in data types and automatically convert them into the proper internal format. It is much like the reverse of **printf( )**.

The control string pointed to by *format* consists of three classifications of characters:

- Format specifiers
- White-space characters
- Non-white-space characters

The input format specifiers are preceded by a percent sign and tell **scanf( )** what type of data is to be read next. These codes are listed in Table 16-3. For example, **%s** reads a string, while **%d** reads an integer.

The format string is read left to right, and the format codes are matched, in order, with the arguments in the argument list.

Code	Meaning
%c	Read a single character
%d	Read a decimal integer
%i	Read a decimal integer
%e	Read a floating-point number
%f	Read a floating-point number
%h	Read a short integer
%o	Read an octal number
%s	Read a string
%x	Read a hexadecimal number
%p	Read a pointer
%n	Receive an integer value equal to the number of characters read so far

Table 16-3.   **scanf( )** *Format Codes*

A white-space character in the control string causes **scanf( )** to skip over one or more white-space characters in the input stream. A white-space character is either a space, a tab, or a newline. In essence, one white-space character in the control string causes **scanf( )** to read, but not store, any number (including 0) of white-space characters up to the first non-white-space character.

A non-white-space character causes **scanf( )** to read and discard a matching character. For example, **"%d,%d"** causes **scanf( )** first to read an integer, then to read and discard a comma, and finally to read another integer. If the specified character is not found, **scanf( )** terminates.

All the variables used to receive values through **scanf( )** must be passed by their addresses. This means that all arguments must be pointers to the variables used as arguments. This is C's way of creating a "call by reference," and it allows a function to alter the contents of an argument. For example, if you wish to read an integer into the variable **count**, you would use the following **scanf( )** call.

```
scanf("%d",&count);
```

Strings will be read into character arrays, and the array name, without any index, is the address of the first element of the array. So, to read a string into the character array **address**, you would use

```
scanf("%s",address);
```

In this case, **address** is already a pointer and need not be preceded by the **&** operator.

The input data items must be separated by spaces, tabs, or newlines. Commas, semicolons, and other punctuation marks do not count as separators. This means that

```
scanf("%d%d",&r,&c);
```

will accept an input of **10 20**, but fail with **10,20**. As in **printf( )**, the **scanf( )** format codes are matched in order with the variables receiving the input in the argument list.

An * placed after the % and before the format code will read data of the specified type but suppress its assignment. Thus, given the input **10/20**,

```
scanf("%d%*c%d",&x,&y);
```

places the value 10 into **x**, discards the divide sign, and gives **y** the value 20.

The format commands can specify a maximum field-length modifier. This is an integer number placed between the % and the format-command code that limits the number of characters read for any field. For example, if you wish to read no more than 20 characters into **address**, you write

```
scanf("%20s",address);
```

If the input stream contains a value greater than twenty characters, a subsequent call to input would begin where this call left off. For example, if ABCDEFGHIJKLMNOPQRSTUVWXYZ had been entered as the response to the earlier **scanf( )** call, only the first 20 characters—up to the T—would have been placed into **address** because of the maximum size specifier. This means that the remaining six characters, UVWXYZ, have not yet been used. If another **scanf( )** call is made, such as

```
scanf("%s", str);
```

UVWXYZ will be placed into **str**. Input for a field can terminate before the maximum field length is reached if a white-space character is encountered. In this case, **scanf( )** moves on to the next field.

Although spaces, tabs, and newlines are used as field separators, when reading a single character they are read like any other character. For example, with an input stream of **x y**,

```
scanf("%c%c%c", &a, &b, &c);
```

returns the character x in **a**, a space in **b**, and y in **c**.

Any other characters in the control string—including spaces, tabs, and newlines—
are used to match and discard characters from the input stream. Any character that
matches is discarded. For example, given the input stream **10t20,**

```
scanf("%st%s", &x, &y);
```

places 10 into **x** and 20 into **y**. The t is discarded because of the **t** in the control string.
As another example,

```
scanf("%s ", name);
```

does *not* return until you type a character *after* you type a terminator because the space
after the **%s** has instructed **scanf( )** to read and discard spaces, tabs, and newline characters.
      Another feature of **scanf( )** is the *scanset*. A scanset defines a list of characters that
will be matched by **scanf( )** and stored in a character array variable. The **scanf( )**
function inputs characters, putting them into the corresponding character array, as
long as they are members of the scanset. When a character is entered that does not
match any in the scanset, **scanf( )** null-terminates the corresponding array and moves
on to the next (if any) field.
      A scanset is defined by putting a list of the characters you want to scan for inside
square brackets. The beginning square bracket must be prefixed by a percent sign.
For example, this scanset tells **scanf( )** to read only the characters []{ }:

```
%[[]{ }]
```

The argument corresponding to the scanset must be a pointer to a character array. Upon
return from **scanf( )**, the array contains a null-terminated string comprising the characters read. For example, the following program uses a scanset to read punctuation into
s1. As soon as a non-punctuation character is entered, **s1** is null-terminated and
characters are read into **s2** until the next white-space character is entered.

```
/* A simple scanset example. */
#include <stdio.h>

main(void)
{
  char s1[80], s2[80];

  printf("Enter punctuation, then some letters\n");
  scanf("%[,.;'!:?]%s", s1, s2);
  printf("%s %s", s1, s2);
  return 0;
}
```

You can specify a range inside a scanset using a hypen. For example, this tells **scanf( )** to accept the characters A through Z:

```
%[A-Z]
```

You can specify more than one range within a scanset. For example, this scanset reads both upper- and lowercase letters:

```
%[A-Za-z]
```

You can specify an inverted set if the first character in the set is a ^. When the ^ is present, it instructs **scanf( )** to accept any character that *is not* defined by the scanset. Here, the previous scanset uses the ^ to invert the type of characters the scanset will read. This means that it will match all characters that are *not* letters of the alphabet.

```
%[^a-zA-Z]
```

The **scanf( )** function returns a number equal to the number of fields that were successfully assigned values. This number does not include fields that were read but not assigned using the * modifier to suppress the assignment. A value of **EOF** is returned if an attempt is made to read at the end-of-file mark. A 0 is returned if no fields were assigned.

You can override the default memory model used to compile your program by explicitly specifying the size of each pointer used in a call to **scanf( )**. To specify a **near** pointer, use the **N** modifier. To specify a **far** pointer, use the **F** modifier. (You cannot use the **N** modifier if your program was compiled for the **huge** memory model.)

Example

The operation of the following **scanf( )** statements are explained in their comments.

```
char str[80];
int i;

/* read a string and an integer */
scanf("%s%d", str, &i);

/* read up to 79 chars into str */
scanf("%79s", str);

/* skip the integer between the two strings */
scanf("%s%*d%s", str, &i, str);
```

Related Functions

printf( ), **fscanf( )**

void setbuf(FILE *stream, char *buf)

Description

The prototype to **setbuf( )** is found in **stdio.h**.

The **setbuf( )** function is used either to specify the buffer the specified stream will use or, if called with *buf* set to null, to turn off buffering. If a programmer-defined buffer is to be specified, it must be **BUFSIZ** characters long. **BUFSIZ** is defined in **stdio.h**.

The **setbuf( )** function returns no value.

Example

This following fragment associates a programmer-defined buffer with the stream pointed to by **fp**:

```
char buffer[BUFSIZ];
   .
   .
   .
setbuf(fp,buffer);
```

Related Functions

fopen( ), **fclose( )**, **setvbuf( )**

int setmode(int handle, int mode)

Description

The prototype to **setmode( )** is found in **io.h**.

The **setmode( )** function is not defined by the ANSI C standard. It is used to reset the mode of an already open file given its file descriptor and the new mode desired. The only valid modes are **O_BINARY** and **O_TEXT**.

It returns 0 on success, –1 on error. If an error occurs, **errno** is set to **EINVAL** (invalid argument).

Example

This line of code sets the file associated with **fd** to text-only operation.

```
setmode(fd, O_TEXT)
```

Related Functions

open( ), **creat( )**

int setvbuf(FILE *stream, char *buf, int mode, size_t size)

Description

The prototype for **setvbuf( )** is found in **stdio.h**.

The **setvbuf( )** function allows the programmer to specify the buffer, its size, and its mode for the specified stream. The character array pointed to by *buf* is used as *stream*'s buffer for I/O operations. The size of the buffer is set by *size,* and *mode* determines how buffering will be handled. If *buf* is null, no buffering takes place.

The legal values of *mode* are **_IOFBF**, **_IONBF**, and **_IOLBF**. These are defined in **stdio.h**. When the mode is set to **_IOFBF** full buffering takes place. This is the default setting. When set to **_IONBF**, the stream is unbuffered regardless of the value *buf.* If *mode* is **_IOLBF**, the stream is line-buffered, which means that the buffer is flushed each time a newline character is written for output streams; for input streams an input request reads all characters up to a newline. In either case, the buffer is also flushed when full.

The value of *size* must be greater than 0 and less than 32,768.

The **setvbuf( )** function returns 0 on success, non-0 on failure.

Example

This fragment sets the stream **fp** to line-buffered mode with a buffer size of 128:

```
#include <stdio.h>
char buffer[128];
 .
 .
 .
setvbuf(fp, buffer, _IOLBF, 128);
```

Related Functions

setbuf( )

int sopen(const char *filename, int access, int shflag, int mode)

Description

The prototype for **sopen( )** is found in **io.h**. The **sopen( )** macro is part of the UNIX-like file system.

The **sopen( )** macro opens a file for shared-mode access using a network. It is defined as

open(*filename*, (*access* | *shflag*), *mode*)

The **sopen( )** macro opens a file with the name *filename* and sets its access mode as specified by *access* and its share mode as specified by *shflag*. You can think of *access* as being constructed of a base mode of operation plus modifiers. The following base modes are allowed:

Base	Meaning
O_RDONLY	Open for read only
O_WRONLY	Open for write only
O_RDWR	Open for read/write

After selecting one of these values, you may **OR** it with one or more of the following access modifiers:

Modifiers	Meaning When Set
O_NDELAY	Not used; included for UNIX compatibility
O_APPEND	Causes the file pointer to be set to the end of the file prior to each write operation
O_CREAT	If the file does not exist, it is created with its attribute set to the value of *mode*
O_TRUNC	If the file exists, it is truncated to length 0 but retains its file attributes
O_EXCL	When used with **O_CREAT**, will not create output file if a file by that name already exists
O_BINARY	Opens a binary file
O_TEXT	Opens a text file

The *shflag* argument defines the type of sharing allowed on this file and can be one of these values:

shflag	Meaning
SH_COMPAT	Compatibility mode
SH_DENYRW	No read or write
SH_DENYWR	No write
SH_DENYRD	No read
SH_DENYNONE	Allow read/write
SH_DENYNO	Allow read/write

The *mode* argument is only required if the **O_CREAT** modifier is used. In this case, *mode* can be one of these values:

Mode	Meaning
S_IWRITE	Write access
S_IREAD	Read access
S_IWRITE I S_IREAD	Read/write access

A successful call to **sopen( )** returns a positive integer that is the file descriptor associated with the file. A return value of –1 means that the file cannot be opened, and **errno** will be set to one of these values:

ENOENT	File does not exist
EMFILE	Too many open files
EACCES	Access denied
EINVACC	Invalid access code

Example

You will usually see the call to **sopen( )** like this:

```
if((fd=sopen(filename, access, shflag, mode)) ==-1)  {
  printf("cannot open file\n");
  exit(1);
}
```

Related Functions

open( ), **_open( )**, **close( )**

int sprintf(char *buf, const char *format, arg-list)

Description

The prototype for **sprintf( )** is found in **stdio.h**.

The **sprintf( )** function is identical to **printf( )** except that the output generated is placed into the array pointed to by *buf*. See the **printf( )** function.

The return value is equal to the number of characters actually placed into the array.

Example

After this code fragment executes, **str** holds **one 2 3**:

```
char str[80];
sprintf(str,"%s %d %c","one",2,'3');
```

Related Functions

printf( ), **fsprintf( )**

int sscanf(char *buf, const char *format, arg-list)

Description

The prototype for **sscanf( )** is found in **stdio.h**.

The **sscanf( )** function is identical to **scanf( )** except that data is read from the array pointed to by *buf* rather than **stdin**. See **scanf( )**.

The return value is equal to the number of fields that were actually assigned values. This number does not include fields that were skipped through the use of the * format-command modifier. A value of 0 means that no fields were assigned, and **EOF** indicates that a read was attempted at the end of the string.

Example

This program prints the message "hello 1" on the screen:

```
#include <stdio.h>

main(void)
{
    char str[80];
    int i;
```

```
  sscanf("hello 1 2 3 4 5","%s%d",str,&i);
  printf("%s %d",str,i);
  return 0;
}
```

Related Functions

scanf( ), **fscanf( )**

int stat(char *filename, struct stat *statbuf)

Description

The prototype to **stat( )** is found in **sys\stat.h**.

The **stat( )** function fills the structure *statbuf* with information on the file associated with *filename*. The **stat** structure is defined in **sys\stat.h**.

Upon successfully filling the **stat** structure, 0 is returned. If unsuccessful, −1 is returned and **errno** is set to **ENOENT**.

Example

The following example opens a file, fills the **stat** structure, and prints out one of its fields:

```
#include <stdio.h>
#include <sys\stat.h>
#include <stdlib.h>

main(void)
{
  FILE *fp;
  struct stat buff;

  if(!(fp=fopen("test","rb"))) {
    printf("cannot open file\n");
    exit(1);
  }

  /* fill the stat structure */
  stat("test", &buff);

  printf("size of the file is: %ld\n", buff.st_size);
  fclose(fp);
  return 0;
}
```

Related Functions

fstat( ), **access( )**

long tell(int fd)

Description

The prototype for **tell( )** is found in **io.h**.

The **tell( )** function is part of the UNIX-like I/O system and is not defined by the ANSI C standard.

The **tell( )** function returns the current value of the file-position indicator associated with the file descriptor *fd*. This value is the number of bytes the position indicator is from the start of the file. A return value of −1L indicates an error and **errno** is set to EBADF (bad file handle).

Example

This fragment prints the current value of the position indicator for the file described by **fd**:

```
long pos;
   .
   .
   .
pos = tell(fd);
printf("Position indicator is %ld bytes from the start", pos);
```

Related Functions

lseek( ), **open( )**, **close( )**, **read( )**, **write( )**

FILE *tmpfile(void)

Description

The prototype for the **tmpfile( )** function is found in **stdio.h**.

The **tmpfile( )** function opens a temporary file for update and returns a pointer to the stream. The function automatically uses a unique file name to avoid conflicts with existing files.

The **tmpfile( )** function returns a null pointer on failure; otherwise it returns a pointer to the stream.

The temporary file created by **tmpfile( )** is automatically removed when the file is closed or when the program terminates.

Example

This fragment creates a temporary working file:

```
FILE *temp;

if(!(temp=tmpfile())) {
  printf("cannot open temporary work file\n");
  exit(1);
}
```

Related Functions

tmpnam( )

char *tmpnam(char *name)

Description

The prototype for **tmpnam( )** is found in **stdio.h**.

The **tmpnam( )** function is defined by the ANSI C standard. It generates a unique file name and stores it in the array pointed to by *name*. The main purpose of **tmpnam( )** is to generate a temporary file name that is different from any other file name in the directory.

The function may be called up to **TMP_MAX** times, defined in **stdio.h**. Each time it generates a new temporary file name.

A pointer to *name* is returned. If *name* is null, a pointer to an internal string is returned.

Example

This program displays three unique temporary file names:

```
#include <stdio.h>

main(void)
{
  char name[40];
  int i;
  for(i=0; i<3; i++) {
    tmpnam(name);
    printf("%s ", name);
  }
```

```
   return 0;
}
```

Related Functions

tmpfile( )

int ungetc(int ch, FILE *stream)

Description

The prototype for **ungetc( )** is found in **stdio.h**.

The **ungetc( )** function returns the character specified by the low-order byte of *ch* back into the input *stream*. This character is then returned by the next read operation on *stream*. A call to **fflush( )** or **fseek( )** undoes an **ungetc( )** operation and discards the character put back.

Only one character can be put back between subsequent read operations.

You cannot unget an **EOF**.

A call to **ungetc( )** clears the end-of-file flag associated with the specified stream. The value of the file-position indicator for a text stream is undefined until all pushed-back characters are read, in which case it is the same as it was prior to the first **ungetc( )** call. For binary streams, each **ungetc( )** call decrements the file-position indicator.

The return value is equal to *ch* on success and **EOF** on failure.

Example

This function reads words from the input stream pointed to by **fp**. The terminating character is returned to the stream for later use. For example, given input of **count/10**, the first call to **read_word( )** returns **count** and puts the / back on the input stream.

```
read_word(FILE *fp, char *token)
{

  while(isalpha(*token=getc(fp))) token++;

  ungetc(fp, *token);
}
```

Related Functions

getc( )

int ungetch(int ch)

Description

The prototype for **ungetch( )** is in **conio.h**. This function is not defined by the ANSI C standard.

The **ungetch( )** function returns the character specified in the low-order byte of *ch* back into the console input buffer. This character is then returned by the next call to a console input function. Only one character can be put back between subsequent input operations.

The return value is equal to *ch* on success and **EOF** on failure.

Example

This program inputs a key, displays it, returns it to the input buffer, and reads and displays it again:

```
#include <stdio.h>
#include <conio.h>

main()
{
  char ch;

  ch = getch(); // get keypress
  putch(ch); // show the key
  ungetch(ch);  // return to buffer
  ch = getch(); // get same key again
  putch(ch); // show the key again

  return 0;
}
```

Related Function

ungetc( )

int unlink(const char *fname)

Description

The prototype to **unlink( )** is found in **dos.h**.

The **unlink( )** function is part of the UNIX-like I/O system and is not defined by the ANSI C standard.

The **unlink( )** function removes the specified file from the directory. It returns 0 on success and –1 on failure and sets **errno** to one of the following values:

Error	Meaning
ENOENT	Invalid path or file name
EACCES	Access denied

Example

This program deletes the file specified as the first command-line argument:

```
#include <stdio.h>
#include <dos.h>

main(int argc, char *argv[])
{
  if(unlink(argv[1])==-1)
    printf("cannot remove file");
  return 0;
}
```

Related Functions

open( ), **close( )**

int unlock(int handle, long offset, long length)

Description

The prototype for **unlock( )** is found **io.h**.

The **unlock( )** function is not defined by the ANSI C standard. It is used to unlock a portion of a locked file, thus allowing another program to use it until a new lock is placed on the file. To lock a file, use **lock( )**. These functions provide control for file sharing in network environments.

The file to be unlocked is associated with *handle*. The portion of the file to be unlocked is determined by the starting *offset* from the beginning of the file and the *length*.

If **unlock( )** is successful, 0 is returned. If it is unsuccessful, –1 is returned.

Example

This fragment unlocks the first 128 bytes of the file associated with **fd**:

```
unlock(fd, 0, 128);
```

Related Functions

lock( ), **sopen( )**

int vprintf(const char *format, va_list arg_ptr)
int vfprintf(FILE *stream, const char *format, va_list arg_ptr)
int vsprintf(char *buf, const char *format, va_list arg_ptr)

Description

The prototypes for these functions require the files **stdio.h** and **stdarg.h**.

The functions **vprintf( )**, **vfprintf( )**, and **vsprintf( )** are functionally equivalent to **printf( )**, **fprintf( )**, and **sprintf( )**, respectively, except that the argument list has been replaced by a pointer to a list of arguments. This pointer must be of type **va_list**, which is defined in **stdarg.h**. See the proper related function. Also see **va_arg( )**, **va_start( )**, and **va_end( )** in Chapter 24 for further information.

Example

This fragment shows how to set up a call to **vprintf( )**. The call to **va_start( )** creates a variable-length argument pointer to the start of the argument list. This pointer must be used in the call to **vprintf( )**. The call to **va_end( )** clears the variable-length argument pointer.

```
#include <stdio.h>
#include <stdarg.h>

void print_message(char *, ...);

main(void)
{
  print_message("cannot open file %s","test");
  return 0;
}

void print_message( char *format, ...)
{
  va_list ptr; /* get an arg ptr */

  /* initialize ptr to point to the first argument after the
     format string
  */
```

```
  va_start(ptr, format);
  /* print out message */
  vprintf(format, ptr);
  va_end(ptr);
}
```

Related Functions

va_list( ), **va_start( )**, **va_end( )**

int vscanf(const char *format, va_list arg_ptr)
int vfscanf(FILE *stream, const char *format, va_list arg_ptr)
int vsscanf(const char *buf, const char *format, va_list arg_ptr)

Description

The prototypes for these functions require the files **stdio.h** and **stdarg.h**.

The functions **vscanf( )**, **vfscanf( )**, and **vsscanf( )** are functionally equivalent to **scanf( )**, **fscanf( )**, and **sscanf( )**, respectively, except that the argument list has been replaced by a pointer to a list of arguments. This pointer must be of type **va_list**, which is defined in **stdarg.h**. See the proper related function. Also see **va_arg( )**, **va_start( )**, and **va_end( )** in Chapter 24 for further information.

Example

This fragment shows how to set up a call to **vscanf( )**. The call to **va_start( )** creates a variable-length argument pointer to the start of the argument list. It is this pointer that must be used in the call to **vscanf( )**. The call to **va_end( )** clears the variable-length argument pointer.

```
#include <stdio.h>
#include <stdarg.h>

void read_int(char *, ...);

main(void)
{
  read_int("%d","test");
  return 0;
}

void read_int( char *format, ...)
{
  va_list ptr; /* get an arg ptr */
```

```
/* initialize ptr to point to the first argument after the
   format string
*/
 va_start(ptr, format);

/* read in an int */
vscanf(format, &ptr);
va_end(ptr);
}
```

Related Functions

va_list( ), **va_start( )**, **va_end( )**

int write(int handle, void *buf, int count)
int _write(int handle, void *buf, int count)

Description

The prototypes for **write( )** and **_write( )** are found in **io.h**.

The **write( )** function is part of the UNIX-like I/O system and is not defined by the ANSI C standard.

The **write( )** function writes *count* number of bytes to the file described by *handle* from the buffer pointed to by *buf*. The file-position indicator is incremented by the number of bytes written. If the file is opened in text mode, linefeeds are automatically expanded to carriage return, linefeed combinations. However, **_write( )** does not perform this expansion.

The return value is the number of bytes actually written. This number may be smaller than *count* if an error is encountered. A value of –1 means an error has occurred, and **errno** is set to one of these values:

Value	Meaning
EACCES	Access denied
EBADF	Bad file number

Example

This program writes the 100 bytes from **buffer** to the file **test**.

```
#include <stdio.h>
#include <io.h>
#include <fcntl.h>
#include <stdlib.h>
```

```
main(void)
{
  int fd;
  char buffer[100];

  if((fd=open("test", O_WRONLY)==-1) {
    printf("cannot open file\n");
    exit(1);
  }

  gets(buffer);

  if(write(fd, buffer, 100)!=100)
    printf("write error");
  close(fd);

  return 0;
}
```

Related Functions

read( ), **close( )**, **lseek( )**

Chapter 17

String, Memory, and Character Functions

The Turbo/Borland C/C++ standard library has a rich and varied set of string-, memory-, and character-handling functions. A string is a null-terminated array of characters, memory is a block of contiguous RAM, and a character is a single byte value. The string functions require the header file **string.h** to provide their prototypes. The memory manipulation functions use **mem.h**, but several may also use **string.h**. The character functions use **ctype.h** as their header file.

Because C/C++ has no bounds checking on array operations, it is the programmer's responsibility to prevent an array overflow. As the ANSI C standard puts it, if an array has overflowed, "the behavior is undefined," which is a nice way of saying that your program is about to crash!

In Turbo/Borland C/C++, a *printable character* is one that can be displayed on a terminal. These are the characters between a space (0x20) and tilde (0xFE). *Control characters* have values between (0) and (0x1F) as well as DEL (0x7F). The ASCII characters are between 0 and 0x7F.

The character functions are declared to take an integer argument. While this is true, only the low-order byte is used by the function. Therefore, you are free to use a character argument because it is automatically elevated to **int** at the time of the call.

Most of the functions described in this chapter are defined by the ANSI C standard and are fully portable. The major exception to this is that Turbo/Borland C/C++ includes several FAR versions of many string functions. These will be discussed along with their normal versions. (The FAR versions are not defined by the ANSI C standard.)

Several functions use the **size_t** data type. This type is defined in the various header files used by the functions described here and is an integer type.

int isalnum(int ch)

Description

The prototype for **isalnum( )** is found in **ctype.h**.

The **isalnum( )** macro returns non-0 if its argument is either a letter of the alphabet (upper- or lowercase) or a digit. If the character is not alphanumeric, 0 is returned.

Example

This program checks each character read from **stdin** and reports all alphanumeric ones:

```
#include <ctype.h>
#include <stdio.h>

main(void)
{
  char ch;

  for(;;) {
    ch = getchar();
    if(ch==' ') break;
    if(isalnum(ch)) printf("%c is alphanumeric\n", ch);
  }
  return 0;
}
```

Related Functions

isalpha( ), isdigit( ), iscntrl( ), isgraph( ), isprint( ), ispunct( ), isspace( )

int isalpha(int ch)

Description

The prototype for **isalpha( )** is found in **ctype.h**.

The **isalpha( )** macro returns non-0 if *ch* is a letter of the alphabet (upper- or lowercase); otherwise it returns 0.

Example

This program checks each character read from **stdin** and reports all those that are letters of the alphabet:

```
#include <ctype.h>
#include <stdio.h>

main(void)
{
  char ch;

  for(;;) {
    ch = getchar();
    if(ch==' ') break;
    if(isalpha(ch)) printf("%c is a letter\n", ch);
  }
  return 0;
}
```

Related Functions

isalnum( ), **isdigit( )**, **iscntrl( )**, **isgraph( )**, **isprint( )**, **ispunct( )**, **isspace( )**

int isascii(int ch)

Description

The prototype for **isascii( )** is found in **ctype.h** and is not defined by the ANSI C standard.

The **isascii( )** macro returns non-0 if *ch* is in the range 0 through 0x7F; otherwise it returns 0.

Example

This program checks each character read from **stdin** and reports all those that are defined by ASCII:

```
#include <ctype.h>
#include <stdio.h>

main(void)
{
  char ch;

  for(;;) {
    ch = getchar();
    if(ch==' ') break;
    if(isascii(ch)) printf("%c is ASCII defined\n", ch);
```

```
    }
    return 0;
}
```

Related Functions

isalnum( ), **isdigit( )**, **iscntrl( )**, **isgraph( )**, **isprint( )**, **ispunct( )**, **isspace( )**

int iscntrl(int ch)

Description

The prototype for **iscntrl( )** is found in **ctype.h**.

   The **iscntrl( )** macro returns non-0 if *ch* is between 0 and 0x1F or is equal to 0x7F (DEL); otherwise it returns 0.

Example

This program checks each character read from **stdin** and reports all those that are control characters:

```
#include <ctype.h>
#include <stdio.h>    `

main(void)
{
  char ch;

  for(;;) {
    ch = getchar();
    if(ch==' ') break;
    if(iscntrl(ch)) printf("%c is a control character\n", ch);
  }
  return 0;
}
```

Related Functions

isalnum( ), **isdigit( )**, **isalpha( )**, **isgraph( )**, **isprint( )**, **ispunct( )**, **isspace( )**

int isdigit(int ch)

Description

The prototype for **isdigit( )** is found in **ctype.h**.

The **isdigit( )** macro returns non-0 if *ch* is a digit, that is, 0 through 9; otherwise it returns 0.

Example

This program checks each character read from **stdin** and reports all those that are digits:

```
#include <ctype.h>
#include <stdio.h>

main(void)
{
  char ch;

  for(;;) {
    ch = getchar();
    if(ch==' ') break;
    if(isdigit(ch)) printf("%c is a digit\n", ch);
  }
  return 0;
}
```

Related Functions

isalnum( ), **iscntrl( )**, **isalpha( )**, **isgraph( )**, **isprint( )**, **ispunct( )**, **isspace( )**

int isgraph(int ch)

Description

The prototype for **isgraph( )** is found in **ctype.h**.

The **isgraph( )** macro returns non-0 if *ch* is any printable character other than a space; otherwise it returns 0. Printable characters are in the range 0x21 through 0x7E.

Example

This program checks each character read from **stdin** and reports all those that are printable characters:

```
#include <ctype.h>
#include <stdio.h>
```

```
main(void)
{
  char ch;

  for(;;) {
    ch = getchar();
    if(ch==' ') break;
    if(isgraph(ch)) printf("%c is a printing character\n", ch);
  }
  return 0;
}
```

Related Functions

isalnum( ), **iscntrl( )**, **isalpha( )**, **isdigit( )**, **isprint( )**, **ispunct( )**, **isspace( )**

int islower(int ch)

Description

The prototype for **islower( )** is found in **ctype.h**.

The **islower( )** macro returns non-0 if *ch* is a lowercase letter ("a" through "z"); otherwise it returns 0.

Example

This program checks each character read from **stdin** and reports all those that are lowercase letters:

```
#include <ctype.h>
#include <stdio.h>

main(void)
{
  char ch;

  for(;;) {
    ch = getchar();
    if(ch==' ') break;
    if(islower(ch)) printf("%c is lowercase\n", ch);
  }
  return 0;
}
```

Related Function

isupper( )

int isprint(int ch)

Description

The prototype for **isprint( )** is found in **ctype.h**.

The **isprint( )** macro returns non-0 if *ch* is a printable character, including a space; otherwise it returns 0. The printable characters are in the range 0x20 through 0x7E.

Example

This program checks each character read from **stdin** and reports all those that are printable:

```
#include <ctype.h>
#include <stdio.h>

main(void)
{
  char ch;

  for(;;) {
    ch = getchar();
    if(ch==' ') break;
    if(isprint(ch)) printf("%c is printable\n", ch);
  }
  return 0;
}
```

Related Functions

isalnum( ), iscntrl( ), isalpha( ), isdigit( ), isgraph( ), ispunct( ), isspace( )

int ispunct(int ch)

Description

The prototype for **ispunct( )** is found in **ctype.h**.

The **ispunct( )** macro returns non-0 if *ch* is a punctuation character or a space; otherwise it returns 0.

Example

This program checks each character read from **stdin** and reports all those that are punctuation:

```
#include <ctype.h>
#include <stdio.h>

main(void)
{
  char ch;

  for(;;) {
    ch = getchar();
    if(ch==' ') break;
    if(ispunct(ch)) printf("%c is punctuation\n", ch);
  }
  return 0;
}
```

Related Functions

isalnum( ), iscntrl( ), isalpha( ), isdigit( ), isgraph( ), isspace( )

int isspace(int ch)

Description

The prototype for **isspace( )** is found in **ctype.h**.

The **isspace( )** macro returns non-0 if *ch* is either a space, carriage return, horizontal tab, vertical tab, form feed, or newline character; otherwise it returns 0.

Example

This program checks each character read from **stdin** and reports all those that are white-space characters:

```
#include <ctype.h>
#include <stdio.h>

main(void)
{
  char ch;
```

```
for(;;) {
  ch = getchar();
  if(ch=='$') break;
  if(isspace(ch)) printf("%c is white-space\n", ch);
}
return 0;
}
```

Related Functions

isalnum( ), iscntrl( ), isalpha( ), isdigit( ), isgraph( ), ispunct( )

int isupper(ch)

Description

The prototype for **isupper( )** is found in **ctype.h**.

The **isupper( )** macro returns non-0 if *ch* is an uppercase letter ("A" through "Z"); otherwise it returns 0.

Example

This program checks each character read from **stdin** and reports all those that are uppercase letters:

```
#include <ctype.h>
#include <stdio.h>

main(void)
{
  char ch;

  for(;;) {
    ch = getchar();
    if(ch==' ') break;
    if(isupper(ch)) printf("%c is upper-case\n", ch);
  }
  return 0;
}
```

Related Function

islower( )

int isxdigit(int ch)

Description

The prototype for **isxdigit( )** is found in **ctype.h**.

The **isxdigit( )** macro returns non-0 if *ch* is a hexadecimal digit; otherwise it returns 0. A hexadecimal digit will be in one of these ranges: "A" through "F", "a" through "f", or "0" through "9".

Example

This program checks each character read from **stdin** and reports all those that are hexadecimal digits:

```
#include <ctype.h>
#include <stdio.h>

main(void)
{
  char ch;

  for(;;) {
    ch = getchar();
    if(ch==' ') break;
    if(isxdigit(ch)) printf("%c is hexadecimal \n", ch);
  }
  return 0;
}
```

Related Functions

isalnum( ), **iscntrl( )**, **isalpha( )**, **isdigit( )**, **isgraph( )**, **isspace( )**, **ispunct( )**

void *memccpy(void *dest, const void *source, int ch, size_t count)
void far * far _fmemccpy(void far *dest, const void far *source, int ch, size_t count)

Description

The prototype for **memccpy( )** is found in both **string.h** and **mem.h** and is not defined by the ANSI C standard.

The **memccpy( )** function copies the contents of the memory pointed to by *source* into the memory pointed to by *dest*. The copy operation stops when either *count* number of bytes have been copied or after the first occurrence of *ch* has been copied. It returns a pointer to the end of *dest* if *ch* is found or null if *ch* is not part of *source*.

_fmemccpy( ) is the FAR version of **memccpy( )**.

Example

After this fragment has executed, the word "hello" will be in array **out** because the space is used to terminate the copy operation:

```
char str[20], out[20];

strcpy(str, "hello there");

memccpy(out, str,' ', 20);
```

Related Functions

memcpy( ), **strcpy( )**

void *memchr(const void *buffer, int ch, size_t count)
void far * far _fmemchr(const void far *buffer, int ch, size_t count)

Description

The prototype for the **memchr( )** function is found in both **string.h** and **mem.h**.

The **memchr( )** function searches *buffer* for the first occurrence of *ch* in the first *count* characters.

The **memchr( )** function returns a pointer to the first occurrence of *ch* in *buffer*, or a null pointer if *ch* is not found.

_fmemchr( ) is the FAR version of **memchr( )**.

Example

This program prints " is a test" on the screen:

```
#include <stdio.h>
#include <string.h>

main(void)
{
  void *p;

  p = memchr("this is a test",' ', 14);
```

```
    printf((char *) p);
    return 0;
}
```

Related Functions

memmove( ), memcpy( )

int memcmp(const void *buf1, const void *buf2, size_t count)
int memicmp(const void *buf1, const void *buf2, size_t count)
int far _fmemcmp(const void far *buf1, const void far *buf2,
                        size_t count)
int far _fmemicmp(const void far *buf1, const void far *buf2,
                        size_t count)

Description

The prototype for the **memcmp( )** function is found in both **string.h** and **mem.h**. The
memicmp( ) function is not defined by the ANSI C standard.

The **memcmp( )** function compares the first *count* characters of the arrays pointed
to by *buf1* and *buf2*. The comparison is done lexicographically.

The **memcmp( )** function returns an integer that is interpreted as indicated here:

Value	Meaning
Less than 0	*buf1* is less than *buf2*
0	*buf1* is equal to *buf2*
Greater than 0	*buf1* is greater than *buf2*

The **memicmp( )** function is identical to **memcmp( )** except that case is ignored
when comparing letters.

_fmemcmp( ) and **_fmemicmp( )** are the FAR versions of these functions.

Example

This program shows the outcome of a comparison of its two command-line arguments:

```
#include <stdio.h>
#include <string.h>

main(int argc, char *argv[])
```

```
{
  int outcome;
  size_t len, l1, l2;

  /* find the length of shortest */
  len=(l1=strlen(argv[1]))<(l2=strlen(argv[2])) ? l1:l2;

  outcome = memcmp(argv[1], argv[2], len);
  if(!outcome) printf("equal");
  else if(outcome<0) printf("first less than second");
  else printf("first greater than second");
  return 0;
}
```

Related Functions

memcpy( ), memchr( ), strcmp( )

void *memcpy(void *dest, const void *source, size_t count)
void far * far _fmemcpy(void far *dest, const void far *source, size_t count)

Description

The prototype for **memcpy( )** is found in both **string.h** and **mem.h**.

   The **memcpy( )** function copies *count* characters from the array pointed to by *source* into the array pointed to by *dest*. If the arrays overlap, the behavior of **memcpy( )** is undefined.

   The **memcpy( )** function returns a pointer to *dest*.

   _fmemcpy( ) is the FAR version of this function.

Example

This program copies the contents of **buf1** into **buf2** and displays the result:

```
#include <stdio.h>
#include <string.h>
#define SIZE 80

main(void)
{
  char buf1[SIZE], buf2[SIZE];
```

```
strcpy(buf1, "When, in the course of...");
memcpy(buf2, buf1, SIZE);
printf(buf2);
return 0;
}
```

Related Function

memmove( )

void *memmove(void *dest, const void *source, size_t count)

Description

The prototype for **memmove( )** is found in both **string.h** and **mem.h**.

The **memmove( )** function copies *count* characters from the array pointed to by *source* into the array pointed to by *dest*. If the arrays overlap, the copy takes place correctly, placing the correct contents into *dest* but leaving *source* modified.

The **memmove( )** function returns a pointer to *dest*.

Example

This program copies the contents of *str1* into *str2* and displays the result:

```
#include <stdio.h>
#include <string.h>

main(void)
{
  char str1[20], str2[20];

  strcpy(str1,"Born to code in C.");
  memmove(str2, str1, 20);
  printf(str2);
  return 0;
}
```

Related Functions

memcpy( ), movedata( ), movemem( )

void *memset(void *buf, int ch, size_t count)
void far * far _fmemset(void far *buf, int ch, size_t count)

Description

The prototype for **memset( )** is found in both **string.h** and **mem.h**.

The **memset( )** function copies the low-order byte of *ch* into the first *count* characters of the array pointed to by *buf*. It returns *buf*.

The most common use of **memset( )** is to initialize a region of memory to some known value.

_fmemset( ) is the FAR version of this function.

Example

This fragment first initializes to null the first 100 bytes of the array pointed to by *buf* and then sets the first 10 bytes to '**X**' and displays the string "XXXXXXXXXX":

```
memset(buf, '\0', 100);
memset(buf, 'X', 10);
printf((char *) buf);
```

Related Functions

memcpy( ), **memcmp( )**, **memmove( )**

void movedata(unsigned sourceseg, unsigned sourceoff, unsigned destseg, unsigned destoff, size_t count)

Description

The prototype for **movedata( )** is found in both **string.h** and **mem.h**. The **movedata( )** function is not defined by the ANSI C standard.

The **movedata( )** function copies *count* characters from the memory at location *sourceseg:sourceoff* into the memory location *destseg:destoff*. The **movedata( )** function works regardless of which memory model is selected.

Example

This program copies the first 25 bytes of the data segment into the array **buff**.

```
#include <stdio.h>
#include <string.h>
#include <dos.h>

main(void)
{
  char buff[25];

  movedata(_DS, 0, FP_SEG(buff), FP_OFF(buff), 25);
  return 0;
}
```

Related Functions

memcpy( ), movemem( ), memmove( )

void movemem(void *source, void *dest, unsigned count)

Description

The prototype for **movemem( )** is found in **mem.h**. The function **movemem( )** is not defined by the ANSI C standard.

The **movemem( )** function copies *count* characters from the array pointed to by *source* into the array pointed to by *dest*. If the arrays overlap, the copy takes place correctly, placing the correct contents into *dest* but leaving *source* modified.

The **movemem( )** function is equivalent to the **memmove( )** function except that the **movemem( )** function has no return value and is not defined by the ANSI C standard.

Related Functions

memcpy( ), movedata( ), memmove( )

void setmem(void *buf, unsigned count, char ch)

Description

The prototype for **setmem( )** is found in **mem.h**. The **setmem( )** function is not defined by the ANSI C standard.

The **setmem( )** function copies *ch* into the first *count* characters of the array pointed to by *buf*.

The **setmem( )** function is equivalent to the **memset( )** function except that the **setmem( )** function has no return value and is not defined by the ANSI C standard.

Related Functions

memcpy( ), memset( ), memmove( )

char *stpcpy(char *str1, const char *str2)

Description

The prototype for **stpcpy( )** is found in **string.h** and is not defined by the ANSI C standard.

The **stpcpy( )** function is used to copy the contents of *str2* into *str1*. *str2* must be a pointer to a null-terminated string. The **stpcpy( )** function returns a pointer to the end of *str1*.

Example

The following code fragment copies "hello" into string **str**:

```
char str[8];
stpcpy(str, "hello");
```

Related Functions

strcpy( )

char *strcat(char *str1, const char *str2)
char far * far _fstrcat(char far *str1, const char *str2)

Description

The prototype for **strcat( )** is found in **string.h**.

The **strcat( )** function concatenates a copy of *str2* to *str1* and terminates *str1* with a null. The null terminator originally ending *str1* is overwritten by the first character of *str2*. The string *str2* is untouched by the operation.

The **strcat( )** function returns *str1*.

Remember that no bounds checking takes place, so it is the programmer's responsibility to ensure that *str1* is large enough to hold both its original contents and the contents of *str2*.

_fstrcat( ) is the FAR version of this function.

Example

This program appends the first string read from **stdin** to the second. For example, assuming the user enters "hello" and "there", the program prints "therehello".

```
#include <stdio.h>
#include <string.h>

main(void)
{
  char s1[80], s2[80];

  gets(s1);
  gets(s2);

  strcat(s2, s1);
  printf(s2);
  return 0;
}
```

Related Functions

strchr( ), strcmp( ), strcpy( )

char *strchr(const char *str, int ch)
char far * far _fstrchr(const char far *str, int ch)

Description

The prototype for **strchr( )** is found in **string.h**.

The **strchr( )** function returns a pointer to the first occurrence of *ch* in the string pointed to by *str*. If no match is found, it returns a null pointer.

_fstrchr( ) is the FAR version of this function.

Example

This program prints the string " is a test":

```
#include <stdio.h>
#include <string.h>

main(void)
{
  char *p;

  p = strchr("this is a test", ' ');
  printf(p);
  return 0;
}
```

Related Functions

strpbrk( ), **strstr( )**, **strtok( )**, **strspn( )**

int strcmp(const char *str1, const char *str2)

Description

The prototype for the **strcmp( )** function is found in **string.h**.

The **strcmp( )** function lexicographically compares two null-terminated strings and returns an integer based on the outcome, as shown here:

Value	Meaning
Less than 0	*str1* is less than *str2*
0	*str1* is equal to *str2*
Greater than 0	*str1* is greater than *str2*

Example

The following function can be used as a password-verification routine. It returns 0 on failure and 1 on success.

```
password()
{
  char s[80];

  printf("enter password: ");
  gets(s);

  if(strcmp(s, "pass")) {
    printf("invalid password\n");
    return 0;
  }
  return 1;
}
```

Related Functions

strchr( ), **strcpy( )**, **strncmp( )**

int strcoll(char *str1, char *str2)

Description

The prototype for the **strcoll( )** function is found in **string.h**.

The **strcoll( )** function is equivalent to the **strcmp( )** function. Please refer to strcmp( ) for a description.

Related Functions

strncmp( ), stricmp( )

char *strcpy(char *str1, const char *str2)

Description

The prototype for **strcpy( )** is found in **string.h**.

The **strcpy( )** function is used to copy the contents of *str2* into *str1*; *str2* must be a pointer to a null-terminated string. The **strcpy( )** function returns a pointer to *str1*.

If *str1* and *str2* overlap, the behavior of **strcpy( )** is undefined.

Example

The following code fragment copies "hello" into string **str**.

```
char str[80];
strcpy(str, "hello");
```

Related Functions

strchr( ), strcmp( ), memcpy( ), strncmp( )

size_t strcspn(const char *str1, const char *str2)
size_t far _fstrcspn(const char far *str1, const char far *str2)

Description

The prototype for the **strcspn( )** function is found in **string.h**.

The **strcspn( )** function returns the length of the initial substring of the string pointed to by *str1* that is made up of only those characters not contained in the string pointed to by *str2*. Stated differently, **strcspn( )** returns the index of the first character in the string pointed to by *str1* that matches any of the characters in the string pointed to by *str2*.

_fstrcspn( ) is the FAR version of this function.

Example

This program prints the number 8:

```
#include <stdio.h>
#include <string.h>

main(void)
{
  int len;

  len = strcspn("this is a test", "ab");
  printf("%d", len);
  return 0;
}
```

Related Functions

strpbrk( ), strstr( ), strtok( ), strrchr( )

char *strdup(const char *str)
char far * far _fstrdup(const char far *str)

Description

The prototype for **strdup( )** is found in **string.h**. The **strdup( )** function is not defined by the ANSI C standard.

The **strdup( )** function allocates enough memory, via a call to **malloc( )**, to hold a duplicate of the string pointed to by *str* and then copies that string into the allocated region and returns a pointer to it.

_fstrdup( ) is the FAR version of this function.

Example

This fragment duplicates the string **str**.

```
char str[80], *p;

strcpy(str, "this is a test");

p = strdup(str);
```

Related Function

strcpy( )

char *_strerror(const char *str)

Description

The prototype for the **_strerror( )** function is found in **stdio.h** and **string.h**.

The **_strerror( )** function lets you display your own error message followed by a colon and the most recent error message generated by the program. It returns a pointer to the entire string.

The **_strerror( )** function is equivalent to **strerror( )** in version 1.0 of Turbo C. The **_strerror( )** function is not defined by the ANSI C standard.

Example

This fragment prints a message stating that the function called **swap( )** encountered an error:

```
swap()
{
  .
  .
  .

  if(error) printf(_strerror("error in swap"));
```

Related Functions

perror( ), **strerror( )**

char *strerror(int num)

Description

The prototype for the **strerror( )** function is found in **stdio.h** and **string.h**.

The **strerror( )** function returns a pointer to the error message associated with an error number.

The operation of **strerror( )** changed after release 1.0 of Turbo C. The original **strerror( )** is implemented as **_strerror( )**, which is not defined by the ANSI C standard.

Example

This fragment prints the error message associated with the global variable **errno** if an error has occurred.

```
          .
          .
          .

if(errno) printf(strerror(errno));
```

Related Functions

perror( ), _strerror( )

int stricmp(const char *str1, const char *str2)
int strcmpi(const char *str1, const char *str2)
int far _fstricmp(const char far *str1, const char far *str2)

Description

The prototypes for the **stricmp( )** function and **strcmpi( )** macro are found in **string.h**. Neither of these are defined by the ANSI C standard.

The **stricmp( )** function lexicographically compares two null-terminated strings while ignoring case; **strcmpi( )** is a macro that translates to a **stricmp( )** call.

Both functions return an integer based on the outcome, as shown here:

Value	Meaning
Less than 0	*str1* is less than *str2*
0	*str1* is equal to *str2*
Greater than 0	*str1* is greater than *str2*

_fstricmp( ) is the FAR version of this stricmp( ).

Example

The following function compares the two file names specified on the command line to determine if they are the same:

```
#include <stdio.h>
#include <string.h>

main(int argc, char *argv[])
{
  if(!stricmp(argv[1], argv[2]))
    printf("the filenames are the same\n");
```

```
   return 0;
}
```

Related Functions

strnchr( ), strcmp( ), strncpy( )

size_t strlen(const char *str)
size_t _fstrlen(const char far *str)

Description

The prototype for **strlen( )** is found in **string.h**.

The **strlen( )** function returns the length of the null-terminated string pointed to by *str*. The null is not counted.

_fstrlen( ) is the FAR version of this function.

Example

This code fragment prints the number 5 on the screen:

```
strcpy(s, "hello");
printf("%d", strlen(s));
```

Related Functions

strchr( ), strcmp( ), memcpy( ), strncmp( )

char *strlwr(char *str)
char far * far _fstrlwr(char far *str)

Description

The prototype for **strlwr( )** is found in **string.h**. The **strlwr( )** function is not defined by the ANSI C standard.

The **strlwr( )** function converts the string pointed to by *str* to lowercase. It returns *str*.

_fstrlwr( ) is the FAR version of this function.

Example

This program prints "this is a test" on the screen:

```
#include <stdio.h>
#include <string.h>

main(void)
{
  char s[80];

  strcpy(s, "THIS IS A TEST");

  strlwr(s);

  printf(s);

  return 0;
}
```

Related Function

strupr( )

char *strncat(char *str1, const char *str2, size_t count)
char far * far _fstrncat(char far *str1, const char far *str2, size_t count)

Description

The prototype for the **strncat( )** function is found in **string.h**.

The **strncat( )** function concatenates no more than *count* characters of the string pointed to by *str2* to the string pointed to by *str1* and terminates *str1* with a null. The null terminator originally ending *str1* is overwritten by the first character of *str2*. The string *str2* is untouched by the operation.

The **strncat( )** function returns *str1*.

Remember, no bounds checking takes place, so it is the programmer's responsibility to ensure that *str1* is large enough to hold both its original contents and those of *str2*.

_fstrncat( ) is the FAR version of this function.

Example

This program appends the first string read from **stdin** to the second and prevents an array overflow from occurring in *str1*. For example, if the user enters "hello" and "there", the program prints "therehello":

```
#include <stdio.h>
#include <string.h>

main(void)
{
  char s1[80], s2[80];
  size_t len;

  gets(s1);
  gets(s2);

  /* compute how many chars will actually fit */
  len = 79-strlen(s2);

  strncat(s2, s1, len);
  printf(s2);
  return 0;
}
```

Related Functions

strnchr( ), **strncmp( )**, **strncpy( )**, **strcat( )**

int strncmp(const char *str1, const char *str2, size_t count)
int strnicmp(const char *str1, const char *str2, size_t count)
int strncmpi(const char *str1, const char *str2, size_t count)
int far _fstrncmp(const char far *str1, const char far *str2, size_t count)
int far _fstrnicmp(const char far *str1, const char far *str2, size_t count)

Description

The prototypes for the **strncmp( )** and **strnicmp( )** functions, and the **strncmpi( )** macro are found in **string.h**. Of these, only **strncmp( )** is defined by the ANSI C standard.

The **strncmp( )** function lexicographically compares no more than *count* characters from the two null-terminated strings. The functions **strnicmp( )** and **strncmpi( )** perform the same comparison while ignoring case; **strncmpi( )** is a macro that translates to a **strnicmp( )** call.

All three functions return an integer based on the outcome, as shown here:

Value	Meaning
Less than 0	*str1* is less than *str2*
0	*str1* is equal to *str2*
Greater than 0	*str1* is greater than *str2*

If there are fewer than *count* characters in either string, the comparison ends when the first null is encountered.

_fstrncmp( ) is the FAR version of **strncmp( )**.

_fstrnicmp( ) is the FAR version of **strnicmp( )**.

Example

The following function compares the first eight characters of the two file names specified on the command line to determine if they are the same:

```
#include <stdio.h>
#include <string.h>

main(int argc, char *argv[])
{
  if(!strnicmp(argv[1], argv[2], 8))
    printf("the file names are the same\n");
  return 0;
}
```

Related Functions

strnchr( ), strcmp( ), strncpy( )

char *strncpy(char *dest, const char *source, size_t count)
char far * far _fstrncpy(char far *dest, const char far *source, size_t count)

Description

The prototype for **strncpy( )** is found in **string.h**.

The **strncpy( )** function is used to copy up to *count* characters from the string pointed to by *source* into the string pointed to by *dest*. The *source* must be a pointer to a null-terminated string. The **strncpy( )** function returns a pointer to *dest*.

If *dest* and *source* overlap, the behavior of **strncpy( )** is undefined.

If the string pointed to by *source* has fewer than *count* characters, nulls are appended to the end of *dest* until *count* characters have been copied.

Alternately, if the string pointed to by *source* is longer than *count* characters, the resulting string pointed to by *dest* is not null-terminated.

_fstrncpy( ) is the FAR version of this function.

Example

The following code fragment copies at most 79 characters of *str1* into *str2*, thus ensuring that no array boundary overflow will occur:

```
char str1[128], str2[80];
gets(str1);
strncpy(str2, str1, 79);
```

Related Functions

strchr( ), strncmp( ), memcpy( ), strncat( )

char *strnset(char *str, int ch, size_t count)
char far * far _fstrnset(char far *str, int ch, size_t count)

Description

The prototype for **strnset( )** is found in **string.h**.

   The **strnset( )** function sets the first *count* characters in the string pointed to by *str* to the value of *ch*. It returns *str*.

   _fstrnset( ) is the FAR version of this function.

Example

This fragment sets the first 10 characters of *str* to the value **x**:

```
strnset(str, 'x', 10);
```

Related Function

strset( )

char *strpbrk(const char *str1, const char *str2)
char far * far _fstrpbrk(const char far *str1, const char far *str2)

Description

The prototype to **strpbrk( )** is found in **string.h**.

   The **strpbrk( )** function returns a pointer to the first character in the string pointed to by *str1* that matches any character in the string pointed to by *str2*. The null terminators are not included. If there are no matches, a null pointer is returned.

   _fstrpbrk( ) is the FAR version of this function.

Example

This program prints the message "s is a test" on the screen:

```
#include <stdio.h>
#include <string.h>

main(void)
{
  char *p;

  p = strpbrk("this is a test", " absj");
  printf(p);
  return 0;
}
```

Related Functions

strrchr( ), strstr( ), strtok( ), strspn( )

char *strrchr(const char *str, int ch)
char far * far _fstrrchr(const char far *str, int ch)

Description

The prototype to **strrchr( )** is found in **string.h**.

The **strrchr( )** function returns a pointer to the last occurrence of the low-order byte of *ch* in the string pointed to by *str*. If no match is found, it returns a null pointer.

_fstrrchr( ) is the FAR version of this function.

Example

This program prints the string "is a test":

```
#include <stdio.h>
#include <string.h>

main(void)
{
  char *p;
```

```
  p = strrchr("this is a test", 'i');
  printf(p);
  return 0;
}
```

Related Functions

strpbrk( ), strstr( ), strtok( ), strspn( )

char *strrev(char *str)
char far * far _fstrrev(char far *str)

Description

The prototype for **strrev( )** is found in **string.h**. The **strrev( )** function is not defined by the ANSI C standard.

   The **strrev( )** function reverses all characters, except the null terminator, in the string pointed to by *str*. It returns *str*.

   _fstrrev( ) is the FAR version of this function.

Example

This program prints "hello" backwards on the screen:

```
#include <stdio.h>
#include <string.h>

char s[] = "hello";

main(void)
{
  strrev(s);

  printf(s);

  return 0;
}
```

Related Function

strset( )

char *strset(char *str, int ch)
char far * far _fstrset(char far *str, int ch)

Description

The prototype for **strset( )** is found in **string.h**. The **strset( )** function is not defined by the ANSI C standard.

The **strset( )** function sets all characters in the string pointed to by *str* to the value of *ch*. It returns **str**.

_fstrset( ) is the FAR version of this function.

Example

This fragment fills the string *str* with the value **x**.

```
strset(str, 'x');
```

Related Function

strnset( )

size_t strspn(const char *str1, const char *str2)
size_t far _fstrspn(const char far *str1, const char far *str2)

Description

The **strspn( )** function returns the length of the initial substring of the string pointed to by *str1* that is made up of only those characters contained in the string pointed to by *str2*. Stated differently, **strspn( )** returns the index of the first character in the string pointed to by *str1* that does not match any of the characters in the string pointed to by *str2*.

_fstrspn( ) is the FAR version of this function.

Example

This program prints the number 8:

```
#include <stdio.h>
#include <string.h>

main(void)
{
```

```
    int len;

    len = strspn("this is a test", "siht ");
    printf("%d",len);
    return 0;
}
```

Related Functions

strpbrk( ), strstr( ), strtok( ), strrchr( )

char *strstr(const char *str1, const char *str2)
char far * far _fstrstr(const char far *str1, const char far *str2)

Description

The prototype for **strstr( )** is found in **string.h**.

The **strstr( )** function returns a pointer to the first occurrence in the string pointed to by *str1* of the string pointed to by *str2* (except *str2*'s null terminator). It returns a null pointer if no match is found.

_fstrstr( ) is the FAR version of this function.

Example

This program displays the message "is is a test":

```
#include <stdio.h>
#include <string.h>

main(void)
{
  char *p;

  p = strstr("this is a test", "is");
  printf(p);
  return 0;
}
```

Related Functions

strpbrk( ), strspn( ), strtok( ), strrchr( ), strchr( ), strcspn( )

char *strtok(char *str1, const char *str2)
char far * far _fstrtok(char far *str1, const char far *str2)

Description

The prototype for **strtok( )** is in **string.h**.

The **strtok( )** function returns a pointer to the next token in the string pointed to by *str1*. The characters making up the string pointed to by *str2* are the delimiters that determine the token. A null pointer is returned when there is no token to return.

The first time **strtok( )** is called, *str1* is actually used in the call. Subsequent calls use a null pointer for the first argument. In this way the entire string can be reduced to its tokens.

It is important to understand that the **strtok( )** function modifies the string pointed to by *str1*. Each time a token is found, a null is placed where the delimiter was found. In this way **strtok( )** continues to advance through the string.

It is possible to use a different set of delimiters for each call to **strtok( )**.

_fstrtok( ) is the FAR version of this function.

Example

This program tokenizes the string "The summer soldier, the sunshine patriot" with spaces and commas as the delimiters. The output is "The|summer|soldier|the|sunshine|patriot".

```
#include <stdio.h>
#include <string.h>

main(void)
{
  char *p;

  p = strtok("The summer soldier, the sunshine patriot"," ");
  printf(p);
  do {
    p=strtok('\0', ", ");
    if(p) printf("|%s", p);
  } while(p);
  return 0;
}
```

Related Functions

strpbrk( ), strspn( ), strtok( ), strrchr( ), strchr( ), strcspn( )

char *strupr(char *str)
char far * far _fstrupr(char far *str)

Description

The prototype for **strupr( )** is found in **string.h**. The **strupr( )** function is not defined by the ANSI C standard.

The **strupr( )** function converts the string pointed to by *str* to uppercase. It returns *str*.

_fstrupr( ) is the FAR version of this function.

Example

This program prints "THIS IS A TEST" on the screen:

```
#include <stdio.h>
#include <string.h>

main(void)
{
  char s[80];

  strcpy(s, "this is a test");

  strupr(s);

  printf(s);

  return 0;
}
```

Related Function

strlwr( )

size_t strxfrm(char *dest, const char *source, size_t count)

Description

The prototype for **strxfrm( )** is found in **string.h**.

The **strxfrm( )** function is used to copy up to *count* characters from the string pointed to by *source* into the string pointed to by *dest*. The *source* must be a pointer to a null-terminated string. In the process, any country-related items are transformed into the proper format for the current country. The **strxfrm( )** function returns the length of the string pointed to by *source.*

The **strxfrm( )** function is equivalent to the **strncpy( )** function.

Related Functions

strncpy( ), **movedata( )**, **memcpy( )**, **strncat( )**

int tolower(int ch)
int _tolower(int ch)

Description

The prototype for **tolower( )** and the definition of the macro **_tolower( )** are found in **ctype.h**. The **_tolower( )** macro is not defined by the ANSI C standard.

The **tolower( )** function returns the lowercase equivalent of *ch* if *ch* is an uppercase letter; otherwise it returns *ch* unchanged. The **_tolower( )** macro is equivalent, but should only be used when *ch* is an uppercase letter; otherwise the results are undefined.

Example

This code fragment displays a "q".

```
putchar(tolower('Q'));
```

Related Function

toupper( )

int toupper(int ch)
int _toupper(int ch)

Description

The prototype for **toupper( )** and the macro **_toupper( )** are found in **ctype.h**. The **_toupper( )** macro is not defined by the ANSI C standard.

The **toupper( )** function returns the uppercase equivalent of *ch* if *ch* is a letter; otherwise it returns *ch* unchanged. The **_toupper( )** macro is equivalent, but should only be used when *ch* is a lowercase letter; otherwise the results are undefined.

Example

This displays an "A".

```
putchar(toupper('a'));
```

Related Function

tolower( )

Chapter *18*

Mathematical Functions

The ANSI C standard defines 22 mathematical functions that fall into the following categories:

- Trigonometric functions

- Hyperbolic functions

- Exponential and logarithmic functions

- Miscellaneous

Turbo/Borland C/C++ implements all of these functions and includes several of its own mathematical functions. Many of the functions added by Borland are **long double** versions of the standard functions. All mathematical functions provided by the Turbo/Borland C/C++ are discussed here.

All the math functions require the header **math.h** to be included in any program using them. In addition to declaring the math functions, this header defines three macros called **EDOM**, **ERANGE**, and **HUGE_VAL**. If an argument to a math function is not in the domain for which it is defined, an implementation-defined value is returned and the global **errno** is set equal to **EDOM**. If a routine produces a result that is too large to be represented, an overflow happens. This causes the routine to return **HUGE_VAL** and **errno** is set to **ERANGE**, indicating a range error. (If the function returns a **long double**, then it returns **_LHUGE_VAL**.) If an underflow happens, the routine returns 0 and sets **errno** to **ERANGE**.

double acos(double arg)
long double acosl(long double arg)

Description

The prototype for **acos( )** is in **math.h**.

The **acos( )** function returns the arc cosine of *arg*. The argument to **acos( )** must be in the range −1 to 1; otherwise a domain error occurs. The return value is in the range 0 to π. The value of *arg* is specified in radians and the return value is in radians.

acosl( ) is the **long double** version of this function.

Example

This program prints the arc cosines, in one-tenth increments, of the values −1 through 1:

```
#include <stdio.h>
#include <math.h>

main(void)
{
  double val = -1.0;

  do {
    printf("arc cosine of %lf is %lf\n", val, acos(val));
    val += 0.1;
  } while(val <= 1.0);
  return 0;
}
```

Related Functions

asin( ), atan( ), atan2( ), sin( ), cos( ), tan( ), sinh( ), cosh( ), tanh( )

double asin(double arg)
long double asinl(long double arg)

Description

The prototype for **asin( )** is in **math.h**.

The **asin( )** function returns the arc sine of *arg*. The argument to **asin( )** must be in the range −1 to 1; otherwise a domain error occurs. Its return value is in the range −$\pi/2$ to $\pi/2$. The value of *arg* is specified in radians.

asinl( ) is the **long double** version of this function.

Example

This program prints the arc sines, in one-tenth increments, of the values –1 through 1:

```
#include <stdio.h>
#include <math.h>

main(void)
{
  double val = -1.0;

  do {
    printf("arc sine of %lf is %lf\n", val, asin(val));
    val += 0.1;
  } while(val <= 1.0);
  return 0;
}
```

Related Functions

atan( ), **atan2( )**, **sin( )**, **cos( )**, **tan( )**, **sinh( )**, **cosh( )**, **tanh( )**

double atan(double arg)
long double atanl(long double arg)

Description

The prototype for **atan( )** is in **math.h**.

The **atan( )** function returns the arc tangent of *arg*. The value of *arg* must be in the range –1 to 1; otherwise a domain error occurs. The value of *arg* is specified in radians.

atanl( ) is the **long double** version of this function.

Example

This program prints the arc tangents, in one-tenth increments, of the values –1 through 1.

```
#include <stdio.h>
#include <math.h>

main(void)
{
  double val = -1.0;
```

```
do {
  printf("arc tangent of %lf is %lf\n", val, atan(val));
  val += 0.1;
} while(val <= 1.0);
return 0;
}
```

Related Functions

asin( ), acos( ), atan2( ), tan( ), cos( ), sin( ), sinh( ), cosh( ), tanh( )

double atan2(double y, double x)
long double atan2l(long double y, long double x)

Description

The prototype for **atan2( )** is in **math.h**.

The **atan2( )** function returns the arc tangent of *y/x*. It uses the signs of its arguments to compute the quadrant of the return value. The value of *arg* is specified in radians.

atan2l( ) is the **long double** version of this function.

Example

This program prints the arc tangents, in one-tenth increments of *y*, from –1 through 1:

```
#include <stdio.h>
#include <math.h>

main(void)
{
  double y = -1.0;

  do {
    printf("atan2 of %lf is %lf\n", y, atan2(y, 1.0));
    y += 0.1;
  } while(y <= 1.0);
  return 0;
}
```

Related Functions

asin( ), acos( ), atan( ), tan( ), cos( ), sin( ), sinh( ), cosh( ), tanh( )

double cabs(struct complex znum)
long double cabsl(struct _complex znum)

Description

The prototype for **cabs( )** is in **math.h**. This macro is not defined by the ANSI C standard.

The **cabs( )** macro returns the absolute value of a complex number. The structure **complex** is defined as

```
struct complex {
    double x;
    double y;
};
```

If an overflow occurs, **HUGE_VAL** is returned and **errno** is set to **ERANGE** (out of range).

cabsl( ) is the **long double** version of this macro and **_complex** is the **long double** equivalent of **complex**.

Example

This code prints the absolute value of a complex number that has a real part equal to 1 and an imaginary part equal to 2:

```
#include <stdio.h>
#include <math.h>

main(void)
{
    struct complex z;

    z.x = 1;
    z.y = 2;

    printf("%lf", cabs(z));
    return 0;
}
```

Related Function

abs( )

double ceil(double num)
long double ceill(long double num)

Description

The prototype for **ceil( )** is in **math.h**.

The **ceil( )** function returns the smallest integer (represented as a **double**) not less than *num*. For example, given 1.02, **ceil( )** returns 2.0. Given –1.02, **ceil( )** returns –1.

ceill( ) is the **long double** version of **ceil( )**.

Example

This fragment prints the value "10" on the screen:

```
printf("%lf", ceil(9.9));
```

Related Functions

floor( ), **fmod( )**

double cos(double arg)
long double cosl(long double arg)

Description

The prototype for **cos( )** is in **math.h**.

The **cos( )** function returns the cosine of *arg*. The value of *arg* must be in radians. The return value is in the range –1 to 1.

cosl( ) is the **long double** version of this function.

Example

This program prints the cosines, in one-tenth increments, of the values –1 through 1:

```
#include <stdio.h>
#include <math.h>

main(void)
{
  double val = -1.0;
```

```
do {
    printf("cosine of %lf is %lf\n", val, cos(val));
    val += 0.1;
} while(val <= 1.0);
return 0;
}
```

Related Functions

asin( ), acos( ), atan2( ), atan( ), tan( ), sin( ), sinh( ), cosh( ), tanh( )

double cosh(double arg)
long double coshl(long double arg)

Description

The prototype for **cosh( )** is in **math.h**.

The **cosh( )** function returns the hyperbolic cosine of *arg*. The value of *arg* must be in radians.

coshl( ) is the **long double** version of this function.

Example

This program prints the hyperbolic cosines, in one-tenth increments, of the values −1 through 1:

```
#include <stdio.h>
#include <math.h>

main(void)
{
    double val = -1.0;

    do {
        printf("hyperbolic cosine of %lf is %lf\n", val, cosh(val));
        val += 0.1;
    } while(val <= 1.0);
    return 0;
}
```

Related Functions

asin( ), acos( ), atan2( ), atan( ), tan( ), cos( ), sin( ), tanh( )

double exp(double arg)
long double expl(long double arg)

Description

The prototype for **exp( )** is in **math.h**.
The **exp( )** function returns the natural logarithm *e* raised to the *arg* power.
expl( ) is the **long double** version of **exp( )**.

Example

This fragment displays the value of e (rounded to 2.718282).

```
printf("value of e to the first: %lf", exp(1.0));
```

Related Function

log( )

double fabs(double num)
long double fabsl(long double num)

Description

The prototype for **fabs( )** is in **math.h**.
The **fabs( )** function returns the absolute value of *num*.
fabsl( ) is the **long double** version of this function.

Example

This program prints "1.0 1.0" on the screen:

```
#include <stdio.h>
#include <math.h>

main(void)
{
  printf("%1.1lf %1.1lf", fabs(1.0), fabs(-1.0));
  return 0;
}
```

Related Function

abs( )

double floor(double num)
long double floorl(long double num)

Description

The prototype for **floor( )** is in **math.h**.

The **floor( )** function returns the largest integer (represented as a **double**) that is not greater than *num*. For example, given 1.02, **floor( )** returns 1.0. Given –1.02, **floor( )** returns –2.0.

floor( ) is the **long double** version of this function.

Example

This fragment prints "10" on the screen:

```
printf("%lf",floor(10.9));
```

Related Function

fmod( )

double fmod(double x, double y)
long double fmodl(long double x, long double y)

Description

The prototype for **fmod( )** is in **math.h**.

The **fmod( )** function returns the remainder of *x/y*.

fmodl( ) is the **long double** version of this function.

Example

This program prints "1.0" on the screen, which represents the remainder of 10/3:

```
#include <stdio.h>
#include <math.h>

main(void)
{
  printf("%1.1lf", fmod(10.0, 3.0));
```

```
    return 0;
}
```

Related Functions

ceil( ), floor( ), fabs( )

double frexp(double num, int *exp)
long double frexpl(long double num, int *exp)

Description

The prototype for **frexp( )** is in **math.h**.

The **frexp( )** function decomposes the number *num* into a mantissa in the range 0.5 to less than 1, and an integer exponent such that $num=mantissa*2^{exp}$. The mantissa is returned by the function, and the exponent is stored at the variable pointed to by *exp*.

frexpl( ) is the **long double** version of this function.

Example

This code fragment prints "0.625" for the mantissa and "4" for the exponent:

```
int e;
double f;

f = frexp(10.0, &e);
printf("%lf %d", f, e);
```

Related Function

ldexp( )

double hypot(double x, double y)
long double hypotl(long double x, long double y)

Description

The prototype for **hypot( )** is in **math.h**. This function is not defined by the ANSI C standard.

The **hypot( )** function returns the length of the hypotenuse of a right triangle given the lengths of the other two sides.

hypotl( ) is the **long double** version of this function.

Example

This code fragment prints the value "2.236068":

```
printf("%lf", hypot(2, 1));
```

double ldexp(double num, int exp)
long double ldexpl(long double num, int exp)

Description

The prototype for **ldexp( )** is in **math.h**.

The **ldexp( )** function returns the value of $num * 2^{exp}$. If overflow occurs, **HUGE_VAL** is returned.

ldexpl( ) is the **long double** version of this function.

Example

This program displays the number "4":

```
#include <stdio.h>
#include <math.h>

main(void)
{
  printf("%lf", ldexp(1, 2));
  return 0;
}
```

Related Functions

frexp( ), **modf( )**

double log(double num)
long double logl(long double num)

Description

The prototype for **log( )** is in **math.h**.

The **log( )** function returns the natural logarithm for *num*. A domain error occurs if *num* is negative and a range error occurs if the argument is 0.

logl( ) is the **long double** version of this function.

Example

This program prints the natural logarithms for the numbers 1 through 10:

```
#include <stdio.h>
#include <math.h>

main(void)
{
  double val = 1.0;

  do {
    printf("%lf %lf\n", val, log(val));
    val++;
  } while (val < 11.0);
  return 0;
}
```

Related Function

log10( )

double log10(double num)
long double log10l(long double num)

Description

The prototype for **log10( )** is in **math.h**.

The **log10( )** function returns the base 10 logarithm for *num*. A domain error occurs if *num* is negative, and a range error occurs if the argument is 0.

log10l( ) is the **long double** version of this function.

Example

This program prints the base 10 logarithms for the numbers 1 through 10:

```
#include <stdio.h>
#include <math.h>

main(void)
{
  double val = 1.0;

  do {
```

```
      printf("%lf %lf\n", val, log10(val));
      val++;
   } while (val < 11.0);
   return 0;
}
```

Related Function

log( )

int matherr(struct exception *err)
int _matherr(struct _exception *err)

Description

The prototype for **matherr( )** is in **math.h**. This function is not defined by the ANSI C standard.

The **matherr( )** function allows you to create custom math error handling routines. The function must perform as follows. When the **matherr( )** function can resolve a problem, it returns non-0 and no message is printed. Also, the **errno** built-in variable is not altered. However, if **matherr( )** cannot resolve the problem, it returns 0, the appropriate error message is printed, and the value of **errno** is changed. By default, Turbo/Borland C/C++ provides a dummy **matherr( )** function that returns 0.

The **matherr( )** function is called with an argument of type **exception**, which is shown here.

```
struct exception {
  int type;
  char *name;
  double arg1, arg2;
  double retval;
};
```

The *type* element holds the type of the error that occurred. Its value will be one of the following enumerated values.

Symbol	Meaning
DOMAIN	Domain error
SING	Result is a singularity
OVERFLOW	Overflow error
UNDERFLOW	Underflow error
TLOSS	Total loss of significant digits

The *name* element holds a pointer to a string that holds the name of the function in which the error took place. The *arg1* and *arg2* elements hold the arguments to the function that caused the error. If the function only takes one argument, it will be in *arg1*. Finally, *retval* holds the default return value for **matherr( )**. It is this value that you can modify.

   _matherr is used with the **long double** math functions. In this case, in **_exception**, elements *arg1, arg2,* and *retval* are **long doubles**.

double modf(double num, double *i)
long double modfl(long double num, long double *i)

Description

The prototype for **modf( )** is in **math.h**.

   The **modf( )** function decomposes *num* into its integer and fractional parts. It returns the fractional portion and places the integer part in the variable pointed to by *i.*

   modfl( ) is the **long double** version of this function.

Example

This fragment prints "10" and "0.123" on the screen:

```
int i;
double f;

f = modf(10.123, &i);
printf("%d %lf", i, f);
```

Related Functions

frexp( ), ldexp( )

double poly(double x, int n, double c[])
long double polyl(long double x, int n, long double c[])

Description

The prototype for **poly( )** is in **math.h**. This function is not defined by the ANSI C standard.

   The **poly( )** function evaluates a polynomial in *x* of degree *n* with coefficients *c[0]* through *c[n]* and returns the result. For example, if *n*=3, the polynomial evaluated is

$$c[3]x^3 + c[2]x^2 + c[1]x + c[0]$$

polyl( ) is the **long double** version of this function.

Example

This program prints 47 on the screen.

```
#include <stdio.h>
#include <math.h>

main(void)
{
  double c[2];

  c[1] = 2;
  c[0] = 45;

  printf("%lf", poly(1, 2, c));
  return 0;
}
```

Related Function

hypot( )

double pow(double base, double exp)
long double powl(long double base, long double exp)

Description

The prototype for **pow( )** is in **math.h**.

The **pow( )** function returns *base* raised to the *exp* power ($base^{exp}$). An overflow produces a range error.

powl( ) is the **long double** version of this function.

Example

This program prints the first 11 powers of 12.

```
#include <stdio.h>
#include <math.h>
```

```
main(void)
{
  double x=12.0, y=0.0;

  do {
    printf("%lf", pow(x, y));
    y++;
  } while(y<11);
  return 0;
}
```

Related Functions

exp( ), log( ), sqrt( ), pow10( )

double pow10(int n)
long double pow10l(int n)

Description

The prototype for **pow10( )** is in **math.h**. This function is not defined by the ANSI C standard.

The **pow10( )** function returns 10 raised to the power *n*. Overflow and underflow are the only possible errors.

pow10l( ) is the **long double** version of this function.

Example

This program prints the first 11 powers of 10:

```
#include <stdio.h>
#include <math.h>

main(void)
{
  int x=0;

  while(x < 11)
    printf("%lf", pow10(x++));
  return 0;
}
```

Related Functions

exp( ), **log( )**, **sqrt( )**, **pow( )**

double sin(double arg)
long double sinl(long double arg)

Description

The prototype to **sin( )** is in **math.h**.
   The **sin( )** function returns the sine of *arg*. The value of *arg* must be in radians.
   sinl( ) is the **long double** version of this function.

Example

This program prints the sines, in one-tenth increments, of the values –1 through 1:

```
#include <stdio.h>
#include <math.h>

main(void)
{
  double val = -1.0;

  do {
    printf("sine of %lf is %lf\n", val, sin(val));
    val += 0.1;
  } while(val <= 1.0);
  return 0;
}
```

Related Functions

asin( ), **acos( )**, **atan2( )**, **atan( )**, **tan( )**, **cos( )**, **sinh( )**, **cosh( )**, **tanh( )**

double sinh(double arg)
long double sinhl(long double arg)

Description

The prototype for **sinhl( )** is in **math.h**.

The **sinh( )** function returns the hyperbolic sine of *arg*. The value of *arg* must be in radians.

sinhl( ) is the **long double** version of this function.

Example

This program prints the hyperbolic sines, in one-tenth increments, of the values –1 through 1:

```
#include <stdio.h>
#include <math.h>

main(void)
{
  double val = -1.0;

  do {
    printf("hyperbolic sine of %lf is %lf\n", val, sinh(val));
    val += 0.1;
  } while(val <= 1.0);
    return 0;
}
```

Related Functions

asin( ), **acos( )**, **atan2( )**, **atan( )**, **tan( )**, **cos( )**, **tanh( )**, **cosh( )**

double sqrt(double num)
long double sqrtl(long double num)

Description

The prototype for **sqrt( )** is in **math.h**.

The **sqrt( )** function returns the square root of *num*. If called with a negative argument, a domain error occurs.

sqrtl( ) is the **long double** version of this function.

Example

This fragment prints "4" on the screen:

```
printf("%lf", sqrt(16.0));
```

```
    int tm_year; /* years from 1900 */
    int tm_wday; /* days since Sunday, 0-6 */
    int tm_yday; /* days since Jan 1, 0-365 */
    int tm_isdst /* daylight saving time indicator */
};
```

The value of **tm_isdst** will be positive if daylight saving time is in effect, 0 if it is not in effect, and negative if there is no information available. This form of the time and date is called the *broken-down time*.

Turbo/Borland C/C++ also includes some nonstandard time and date functions that bypass the normal time and date system and interface more closely with DOS. The functions use structures of either type **time** or **date**, which are defined in **dos.h**. Their declarations are shown here.

```
struct date {
    int da_year; /* year */
    char da_day; /* day of month */
    char da_mon; /* month, Jan=1 */
};

struct time {
    unsigned char ti_min;  /* minutes */
    unsigned char ti_hour; /* hours */
    unsigned char ti_hund; /* hundredths of seconds */
    unsigned char ti_sec;  /* seconds */
};
```

The DOS interfacing functions require the header **dos.h**. The file **dos.h** defines a union that corresponds to the registers of the 8086 family of CPUs and is used by some of the system interfacing functions. It is defined as the union of two structures to allow each register to be accessed by either word or byte.

```
/*
    Copyright (c) 1987, 1988, 1990, 1991 by
    Borland International. All Rights Reserved.
*/


struct WORDREGS
{
    unsigned int  ax, bx, cx, dx, si, di, cflag;
```

Related Functions

exp( ), **log( )**, **pow( )**

double tan(double arg)
long double tanl(long double arg)

Description

The prototype for **tan( )** is in **math.h**.

The **tan( )** function returns the tangent of *arg*. The value of *arg* must be in radians.

tanl( ) is the **long double** version of this function.

Example

This program prints the tangent, in one-tenth increments, of the values –1 through 1:

```
#include <stdio.h>
#include <math.h>

main(void)
{
    double val = -1.0;

    do {
        printf("tangent of %lf is %lf\n", val, tan(val));
        val += 0.1;
    } while(val <= 1.0);
    return 0;
}
```

Related Functions

asin( ), **atan( )**, **atan2( )**, **cos( )**, **sin( )**, **sinh( )**, **cosh( )**, **tanh( )**

double tanh(double arg)
long double tanhl(long double arg)

Description

The prototype for **tanh( )** is in **math.h**.

The **tanh( )** function returns the hyperbolic tangent of *arg*. The value of *arg* must be in radians.

tanhl( ) is the **long double** version of this function.

Example

This program prints the hyperbolic tangent, in one-tenth increments, of the values −1 through 1:

```
#include <stdio.h>
#include <math.h>

main(void)
{
  double val = -1.0;

  do {
    printf("Hyperbolic tangent of %lf is %lf\n", val, tanh(val));
    val += 0.1;
  } while(val <= 1.0);
  return 0;
}
```

Related Functions

asin( ), **atan( )**, **atan2( )**, **cos( )**, **sin( )**, **cosh( )**, **sinh( )**

Chapter **19**

Time-, Date-, and System-Related Functions

This chapter covers those functions that in one way or another are more operating system sensitive than others. Of the functions defined by the ANSI C standard, these include the time and date functions, which relate to the operating system by using its time and date information.

Also discussed in this chapter is a category of functions that allow direct operating system interfacing. None of these functions is defined by the ANSI C standard because each operating environment is different. However, Turbo/Borland C/C++ provides extensive DOS and BIOS interfacing functions that allow you to wring every ounce of performance out of the computer.

The functions that deal with the system time and date require the header file **time.h** for their prototypes. This header also defines two types. The type **time_t** is capable of representing the system time and date as a long integer. This is referred to as the *calendar time*. The structure type **tm** holds the date and time broken down into its elements. The **tm** structure is defined as shown here:

```
struct tm {
    int tm_sec;   /* seconds, 0-59 */
    int tm_min;   /* minutes, 0-59 */
    int tm_hour;  /* hours, 0-23 */
    int tm_mday;  /* day of the month, 1-31 */
    int tm_mon;   /* months since Jan, 0-11 */
```

```
};

struct BYTEREGS
{
    unsigned char  al, ah, bl, bh, cl, ch, dl, dh;
};

union  REGS {
    struct  WORDREGS x;
    struct  BYTEREGS h;
};
```

Also defined in **dos.h** is the structure type **SREGS**, which is used by some functions to set the segment registers. It is defined as:

```
struct    SREGS    {
    unsigned int    es;
    unsigned int    cs;
    unsigned int    ss;
    unsigned int    ds;
};
```

Several of the functions described here interface directly to the ROM-BIOS—the lowest level of the operating system. These functions require the header **bios.h**.

A few functions require predefined structures that have not been discussed. Definitions for these structures will be described as needed.

Microsoft Compatibility Functions

Turbo/Borland C/C++ includes several redundant DOS and BIOS interface functions. This is for compatibility with Microsoft C/C++. Although Turbo/Borland C/C++ defines its own complete set of DOS and BIOS interface functions, it also supplies versions of these functions that are compatible with Microsoft C/C++. The Microsoft versions all begin with **_dos** or **_bios**. Aside from portability issues, it doesn't matter which versions you use.

You will also find some other apparently redundant functions with slightly different names. Again, the reason for this is to provide compatibility with Microsoft C/C++. In general, the Microsoft versions of these functions begin with an underscore. For example, **enable( )** is a Turbo/Borland function and **_enable( )** is the name of the Microsoft version included for compatibility.

int absread(int drive, int numsects, long sectnum, void *buf)
int abswrite(int drive, int numsects, long sectnum, void *buf)

Description

The prototypes for **absread( )** and **abswrite( )** are in **dos.h**. These functions are not defined by the ANSI C standard.

The functions **absread( )** and **abswrite( )** perform absolute disk read and write operations respectively. They bypass the logical structure of the disk and ignore files or directories. Instead they operate on the disk at the sector specified in *sectnum*. The drive is specified in *drive* with drive A being equal to 0. The number of sectors to read or write is specified in *numsects* and the information is read into or from the region of memory pointed to by *buf*.

Upon success, these functions return 0; they return non-0 on failure. When a failure occurs, the built-in variable **errno** is set to the error value returned by DOS. You will need DOS technical documentation to determine the nature of any error that occurs.

You must use great caution when calling **abswrite( )** because it is very easy to corrupt the disk directory or a file.

Example

This program displays the contents of the specified disk sector in both hexadecimal and character form:

```
#include <stdio.h>
#include <dos.h>
#include <stdlib.h>

main(void)
{
  char buf[512];
  int sector, i, j;

  for(;;) {
    printf("Enter sector: ");
    scanf("%d", &sector);
      if(sector==-1) return 0;
      absread(3, 1, sector, buf); /* read drive D*/
      for(i=0, j=0; i<512; i++) {
          printf("%x ", buf[i]);
          if(!(i%16)) {
      for( ; j<i; j++) printf("%c", buf[j]);
          printf("\n");
        }
```

```
      }
    }
  }
```

Related Functions

read( ), **fread( )**, **write( )**, **fwrite( )**

char *asctime(const struct tm *ptr);

Description

The prototype for **asctime( )** is in **time.h**.

The **asctime( )** function returns a pointer to a string representing the information stored in the structure pointed to by *ptr* that is converted into the following form:

day month date hours:minutes:seconds year\n\0

For example:

Wed Jun 19 12:05:34 1999

The structure pointer passed to **asctime( )** is generally obtained from either **localtime( )** or **gmtime( )**.

The buffer used by **asctime( )** to hold the formatted output string is a statically allocated character array and is overwritten each time the function is called. If you wish to save the contents of the string, it is necessary to copy it elsewhere.

Example

This program displays the local time defined by the system:

```
#include <stdio.h>
#include <time.h>

main(void)
{
  struct tm *ptr;
  time_t lt;

  lt = time(NULL);
  ptr = localtime(&lt);
  printf(asctime(ptr));
```

```
  return 0;
}
```

Related Functions

localtime( ), **gmtime( )**, **time( )**, **ctime( )**

int bdos(int fnum, unsigned dx, unsigned al)
int bdosptr(int fnum, void *dsdx, unsigned al)

Description

The prototypes for **bdos( )** and **bdosptr( )** are in **dos.h**. These functions are not defined by the ANSI C standard.

The **bdos( )** function is used to access the DOS system call specified by *fnum*. It first places the values *dx* into the DX register and *al* into the AL register and then executes an INT 0x21 instruction.

If you will be passing a pointer argument to DOS, use the **bdosptr( )** function instead of **bdos( )**. Although for the tiny, small, and medium memory models, the two functions are operationally equivalent, when the larger memory models are used, 20-bit pointers are required. When this is the case, the pointer will be passed in DS:DX.

Both the **bdos( )** and **bdosptr( )** functions return the value of the AX register which is used by DOS to return information.

Example

This program reads characters directly from the keyboard, bypassing all of C's I/O functions, until a "q" is typed:

```
/* Do raw keyboard reads. */
#include <dos.h>

main(void)
{
  char ch;

  while((ch=bdos(1, 0, 0))!='q') ;
  /* ... */
  return 0;
}
```

Related Functions

intdos( ), intdosx( )

int bioscom(int cmd, char byte, int port)
unsigned _bios_serialcom(int cmd, int port, char byte)

Description

The prototypes for **bioscom( )** and **_bios_serialcom( )** are in **bios.h**. These functions are not defined by the ANSI C standard.

The **bioscom( )** and **_bios_serialcom( )** functions are used to manipulate the RS232 asynchronous communication port specified in *port*. Their operation is determined by the value of *cmd*, whose values are shown here, along with their macro equivalents defined in **bios.h**.

cmd	Macro	Meaning
0	_COM_INIT	Initialize the port
1	_COM_SEND	Send a character
2	_COM_RECEIVE	Receive a character
3	_COM_STATUS	Return the port status

Before using the serial port you will probably want to initialize it to something other than its default setting. To do this, set *cmd* equal to 0. The exact way the port will be set up is determined by the value of *byte*, which is encoded with initialization parameters as shown here:

```
Bit Numbers:    7 6 5    4 3  2   1 0

baud  _____|
parity _____|
stop bits _____|
data bits _____|
```

The baud is encoded as shown here:

Baud	Bit Pattern
9600	1 1 1
4800	1 1 0
2400	1 0 1
1200	1 0 0

600	0 1 1
300	0 1 0
150	0 0 1
110	0 0 0

The parity bits are encoded as shown here:

Parity	Bit Pattern
No parity	0 0
Odd	0 1
Even	1 1

The number of stop bits is determined by bit 2 of the serial port initialization byte. If it is 1, two stop bits are used; otherwise one stop bit is used. Finally, the number of data bits is set by the code in bits 1 and 0 of the initialization byte. Of the four possible bit patterns, only two are valid. If bits 1 and 0 contain the pattern 1 0, 7 data bits are used. If they contain 1 1, then 8 data bits are used.

For example, if you want to set the port to 9600 baud, even parity, 1 stop bit, and 8 data bits, you would use this bit pattern:

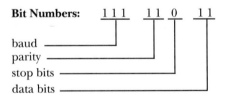

In decimal, this works out to 251.

The return value of **bioscom( )** and **_bios_serialcom( )** is always a 16-bit quantity. The high-order byte contains the status bits and they have the following values:

Meaning When Set	Bit
Data ready	0
Overrun error	1
Parity error	2
Framing error	3
Break-detect error	4
Transfer holding register empty	5
Transfer shift register empty	6
Time-out error	7

If *cmd* is set to 0, 1, or 3, the low-order byte is encoded as shown here:

Meaning When Set	Bit
Change in clear-to-send	0
Change in data-set-ready	1
Trailing-edge ring detector	2
Change in line signal	3
Clear-to-send	4
Data-set-ready	5
Ring indicator	6
Line signal detected	7

When *cmd* has a value of 2, the lower-order byte contains the value received by the port.

Example

This initializes port 0 to 9600 baud, even parity, 1 stop bit, and 8 data bits:

```
bioscom(0, 251, 0);
```

Related Function

bioskey( )

int biosdisk(int cmd, int drive, int head, int track, int sector, int nsects, void *buf)

Description

The prototype for **biosdisk( )** is in **bios.h**. This function is not defined by the ANSI C standard.

The **biosdisk( )** function performs BIOS-level disk operations using interrupt 0x13. These operations ignore the logical structure of the disk including files. All operations take place on sectors.

The drive affected is specified in *drive* with 0 corresponding to A, 1 to B, and so on for floppy drives. The first fixed disk is drive 0x80, the second 0x81, and so on. The part of the disk that is operated on is specified in *head, track,* and *sector.* This function returns the outcome of the operation. You should refer to a PC technical reference manual for details of the operation and options of the BIOS-level disk routines. Keep in mind that direct control of the disk requires thorough and intimate knowledge of both the hardware as well as DOS. It is best avoided except in unusual situations.

Related Functions

absread( ), **abswrite( )**, **_bios_disk( )**

unsigned _bios_disk(unsigned cmd, struct diskinfo_t *info)

Description

The prototype for **_bios_disk( )** is in **bios.h**. This function is not defined by the ANSI C standard.

The **_bios_disk( )** function performs BIOS-level disk operations using interrupt 0x13. These operations ignore the logical structure of the disk including files. All operations take place on sectors.

The **diskinfo_t** structure looks like this:

```
struct diskinfo_t {
    unsigned drive;
    unsigned head;
    unsigned track;
    unsigned sector;
    unsigned nsectors;
    void far *buffer;
};
```

The drive affected is specified in *drive* with 0 corresponding to A, 1 to B, and so on for floppy drives. The first fixed disk is drive 0x80, the second 0x81, and so on. The part of the disk that is operated on is specified in *head, track,* and *sector.* The *nsector* field specifies the number of sectors to read or write and *buffer* points to a buffer that will hold information written to or read from the disk. This function returns the outcome of the operation. You should refer to a PC reference manual for details of the operation and options of the BIOS-level disk routines. Keep in mind that direct control of the disk requires thorough and intimate knowledge of both the hardware as well as DOS and BIOS. It is best avoided except in unusual situations.

Related Functions

absread( ), **abswrite( )**, **biosdisk( )**

int biosequip(void)
unsigned _bios_equiplist(void)

Description

The prototypes for **biosequip( )** and **_bios_equiplist( )** are found in **bios.h**. These functions are not defined by the ANSI C standard.

Both **biosequip( )** and **_bios_equiplist( )** functions return what equipment is in the computer encoded as a 16-bit value. This value is encoded as shown here:

Bit	Equipment
0	Must boot from the floppy drive
1	80x87 math coprocessor installed
2, 3	Motherboard RAM size
	0 0: 16k
	0 1: 32k
	1 0: 48k
	1 1: 64k
4, 5	Initial video mode
	0 0: unused
	0 1: 40x25 BW, color adapter
	1 0: 80x25 BW, color adapter
	1 1: 80x25, monochrome adapter
6, 7	Number of floppy drives
	0 0: one
	0 1: two
	1 0: three
	1 1: four
8	0 if DMA chip installed; 1 otherwise
9, 10, 11	Number of serial ports
	0 0 0: zero
	0 0 1: one
	0 1 0: two
	0 1 1: three
	1 0 0: four
	1 0 1: five
	1 1 0: six
	1 1 1: seven

12	Game adapter installed
13	Serial printer installed (PCjr only)
14, 15	Number of printers
	0 0: zero
	0 1: one
	1 0: two
	1 1: three

Example

This program displays the number of floppy drives installed in the computer:

```
#include <stdio.h>
#include <bios.h>

main(void)
{
  unsigned eq;

  eq = biosequip();

  eq >>= 6; /* shift bits 6 and 7 into lowest position */

  printf("number of disk drives: %d", (eq & 3) + 1);

  return 0;
}
```

Related Function

bioscom( )

int bioskey(int cmd)
unsigned _bios_keybrd(unsigned cmd)

Description

The prototypes for **bioskey( )** and **_bios_keybrd( )** are in **bios.h**. These functions are not defined by the ANSI C standard. The **bios.h** file also contains several macros that can be used as parameters to these functions.

The **bioskey( )** and **_bios_keybrd( )** functions perform direct keyboard operations. The value of *cmd* determines what operation is executed.

If *cmd* is 0 or the macro **_KEYBRD_READ**, both functions return the next key struck on the keyboard. (They will wait until a key is pressed.) Both return a 16-bit quantity that consists of two different values. The low-order byte contains the ASCII character code if a "normal" key is pressed. It will contain 0 if a "special" key is pressed. Special keys include the arrow keys, the function keys, and the like. The high-order byte contains the position code of the key.

If *cmd* is 1 or the macro **_KEYBRD_READY**, both functions check to see if a key has been pressed. They return the value of key pressed (–1 for CTRL-BRK), which is non-0, if a key has been pressed; 0 otherwise. In no situation is the keystroke removed from the keyboard buffer.

When *cmd* is 2 or the macro **_KEYBRD_SHIFTSTATUS**, the shift status is returned. The status of the various keys that shift a state are encoded into the low-order part of the return value as shown here:

Bit	Meaning
0	Right SHIFT pressed
1	Left SHIFT pressed
2	CTRL key pressed
3	ALT pressed
4	SCROLL LOCK on
5	NUM LOCK on
6	CAPS LOCK on
7	INS on

For **_bios_keybrd( )** only: If *cmd* is **_NKEYBRD_READ**, the function reads the position codes for extended keyboards. If *cmd* is **_NKEYBRD_READY**, additional keys are checked on extended keyboards. Finally, if *cmd* is **_NKEYBRD_SHIFTSTATUS**, then the following status information is also returned in the high-order byte of the return value, as shown here:

Bit	Meaning
8	Left CTRL pressed
9	Left ALT pressed
10	Right CTRL pressed
11	Right ALT pressed
12	SCROLL LOCK pressed
13	NUM LOCK pressed
14	CAPS LOCK pressed
15	SYS REQ pressed

Example

This fragment generates random numbers until a key is pressed:

```
while(!bioskey(1)) rand();
```

Related Functions

getche( ), **kbhit( )**

int biosmemory(void)
unsigned _bios_memsize(void)

Description

The prototypes for **biosmemory( )** and **_bios_memsize( )** are in **bios.h**. These functions are not defined by the ANSI C standard.

The **biosmemory( )** and **_bios_memsize( )** functions return the amount of memory (in units of 1K) installed in the system.

Example

This program reports the amount of memory in the system:

```
#include <stdio.h>
#include <bios.h>

main(void)
{
  printf("%dK bytes of ram", biosmemory());

  return 0;
}
```

Related Function

biosequip( )

int biosprint(int cmd, int byte, int port)
unsigned _bios_printer(int cmd, int port, int byte)

Description

The prototypes for **biosprint( )** and **_bios_printer( )** are in **bios.h**. These functions are not defined by the ANSI C standard.

The **biosprint( )** and **_bios_printer( )** functions control the printer port specified in *port*. If *port* is 0 then LPT1 is used; if *port* is 1, LPT2 is accessed, and so on. The exact function performed is contingent upon the value of *cmd*. The legal values for *cmd* are shown here, along with macro equivalents defined in **bios.h**.

Value	Macro	Meaning
0	_PRINTER_WRITE	Print the character in *byte*
1	_PRINTER_INIT	Initialize the printer *port*
2	_PRINTER_STATUS	Return the status of the port

These functions return printer port status as encoded into the low-order byte of the return value as shown here:

Bit	Meaning
0	Time-out error
1	Unused
2	Unused
3	I/O error
4	Printer selected
5	Out-of-paper error
6	Acknowledge
7	Printer not busy

Example

This fragment prints the string "hello" on the printer connected to LPT1:

```
char p[]="hello";

while(*p) biosprint(0, *p++, 0);
```

Related Function

bioscom( )

long biostime(int cmd, long newtime)

Description

The prototype for **biostime( )** is in **bios.h**. This function is not defined by the ANSI C standard.

The **biostime( )** function reads or sets the system clock. The system clock ticks at a rate of about 18.2 ticks per second. Its value is 0 at midnight and increases until reset at midnight again or manually set to some value. If *cmd* is 0, **biostime( )** returns the current timer value, in clock ticks. If *cmd* is 1, the timer is set to the value of *newtime*, specified in clock ticks.

Example

This program prints the current value of the timer:

```
#include <stdio.h>
#include <bios.h>

main(void)
{
  printf("The current timer value is %ld", biostime(0,0));
  return 0;
}
```

Related Functions

time( ), **ctime( )**, **_bios_timeofday( )**

unsigned _bios_timeofday(int cmd, long *newtime)

Description

The prototype for **_bios_timeofday( )** is in **bios.h**. This function is not defined by the ANSI C standard.

The **_bios_timeofday( )** function reads or sets the system clock, which ticks about 18.2 times a second. If *cmd* is 0, then the function reads the current time. If *cmd* is 1, then the time is set. (You may also use the macros **_TIME_GETCLOCK** and **_TIME_SETCLOCK**, respectively, for this parameter.)

When setting the clock, the new time, in clock ticks, is passed in the variable pointed to by *newtime*. There is no meaningful return value when setting the time.

When reading the system time, the variable pointed to by *newtime* will contain the system time, in clock ticks, after the function has returned. The function returns 1 if the timer has not been read since midnight. It returns 0 otherwise.

Example

This resets the system timer:

```
_bios_timeofday(_TIME_SETCLOCK, 0L);
```

Related Functions

time( ), **biostime( )**

void _chain_intr(void (interrupt far *newintr)( ))

Description

The prototype for **_chain_intr( )** is in **dos.h**. This function is not defined by the ANSI C standard.

The **_chain_intr( )** function is primarily for use in DOS TSR (Terminate and Stay-Resident) programs and interrupt handlers. It is used to pass control from a currently executing interrupt handler or TSR to another. The address of the new interrupt handler or TSR is specified in *newintr.* The new interrupt handler uses the registers that are on the stack, not the current state of the registers at the time of the call to **_chain_intr( )**.

The reason **_chain_intr( )** is often used with TSRs is that it facilitates the inclusion of a new TSR in a chain of existing TSRs or interrupt handlers.

Because of the complex nature of TSRs and interrupt handlers, no example is given.

Related Functions

getvect( ), **setvect( )**

clock_t clock(void);

Description

The prototype for **clock( )** is in **time.h**.

The **clock( )** function returns the amount of time elapsed since the program that called **clock( )** started running. If a clock is not available, –1 is returned. To convert the return value to seconds, divide it by the macro **CLK_TCK**.

Example

This program times the number of seconds that it takes for the empty **for** loop to go from 0 to 500000:

```
#include <stdio.h>
#include <time.h>
```

```
main(void)
{
  clock_t start, stop;
  unsigned long t;

  start = clock();
  for(t=0; t<500000L; t++);
  stop = clock();
  printf("loop required %f seconds\n",
         (stop - start) / CLK_TCK);

  return 0;
}
```

Related Functions

localtime( ), **gmtime( )**, **time( )**, **asctime( )**

struct COUNTRY *COUNTRY(int countrycode, struct COUNTRY *countryptr)

Description

The prototype for **country( )** is in **dos.h**. This function is not defined by the ANSI C standard.

The **country( )** function sets several country-dependent items, such as the currency symbol and the way the date and time are displayed.

The structure **COUNTRY** is defined like this:

```
struct COUNTRY {
  int co_date;          /* date format */
  char co_curr[5];      /* currency symbol */
  char co_thsep[2];     /* thousand separator */
  char co_desep[2];     /* decimal separator */
  char co_dtsep[2];     /* date separator */
  char co_tmsep[2];     /* time separator */
  char co_currstyle;    /* currency style */
  char co_digits;       /* significant digits in currency */
  char co_time;         /* format of time */
  long co_case;         /* case map */
  char so_dasep[2];     /* data separator */
  char co_fill[10];     /* filler */
}
```

If *countrycode* is set to 0, the country-specific information is put in the structure pointed to by *countryptr*. If *countrycode* is non-0, the country-specific information is set to the value of the structure pointed to by *countryptr*.

The value of **co_date** determines the date format. If it is 0, US style (month, day, year) format is used. If it is 1, the European style (day, month, year) is used. Finally, if it is 2, the Japanese style (year, month, day) is used.

The way currency is displayed is determined by the value of **co_currstyle**. The legal values for **co_currstyle** are shown here.

0   Currency symbol immediately precedes the value

1   Currency symbol immediately follows the value

2   Currency symbol precedes the value with a space between the symbol and the value

3   Currency symbol follows the value with a space between the symbol and the value

The function returns a pointer to the *countryptr* argument.

Example

This program displays the currency symbol:

```
#include <stdio.h>
#include <dos.h>

main(void)
{
  struct COUNTRY c;

  country(0, &c);

  printf(c.co_curr);

  return 0;
}
```

char *ctime(const time_t *time)

Description

The prototype for **ctime( )** is in **time.h**.

The **ctime( )** function returns a pointer to a string of the form *day month date hours:minutes:seconds year\n\0*

given a pointer to the calendar time. The calendar time is generally obtained through a call to **time( )**. The **ctime( )** function is equivalent to

```
asctime(localtime(time))
```

The buffer used by **ctime( )** to hold the formatted output string is a statically allocated character array and is overwritten each time the function is called. If you wish to save the contents of the string, it is necessary to copy it elsewhere.

Example

This program displays the local time defined by the system:

```
#include <stdio.h>
#include <time.h>
#include <stddef.h>

main(void)
{
  time_t lt;

  lt = time(NULL);
  printf(ctime(&lt));
  return 0;
}
```

Related Functions

localtime( ), **gmtime( )**, **time( )**, **asctime( )**

void ctrlbrk(int (*fptr)(void))

Description

The prototype for **ctrlbrk( )** is in **dos.h**. This function is not defined by the ANSI C standard.

The **ctrlbrk( )** function is used to replace the control-break handler called by DOS with the one pointed to by *fptr.* This routine is called each time the CTRL-BRK key combination is pressed. A control-break generates an interrupt 0x23.

Turbo/Borland C/C++ automatically replaces the old control-break handler when your program exits.

The new control-break routine should return non-0 if the program is to continue running. If it returns 0, the program will be terminated.

Example

This program prints the numbers 0 to 31,999 unless the CTRL-BRK key is pressed, which causes the program to abort.

```
#include <stdio.h>
#include <dos.h>

int break_handler(void);

main(void)
{
  register int i;

  ctrlbrk(break_handler);

  for(i=0; i<32000; i++)  printf("%d ", i);

  return 0;
}

break_handler(void)
{
  printf("this is the new break handler");
  return 0;
}
```

Related Function

geninterrupt( )

void delay(unsigned time)

Description

The prototype for **delay( )** is in **dos.h**. This function is not defined by the ANSI C standard.

The **delay( )** function halts program execution for *time* number of milliseconds.

Example

This program displays a message and beeps twice:

```
#include <stdio.h>
#include <dos.h>

main(void)
{
  printf("beep beep \n");

  sound(500);
  delay(600);
  nosound();
  delay(300);
  sound(500);
  delay(600);
  nosound();

  return 0;
}
```

Related Function

sleep( )

double difftime(time_t time2, time_t time1)

Description

The prototype for **difftime( )** is in **time.h**.

  The **difftime( )** function returns the difference, in seconds, between *time1* and *time2*. That is, it returns *time2–time1*.

Example

This program times the number of seconds that it takes for the empty **for** loop to go from 0 to 500000:

```
#include <stdio.h>
#include <time.h>
#include <stddef.h>

main(void)
```

```
{
  time_t start,end;
  long unsigned int t;

  start = time(NULL);
  for(t=0; t<500000L; t++) ;
  end = time(NULL);
  printf("loop required %f seconds\n", difftime(end, start));

  return 0;
}
```

Related Functions

localtime( ), **gmtime( )**, **time( )**, **asctime( )**

void disable(void)
void _disable(void)

Description

The prototypes for **disable( )** and **_disable( )** are in **dos.h**. These macros are not defined by the ANSI C standard.

The **disable( )** and **_disable( )** macros disable interrupts. The only interrupt that they allow is the NMI (nonmaskable interrupt). Use this function with care because many devices in the system use interrupts.

Related Functions

enable( ), **geninterrupt( )**

unsigned _dos_close(int fd)

Description

The prototype for **_dos_close( )** is in **dos.h**. This function is not defined by the ANSI C standard.

The **_dos_close( )** function closes the file specified by the file descriptor *fd*. The file must have been opened using a call to either **_dos_creat( )**, **_dos_open( )**, or **_dos_creatnew( )**. The function returns 0 if successful. Otherwise, non-0 is returned and **errno** is set to **EBADF** (bad file descriptor).

Example

This fragment closes the file associated with the file descriptor **fd**:

```
_dos_close(fd);
```

Related Functions

_dos_creat( ), **_dos_open( )**

unsigned _dos_creat(const char *fname, unsigned attr, int *fd)
unsigned _dos_creatnew(const char *fname, unsigned attr, int *fd)

Description

The prototypes for **_dos_creat( )** and **_dos_creatnew( )** are in **dos.h**. These functions are not defined by the ANSI C standard.

The **_dos_creat( )** function creates a file by the name pointed to by *fname* with the attributes specified by *attr*. It returns a file descriptor to the file in the integer pointed to by *fd*. If the file already exists, it will be erased. The **_dos_creatnew( )** function is the same as **_dos_creat( )** except that if the file already exists, it will not be erased and **_dos_creatnew( )** will return an error.

The valid values for *attr* are shown here. (The macros are defined in **dos.h**.)

Macro	Meaning
_A_NORMAL	Normal file
_A_RDONLY	Read only file
_A_HIDDEN	Hidden file
_A_SYSTEM	System file
_A_VOLID	Volume label
_A_SUBDIR	Subdirectory
_A_ARCH	Archive byte set

Both functions return 0 if successful and non-0 on failure. On failure, **errno** will contain one of these values: **ENOENT** (file not found), **EMFILE** (too many open files), **EACCES** (access denied), or **EEXIST** (file already exists).

Example

This fragment opens a file called TEST.TST for output:

```
int fd;

if(_dos_creat("test.tst", _A_NORMAL, &fd))
  printf("cannot open file");
```

Related Function

_dos_open( )

int dosexterr(struct DOSERROR *err)

Description

The prototype for **dosexterr( )** is in **dos.h**. This function is not defined by the ANSI C standard.

The **dosexterr( )** function fills the structure pointed to by *err* with extended error information when a DOS call fails. The **DOSERROR** structure is defined like this:

```
struct DOSERROR {
  int de_exterror; /* error code */
  int de_class;    /* class of error */
  char de_action   /* suggested action */
  char de_locus;   /* location of error */
};
```

For the proper interpretation of the information returned by DOS, refer to the DOS technical reference manual.

Related Function

ferror()

void _dos_getdate(struct dosdate_t *d)
void _dos_gettime(struct dostime_t *t)

Description

The prototypes for **_dos_getdate( )** and **_dos_gettime( )** are in **dos.h**. These functions are not defined by the ANSI C standard.

The **_dos_getdate( )** function returns the DOS system date in the structure pointed to by *d*. The **_dos_gettime( )** function returns the DOS system time in the structure pointed to by *t*.

The **dosdate_t** structure is defined like this:

```
struct dosdate_t {
  unsigned char day;
  unsigned char month;
  unsigned int year;
  unsigned char dayofweek;   /* Sunday is 0 */
};
```

The **dostime_t** structure is defined as shown here:

```
struct dostime_t {
  unsigned char hour;
  unsigned char minute;
  unsigned char second;
  unsigned char hsecond; /* hundredths of second */
};
```

Example

This displays the system time and date:

```
#include <stdio.h>
#include <dos.h>

main(void)
{
  struct dosdate_t d;
  struct dostime_t t;

  _dos_getdate(&d);
  _dos_gettime(&t);

  printf("Time and date: %d:%d:%d, %d/%d/%d\n",
         t.hour, t.minute, t.second, d.month, d.day,
         d.year);

  return 0;
}
```

Related Functions

_dos_settime( ), **_dos_setdate( )**

unsigned _dos_getdiskfree(unsigned char drive, struct diskfree_t *dfptr)

Description

The prototype for **_dos_getdiskfree( )** is in **dos.h**. This function is not defined by the ANSI C standard.

The **_dos_getdiskfree( )** function returns the amount of free disk space in the structure pointed to by *dfptr* for the drive specified by *drive*. The drives are numbered from 1 beginning with A. You can specify the default drive by giving *drive* the value 0. The **diskfree_t** structure is defined like this:

```
struct diskfree_t {
  unsigned total_clusters;
  unsigned avail_clusters;
  unsigned sectors_per_cluster;
  unsigned bytes_per_sector;
};
```

The function returns 0 if successful. If an error occurs, it returns non-0 and **errno** is set to **EINVAL** (invalid drive).

Example

This program prints the number of free clusters available for use on drive C:

```
#include <dos.h>
#include <stdio.h>

main(void)
{
  struct diskfree_t p;

  _dos_getdiskfree(3, &p); /* drive C */

  printf("Number of free clusters is %d.",
         p.avail_clusters);

  return 0;
}
```

Related Function

getdfree( )

void _dos_getdrive(unsigned *drive);

Description

The prototype for **_dos_getdrive( )** is in **dos.h**. This function is not defined by the ANSI C standard.

The **_dos_getdrive( )** function returns the number of the currently logged in disk drive in the integer pointed to by *drive*. Drive A is encoded as 1, drive B as 2, and so on.

Example

This fragment displays the current disk drive:

```
unsigned d;

_dos_getdrive(&d);
printf("drive is %c", d-1+'A');
```

Related Function

_dos_setdrive( )

unsigned _dos_getfileattr(const char *fname, unsigned *attrib)

Description

The prototype for **_dos_getfileattr( )** is in **dos.h**. This function is not defined by the ANSI C standard.

The **_dos_getfileattr( )** returns the attribute of the file specified by *fname* in the unsigned integer pointed to by *attrib*, which may be one or more of these values. (The macros are defined in **dos.h**.)

Macro	Meaning
_A_NORMAL	Normal file
_A_RDONLY	Read only file
_A_HIDDEN	Hidden file
_A_SYSTEM	System file
_A_VOLID	Volume label
_A_SUBDIR	Subdirectory
_A_ARCH	Archive byte set

The **_dos_getfileattr( )** function returns 0 if successful; it returns non-0 otherwise. If failure occurs, **errno** is set to **ENOENT** (file not found).

Example

This fragment determines if the file TEST.TST is a normal file:

```
unsigned attr;

if(_dos_getfileattr("test.tst", &attr))
  printf("file error");

if(attr & _A_NORMAL) printf("file is normal");
```

Related Function

_dos_setfileattr( )

unsigned _dos_getftime(int fd, unsigned *fdate, unsigned *ftime)

Description

The prototype for **_dos_getftime( )** is in **dos.h**. This function is not defined by the ANSI C standard.

The function **_dos_getftime( )** returns the time and date of creation for the file associated with file descriptor *fd* in the integers pointed to by *ftime* and *fdate*. The file must have been opened using either **_dos_open( )**, **_dos_creatnew( )**, or **_dos_creat( )**.

The bits in the object pointed to by *ftime* are encoded as shown here:

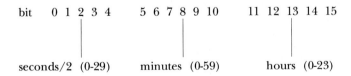

The bits in the object pointed to by *fdate* are encoded like this:

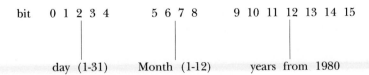

As indicated, the year is represented as the number of years from 1980. Therefore, if the year is 2000, the value of bits 9 through 15 will be 20. The **_dos_getftime()** function returns 0 if successful. If an error occurs, non-0 is returned and **errno** is set to **EBADF** (bad file handle).

Example

This program prints the year the file TEST.TST was created:

```
#include <io.h>
#include <dos.h>
#include <fcntl.h>
#include <stdio.h>
#include <stdlib.h>

main(void)
{
  struct {
    unsigned day: 5;
    unsigned month: 4;
    unsigned year: 7;
  } d;

  unsigned t;
  int fd;

  if(_dos_open("TEST.TST", O_RDONLY, &fd)) {
    printf("cannot open file");
    exit(1);
  }

  _dos_getftime(fd, (unsigned *) &d, &t);

  printf("date of creation: %u", d.year+1980);

  return 0;
}
```

Related Function

_dos_setftime( )

void interrupt (far *_dos_getvect(unsigned intr))( )

Description

The prototype for **_dos_getvect( )** is in **dos.h**. This function is not defined by the ANSI C standard.

The **_dos_getvect( )** function returns the address of the interrupt service routine associated with the interrupt specified in *intr*. This value is returned as a **far** pointer.

Example

This fragment returns the address of the print screen function, which is associated with interrupt 5:

```
void interrupt (*p)(void);

p = _dos_getvect(5);
```

Related Function

setvect( )

unsigned _dos_open(const char *fname, unsigned mode, int *fd)

Description

The prototype for **_dos_open( )** is in **dos.h**. This function is not defined by the ANSI C standard.

The **_dos_open( )** function opens the file whose name is pointed to by *fname* in the mode specified by *mode* and returns a file descriptor to the file in the integer pointed to by *fd*.

The foundation values for the *mode* parameter are shown below. (These macros are defined in **dos.h**.)

Value	Meaning
O_RDONLY	Read only
O_WRONLY	Write only
O_RDWR	Read/write

You may add the following file sharing attributes to *mode* by ORing them to the foundation value. (These macros are defined in **share.h**.)

Value	Meaning
SH_COMPAT	Compatibility mode only
SH_DENYNO	Allow reading and writing
SH_DENYRD	Deny reading
SH_DENYRW	Deny reading and writing
SH_DENYWR	Deny writing

You may also specify that the file cannot be inherited by a child process by ORing the macro **O_NOINHERIT**. This macro is defined in **fcntl.h**.

The **_dos_open( )** function returns 0 if successful and non-0 on failure. If an error occurs, **errno** is set to one of these values:

EACCES	Access denied
EINVACC	Invalid access attempted (for example, trying to read a file opened for write operations)
EMFILE	Too many open files
ENOENT	File not found

Example

This fragment opens a file called TEST.TST for read/write operations:

```
int fd;

if(_dos_open("test.tst", O_RDWR, &fd))
   printf("error opening file");
```

Related Functions

_dos_creat( ), **_dos_creatnew( )**, **_dos_close( )**

unsigned _dos_read(int fd, void far *buf, unsigned count, unsigned *numread)

Description

The prototype for **_dos_read( )** is in **dos.h**. This function is not defined by the ANSI C standard.

The **_dos_read( )** function reads up to *count* bytes from the file specified by the file descriptor *fd* into the buffer pointed to by *buf*. The number of bytes actually read are returned in *numread*, which may be less than *count* if the end of the file is reached before the specified number of bytes have been input. The file must have been opened using a call to **_dos_creat( )**, **_dos_creatnew( )**, or **_dos_open()**. Also, **_dos_read()** treats all files as binary.

Upon success, **_dos_read( )** returns 0; non-0 on failure. On failure, **errno** is set to either **EACCES** (access denied) or **EBADF** (bad file handle). Also, when a failure occurs, the return value is determined by DOS and you will need DOS technical documentation to determine the exact nature of the error, if one should occur.

Example

This fragment reads up to 128 characters from the file described by **fd**:

```
int fd;
unsigned count
char *buf[128];
.
.
.
if(_dos_read(fd, buf, 128, &count))
  printf("error reading file");
```

Related Function

_dos_write( )

unsigned _dos_setdate(struct dosdate_t *d)
unsigned _dos_settime(struct dostime_t *t)

Description

The prototypes for **_dos_setdate( )** and **_dos_settime( )** are in **dos.h**. These functions are not defined by the ANSI C standard.

The **_dos_setdate( )** function sets the DOS system date as specified in the structure pointed to by *d*. The **_dos_settime( )** function sets the DOS system time as specified in the structure pointed to by *t*.

The **dosdate_t** structure is defined like this:

```
struct dosdate_t {
  unsigned char day;
  unsigned char month;
  unsigned int year;
  unsigned char dayofweek;   /* Sunday is 0 */
};
```

The **dostime_t** structure is defined as shown here:

```
struct dostime_t {
  unsigned char hour;
  unsigned char minute;
  unsigned char second;
  unsigned char hsecond; /* hundredths of second */
};
```

Both functions return 0 if successful. On failure they return a non-0 DOS error code and **errno** is set to **EINVAL** (invalid time or date).

Example

The following program sets the system time to 10:10:10.0.

```
struct dostime_t t;

t.hour = 10;
t.minute  = 10;
t.second  = 10;
t.hsecond = 0;

_dos_settime(&t);
```

Related Functions

_dos_gettime( ), **_dos_getdate( )**

void _dos_setdrive(unsigned drive, unsigned *num)

Description

The prototype for **_dos_setdrive( )** is in **dos.h**. This function is not defined by the ANSI C standard.

The **_dos_setdrive( )** function changes the current disk drive to the one specified by *drive*. Drive A corresponds to 1, drive B to 2, and so on. The number of drives in the system is returned in the integer pointed to by *num*.

Example

This fragment makes drive B the current drive:

```
unsigned num;

_dos_setdrive(2, &num);
```

Related Function

_dos_getdrive( )

unsigned _dos_setfileattr(const char *fname, unsigned attrib)

Description

The prototype for **_dos_setfileattr( )** is in **dos.h**. This function is not defined by the ANSI C standard.

The **_dos_setfileattr( )** sets the attributes of the file specified by *fname* to that specified by *attrib,* which must be one (or more) of these values. When using more than one, OR them together. (The macros are defined in **dos.h**.)

Macro	Meaning
_A_NORMAL	Normal file
_A_RDONLY	Read only file
_A_HIDDEN	Hidden file
_A_SYSTEM	System file
_A_VOLID	Volume label
_A_SUBDIR	Subdirectory
_A_ARCH	Archive byte set

The **_dos_setfileattr( )** function returns 0 if successful; it returns non-0 otherwise. If failure occurs, **errno** is set to **ENOENT** (invalid file).

Example

This fragment sets the file TEST.TST to read only:

```
unsigned attr;

attr = _A_RDONLY;

if(_dos_setfileattr("test.tst", attr))
  printf("file error");
```

Related Function

_dos_getfileattr( )

unsigned _dos_setftime(int fd, unsigned fdate, unsigned ftime)

Description

The prototype for **_dos_setftime( )** is in **dos.h**. This function is not defined by the ANSI C standard.

The **_dos_setftime( )** sets the date and time of the file specified by *fd,* which must be a valid file descriptor obtained through a call to either **_dos_open( )**, **_dos_creat( )**, or **_dos_creatnew( )**.

The bits in *ftime* are encoded as shown here:

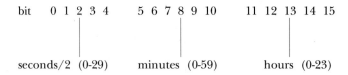

The bits in *fdate* are encoded like this:

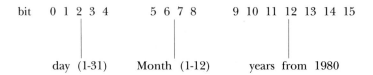

As indicated, the year is represented as the number of years from 1980. Therefore, to set the year to 2000, the value of bits 9 through 15 must be 20. The **_dos_setftime( )** function returns 0 if successful. If an error occurs, non-0 is returned and **errno** is set to **EBADF** (bad file handle).

Example

This changes the year of the file's creation date to 2000:

```
#include <stdio.h>
#include <io.h>
#include <dos.h>
#include <fcntl.h>
#include <stdlib.h>
```

```
main(void)
{
  struct dt {
    unsigned day: 5;
    unsigned month: 4;
    unsigned year: 7;
  } ;

  union {
    struct dt date_time;
    unsigned u;
  } d;

  unsigned t;
  int fd;

  if(_dos_open("TEST.TST", O_RDONLY, &fd)) {
    printf("cannot open file");
    exit(1);
  }

  _dos_getftime(fd, &d.u, &t);
  d.date_time.year = 20;

  _dos_setftime(fd, d.u, t);

  return 0;
}
```

Related Function

_dos_getftime()

void _dos_setvect(unsigned intr, void interrupt (far *isr)( ))

Description

The prototype for **_dos_setvect( )** is in **dos.h**. This function is not defined by the ANSI C standard.

The **_dos_setvect( )** puts the address of the interrupt service routine pointed to by *isr* into the vectored interrupt table at the location specified by *intr*.

Because of the specialized nature of rerouting interrupt vectors, no example is shown.

Related Function

getvect( )

long dostounix(struct date *d, struct time *t)

Description

The prototype for **dostounix( )** is in **dos.h**. This function is not defined by the ANSI C standard.

The function **dostounix( )** returns the system time as returned by **gettime( )** and **getdate( )** into a form compatible with the UNIX time format, which is also compatible with the ANSI standard's format.

Example

See **getdate( )** for an example.

Related Functions

unixtodos( ), **ctime( )**, **time( )**

unsigned _dos_write(int fd, void far *buf, unsigned count, unsigned *numwritten)

Description

The prototype for **_dos_write( )** is in **dos.h**. This function is not defined by the ANSI C standard.

The **_dos_write( )** function writes up to *count* bytes to the file specified by the file descriptor *fd* from the buffer pointed to by *buf*. The number of bytes actually written are returned in *numwritten*, which may be less than requested if the disk becomes full. All files are treated as binary and no character translations will occur.

Upon success, **_dos_write( )** returns 0; it returns non-0 on failure. The return value is determined by DOS and you will need DOS technical documentation to determine the nature of the error, if one should occur. Also, if an error occurs, **errno** will be set to either **EACCES** (Access denied) or **EBADF** (Bad file handle).

Example

This fragment writes 128 characters from the file described by **fd**:

```
int fd;
unsigned count
char *buf[128];
    .
    .
    .
if(_dos_write(fd, buf, 128, &count))
  printf("error writing file");
```

Related Function

_dos_read( )

void enable(void)
void _enable(void)

Description

The prototypes for **enable( )** and **_enable( )** are in **dos.h**. These functions are not defined by the ANSI C standard.

The **enable( )** and **_enable( )** functions enable interrupts.

Related Functions

disable( ), **geninterrupt( )**

unsigned FP_OFF(void far *ptr)
unsigned FP_SEG(void far *ptr)

Description

The prototypes for **FP_OFF( )** and **FP_SEG( )** are in **dos.h**. These macros are not defined by the ANSI C standard.

The **FP_OFF( )** macro returns the offset portion of the far pointer *ptr*. The **FP_SEG( )** macro returns the segment of the far pointer *ptr*.

Example

This program prints the segment and offset of the far pointer *ptr:*

```
#include <stdio.h>
#include <dos.h>
#include <stdlib.h>
```

```
main(void)
{
  char far *ptr;

  ptr = (char far *) malloc(100);

  printf("segment:offset of ptr: %u %u", FP_SEG(ptr),
         FP_OFF(ptr));

  return 0;
}
```

Related Function

MK_FP( )

void ftime(struct timeb *time)

Description

The prototype for **ftime( )** is in **sys\timeb.h**. This function is not defined by the ANSI C standard.

The **ftime( )** function fills the **timeb** structure with system time information. Specifically, it retrieves the elapsed time in seconds since January 1, 1970 (GMT), the fractional part of any elapsed second in milliseconds, the difference between GMT and local time in minutes, and whether daylight saving time is in effect.

The **timeb** structure looks like this:

```
struct timeb {
  long time; /* time in seconds from Jan. 1, 1970 */
  short millitm; /* milliseconds */
  short timezone; /* difference between GMT and local time */
  short dstflag; /* non-0 if daylight saving time is in effect */
};
```

Example

This program displays the number of seconds that have elapsed since January 1, 1970, Greenwich mean time:

```
#include <stdio.h>
#include <sys\timeb.h>

main(void)
```

```
{
  struct timeb lt;

  ftime(&lt);
  printf("%ld seconds %d milliseconds.\n",lt.time,lt.millitm);
  return 0;
}
```

Related Functions

localtime( ), **gmtime( )**, **ctime( )**, **asctime( )**

void geninterrupt(int intr)

Description

The prototype for **geninterrupt( )** is in **dos.h**. This function is not defined by the ANSI C standard.

The **geninterrupt( )** macro generates a software interrupt. The number of the interrupt generated is determined by the value of *intr*.

Example

This generates interrupt 5, the print screen function:

```
#include <dos.h>

main(void)
{
  geninterrupt(5); /* print screen function */
  return 0;
}
```

Related Functions

enable( ), **disable( )**

int getcbrk(void)

Description

The prototype for **getcbrk( )** is in **dos.h**. This function is not defined by the ANSI C standard.

The **getcbrk( )** function returns 0 if extended control-break checking is off and 1 if extended control-break checking is on. When extended control-break checking is off, the only time DOS checks to see if the CTRL-BRK key combination has been pressed is when console, printer, or auxiliary communication devices are performing I/O operations. When the extended checking is on, the control-break combination is checked for by each DOS call.

Example

This prints the current state of control-break checking:

```
printf("The current cbrk setting is %d", getcbrk());
```

Related Function

setcbrk( )

void getdate(struct date *d)
void gettime(struct time *t)

Description

The prototypes for **getdate( )** and **gettime( )** are in **dos.h**. These functions are not defined by the ANSI C standard.

The **getdate( )** function fills the **date** structure pointed to by *d* with the DOS form of the current system date. The **gettime( )** function fills the **time** structure pointed to by *t* with the DOS form of the current system time.

Example

This converts the DOS version of time and date into the form that can be used by the standard ANSI C time and date routines and displays the time and date on the screen:

```
#include <stdio.h>
#include <time.h>
#include <dos.h>

main(void)
{
  time_t t;
  struct time dos_time;
  struct date dos_date;
```

```
struct tm *local;

getdate(&dos_date);
gettime(&dos_time);

t = dostounix(&dos_date, &dos_time);
local = localtime(&t);
printf("time and date: %s\n", asctime(local));

return 0;
}
```

Related Functions

settime( ), **setdate( )**

void getdfree(unsigned char drive, struct dfree *dfptr)

Description

The prototype for **getdfree( )** is in **dos.h**. This function is not defined by the ANSI C standard.

The **getdfree( )** function assigns information about the amount of free disk space to the structure pointed to by *dfptr* for the drive specified by *drive*. The drives are numbered from 1 beginning with drive A. You can specify the default drive by calling **getdfree( )** with a value of 0. The **dfree** structure is defined like this:

```
struct dfree {
  unsigned df_avail;   /* unused clusters */
  unsigned df_total;   /* total number of clusters */
  unsigned df_bsec;    /* number of bytes per sector */
  unsigned df_sclus;   /* number of sectors per cluster */
};
```

If an error occurs, the **df_sclus** field is set to –1.

Example

This program prints the number of free clusters available for use on drive C:

```
#include <stdio.h>
#include <dos.h>

main(void)
```

```
{
  struct dfree p;

  getdfree(3, &p); /* drive C */

  printf("Number of free clusters is %d.", p.df_avail);

  return 0;
}
```

Related Functions

getfat( ), _dos_getdiskfree( )

char far *getdta(void)

Description

The prototype for **getdta( )** is in **dos.h**. This function is not defined by the ANSI C standard.

    The **getdta( )** function returns a pointer to the disk transfer address (DTA). A **far** pointer is returned because you cannot assume, in all circumstances, that the disk transfer address will be located within the data segment of your program.

Example

This assigns the DTA to the **far** pointer *ptr*:

```
char far *ptr;

ptr = getdta();
```

Related Function

setdta( )

void getfat(unsigned char drive, struct fatinfo *fptr)
void getfatd(struct fatinfo *fptr)

Description

The prototypes for **getfat( )** and **getfatd( )** are in **dos.h**. These functions are not defined by the ANSI C standard.

The **getfat( )** function returns various information about the disk in *drive*, which is gathered from that drive's file allocation table (FAT). If the value *drive* is 0, the default drive is used. Otherwise, 1 is used for drive A, 2 for B, and so on. The structure pointed to by **fptr** is loaded with the information from the FAT. The structure **fatinfo** is defined as

```
struct fatinfo {
  char fi_sclus; /* number of sectors per cluster */
  char fi_fatid; /* FAT ID */
  int fi_nclus;  /* total number of clusters */
  int fi_bysec;  /* number of bytes per sector */
};
```

The **getfatd( )** function is the same as **getfat( )** except that the default drive is always used.

Example

This program displays the total storage capacity, in bytes, of the default drive:

```
#include <stdio.h>
#include <dos.h>

main(void)
{
  long total;
  struct fatinfo p;

  getfat(0, &p);

  total = (long) p.fi_sclus * (long) p.fi_nclus *
          (long) p.fi_bysec;

  printf("total storage capacity: %ld.", total);

  return 0;
}
```

Related Function

getdfree( )

int getftime(int handle, struct ftime *ftptr)

Description

The prototype for **getftime( )** is in **io.h**. This function is not defined by the ANSI C standard.

The function **getftime( )** returns time and date of creation for the file associated with *handle*. The information is loaded into the structure pointed to by *ftptr*. The bit-field structure **ftime** is defined like this:

```
struct ftime {
  unsigned ft_tsec:  5; /* seconds */
  unsigned ft_min:   6; /* minutes */
  unsigned ft_hour:  5; /* hours */
  unsigned ft_day:   5; /* days */
  unsigned ft_month: 4; /* month */
  unsigned ft_year:  7; /* year from 1980 */
}
```

The **getftime( )** function returns 0 if successful. If an error occurs, –1 is returned and **errno** is set to either **EINVFNC** (invalid function number) or **EBADF** (bad file number).

Example

This program prints the year the file TEST.TST was created:

```
#include <stdio.h>
#include <io.h>
#include <dos.h>
#include <fcntl.h>
#include <stdlib.h>

main(void)
{
  struct ftime p;
  int fd;

  if((fd=open("TEST.TST", O_RDONLY))==-1) {
    printf("cannot open file");
   exit(1);
  }

  getftime(fd, &p);
```

```
    printf("%d", p.ft_year + 1980);

    return 0;
}
```

Related Functions

open( ), **_dos_open( )**

unsigned getpsp(void)

Description

The prototype for **getpsp( )** is in **dos.h**. This function is not defined by the ANSI C standard.

The **getpsp( )** function returns the segment of the program segment prefix (PSP). This function works only with DOS version 3.0 or later.

The PSP is also set in the global variable **_psp**, which may be used with versions of DOS more recent than 2.0.

Related Function

biosdisk( )

void interrupt(*getvect(int intr))( )

Description

The prototype for **getvect( )** is in **dos.h**. This function is not defined by the ANSI C standard.

The **getvect( )** function returns the address of the interrupt service routine associated with the interrupt specified in *intr.* This value is returned as a **far** pointer.

Example

This fragment returns the address of the print screen function, which is associated with interrupt 5:

```
void interrupt (*p)(void);

p = getvect(5);
```

Related Function

setvect( )

int getverify(void)

Description

The prototype for **getverify( )** is in **dos.h**. This function is not defined by the ANSI C standard.

The **getverify( )** function returns the status of the DOS verify flag. When this flag is on, all disk writes are verified against the output buffer to ensure that the data was properly written. If the verify flag is off, no verification is performed.

If the verify flag is off, 0 is returned; otherwise, 1 is returned.

Example

This program prints the value of the DOS verify flag:

```
#include <stdio.h>
#include <dos.h>

main(void)
{
  printf("The verify flag is set to %d.", getverify());

  return 0;
}
```

Related Function

setverify( )

struct tm *gmtime(const time_t *time)

Description

The prototype for **gmtime( )** is in **time.h**.

The **gmtime( )** function returns a pointer to the broken-down form of *time* in the form of a **tm** structure. The time is represented in Greenwich mean time. The *time* value is generally obtained through a call to **time( )**.

The structure used by **gmtime( )** to hold the broken-down time is statically allocated and is overwritten each time the function is called. If you wish to save the contents of the structure, it is necessary to copy it elsewhere.

Example

This program prints both the local time and the Greenwich mean time of the system:

```
#include <stdio.h>
#include <time.h>
#include <stddef.h>

/* print local and GM time */
main(void)
{
  struct tm *local, *gm;
  time_t t;

  t = time(NULL);
  local = localtime(&t);
  printf("Local time and date: %s", asctime(local));
  gm = gmtime(&t);
  printf("Greenwich mean time and date: %s", asctime(gm));

  return 0;
}
```

Related Functions

localtime( ), **time( )**, **asctime( )**

void harderr(int (*handler)( ))
void _harderr(int (far *handler)( ))
void hardresume(int code)
void _hardresume(int code)
void hardretn(int code)
void _hardretn(int code)

Description

The prototypes for **harderr( )**, **_harderr( )**, **hardresume( )**, **_hardresume( )**, **hardretn( )**, and **_hardretn( )** are in **dos.h**. These functions are not defined by the ANSI C standard.

The functions **harderr( )** and **_harderr( )** allow you to replace DOS's default hardware error handler with one of your own. The function is called with the address of the function that is to become the new error-handling routine. It will be executed each time an interrupt 0x24 occurs.

For **harderrr( )**, the error-handling function pointed to by *handler* must have the following prototype:

void *err_handler*(int *errnum*, int *ax*, int *bp*, int *si*);

Here, *errnum* is DOS's error code and *ax, bp, si* contain the values of the AX, BP, and SI registers. If *ax* is nonnegative, a disk error has occurred. When this is the case, ANDing *ax* with 0xFF yields the number of the drive that failed with drive A being equal to 0. If *ax* is negative, a device failed. You must consult a DOS technical reference guide for complete interpretation of the error codes. The *bp* and *si* registers contain the address of the device driver from the device that sustained the error.

When using **_harderr( )**, the error handler pointed to by *handler* must be a FAR function and have this prototype:

void far *err_handler*(unsigned *err*, unsigned *errnum*,
                    unsigned far **devptr*)

Here, *err* receives a code that indicates what device has failed. If *err* is nonnegative, a disk error has occurred. When this is the case, ANDing *err* with 0xFF yields the number of the drive that failed with drive A being equal to 0. If *err* is negative, a device failed. You must consult a DOS technical reference guide for complete interpretation of the error codes. The *errnum* value is the actual device error code passed to the handler. The contents of *devptr* contain the address of the device driver that sustained the error.

There are two very important rules that you must follow when creating your own error handlers. First, the interrupt handler must not use any of the standard or UNIX-like I/O functions. Attempting to do so will crash the computer. Second, you may use only DOS calls numbers 1 through 12.

The error interrupt handler can exit in one of two ways. First, the **hardresume( )** (and **_hardresume( )**) function causes the handler to exit to DOS, returning the value of *code*. Second, the handler can return to the program via a call to **hardretn( )** (or **_hardretn( )**) with a return value of *code*. For **hardresume( )** and **_hardresume( )**, the value returned must be one of the following. (The macro equivalents are defined in **dos.h**.)

Value	Macro	Meaning
0	_HARDERR_IGNORE	Ignore
1	_HARDERR_RETRY	Retry
2	_HARDERR_ABORT	Abort
3	_HARDERR_FAIL	Fail

Due to the complex nature of interrupt service functions, no example is shown.

Related Function

geninterrupt( )

int inp(unsigned port)
int inport(int port)
unsigned inpw(unsigned port)
unsigned char inportb(int port)

Description

The prototypes for **inp( )**, **inpw( )**, **inport( )** and **inportb( )** are in **dos.h**. These functions are not defined by the ANSI C standard.

The **inport( )** and **inpw( )** functions return the word value read from the port specified in *port*.

The **inportb( )** and **inp( )** macros return a byte read from the specified port.

Example

The following fragment reads a word from port 1:

```
unsigned int i;

i = inport(1);
```

Related Functions

outport( ), **outportb( )**, **outp( )**, **outpw( )**

int int86(int int_num, union REGS *in_regs,
        union REGS *out_regs)
int int86x(int int_num, union REGS *in_regs,
        union REGS *out_regs, struct SREGS *segregs)

Description

The prototypes for **int86( )** and **int86x( )** are in **dos.h**. These functions are not defined by the ANSI C standard.

The **int86( )** function is used to execute a software interrupt specified by *int_num*. The contents of the union *in_regs* are first copied into the registers of the processor and then the proper interrupt is executed.

Upon return, the union *out_regs* contains the values of the registers that the CPU has upon return from the interrupt. If the carry flag is set, an error has occurred. The value of the AX register is returned.

The **int86x()** copies the values of *segregs->ds* into the DS register and *segregs->es* into the ES register. This allows programs compiled for the large data model to specify which segments to use during the interrupt.

REGS and **SREGS** are defined in the header **dos.h**.

Example

The **int86( )** function is often used to call ROM routines in the PC. For example, this function executes an INT 0x10, function code 0, that causes the video mode to be set to the value specified by the argument **mode**:

```
#include <dos.h>

/* Set the video mode */
void set_mode(char mode)
{
  union REGS in, out;

  in.h.al = mode;
  in.h.ah = 0;  /* set mode function number */

  int86(0x10, &in, &out);
}
```

Related Functions

intdos( ), bdos( )

int intdos(union REGS *in_regs, union REGS *out_regs)
int intdosx(union REGS *in_regs, union REGS *out_regs,
struct SREGS *segregs)

Description

The prototypes for **intdos( )** and **intdosx( )** are in **dos.h**. These functions are not defined by the ANSI C standard.

The **intdos( )** function is used to access the DOS system call specified by the contents of the union pointed to by *in_regs*. It executes an INT 0x21 instruction and places the outcome of the operation in the union pointed to by *out_regs*. The **intdos( )**

function returns the value of the AX register that is used by DOS to return information. Upon return, if the carry flag is set, an error has occurred.

The **intdos( )** function is used to access those system calls that either require arguments in registers other than only DX and/or AL or that return information in a register other than AX.

The union **REGS** defines the registers of the 8088/86 family of processors and is found in the **dos.h** header file.

For **intdosx( )**, the value of *segregs* specifies the DS and ES registers. This is principally for use in programs compiled using the large data models.

Example

This program reads the time directly from the system clock, bypassing all of C's time functions:

```
#include <stdio.h>
#include <dos.h>

main(void)
{
  union REGS in, out;

  in.h.ah=0x2c;  /* get time function number */
  intdos(&in, &out);
  printf("time is %.2d:%.2d:%.2d", out.h.ch, out.h.cl, out.h.dh);

  return 0;
}
```

Related Functions

bdos( ), **int86( )**

void intr(int intr_num, struct REGPACK *reg)

Description

The prototype for **intr( )** is in **dos.h**. This function is not defined by the ANSI C standard.

The **intr( )** function executes the software interrupt specified by *intr_num*. It provides an alternative to the **int86( )** function, but does not contain any expanded functionality.

The values of the registers in the structure pointed to by *reg* are copied into the CPU registers before the interrupt occurs. After the interrupt returns, the structure contains the values of the registers as set by the interrupt service routine. The structure **REGPACK** is defined as shown here:

```
struct REGPACK {
  unsigned r_ax, r_bx, r_cx, r_dx;
  unsigned r_bp, r_si, r_di, r_ds, r_es;
  unsigned r_flags;
};
```

Any registers not used by the interrupt are ignored.

Example

This program prints the screen using interrupt 5, the print screen interrupt:

```
#include <dos.h>

main(void)
{
  struct REGPACK r;

  intr(5, &r);

  return 0;
}
```

Related Functions

int86( ), **intdos( )**

int ioctl(int device, int cmd, void *dx, void *cx)

Description

The prototype for **ioctl( )** is in **io.h**. This function is not defined by the ANSI C standard.

The **ioctl( )** function is essentially a UNIX-based function that Turbo/Borland C/C++ compilers include for compatibility, although the parameters supported by Turbo/Borland C/C++ are not portable to UNIX or vice versa. It executes a call to DOS function 0x44, which controls the device specified by *device*. Refer to a DOS technical reference manual for details of its operation.

The function returns the outcome of the 0x44 DOS function.

int kbhit(void)

Description

The prototype for **kbhit( )** is in **conio.h**. This function is not defined by the ANSI C standard.

The **kbhit( )** function returns true if a key has been pressed on the keyboard. It returns 0 otherwise. In no situation is the key removed from the input buffer.

Example

This fragment loops until a key is pressed:

```
while(!kbhit());  /* wait for keypress */
```

Related Functions

bioskey( ), **_bios_keybrd( )**

void keep(unsigned char status, unsigned size)
void _dos_keep(unsigned char status, unsigned size)

Description

The prototypes for **keep( )** and **_dos_keep( )** are in **dos.h**. These functions are not defined by the ANSI C standard.

The **keep( )** and **_dos_keep( )** functions execute an interrupt 0x31 which causes the current program to terminate, but stay resident. The value of *status* is returned to DOS as a return code. The size of the program that is to stay resident is specified in *size*. The rest of the memory is freed for use by DOS.

Because the subject of terminate and stay resident programs is quite complex, no example is presented here. However, the interested reader is referred to *The Art of C* (Herbert Schildt, Osborne/McGraw-Hill, 1992), which provides coverage of this topic.

Related Function

geninterrupt( )

struct tm *localtime(const time_t *time)

Description

The prototype for **localtime( )** is in **time.h**

The **localtime( )** function returns a pointer to the broken-down form of *time* in the form of a **tm** structure. The time is represented in local time. The *time* value is generally obtained through a call to **time( )**.

The structure used by **localtime( )** to hold the broken-down time is statically allocated and is overwritten each time the function is called. To save the contents of the structure, it is necessary to copy it elsewhere.

Example

This program prints both the local time and the Greenwich mean time of the system:

```
#include <stdio.h>
#include <time.h>
#include <stddef.h>

/* Print local and Greenwich mean time. */
main(void)
{
  struct tm *local, *gm;
  time_t t;

  t = time(NULL);
  local = localtime(&t);
  printf("Local time and date: %s", asctime(local));
  gm = gmtime(&t);
  printf("Greenwich mean time and date: %s", asctime(gm));

  return 0;
}
```

Related Functions

gmtime( ), **time( )**, **asctime( )**

time_t mktime(struct tm *p)

Description

The prototype for **mktime( )** is in **time.h**.

The **mktime( )** function converts the time pointed to by *p* into calendar time.

The **mktime( )** returns the time as a value of type **time_t**. If no time information is available, then −1 is returned.

Example

This program displays the day of the week for the given year, month, and day:

```
#include <stdio.h>
#include <time.h>

main(void)
{
  struct tm t;

  t.tm_year = 90;  /* year 1990   */
  t.tm_mon  =  1;  /* month - 1 */
  t.tm_mday =  7;
  mktime(&t);
  printf("The day of the week is %d\n", t.tm_wday);

  return 0;
}
```

Related Functions

localtime( ), **time( )**, **asctime( )**

void far *MK_FP(unsigned seg, unsigned off)

Description

The prototype for **MK_FP( )** is in **dos.h**. This macro is not defined by the ANSI C standard.

The **MK_FP( )** macro returns a **far** pointer given the segment *seg* and the offset *off*.

Example

This returns the appropriate **far** pointer given a segment value of 16 and an offset of 101:

```
void far *p;

p = MK_FP(16, 101);
```

Related Functions

FP_OFF( ), **FP_SEG( )**

void outport(int port, int word)
unsigned outpw(unsigned port, unsigned word)
void outportb(int port, unsigned char byte)
int outp(unsigned port, int byte)

Description

The prototypes for **outport( )**, **outportb( )**, **outp( )**, and **outpw( )** are in **dos.h**. These functions are not defined by the ANSI C standard.

The **outport( )** and **outpw( )** functions output the value of *word* to the port specified in port.

The macros **outportb( )** and **outp( )** output the specified byte to the specified port.

The **outp( )** and **outpw( )** functions return the value sent to the port.

Example

This fragment writes the value 0xFF to port 0x10:

```
outport(0x10, 0xFF);
```

Related Functions

inport( ), **inportb( )**, **inp( )**, **inpw( )**

char *parsfnm(const char *fname, struct fcb *fcbptr, int option)

Description

The prototype for **parsfnm( )** is in **dos.h**. This function is not defined by the ANSI C standard.

The **parsfnm( )** function converts a file name contained in a string pointed to by *fname* into the form required by the file control block (FCB) and places it into the one pointed to by *fcbptr*. This function is frequently used with command line arguments. The function uses DOS function 0x29. The *option* parameter is used to set the AL register prior to the call to DOS. Refer to a DOS programmer's manual for complete information on the 0x29 function. The **fcb** structure is defined as

```
struct  fcb  {
  char    fcb_drive;     /* 0 = default, 1 = A, 2 = B */
  char    fcb_name[8];   /* File name */
  char    fcb_ext[3];    /* File extension */
  short   fcb_curblk;    /* Current block number */
  short   fcb_recsize;   /* Logical record size in bytes */
```

```
  long   fcb_filsize;   /* File size in bytes */
  short  fcb_date;      /* Date file was last written */
  char   fcb_resv[10];  /* Reserved for DOS */
  char   fcb_currec;    /* Current record in block */
  long   fcb_random;    /* Random record number */
};
```

If the call to **parsfnm( )** is successful, a pointer to the next byte after the file name is returned. If there is an error, 0 is returned.

Related Function

fopen( )

int peek(unsigned seg, unsigned offset)
char peekb(unsigned seg, unsigned offset)
void poke(unsigned seg, unsigned offset, int word)
void pokeb(unsigned seg, unsigned offset, char byte)

Description

The prototypes for **peek( )**, **peekb( )**, **poke( )**, and **pokeb( )** are in **dos.h**. These macros are not defined by the ANSI C standard.

The **peek( )** macro returns the 16-bit value at the location in memory pointed to by *seg:offset*.

The **peekb( )** macro returns the 8-bit value at the location in memory pointed to by *seg:offset*.

The **poke( )** macro stores the 16-bit value of *word* at the address pointed to by *seg:offset*.

The **pokeb( )** macro stores the 8-bit value of *byte* at the address pointed to by *seg:offset*.

Example

The following program displays the value of the byte stored at location 0000:0100.

```
#include <stdio.h>
#include <dos.h>

main(void)
{
  printf("%d", peekb(0, 0x0100));
```

```
   return 0;
}
```

Related Functions

FP_OFF( ), FP_SEG( ), MK_FP( )

int randbrd(struct fcb *fcbptr, int count)
int randbwr(struct fcb *fcbptr, int count)

Description

The prototypes for **randbrd( )** and **randbwr( )** are in **dos.h**. These functions are not defined by the ANSI C standard.

The **randbrd( )** function reads *count* number of records into the memory at the current disk transfer address. The actual records read are determined by the values of the structure pointed to by *fcbptr.* The **fcb** structure is defined as

```
struct  fcb  {
  char    fcb_drive;       /* 0 = default, 1 = A, 2 = B */
  char    fcb_name[8];     /* File name */
  char    fcb_ext[3];      /* File extension */
  short   fcb_curblk;      /* Current block number */
  short   fcb_recsize;     /* Logical record size in bytes */
  long    fcb_filsize;     /* File size in bytes */
  short   fcb_date;        /* Date file was last written */
  char    fcb_resv[10];    /* Reserved for DOS */
  char    fcb_currec;      /* Current record in block */
  long    fcb_random;      /* Random record number */
};
```

The **randbrd( )** function uses DOS function 0x27 to accomplish its operation. Refer to a DOS programmer's guide for details.

The **randbwr( )** function writes *count* records to the file associated with the **fcb** structure pointed to by **fcbptr**. The **randbwr( )** uses DOS function 0x28 to accomplish its operation. Refer to a DOS programmer's guide for details.

The following values are returned by the functions.

0	All records successfully transferred
1	EOF encountered but the last record transferred is complete
2	Too many records, but those records transferred are complete
3	EOF encountered and the last record is incomplete. (Applies to **randbrd( )** only.)

Related Function

parsfnm( )

void segread(struct SREGS *sregs)

Description

The prototype for **segread( )** is in **dos.h**. This function is not defined by the ANSI C standard.

The **segread( )** function copies the current values of the segment registers into the structure of type **SREGS** pointed to by *sregs*. This function is intended for use by the **intdosx( )** and **int86x( )** functions. Refer to these functions for further information.

int setcbrk(int cb)

Description

The prototype for **setcbrk( )** is in **dos.h**. This function is not defined by the ANSI C standard.

The **setcbrk( )** function turns extended control-break checking on and off. If *cb* is 1, extended control-break checking is turned on; if it is 0, extended control-break checking is turned off. When extended control-break checking is off, the only time DOS checks to see if the CTRL-BRK key combination has been pressed is when performing standard I/O operations. When extended checking is on, the control-break combination is checked for each time a DOS function is accessed.

The **setcbrk( )** function returns *cb*.

Example

This program toggles extended control-break checking:

```
#include <stdio.h>
#include <dos.h>

main(void)
{
  if (getcbrk() == 0)
    setcbrk(1);
  else
    setcbrk(0);

  printf("BREAK is %s\n", (getcbrk()) ? "on" : "off");
```

```
    return 0;
}
```

Related Functions

getcbrk( ), **enable( )**, **disable( )**

void setdate(struct date *d)
void settime(struct time *t)

Description

The prototypes for **setdate( )** and **settime( )** are in **dos.h**. These functions are not defined by the ANSI C standard.

The **setdate( )** function sets the DOS system date as specified in the structure pointed to by *d*. The **settime( )** function sets the DOS system time as specified in the structure pointed to by *t*.

Example

The following program sets the system time to 10:10:10.0.

```
struct time t;

t.ti_hour = 10;
t.ti_min  = 10;
t.ti_sec  = 10;
t.ti_hund = 0;

settime(&t);
```

Related Functions

gettime( ), **getdate( )**

void setdta(char far *dta)

Description

The prototype for **setdta( )** is in **dos.h**. This function is not defined by the ANSI C standard.

The **setdta( )** function sets disk transfer address (DTA) to that specified by *dta*.

Example

The following fragment sets the disk transfer address to location A000:0000.

```
char far *p;

p = MK_FP(0xA000, 0)
setdta(p);
```

Related Function

getdta( )

int setftime(int handle, struct ftime *t)

Description

The prototype to **setftime( )** is found in **io.h**. This function is not defined by the ANSI C standard.

The **setftime( )** function is used to set the date and time associated with a disk file. It changes the date and time of the file linked to *handle* using the information found in the structure pointed to by *t*. The **ftime** structure is shown here:

```
struct ftime {
  unsigned ft_tsec:  5; /* seconds */
  unsigned ft_min:   6; /* minutes */
  unsigned ft_hour:  5; /* hours */
  unsigned ft_day:   5; /* days */
  unsigned ft_month: 4; /* month */
  unsigned ft_year:  7; /* year from 1980 */
}
```

Since a file's date and time are generally used to indicate the time of the file's last modification, you should use **setftime( )** carefully.

If **setftime( )** is successful, 0 is returned. If an error occurs, −1 is returned and **errno** is set to one of the following:

EINVFNC	Invalid function number
EBADF	Bad file handle

Example

This line of code sets the file to the date and time specified in the **ftime** structure:

```
setftime(fd, &t);
```

Related Function

getftime( )

void setvect(int intr, void interrupt(*isr)( ))

Description

The prototype for **setvect( )** is in **dos.h**. This function is not defined by the ANSI C standard.

The **setvect( )** function puts the address of the interrupt service routine, pointed to by *isr,* into the vectored interrupt table at the location specified by *intr.*

Related Function

getvect( )

void setverify(int value)

Description

The prototype for **setverify( )** is in **dos.h**. This function is not defined by the ANSI C standard.

The **setverify( )** function sets the state of the DOS verify flag. When this flag is on, all disk writes are verified against the output buffer to ensure that the data was properly written. If the verify flag is off, no verification is performed.

To turn on the verify flag call **setverify( )** with *value* set to 1. Set *value* to 0 to turn it off.

Example

This program turns on the DOS verify flag:

```
#include <stdio.h>
#include <dos.h>

main(void)
{
  printf("Turning the verify flag on.");
  setverify(1);
```

```
    return 0;
}
```

Related Function

getverify( )

void sleep(unsigned time)

Description

The prototype for **sleep( )** is in **dos.h**. This function is not defined by the ANSI C standard.

The **sleep( )** function suspends program execution for *time* number of seconds.

Example

This program waits 10 seconds between messages:

```
#include <stdio.h>
#include <dos.h>

main(void)
{
  printf("hello");

  sleep(10);

  printf(" there");

  return 0;
}
```

Related Functions

time( ), delay( )

int stime(time_t *t)

Description

The prototype for **stime( )** is in **time.h**. This function is not defined by the ANSI C standard.

The **stime( )** function sets the current system time to the value pointed to by *t*. This value must specify the time as the number of seconds since January 1, 1970, Greenwich mean time.

The **stime( )** function always returns 0.

Example

This program sets the time to January 1, 1970:

```
#include <stdio.h>
#include <time.h>

main(void)
{
  time_t t;

  t = 0;
  stime(&t);
  return 0;
}
```

Related Functions

settime( ), gettime( ), time( )

char *_strdate(char *buf)
char *_strtime(char *buf)

Description

The prototypes for **_strdate( )** and **_strtime( )** are in **time.h**. These functions are not defined by the ANSI C standard.

The **_strdate( )** function converts the system date into a string and copies it into the character array pointed to by *buf*. The date will have the form MM/DD/YY. The array pointed to by *buf* must be at least 9 characters long. **_strdate( )** returns *buf*.

The **_strtime( )** function converts the system time into a string and copies it into the array pointed to *buf*. The time will have this form: HH:MM:SS. The array pointed to by *buf* must be at least 9 characters long. **_strtime( )** returns a pointer to *buf*.

Example

This program displays the current system time and date:

```
#include <stdio.h>
#include <time.h>

main(void)
{
  char str[9];

  _strtime(str);
  printf("Time: %s", str);

  _strdate(str);
  printf(", Date: %s\n", str);

  return 0;
}
```

Related Functions

time( ), **clock( )**

size_t strftime(char *str, size_t maxsize, char const *fmt, const struct tm *time);

Description

The prototype for **strftime( )** is in **time.h**. It stores time and date information, along with other information, into the string pointed to by *str* according to the format commands found in the string pointed to by *fmt* and using the time specified in *time*. A maximum of *maxsize* characters will be placed into *str*.

The **strftime( )** function works a little like **sprintf( )** in that it recognizes a set of format commands that begin with the percent sign (%) and it places its formatted output into a string. The format commands are used to specify the exact way various time and date information is represented in *str*. Any other characters found in the format string are placed into *str* unchanged. The time and date displayed are in local time. The format commands are shown in Table 19-1. Notice that many of the commands are case sensitive.

The **strftime( )** function returns the number of characters placed in the string pointed to by *str*, or 0 if an error occurs.

Example

Assuming that **ltime** points to a structure that contains 10:00:00 AM, Jan 2, 1994, then this fragment will print "It is now 10 AM".

```
strftime(str, 100, "It is now %H %p", ltime)
printf(str);
```

Related Functions

time( ), **localtime( )**, **gmtime( )**

time_t time(time_t *time)

Description

The prototype for **time( )** is in **time.h**.

Command	Replaced By
%a	Abbreviated weekday name
%A	Full weekday name
%b	Abbreviated month name
%B	Full month name
%c	Standard date and time string
%d	Day-of-month as a decimal (1-31)
%H	Hour, range (0-23)
%I	Hour, range (1-12)
%j	Day-of-year as a decimal (1-366)
%m	Month as decimal (1-12)
%M	Minute as decimal (0-59)
%p	Locale equivalent of AM or PM
%S	Second as decimal (0-59)
%U	Week-of-year, Sunday being first day (0-53)
%w	Weekday as a decimal (0-6, Sunday being 0)
%W	Week-of-year, Monday being first day (0-53)
%x	Standard date string
%X	Standard time string
%y	Year in decimal without century (00-99)
%Y	Year including century as decimal
%Z	Time zone name
%%	The percent sign

Table 19-1.   *The strftime( ) format commands*

The **time( )** function returns the current calendar time of the system.

The **time( )** function can be called either with a null pointer or with a pointer to a variable of type **time_t**. If the latter is used, then the argument is also assigned the calendar time.

Example

This program displays the local time defined by the system:

```
#include <stdio.h>
#include <time.h>

main(void)
{
  struct tm *ptr;
  time_t lt;

  lt = time(NULL);
  ptr = localtime(&lt);
  printf(asctime(ptr));

  return 0;
}
```

Related Functions

localtime( ), **gmtime( )**, **strftime( )**, **ctime( )**

void tzset(void)

Description

The prototype for **tzset( )** is in **time.h**. This function is not defined by the ANSI C standard.

The **tzset( )** function sets Turbo/Borland C/C++'s built-in variables **daylight** (daylight saving time indicator), **timezone** (time zone number), and **tzname** (time zone name) using the environmental variable **TZ**. Since the ANSI C standard time functions provide complete access and control over the system time and date, there is no reason to use **tzset( )**. The **tzset( )** function is included for UNIX compatibility.

void unixtodos(long utime, struct date *d, struct time *t)

Description

The prototype for **unixtodos( )** is in **dos.h**. This function is not defined by the ANSI C standard.

The **unixtodos( )** function converts the UNIX-like time format into a DOS format. The UNIX and ANSI standard time formats are the same. The *utime* argument holds the UNIX time format. The structures pointed to by *d* and *t* are loaded with the corresponding DOS date and time.

Example

This converts the time contained in **timeandday** into its corresponding DOS format:

```
struct time t;
struct date d;

unixtodos(timeandday, &d, &t)
```

Related Function

dostounix( )

Chapter 20

Dynamic Allocation

There are two primary ways in which your program can store information in the main memory of the computer. The first uses *global* and *local variables*—including arrays and structures. In the case of global and static local variables, the storage is fixed throughout the run-time of your program. For local variables, storage is allocated from the stack space of the computer. Although these variables are implemented efficiently in Turbo/Borland C/C++, they require the programmer to know in advance the amount of storage needed for every situation.

The second way information can be stored is through the use of Turbo/Borland C/C++'s dynamic allocation system. In this method, storage for information is allocated from the free memory area as it is needed and returned to free memory when it has served its purpose. The free memory region lies between your program's permanent storage area and the stack. This region, called the *heap,* is used to satisfy a dynamic allocation request. The heap is contained in the data segment.

One advantage to using dynamically allocated memory to hold data is that the same memory can be used for several different things in the course of a program's execution. Because memory can be allocated for one purpose and freed when that use has ended, it is possible for another part of the program to use the same memory for something else at a different time. Another advantage of dynamically allocated storage is that it allows the creation of linked lists.

At the core of C's dynamic allocation system are the functions **malloc( )** and **free( )**, which are part of the standard library. Each time a **malloc( )** memory request is made, a portion of the remaining free memory is allocated. Each time a **free( )** memory release call is made, memory is returned to the system.

The ANSI C standard defines only four functions for the dynamic allocation system: **calloc( )**, **malloc( )**, **free( )**, and **realloc( )**. However, Turbo/Borland C/C++ contains several other dynamic allocation functions. Some of these additional functions are necessary to efficiently support the segmented architecture of the 8086 family of processors.

C++ also defines two dynamic allocation operators called **new** *and* **delete**. *These are discussed in Part Four of this book.*

The ANSI C standard specifies that the header information necessary to the dynamic allocation functions defined by the standard be in **stdlib.h**. Turbo/Borland C/C++ lets you use either **stdlib.h** or **alloc.h**. This guide uses **stdlib.h** because it is more portable. Some of the other dynamic allocation functions require the header **alloc.h**, and others require the **dos.h** header. You should pay special attention to which header file is used with each function.

Some of the allocation functions allocate memory from the *far heap,* which lies outside the program's default data segment. This provides two very important features:

1. All the RAM in the system can be allocated—not just that within the data segment.

2. Blocks of memory larger than 64KB can be allocated.

Memory in the far heap must be accessed with **far** pointers.

void *alloca(size_t size)

Description

The prototype for **alloca( )** is in **malloc.h**. This function is not defined by the ANSI C standard.

The **alloca( )** function allocates *size* bytes of memory from the system stack (not the heap) and returns a character pointer to it. A null pointer is returned if the allocation request cannot be honored.

Memory allocated using **alloca( )** is automatically released when the function that called **alloca( )** returns. This means that you should never use a pointer generated by **alloca( )** as an argument to **free( )**.

For technical reasons, to ensure that the stack is not corrupted, any function that executes a call to **alloca()** *must contain at least one local variable that is assigned a value.*

Example

The following allocates 80 bytes from the stack using **alloca( )**.

```
#include <malloc.h>
#include <stdio.h>
#include <stdlib.h>

main(void)
{
  int i=10;
  char *str;

  if(!(str=alloca(80))) {
    printf("Allocation error - aborting.");
    exit(1);
  }
  .
  .
  .
  return 0;
}
```

Related Function

malloc( )

int allocmem(unsigned size, unsigned *seg)

Description

The prototype for **allocmem( )** is in **dos.h**. This function is not defined by the ANSI C standard.

The **allocmem( )** function executes a DOS 0x48 function call to allocate a paragraph-aligned block of memory. It puts the segment address of the block into the unsigned integer pointed to by *seg*. The *size* argument specifies the number of paragraphs to be allocated. (A paragraph is 16 bytes.)

If the requested memory can be allocated, a −1 is returned. If insufficient free memory exists, no assignment is made to the unsigned integer pointed to by *seg*, and the size of the largest available block is returned. Also, **errno** is set to **ENOMEM** (insufficient memory).

Example

This fragment allocates 100 paragraphs of memory:

```
unsigned i;
```

```
i = 0;

if((i=allocmem(100, &i)==-1) printf("allocate successful");
else
  printf("allocation failed, only %u paragraphs available", i);
```

Related Functions

freemem( ), setblock( ), _dos _allocmem( )

int brk(void *eds)

Description

The prototype for **brk( )** is in **alloc.h**. This function is not defined by the ANSI C standard.

The **brk( )** function dynamically changes the amount of memory for use by the data segment. If successful, the end of the data segment is set to *eds* and 0 is returned. If unsuccessful, −1 is returned and **errno** is set to **ENOMEM** (insufficient memory).

Because the application of **brk( )** is highly specialized, no example is presented here.

Related Function

sbrk( )

void *calloc(size_t num, size_t size)

Description

The prototype for **calloc( )** is in **stdlib.h**.

The **calloc( )** function returns a pointer to the allocated memory. The amount of memory allocated is equal to *num**size where *size* is in bytes. That is, **calloc( )** allocates sufficient memory for an array of *num* objects of *size* bytes.

The **calloc( )** function returns a pointer to the first byte of the allocated region. If there is not enough memory to satisfy the request, a null pointer is returned. It is always important to verify that the return value is not a null pointer before attempting to use the pointer.

Example

This function returns a pointer to a dynamically allocated array of 100 **floats**:

```
#include <stdlib.h>
#include <stdio.h>

float *get_mem(void)
{
  float *p;

  p = (float *) calloc(100, sizeof(float));
  if(!p) {
    printf("allocation failure - aborting");
    exit(1);
  }
  return p;
}
```

Related Functions

malloc( ), realloc( ), free( )

unsigned coreleft(void) /* small data models */
unsigned long coreleft(void) /* large data models */

Description

The prototype for **coreleft( )** is in **alloc.h**. This function is not defined by the ANSI C standard.

The **coreleft( )** function returns the number of bytes of unused memory left on the heap. For programs compiled using a small memory model, the function returns an **unsigned** integer. For programs compiled using a large data model, **coreleft( )** returns an **unsigned long** integer.

Example

This program displays the size of the heap when compiled for a small data model:

```
#include <alloc.h>
#include <stdio.h>

main(void)
{
  printf("The size of the heap is %u", coreleft());
  return 0;
}
```

Related Function

malloc( )

unsigned _dos_allocmem(unsigned size, unsigned *seg)

Description

The prototype for **_dos_allocmem( )** is in **dos.h**. This function is not defined by the ANSI C standard.

The **_dos_allocmem( )** function executes a DOS 0x48 function call to allocate a paragraph-aligned block of memory. It puts the segment address of the block into the unsigned integer pointed to by *seg*. The *size* argument specifies the number of paragraphs to be allocated. (A paragraph is 16 bytes.)

If successful, **_dos_allocmem()** returns 0. If the requested memory cannot be allocated, the appropriate DOS error code is returned and the size of the largest available block (in paragraphs) is put into the **unsigned** integer pointed to by *seg*. On failure, **errno** is also set to **ENOMEM** (insufficient memory).

Example

This fragment allocates 100 paragraphs of memory.

```
unsigned i;

i = 0;

if(!_dos_allocmem(100, &i)) printf("allocate successful");
else
  printf("Failure - only %u paragraphs available", i);
```

Related Functions

_dos_freemem( ), _dos_setblock( )

int _dos_freemem(unsigned seg)

Description

The prototype for **_dos_freemem( )** is in **dos.h**. This function is not defined by the ANSI C standard.

The **_dos_freemem( )** function frees the block of memory whose first byte is at the segment specified by *seg*. This memory must have been previously allocated using

_dos_allocmem( ). The function returns 0 on success. Upon failure, the DOS error code is returned and **errno** is set to **ENOMEM** (insufficient memory).

Example

This illustrates how to allocate and free memory using **_dos_allocmem( )** and **_dos_freemem( )**.

```
unsigned i;

if(_dos_allocmem(some, &i))
  printf("allocation error");
  /* ... */

_dos_freemem(i); /* free memory */
```

Related Functions

_dos_allocmem( ), _dos_setblock( )

unsigned _dos_setblock(unsigned size, unsigned seg, unsigned *max)

Description

The prototype for **_dos_setblock( )** is in **dos.h**. This function is not defined by the ANSI C standard.

The **_dos_setblock( )** function changes the size of the block of memory whose segment address is *seg*. The new size *size* is specified in paragraphs (16 bytes). The block of memory must have been previously allocated using **_dos_allocmem( )**.

If successful, **_dos_setblock( )** returns 0. However, if the size adjustment cannot be made, **_dos_setblock( )** returns a DOS error code and sets the unsigned integer pointed to by *max* to the size (in paragraphs) of the largest block that can be allocated. Also, on failure, **errno** is set to **ENOMEM** (insufficient memory).

Example

This attempts to resize the block of memory whose segment address is in **seg** to 100 paragraphs.

```
unsigned max;
if(_dos_setblock(100, seg, &max)) printf("resize error");
```

Related Functions

_dos_allocmem( ), _dos_freemem( )

void far *farcalloc(unsigned long num, unsigned long size)

Description

The prototype for **farcalloc( )** is in **alloc.h**. This function is not defined by the ANSI C standard.

The **farcalloc( )** function is the same as **calloc( )** except that memory is allocated from outside the current data segment using the far heap.

See **calloc( )** for additional details.

unsigned long farcoreleft(void)

Description

The prototype for **farcoreleft( )** is in **alloc.h**. This function is not defined by the ANSI C standard.

The function **farcoreleft( )** returns the number of bytes of free memory left in the far heap.

Example

This program prints the number of bytes of available memory left in the far heap:

```
#include <alloc.h>
#include <stdio.h>

main(void)
{
  printf("far heap free memory: %ld", farcoreleft());
  return 0;
}
```

Related Function

coreleft( )

void farfree(void far *ptr)

Description

The prototype for **farfree( )** is in **alloc.h**. This function is not defined by the ANSI C standard.

The function **farfree( )** is used to release memory allocated from the far heap via a call to **farmalloc( )** or **farcalloc( )**.

You must use great care to call **farfree( )** only with a valid pointer into the far heap. Doing otherwise will corrupt the far heap. You cannot free a far heap pointer with the **free( )** function or a regular heap pointer with **farfree( )**.

Example

This program allocates and then frees a 100-byte region in the far heap:

```
#include <alloc.h>

main(void)
{
  char far *p;

  p = farmalloc(100);

  /* only free it if there was no allocation error */
  if(p) farfree(p);
  return 0;
}
```

Related Function

free( )

void far *farmalloc(unsigned long size)

Description

The prototype for **farmalloc( )** is in **alloc.h**. This function is not defined by the ANSI C standard.

The **farmalloc( )** function returns a pointer into the far heap that is the first byte in a region of memory *size* bytes long. It is the same as **malloc( )** except that the far heap is used instead of the heap within the default data segment.

See **malloc( )** for further details.

void far *farrealloc(void far *ptr, unsigned long newsize)

Description

The prototype for **farrealloc( )** is in **alloc.h**. This function is not defined by the ANSI C standard.

The **farrealloc( )** function resizes the block of memory previously allocated from the far heap and pointed to by *ptr* to the new size specified in *newsize*. It is functionally equivalent to **realloc( )** except that it operates on the far heap instead of the heap within the default data segment.

See **realloc( )** for further details.

void free(void *ptr)

Description

The prototype for **free( )** is in **stdlib.h**.

The **free( )** function returns the memory pointed to by *ptr* back to the heap. This makes the memory available for future allocation.

It is imperative that **free( )** be called only with a pointer that was previously allocated using one of the dynamic allocation system's functions, such as **malloc( )** or **calloc( )**. Using an invalid pointer in the call most likely will destroy the memory-management mechanism and cause a system crash.

Example

This program first allocates room for strings entered by the user and then frees them:

```
#include <stdlib.h>
#include <stdio.h>

main(void)
{
  char *str[100];
  int i;

  for(i=0; i<100; i++) {
    if((str[i]=(char *)malloc(128))==NULL) {
      printf("allocation error - aborting");
      exit(0);
    }
    gets(str[i]);
  }

  /* now free the memory */
  for(i=0; i<100; i++) free(str[i]);
  return 0;
}
```

Related Functions

malloc( ), **realloc( )**, **calloc( )**

int freemem(unsigned seg)

Description

The prototype for **freemem( )** is in **dos.h**. This function is not defined by the ANSI C standard.

The **freemem( )** function frees the block of memory whose first byte is at *seg*. This memory must have been previously allocated using **allocmem( )**. The function returns 0 on success. On failure, it returns –1 and **errno** is set to **ENOMEM** (insufficient memory).

Example

This fragment illustrates how to allocate and free memory using **allocmem( )** and **freemem( )**:

```
unsigned i;

if(allocmem(some, &i)!=-1)
  printf("allocation error");
else
  freemem(i);
```

Related Functions

allocmem( ), setblock( ), _dos_freemem( )

int heapcheck(void)
int farheapcheck(void)

Description

The prototypes for **heapcheck( )** and **farheapcheck( )** are in **alloc.h**. These functions are not defined by the ANSI C standard, and are specific to Turbo C++.

The **heapcheck( )** and **farheapcheck( )** functions examine the heap for errors. The **heapcheck( )** function checks the normal heap and the **farheapcheck( )** function checks the far heap. Both functions return one of these values:

Value	Meaning
_HEAPOK	No errors
_HEAPEMPTY	No heap present
_HEAPCORRUPT	Error found in the heap

Example

This fragment illustrates how to check the heap for errors:

```
if(heapcheck() == _HEAPOK)
  printf("heap is correct");
else
  printf("error in heap");
```

Related Functions

heapwalk( ), heapchecknode( )

int heapcheckfree(unsigned fill)
int farheapcheckfree(unsigned fill)

Description

The prototypes for **heapcheckfree( )** and **farheapcheckfree( )** are in **alloc.h**. These functions are not defined by the ANSI C standard, and are specific to Turbo C++.

The **heapcheckfree( )** and **farheapcheckfree( )** functions verify that the free area is filled with the specified value *fill*. The **heapcheckfree( )** function checks the normal heap and the **farheapcheckfree( )** function checks the far heap. Both functions return one of these values:

Value	Meaning
_HEAPOK	No errors
_HEAPEMPTY	No heap present
_HEAPCORRUPT	Error found in the heap
_BADVALUE	A value other than *fill* was found

Example

The following code illustrates how to check the heap for the specified value after filling the heap with that value.

```
int status;

heapfillfree(1);
status = heapcheckfree(1)

if(status == _HEAPOK)
  printf("heap is filled correctly\n");
```

```
else
  if(status == _BADVALUE)
    printf("heap not filled with correct value\n");
```

Related Functions

heapfillfree( ), heapchecknode( )

int heapchecknode(void *ptr)
int farheapchecknode(void far *ptr)

Description

The prototypes for **heapchecknode( )** and **farheapchecknode( )** are in **alloc.h**. These functions are not defined by the ANSI C standard, and are specific to Turbo C++.

The **heapchecknode( )** and **farheapchecknode( )** functions check the status of a single node in the heap pointed to by *ptr*. The **heapchecknode( )** function checks the normal heap and **farheapchecknode( )** checks the far heap. Both functions return one of these values:

Value	Meaning
_BADNODE	The specified node could not be located
_FREEENTRY	The specified node is free memory
_HEAPCORRUPT	Error found in the heap
_HEAPEMPTY	No heap present
_USEDENTRY	The specified node is being used

If either function is called with a pointer to a node that has been freed, **_BADNODE** could be returned because adjacent free memory is sometimes merged.

Example

The following code illustrates how to check a node on the heap.

```
#include <stdio.h>
#include <stdlib.h>
#include <alloc.h>

main(void)
{
  char *ptr;
  int status;
```

```
if((ptr=malloc(10)) == NULL)
  exit(1);

status = heapchecknode(ptr);

if(status == _USEDENTRY)
  printf("node is being used\n");
else
  printf("error in heap\n");

free(ptr);
return 0;
}
```

Related Functions

heapcheck( ), heapcheckfree( )

int heapfillfree(unsigned fill)
int farheapfillfree(unsigned fill)

Description

The prototypes for **heapfillfree( )** and **farheapfillfree( )** are in **alloc.h**. These functions are not defined by the ANSI C standard, and are specific to Turbo C++.

   The **heapfillfree( )** and **farheapfillfree( )** functions fill the free blocks of memory in the heap with *fill*. The **heapfillfree( )** function operates on the normal heap and **farheapfillfree( )** works with the far heap. You may want to use one of these functions to give allocated memory a known initial value.

   Both functions return one of these values:

Value	Meaning
_HEAPOK	No errors
_HEAPEMPTY	No heap present
_HEAPCORRUPT	Error found in the heap

Example

This code illustrates how to fill the heap with a desired value:

```
int status;
```

```
status = heapfillfree(0);
if(status == _HEAPOK)
  printf("heap is correct");
else
  printf("error in heap");
```

Related Function

heapcheckfree( )

int heapwalk(struct heapinfo *hinfo)
int farheapwalk(struct farheapinfo *hinfo)

Description

The prototypes for **heapwalk( )** and **farheapwalk( )** are in **alloc.h**. These functions are not defined by the ANSI C standard, and are specific to Turbo C++.

The **heapwalk( )** and **farheapwalk( )** functions fill the structure pointed to by *hinfo*. Each call to **heapwalk( )** or **farheapwalk( )** steps to the next node in the heap and returns information on that node. When there are no more nodes on the heap, **_HEAPEND** is returned. If there is no heap, **_HEAPEMPTY** is returned. Each time a valid block is examined, **_HEAPOK** is returned.

The **heapwalk( )** function operates on the normal heap and the **farheapwalk( )** function works with the far heap.

The **heapinfo** and **farheapinfo** structures contain three fields: a pointer to a block, the size of the block, and a flag that is set if the block is being used. These structures are shown here:

```
struct farheapinfo {
  void huge *ptr; /* pointer to block */
  unsigned long size; /* size of block, in bytes */
  int in_use; /* set if block is in use */
};

struct heapinfo {
  void *ptr; /* pointer to block */
  unsigned int size; /* size of block, in bytes */
  int in_use; /* set if block is in use */
};
```

On the first call to either function, you must set the *ptr* field to **NULL** before the first call to **heapwalk( )** or **farheapwalk( )**.

Because of the way Turbo/Borland C/C++ organizes the dynamic allocation system, the size of an allocated block of memory is slightly larger than the amount requested when it is allocated.

These functions assume the heap is not corrupted. Always call **heapcheck( )** or **farheapcheck( )** before beginning a walk through the heap.

Example

This program walks through the heap, printing the size of each allocated block:

```
#include <stdio.h>
#include <stdlib.h>
#include <alloc.h>

main(void)
{
  struct heapinfo hinfo;
  char *p1, *p2;

  if((p1 = (char *) malloc(80)) == NULL)
    exit(1);

  if((p2 = (char *) malloc(20)) == NULL)
    exit(1);

  if(heapcheck() < 0) { /* always check heap before walk */
    printf("heap corrupt, aborting");
    exit(1);
  }

  hinfo.ptr = NULL;  /* set ptr to null before first call */

  /* examine first block */
  if(heapwalk(&hinfo) == _HEAPOK)
    printf("size of p1's block is %d\n", hinfo.size);

  /* examine second block */
  if(heapwalk(&hinfo) == _HEAPOK)
    printf("size of p2's block is %d\n", hinfo.size);

  free(p1);
  free(p2);
  return 0;
}
```

Related Function

heapcheck( )

void *malloc(size_t size)

Description

The prototype for **malloc( )** is in **stdlib.h**.

The **malloc( )** function returns a pointer to the first byte of a region of memory *size* bytes long that has been allocated from the heap. If there is insufficient memory in the heap to satisfy the request, **malloc( )** returns a null pointer. It is always important to verify that the return value is not a null pointer before attempting to use the pointer. Attempting to use a null pointer usually causes a system crash.

Example

This function allocates sufficient memory to hold structures of type **addr**:

```
#include <stdlib.h>

struct addr {
  char name[40];
  char street[40];
  char city[40];
  char state[3];
  char zip[10];
};
     .
     .
     .
struct addr *get_struct(void)
{
  struct addr *p;

  if(!(p=(struct addr *)malloc(sizeof(addr)))) {
    printf("allocation error - aborting");
    exit(0);
  }
  return p;
}
```

Related Functions

free( ), realloc( ), calloc( )

void *realloc(void *ptr, size_t newsize)

Description

The prototype for **realloc( )** is in **stdlib.h**.

The **realloc( )** function changes the size of the allocated memory pointed to by *ptr* to that specified by *newsize*. The value of *newsize* specified in bytes can be greater or less than the original. A pointer to the memory block is returned because it may be necessary for **realloc( )** to move the block to increase its size. If this occurs, the contents of the old block are copied into the new block and no information is lost.

If there is not enough free memory in the heap to allocate *newsize* bytes, a null pointer is returned.

Example

The following program allocates 17 characters of memory, copies the string "this is 16 chars" into them, and then uses **realloc( )** to increase the size to 18 in order to place a period at the end.

```
#include <stdlib.h>
#include <stdio.h>
#include <string.h>

main(void)
{
  char *p;

  p = (char *) malloc(17);
  if(!p) {
    printf("allocation error - aborting");
    exit(1);
  }

  strcpy(p, "this is 16 chars");

  p = (char *) realloc(p,18);
  if(!p) {
    printf("allocation error - aborting");
    exit(1);
  }

  strcat(p, ".");

  printf(p);
```

```
   free(p);

   return 0;
}
```

Related Functions

free( ), **malloc( )**, **calloc( )**

void *sbrk(int amount)

Description

The prototype for **sbrk( )** is in **alloc.h**. This function is not defined by the ANSI C standard.

The **sbrk( )** function increments (or decrements if a negative value is used) the amount of memory allocated to the data segment by *amount* number of bytes. If successful, it returns a pointer to the old break address. Otherwise, it returns −1 and **errno** is set to **ENOMEM** (insuficient memory).

Because the use of **sbrk( )** is highly specialized, no example is given.

Related Function

brk( )

int setblock(unsigned seg, unsigned size)

Description

The prototype for **setblock( )** is in **dos.h**. This function is not defined by the ANSI C standard.

The **setblock( )** function changes the size of the block of memory whose segment address is seg to *size*, which is specified in paragraphs (16 bytes). The block of memory must have been previously allocated using **allocmem( )**.

If the size adjustment cannot be made, **setblock( )** returns the largest block that can be allocated. On success, it returns −1.

Example

This fragment attempts to resize to 100 paragraphs the block of memory whose segment address is in **seg**:

```
if(setblock(seg, 100)!=-1) printf("resize error");
```

Related Functions

allocmem( ), **freemem( )**, **_dos_setblock( )**

Chapter *21*

Directory Functions

Turbo/Borland C/C++ has a number of directory-manipulation functions in its library. Although none of these functions is defined by the ANSI standard, they are included to allow easy access to DOS directories.

int chdir(const char *path)

Description

The prototype for **chdir( )** is in **dir.h**. This function is not defined by the ANSI C standard.

The **chdir( )** function causes the directory whose path name is pointed to by *path* to become the current directory. The path name may include a drive specifier. The directory must exist.

If successful, **chdir( )** returns 0.

If unsuccessful, it returns −1 and sets **errno** to **ENOENT** (invalid path name).

Example

This fragment makes the WP\FORMLETdirectory on drive C the current working directory:

```
chdir("C:\\WP\\FORMLET");
```

Related Functions

mkdir( ), rmdir( )

int _chdrive(int drivenum)

Description

The prototype for **_chdrive( )** is in **direct.h.** This function is not defined by the ANSI C standard.

The **_chdrive( )** function changes the currently logged in drive to the one specified by *drivenum*, with A being 1, B being 2, and so on.

The **_chrdrive( )** function returns 0 if successful. Otherwise, –1 is returned.

Example

This changes the currently logged in drive to C.

```
_chdrive(3); /* switch to C */
```

Related Functions

setdrive( ), getdrive( )

void closedir(DIR *ptr)
DIR *opendir(char *dirname)
struct dirent readdir(DIR *ptr)
void rewinddir(DIR *ptr)

Description

The prototypes for **closedir( )**, **opendir( )**, **readdir( )**, and **rewinddir( )** are found in **dirent.h.** These functions are not defined by the ANSI C standard. These functions are included for UNIX compatibility.

The **closedir( )** function closes a directory that was previously opened using **opendir( )**. The **opendir( )** function opens a directory stream and returns a pointer to a structure of type **DIR**, which maintains information about the directory. You should not modify the contents of this structure. The **closedir( )** function closes the directory stream pointed to by *ptr*.

The **readdir( )** function returns the name of the next file in the directory. That is, **readdir( )** reads the contents of the directory a file at a time. The parameter *ptr* must point to a directory stream opened by **opendir( )**. The **dirent** structure is defined as shown on the following pages.

```
struct dirent
{
  char d_name[13];
}
```

Therefore, **d_name** contains the name of the next file in the directory after a call to **readdir( )** has returned.

The **rewinddir( )** function causes the directory pointed to by *ptr* (and previously obtained using **opendir( )**) to return to the start (that is, to the first entry in the specified directory). This allows the directory to be reread.

The **closedir( )** function returns 0 if successful; it returns –1 otherwise. On failure, it also sets **errno** to **EBADF** (invalid directory). The **opendir( )** function returns null if the directory cannot be opened and **errno** is set to either **ENOENT** (directory not found) or **ENOMEM** (insufficient memory). The **readdir( )** function returns null when the end of the directory is reached.

Because these functions are primarily included for compatibility with UNIX (and better ways exist under DOS to access directories), no examples are given.

Related Functions

findfirst( ), **findnext( )**

unsigned _dos_findfirst(const char *fname, int attr, struct find_t *ptr)
unsigned _dos_findnext(struct find_t *ptr)

Description

The prototypes for **_dos_findfirst( )** and **_dos_findnext( )** are in **dos.h**. These functions are not defined by the ANSI C standard.

The **_dos_findfirst( )** function searches for the first file name that matches that pointed to by *fname*. The file name may include both a drive specifier and a path name. Also, the file name may include the wild card characters * and ?. If a match is found, the structure pointed to by *ptr* is filled with information about the file.

The **find_t** structure is defined like this:

```
struct find_t {
  char reserved[21];/* used by DOS */
  char attrib;       /* attribute of file */
  unsigned wr_time; /* last time file was written to */
  unsigned wr_date; /* last date file was written to */
  long size;         /* size in bytes */
  char name[13];     /* filename */
};
```

The *attrib* parameter determines what type of files will be found by **_dos_findfirst( )**. The *attrib* can be one or more of the following macros (defined in **dos.h**):

Macro	Meaning
_A_NORMAL	normal file
_A_RDONLY	read only file
_A_HIDDEN	hidden file
_A_SYSTEM	system file
_A_VOLID	volume label
_A_SUBDIR	subdirectory
_A_ARCH	archive

The **_dos_findnext( )** function continues a search started by **_dos_findfirst( )**. The buffer pointed to by *ptr* must be the one used in the call to **findfirst( )**.

Both the **_dos_findfirst( )** and **_dos_findnext( )** functions return 0 on success and non-0 on failure or when no more matches are found. On failure, **errno** will be set to **ENOENT** (file not found).

Example

This program displays all normal files and their sizes in the current directory with a ".C" extension.

```
#include <dos.h>
#include <stdio.h>

main(void)
{
  struct find_t f;
  register int done;

  done = _dos_findfirst("*.c", _A_NORMAL, &f);
  while(!done) {
    printf("%s %ld\n", f.name, f.size);
    done = _dos_findnext(&f);
  }
  return 0;
}
```

Related Functions

findfirst( ), **findnext( )**

int findfirst(const char *fname, struct ffblk *ptr, int attrib)
int findnext(struct ffblk *ptr)

Description

The prototypes for **findfirst( )** and **findnext( )** are in **dir.h**. However, you also need to include the **dos.h** header, which contains macros that can be used as values for *attrib*. These functions are not defined by the ANSI C standard.

The **findfirst( )** function searches for the first file name that matches that pointed to by *fname*. The file name may include both a drive specifier and a path name. The file name may also include the wild-card characters * and ?. If a match is found, the structure pointed to by *ptr* is filled with information about the file, and the DTA is set to the address of the **ffblk** structure.

The **ffblk** structure is defined like this:

```
struct ffblk {
  char ff_reserved[2];        /* used by DOS */
  char ff_attrib              /* attribute of file */
  int ff_ftime;               /* creation time */
  int ff_fdate;               /* create date */
  long ff_fsize;              /* size in bytes */
  char ff_name[13];           /* file name */
};
```

The *attrib* parameter determines the type of files to be found by **findfirst( )**. If *attrib* is 0, all types of files that match the desired file name are acceptable. To cause a more selective search, *attrib* can be one the following macros:

Macro	Meaning
FA_RDONLY	Read-only file
FA_HIDDEN	Hidden file
FA_SYSTEM	System file
FA_LABEL	Volume label
FA_DIREC	Subdirectory
FA_ARCH	Archive byte set

The **findnext( )** function continues a search started by **findfirst( )**.

Both the **findfirst( )** and **findnext( )** functions return 0 on success and −1 on failure. On failure, **errno** is set to either **ENOENT** (file name not found) or **ENMFILE** (no more files in directory).

Example

This program displays all files with a .C extension (and their sizes) in the current working directory:

```
#include <stdio.h>
#include <dos.h>
#include <dir.h>

main(void)
{
  struct ffblk f;
  register int done;

  done = findfirst("*.c", &f, 0);
  while(!done) {
    printf("%s %ld\n", f.ff_name, f.ff_fsize);
    done = findnext(&f);
  }
  return 0;
}
```

Related Function

fnmerge( )

void fnmerge(char *path, const char *drive, const char *dir, const char *fname, const char *ext)
int fnsplit(const char *path, char *drive, char *dir, char *fname, char *ext)

Description

The prototypes for **fnmerge( )** and **fnsplit( )** are in **dir.h**. These functions are not defined by the ANSI C standard.

The **fnmerge( )** function constructs a file name from the specified individual components and puts that name into the string pointed to by *path*. For example, if *drive* is C:, *dir* is \TC\, *fname* is TEST, and *ext* is .C, the file name produced is C:\TC\TEST.C.

The **fnsplit( )** decomposes the file name pointed to by *path* into its component parts.

The array size needed for each parameter is shown here, along with a macro defined in **dir.h** that can be used in place of the actual number:

Parameter	Size	Macro Name
path	80	MAXPATH
drive	3	MAXDRIVE
dir	66	MAXDIR
fname	9	MAXFILE
ext	5	MAXEXT

The **fnsplit( )** function puts the colon after the drive specifier in the string pointed to by *drive*. It puts the period preceding the extension into the string pointed to by *ext*. Leading and trailing backslashes are retained.

The two functions **fnmerge( )** and **fnsplit( )** are complementary—the output from one can be used as input to the other.

The **fnsplit( )** function returns an integer than has five flags encoded into it. The flags have these macro names associated with them (defined in **dir.h**):

Macro Name	Meaning When Set
EXTENSION	Extension present
FILENAME	File name present
DIRECTORY	Directory path present
DRIVE	Drive specifier present
WILDCARD	One or more wild-card characters present

To determine if a flag is set, AND the flag macro with the return value and test the result. If the result is 1, the flag is set; otherwise it is off.

Example

This program illustrates how **fnmerge( )** encodes a file name. Its output is "C:TEST.C":

```
#include <stdio.h>
#include <dir.h>

main(void)
{
  char path[MAXPATH];
  fnmerge(path, "C:", "", "TEST", ".C");
  printf(path);
  return 0;
}
```

Related Functions

findfirst( ), findnext( )

char *_fullpath(char *fpath, const char *rpath, int len)

Description

The prototype for **_fullpath( )** is in **stdlib.h**. This function is not defined by the ANSI C standard.

The **_fullpath( )** function constructs a full path name given a relative path name. The relative path name is pointed to by *rpath*. The full path name is put into the array pointed to by *fpath*. The size of the array pointed to by *fpath* is specified by *len*. If *fpath* is null, then an array will be dynamically allocated. (In this case, the array must be freed manually using **free( )**.)

The **_fullpath( )** function returns a pointer to *fpath*, or null if an error occurs.

Example

This program displays the full path to the \INCLUDE directory.

```
#include <stdio.h>
#include <stdlib.h>

main(void)
{
  char fpath[80];

  _fullpath(fpath, "\INCLUDE", 80);

  printf("Full path: %s\n", fpath);

  return 0;
}
```

Related Functions

_makepath( ), **mkdir( )**, **getcwd( )**

int getcurdir(int drive, char *dir)

Description

The prototype for **getcurdir( )** is in **dir.h**. This function is not defined by the ANSI C standard.

The **getcurdir( )** function copies the name of the current working directory of the drive specified in *drive* into the string pointed to by *dir*. A 0 value for *drive* specifies the default drive. For drive A, use 1; for B, use 2; and so on.

The string pointed to by *dir* must be at least **MAXDIR** bytes in length. **MAXDIR** is a macro defined in **dir.h**. The directory name will not contain the drive specifier and will not include leading backslashes.

The **getcurdir( )** function returns 0 if successful, –1 on failure.

Example

The following program prints the current directory on the default drive:

```
#include <stdio.h>
#include <dir.h>

main(void)
{
  char dir[MAXDIR];

  getcurdir(0, dir);
  printf("current directory is %s", dir);
  return 0;
}
```

Related Function

getcwd( )

char *getcwd(char *dir, int len)

Description

The prototype for **getcwd( )** is in **dir.h**. This function is not defined by the ANSI C standard.

The **getcwd( )** function copies the full path name (up to *len* characters) of the current working directory into the string pointed to by *dir*. An error occurs if the full path name is longer than *len* characters. The **getcwd( )** function returns a pointer to *dir*.

If **getcwd( )** is called with *dir*'s value being null, **getcwd( )** automatically allocates a buffer using **malloc( )** and returns a pointer to this buffer. You can free the memory allocated by **getcwd( )** using **free( )**.

On failure, **getcwd( )** returns null and **errno** is set to either **ENODEV** (non-existent device), **ENOMEM** (insufficient memory), or **ERANGE** (out-of-range).

Example

This program prints the full path name of the current working directory:

```
#include <stdio.h>
#include <dir.h>

main(void)
{
  char dir[MAXDIR];
  getcwd(dir, MAXDIR);
  printf("current directory is %s", dir);   return 0;
}
```

Related Function

getcurdir( )

char *_getdcwd(int drive, char *path, int len)

Description

The prototype for **_getdcwd( )** is in **direct.h**. This function is not defined by the ANSI C standard.

The **_getdcwd( )** function obtains the path name of the current directory of the drive specified by *drive,* with A being 1, B being 2, and so on. (The default drive is specified as 0.) It copies the path name into the array pointed to by *path*. The size of *path* is specified by *len*. If *path* is null, then an array will be dynamically allocated. (In this case, the array must be freed manually using **free( )**.)

The **_getdcwd( )** funtion returns *path*. On failure, a null pointer is returned and **errno** contains either **ENOMEM** (insufficient memory) or **ERANGE** (path name exceeds array size).

Example

This program displays the current directory of drive D.

```
#include <stdio.h>
#include <direct.h>

main(void)
{
  char path[80];
```

```
_getdcwd(4, path, 80);

  printf("Current directory of drive D is %s\n", path);

  return 0;
}
```

Related Functions

mkdir( ), chdir( ), _fullpath( )

int getdisk(void)

Description

The prototype for **getdisk( )** is in **dir.h**. This function is not defined by the ANSI C standard.

The **getdisk( )** function returns the number of the current drive. Drive A corresponds to 0, drive B is 1, and so on.

Example

This program displays the name of the current drive:

```
#include <stdio.h>
#include <dir.h>

main(void)
{
  printf("current drive is %c", getdisk( )+'A');
  return 0;
}
```

Related Functions

setdisk( ), getcwd( )

int _getdrive(void)

Description

The prototype for **_getdrive( )** is in **direct.h**. This function is not defined by the ANSI C standard.

The **_getdrive( )** function returns the number of the current drive, with A being 1, B being 2, and so on.

Example

This statement displays the number of the current drive.

```
printf("Current drive is %d.", _getdrive( ));
```

Related Functions

getcwd( )

void _makepath(char *pname, const char *drive, const char *directory, const char *fname, cont char *extension)

Description

The prototype for **_makepath( )** is in **stdlib.h**. This function is not defined by the ANSI C standard.

The **_makepath( )** function constructs a full path name from the elements specified in its parameters and places the result in the array pointed to by *pname*. The drive is specified in the string pointed to by *drive*. The directory (and any subdirectories) are specified in the string pointed to by *directory*. The file name is pointed to by *fname* and the extension is pointed to by *extension*. Any of these strings may be empty.

Example

This program constructs a full path name from its elements. Next, it displays the path and then dissects it into its components using **_splitpath( )**, which is the complement to **_makepath( )**.

```
#include <stdio.h>
#include <stdlib.h>

main(void)
{
  char fpath[80];
  char fname[9];
  char dir[64];
  char drive[3];
  char ext[5];
```

```
_makepath(fpath, "B:", "MYDIR", "MYFILE", "DAT");
printf("%s\n", fpath);

_splitpath(fpath, drive, dir, fname, ext);
printf("%s %s %s %s\n", drive, dir, fname, ext);

return 0;
}
```

Related Function

_splitpath( ), fnmerge( ), fnsplit( )

int mkdir(const char *path)

Description

The prototype for **mkdir( )** is in **dir.h**. This function is not defined by the ANSI C standard.

The **mkdir( )** function creates a directory using the path name pointed to by *path*.

The **mkdir( )** function returns 0 if successful. If unsuccessful, it returns −1 and sets **errno** to either **EACCESS** (access denied) or **ENOENT** (invalid path name).

Example

This program creates a directory called FORMLET:

```
#include <dir.h>

main(void)
{
  mkdir("FORMLET");
  return 0;
}
```

Related Function

rmdir( )

char *mktemp(char *fname)

Description

The prototype for **mktemp( )** is in **dir.h**. This function is not defined by the ANSI C standard.

The **mktemp( )** function creates a unique file name and copies it into the string pointed to by *fname*. When you call **mktemp( )**, the string pointed to by *fname* must contain six "X"s followed by a null terminator. The **mktemp( )** function transforms that string into a unique file name. It does not create the file, however.

If successful, **mktemp( )** returns a pointer to *fname;* otherwise, it returns a null.

Example

This program displays a unique file name:

```
#include <stdio.h>
#include <dir.h>

char fname[7] = "XXXXXX";

main(void)
{
  mktemp(fname);
  printf(fname);
  return 0;
}
```

Related Functions

findfirst( ), findnext( )

int rmdir(const char *path)

Description

The prototype for rmdir( ) is in dir.h. This function is not defined by the ANSI C standard.

The **rmdir( )** function removes the directory whose path name is pointed to by *path*. To be removed, a directory must be empty, must not be the current directory, and must not be the root.

If **rmdir( )** is successful, 0 is returned. Otherwise, −1 is returned and **errno** is set to either **EACCESS** (access denied) or **ENOENT** (invalid path name).

Example

This removes the directory called FORMLET:

```
#include <stdio.h>
#include <dir.h>
```

```
main(void)
{
  if(!rmdir("FORMLET")) printf("FORMLET removed");
  return 0;
}
```

Related Function

mkdir( )

char *searchpath(const char *fname)

Description

The prototype for **searchpath( )** is in **dir.h**. This function is not defined by the ANSI C standard.

The **searchpath( )** function tries to find the file whose name is pointed to by *fname* using the DOS PATH environmental variable. If it finds the file, it returns a pointer to the entire path name. This string is statically allocated and is overwritten by each call to **searchpath( )**. If the file cannot be found, a null is returned.

Example

This program displays the path name for the file TCC.EXE:

```
#include <stdio.h>
#include <dir.h>

main(void)
{
  printf(searchpath("TCC.EXE"));
  return 0;
}
```

Related Function

mktemp( )

int setdisk(int drive)

Description

The prototype for **setdisk( )** is in **dir.h**. This function is not defined by the ANSI C standard.

The **setdisk( )** function sets the current drive to that specified by *drive*. Drive A corresponds to 0, drive B to 1, and so on. It returns the total number of drives in the system.

Example

This program switches to drive A and reports the total number of drives in the system:

```
#include <stdio.h>
#include <dir.h>

main(void)
{
  printf("%d drives", setdisk(0));
  return 0;
}
```

Related Function

getdisk( )

void _splitpath(const char *fpath, char *drive, char *directory char *fname, char *extension)

Description

The prototype for **_splitpath( )** is in **stdlib.h**. This function is not defined by the ANSI C standard.

The **_splitpath( )** function dissects the full path name specified in the string pointed to by *fpath*. The drive letter is put in the string pointed to by *drive*. The directory (and any subdirectories) is put in the string pointed to by *directory*. The file name is put in the string pointed to by *fname* and the extension is put in the string pointed to by *extension*.

Example

This program displays the elements of this full path: B:\MYDIR\MYFILE.DAT.

```
#include <stdio.h>
#include <stdlib.h>

main(void)
{
```

```
  char fname[9];
  char dir[64];
  char drive[3];
  char ext[5];

  _splitpath("B:\\MYDIR\\MYFILE.DAT", drive, dir, fname, ext);

  printf("%s %s %s %s\n", drive, dir, fname, ext);

  return 0;
}
```

Related Function

_makepath( ), fnsplit( ), fnmerge( )

Chapter 22

Process Control Functions

This chapter covers a number of functions that are used to control the way a program executes, terminates, or invokes the execution of another program. Aside from **abort( )**, **atexit( )**, and **exit( )**, none of the functions described here is defined by the ANSI C standard. However, all allow your program greater flexibility in its execution.

The process control functions have their prototypes in **process.h**. However, those functions defined by the ANSI standard also have their prototypes in the **stdlib.h** header file.

void abort(void)

Description

The prototype for **abort( )** is in **process.h** and **stdlib.h**.

The **abort( )** function causes immediate termination of a program. No files are flushed. It returns a value of 3 to the calling process (usually the operating system).

The primary use of **abort( )** is to prevent a runaway program from closing active files.

Example

This program terminates if the user enters an "A":

```
#include <process.h>
#include <conio.h>

main(void)
{
  for(;;)
    if(getch()=='A') abort();
  return 0;
}
```

Related Functions

exit( ), atexit( )

int atexit(void (*func)( ))

Description

The prototype for **atexit( )** is in **stdlib.h**.

The **atexit( )** function establishes the function pointed to by *func* as the function to be called upon normal program termination. That is, the specified function is called at the end of a program run. The act of establishing the function is referred to as *registration* by the ANSI standard.

The **atexit( )** function returns 0 if the function is registered as the termination function, and non-0 otherwise.

Up to 32 termination functions can be established. They are called in the reverse order of their establishment: first in, last out.

Example

This program prints "hello there" on the screen:

```
#include <stdio.h>
#include <stdlib.h>

/* example using atexit() */
```

```
main(void)
{
  void done();

  if(atexit(done)) printf("error in atexit()");
  return 0;
}

void done()
{
  printf("hello there");
}
```

Related Functions

exit( ), abort( )

void _c_exit(void)
void _cexit(void)

Description

The prototypes for **_c_exit( )** and **_cexit( )** are in **process.h**. These functions are defined by the ANSI C standard.

The **_c_exit( )** function performs the same actions as **_exit( )** except that the program is not terminated.

The **_cexit( )** function performs the same actions as **exit( )** except that the program is not terminated and open files are not closed. However, all buffers are flushed and any termination functions are executed.

Example

This statement performs program shut-down procedures except that the program is not terminated and no files are closed.

```
_cexit();
```

Related Functions

exit( ), _exit( ), atexit( )

int execl(char *fname, char *arg0, . . ., char *argN, NULL)
int execle(char *fname, char *arg0, . . ., char *argN,
NULL, char *envp[])
int execlp(char *fname, char *arg0, . . ., char *argN, NULL)
int execlpe(char *fname, char *arg0, . . ., char *argN,
NULL, char *envp[])
int execv(char *fname, char *arg[])
int execve(char *fname, char *arg[], char *envp[])
int execvp(char *fname, char *arg[])
int execvpe(char *fname, char *arg[], char *envp[])

Description

The prototypes for these functions are in **process.h**. These functions are not defined by the ANSI C standard.

The **exec** group of functions is used to execute another program. This other program, called the *child process*, is loaded over the one that contains the **exec** call. The name of the file that contains the child process is pointed to by *fname*. Any arguments to the child process are pointed to either individually by *arg0* through *argN* or by the array *arg[]*. An environment string must be pointed to by *envp[]*. (The arguments are pointed to by **argv** in the child process.)

If no extension or period is part of the string pointed to by *fname,* a search is first made for a file by that name. If that fails, the .COM extension is added and the search is tried again. If that fails, the .EXE extension is added and the search is tried again. When an extension is specified, only an exact match will satisfy the search. Finally, if a period but no extension is present, a search is made for only the file specified by the left side of the file name.

The exact way the child process is executed depends on which version of **exec** you use. You can think of the **exec** function as having different suffixes that determine its operation. A suffix can consist of either one or two characters.

Functions that have a **p** in the suffix search for the child process in the directories specified by the DOS PATH command. If a **p** is not in the suffix, only the current and root directories are searched.

An **l** in the suffix specifies that pointers to the arguments to the child process will be passed individually. You use this method when you know in advance how many arguments will be passed. Notice that the last argument must be **NULL**. (**NULL** is defined in **stdio.h**.)

A **v** in the suffix means that pointers to the arguments to the child process will be passed in an array. This is the way you must pass arguments when you do not know in advance how many there will be. Typically, the end of the array is signaled by a null pointer.

An **e** in the suffix specifies that one or more environmental strings will be passed to the child process. The *envp* parameter is an array of string pointers. Each string pointed to by the array must have the form *environment variable = value*

The last pointer in the array must be **NULL**. If the first element in the array is **NULL**, the child retains the same environment as the parent.

It is important to remember that files open at the time of an **exec** call are also open in the child program.

When successful, the **exec** functions return no value. On failure, they return –1 and set **errno** to one of the following values.

Macro	Meaning
E2BIG	Too many arguments
EACCES	Access to child process file denied
EMFILE	Too many open files
ENOENT	File not found
ENOEXEC	**exec** format error
ENOMEM	Not enough free memory to load child process

Example

The first of the following programs invokes the second, which displays its arguments. Remember, both programs must be in separate files.

```
/* first file  - parent */

#include <stdio.h>
#include <process.h>

main(void)
{
  execl("test.exe", "test.exe", "hello", "10", NULL);
  return 0;
}

/* second file - child */
main(int argc, char *argv[])
{
  printf("this program is executed with these command line ");
  printf("arguments: ");
  printf(argv[1]);
  printf(" %d", atoi(argv[2]));
  return 0;
}
```

Related Function

spawn( )

void exit(int status)
void _exit(int status)

Description

The prototypes for **exit( )** and **_exit( )** are in **process.h** and **stdlib.h**.

The **exit( )** function causes immediate, normal termination of a program. The value of *status* is passed to the calling process. By convention, if the value of *status* is 0, normal program termination is assumed. A non-0 value can be used to indicate an implementation-defined error. Calling **exit( )** flushes and closes all open files, writes any buffered output, and calls any program termination functions registered using **atexit( )**.

The **_exit( )** program does not close any files, flush any buffers, or call any termination functions. This function is not defined by the ANSI C standard.

Example

This function performs menu selection for a mailing-list program. If Q is pressed, the program is terminated.

```
char menu(void)
{
  char ch;

  do {
    printf("Enter names (E)\n");
    printf("Delete name (D)\n");
    printf("Print (P)\n");
    printf("Quit (Q)\n");
  } while(!strchr("EDPQ",toupper(ch)));
  if(ch=='Q') exit(0);
  return ch;
}
```

Related Functions

atexit( ), abort( )

int spawnl(int mode, char *fname, char *arg0, . . .,
         char *argN, NULL)
int spawnle(int mode, char *fname, char *arg0, . . .,
          char *argN, NULL, char *envp[])
int spawnlp(int mode, char *fname, char *arg0, . . .,
          char *argN, NULL)
int spawnlpe(int mode, char *fname, char *arg0, . . .,
          char *argN, NULL, char *envp[])
int spawnv(int mode, char *fname, char *arg[])
int spawnve(int mode, char *fname, char *arg[], char *envp[])
int spawnvp(int mode, char *fname, char *arg[])
int spawnvpe(int mode, char *fname, char *arg[], char *envp[])

Description

The prototypes for these functions are in **process.h**. These functions are not defined by the ANSI C standard.

The **spawn** group of functions is used to execute another program. This other program, the *child process,* does not necessarily replace the parent program (unlike the child process executed by the **exec** group of functions). The name of the file that contains the child process is pointed to by *fname.* The arguments to the child process, if any, are pointed to either individually by *arg0* through *argN* or by the array *arg[].* If you pass an environment string, it must be pointed to by *envp[].* (The arguments will be pointed to by **argv** in the child process.) The *mode* parameter determines how the child process will be executed. It can have one of these three values (defined in **process.h**).

Macro	Execution Mode
P_WAIT	Suspends parent process until the child has finished executing
P_NOWAIT	Executes both the parent and the child concurrently— not implemented in Turbo/Borland C/C++
P_OVERLAY	Replaces the parent process in memory

Since the **P_NOWAIT** option is currently unavailable, you will almost always use **P_WAIT** as a value for *mode.* (If you want to replace the parent program, it is better to use the **exec** functions instead.) If you use the **P_WAIT** option, when the child process terminates, the parent process is resumed at the line after the call to **spawn**.

If no extension or period is part of the string pointed to by *fname,* a search is made for a file by that name. If that fails, then a .COM extension is tried. If that fails, the

.EXE extension is added and the search is tried again. If an extension is specified, only an exact match satisfies the search. If a period but no extension is present, a search is made for only the file specified by the left side of the file name.

The exact way the child process is executed depends on which version of **spawn** you use. You can think of the **spawn** function as having different suffixes that determine its operation. A suffix can consist of either one or two characters.

Those functions that have a **p** in the suffix search for the child process in the directories specified by the DOS PATH command. If a **p** is not in the suffix, only the current and root directories are searched.

An **l** in the suffix specifies that pointers to the arguments to the child process will be passed individually. You use this method when you know in advance how many arguments will be passed. Notice that the last argument must be **NULL**. (**NULL** is defined in **stdio.h**.)

A **v** in the suffix means that pointers to the arguments to the child process will be passed in an array. This is the way you must pass arguments when you do not know in advance how many there will be. Typically, the end of the array is signaled by a null pointer.

An **e** in the suffix specifies that one or more environmental strings will be passed to the child process. The *envp[]* parameter is an array of string pointers. Each string pointed to by the array must have the form:

environment variable = value

The last pointer in the array must be **NULL**. If the first element in the array is **NULL**, the child retains the same environment as the parent.

It is important to remember that files open at the time of a **spawn** call are also open in the child process.

When successful, the **spawn**ed functions return 0. On failure, they return −1 and set **errno** to one of the following values:

Macro	Meaning
EINVAL	Bad argument
E2BIG	Too many arguments
ENOENT	File not found
ENOEXEC	**spawn** format error
ENOMEM	Not enough free memory to load child process

A **spawn**ed process can **spawn** another process. The level of nested **spawn**s is limited by the amount of available RAM and the size of the programs.

Example

The first of the following programs invokes the second, which displays its arguments and invokes a third program. After the third program terminates, the second is resumed. When the second program terminates, the parent program is resumed. Remember that the three programs must be in separate files.

```
/* parent process */

#include <stdio.h>
#include <process.h>

main(void)
{
  printf("In parent\n");
  spawnl(P_WAIT, "test.exe", "test.exe", "hello", "10", NULL);
  printf("\nBack in parent");
  return 0;
}


/* first child */
#include <stdio.h>
#include <process.h>

main(int argc, char *argv[])
{
  printf("First child process executing ");
  printf("with these command line arguments: ");
  printf(argv[1]);
  printf(" %d\n", atoi(argv[2]));
  spawnl(P_WAIT, "test2.exe", NULL);
  printf("\nBack in first child process.");
  return 0;
}


/* second child */
main(void)
{
  printf("In second child process.");
  return 0;
}
```

Related Function

exec( )

Chapter *23*

Text and Graphics Functions

The ANSI C standard doesn't define any text or graphics functions, mainly because the capabilities of diverse hardware environments preclude standardization across a wide range of machines. However, Turbo/Borland C/C++ provides extensive screen and graphics support systems for the PC environment. If you will not be porting your code to a different computer system, you should feel free to use them because they can add substantial appeal to any application. In fact, intensive screen control is a must for most successful commercial programs.

The prototypes and header information for the text handling functions are in **conio.h**. The prototypes and related information for the graphics system are in **graphics.h**.

The graphics system requires that the **graphics.lib** library be linked with your program. If you are using the command-line version, you need to include its name on the command line. For example, if your program is called **test**, and you are using Turbo C, the command line looks like this:

```
tcc test graphics.lib
```

If you use the integrated development environment in its default configuration, the **graphics.lib** library may or may not be linked automatically with any program that uses graphics functions. You can set this option using the **Options** menu.

Central to both the text and graphics functions is the concept of the *window,* the active part of the screen within which output is displayed. A window can be as large as the entire screen, as it is by default, or as small as your specific needs require.

Turbo/Borland C/C++ uses slightly different terminology between the text and graphics systems to help keep the two systems separate. The text functions refer to *windows;* the graphics system refers to *viewports.* However, the concept is the same.

It is important to understand that most of the text and graphics functions are window (viewport) relative. For example, the **gotoxy( )** cursor location function sends the cursor to the specified *x,y* position relative to the window, not the screen.

All of the graphics functions are **far** functions.

One last point: When the screen is in a text mode, the upper left corner is location 1,1. In a graphics mode, the upper left corner is 0,0.

For an overview of how the text and graphics systems operate as well as background material on the various video modes, refer to Chapter 11.

None of the functions described in this chapter are defined by the ANSI C standard.

void far arc(int x, int y, int start, int end, int radius)

Description

The prototype for **arc( )** is in **graphics.h**.

The **arc( )** function draws an arc from *start* to *end* (given in degrees), along the invisible circle centered at *x,y,* with the radius *radius.* The color of the arc is determined by the current drawing color.

Example

This code draws an arc from 0 to 90 degrees on an imaginary circle located at 100,100 with the radius 20:

```
#include <graphics.h>
#include <conio.h>

main(void)
{
  int driver, mode;

  driver = DETECT; /* autodetect */
  mode = 0;
  initgraph(&driver, &mode, "");

  setcolor(WHITE);
  arc(100, 100, 0, 90, 20);
```

```
getch(); /* wait until keypress */
restorecrtmode();

return 0;
}
```

Related Functions

circle( ), **ellipse( )**, **getarccoords( )**

void far bar(int left, int top, int right, int bottom)
void far bar3d(int left, int top, int right, int bottom,
int depth, int topflag)

Description

The prototypes for **bar( )** and **bar3d( )** are in **graphics.h**.

The **bar( )** function draws a rectangular bar that has its upper left corner defined by *left,top* and its lower right corner defined by *right,bottom*. The bar is filled with the current fill pattern and color. (You set the current fill pattern and color using **setfillpattern( )**.) The bar is not outlined.

The **bar3d( )** function is the same as **bar( )** except that it produces a three-dimensional bar of *depth* pixels. The bar is outlined in the current drawing color. This means that if you want a two-dimensional bar that is outlined, use **bar3d( )** with a depth of 0. If *topflag* is non-0, a top is added to the bar; otherwise, the bar has no top.

Example

This program draws a two-dimensional and a three-dimensional bar:

```
#include <graphics.h>
#include <conio.h>

main(void)
{
  int driver, mode;
  driver = DETECT; /* autodetect */
  mode = 0;
  initgraph(&driver, &mode, "");

  /* display a green 2-d bar */
  setfillstyle(SOLID_FILL, GREEN);
  bar(100, 100, 120, 200);
```

```
/* now show a red 3-d bar */
setfillstyle(SOLID_FILL, RED);
bar3d(200, 100, 220, 200, 10, 1);

getch();
restorecrtmode();
return 0;
}
```

Related Function

rectangle( )

void far circle(int x, int y, int radius)

Description

The prototype for **circle( )** is in **graphics.h**.

The **circle( )** function draws a circle centered at *x,y* with radius *radius* (expressed in pixels) in the current drawing color.

Example

This program draws five concentric circles at location 200,200:

```
#include <graphics.h>
#include <conio.h>

main(void)
{
  int driver, mode;
  driver = DETECT; /* autodetect */
  mode = 0;
  initgraph(&driver, &mode, "");

  circle(200, 200, 20);
  circle(200, 200, 30);
  circle(200, 200, 40);
  circle(200, 200, 50);
  circle(200, 200, 60);

  getch();
  restorecrtmode();
```

```
    return 0;
}
```

Related Functions

arc( ), **ellipse( )**

void far cleardevice(void)
void far clearviewport(void)

Description

The prototypes for **cleardevice( )** and **clearviewport( )** are in **graphics.h**.

The **cleardevice( )** function clears the screen and resets the current position (CP) to 0,0. This function is used only with the graphics screen modes.

The **clearviewport( )** function clears the current viewport and resets the current position (CP) to 0,0. After **clearviewport( )** has executed, the viewport no longer exists.

Example

This program creates a viewport, writes some text into it, and then clears it:

```
#include <graphics.h>
#include <conio.h>

void box(int, int, int, int, int);

main(void)
{
  int driver, mode;

  driver = DETECT; /* autodetect */
  mode = 0;
  initgraph(&driver, &mode, "");

  /* frame the screen for perspective */
  box(0, 0, 639, 349, WHITE);

  setviewport(20, 20, 200, 200, 1);
  box(0, 0, 179, 179, RED);

  outtext("this is a test of the viewport");
```

```
    outtextxy(20, 10, "press a key");
    getch();
    /* clear the current viewport but not the entire screen */
    clearviewport();

    getch();
    restorecrtmode();
    return 0;
}

/* Draw a box given the coordinates of its two corners. */
void box(int startx, int starty, int endx, int endy,
         int color)
{
    setcolor(color);
    line(startx, starty, startx, endy);
    line(startx, starty, endx, starty);
    line(endx, starty, endx, endy);
    line(endx, endy, startx, endy);
}
```

Related Function

getviewsettings( )

void far closegraph(void)

Description

The prototype for **closegraph( )** is in **graphics.h**.

The **closegraph( )** function deactivates the graphics environment, which includes returning to the system memory that was used to hold the graphics drivers and fonts. This function should be used when your program uses both graphics and nongraphics output. It also returns the system video mode to what it was prior to the call to **initgraph( )**. You may also use **restorecrtmode( )** in place of **closegraph( )** if your program is terminating. In this case, any allocated memory is automatically freed.

Example

This fragment turns off the graphics system:

```
closegraph();
cprintf("this is not in graphics");
```

Related Function

initgraph( )

void clreol(void)
void clrscr(void)

Description

The prototypes for **clreol( )** and **clrscr( )** are in **conio.h**.

The **clreol( )** function clears from the current cursor position to the end of the line in the active text window. The cursor position remains unchanged.

The **clrscr( )** function clears the entire active text window and locates the cursor in the upper left corner (1,1).

Example

This program illustrates **clreol( )** and **clrscr( )**:

```c
#include <conio.h>

main(void)
{
  register int i;

  gotoxy(10, 10);
  cprintf("This is a test of the clreol() function.");
  getch();
  gotoxy(10, 10);
  clreol();

  for(i=0; i<20; i++) cprintf("Hello there\n");
  getch();

  /* clear the screen */
  clrscr();
  return 0;
}
```

Related Functions

delline( ), **window( )**

int cprintf(const char *fmt, . . .)

Description

The prototype for **cprintf( )** is in **conio.h**.

The **cprintf( )** function works like the **printf( )** function except that it writes to the current text window instead of **stdout**. Its output may not be redirected and it automatically prevents the boundaries of the window from being overrun. See the **printf( )** function for details.

The **cprintf( )** function does not translate the newline (\n) into the linefeed, carriage return pair as does the **printf( )** function, so it is necessary to explicitly put the carriage return (\r) where desired.

The **cprintf( )** function returns the number of characters actually printed. A negative return value indicates that an error has taken place.

Example

This program displays the output shown in its comments:

```
#include <conio.h>

main(void)
{
  /* This prints "this is a test" left justified
     in 20 character field.
  */
  cprintf("%-20s", "this is a test");

  /* This prints a float with 3 decimal places in a 10
     character field. The output will be "    12.235".
  */
  cprintf("%10.3f\n\r", 12.234657);
  return 0;
}
```

Related Functions

cscanf( ), **cputs( )**

int cputs(const char *str)

Description

The prototype for **cputs( )** is in **conio.h**.

The **cputs( )** function outputs the string pointed to by *str* to the current text window. Its output cannot be redirected, and it automatically prevents the boundaries of the window from being overrun.

It returns the last character written if successful and EOF if unsuccessful.

Example

This program creates a window and uses **cputs( )** to write a line longer than will fit in the window. The line is automatically wrapped at the end of the window instead of spilling over into the rest of the screen.

```c
#include <conio.h>

void border(int, int, int, int);

main(void)
{
  clrscr();
  /* create first window */
  window(3, 2, 40, 9);
  border(3, 2, 40, 9);
  gotoxy(1,1);
  cputs("This line will be wrapped at the end of the window.");
  getche();
  return 0;
}

/* Draws a border around a text window. */
void border(startx, starty, endx, endy)
int startx, starty, endx, endy;
{
  register int i;

  gotoxy(1, 1);
  for(i=0; i<=endx-startx; i++)
    putch('-');

  gotoxy(1, endy-starty);
  for(i=0; i<=endx-startx; i++)
    putch('-');

  for(i=2; i<endy-starty; i++) {
    gotoxy(1, i);
    putch('|');
```

```
    gotoxy(endx-startx+1, i);
    putch('|');
  }
}
```

Related Functions

cprintf( ), **window( )**

int cscanf(char *fmt, . . .)

Description

The prototype for **cscanf( )** is in **conio.h**.

The **cscanf( )** function works like the **scanf( )** function except that it reads the information from the console instead of **stdin**. It cannot be redirected. See the **scanf( )** function for details.

The **cscanf( )** function returns the number of arguments that are actually assigned values. This number does not include skipped fields. The **cscanf( )** function returns the value **EOF** if an attempt is made to read past end-of-file.

Example

This code fragment reads a string and a **float** number from the console:

```
char str[80];
float f;

cscanf("%s%f", str, &f);
```

Related Functions

scanf( ), **cprintf( )**, **sscanf( )**

void delline(void)

Description

The prototype for **delline( )** is in **conio.h**.

The **delline( )** function deletes the line in the active window that contains the cursor. All lines below the deleted line are moved up to fill the void. Remember that if the current window is smaller than the entire screen, only the text inside the window is affected.

Example

This program prints 24 lines on the screen and then deletes line 3:

```
#include <conio.h>

main(void)
{
  register int i;

  clrscr();

  for(i=0; i<24; i++) cprintf("line %d\n\r", i);
  getch();
  gotoxy(1, 3);
  delline();

  getch();
  return 0;
}
```

Related Functions

clreol( ), insline( )

void far detectgraph(int far *driver, int far *mode)

Description

The prototype for **detectgraph( )** is in **graphics.h**.

The **detectgraph( )** function determines what type of graphics adapter, if any, the computer contains. If the system has a graphics adapter, **detectgraph( )** returns the number of the appropriate graphics driver for the adapter in the integer pointed to by *driver*. It sets the variable pointed to by *mode* to the highest resolution supported by the adapter. If no graphics hardware is in the system, the variable pointed to by *driver* contains a –2.

You can use **detectgraph( )** to determine what type of video graphics hardware is in the system.

Example

This fragment tests for the presence of a video adapter:

```
int driver, mode;
detectgraph(&driver, &mode);

if(driver==-2) {
  cprintf("no graphics adapter in the system.");
  exit(1);
}
```

Related Function

initgraph( )

void far drawpoly(int numpoints, int far *points)

Description

The prototype for **drawpoly( )** is in **graphics.h**.

The **drawpoly( )** function draws a polygon using the current drawing color. The number of end points in the polygon are equal to *numpoints*. Since each point consists of both *x* and *y* coordinates, the integer array pointed to by *points* must be at least as large as two times the number of points. Within this array, each point is defined by its *x,y* coordinate pair with the *x* coordinate first.

Example

This program draws the polygon defined in the array **shape**:

```
#include <graphics.h>
#include <conio.h>

main(void)
{
  int driver, mode;
  int shape[10] = { /* five points * 2 */
    10, 10,
    100, 80,
    200, 200,
    350, 90,
    0, 0
  };

  driver = DETECT; /* autodetect */
  mode = 0;
  initgraph(&driver, &mode, "");
```

```
    drawpoly(5, shape);
    getch();
    restorecrtmode();
    return 0;
}
```

Related Functions

fillpoly( ), line( ), circle( )

void far ellipse(int x, int y, int start, int end, int xradius, int yradius)

Description

The prototype for **ellipse( )** is in **graphics.h**.

The **ellipse( )** function draws an ellipse in the current drawing color. The center of the ellipse is at *x,y*. The length of the *x* and *y* radii are specified by *xradius* and *yradius*. The amount of the ellipse actually displayed is determined by the values for *start* and *end,* which are specified in degrees. If *start* equals 0 and *end* equals 360, the entire ellipse is shown.

Example

This program draws an egg-shaped ellipse on the screen.

```
#include <graphics.h>
#include <conio.h>

main(void)
{   int driver, mode;

    driver = DETECT; /* autodetect */
    mode = 0;
    initgraph(&driver, &mode, "");

    ellipse(100, 100, 0, 360, 80, 40);

    getch();
    restorecrtmode();
    return 0;
}
```

Related Functions

circle( ), **arc( )**

void far fillellipse(int x, int y, int xr, int yr)

Description

The prototype for **fillellipse( )** is in **graphics.h**.

The **fillellipse( )** function draws and fills an ellipse using the current fill color and pattern. The outline of the ellipse is drawn in the drawing color. The center of the ellipse is at *x,y*. The length of the *x* and *y* radii are specified by *xr* and *yr*.

Example

This program draws an egg-shaped ellipse on the screen and fills it using the default fill color and pattern.

```
#include <graphics.h>
#include <conio.h>

main(void)
{
  int driver, mode;

  driver = DETECT; /* autodetect */
  mode = 0;
  initgraph(&driver, &mode, "");

  fillellipse(100, 100, 80, 40);

  getch();
  restorecrtmode();
  return 0;
}
```

Related Functions

fillpoly( ), **ellipse( )**, **floodfill( )**

void far fillpoly(int numpoints, int far *points)

Description

The prototype for **fillpoly( )** is in **graphics.h**.

The **fillpoly( )** function first draws the object, in the current drawing color, consisting of *numpoints* points defined by the *x,y* coordinates in the array pointed to by *points*. (See **drawpoly( )** for details on the construction of a polygon.) It then proceeds to fill the object using the current fill pattern and color. The fill pattern can be set by calling **setfillpattern( )**.

Example

This program fills a triangle with magenta interleaving:

```
#include <graphics.h>
#include <conio.h>

main(void)
{
  int driver, mode;

  int shape[] = {
    100, 100,
    100, 200,
    200, 200,
    100, 100
  };

  driver = DETECT; /* autodetect */
  mode = 0;
  initgraph(&driver, &mode, "");

  setfillstyle(INTERLEAVE_FILL, MAGENTA);
  fillpoly(4, shape);

  getch();
  restorecrtmode();
  return 0;
}
```

Related Function

floodfill( )

void far floodfill(int x, int y, int border)

Description

The prototype for **floodfill( )** is in **graphics.h**.

The **floodfill( )** function fills an object with the current fill color and pattern given the coordinates of any point within that object and the color of the border of the object (the color of the lines or arcs that make up the object). You must make sure that the object you are filling is completely enclosed. If it isn't, the area outside the shape will also be filled. The background color is used by default, but you can change the way objects are filled using **setfillstyle( )**.

Example

This program uses **floodfill( )** to fill an ellipse with magenta crosshatching:

```
#include <graphics.h>
#include <conio.h>

main(void)
{
  int driver, mode;

  driver = DETECT; /* autodetect */
  mode = 0;
  initgraph(&driver, &mode, "");

  ellipse(100, 100, 0, 360, 80, 40);

  setfillstyle(XHATCH_FILL, MAGENTA);
  floodfill(100, 100, WHITE);

  getch();
  restorecrtmode();
  return 0;
}
```

Related Function

fillpoly( )

void far getarccoords(struct arccoordstype far *coords)

Description

The prototype for **getarccoords( )** is in **graphics.h**.

The **getarccoords( )** function fills the structure pointed to by *coords* with coordinates related to the last call to **arc( )**. The **arccoordstype** structure is defined as

```
struct arccoordstype {
  int x, y;
  int xstart, ystart, xend, yend;
};
```

Here, **x** and **y** are the center of the imaginary circle about which the arc is drawn. The starting and ending *x,y* coordinates are stored in **xstart**, **ystart** and **xend**, **yend**.

Example

This program draws a quarter of a circle about point 100,100 and then connects a line between the arc's endpoints:

```
#include <graphics.h>
#include <conio.h>

main(void)
{
  int driver, mode;
  struct arccoordstype ac;

  driver = DETECT; /* autodetect */
  mode = 0;
  initgraph(&driver, &mode, "");

  arc(100, 100, 0, 90, 100);

  /* now, draw a line between the endpoints of the arc */
  getarccoords(&ac);  /* get the coordinates */
  line(ac.xstart, ac.ystart, ac.xend, ac.yend);

  getch();
  restorecrtmode();
  return 0;
}
```

Related Functions

line( ), **pieslice( )**

void far getaspectratio(int far *xasp, int far *yasp)

Description

The prototype for **getaspectratio( )** is in **graphics.h**.

The **getaspectratio( )** function copies the *x* aspect ratio into the variable pointed to by *xasp* and the *y* aspect ratio into the variable pointed to by *yasp*. You can manipulate these aspect ratios to alter the way objects are displayed on the screen.

Example

This fragment prints the aspect ratios:

```
int xasp, yasp;

getaspectratio(&xasp, &yasp);

cprintf("X,Y aspect ratios %d %d", xasp, yasp);
```

Related Functions

setaspectratio( ), **circle( )**

int far getbkcolor(void)

Description

The prototype for **getbkcolor( )** is in **graphics.h**.

The **getbkcolor( )** function returns the current background color. The values and their corresponding macros (defined in **graphics.h**) are shown here:

Macro	Integer Equivalent
BLACK	0
BLUE	1
GREEN	2
CYAN	3
RED	4
MAGENTA	5
BROWN	6
LIGHTGRAY	7
DARKGRAY	8
LIGHTBLUE	9
LIGHTGREEN	10
LIGHTCYAN	11
LIGHTRED	12

Macro	Integer Equivalent
LIGHTMAGENTA	13
YELLOW	14
WHITE	15

Example

This fragment displays the current background color:

```
cprintf("background color is %d", getbkcolor());
```

Related Function

setbkcolor( )

int far getcolor(void)

Description

The prototype for **getcolor( )** is in **graphics.h**.
    The **getcolor( )** function returns the current drawing color.

Example

This fragment displays the current drawing color:

```
cprintf("drawing color is %d", getcolor());
```

Related Function

setcolor( )

struct palettetype *far getdefaultpalette(void)

Description

The prototype for **getdefaultpalette( )** is in **graphics.h**.
    The **getdefaultpalette( )** function returns the default palette defined by the graphics driver used in the call to **initgraph( )**. The structure of **palettetype** is defined in **graphics.h** as

```
struct palettetype {
  unsigned char size;
  signed char colors[MAXCOLORS + 1];
};
```

Example

This code illustrates a call to **getdefaultpalette( )**:

```
struct palettetype far *p;
p = getdefaultpalette();
```

Related Functions

setpalette( ), **getpalette( )**

char *far getdrivername(void)

Description

The prototype for **getdrivername( )** is in **graphics.h**.

The **getdrivername( )** function returns the name of the current graphics driver. The name is a string held in a statically allocated character array. The contents of this array are overwritten each time you call the function. If you wish to save the contents of the array, you must copy the string elsewhere.

Example

This program displays the name of the current driver:

```
#include <graphics.h>
#include <conio.h>

main(void)
{
  int driver, mode;
  char *name;
  driver = DETECT; /* autodetect */
  mode = 0;
  initgraph(&driver, &mode, "");

  name = getdrivername();

  outtextxy(10, 10, name);
```

```
  getch();
  restorecrtmode();
  return 0;
}
```

Related Functions

initgraph( ), **getmodename( )**

void far getfillpattern(char far *pattern)

Description

The prototype for **getfillpattern( )** is in **graphics.h**.

The **getfillpattern( )** function fills the array pointed to by *pattern* with the 8 bytes that make up the current fill pattern. The array must be at least 8 bytes long. The pattern is arranged as an 8-bit by 8-byte pattern.

Example

This program displays the bytes that make up the current fill pattern:

```
#include <stdio.h>
#include <graphics.h>
#include <conio.h>

main(void)
{
  int driver, mode;
  char f[8], num[10];
  int i;

  driver = DETECT; /* autodetect */
  mode = 0;
  initgraph(&driver, &mode, "");
  getfillpattern((char far *).&f);

  /* display each byte in fill pattern */
  for(i=0; i<8; i++) {
    sprintf(num, "%d ", f[i]);
    outtext(num);
  }
```

```
getch();
restorecrtmode();
return 0;
}
```

Related Functions

setfillpattern( ), **setfillstyle( )**

void far getfillsettings(struct fillsettingstype far *info)

Description

The prototype for **getfillsettings( )** is in **graphics.h**.

The **getfillsettings( )** function fills the structure pointed to by *info* with the number of the fill pattern and the color currently in use. The **fillsettingstype** structure is defined in **graphics.h** as

```
struct fillsettingstype {
  int pattern;
  int color;
};
```

The values for **pattern** are shown here along with their macro equivalents (defined in **graphics.h**):

Macro	Value	Meaning
EMPTY_FILL	0	Fill with background color
SOLID_FILL	1	Fill with solid color
LINE_FILL	2	Fill with lines
LTSLASH_FILL	3	Fill with light slashes
SLASH_FILL	4	Fill with slashes
BKSLASH_FILL	5	Fill with backslashes
LTBKSLASH_FILL	6	Fill with light backslashes
HATCH_FILL	7	Fill with light hatching
XHATCH_FILL	8	Fill with hatching
INTERLEAVE_FILL	9	Fill with interleaving
WIDE_DOT_FILL	10	Fill with widely spaced dots
CLOSE_DOT_FILL	11	Fill with closely spaced dots
USER_FILL	12	Fill with custom pattern

The color will be one of the colors valid in the video mode currently in use.

Example

This fragment reads the current fill pattern and color:

```
struct fillsettingstype p;

getfillsettings(&p);
```

Related Function

setfillsettings( )

int far getgraphmode(void)

Description

The prototype for **getgraphmode( )** is in **graphics.h**.

The **getgraphmode( )** function returns the current graphics mode. The value returned does *not* correspond to the actual value BIOS associates with the active video mode. Instead, the value returned is relative to the current video driver. The value returned will be one of these values, as defined in **graphics.h**:

Macro	Value	Resolution
CGAC0	0	320×200
CGAC1	1	320×200
CGAC2	2	320×200
CGAC3	3	320×200
CGAHI	4	640×200
MCGAC0	0	320×200
MCGAC1	1	320×200
MCGAC2	2	320×200
MCGAC3	3	320×200
MCGAMED	4	640×200
MCGAHI	5	640×480
EGALO	0	640×200
EGAHI	1	640×350
EGA64LO	0	640×200
EGA64HI	1	640×350

Macro	Value	Resolution
EGAMONOHI	3	640×350
HERCMONOHI	0	720×348
ATT400C0	0	320×200
ATT400C1	1	320×200
ATT400C2	2	320×200
ATT400C3	3	320×200
ATT400MED	4	640×200
ATT400HI	5	640×400
VGALO	0	640×200
VGAMED	1	640×350
VGAHI	2	640×480
PC3270HI	0	720×350
IBM8514HI	1	1024×768
IBM8514LO	0	640×480

Example

This fragment displays the number of the current graphics mode relative to the active graphics driver:

```
printf("graphics mode is %d", getgraphmode());
```

Related Function

setgraphmode( )

void far getimage(int left, int top, int right, int bottom, void far *buf)

Description

The prototype for **getimage( )** is in **graphics.h**.

The **getimage( )** function copies the portion of the graphics screen with upper left corner coordinates *left, top* and lower right corner coordinates *right, bottom* into the region of memory pointed to by *buf*.

To determine the number of bytes needed to store an image, use the **imagesize( )** function. An image stored using **getimage( )** can be written to the screen using the **putimage( )** function.

Example

This program copies a rectangle with two diagonal lines to other screen locations:

```
/* This program demonstrates how a graphics image can be
   moved using getimage(), imagesize(), and putimage().
*/
  #include <conio.h>
  #include <graphics.h>
  #include <stdlib.h>
void box(int, int, int, int, int);

main(void)
{
  int driver, mode;
  unsigned size;
  void *buf;

  driver = DETECT; /* autodetect */
  mode = 0;
  initgraph(&driver, &mode, "");

  box(20, 20, 200, 200, 15);
  setcolor(RED);
  line(20, 20, 200, 200);
  setcolor(GREEN);
  line(20, 200, 200, 20);
  getch();

  /* move the image */

  /* first, get the image's size */
  size = imagesize(20, 20, 200, 200);
  if(size != 0xffff) { /* alloc memory for the image */
    buf = malloc(size);
    if(buf) {
      getimage(20, 20, 200, 200, buf);
      putimage(100, 100, buf, COPY_PUT);
      putimage(300, 50, buf, COPY_PUT);
    }
  }
  outtext("press a key");
  getch();
  restorecrtmode();
  return 0;
```

```
}

/* Draw a box given the coordinates of its two corners. */
void box(int startx, int starty, int endx, int endy,
         int color)
{
  setcolor(color);

  line(startx, starty, startx, endy);
  line(startx, starty, endx, starty);
  line(endx, starty, endx, endy);
  line(endx, endy, startx, endy);
}
```

Related Functions

putimage( ), **imagesize( )**

void far getlinesettings(struct linesettingstype far *info)

Description

The prototype for **getlinesettings( )** is in **graphics.h**.

The **getlinesettings( )** function fills the structure pointed to by *info* with the current line style. The structure **linesettingstype** is defined as

```
struct linesettingstype {
  int linestyle;
  unsigned upattern;
  int thickness;
};
```

The **linestyle** element holds the style of the line. It will be one of these enumerated values (defined in **graphics.h**):

Value	Meaning
SOLID_LINE	Unbroken line
DOTTED_LINE	Dotted line
CENTER_LINE	Centered line (dash-dot-dash)
DASHED_LINE	Dashed line
USERBIT_LINE	User-defined line

If **linestyle** is equal to **USERBIT_LINE**, the 16-bit pattern in **upattern** determines how the line appears. Each bit in the pattern corresponds to one pixel. If that bit is set, the pixel is turned on; otherwise it is turned off.

The **thickness** element will have one of these values:

Value	Meaning
NORM_WIDTH	1 pixel wide
THICK_WIDTH	3 pixels wide

Example

This fragment reads the current line settings:

```
struct linesettingstype info;

getlinesettings(&info);
```

Related Function

setlinestyle( )

int far getmaxcolor(void)

Description

The prototype for **getmaxcolor( )** is in **graphics.h**.

The **getmaxcolor( )** function returns the largest valid color value for the current video mode. For example, in four-color CGA mode, this number will be 3. (The color values for this mode are 0 through 3.)

Example

This program displays the largest valid color value:

```
#include <stdio.h>
#include <graphics.h>
#include <conio.h>

main(void)
{
  int driver, mode;

  driver = DETECT; /* autodetect */
```

```
mode = 0;
initgraph(&driver, &mode, "");

printf("largest color: %d", getmaxcolor());
getch();
restorecrtmode();
return 0;
}
```

Related Functions

getbkcolor( ), **getpalette( )**

int far getmaxmode(void)

Description

The prototype for **getmaxmode( )** is in **graphics.h**.

The **getmaxmode( )** function returns the maximum mode available for the current graphics driver.

Example

This fragment illustrates a call to **getmaxmode( )**:

```
int mode;
mode = getmaxmode();
```

Related Function

getmoderange( )

int far getmaxx(void)
int far getmaxy(void)

Description

The prototypes for **getmaxx( )** and **getmaxy( )** are in **graphics.h**.

The **getmaxx( )** function returns the largest valid x value for the current graphics mode.

The **getmaxy( )** function returns the largest valid y value for the current graphics mode.

Example

This code displays the maximum *x* and *y* coordinates supported by the graphics hardware in the system:

```
#include <stdio.h>
#include <graphics.h>
#include <conio.h>

main(void)
{
  int driver, mode;

  driver = DETECT; /* autodetect */
  mode = 0;
  initgraph(&driver, &mode, "");

  printf("max X,Y: %d,%d", getmaxx(), getmaxy());
  getch();
  restorecrtmode();
  return 0;
}
```

Related Function

getmaxcolor( )

char *far getmodename(int mode)

Description

The prototype for **getmodename( )** is in **graphics.h**.

The **getmodename( )** function returns the name of the specified mode. The value of *mode* is obtained in the call to **initgraph( )** or **getgraphmode( )**.

Example

This program displays the name of the current mode:

```
#include <graphics.h>
#include <conio.h>
main(void)
```

```
{
  int driver, mode;
  char *name;
  driver = DETECT; /* autodetect */
  mode = 0;
  initgraph(&driver, &mode, "");

  name = getmodename(mode);   /* default mode */

  outtextxy(10, 10, name);

  getch();
  restorecrtmode();
  return 0;
}
```

Related Functions

initgraph( ), **getdrivername( )**

void far getmoderange(int driver, int far *lowmode, int far *himode)

Description

The prototype for **getmoderange( )** is in **graphics.h**.

The **getmoderange( )** function determines the lowest and highest modes supported by the graphics driver specified by *driver* and puts these values at the variables pointed to by *lowmode* and *highmode*, respectively. The valid macros for *driver* are shown here (they are defined in **graphics.h**):

Macro

CGA
MCGA
EGA
EGA64
EGAMONO
IBM8514
HERCMONO
ATT400
VGA
PC3270

Example

This program displays the video mode range for the graphics hardware currently installed in the system:

```
#include <stdio.h>
#include <graphics.h>
#include <conio.h>

main(void)
{
  int driver, mode;
  int high, low;

  driver = DETECT; /* autodetect */
  mode = 0;
  initgraph(&driver, &mode, "");

  getmoderange(driver, &low, &high);
  printf("mode range: %d - %d", low, high);
  getch();
  restorecrtmode();
  return 0;
}
```

Related Function

getgraphmode( )

void far getpalette(struct palettetype far *pal)

Description

The prototype for **getpalette( )** is in **graphics.h**.

   The **getpalette( )** function loads the structure pointed to by *pal* with the current palette. The **palettetype** structure is defined as

```
struct palettetype {
  unsigned char size;
  signed char colors[MAXCOLORS + 1];
};
```

The **size** element holds the number of colors available in the current palette. The **colors** array holds the values for the colors available in the palette. The following colors, along with their macro names, are shown here.

CGA codes (background only):

Macro	Value
BLACK	0
BLUE	1
GREEN	2
CYAN	3
RED	4
MAGENTA	5
BROWN	6
LIGHTGRAY	7
DARKGRAY	8
LIGHTBLUE	9
LIGHTGREEN	10
LIGHTCYAN	11
LIGHTRED	12
LIGHTMAGENTA	13
YELLOW	14
WHITE	15

EGA and VGA:

Macro	Value
EGA_BLACK	0
EGA_BLUE	1
EGA_GREEN	2
EGA_CYAN	3
EGA_RED	4
EGA_MAGENTA	5
EGA_BROWN	20
EGA_LIGHTGRAY	7
EGA_DARKGRAY	56
EGA_LIGHTBLUE	57

Macro	Value
EGA_LIGHTGREEN	58
EGA_LIGHTCYAN	59
EGA_LIGHTRED	60
EGA_LIGHTMAGENTA	61
EGA_YELLOW	62
EGA_WHITE	63

Example

This program prints the number of colors supported by the default video mode:

```c
#include <stdio.h>
#include <graphics.h>
#include <conio.h>

main(void)
{
  int driver, mode;
  struct palettetype p;

  driver = DETECT; /* autodetect */
  mode = 0;
  initgraph(&driver, &mode, "");
  getpalette(&p);
  printf("number of colors in palette: %d", p.size);
  getch();
  restorecrtmode();
  return 0;
}
```

Related Function

setpalette( )

int far getpalettesize(void)

Description

The prototype for **getpalettesize( )** is in **graphics.h**.

    The **getpalettesize( )** function returns the number of colors in the current palette.

Example

This program prints the number of colors in the current default palette:

```
#include <graphics.h>
#include <conio.h>
#include <stdio.h>

main(void)
{
  int driver, mode;
  int num;
  char buff[100];

  driver = DETECT; /* autodetect */
  mode = 0;
  initgraph(&driver, &mode, "");

  num = getpalettesize();
  sprintf(buff, "number of colors in palette: %d", num);
  outtextxy(10, 10, buff);

  getch();
  restorecrtmode();
  return 0;
}
```

Related Functions

setpalette( ), **getpalette( )**

unsigned far getpixel(int x, int y)

Description

The prototype for **getpixel( )** is in **graphics.h**.

The **getpixel( )** function returns the color of the pixel located at the specified *x,y* position.

Example

This fragment puts the value of the color at location 10,20 into the variable **color**:

```
color = getpixel(10, 20);
```

Related Function

putpixel( )

int gettext(int left, int top, int right, int bottom, void *buf)

Description

The prototype for **gettext( )** is in **conio.h**.

The **gettext( )** function copies the text from a rectangle with upper left corner coordinates *left,top* and lower right corner coordinates *right,bottom* into the buffer pointed to by *buf*. The coordinates are screen, not window, relative.

The amount of memory needed to hold a region of the screen is computed by the formula **num_bytes = rows × columns × 2**. The reason you must multiply the number of rows times the number of columns by 2 is that each character displayed on the screen requires 2 bytes of storage: 1 for the character itself and 1 for its attributes.

The function returns 1 on success and 0 on failure.

Example

This fragment copies a region of the screen into the memory pointed to by **buf**:

```
buf = malloc(10 * 10 *2);

gettext(10, 10, 20, 20, buf);
```

Related Functions

puttext( ), **movetext( )**

void gettextinfo(struct text_info *info)

Description

The prototype for **gettextinfo( )** is in **conio.h**.

The **gettextinfo( )** function obtains the current text settings and returns them in the structure pointed to by *info*. The **text_info** structure is declared as shown here.

```
struct text_info {
    unsigned char winleft; /* upper left  */
    unsigned char wintop;  /* coordinates */
    unsigned char winright; /* lower right */
    unsigned char winbottom; /* coordinates */
```

```
      unsigned char attribute; /* current attributes */
      unsigned char normattr; /* normal attributes */
      unsigned char currmode; /* active video mode */
      unsigned char screenheight; /* screen */
      unsigned char screenwidth;  /* dimensions */
      unsigned char curx; /* current X and */
      unsigned char cury; /* Y cursor location */
};
```

Example

This fragment obtains the current text settings.

```
struct text_info i;
gettextinfo(&i);
```

Related Functions

textmode(), **gettextsettings()**

void far gettextsettings(struct textsettingstype far *info)

Description

The prototype for **gettextsettings( )** is in **graphics.h**.

   The **gettextsettings( )** function loads the structure pointed to by *info* with information about the current graphics text settings. The structure **textsettingstype** is defined in **graphics.h** and is shown here:

```
struct textsettingstype {
  int font;       /* font type */
  int direction; /* horizontal or vertical */
  int charsize;  /* size of characters */
  int horiz;     /* horizontal justification */
  int vert;      /* vertical justification */
};
```

The **font** element will contain one of these values:

Value	Font
0	Default 8×8 bit-mapped font
1	Stroked triplex font
2	Stroked small font

Value	Font
3	Stroked sans serif font
4	Stroked gothic font
5	Stroked script font
6	Stroked triplex script font
7	Stroked triplex script font
8	Stroked complex font
9	Stroked European font
10	Stroked bold fon

The **direction** element must be set to either **HORIZ_DIR** (the default) for horizontal text or **VERT_DIR** for vertical text. The **charsize** element is a multiplier used to scale the size of the output text. The value of **horiz** and **vert** indicate how text will be justified. They will be one of the following values.

Macro	Meaning
LEFT_TEXT	Left justify
CENTER_TEXT	Center horizontally
RIGHT_TEXT	Right justify
BOTTOM_TEXT	Bottom justify
CENTER_TEXT	Center vertically
TOP_TEXT	Top justify

Example

This fragment reads the current text settings:

```
struct textsettingstype t;

gettextsettings(&t);
```

Related Function

settextstyle( )

void far getviewsettings(struct viewporttype far *info)

Description

The prototype for **getviewsettings( )** is in **graphics.h**.

The **getviewsettings( )** function loads information about the current viewport into the structure pointed to by *info*. The structure **viewporttype** is defined as

```
struct viewporttype {
  int left, top, right, bottom;
  int clip;
};
```

The fields **left**, **top**, **right**, and **bottom** hold the coordinates of the upper left and lower right corners of the viewport. When **clip** is 0, there is no clipping of output that overruns the viewport boundaries. Otherwise, clipping is performed to prevent boundary overrun.

Example

This fragment prints the dimensions of the current screen:

```
struct viewporttype info;

getviewsettings(&info);

printf("view port is %dx%x by %dx%d", info.left, info.right,
        info.top, info.bottom);
```

Related Function

setviewport( )

int far getx(void)
int far gety(void)

Description

The prototypes for **getx( )** and **gety( )** are in **graphics.h**.

The functions **getx( )** and **gety( )** return the current position's (CP's) *x* and *y* location on the graphics screen.

Example

This fragment displays the CP's current location:

```
printf("CP's loc: %d, %d", getx(), gety());
```

Related Function

moveto( )

void gotoxy(int x, int y)

Description

The prototype for **gotoxy( )** is in **conio.h**.

The **gotoxy( )** function sends the text screen cursor to the location specified by *x,y*. If either or both of the coordinates are invalid, no action takes place.

Example

This program prints **X**s diagonally across the screen:

```
#include <conio.h>

main(void)
{
  register int i, j;

  clrscr();

  /* print diagonal Xs */
  for(i=1, j=1; j<24; i+=3, j++) {
    gotoxy(i, j);
    cprintf("X");
  }
  getche();
  clrscr();
  return 0;
}
```

Related Functions

wherex( ), **wherey( )**

void far graphdefaults(void)

Description

The prototype for **graphdefaults( )** is in **graphics.h**.

The **graphdefaults( )** function resets the graphics system to its default settings. Specifically, the entire screen becomes the viewport with the CP located at 0,0. The palette, drawing color, and background color are reset; the fill style, fill pattern, text font, and justification are returned to their original values.

Example

This fragment resets the graphics system:

```
graphdefaults();
```

Related Functions

initgraph( ), **setpalette( )**

char *far grapherrormsg(int errcode)

Description

The prototype for **grapherrormsg( )** is in **graphics.h**.

The **grapherrormsg( )** function returns a pointer to the error message that corresponds to *errcode*. The error code is obtained by a call to **graphresult( )**.

See **graphresult( )** for details of the error conditions.

Example

Assuming that **errcode** was returned by a call to **graphresult( )**, this fragment displays in text form the error message associated with that code:

```
printf("%s", grapherrormsg(graphresult()));
```

Related Function

graphresult( )

void far _graphfreemem(void far *ptr, unsigned size)
void far *far _graphgetmem(unsigned size)

Description

The prototypes for **_graphfreemem( )** and **_graphgetmem( )** are in **graphics.h**.

The **_graphgetmem( )** function is called by the graphics system to allocate memory for the graphics drivers and other graphics system needs. The **_graphfreemem( )** function frees this memory.

These functions should not generally be called directly by your programs.

int far graphresult(void)

Description

The prototype for **graphresult( )** is in **graphics.h**.

The **graphresult( )** function returns a value that represents the outcome of the last graphics operation. This value will be one of the following enumerated values:

Name	Value	Meaning
grOk	0	Successful
grNoInitGraph	−1	No driver installed
grNotDetected	−2	No graphics hardware in system
grFileNotFound	−3	Driver file not found
grInvalidDriver	−4	Invalid driver file
grNoLoadMem	−5	Not enough memory
grNoScanMem	−6	Insufficient memory for scan fill
grNoFloodMem	−7	Insufficient memory for flood fill
grFontNotFound	−8	Font file not found
grNoFontMem	−9	Insufficient memory for font
grInvalidMode	−10	Invalid mode
grError	−11	General graphics error
grIOerror	−12	I/O error
grInvalidFont	−13	Invalid font file
grInvalidFontNum	−14	Invalid font number
grInvalidDeviceNum	−15	Invalid device number
grInvalidVersion	−18	Invalid version number

Use **grapherrormsg( )** to display a graphics error message given its error number.

Example

This fragment displays the outcome of the last graphics operation:

```
printf("%s", grapherrormsg(graphresult()));
```

Related Function

grapherrormsg( )

void highvideo(void)

Description

The prototype for **highvideo( )** is in **conio.h**.

After a call to **highvideo( )**, characters written to the screen are displayed in high-intensity video. This function works only for text screens.

Example

This fragment turns on high-intensity output:

```
highvideo();
```

Related Functions

lowvideo( ), **normvideo( )**

unsigned far imagesize(int left, int top, int right, int bottom)

Description

The prototype for **imagesize( )** is in **graphics.h**.

The **imagesize( )** function returns the number of bytes of storage necessary to hold a portion of the screen with upper left corner coordinates *left,top* and lower right corner coordinates *right,bottom*. This function is generally used in conjunction with **getimage( )**. The **imagesize( )** function works only in graphic modes.

Example

This fragment determines the number of bytes needed to hold a graphics image at the specified location:

```
unsigned size;

size = imagesize(10, 10, 100, 100);
```

Related Function

getimage( )

void far initgraph(int far *driver, int far *mode, char far *path)

Description

The prototype for **initgraph( )** is in **graphics.h**.

The **initgraph( )** function is used to initialize the graphics system and to load the appropriate graphics driver. The **initgraph( )** function loads into memory a graphics driver that corresponds to the number pointed to by *driver*. Without a graphics driver loaded into memory, no graphics functions can operate. The video mode used by the graphics functions is specified by an integer pointed to by *mode*. Finally, a path to the driver can be specified in the string pointed to by *path*. If no path is specified, the current working directory is searched.

The graphics drivers are contained in .BGI files, which must be available on the system. However, you need not worry about the actual name of the file because you only have to specify the driver by its number. The header **graphics.h** defines several macros that you can use for this purpose. They are shown here:

Macro	Equivalent
DETECT	0
CGA	1
MCGA	2
EGA	3
EGA64	4
EGAMONO	5
IBM8514	6
HERCMONO	7
ATT400	8
VGA	9
PC3270	10

When you use **DETECT**, **initgraph( )** automatically detects the type of video hardware present in the system and selects the video mode with the greatest resolution. In this case, *driver* will contain the video mode when the function returns.

The value of *mode* must be one of the graphics modes shown here. Notice that the value pointed to by *mode* is not the same as the value recognized by the BIOS routine that actually sets the mode. Instead the value used to call BIOS to initialize a video mode is created by **initgraph( )** using both the driver and the mode.

Driver	Mode	Equivalent	Resolution
CGA	CGAC0	0	320×200
	CGAC1	1	320×200
	CGAC2	2	320×200
	CGAC3	3	320×200
	CGAHI	4	640×200
MCGA	MCGAC0	0	320×200
	MCGAC1	1	320×200

Driver	Mode	Equivalent	Resolution
	MCGAC2	2	320×200
	MCGAC3	3	320×200
	MCGAMED	4	640×200
	MCGAHI	5	640×480
EGA	EGALO	0	640×200
	EGAHI	1	640×350
EGA64	EGA64LO	0	640×200
	EGA64HI	1	640×350
EGAMONO	EGAMONOHI	3	640×350
HERC	HERCMONOHI	0	720×348
ATT400	ATT400C0	0	320×200
	ATT400C1	1	320×200
	ATT400C2	2	320×200
	ATT400C3	3	320×200
	ATT400MED	4	640×200
	ATT400HI	5	640×400
VGA	VGALO	0	640×200
	VGAMED	1	640×350
	VGAHI	2	640×480
PC3270	PC3270HI	0	720×350
IBM8514	IBM8514HI	1	1024×768
	IBM8514LO	0	640×480

Example

This fragment uses **initgraph( )** to autodetect the graphics hardware and to select the mode of greatest resolution:

```
int driver, mode;

driver = DETECT; /* autodetect */
mode = 0;
initgraph(&driver, &mode, "");
```

Related Function

getgraphmode( )

void insline(void)

Description

The prototype for **insline( )** is in **conio.h**.

The **insline( )** function inserts a blank line at the current cursor position. All lines below the cursor move down. This function is for text mode only, and it operates relative to the current text window.

Example

The following program illustrates the use of **insline( )**.

```
#include <conio.h>

main(void)
{
  register int i;

  clrscr();

  for(i=1; i<24; i++) {
    gotoxy(1, i);
    cprintf("this is line %d\n\r", i);
  }
  getche();
  gotoxy(1, 10);
  insline();
  getch();
  return 0;
}
```

Related Function

delline( )

int far installuserdriver(char far *drivername, int huge (*func)(void))

Description

The prototype for **installuserdriver( )** is in **graphics.h**.

The **installuserdriver( )** function allows you to install third-party BGI drivers. The *drivername* parameter specifies the driver name. The *func* parameter is a pointer to the function that provides autodetection of the required hardware for the installed driver. This parameter is optional and if not used, **func** must be NULL.

The **installuserdriver( )** function returns the graphics driver's value, which you can then use to call **initgraph( )**.

Example

This following fragment assumes you have acquired a new BGI driver named **newdriver.bgi**.

```
int driver, mode;

driver = installuserdriver("newdriver", NULL);
mode = 0;
initgraph(&driver, &mode, "");
```

Related Function

installuserfont( )

int far installuserfont(char far *fontname)

Description

The prototype for **installuserfont( )** is in **graphics.h**.

The **installuserfont( )** function allows you to install third-party stroked-character fonts. The parameter *fontname* is a pointer to the name of the file that contains the font. All font files must use the .CHR extension.

The **installuserfont( )** function returns the ID number associated with the font, which can then be used in a call to **settextstyle( )** to activate the font. If the font table is full, **grError** is returned and the new font cannot be loaded. (Up to 20 fonts can be loaded at a time.)

Example

This fragment loads a .CHR font file named **newfont.chr**:

```
int fontnumber;

fontnumber = installuserfont("newfont.chr");
settextstyle(fontnumber, HORIZ_DIR, 1);
```

Related Function

installuserdriver( )

void far line(int startx, int starty, int endx, int endy)
void far lineto(int x, int y);
void far linerel(int deltax, int deltay)

Description

The prototypes for **line( )**, **lineto( )**, and **linerel( )** are in **graphics.h**.

The **line( )** function draws a line in the current drawing color from *startx,starty* to *endx,endy*. The current position is unchanged.

The **lineto( )** function draws a line in the current drawing color from the current position (CP) to *x,y* and locates the CP at *x,y*.

The **linerel( )** function draws a line from the CP to the location that is *deltax* units away in the *x* direction and *deltay* units away in the *y* direction. The CP is moved to the new location.

Example

This program illustrates the line functions:

```
#include <graphics.h>
#include <conio.h>

main(void)
{
  int driver, mode;

  driver = DETECT; /* autodetect */
  mode = 0;
  initgraph(&driver, &mode, "");

  line(100, 100, 200, 200);

  lineto(100, 50);

  linerel(30, 40);

  getch();
  restorecrtmode();
  return 0;
}
```

Related Functions

circle( ), **drawpoly( )**

void lowvideo(void)

Description

The prototype for **lowvideo( )** is in **conio.h**.

After a call to **lowvideo( )**, characters written to the screen are displayed in low-intensity video. This function works only for text screens.

Example

This fragment turns on low-intensity output:

```
lowvideo();
```

Related Functions

highvideo( ), **normvideo( )**

void far moverel(int deltax, int deltay)

Description

The prototype for **moverel( )** is in **graphics.h**.

The **moverel( )** function advances the current position (CP) on a graphics screen by the magnitudes of *deltax* and *deltay*.

Example

If the CP is at location 10,10 prior to execution of the following statement, it will be at 20,30 after the statement executes:

```
moverel(10, 20);
```

Related Function

moveto( )

int movetext(int left, int top, int right, int bottom, int newleft, int newtop)

Description

The prototype for **movetext( )** is in **conio.h**.

The **movetext( )** function moves the portion of a text screen with the upper left corner at *left,top* and lower right corner at *right,bottom* to the region of the screen that has *newleft,newtop* as the coordinates of its upper left corner. This function is screen, not window, relative.

The **movetext( )** function returns 0 if one or more coordinates are out of range and non-0 otherwise.

Example

This fragment moves the contents of the rectangle with upper left corner coordinates of 1,1 and lower right corner coordinates of 8,8 to 10,10:

```
movetext(1, 1, 8, 8, 10, 10);
```

Related Function

gettext( )

void far moveto(int x, int y)

Description

The prototype for **moveto( )** is in **graphics.h**.

The **moveto( )** function moves the current position (CP) to the location specified by *x,y* relative to the current viewport.

The **moveto( )** graphics function corresponds to the text **gotoxy( )** function in operation.

Example

This fragment moves the CP to location 100,100:

```
moveto(100, 100);
```

Related Function

moverel( )

void normvideo(void)

Description

The prototype for **normvideo( )** is in **conio.h**.

After a call to **normvideo( )**, characters written to the screen are displayed in normal-intensity video. This function works only for text screens.

Example

This fragment turns on normal-intensity output:

```
normvideo();
```

Related Functions

highvideo( ), **lowvideo( )**

void far outtext(char far *str)
void var outtextxy(int x, int y, char *str)

Description

The prototypes for **outtext( )** and **outtextxy( )** are in **graphics.h**.

The **outtext( )** function displays a text string on a graphics mode screen at the current position (CP) using the active text settings (direction, font, size, and justification). If the active direction is horizontal, the CP is increased by the length of the string; otherwise no change is made in the CP. In graphics modes, there is no visible cursor, but the current position on the screen is maintained as if there were an invisible cursor.

The **outtextxy( )** function is similar to **outtext( )** except that it displays the string beginning at the location specified by *x,y*. These coordinates are relative to the current viewport.

To change the style of the text refer to **settextstyle( )**.

Example

This program illustrates the use of **outtext( )** and **outtextxy( )**:

```
#include <graphics.h>
#include <conio.h>

main(void)
{
  int driver, mode;
  int i;

  driver = DETECT; /* autodetect */
```

```
  mode = 0;
  initgraph(&driver, &mode, "");

  /* write two lines at CP */
  outtext("this is an example ");
  outtext("another line");

  /* use "cursor" positioning */
  for(i=100; i<200; i+=8) outtextxy(200, i, "hello");

  getch();
  restorecrtmode();
  return 0;
}
```

Related Function

settextstyle( )

void far pieslice(int x, int y, int start, int end, int radius)

Description

The prototype for **pieslice( )** is in **graphics.h**.

The **pieslice( )** function draws a pie slice, using the current drawing color, covering an angle equal to *end–start*. The beginning and ending points of the angle are specified in degrees. The center of the "circle" that the slice is "cut" from is at *x,y* and has a radius equal to *radius*. The slice is filled with the current fill pattern and color.

Example

This program prints a full circle of pie slices, each 45 degrees wide and each in a different color. (This program requires EGA or VGA.)

```
#include <graphics.h>
#include <conio.h>

main(void)
{
  int driver, mode;
  int i, start, end;

  driver = DETECT; /* autodetect */
  mode = 0;
```

```
initgraph(&driver, &mode, "");

/* demonstrate pieslice() */

start = 0; end = 45;
for(i=0; i<8; i++) {
  setfillstyle(SOLID_FILL, i);
  pieslice(300, 200, start, end, 100);
  start += 45;
  end += 45;
}

getch();
restorecrtmode();
return 0;
}
```

Related Functions

arc( ), **circle( )**

void far putimage(int x, int y, void far *buf, int op)

Description

The prototype for **putimage( )** is in **graphics.h**.

The **putimage( )** function copies an image previously saved (by using **getimage( )**) in the memory location pointed to by *buf* to the screen beginning at location *x,y*. The value of *op* determines exactly how the image is written to the screen. Its valid enumerated values are

Name	Value	Meaning
COPY_PUT	0	Copy as is
XOR_PUT	1	Exclusive-OR with destination
OR_PUT	2	Inclusive-OR with destination
AND_PUT	3	AND with destination
NOT_PUT	4	Invert source image

Example

The following program demonstrates the **getimage( )**, **imagesize( )**, and **putimage( )** functions:

```
/* This program demonstrates how a graphics image can be
   moved using getimage(), imagesize(), and putimage().
*/
  #include <conio.h>
  #include <graphics.h>
  #include <stdlib.h>

void box(int, int, int, int, int);

main(void)
{
  int driver, mode;
  unsigned size;
  void *buf;

  driver = DETECT; /* autodetect */
  mode = 0;
  initgraph(&driver, &mode, "");

  box(20, 20, 200, 200, 15);

  setcolor(RED);
  line(20, 20, 200, 200);
  setcolor(GREEN);
  line(20, 200, 200, 20);
  getch();

  /* move the image */

  /* first, get the image's size */
  size = imagesize(20, 20, 200, 200);
  if(size != 0xffff) { /* alloc memory for the image */
    buf = malloc(size);
    if(buf) {
      getimage(20, 20, 200, 200, buf);
      putimage(100, 100, buf, COPY_PUT);
      putimage(300, 50, buf, COPY_PUT);
    }
  }
  outtext("press a key");
  getch();
  restorecrtmode();
  return 0;
}
```

```
/* Draw a box given the coordinates of its two corners. */
void box(int startx, int starty, int endx, int endy,
         int color)
{
  setcolor(color);

  rectangle(startx, starty, endx, endy);
}
```

Related Functions

getimage( ), **imagesize( )**

void far putpixel(int x, int y, int color)

Description

The prototype for **putpixel( )** is in **graphics.h**.

    The **putpixel( )** function writes the color specified by *color* to the pixel at location *x,y*.

Example

This fragment makes the pixel at location 10,20 green, assuming that green is supported by the current video mode:

```
putpixel(10, 20, GREEN);
```

Related Function

getpixel( )

int puttext(int left, int top, int right, int bottom void *buf)

Description

The prototype for **puttext( )** is in **conio.h**.

    The **puttext( )** function copies text previously saved by **gettext( )** from the buffer pointed to by *buf* into the region with upper left and lower right corners specified by *left,top* and *right,bottom*.

    The **puttext( )** function uses screen-absolute, not window-relative, coordinates. It returns 0 if the coordinates are out-of-range, non-0 otherwise.

Example

This fragment copies a region of the screen into the memory pointed to by *buf* and puts that text in a new location:

```
buf = malloc(10 * 10 *2);
gettext(10, 10, 20, 20, buf);
puttext(0, 0, 30, 30, buf);
```

Related Functions

gettext( ), **movetext( )**

void far rectangle(int left, int top, int right, int bottom)

Description

The prototype for **rectangle( )** is in **graphics.h**.

   The **rectangle( )** function draws a box as defined by the coordinates *left,top* and *right,bottom* in the current drawing color.

Example

This program draws some sample rectangles:

```
#include <graphics.h>
#include <conio.h>

main(void)
{
  int driver, mode;

  driver = DETECT; /* autodetect */
  mode = 0;
  initgraph(&driver, &mode, "");

  rectangle(100, 100, 300, 300);
  rectangle(150, 90, 34, 300);
  rectangle(0, 0, 2, 2);

  getch();
  restorecrtmode();
  return 0;
}
```

Related Functions

bar( ), **bar3d( )**, **line( )**

int registerbgidriver(void (*driver)(void))
int registerbgifont(void (*font)(void))

Description

The prototypes for **registerbgidriver( )** and **registerbgifont( )** are in **graphics.h**.

These functions are used to notify the graphics system that either a graphics driver, a font, or both have been linked in and there is no need to look for a corresponding disk file.

The actual registration process is somewhat difficult, and you should consult your user manual for details as they relate to your version of Turbo/Borland C/C++.

void far restorecrtmode(void)

Description

The prototype for **restorecrtmode( )** is in **graphics.h**.

The **restorecrtmode( )** function restores the screen to the mode that it had prior to the call to **initgraph( )**.

Example

This fragment restores the screen to its original video mode:

```
restorecrtmode();
```

Related Function

initgraph( )

void far sector(int x, int y, int start, int end, int xr, int yr)

Description

The prototype for **sector( )** is in **graphics.h**.

The **sector( )** function draws an elliptical pie slice using the current drawing color and fills it using the current fill color and fill pattern. The slice covers an angle equal to *end–start*. The beginning and ending points of the angle are specified in degrees using the Cartesian coordinate plane as shown in Figure 23-1. The center of the

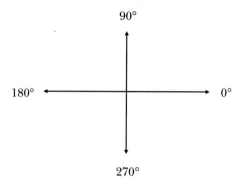

Figure 23-1. *The Cartesian coordinate plane*

"ellipse" that the slice is "cut" from is at *x,y.* It has horizontal and vertical radii equal to *xr* and *yr.*

Example

This program prints a full ellipse of pie slices, each 45 degrees wide and each in a different color. (This program requires EGA or VGA.)

```
#include <graphics.h>
#include <conio.h>

main(void)
{
  int driver, mode;
  int i, start, end;

  driver = DETECT; /* autodetect */
  mode = 0;
  initgraph(&driver, &mode, "");

  /* demonstrate sector() */

  start = 0; end = 45;
  for(i=0; i<8; i++) {
  setfillstyle(SOLID_FILL, i);
```

```
   sector(300, 200, start, end, 100, 200);
   start += 45;
   end += 45;
}

   getch();
   restorecrtmode();
   return 0;
}
```

Related Functions

pieslice( ), **ellipse( )**, **fillellipse( )**

void far setactivepage(int page)

Description

The prototype for **setactivepage( )** is in **graphics.h**.

The **setactivepage( )** function determines the video page that will receive the output of the graphics functions. Turbo/Borland C/C++ uses video page 0 by default. If you call **setactivepage( )** with another page, subsequent graphics output is written to the new page, not necessarily the one currently displayed. In graphics modes, only the EGA, VGA, and Hercules adapters support multiple pages. However, even for these adapters, not all modes have multiple pages.

Example

This fragment makes page 1 the active page:

```
setactivepage(1);
```

Related Function

setvisualpage( )

void far setallpalette(struct palettetype far *pal)

Description

The prototype for **setallpalette( )** is in **graphics.h**.

The **setallpalette( )** function changes all the colors in an EGA/VGA palette. The structure **palettetype** is defined as

```
struct palettetype {
  unsigned char size;
  signed char colors[MAXCOLORS+1];
};
```

You must set *size* to the number of colors in the palette of the currently active graphics mode, and set each element of *colors* to its corresponding color. (Refer to **setpalette( )** for the valid colors for the various video adapters.) To leave a specific color unchanged, use the value −1.

If you call **setallpalette( )** with incorrect values, no change to the current palette takes place.

Example

This fragment changes the 16-color palette for an EGA/VGA adapter to the first 16 colors:

```
struct palettetype p;
int i;

for(i=0; i<16; i++) p.colors[i] = i;
p.size = 16;

setallpalette(&p);
```

Related Function

setpalette( )

void far setaspectratio(int xaspect, int yaspect)

Description

The prototype for **setaspectratio( )** is in **graphics.h**.

The **setaspectratio( )** function sets the *x* aspect ratio to the value pointed to by *xaspect* and the *y* aspect ratio to the value pointed to by *yaspect*. By default, the aspect ratios of the graphics system are set so that circles are round. However, you can manipulate the aspect ratios to alter the shape of objects that are displayed on the screen. (The **getaspectratio( )** function is used to get the current aspect ratios.)

Example

This fragment increases the *y* aspect ratio and prints the values of both the *x* and *y* aspect ratios:

```
int xaspect, yaspect;

getaspectratio(&xaspect, &yaspect);
yaspect += 1;
setaspectratio(&xaspect, &yaspect);

cprintf("X,Y aspect ratios are now %d %d",
        xaspect, yaspect);
```

Related Function

getaspectratio( )

void far setbkcolor(int color)

Description

The prototype for **setbkcolor( )** is in **graphics.h**.

The **setbkcolor( )** function changes the background color to the color specified in *color*. The valid values for *color* are

Number	Macro Name
0	BLACK
1	BLUE
2	GREEN
3	CYAN
4	RED
5	MAGENTA
6	BROWN
7	LIGHTGRAY
8	DARKGRAY
9	LIGHTBLUE
10	LIGHTGREEN
11	LIGHTCYAN
12	LIGHTRED
13	LIGHTMAGENTA
14	YELLOW
15	WHITE

Example

This program sets the background to light gray before drawing some rectangles:

```
#include <graphics.h>
#include <conio.h>

main(void)
{
  int driver, mode;

  driver = DETECT; /* autodetect */
  mode = 0;
  initgraph(&driver, &mode, "");

  setbkcolor(LIGHTGRAY);

  rectangle(100, 100, 300, 300);
  rectangle(150, 90, 34, 300);
  rectangle(0, 0, 2, 2);

  getch();
  restorecrtmode();
  return 0;
}
```

Related Function

setcolor( )

void far setcolor(int color)

Description

The prototype for **setcolor( )** is in **graphics.h**.

The **setcolor( )** function sets the current drawing color to the color specified by *color.* For the valid colors for each video adapter refer to **setpalette( )**.

Example

Assuming an EGA/VGA adapter, this program prints 16 line segments in 16 different colors. (The first is the same color as the background.)

```
#include <graphics.h>
#include <conio.h>

main(void)
{
  int driver, mode;
  int i;

  driver = DETECT; /* autodetect */
  mode = 0;
  initgraph(&driver, &mode, "");

  moveto(0, 200);

  for(i=0; i<16; i++) {
    setcolor(i);
    linerel(20, 0);
  }

  getch();
  restorecrtmode();
  return 0;
}
```

Related Function

setpalette( )

void far setfillpattern(char far *pattern, int color)

Description

The prototype for **setfillpattern( )** is in **graphics.h**.

The **setfillpattern( )** function sets the fill pattern used by various functions, such as **floodfill( )**, to the pattern pointed to by *pattern*. The array must be at least 8 bytes long. The pattern is arranged as an 8-bit by 8-byte pattern. When a bit is on, the color specified by *color* is displayed; otherwise the background color is used.

Example

This program creates an unusual fill pattern and uses it to fill a rectangle:

```
#include <graphics.h>
#include <conio.h>
```

```
main(void)
{
  int driver, mode;
  /* define a fill pattern */
  char p[8] = {1, 2, 3, 4, 5, 6, 7};

  driver = DETECT; /* autodetect */
  mode = 0;
  initgraph(&driver, &mode, "");

  setcolor(GREEN);
  rectangle(100, 200, 200, 300);

  setfillpattern(p, RED);
  floodfill(150, 250, GREEN);

  getch();
  restorecrtmode();
  return 0;
}
```

Related Function

setfillstyle( )

void far setfillstyle(int pattern, int color)

Description

The prototype for **setfillstyle( )** is in **graphics.h**.

The **setfillstyle( )** function sets the style and color of the fill used by various graphics functions. The value of *color* must be valid for the current video mode. The values for *pattern* are shown here along with their macro equivalents (defined in **graphics.h**):

Macro	Value	Meaning
EMPTY_FILL	0	Fill with background color
SOLID_FILL	1	Fill with solid color
LINE_FILL	2	Fill with lines
LTSLASH_FILL	3	Fill with light slashes
SLASH_FILL	4	Fill with slashes
BKSLASH_FILL	5	Fill with backslashes

Macro	Value	Meaning
LTBKSLASH_FILL	6	Fill with light backslashes
HATCH_FILL	7	Fill with light hatching
XHATCH_FILL	8	Fill with hatching
INTERLEAVE_FILL	9	Fill with interleaving
WIDE_DOT_FILL	10	Fill with widely spaced dots
CLOSE_DOT_FILL	11	Fill with closely spaced dots
USER_FILL	12	Fill with custom pattern

You define a custom fill pattern using **setfillpattern( )**.

Example

This program fills a box using **LINE_FILL** in the color red:

```
#include <graphics.h>
#include <conio.h>

main(void)
{
  int driver, mode;

  driver = DETECT; /* autodetect */
  mode = 0;
  initgraph(&driver, &mode, "");

  setcolor(GREEN);
  rectangle(100, 200, 200, 300);

  setfillstyle(LINE_FILL, RED);
  floodfill(150, 250, GREEN);

  getch();
  restorecrtmode();
  return 0;
}
```

Related Function

setfillpattern( )

unsigned far setgraphbufsize(unsigned size)

Description

The prototype for **setgraphbufsize( )** is in **graphics.h**.

The **setgraphbufsize( )** function is used to set the size of the buffer used by many of the graphics functions. You generally do not need to use this function. If you do use it, you must call it before **initgraph( )**. This function returns the size of the previous buffer.

Related Function

_getgraphmem( )

void far setgraphmode(int mode)

Description

The prototype for **setgraphmode( )** is in **graphics.h**.

The **setgraphmode( )** function sets the current graphics mode to that specified by *mode*, which must be a valid mode for the graphics driver.

Example

This fragment sets a CGA adapter to CGAHI mode:

```
/* after graphics system has been initialized */
setgraphmode(CGAHI);
```

Related Function

getmoderange( )

void far setlinestyle(int style, unsigned pattern, int width)

Description

The prototype for **setlinestyle( )** is in **graphics.h**.

The **setlinestyle( )** function determines the way a line looks when drawn with any graphics function that draws lines.

The *style* element holds the style of the line. It will be one of these enumerated values (defined in **graphics.h**):

Value	Meaning
SOLID_LINE	Unbroken line
DOTTED_LINE	Dotted line
CENTER_LINE	Centered line (dash-dot-dash)
DASHED_LINE	Dashed line
USERBIT_LINE	User-defined line

If *style* is equal to **USERBIT_LINE**, the 16-bit pattern in *pattern* determines how the line appears. Each bit in the pattern corresponds to one pixel. If that bit is set, the pixel is turned on; otherwise it is turned off.

The *width* element will have one of these values:

Value	Meaning
NORM_WIDTH	1 pixel wide
THICK_WIDTH	3 pixels wide

The value of *pattern* is important only if **USERBIT_LINE** is the value of *style*. When it is, each bit in *pattern* that is set will cause a pixel to be turned on. Each 0 bit causes a pixel to be turned off. The pattern then repeats as necessary.

Example

This program displays the built-in line styles:

```
#include <graphics.h>
#include <conio.h>

main(void)
{
  int driver, mode;
  int i;

  driver = DETECT; /* autodetect */
  mode = 0;
  initgraph(&driver, &mode, "");

  for(i=0; i<4; i++) {
    setlinestyle(i, 0, 1);
    line(i*50, 100, i*50+50, 100);
  }

  getch();
```

```
   restorecrtmode();
   return 0;
}
```

Related Function

setfillstyle( )

void far setpalette(int index, int color)

Description

The prototype for **setpalette( )** is in **graphics.h**.

The **setpalette( )** function changes the colors displayed by the video system. The operation of this function is a little difficult to understand at first. Essentially, it associates the value of *color* with an index into a table that Turbo/Borland C/C++ uses to map the color actually shown on the screen with the color being requested. The values for the *color* codes are shown here:

CGA codes (background only):

Macro	Value
BLACK	0
BLUE	1
GREEN	2
CYAN	3
RED	4
MAGENTA	5
BROWN	6
LIGHTGRAY	7
DARKGRAY	8
LIGHTBLUE	9
LIGHTGREEN	10
LIGHTCYAN	11
LIGHTRED	12
LIGHTMAGENTA	13
YELLOW	14
WHITE	15

EGA and VGA:

Macro	Value
EGA_BLACK	0
EGA_BLUE	1
EGA_GREEN	2
EGA_CYAN	3
EGA_RED	4
EGA_MAGENTA	5
EGA_BROWN	20
EGA_LIGHTGRAY	7
EGA_DARKGRAY	56
EGA_LIGHTBLUE	57
EGA_LIGHTGREEN	58
EGA_LIGHTCYAN	59
EGA_LIGHTRED	60
EGA_LIGHTMAGENTA	61
EGA_YELLOW	62
EGA_WHITE	63

Only the background color can be changed for CGA modes. The background color is always index 0. For CGA modes, this code changes the background color to green:

```
setpalette(0, GREEN);
```

EGA modes can display 16 colors at a time. You can use **setpalette( )** to map a color onto one of the 16 different indexes.

Example

This fragment sets the value of color 5 to cyan:

```
setpalette(5, EGA_CYAN);
```

Related Function

setcolor( )

void far setrgbpalette(int color, int r, int g, int b)

Description

The prototype for **setrgbpalette( )** is in **graphics.h**.

The **setrgbpalette( )** function changes the colors displayed by the video system. It is for use with graphics systems that support RGB displays, such as the IBM 8514 and VGA, only.

The *color* parameter must be a valid entry in the current palette. The other three parameters (*r*, *g*, and *b*) correspond to the desired red, green, and blue settings of the palette entry. You can mix different proportions of these colors (that is, you specify a color mix for each entry in the palette). The values of *r*, *g*, and *b* must be in the range 0 through 31. (Only the upper 6 most significant bits of the lower byte are used.)

Example

This fragment sets the 15th color to equal amounts of red, green, and blue:

```
setrgbpalette(15, 16, 16, 16);   /* the upper 6 bits = 4 */
```

Related Functions

setpalette( ), **getpalette( )**

void far settextjustify(int horiz, int vert)

Description

The prototype for **settextjustify( )** is in **graphics.h**.

The **settextjustify( )** function sets the way text is aligned relative to the CP. The values of *horiz* and *vert* determine the effect of **settextjustify( )**, as shown here (the macros are defined in **graphics.h**):

Macro	Value	Meaning
LEFT_TEXT	0	CP at left
CENTER_TEXT	1	CP in the center
RIGHT_TEXT	2	CP at right
BOTTOM_TEXT	0	CP at the bottom
TOP_TEXT	2	CP at the top

The default settings are **LEFT_TEXT** and **TOP_TEXT**.

Example

This fragment places the CP on the right:

```
settextjustify(RIGHT_TEXT, TOP_TEXT);
```

Related Function

settextstyle( )

void far settextstyle(int font, int direction, int size)

Description

The prototype for **settextstyle( )** is in **graphics.h**.

The **settextstyle( )** function sets the active font used by the graphics text output functions. It also sets the direction and size of the characters.

The *font* parameter determines the type of font used. The default is the hardware-defined 8×8 bit-mapped font. You can give *font* one of these values (the macros are defined in **graphics.h**):

Macro	Value	Font
DEFAULT_FONT	0	Default 8×8 bit-mapped font
TRIPLEX_FONT	1	Stroked triplex font
SMALL_FONT	2	Stroked small font
SANS_SERIF_FONT	3	Stroked sans serif font
GOTHIC_FONT	4	Stroked gothic font
SCRIPT_FONT	5	Stroked script font
SIMPLEX_FONT	6	Stroked triplex script font
TRIPLEX_SCR_FONT	7	Stroked triplex script font
COMPLEX_FONT	8	Stroked complex font
EUROPEAN_FONT	9	Stroked European font
BOLD_FONT	10	Stroked bold font

The direction in which the text is displayed—either left to right or bottom to top—is determined by the value of *direction,* which can be either **HORIZ_DIR** (0) or **VERT_DIR** (1).

The *size* parameter is a multiplier that increases the character size. It can have a value of 0 through 10.

Example

The following program illustrates the use of the **settextstyle( )** function:

```
/* Demonstrate some different text fonts and sizes. */

#include <graphics.h>
#include <conio.h>

main(void)
{
  int driver, mode;

  driver = DETECT; /* autodetect */
  mode = 0;
  initgraph(&driver, &mode, "");

  outtext("Normal ");

  /* Gothic font, twice normal size */
  settextstyle(GOTHIC_FONT, HORIZ_DIR, 2);
  outtext("Gothic ");

  /* Triplex font, twice normal size */
  settextstyle(TRIPLEX_FONT, HORIZ_DIR, 2);
  outtext("Triplex ");

  /* Sans serif font, 7 times normal size*/
  settextstyle(SANS_SERIF_FONT, HORIZ_DIR, 7);
  outtext("Sans serif");
  getch();
  restorecrtmode();
  return 0;
}
```

Related Function

settextjustify( )

void far setusercharsize(int mulx, int divx, int muly, int divy)

Description

The prototype for **setusercharsize( )** is in **graphics.h**.

The **setusercharsize( )** function specifies multipliers and divisors that scale the size of graphics stroked fonts. In essence, after a call to **setusercharsize( )**, each character displayed on the screen has its default size multiplied by *mulx/divx* for its *x* dimension and *muly/divy* for its *y* dimension.

Example

This code writes text in both normal and large letters:

```
#include <graphics.h>
#include <conio.h>

main(void)
{
  int driver, mode;

  driver = DETECT; /* autodetect */
  mode = 0;
  initgraph(&driver, &mode, "");

  outtext("normal ");
  settextstyle(TRIPLEX_FONT, HORIZ_DIR, USER_CHAR_SIZE);

  /* make very big letters */
  setusercharsize(5, 1, 5, 1);
  outtext("big");

  getch();
  restorecrtmode();
  return 0;
}
```

Related Function

gettextsettings( )

void far setviewport(int left, int top, int right, int bottom, int clip)

Description

The prototype for **setviewport( )** is in **graphics.h**.

    The **setviewport( )** function creates a new viewport using the upper left and lower right corner coordinates specified by *left*, *top*, *right*, and *bottom*. If *clip* is 1, output is automatically clipped at the edge of the viewport and prevented from spilling into other parts of the screen. If *clip* is 0, no clipping takes place.

Example

This fragment creates a viewport with corners at 10,10 and 40,40 with clipping:

```
setviewport(10, 10, 40, 40, 1);
```

Related Function

clearviewport( )

void far setvisualpage(int page)

Description

The prototype for **setvisualpage( )** is in **graphics.h**.

For some video modes, there is enough memory in video adapters to have two or more complete screens' worth of information stored at the same time. The RAM that holds the information displayed on the screen is called a *page*. Turbo/Borland C/C++ uses page 0 by default. However, you can use any of the video pages supported by your hardware, switching between them as desired. Although only one screen of data can be displayed at one time, it is occasionally useful to build an image as a background task in a page that is not currently displayed so that it is ready when needed without delay. To activate the image, simply switch to that display page. This method is particularly useful in cases where complex images take a long time to construct. To support this sort of approach, Turbo/Borland C/C++ supplies the functions **setactivepage( )** and **setvisualpage( )**.

The **setactivepage( )** function determines the video page to which output of Turbo/Borland C/C++'s graphics functions is directed. If you call **setactivepage( )** with a different page than is currently being displayed, subsequent graphics output is written to the new page, not necessarily the one currently displayed. To actually display a different page, use the **setvisualpage( )** function. For example, to display video page 1 you would call **setvisualpage( )** with an argument of 1.

Example

This fragment selects page 1 to be displayed:

```
setvisualpage(1);
```

Related Function

setactivepage( )

void far setwritemode(int wmode)

Description

The prototype for **setwritemode( )** is in **graphics.h**.

The **setwritemode( )** function determines how **line( )**, **linerel( )**, **lineto( )**, **rectangle( )**, and **drawpoly( )** display their output on the screen. The value of *wmode* must be one of these two macros (defined in **graphics.h**): **COPY_PUT** and **XOR_PUT**. Calling **setwritemode( )** using **COPY_PUT** causes subsequent output to overwrite any image on the screen. However, if you call **setwritemode( )** using **XOR_PUT**, subsequent output is XORed with any preexisting image. The advantage of using the **XOR_PUT** mode is that you can restore the original screen by outputting the same object a second time.

Example

This program illustrates the **setwritemode( )** function:

```
#include <graphics.h>
#include <conio.h>

main(void)
{
  int driver, mode;

  driver = DETECT; /* autodetect */
  mode = 0;
  initgraph(&driver, &mode, "");

  setwritemode(COPY_PUT);  /* set for overwrite */
  setcolor(BLUE);
  rectangle(10, 10, 100, 100);
  getch();

  setwritemode(XOR_PUT);  /* set for combining */

  setcolor(RED);
  rectangle(30, 30, 80, 80); /* draw inside first rectangle */
  getch();
```

```
rectangle(30, 30, 80, 80); /* now erase it */
getch();

restorecrtmode();
return 0;
}
```

Related Function

setlinestyle( )

void textattr(int attr)

Description

The prototype for **textattr( )** is in **conio.h**.

The **textattr( )** function sets both the foreground and background colors in a text screen at one time. The value of *attr* represents an encoded form of the color information, as shown here.

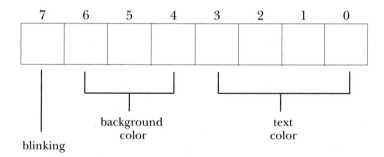

If bit **7** is set, the text blinks. Bits 6 through 4 determine the background color. Bits 3 through 0 set the color for the text. The easiest way to encode the background color into the attribute byte is to multiply the number of the color you desire by 16 and then OR that with the text color. For example, to create a green background with blue text you would use **GREEN * 16 | BLUE**. To cause the text to blink, OR the text color, background color, and **BLINK** (128) together.

Example

This fragment displays the text in blinking red with a blue background:

```
textattr(RED | BLINK | BLUE*16);
```

Related Functions

textbackground( ), **textcolor( )**

void textbackground(int color)

Description

The prototype for **textbackground( )** is in **conio.h**.

The **textbackground( )** function sets the background color of a text screen. A call to **textbackground( )** affects only the background color of subsequent write operations. The valid colors are shown here along with their macro names (defined in **conio.h**):

Macro	Integer Equivalent
BLACK	0
BLUE	1
GREEN	2
CYAN	3
RED	4
MAGENTA	5
BROWN	6
LIGHTGRAY	7

The new background color takes effect after the call to **textbackground( )**. The background of characters currently on the screen is not affected.

Example

This fragment sets the background color of a text screen to cyan.

```
textbackground(CYAN);
```

Related Function

textcolor( )

void textcolor(int color)

Description

The prototype of **textcolor( )** is in **conio.h**.

The **textcolor( )** function sets the color in which characters are displayed in a text screen. It can also be used to specify blinking characters. The valid values for *color* are shown here, along with their macro names (defined in **conio.h**):

Macro	Integer Equivalent
BLACK	0
BLUE	1
GREEN	2
CYAN	3
RED	4
MAGENTA	5
BROWN	6
LIGHTGRAY	7
DARKGRAY	8
LIGHTBLUE	9
LIGHTGREEN	10
LIGHTCYAN	11
LIGHTRED	12
LIGHTMAGENTA	13
YELLOW	14
WHITE	15
BLINK	128

The color of characters on the screen is not changed by **textcolor( )**; it affects only those written after **textcolor( )** has executed.

Example

This fragment displays subsequent output in blinking characters:

```
textcolor(BLINK);
```

Related Function

textattr( )

int far textheight(char far *str)

Description

The prototype for **textheight( )** is in **graphics.h**.

The **textheight( )** function returns the height, in pixels, of the string pointed to by *str* relative to the current font and size.

Example

This program displays the number 8 for the text height:

```
#include <stdio.h>
#include <graphics.h>
#include <conio.h>

main(void)
{
  int driver, mode;

  driver = DETECT; /* autodetect */
  mode = 0;
  initgraph(&driver, &mode, "");

  printf("height: %d", textheight("hello"));

  getch();
  restorecrtmode();
  return 0;
}
```

Related Function

textwidth( )

void textmode(int mode)

Description

The prototype for **textmode( )** is in **conio.h**.

The **textmode( )** function is used to change the video mode of a text screen. The argument *mode* must be one of the values shown in the following table. You can use either the integer value or the macro name (the macros are defined in **conio.h**):

Macro Name	Integer Equivalent	Description
BW40	0	40 column black and white
C40	1	40 column color
BW80	2	80 column black and white

Macro Name	Integer Equivalent	Description
C80	3	80 column color
MONO	7	80 column monochrome
LASTMODE	−1	Previous mode

After a call to **textmode( )** the screen is reset and all text screen attributes are returned to their default settings.

Example

This fragment puts the video hardware into 80 column color mode:

```
textmode(C80);
```

Related Function

gettextinfo( )

int far textwidth(char far *str)

Description

The prototype for **textwidth( )** is in **graphics.h**.

The **textwidth( )** function returns the width, in pixels, of the string pointed to by *str* relative to the current font and size.

Example

This program displays 40 as the pixel length of the string "hello":

```
#include <stdio.h>
#include <graphics.h>
#include <conio.h>

main(void)
{
  int driver, mode;

  driver = DETECT; /* autodetect */
  mode = 0;
  initgraph(&driver, &mode, "");
```

```
printf("width: %d", textwidth("hello"));

getch();
restorecrtmode();
return 0;
}
```

Related Function

textheight( )

int wherex(void)
int wherey(void)

Description

The prototypes for **wherex( )** and **wherey( )** are in **conio.h**.

The **wherex( )** and **wherey( )** functions return the current *x* and *y* cursor coordinates relative to the current text window.

Example

This fragment loads the variables **xpos** and **ypos** with the current *x,y* coordinates:

```
int xpos, ypos;

xpos = wherex();
ypos = wherey();
```

Related Function

gotoxy( )

void window(int left, int top, int right, int bottom)

Description

The prototype for **window( )** is in **conio.h**.

The **window( )** function is used to create a rectangular text window with upper left and lower right coordinates specified by *left, top* and *right, bottom*. If any coordinate is invalid, **window( )** takes no action. Once a call to **window( )** has been successfully completed, all references to location coordinates are interpreted relative to the window, not the screen.

Example

This fragment creates a window and writes a line of text at location 2,3 inside that window:

```
window(10, 10, 60, 15);
gotoxy(2, 3);
cprintf("at location 2, 3");
```

Related Function

clrscr( )

Chapter 24

Miscellaneous Functions

The functions discussed in this chapter are all the functions that don't fit easily in any other category. They include various conversion, variable-length argument processing, sorting, and other functions.

Many of the functions covered here require the use of the header **stdlib.h**. This header defines two types: **div_t** and **ldiv_t** which are the types of the values returned by **div( )** and **ldiv( )**, respectively. These macros are also defined:

Macro	Meaning
ERANGE	The value assigned to **errno** if a range error occurs
HUGE_VAL	The largest value representable by the floating-point routines
RAND_MAX	The maximum value that can be returned by the **rand( )** function

Different header files will be discussed in the descriptions of the functions that require them.

int abs(int num)

Description

The prototype for **abs( )** is in both **stdlib.h** and **math.h**. For maximum portability, use **stdlib.h**.

The **abs( )** function returns the absolute value of the integer *num*.

Example

This function converts a user-entered number into its absolute value:

```
#include <stdio.h>
#include <stdlib.h>

int get_abs()
{
  char num[80];

  gets(num);

  return abs(atoi(num));
}
```

Related Function

labs( )

void assert(int exp)

Description

The prototype for **assert( )** is in **assert.h**.

The **assert( )** macro writes error information to **stderr** and aborts program execution if the expression *exp* evaluates to 0. Otherwise, **assert( )** does nothing. The output of the function is in this general form:

Assertion failed: *exp*, file *<file>*, line *<linenum>*

The **assert( )** macro is generally used to help verify that a program is operating correctly; the expression is devised so that it evaluates true only when no errors have taken place.

It is not necessary to remove the **assert( )** statements from the source code once a program is debugged because if the macro **NDEBUG** is defined (as anything), the **assert( )** macros are ignored.

Example

This code fragment is used to test whether the data read from a serial port is ASCII (that is, that it does not use the 7th bit):

```
  .
  .
  .
ch = read_port();
assert(!(ch & 128)); /* check bit 7 */
  .
  .
  .
```

Related Function

abort( )

double atof(const char *str)
long double _atold(const char *str)

Description

The prototypes for **atof( )** and **_atold( )** are in **stdlib.h** and **math.h**. For compatibility with the ANSI C standard, use **stdlib.h**.

The **atof( )** function converts the string pointed to by *str* into a **double** value. The string must contain a valid floating-point number. If this is not the case, 0 is returned and **errno** is set to **ERANGE**.

The number can be terminated by any character that cannot be part of a valid floating-point number. This includes white space, punctuation (other than periods), and characters other than "E" or "e". This means that if **atof( )** is called with "100.00HELLO", the value 100.00 is returned.

_atold( ) is the **long double** version of **atof( )**.

Example

This program reads two floating-point numbers and displays their sum:

```
#include <stdio.h>
#include <stdlib.h>

main(void)
{
  char num1[80], num2[80];

  printf("enter first: ");
  gets(num1);
  printf("enter second: ");
  gets(num2);
```

```
printf("the sum is: %f",atof(num1)+atof(num2));
return 0;
}
```

Related Functions

atoi( ), atol( )

int atoi(const char *str)

Description

The prototype for **atoi( )** is in **stdlib.h**.

The **atoi( )** function converts the string pointed to by *str* into an **int** value. The string must contain a valid integer number. If this is not the case, 0 is returned.

The number can be terminated by any character that cannot be part of an integer number. This includes white space, punctuation, and characters other than "E" or "e". This means that if **atoi( )** is called with **123.23**, the integer value 123 is returned and the 0.23 ignored.

Example

This program reads two integer numbers and displays their sum:

```
#include <stdio.h>
#include <stdlib.h>

main(void)
{
  char num1[80], num2[80];

  printf("enter first: ");
  gets(num1);
  printf("enter second: ");
  gets(num2);
  printf("the sum is: %d",atoi(num1)+atoi(num2));
  return 0;
}
```

Related Functions

atof( ), atol( )

long atol(const char *str)

Description

The prototype for **atol( )** is in **stdlib.h**.

The **atol( )** function converts the string pointed to by *str* into a **long int** value. The string must contain a valid **long** integer number. If this is not the case, 0 is returned.

The number can be terminated by any character that cannot be part of an integer number. This includes white space, punctuation, and characters other than "E" or "e". This means that if **atol( )** is called with **123.23**, the integer value 123 is returned and the 0.23 ignored.

Example

This program reads two **long** integer numbers and displays their sum:

```
#include <stdio.h>
#include <stdlib.h>

main(void)
{
  char num1[80], num2[80];

  printf("enter first: ");
  gets(num1);
  printf("enter second: ");
  gets(num2);
  printf("the sum is: %ld",atol(num1)+atol(num2));
  return 0;
}
```

Related Functions

atof( ), **atoi( )**

void *bsearch(const void *key, const void *base, size_t num, size_tsize, int (*compare)(const void *, const void *))

Description

The prototype for **bsearch( )** is in **stdlib.h**.

The **bsearch( )** function performs a binary search on the sorted array pointed to by *base* and returns a pointer to the first member that matches the key pointed to by *key.* The number of elements in the array is specified by *num,* and the size (in bytes) of each element is described by *size.*

The type **size_t** is defined as an **unsigned int** in **stdlib.h**.

The function pointed to by *compare* compares an element of the array with the key. The form of the *compare* function must be

> *func_name*(const void **arg1,* const void **arg2*)

It must return the following values:

- If *arg1* is less than *arg2,* return less than 0
- If *arg1* is equal to *arg2,* return 0
- If *arg1* is greater than *arg2,* return greater than 0

The array must be sorted in ascending order with the lowest address containing the lowest element.

If the array does not contain the key, a null pointer is returned.

Example

This program reads characters entered at the keyboard and determines whether they belong to the alphabet:

```
#include <stdio.h>
#include <stdlib.h>
#include <ctype.h>

char *alpha="abcdefghijklmnopqrstuvwxyz";
int comp(const char *, const char *);

main(void)
{
  char ch;
  char *p;

  do {
    printf("enter a character: ");
    scanf("%c%*c", &ch);
    ch = tolower(ch);
    p = bsearch(&ch,alpha, 26, 1, comp);
    if(p) printf("is in alphabet\n");
    else printf("is not in alphabet\n");
  } while(p);
```

```
  return 0;
}

/* compare two characters */
int comp(const char *ch, const char *s)
{
  return *ch-*s;
}
```

Related Function

qsort( )

unsigned int _clear87(void)

Description

The prototype for **_clear87( )** is in **float.h**. This function is not defined by the ANSI C standard.

The **_clear87( )** function resets the 80x87 hardware floating-point coprocessor's status word. The function returns the previous status word.

You must have an 80x87 math coprocessor installed in your system in order to use any of the 80x87-based functions.

Related Function

_status87( )

unsigned int _control87(unsigned fpword, unsigned fpmask)

Description

The prototype for **_control87( )** is in **float.h**. This function is not defined by the ANSI C standard.

The **_control87( )** function returns or modifies the value of the 80x87 control word that controls the behavior of the chip. You must have an 80x87 math coprocessor installed in the computer before using this function.

The parameter *fpmask* determines which bits of the control word will be modified. Each bit in *fpmask* corresponds with each bit in *fpword* and the bits in the floating-point control word. If the bit in *fpmask* is non-0, the control word at the corresponding bit position is set to the value of the corresponding position in *fpword*.

The **_control87( )** function returns the modified control word. However, if *fpmask* contains 0, the control word is unchanged, and the current value of the control word is returned.

For a complete description of what each bit controls, consult the header file **float.h**.

Related Functions

_clear87( ), _fpreset( )

div_t div(int numer, int denom)

Description

The prototype for **div( )** is in **stdlib.h**.

The **div( )** function returns the quotient and the remainder of the operation *numer/denom*.

The structure type **div_t** is defined in **stdlib.h** and has these two fields.

```
int quot;  /* the quotient */
int rem;   /* the remainder */
```

Example

This program displays the quotient and the remainder of 10/3:

```
#include <stdio.h>
#include <stdlib.h>

main(void)
{
  div_t n;

  n=div(10,3);

  printf("quotient and remainder: %d %d\n", n.quot, n.rem);

  return 0;
}
```

Related Function

ldiv( )

char *ecvt(double value, int ndigit, int *dec, int *sign)

Description

The prototype for **ecvt( )** is in **stdlib.h**. This function is not defined by the ANSI C standard.

The **ecvt( )** function converts *value* into a string *ndigit* long. After the call, the value of the variable pointed to by *dec* indicates the position of the decimal point. If the decimal point is to the left of the number, the number pointed to by *dec* is negative. The decimal point is not actually stored in the string. If *value* is positive, *sign* is 0. If the number is negative, *sign* is non-0.

The **ecvt( )** function returns a pointer to a static data area that holds the string representation of the number.

Example

This call converts the number 10.12 into a string:

```
int decpnt, sign;
char *out;

out = ecvt(10.12, 5, &decpnt, &sign);
```

Related Functions

fcvt( ), **gcvt( )**

void _ _emit_ _(arg, . . .)

Description

The prototype for _ _**emit**_ _( ) is in **dos.h**. This function is not defined by the ANSI C standard.

The _ _**emit**_ _( ) function is used to insert one or more values directly into the executable code of your program at the point at which _ _**emit**_ _( ) is called. These values generally will be 8086 (family) machine instructions. If a value fits into a byte, it is treated as a byte quantity. Otherwise, it is treated as a word quantity. You can only pass _ _**emit**_ _( ) byte or word values.

You must be an expert 8086 assembly language programmer to use _ _**emit**_ _( ). If you insert incorrect values, your program will crash.

char *fcvt(double value, int ndigit, int *dec, int *sign)

Description

The prototype for **fcvt( )** is in **stdlib.h**. This function is not defined by the ANSI C standard.

The **fcvt( )** function is the same as **ecvt( )** except that the output is rounded to the number of digits specified by *ndigit*.

The **fcvt( )** function returns a pointer to a static data area that holds the string representation of the number.

Example

This call converts the number 10.12 into a string:

```
int decpnt, sign;
char *out;

out = fcvt(10.12, 5, &decpnt, &sign);
```

Related Functions

ecvt( ), **gcvt( )**

void _fpreset(void)

Description

The prototype for **_fpreset( )** is in **float.h**. This function is not defined by the ANSI C standard.

The **_fpreset( )** function resets the the floating-point arithmetic system. You may need to reset the floating-point routines after a **system( )**, **exec( )**, **spawn( )**, or **signal( )** function executes. Refer to the user manuals for specific details.

Example

This fragment ensures that the floating-point arithmetic routines are reset after **system( )** returns:

```
/* compute and print payroll checks */
system("payroll");

_fpreset();
```

Related Function

_status87( )

char *gcvt(double value, int ndigit, char *buf)

Description

The prototype for **gcvt( )** is in **stdlib.h**. This function is not defined by the ANSI C standard.

The **gcvt( )** function converts *value* into a string *ndigit* long. The converted string output is stored in the array pointed to by *buf* in FORTRAN F-format if possible, E-format otherwise. A pointer to *buf* is returned.

Example

This call converts the number 10.12 into a string:

```
char buf[80];

gcvt(10.12, 5, buf);
```

Related Functions

fcvt( ), ecvt( )

char *getenv(const char *name)

Description

The prototype for **getenv( )** is in **stdlib.h**.

The **getenv( )** function returns a pointer to environmental information associated with the string pointed to by *name* in the DOS environmental information table. The string returned must never be changed by the program.

The environment of a program can include such things as path names and devices on-line. The exact meaning of this data is defined by DOS.

If a call is made to **getenv( )** with an argument that does not match any of the environmental data, a null pointer is returned.

Example

Assuming that a specific compiler maintains environmental information on the devices connected to the system, the following fragment returns a pointer to the list of devices.

.
.
.

```
p = getenv("DEVICES");
```

.
.
.

Related Functions

putenv( ), **system( )**

char *getpass(const char *str)

Description

The prototype for **getpass( )** is in **conio.h**. This function is not defined by the ANSI C standard.

    After displaying the prompt *str* on the screen, the **getpass( )** function returns a pointer to a null-terminated string of not more than eight characters. This string is statically allocated by **getpass( )** and is overwritten each time the function is called. If you want to save the string, you must copy it elsewhere. Keystrokes are not echoed when the password is entered.

Example

This function waits until the proper password is entered:

```
#include <conio.h>
#include <string.h>

void pswd (char *pw)

{
  char *input;

  do {
    input=getpass("Enter your password:");
  }while (!strcmp("starbar", input));

  printf("You're in!");
}
```

unsigned getpid(void)

Description

The prototype for **getpid( )** is in **process.h**. This function is not defined by the ANSI C standard.

   The **getpid( )** function returns the process ID number associated with a program. This value is also the segment address of the PSP (program segment prefix) for the program.

Example

This fragment displays the process ID number:

```
printf("This process ID of this program is %d\n", getpid());
```

Related Function

getpsp( )

char *itoa(int num, char *str, int radix)

Description

The prototype for **itoa( )** is in **stdlib.h**. This function is not defined by the ANSI C standard.

   The **itoa( )** function converts the integer *num* into its string equivalent and places the result in the string pointed to by *str.* The base of the output string is determined by *radix,* which can be in the range 2 through 36.

   The **itoa( )** function returns a pointer to *str.* There is no error return value. Be sure to call **itoa( )** with a string of sufficient length to hold the converted result. The maximum length needed is 17 bytes.

Example

This program displays the value of 1423 in hexadecimal (58F):

```
#include <stdio.h>
#include <stdlib.h>

main(void)
{
  char p[17];
```

```
  itoa(1423, p, 16);

  printf(p);

  return 0;
}
```

Related Functions

atoi( ), sscanf( )

long labs(long num)

Description

The prototype for **labs( )** is in **stdlib.h** and **math.h**. For the ANSI C standard compatibility, use **stdlib.h**.

The **labs( )** function returns the absolute value of the **long int** *num*.

Example

This function converts the user-entered numbers into their absolute values:

```
#include <stdio.h>
#include <stdlib.h>
long int get_labs()
{
  char num[80];

  gets(num);

  return labs(atol(num));
}
```

Related Function

abs( )

ldiv_t ldiv(long numer, long denom)

Description

The prototype for **ldiv( )** is in **stdlib.h**.

The **ldiv( )** function returns the quotient and the remainder of the operation *numer/denom.*

The structure type **ldiv_t** is defined in **stdlib.h** and has these two fields:

```
long quot;   /* the quotient */
long rem;    /* the remainder */
```

Example

This program displays the quotient and the remainder of 100000L/3L:

```
#include <stdio.h>
#include <stdlib.h>

main(void)
{
  ldiv_t n;

  n = ldiv(100000L,3L);

  printf("quotient and remainder: %ld %ld\n", n.quot, n.rem);

  return 0;
}
```

Related Function

div( )

void *lfind(const void *key, const void *base, size_t *num, size_t size, int (*compare)(const void *, const void *))
void *lsearch(const void *key, void *base, size_t *num, size_t size, int (*compare)(const void *, const void *))

Description

The prototypes for **lfind( )** and **lsearch( )** are in **stdlib.h**. These functions are not defined by the ANSI C standard.

The **lfind( )** and **lsearch( )** functions perform a linear search on the array pointed to by *base* and return a pointer to the first element that matches the key pointed to by *key*. The number of elements in the array is pointed to by *num,* and the size (in bytes) of each element is described by *size*.

The type **size_t** is defined as an **unsigned int** in **stdlib.h**.

The function pointed to by *compare* compares an element of the array with the key. The form of the *compare* function must be

func_name(const void **arg1,* const void **arg2*)

It must return the following values:

- If *arg1* does not equal *arg2*, return non-0
- If *arg1* is equal to *arg2*, return 0

The array being searched does not have to be sorted.
If the array does not contain the key, a null pointer is returned.
The difference between **lfind( )** and **lsearch( )** is that if the item being searched for does not exist in the array, **lsearch( )** adds it to the end of the array; **lfind( )** does not.

Example

This program reads characters entered at the keyboard and determines whether they belong to the alphabet:

```
#include <stdlib.h>
#include <ctype.h>
#include <stdio.h>

char *alpha="abcdefghijklmnopqrstuvwxyz";

int comp(const char *, const char *);

main(void)
{
  char ch;
  char *p;
  size_t num=26;

  do {
    printf("enter a character: ");
    scanf("%c%*c", &ch);
    ch = tolower(ch);
    p = lfind(&ch, alpha, &num, 1, comp);
    if(p) printf("is in alphabet\n");
    else printf("is not in alphabet\n");
  } while(p);
```

```
  return 0;
}

/* compare two characters */
int comp(const char *ch, const char *s)
{
  return *ch-*s;
}
```

Related Function

qsort( )

struct lconv *localeconv(void)

Description

The prototype for **localeconv( )** is in **locale.h**. It returns a pointer to a structure of type **lconv**, which contains various country-specific environmental information relating to the way numbers are formatted. The **lconv** structure is organized as shown here.

```
struct lconv {
  char *decimal_point; /* decimal point character
                          for non-monetary values */
  char *thousands_sep; /* thousands separator
                          for non-monetary values */
  char *grouping; /* specifies grouping for
                     non-monetary values */
  char int_curr_symbol; /* international currency symbol */
  char *currency_symbol; /* local currency symbol */
  char *mon_decimal_point; /* decimal point character
                             for monetary values */
  char *mon_thousands_sep; /* thousands separator
                             for monetary values */
  char *mon_grouping; /* specifies grouping for
                        monetary values */
  char *positive_sign; /* positive value indicator
                          for monetary values */
  char *negative_sign; /* negative value indicator
                          for monetary values */
  char int_frac_digits; /* number of digits displayed
                           to the right of the decimal
                           point for monetary values
```

```
                                displayed using international
                                format */
     char frac_digits; /* number of digits displayed
                                to the right of the decimal
                                point for monetary values
                                displayed using local format */
     char p_cs_precedes; /* 1 if currency symbol precedes
                                positive value,
                                0 if currency symbol
                                follows value *.
     char p_sep_by_space; /* 1 if currency symbol is
                                separated from value by a
                                space, 0 otherwise */
     char n_cs_precedes; /* 1 if currency symbol precedes
                                a negative value, 0 if
                                currency symbol follows value */
     char n_sep_by_space; /* 1 if currency symbol is
                                separated from a negative
                                value by a space, 0 if
                                currency symbol follows value */
     char p_sign_posn; /* indicates position of positive
                                value symbol */
     char n_sign_posn; /* indicates position of negative
                                value symbol */
}
```

Related Function

setlocale( )

void longjmp(jmp_buf envbuf, int val)

Description

The prototype for **longjmp( )** is in **setjmp.h**.

The **longjmp( )** instruction causes program execution to resume at the point of the last call to **setjmp( )**. These two functions create a way to jump between functions.

The **longjmp( )** function operates by resetting the stack to the state defined in *envbuf*, which must have been set by a prior call to **setjmp( )**. This causes program execution to resume at the statement following the **setjmp( )** invocation. That is, the computer is "tricked" into thinking that it never left the function that called **setjmp( )**. (As a somewhat graphic explanation, the **longjmp( )** function "warps" across time and space (memory) to a previous point in your program without having to perform the normal function-return process.)

The buffer *envbuf* is of type **jmp_buf**, which is defined in the header **setjmp.h**. The buffer must have been set through a call to **setjmp( )** prior to calling **longjmp( )**.

The value of *val* becomes the return value of **setjump( )** and can be interrogated to determine where the long jump came from. The only value not allowed is 0.

It is important to understand that the **longjmp( )** function must be called before the function that called **setjmp( )** returns. If not, the result is technically undefined. (Actually, a crash will almost certainly occur.)

By far, the most common use of **longjmp( )** is to return from a deeply nested set of routines when a catastrophic error occurs.

Example

This program prints "1 2 3":

```
#include <stdio.h>
#include <setjmp.h>

jmp_buf ebuf;
void f2(void);

main(void)
{
  char first=1;
  int i;

  printf("1 ");
  i = setjmp(ebuf);
  if(first) {
    first =! first;
    f2();
    printf("this will not be printed");
  }
  printf("%d", i);
  return 0;
}

void f2(void)
{
  printf("2 ");
  longjmp(ebuf, 3);
}
```

Related Function

setjmp( )

char *ltoa(long num, char *str, int radix)
char *ultoa(unsigned long num, char *str, int radix)

Description

The prototype for **ltoa( )** and **ultoa( )** are in **stdlib.h**. These functions are not defined by the ANSI C standard.

The **ltoa( )** function converts the long integer *num* into its string equivalent and places the result in the string pointed to by *str*. The base of the output string is determined by *radix*, which must be in the range 2 through 36. The **ultoa( )** function performs the same conversion, but on an **unsigned long** integer.

The **ltoa( )** and **ultoa( )** functions return a pointer to *str*. There is no error return value. Be sure *str* is of sufficient length to hold the converted result. The longest array you need is 34 bytes.

Example

This program displays the value of 1423 in hexadecimal (58F):

```
#include <stdio.h>
#include <stdlib.h>

main(void)
{
  char p[34];

  ltoa(1423, p, 16);

  printf(p);

  return 0;
}
```

Related Functions

itoa( ), sscanf( )

unsigned long _lrotl(unsigned long l, int i)
unsigned long _lrotr(unsigned long l, int i)

Description

The prototypes for **_lrotl( )** and **_lrotr( )** are in **stdlib.h**. These functions are not defined by the ANSI C standard.

The **_lrotl( )** and **_lrotr( )** functions rotate the bits of the long value *l*, *i* number of bits to the left or right, respectively and returns the result. When a rotate is performed, bits rotated off one end are inserted onto the other end. For example, given the value

1111 0000 0000 1111 1111 0000 1010 0101

rotating it left by one bit, produces the value

1110 0000 0001 1111 1110 0001 0100 1011

Example

The following program shows the effect of left and right rotation.

```
#include <stdio.h>
#include <stdlib.h>

main(void)
{
  unsigned long l = 1;

  printf("1 rotated left 2 bits = %ld\n", _lrotl(1,2));
  printf("1 rotated right 2 bits = %ld\n", _lrotr(1,2));

  return 0;
}
```

Related Functions

_rotl( ), _rotr( )

max(x,y)
min(x,y)

Description

The **max( )** and **min( )** macros are defined in **stdlib.h**. These functions are not defined by the ANSI C standard.

The **max( )** macro returns the larger of the two values and the **min( )** returns the smaller of the two values. The **max( )** and **min( )** macros return the same type as passed to them; both arguments passed must be of the same type.

Example

This program illustrates the **min( )** and **max( )** macros:

```
#include <stdlib.h>
#include <stdio.h>

main (void)
{
  printf("max of 10, 20 is %d\n", max (10, 20));
  printf("min of 10, 20 is %d\n", min (10, 20));

return 0;
}
```

int mblen(const char *str, size_t size)

Description

The prototype for **mblen( )** is in **stdlib.h**.

This function returns the length of a multibyte character pointed to by *str*. Only the first *size* number of characters are examined.

If *str* is null, then **mblen( )** returns non-0 if multibyte characters have shift-state dependencies. If they do not, 0 is returned.

Example

This statement displays the length of the multibyte character pointed to by **mb**.

```
printf("%d", mblen(mb, 2));
```

Related Functions

mbtowc( ), wctomb( )

size_t mbstowcs(wchar_t *out, const char *in, size_t size)

Description

The prototype for **mbstowcs( )** is in **stdlib.h**.

The **mbstowcs( )** converts the multibyte string pointed to by *in* into a standard string and puts that result in the array pointed to by *out*. The type **wchar_t** is a **typdef** that is the same as **char**. Only *size* number of bytes will be stored in *out*.

The **mbstowcs( )** function returns the number of multibyte characters that are converted. If an error occurs, the function returns –1.

Example

This statement converts the first four characters in the multibyte string pointed to by **mb** and puts the result in **str**.

```
mbstowcs(str, mb, 4);
```

Related Functions

wcstombs( ), **mbtowc( )**

int mbtowc(wchar_t *out, const char *in, size_t size)

Description

The prototype for **mbtowc( )** is in **stdlib.h**.

The **mbtowc( )** function converts the multibyte character in the array pointed to by *in* into its normal character equivalent and puts that result in the array pointed to by *out*. The type **wchar_t** is **typdef**ed as a character. Only *size* number of characters will be examined.

This function returns the number of bytes that are put into *out*. −1 is returned if an error occurs.

If *in* is null, then **mbtowc( )** returns non-0 if multibyte characters have shift-state dependencies. If they do not, 0 is returned.

Example

This statement converts the multibyte character in **mbstr** into its equivalent normal characters and puts the result in the array pointed to by **normstr**. (Only the first 2 bytes of **mbstr** are examined.)

```
mbtowc(normstr, mbstr, 2);
```

Related Functions

mblen( ), **wctomb( )**

void nosound(void)

Description

The prototype for **nosound( )** is in **dos.h**. This function is not defined by the ANSI C standard.

The **nosound( )** function turns off the PC's speaker. This function normally follows a call to the **sound( )** function.

Example

This program makes the speaker beep and then stop:

```
#include <dos.h>

main(void)
{
  sound(1000);
  sleep(2);
  nosound();

  return 0;
}
```

Related Function

sound( )

int cdecl far _OvrInitEms(unsigned handle, unsigned page, unsigned num)
int cdecl far _OvrInitExt(unsigned long address, unsigned long len)

Description

The prototypes for **_OvrInitEms( )** and **_OvrInitExt( )** are in **dos.h**. These functions are not defined by the ANSI C standard.

The **_OvrInitEms( )** function prepares the expanded memory of the computer, if it exists, so that it can be used by the overlay manager. The value of *handle* must be a valid EMS handle. Or, it may be 0, in which case, the overlay manager simply allocates its own memory. The value of *page* is only meaningful when *handle* is non-0, in which case it specifies the first page of memory to use for swapping. The value of *len* specifies the number of pages to be used by the overlay manager. This function returns 0 if successful and non-0 otherwise.

The **_OvrInitExt( )** function prepares the extended memory of the computer, if it exists, so that it can be used by the overlay manager. The value of *address* determines the beginning address of extended memory to use. If *address* is 0, then the function will determine the beginning address of extended memory. The value of *len* determines how many bytes of memory may be used. If this value is 0, then the overlay manager is free to use all of extended memory. This function returns 0 if successful and non-0 if an error occurs.

Example

This program initializes all of extended memory for use by the overlay manager.

```
#include <dos.h>
#include <stdio.h>

main(void)
{
  int result;

  result = _OvrInitExt(NULL, 0);
  if(result)
    printf("Cannot use extended memory for overlays.\n");

  return 0;
}
```

int putenv(const char *evar)

Description

The prototype for **putenv( )** is in **stdlib.h**. This function is not defined by the ANSI C standard.

The **putenv( )** function puts an environmental variable into DOS. It returns 0 if successful; –1 if unsuccessful. Refer to **getenv( )** and to a DOS manual for information about DOS environmental variables.

Related Function

getenv( )

void qsort(void *base, size_t num, size_t size, int (*compare) (const void *, const void *))

Description

The prototype for **qsort( )** is in **stdlib.h**.

The **qsort( )** function sorts the array pointed to by *base* using a *quicksort,* a general-purpose sorting algorithm (developed by C.A.R. Hoare). Upon termination, the array is sorted. The number of elements in the array is specified by *num,* and the size (in bytes) of each element is described by *size.*

The function pointed to by *compare* compares an element of the array with the key. The form of the *compare* function must be int *func_name*(const void *arg1*, const void *arg2*)

It must return the following values:

- If *arg1* is less than *arg2*, return less than 0
- If *arg1* is equal to *arg2*, return 0
- If *arg1* is greater than *arg2*, return greater than 0

The array is sorted into ascending order with the lowest address containing the lowest element.

Example

This program sorts a list of integers and displays the result:

```
#include <stdio.h>
#include <stdlib.h>

int num[10]= {
  1,3,6,5,8,7,9,6,2,0
};

int comp(const int *, const int *);

main(void)
{
  int i;

  printf("original array: ");
  for(i=0; i<10; i++) printf("%d ",num[i]);

  qsort(num, 10, sizeof(int),
        (int(*)(const void *, const void *)) comp);

  printf("sorted array: ");
  for(i=0; i<10; i++) printf("%d ", num[i]);

  return 0;
}

/* compare the integers */
int comp(const int *i, const int *j)
```

```
{
  return *i-*j;
}
```

Related Function

bsearch( )

int raise(int signal)

Description

The prototype for **raise( )** is in **signal.h**. The **raise( )** function sends the signal specified by *signal* to the currently executing program.

The following signals are defined in **signal.h**:

Macro	Meaning
SIGABRT	Termination error
SIGFPE	Floating-point error
SIGILL	Bad instruction
SIGINT	Control break
SIGSEGV	Illegal memory access
SIGTERM	Terminate program

On success, **raise( )** returns 0.

You will often use this function in conjunction with the **signal( )** function.

Example

This program raises the **SIGTERM** signal, which causes **myhandler( )** to be executed:

```
#include <signal.h>
#include <stdio.h>
#include <stdlib.h>

void myhandler(void);
main(void)
{
  signal(SIGTERM, myhandler);
  raise(SIGTERM);
  printf("This line will not be executed.\n");
  return 0;
}
```

```
void myhandler(void)
{
  printf("Program terminated.\n");
  exit(1);
}
```

Related Function

signal( )

int rand(void)

Description

The prototype for **rand( )** is in **stdlib.h**.

The **rand( )** function generates a sequence of pseudorandom numbers. Each time it is called it returns an integer between 0 and **RAND_MAX**.

Example

This program displays ten pseudorandom numbers:

```
#include <stdio.h>
#include <stdlib.h>

main(void)
{
  int i;

  for(i=0; i<10; i++)
    printf("%d ", rand());
  return 0;
}
```

Related Function

srand( )

int random(int num)
void randomize(void)

Description

The prototypes for **random( )** and **randomize( )** are in **stdlib.h**. These functions are not defined by the ANSI C standard.

The **random( )** macro returns a random number in the range 0 through *num*−1.

The **randomize( )** macro initializes the random number generator to some random value. It uses the **time( )** function, so you should include **time.h** in any program that uses **randomize( )**.

Example

This program prints ten random numbers between 0 and 24:

```
#include <time.h>
#include <stdio.h>
#include <stdlib.h>

main(void)
{
  int i;

  randomize();

  for(i=0; i<10; i++) printf("%d ", random(25));

  return 0;
}
```

Related Functions

rand( ), srand( )

unsigned _rotl(unsigned val, int num)
unsigned _rotr(unsigned val, int num)

Description

The prototypes for **_rotl( )** and **_rotr( )** are in **stdlib.h**. These functions are not defined by the ANSI C standard.

The **_rotl( )** and **_rotr( )** functions rotate the bits of the value *val*, *num* number of bits to the left or right, respectively and return the result. When a rotate is performed, bits rotated off one end are inserted onto the other end. For example, given the value

1111 0000 0000 1111

rotating it left by one bit produces the value

1110 0000 0001 1111

Example

The following program prints the value of 64 after it is rotated left and it is rotated right:

```
#include <stdio.h>
#include <stdlib.h>

main(void)
{
  unsigned val = 64;

  printf("rotated left 2 bits = %d\n", _rotl(val,2));
  printf("rotated right 2 bits = %d\n", _rotr(val,2));

  return 0;
}
```

Related Functions

_lrotl( ), _lrotr( )

void _setcursortype(int type)

Description

The prototype for **_setcursortype( )** is in **conio.h**. This function is not defined by the ANSI C standard.

The **_setcursortype( )** function changes how the cursor is displayed. It can be called with one of three macros (defined in **conio.h**). Calling **_setcursortype( )** with **_NOCURSOR** turns off the cursor. Using **_SOLIDCURSOR** makes a block cursor, and **_NORMALCURSOR** creates an underscore cursor.

Example

This fragment changes the cursor type to a block:

```
_setcursortype(_SOLIDCURSOR);
```

Related Function

setcolor( )

int setjmp(jmp_buf envbuf)

Description

The prototype for **setjmp( )** is in **setjmp.h**.

The **setjmp( )** function saves the contents of the system stack in the buffer *envbuf* for later use by **longjmp( )**.

The **setjmp( )** function returns 0 upon invocation. However, when **longjmp( )** executes, it passes an argument (always non-0) to **setjmp( )**, which appears to be **setjmp( )**'s return value.

See **longjmp( )** for additional information.

Example

This program prints "1 2 3":

```
#include <stdio.h>
#include <setjmp.h>

jmp_buf ebuf;
void f2(void);

main(void)
{
  char first=1;
  int i;

  printf("1 ");
  i = setjmp(ebuf);
  if(first) {
    first =! first;
    f2();
    printf("this will not be printed");
  }
  printf("%d", i);
  return 0;
}

void f2(void)
{
  printf("2 ");
  longjmp(ebuf, 3);
}
```

Related Function

longjmp( )

void _searchenv(const char *fname, const char *ename, char *fpath)

Description

The prototype for **_searchenv( )** is in **stdlib.h**. The function is not defined by the ANSI C standard.

The **_searchenv( )** searches for the file whose name is pointed to by *fname* using the path defined by the DOS environmental name pointed to by *ename*. If the file is found, its full path is put into the string pointed to by *fpath*.

Example

This program searches for the specified file using the specified path. If it finds the file, it displays the full path.

```
#include <stdlib.h>
#include <stdio.h>

main(int argc, char *argv[])
{
  char fpath[64];

  if(argc!=3) {
    printf("Usage: FINDFILE <fname> <ename>\n");
    return 1;
  }

  _searchenv(argv[1], argv[2], fpath);

  /* fpath will contain path if file is found */
  if(*fpath) printf("Path: %s", fpath);

  return 0;
}
```

Related Function

searchpath( )

char *setlocale(int type, const char *locale)

Description

The prototype for **setlocale( )** is in **locale.h**. This function allows certain parameters that are sensitive to the geopolitical location of a program's execution to be queried or set. For example, in Europe, the comma is used in place of the decimal point.

If *locale* is null, then **setlocale( )** returns a pointer to the current localization string. Otherwise, **setlocale( )** attempts to use the specified localization string to set the locale parameters as specified by *type*.

At the time of the call, *type* must be one of the following macros:

```
LC_ALL
LC_COLLATE
LC_CTYPE
LC_MONETARY
LC_NUMERIC
LC_TIME
```

LC_ALL refers to all localization categories. **LC_COLLATE** affects the operation of the **strcoll( )** function. **LC_CTYPE** alters the way the character functions work. **LC_MONETARY** determines the monetary format. **LC_NUMERIC** changes the decimal-point character for formatted input/output functions. Finally, **LC_TIME** determines the behavior of the **strftime( )** function.

The ANSI C standard defines two possible strings for *locale*. The first is **"C"**, which specifies a minimal environment for C compilation. The second is **""**, the null string, which specifies the implementation-defined default environment, which for Turbo/Borland C/C++ is the same as the **"C"** locale. Turbo/Borland C/C++ defines no other locales.

The **setlocale( )** function returns a pointer to a string associated with the *type* parameter. It returns null if an error occurs.

Since no other locales are available, it is currently pointless to call this function and no example is presented.

Related Functions

localeconv( ), **time( )**, **strcoll( )**, **strftime( )**

void (*set_new_handler(void (* newhand)( )))( )

Description

The prototype for **set_new_handler( )** is in **new.h**. This function is not defined by the ANSI C standard.

The **set_new_handler( )** function allows you to determine which function is called when a **new** memory allocation request fails. The address of this function is passed in *newhand*. To deactivate your function and return to the default processing of allocation request failures, call **set_new_handler( )** with *newhand* being **NULL**.

In general, you should not use this function. Its use is highly specialized and no example is given.

Related Functions

getvect( ), setvect( )

void (*signal (int signal, void (*sigfunc) (int func)))(int)

Description

The prototype for **signal( )** is in **signal.h**.

The **signal( )** function tells Turbo/Borland C/C++ to execute the function pointed to by *sigfunc* if *signal* is received.

The value for *func* must be one of the following macros, defined in **signal.h**, or the address of a function you created:

Pointer	Meaning
SIG_DFL	Use default signal handling
SIG_IGN	Ignore the signal

If you create your own function, it is executed each time the specified signal is received.

The following signals are defined in **signal.h**. These are the values that can be given to *signal*.

Macro	Meaning
SIGABRT	Termination error
SIGFPE	Floating-point error
SIGILL	Bad instruction
SIGINT	Control break
SIGSEGV	Illegal memory access
SIGTERM	Terminate program

If **signal( )** is activated by a **SIGFPE**, **SIGILL**, or **SIGSEGV**, *func* is called with a second integer parameter that is a pointer to the interrupt handler's stack. The states of the registers prior to the interrupt are stored on the stack in this order:

BP   Top of stack
DI
SI
DS
ES
DX
CX
BX
AX
IP
CS
Flags

To access a register, cast the integer into an integer pointer and use appropriate pointer arithmetic to access the desired register.

On success, **signal( )** returns the address of the previously defined function for the specified signal. On error, **SIG_ERR** is returned, and **errno** is set to **EINVAL**.

Example

This line causes the function **myint( )** to be called if CTRL-C is pressed:

```
signal(SIGINT, myint);
```

Related Function

raise( ) |

void sound(unsigned freq)

Description

The prototype for **sound( )** is in **dos.h**. This function is not defined by the ANSI C standard.

The **sound( )** function causes a tone of *freq* frequency to be sounded on the computer's speaker. The frequency is specified in hertz. The tone continues to be produced until a call to **nosound( )** is made.

Example

This program beeps at 440Hz for one second:

```
#include <dos.h>

main(void)
{
  sound(440);
  sleep(1);
  nosound();

  return 0;
}
```

Related Function

nosound( )

void srand(unsigned seed)

Description

The prototype for **srand( )** is in **stdlib.h**.

The **srand( )** function is used to set a starting point for the sequence generated by **rand( )**. (The **rand( )** function returns pseudorandom numbers.)

The **srand( )** function allows multiple program runs using different sequences of pseudorandom numbers.

Example

This program uses the system time to initialize the **rand( )** function randomly by using **srand( )**.

```
#include <stdio.h>
#include <stdlib.h>
#include <time.h>

/* Seed rand with the system time
   and display the first 100 numbers.
*/
main(void)
{
  int i,stime;
  long  ltime;

  /* get the current calendar time */
```

```
    ltime = time(NULL);
    stime = (unsigned int) ltime/2;
    srand(stime);
    for(i=0; i<10; i++) printf("%d ", rand());
    return 0;
}
```

Related Function

rand( )

unsigned int _status87(void)

Description

The prototype for **_status87( )** is in **float.h**. This function is not defined by the ANSI C standard.

The **_status87( )** function returns the value of the floating-point status word. You must have an 80x87 math coprocessor installed in the computer before using this function.

Related Functions

_clear87( ), **_fpreset( )**

double strtod(const char *start, char **end)
long double _strtold(const char *start, char **end)

Description

The **strtod( )** function converts the string representation of a number stored in the string pointed to by *start* into a **double** and returns the result. Its prototype is in **stdlib.h**

The **strtod( )** function works as follows: First, any leading white space in the string pointed to by *start* is stripped. Next, each character that makes up the number is read. Any character that cannot be part of a floating-point number stops the process. This includes white space, punctuation other than periods, and characters other than "E" or "e". Finally, *end* is set to point to the remainder, if any, of the original string. This means that if **strtod( )** is called with **100.00 Pliers**, the value 100.00 is returned and *end* points to the space that precedes "Pliers".

If a conversion error occurs, **strtod( )** returns either **HUGE_VAL** for overflow, or **–HUGE_VAL** for underflow. If no conversion could take place, 0 is returned.

_strtold( ) is the **long double** version of this function.

Example

This program reads floating-point numbers from a character array:

```
#include <stdio.h>
#include <stdlib.h>
#include <ctype.h>

main(void)
{
  char *end, *start="100.00 pliers 200.00 hammers";

  end = start;
  while(*start) {
    printf("%f, ",strtod(start, &end));
    printf("remainder: %s\n", end);
    start = end;
    /* move past the non-digits */
    while(!isdigit(*start) && *start) start++;
  }
  return 0;
}
```

The output is

```
100.00000, remainder: pliers 200.00 hammers
200.00000, remainder: hammers
```

Related Function

atof( )

long strtol(const char *start, char **end, int radix)
unsigned long strtoul(const char *start, char **end, int radix)

Description

The prototypes for **strtol( )** and **strtoul( )** are in **stdlib.h**.

The **strtol( )** function converts the string representation of a number stored in the string pointed to by *start* into a **long int** and returns the result. The **strtoul( )** function performs the same conversion, but the result is an **unsigned long**. The base of the number is determined by *radix*. If *radix* is 0, the base is determined by rules that govern constant specification. If *radix* is other than 0, it must be in the range 2 through 36.

The **strtol( )** and **strtoul( )** functions work as follows: First, any leading white space in the string pointed to by *start* is stripped. Next, each character that makes up the number is read. Any character that cannot be part of a **long** integer number stops this process. This includes white space, punctuation, and characters. Finally, *end* is set to point to the remainder, if any, of the original string. This means that if **strtol( )** is called with **100 Pliers**, the value 100L is returned and *end* points to the space that precedes "Pliers".

If a conversion error occurs, the return value is **HUGE_VAL** for overflow, or **–HUGE_VAL** for underflow. If no conversion could take place, 0 is returned.

Example

This function reads base 10 numbers from standard input and returns their **long** equivalents:

```
#include <stdio.h>
#include <stdlib.h>

long int read_long()
{
  char start[80], *end;

  printf("enter a number: ");
  gets(start);
  return strtol(start, &end, 10);
}
```

Related Function

atol( )

void swab(char *source, char *dest, int num)

Description

The prototype for **swab( )** is in **stdlib.h**. This function is not defined by the ANSI C standard.

The **swab( )** function copies *num* bytes from the string pointed to by *source* into the string pointed to by *dest*, switching the position of each even/odd pair of bytes as it goes.

Example

This fragment prints "iH":

```
char dest[3];

swab("Hi", dest, 2);
printf(dest);
```

int system(const char *str)

Description

The prototype for **system( )** is in **stdlib.h**.

The **system( )** function passes the string pointed to by *str* as a command to DOS and returns the exit status of the command.

Example

This program displays the contents of the current working directory:

```
#include <stdlib.h>

main(void)
{
  system("dir");
  return 0;
}
```

Related Functions

spawn( ), exec( )

int toascii(int ch)

Description

The prototype for **toascii( )** is in **ctype.h**. This function is not defined by the ANSI C standard.

The **toascii( )** function clears the high order bit in the character in *ch* and returns the result.

Example

This fragment clears the high order bit of the character input from the keyboard.

```
int ch;

ch = getche():

ch = toascii(ch);
```

Related Functions

tolower( ), toupper( )

unsigned umask(unsigned access)

Description

The prototype for **umask( )** is in **io.h**. This function is not defined by the ANSI C standard.

The **umask( )** function modifies the access attribute of a file opened by either **open( )** or **creat( )**. The attribute specified in *access* is removed from the access attribute. The *access* parameter must be one of these two values (which may also be ORed together):

Macro	Meaning
S_IWRITE	file is writable
S_IREAD	file is readable

The **umask( )** function returns the previous access permission mask.

Example

This statement causes subsequent files to be opened as write-only.

```
umask(S_IREAD);
```

Related Functions

creat(), open(), fopen()

int utime(char *fname, struct utimbuf *t)

Description

The prototype for **utime( )** is in **utime.h**. This function is not defined by the ANSI C standard.

The **utime( )** function changes the creation (or last modification) time of the file whose name is pointed to by *fname*. The new time is specified by the structure pointed to by *t*. The **utimbuf** structure is defined like this:

```
struct utimbuf {
        time_t actime;
        time_t modtime;
    }
```

Only **modtime** is actually used—**actime** is not relevant to DOS. If *t* is null, then the file's creation time is set to the current system time.

The **utime( )** function returns 0 if successful. If an error occurs, –1 is returned and **errno** is set to one of these values:

EACCES	Access denied
EMFILE	Too many files are open
ENOENT	Non-existent file

Example

This program sets the specified file's creation time to the current time of the system. (This is a simple version of the common TOUCH utility program.)

```
#include <utime.h>
#include <stdio.h>

main(int argc, char *argv[])
{
  if(argc!=2) {
    printf("Usage: SETTIME <fname>\n");
    return 1;
  }

  /* set to current system time */
  utime(argv[1], NULL);

  return 0;
}
```

Related Functions

time( ), **asctime( )**, **gmtime( )**

void va_start(va_list argptr, last_parm)
void va_end(va_list argptr)
type va_arg(va_list argptr, type)

Description

The prototypes for these macros are in **stdarg.h**.

The **va_arg( )**, **va_start( )**, and **va_end( )** macros work together to allow a variable number of arguments to be passed to a function. The most common example of a function that takes a variable number of arguments is **printf( )**. The type **va_list** is defined by **stdarg.h**.

The general procedure for creating a function that can take a variable number of arguments is as follows: The function must have at least one known parameter, but can have more, prior to the variable parameter list. The rightmost known parameter is called the *last_parm*. The name of the *last_parm* is used as the second parameter in a call to **va_start( )**. Before any of the variable-length parameters can be accessed, the argument pointer *argptr* must be initialized through a call to **va_start( )**. After that, parameters are returned via calls to **va_arg( )** with *type* being the type of the next parameter. Finally, once all the parameters have been read and prior to returning from the function, a call to **va_end( )** must be made to ensure that the stack is properly restored. If **va_end( )** is not called, a program crash is very likely.

Example

This program uses **sum_series( )** to return the sum of a series of numbers. The first argument contains a count of the number of arguments to follow. In this example, the first five elements of the series are

$$\frac{1}{2} + \frac{1}{4} + \frac{1}{8} + \frac{1}{16} \ldots + \frac{1}{2^n}$$

The output displayed is "0.968750".

```
/* Variable length argument example - sum a series.*/

#include <stdio.h>
#include <stdarg.h>
```

```
double sum_series(int, ...);

main(void)
{
  double d;

  d = sum_series(5, 0.5, 0.25, 0.125, 0.0625, 0.03125);

  printf("sum of series is %f\n",d);

  return 0;

}

double sum_series(int num, ...)
{
  double sum = 0.0, t;
  va_list argptr;

  /* initialize argptr */
  va_start(argptr,num);
  /* sum the series */
  for(; num; num--) {
   t = va_arg(argptr,double);
   sum += t;
  }

  /* do orderly shutdown */
  va_end(argptr);
  return sum;
}
```

Related Function

vprintf( )

size_t wcstombs(char *out, const wchar_t *in, size_t size)

Description

The prototype for **wcstombs( )** is in **stdlib.h**.

The **wcstombs( )** converts the string pointed to by *in* into its multibyte equivalent and puts the result in the string pointed to by *out*. Only the first *size* bytes of *in* are converted. Conversion stops before that if the null terminator is encountered.

If successful, **wcstombs( )** returns the number of bytes converted. On failure, –1 is returned.

Related Functions

wctomb( ), **mbstowcs( )**

int wctomb(char *out, wchar_t in)

Description

The prototype for **wctomb( )** is in **stdlib.h**.

The **wctomb( )** converts the character in *in* into its multibyte equivalent and puts the result in the string pointed to by *out*.

If successful, **wctomb( )** returns the number of bytes contained in the multibyte character. On failure, –1 is returned.

If *out* is NULL, then **wctomb( )** returns non-0 if the multibyte character is dependent on the shift-state and 0 if it is not.

Related Functions

wcstombs( ), **mbtowc( )**

Part *IV*

Turbo/Borland C++

Part Four of this book examines Turbo/Borland C++. C++ is essentially a superset of C, so everything you already know about C is applicable to C++. Many of the concepts embodied in C++ will be new, but don't worry—you are starting from a firm base. (Knowledge of the C language is prerequisite to learning C++. If you don't already know C, you must take some time to learn it.)

Chapter *25*

An Overview of C++

Put simply, C++ is an *object-oriented* programming language. The object-oriented features of C++ are interrelated, so it is important to have a general understanding of these features before attempting to learn the details. The purpose of this chapter is to provide an overview of the key concepts embodied in Turbo/Borland C++. The rest of Part Four closely examines specific C++ features.

The first part of this chapter discusses the origin of C++ and describes object-oriented programming. The rest of the chapter introduces the principal C++ concepts.

The Origins of C++

C++ is an expanded version of C. C is flexible yet powerful, and it has been used to create some of the most important software products of the last 15 years. However, when a project exceeds a certain size, C reaches its limits. Depending on the project, a program of 25,000 to 100,000 lines becomes hard to manage because it is difficult to grasp as a totality. In 1980, while working at Bell Laboratories at Murray Hill, New Jersey, Bjarne Stroustrup addressed this problem by adding several extensions to the C language. Initially called "C with Classes," the name was changed to C++ in 1983.

Most additions made to C by Stroustrup support object-oriented programming, sometimes referred to as OOP. (A brief explanation of object-oriented programming follows in the next section.) Stroustrup states that some of C++'s object-oriented features were inspired by another object-oriented language, Simula67. Therefore, C++ represents the blending of two powerful programming methods.

C++ has had two major revisions since it was invented—once in 1985 and again in 1989. Version 2.1 is the version of C++ that Turbo/Borland C++ implements.

Borland began development of C++ in 1988, and released the product in May of 1990.

When he invented C++, Stroustrup knew that it was important to maintain the original spirit of C—including its efficiency, flexibility, and the philosophy that the programmer, not the language, is in charge—while at the same time adding support for object-oriented programming. As you will see, this goal was accomplished. C++ provides the programmer with the freedom and control of C coupled with the power of objects. The object-oriented features in C++, to use Stroustrup's words, "allow programs to be structured for clarity, extensibility, and ease of maintenance without loss of efficiency."

Although C++ was initially designed to aid in the management of very large programs, it is in no way limited to this use. In fact, the object-oriented attributes of C++ can be effectively applied to virtually any programming task. It is not uncommon to see C++ used for projects such as editors, databases, personal file systems, and communication programs. Also, because C++ shares C's efficiency, high-performance systems software can be constructed using C++.

What is Object-Oriented Programming?

Object-oriented programming is a new way of approaching the job of programming. Approaches to programming have changed dramatically since the invention of the computer in order to accommodate the increasing complexity of programs. For example, when computers were first invented, programming was done by toggling in the binary machine instructions using the front panel. As long as programs were just a few hundred instructions long, this approach worked. As programs grew, assembly language was invented so that a programmer could deal with larger, increasingly complex programs using symbolic representations of the machine instructions.

Eventually high-level languages were introduced that gave the programmer more tools with which to handle complexity. The first widely used language was FORTRAN. While FORTRAN was a very impressive first step, it is hardly a language that encourages clear and easily understood programs.

The 1960s gave birth to *structured* programming—the method encouraged by languages such as C and Pascal. For the first time, with structured languages it was possible to write moderately complex programs fairly easily. However, even using structured programming methods, once a project reaches a certain size, its complexity becomes too difficult for a programmer to manage.

At each milestone in the development of programming, methods were created to allow the programmer to deal with increasingly greater complexity. Each step of the way, the new approach took the best elements of the previous methods and moved forward. Today, many projects are near or at the point where the structured approach no longer works. To solve this problem, object-oriented programming was invented.

Object-oriented programming takes the best ideas of structured programming and combines them with powerful, new concepts that encourage you to look at the task of programming in a new light. Object-oriented programming allows you to easily decompose a problem into subgroups of related parts. Then, you can translate these subgroups into self-contained units called objects.

All object-oriented programming languages have three things in common: objects, polymorphism, and inheritance. Let's look at these concepts now.

Objects

The single most important feature of an object-oriented language is the object. Put simply, an *object* is a logical entity containing data and code that manipulates that data. Within an object, some of the code or data may be private to the object and inaccessible by anything outside the object. In this way, an object provides a significant level of protection against accidental modification or incorrect use. The linkage of code and data in this way is often referred to as *encapsulation*.

For all intents and purposes, an object is a variable of a user-defined type. It may seem strange at first to think of an object, which links both code and data, as a variable. However, in object-oriented programming this is precisely the case. When you define an object you are implicitly creating a new data type.

Polymorphism

Object-oriented programming languages support *polymorphism*, which allows one name to be used for several related but slightly different purposes. The purpose of polymorphism is to let one name be used to specify a general class of action. Depending upon what type of data it is dealing with, a specific instance of the general case is executed. For example, you might have a program that defines three different types of stacks: one for integer values, one for floating-point values, and one for **longs**. If you create three sets of functions called **push( )** and **pop( )**, the compiler will select the correct routine depending on the type of data with which it is called.

The first object-oriented programming languages were interpreters, so polymorphism was supported at run-time. However, because C++ is a compiled language, polymorphism is supported at both run-time and compile time.

Inheritance

Inheritance is the process by which one object can acquire the properties of another object. This is important because it supports the concept of classification. If you think about it, most knowledge is made manageable by hierarchical classifications. For example, a Red Delicious apple is part of the *apple* class, which in turn is part of the *fruit* class, which is under the larger *food* class. Without the use of classifications, each object would have to define all of its characteristics explicitly. Using classifications, an object need only define those qualities that make it unique within its class. It is the inheritance mechanism that makes it possible for one object to be a specific instance of a more general case.

Some C++ Fundamentals

Since C++ is a superset of C, most C programs are C++ programs as well. (There are a few minor differences between C and C++ that will prevent a small number of C programs from being compiled by a C++ compiler. These differences will be discussed in Chapter 30.) You can write C++ programs that look just like C programs, but you won't be taking full advantage of C++'s capabilities. Further, although C++ allows you to write C-like programs, most C++ programmers use a style and certain features that are unique to C++. Since it is important to use C++ to its full potential, this section introduces a few of these features before moving on to the "meat" of C++.

Let's begin with an example. Examine this C++ program:

```c++
#include <iostream.h>
#include <stdio.h>

main(void)
{
  int i;
  char str[80];

  cout << "I like Turbo C++.\n";  // this is a single-line comment
  /* you can still use C-style comments, too */

  printf("You can use printf(), but most C++ programs don't.\n");

  // input a number using >>
  cout << "enter a number: ";
  cin >> i;

  // now, output a number using <<
  cout << "your number is " << i << "\n";

  // read a string
  cout << "enter a string: ";
  cin >> str;
  // print it
  cout << str;
```

```
  return 0;
}
```

As you can see, this program looks different from the average C program. The header file, **iostream.h**, is defined by C++ and is used to support C++ I/O operations. The only reason **stdio.h** is included is because of the **printf( )** statement. **stdio.h** is not needed if your C++ program uses only I/O operations specific to C++.

The following line introduces some new C++ features:

```
cout << "I like Turbo C++.\n";  // this is a single line comment
```

The statement

```
cout << "I like Turbo C++.\n";
```

displays "I like Turbo C++." on the screen followed by a carriage return, linefeed combination. In C++, the **<<** has an expanded role. It is still the left-shift operator, but when it is used as shown in this example, it is also an output operator. The word **cout** is an identifier that is linked to the screen. Like C, C++ supports I/O redirection, but for the sake of discussion, we can assume that **cout** refers to the screen. You can use **cout** and the **<<** to output any of the built-in data types plus strings of characters.

It is important to note that you can still use **printf( )** (as the program illustrates) or any other of C's I/O functions, but many programmers feel that using **cout <<** is more in the spirit of C++. More generally, a Turbo/Borland C++ program can use any library function supported by Turbo/Borland C. These functions are described in Part Three of this book. However, in cases where C++ provides an alternate approach, that alternate is generally used instead of a C-like library function (although there is no rule that enforces this).

In the previous example, a C++ comment follows the output expression. In C++, comments are defined two ways. A C-like comment works the same in C++ as in C. However, in C++ you can also define a *single-line comment* using //. When you start a comment using //, whatever follows is ignored by the compiler until the end of the line is reached. In general, use C-like comments when creating multiline comments and C++, single-line comments when only a single-line comment is needed.

Next, the program prompts the user for a number. The number is read from the keyboard using this statement:

```
cin >> i;
```

In C++, the **>>** operator retains its right-shift meaning, but when used as shown, it causes **i** to be given a value read from the keyboard. The identifier **cin** refers to the keyboard. In general you can use **cin >>** to load a variable of any of the basic data types or a string.

Although not illustrated by the program, you are free to use any of C's input functions, such as **scanf( )**, instead of using **cin >>**. However, as with **cout**, many programmers feel that **cin >>** is more in the spirit of C++.

Another interesting line in the program is shown here:

```
cout << "your number is " << i << "\n";
```

This code displays the following phrase (assuming **i** has the value 100):

```
your number is 100
```

followed by a carriage return and linefeed. In general, you can run together as many **<<** output operations as you want.

The rest of the program demonstrates how you can read and write a string using **cin >>** and **cout <<**.

Compiling a C++ Program

Turbo/Borland C++ can compile both C and C++ programs. In general, if a program ends in .CPP it is compiled as a C++ program. If it ends in any other extension, it is compiled as a C program. Therefore, the simplest way to cause Turbo/Borland C++ to compile your C++ program as a C++ program is to give it the .CPP extension.

If you don't want to give your C++ program the .CPP extension, you must either specify the –P option when using the command line or you must change the default settings of the integrated development environment. To do this, first select the **Options** menu, then the **Compiler** option, followed by the **C++** option. You will then be able to set an option that causes the integrated environment to compile all programs as C++ programs.

Introducing C++ Classes

The **class** is at the root of C++. Before you can create an object in C++, you must first define its general form using the keyword **class**. A **class** is similar syntactically to a structure. As an example, this **class** defines a type called **queue**, which is used to create a queue object:

```
// this creates the class queue
class queue {
  int q[100];
```

```
      int sloc, rloc;
public:
   void init(void);
   void qput(int i);
   int qget(void);
};
```

A **class** can contain private as well as public parts. By default, all items defined in the **class** are private. For example, the variables **q, sloc,** and **rloc** are private, meaning they cannot be accessed by any function that is not a member of the **class**. This is how encapsulation is achieved—access to certain items of data may be tightly controlled by keeping them private. Although not shown in this example, you can also define private functions, which can only be called by other members of the **class**.

To make parts of a **class** public (accessible to other parts of your program) you must declare them after the **public** keyword. All variables or functions defined after **public** are accessible by all other functions in the program. Generally, the rest of your program accesses an object through its **public** functions. Although you can have **public** variables, you should try to limit or eliminate their use. Instead, you should make all data private and control access to it through **public** functions. This will help preserve encapsulation. One other point: Notice that the **public** keyword is followed by a colon.

The functions **init( )**, **qput( )**, and **qget( )** are called *member functions* because they are part of the **class queue**. Only member functions have access to the private parts of the **class** in which they are declared.

Once you have defined a **class**, you can create an object of that type using the **class** name. In essence, the **class**'s name becomes a new data type specifier. For example, this code creates an object called **intqueue** of type **queue**:

```
queue intqueue;
```

You can also create objects when defining a **class** by putting the variable names after the closing curly brace, in exactly the same way as you do with a structure.

The general form of a **class** declaration is

```
class class-name{
     private data and functions
public:
     public data and functions
} object name list;
```

Of course, the *object name list* may be empty.

Inside the declaration of **queue**, prototypes to the member functions were used. It is important to understand that in C++, when you need to tell the compiler about a function, you must use its full prototype form. C++ does not support the old, traditional function declaration methods. (Actually, in C++, all functions must be prototyped. Prototypes are not optional.)

When it comes time to actually code a function that is a member of a **class**, you must tell the compiler which **class** the function belongs to. For example, here is one way to code the **qput( )** function:

```
void queue::qput(int i)
{
  if(sloc==100) {
    cout << "queue is full";
    return;
  }
  sloc++;
  q[sloc] = i;
}
```

The **::** is called the *scope resolution operator.* Essentially, it tells the compiler that this version of **qput( )** belongs to the **queue class**. Or, put differently, that this **qput( )** is in **queue**'s scope. In C++, several different **class**es can use the same function names. The compiler knows which function belongs to which class because of the scope resolution operator and the **class** name.

To call a member function from a part of your program that is not part of the **class** you must use an object's name and the dot operator. For example, this fragment calls **init( )** for object **a**:

```
queue a, b;

a.init();
```

It is very important to understand that **a** and **b** are two separate objects. This means that initializing **a** does not cause **b** to be initialized. The only relationship **a** has with **b** is that they are objects of the same type. Further, **a**'s copies of **sloc**, **rloc**, and **a** are completely separate from **b**'s.

Only when a member function is called by code that does not belong to the **class** must the object name and the dot operator be used. Otherwise, one member function can call another member function directly, without using the dot operator.

The program shown here demonstrates all the pieces of **queue class**.

```
#include <iostream.h>

// this creates the class queue
class queue {
  int q[100];
  int sloc, rloc;
```

```
public:
  void init(void);
  void qput(int i);
  int qget(void);
};

void queue::init(void)
{
  rloc = sloc = 0;
}

void queue::qput(int i)
{
  if(sloc==100) {
    cout << "queue is full";
    return;
  }
  sloc++;
  q[sloc] = i;
}

int queue::qget(void)
{
  if(rloc == sloc) {
    cout << "queue underflow";
    return 0;
  }
  rloc++;
  return q[rloc];
}

main(void)
{
  queue a, b;  // create two queue objects

  a.init();
  b.init();

  a.qput(10);
  b.qput(19);

  a.qput(20);
  b.qput(1);

  cout << a.qget() << " ";
```

```
  cout << a.qget() << " ";
  cout << b.qget() << " ";
  cout << b.qget() << "\n";

  return 0;
}
```

Remember that the private parts of an object are accessible only by functions that are members of that object. For example, the statement

```
a.rloc = 0;
```

could not be in the **main( )** function of the previous program because **rloc** is private.

By convention, in most C programs the **main( )** *function is the first function in the program. However, in the* **queue** *program the member functions of* **queue** *are defined before the* **main( )** *function. While there is no rule that dictates this (they could be defined anywhere in the program), this is the most common approach used when writing C++ code. (In fact, the* **class**es *and member functions associated with them are usually contained in a header file in real life.)*

Function Overloading

One way that C++ achieves polymorphism is through the use of *function overloading*. In C++, two or more functions can share the same name as long as their parameter declarations are different. In this situation, the functions that share the same name are said to be *overloaded*. For example, consider this program:

```
#include <iostream.h>

// sqr_it is overloaded three ways
int sqr_it(int i);
double sqr_it(double d);
long sqr_it(long l);

main(void)
{
  cout << sqr_it(10) << "\n";

  cout << sqr_it(11.0) << "\n";

  cout << sqr_it(9L) << "\n";
```

```
    return 0;
}

int sqr_it(int i)
{
  cout << "Inside the sqr_it() function that uses ";
  cout << "an integer argument.\n";

  return i*i;
}

double sqr_it(double d)
{
  cout << "Inside the sqr_it() function that uses ";
  cout << "a double argument.\n";

  return d*d;
}

long sqr_it(long l)
{
  cout << "Inside the sqr_it() function that uses ";
  cout << "a long argument.\n";

  return l*l;
}
```

This program creates three similar but different functions called **sqr_it( )**, each of which returns the square of its argument. As the program illustrates, the compiler knows which function to use in each case because of the type of the argument. The value of overloaded functions is that they allow related sets of functions to be accessed using a common name. In a sense, function overloading lets you create a generic name for an operation; the compiler resolves which function is actually needed to perform the operation.

Function overloading is important because it can help manage complexity. To understand how, consider this example. Turbo/Borland C++ contains the functions **itoa( )**, **ltoa( )**, and **utoa( )** in its standard library. Collectively, these functions convert different types of numbers into their string equivalents. Even though these functions perform almost identical actions, in C three different names must be used to represent these tasks, which makes the situation more complex than it actually is. Even though the underlying concept of each function is the same, the programmer has three things to remember. However, in C++ it is possible to use the same name, such as **numtoa( )**, for all three functions. Thus, the name **numtoa( )** represents the *general action* that is being performed. It is left to the compiler to choose the *specific* version for a particular circumstance; the programmer need only remember the general action being performed. Therefore, by applying polymorphism, three things to remember are reduced to one. If you expand the concept, you can see how polymorphism can help you manage very complex programs.

A more practical example of function overloading is illustrated by the following program. As you know, C (and C++) do not contain any library functions that prompt the user for input and then wait for a response. However, this program creates three functions called **prompt( )** that perform this task for data of types **int**, **double**, and **long**:

```cpp
#include <iostream.h>

void prompt(char *str, int *i);
void prompt(char *str, double *d);
void prompt(char *str, long *l);

main(void)
{
  int i;
  double d;
  long l;

  prompt("Enter an integer: ", &i);
  prompt("Enter a double: ", &d);
  prompt("Enter a long: ", &l);

  cout << i << " " << d << " " << l;

  return 0;
}

void prompt(char *str, int *i)
{
  cout << str;
  cin >> *i;
}

void prompt(char *str, double *d)
{
  cout << str;
  cin >> *d;
}

void prompt(char *str, long *l)
```

```
{
  cout << str;
  cin >> *l;
}
```

You can use the same name to overload unrelated functions, but you should not. For example, you could use the name **sqr_it( )** *to create functions that return the* square *of an* **int** *and the* square root *of a* **double**. *However, these two operations are fundamentally different and applying function overloading in this manner defeats its purpose. In practice, you should only overload closely related operations.*

Operator Overloading

Another way that polymorphism is achieved in C++ is through *operator overloading*. For example, in C++ you can use the **<<** and **>>** operators to perform console I/O operations. This is possible because in the **iostream.h** header file, these operators are overloaded. When an operator is overloaded it takes on an additional meaning relative to a certain **class**. However, it still retains all of its old meanings.

In general, you can overload C++'s operators by defining what they mean relative to a specific **class**. For example, think back to the **queue class** developed earlier in this chapter. It is possible to overload the + operator relative to objects of type **queue** so that it appends the contents of one stack to another. However, the + still retains its original meaning relative to other types of data. You will learn how to overload operators in Chapter 27.

Inheritance

Inheritance is one of the major traits of an object-oriented programming language. In C++, inheritance is supported by allowing one **class** to incorporate another **class** into its declaration. For example, here is a **class**, called **road_vehicle**, that very broadly defines vehicles that travel on the road. It stores the number of wheels a vehicle has and the number of passengers it can carry.

```
class road_vehicle {
  int wheels;
  int passengers;
public:
  void set_wheels(int num);
  int get_wheels(void);
  void set_pass(int num);
```

```
  int get_pass(void);
};
```

We can now use this broad definition of a road vehicle to define specific objects. For example, this declares a **class** called **truck** using **road_vehicle**.

```
class truck : public road_vehicle {
  int cargo;
public:
  void set_cargo(int size);
  int get_cargo(void);
  void show(void);
};
```

Notice how **road_vehicle** is inherited. The general form for inheritance is:

> class *new-class-name* : *access inherited-class* {
>   *// body of new class*
> }

Here, *access* is optional, but if present it must be either **public** or **private**. You will learn more about these options in Chapter 28. For now, all inherited **class**es will use **public**, which means that all the **public** elements of the ancestor are also **public** in the **class** that inherits it. Therefore, in the example, members of the **class truck** have access to the member functions of **road_vehicle** just as if they had been declared inside **truck**. However, the member functions of **truck** *do not* have access to the private parts of **road_vehicle**.

The following program illustrates inheritance by creating two subclasses of **road_vehicle—truck** and **automobile**:

```
#include <iostream.h>

class road_vehicle {
  int wheels;
  int passengers;
public:
  void set_wheels(int num);
  int get_wheels(void);
  void set_pass(int num);
  int get_pass(void);
};

class truck : public road_vehicle {
  int cargo;
```

```
public:
  void set_cargo(int size);
  int get_cargo(void);
  void show(void);
};

enum type {car, van, wagon};

class automobile : public road_vehicle {
  enum type car_type;
public:
  void set_type(enum type t);
  enum type get_type(void);
  void show(void);
};

void road_vehicle::set_wheels(int num)
{
  wheels = num;
}

int road_vehicle::get_wheels(void)
{
  return wheels;
}

void road_vehicle::set_pass(int num)
{
  passengers = num;
}

int road_vehicle::get_pass(void)
{
  return passengers;
}

void truck::set_cargo(int num)
{
  cargo = num;
}

int truck::get_cargo(void)
{
  return cargo;
}
```

```
void truck::show(void)
{
  cout << "wheels: " << get_wheels() << "\n";
  cout << "passengers: " << get_pass() << "\n";
  cout << "cargo capacity in cubic feet: " << cargo << "\n";
}

void automobile::set_type(enum type t)
{
  car_type = t;
}

enum type automobile::get_type(void)
{
  return car_type;
}

void automobile::show(void)
{
  cout << "wheels: " << get_wheels() << "\n";
  cout << "passengers: " << get_pass() << "\n";
  cout << "type: ";
  switch(get_type()) {
    case van: cout << "van\n";
      break;
    case car: cout << "car\n";
      break;
    case wagon: cout << "wagon\n";
  }
}

main(void)
{
  truck t1, t2;
  automobile c;

  t1.set_wheels(18);
  t1.set_pass(2);
  t1.set_cargo(3200);

  t2.set_wheels(6);
  t2.set_pass(3);
  t2.set_cargo(1200);
```

```
   t1.show();
   t2.show();

   c.set_wheels(4);
   c.set_pass(6);
   c.set_type(van);
   c.show();

   return 0;
}
```

As this program illustrates, the major advantage of inheritance is that you can create a base classification that can be incorporated into more specific classes. In this way, each object can represent its own classification precisely.

Notice that both **truck** and **automobile** include member functions called **show( )**, which display information about each object. This is another aspect of polymorphism. Since each **show( )** is linked with its own class, the compiler can easily tell which one to call in any circumstance.

Constructors and Destructors

It is very common for some part of an object to require initialization before it can be used. For example, think back to the **queue class** developed earlier in this chapter. Before **queue** could be used, the variables **rloc** and **sloc** had to be set to 0 using the function **init( )**. Because the requirement for initialization is so common, C++ allows objects to initialize themselves when they are created. This automatic initialization is performed through the use of a constructor function.

A *constructor function* is a special function that is a member of the **class** and has the same name as that **class**. For example, here is how the **queue class** looks when converted to use a constructor function for initialization:

```
// this creates the class queue
class queue {
  int q[100];
  int sloc, rloc;
public:
  queue(void);  // constructor
  void qput(int i);
  int qget(void);
};
```

Notice that the constructor **queue( )** has no return type specified. In C++, constructor functions cannot return values.

The **queue( )** function is coded like this:

```
// This is the constructor function.
queue::queue(void)
{
  sloc = rloc = 0;
  cout << "queue initialized\n";
}
```

Keep in mind that the message "queue initialized" is output as a way to illustrate the constructor. In actual practice, most constructor functions will not output or input anything to the console.

An object's constructor is called each time the object is created (when the object's declaration is executed). Also, for local objects, the constructor is called each time the object declaration is encountered.

The complement of the constructor is the *destructor*. In many circumstances, an object needs to perform some action or actions when it is destroyed. Local objects are created when their block is entered and destroyed when the block is left. Global objects are destroyed when the program terminates. There are many reasons why a destructor function may be needed. For example, an object may need to deallocate memory that it had previously allocated. In C++, it is the destructor function that handles deactivation. The destructor has the same name as the constructor but it is preceded by a ~. The following is an example of **queue** and its constructor and destructor functions. (Keep in mind that the **queue class** does not require a destructor, so the one shown here is just for illustration.)

```
// this creates the class queue
class queue {
  int q[100];
  int sloc, rloc;
public:
  queue(void);  // constructor
  ~queue(void); // destructor
  void qput(int i);
  int qget(void);
};

// This is the constructor function.
queue::queue(void)
{
  sloc = rloc = 0;
  cout << "queue initialized\n";
```

```
}

// This is the destructor function.
queue::~queue(void)
{
  cout << "queue destroyed\n";
}
```

To see how constructors and destructors work, here is a new version of the sample program from earlier in this chapter:

```
#include <iostream.h>

// this creates the class queue
class queue {
  int q[100];
  int sloc, rloc;
public:
  queue(void);  // constructor
  ~queue(void); // destructor
  void qput(int i);
  int qget(void);
};

// This is the constructor function.
queue::queue(void)
{
  sloc = rloc = 0;
  cout << "queue initialized\n";
}

// This is the destructor function.
queue::~queue(void)
{
  cout << "queue destroyed\n";
}

void queue::qput(int i)
{
  if(sloc==100) {
    cout << "queue is full";
    return;
  }
  sloc++;
```

```
  q[sloc] = i;
}

int queue::qget(void)
{
  if(rloc == sloc) {
    cout << "queue underflow";
    return 0;
  }
  rloc++;
  return q[rloc];
}

main(void)
{
  queue a, b;   // create two queue objects

  a.qput(10);
  b.qput(19);

  a.qput(20);
  b.qput(1);

  cout << a.qget() << " ";
  cout << a.qget() << " ";
  cout << b.qget() << " ";
  cout << b.qget() << "\n";

  return 0;
}
```

This program displays the following:

```
queue initialized
queue initialized
10 20 19 1
queue destroyed
queue destroyed
```

The C++ Keywords

In addition to those keywords defined by the C language and those specific to
Turbo/Borland C, C++ contains the keywords shown in Table 25-1. Of these, **catch**

asm	private
catch	protected
class	public
delete	template
friend	this
inline	throw
new	try
operator	virtual
overload	

Table 25-1. *The C++ Keywords*

and **throw** are reserved for future use. You cannot use any of them as names for variables or functions.

Now that you have been introduced to many of Turbo/Borland C++'s major features, the remaining chapters in this section will examine them in greater detail.

Chapter *26*

A Closer Look at Classes and Objects

Classes and objects created using classes are two of C++'s most important features. This chapter examines classes, objects, and related issues in detail.

Parameterized Constructors

Often, when an object is created it is necessary, or desirable, to initialize various data elements with specific values. Using a constructor function it is possible to initialize various variables when the object is created. However, in C++, the concept of object initialization is expanded to allow the initialization of objects using values known only when the object is created. This is accomplished by passing arguments to an object's constructor function. For example, it is possible to enhance the **queue class** that ended the previous chapter to accept an argument that will act as the queue's ID number. First, **queue** is changed to look like this:

```
// this creates the class queue
class queue {
  int q[100];
  int sloc, rloc;
  int who; // holds the queue's ID number
public:
  queue(int id);   // constructor
```

```
~queue(void); // destructor
void qput(int i);
int qget(void);
};
```

The variable **who** is used to hold an ID number that identifies the queue. Its actual value is determined by what is passed to the constructor function in **id** when a variable of type **queue** is created. The **queue( )** constructor function now looks like this:

```
// This is the constructor function.
queue::queue(int id)
{
  sloc = rloc = 0;
  who = id;
  cout << "queue " << who << " initialized\n";
}
```

To pass an argument to the constructor function, you must associate the value or values being passed with an object when it is being declared. C++ supports two ways to accomplish this. The first method

```
queue a = queue(101);
```

creates a queue called **a** and passes the value 101 to it. However, the second method, sometimes called the *shorthand* method, is shorter and more to the point. In the shorthand method the argument or arguments must follow the object's name and be enclosed in parentheses. This code accomplishes the same thing as the previous declaration:

```
queue a(101);
```

Since the shorthand method is used by virtually all C++ programmers, this book uses the shorthand form exclusively. The general form of passing arguments to constructor functions is

   class-type var(*arg-list*);

Here, *arg-list* is a comma-separated list of arguments that are passed to the constructor.

The following version of the **queue** program demonstrates passing arguments to constructor functions:

```
#include <iostream.h>

// this creates the class queue
class queue {
  int q[100];
  int sloc, rloc;
  int who; // holds the queue's ID number
public:
  queue(int id);  // constructor
  ~queue(void); // destructor
  void qput(int i);
  int qget(void);
};

// This is the constructor function.
queue::queue(int id)
{
  sloc = rloc = 0;
  who = id;
  cout << "queue " << who << " initialized\n";
}

// This is the destructor function.
queue::~queue(void)
{
  cout << "queue " << who << " destroyed\n";
}

void queue::qput(int i)
{
  if(sloc==100) {
    cout << "queue is full";
    return;
  }
  sloc++;
  q[sloc] = i;
}

int queue::qget(void)
{
  if(rloc == sloc) {
    cout << "queue underflow";
```

```
      return 0;
  }
  rloc++;
  return q[rloc];
}

main(void)
{
  queue a(1), b(2);   // create two queue objects

  a.qput(10);
  b.qput(19);

  a.qput(20);
  b.qput(1);

  cout << a.qget() << " ";
  cout << a.qget() << " ";
  cout << b.qget() << " ";
  cout << b.qget() << "\n";

  return 0;
}
```

This program produces the following output:

```
queue 1 initialized
queue 2 initialized
10 20 19 1
queue 2 destroyed
queue 1 destroyed
```

As you can see by looking at **main( )**, the queue associated with **a** is given the ID number 1, and the queue associated with **b** is given the number 2.

Although the **queue** example only passes a single argument when an object is created, it is possible to pass several. For example, here, objects of type **widget** are passed two values:

```
#include <iostream.h>

class widget {
  int i;
  int j;
public:
```

```
  widget(int a, int b);
  void put_widget(void);
} ;

widget::widget(int a, int b)
{
  i = a;
  j = b;
}

void widget::put_widget(void)
{
  cout << i << " " << j << "\n";
}

main(void)
{
  widget x(10, 20), y(0, 0);

  x.put_widget();
  y.put_widget();

  return 0;
}
```

This program displays

```
10 20
0 0
```

Friend Functions

It is possible for a nonmember function of a class to have access to the private parts of that class by declaring it as a **friend** of the class. For example, here **frd( )** is declared to be a **friend** of the **class cl**:

```
class cl {
  .
  .
  .
public:
  friend void frd(void);
  .
```

```
       .
       .
       .
};
```

As you can see, the keyword **friend** precedes the entire function declaration.

One reason that **friend** functions are allowed in C++ is to accommodate situations in which, for the sake of efficiency, two classes must share the same function. To see an example, consider a program that defines two classes called **line** and **box**. The **class line** contains all necessary data and code to draw a horizontal dashed line of any specified length, beginning at a specified *x,y* coordinate using a specified color. The **box class** contains all code and data to draw a box at the specified upper left and lower right coordinates in a specified color. Both classes use the **same_color( )** function to determine whether both a line and a box are drawn in the same color. These classes are declared as shown here:

```
class line;

class box {
  int color; // color of box
  int upx, upy; // upper left corner
  int lowx, lowy; // lower right corner
public:
  friend int same_color(line l, box b);
  void set_color(int c);
  void define_box(int x1, int y1, int x2, int y2);
  void show_box(void);
} ;

class line {
  int color;
  int startx, starty;
  int len;
public:
  friend int same_color(line l, box b);
  void set_color(int c);
  void define_line(int x, int y, int l);
  void show_line();
} ;
```

The **same_color( )** function, which is a member of neither class but a **friend** of both, returns true if both the **line** object and the **box** object, which form its arguments, are drawn in the same color; it returns non-0 otherwise. The **same_color( )** function is defined as:

```
// return true if line and box have same color.
int same_color(line l, box b)
{
  if(l.color==b.color) return 1;
  return 0;
}
```

As you can see, the **same_color( )** function needs access to the private parts of both **line** and **box** to perform its task efficiently. Being a **friend** of each class grants it this access privilege. Further, notice that because **same_color( )** is not a member, no scope resolution operator or class name is used in its definition. (Remember that **public** interface functions can be created to return the colors of both **line** and **box**, and any function could have compared their colors. However, such an approach requires extra function calls, which in some cases is inefficient.)

Notice the empty declaration of **line** at the start of the **class** declarations. Since **same_color( )** in **box** references **line** before **line** is declared, **line** must be forward referenced. If this is not done, the compiler will not know what **line** is when encountered in the declaration of **box**. In C++, a forward reference to a class is simply the keyword **class** followed by the type name of the class. Usually, the only time that forward references are needed is when **friend** functions are involved.

Here is a program that demonstrates the **line** and **box** classes and illustrates how a **friend** function can access the private parts of a class:

```
#include <iostream.h>
#include <conio.h>

class line;

class box {
  int color; // color of box
  int upx, upy; // upper left corner
  int lowx, lowy; // lower right corner
 public:
  friend int same_color(line l, box b);
  void set_color(int c);
  void define_box(int x1, int y1, int x2, int y2);
  void show_box(void);
} ;

class line {
  int color;
  int startx, starty;
  int len;
```

```
public:
  friend int same_color(line l, box b);
  void set_color(int c);
  void define_line(int x, int y, int l);
  void show_line();
} ;

// Return true if line and box have same color.
int same_color(line l, box b)
{
  if(l.color==b.color) return 1;
  return 0;
}

void box::set_color(int c)
{
  color = c;
}

void line::set_color(int c)
{
  color = c;
}

void box::define_box(int x1, int y1, int x2, int y2)
{
  upx = x1;
  upy = y1;
  lowx = x2;
  lowy = y2;
}

void box::show_box(void)
{
  int i;

  textcolor(color);

  gotoxy(upx, upy);
  for(i=upx; i<=lowx; i++) cprintf("-");

  gotoxy(upx, lowy-1);
  for(i=upx; i<=lowx; i++) cprintf("-");

  gotoxy(upx, upy);
```

```
  for(i=upy; i<=lowy; i++) {
    cprintf("|");
    gotoxy(upx, i);
  }

  gotoxy(lowx, upy);
  for(i=upy; i<=lowy; i++) {
    cprintf("|");
    gotoxy(lowx, i);
  }
}

void line::define_line(int x, int y, int l)
{
  startx = x;
  starty = y;
  len = l;
}

void line::show_line(void)
{
  int i;

  textcolor(color);

  gotoxy(startx, starty);

  for(i=0; i<len; i++) cprintf("-");
}

main(void)
{
  box b;
  line l;

  b.define_box(10, 10, 15, 15);
  b.set_color(3);
  b.show_box();

  l.define_line(2, 2, 10);
  l.set_color(2);
  l.show_line();

  if(!same_color(l, b)) cout << "not the same";
  cout << "\npress a key";
```

```
getch();

// now, make line and box the same color
l.define_line(2, 2, 10);
l.set_color(3);
l.show_line();

if(same_color(l, b)) cout << "are the same color";

return 0;
}
```

Default Function Arguments

C++ allows a function to assign a default value to a parameter when no argument corresponding to that parameter is specified in a call to that function. The default value is specified in a manner syntactically similar to a variable initialization. For example, this declares **f( )** as taking one integer variable that has a default value of 1:

```
void f(int i = 1)
{
  .
  .
  .
}
```

Now, **f( )** can be called one of two ways as these examples show.

```
f(10);  // pass an explicit value
f();    // let function use default
```

The first call passes the value 10 to **i**. The second call gives **i** the default value 1.

Default arguments in C++ enable a programmer to manage greater complexity. In order to handle the widest variety of situations, a function frequently contains more parameters than are required for its most common use. When using default arguments, you need only specify arguments that are not the defaults in that particular situation.

To better understand the reason for default arguments, let's develop a practical example. One useful function, called **xyout( )**, is shown here:

```
//Output a string at specified X,Y location.
void xyout(char *str, int x = 0, int y = 0)
```

```
{
  if(!x) x = wherex();
  if(!y) y = wherey();
  gotoxy(x, y);
  cout << str;
}
```

This function displays, in text mode, the string pointed to by **str** beginning at the *x,y* location defined by **x** and **y**. However, if neither **x** nor **y** are specified, the string is output at the current text mode *x,y* location. (You can think of this function as an advanced version of **puts( )**.) The functions **wherex( )**, **wherey( )**, and **gotoxy( )** are part of Turbo/Borland C++'s library. The **wherex( )** and **wherey( )** functions return the current *x* and *y* coordinates, respectively. The current *x* and *y* coordinates define where the following output operation will begin. The **gotoxy( )** function moves the cursor to the specified *x,y* location. Chapters 11 and 23 discuss the screen control functions in depth.

The following short program demonstrates how to use **xyout( )**:

```
#include <iostream.h>
#include <conio.h>

void xyout(char *str, int x=0, int y=0)
{
  if(!x) x = wherex();
  if(!y) y = wherey();
  gotoxy(x, y);
  cout << str;
}

main(void)
{
  xyout("hello", 10, 10);
  xyout(" there");
  xyout("I like C++", 40);  // this is still on line 10

  xyout("This is on line 11.\n", 1, 11);
  xyout("This follows on line 12.\n");
  xyout("This follows on line 13.");

  return 0;
}
```

Look closely at how **xyout( )** is called inside **main( )**. This program produces output similar to that shown in Figure 26-1. As this program illustrates, although it is

```
                 hello there           I like C++
        This is on line 11.
        This follows on line 12.
        This follows on line 13.
```

Figure 26-1.   *Sample output from the* **xyout( )** *program*

sometimes useful to specify the exact location where text will be displayed, often, you simply can continue on from the point at which the last output occurred. By using default arguments, you can use the same function to accomplish both goals—there is no need for two separate functions.

Notice that in **main( )**, **xyout( )** is called with either three, two, or one arguments. When called with only one argument, both **x** and **y** default. However, when called with two arguments, only **y** defaults. There is no way to call **xyout( )** with **x** defaulting and **y** being specified. More generally, when a function is called, all arguments are matched to their respective parameters in order from left to right. Once all existing arguments have been matched, any remaining, default arguments are used.

When creating functions that have default argument values the default values must be specified only once and this must be the first time the function is declared within the file. For example, if **xyout( )** is defined after **main( )** (as is the more common case), the default arguments must be declared in **xyout( )**'s prototype, but the values are not repeated in **xyout( )**'s definition. The following program illustrates this:

```
#include <iostream.h>
#include <conio.h>

void xyout(char *str, int x = 0, int y = 0);

main(void)
{
  xyout("hello", 10, 10);
  xyout(" there");
  xyout("I like C++", 40);   // this is still on line 10

  xyout("This is on line 11.\n", 1, 11);
  xyout("This follows on line 12.\n");
  xyout("This follows on line 13.");

  return 0;
```

```
}

/* Since x and y's defaults have already been specified
   in xyout()'s prototype, they cannot
   be repeated here.
*/
void xyout(char *str, int x, int y)
{
  if(!x) x = wherex();
  if(!y) y = wherey();
  gotoxy(x, y);
  cout << str;
}
```

If you try specifying new or even the same default values in **xyout( )**'s definition, the compiler will display an error and not compile your program.

Even though default arguments cannot be redefined, each version of an overloaded function can specify different default arguments.

When defining parameters, it is important to understand that all parameters that take default values must appear to the right of those that do not. That is, you cannot specify a nondefaulting parameter once you have defined a parameter that takes a default value. For example, it would have been incorrect to define **xyout( )** as:

```
// wrong!
void xyout(int x = 0, int y = 0, char *str)
```

Here is another incorrect attempted use of default parameters.

```
// wrong !
int f(int i, int j=10, int k)
```

Once the default parameters begin, no non-defaulting parameter may occur in the list.

You can also use default parameters in an object's constructor function. For example, here is a slightly different version of the **queue( )** constructor function, shown earlier in this chapter.

```
// This is the constructor function that uses
// a default value.
queue::queue(int id=0)
{
  sloc = rloc = 0;
  who = id;
```

```
   cout << "queue " << who << " initialized\n";
}
```

In this version, if an object is declared without any initializing values, **id** defaults to 0. For example,

```
queue a, b(2);
```

creates two objects, **a** and **b**. The **id** value of **a** is 0 and **b** is 2.

Using Default Arguments Correctly

Although default arguments can be very powerful tools when used correctly, they can be misused. Default arguments should allow a function to perform its job efficiently and easily while still allowing considerable flexibility. Toward this end, all default arguments should represent the way the function is used most of the time. For example, using a default argument makes sense if the default value is used 90 percent of the time. However, if a common value occurs in only 10 percent of the calls, and the rest of the time the arguments corresponding to that parameter vary widely, it is not a good idea to provide a default argument. When there is no single value that is normally associated with a parameter, there is no reason for a default argument. In fact, declaring default arguments when there is insufficient basis destructures your code because it misleads and confuses anyone reading your program. At what percentage of frequency you should elect to use a default argument is, of course, subjective. But, 51 percent seems a reasonable break point.

Classes and Structures are Related

In C++ the **struct** has some expanded capabilities compared to its C counterpart. In C++, **class**es and **struct**s are closely related. In fact, with one exception, they are interchangeable because the C++ **struct** can include data and the code that manipulates that data in the same way that a **class** can. Structures may also contain constructor and destructor functions. The only difference is that by default the members of a **class** are **private** while, by default, the members of a **struct** are **public**. Consider this program:

```
#include <iostream.h>

struct cl {
  int get_i(void); // these are public
  void put_i(int j); // by default
```

```
private:
  int i;
} ;

int cl::get_i(void)
{
  return i;
}

void cl::put_i(int j)
{
  i = j;
}

main(void)
{
  cl s;

  s.put_i(10);
  cout << s.get_i();

  return 0;
}
```

This simple program defines a structure type called **cl** in which **get_i( )** and **put_i( )** are **public** and **i** is **private**. Notice that a **struct** uses the keyword **private** to introduce the **private** elements of the structure.

The following program shows an equivalent program using a **class** instead of **struct**.

```
#include <iostream.h>

class cl {
  int i; // private by default
public:
  int get_i(void);
  void put_i(int j);
} ;

int cl::get_i(void)
{
  return i;
}
```

```
void cl::put_i(int j)
{
  i = j;
}

main(void)
{
  cl s;

  s.put_i(10);
  cout << s.get_i();

  return 0;
}
```

For the most part, C++ programmers use **class** to define the form of an object and **struct** in the same way that it is used in C. However, from time to time you will see C++ code that uses the expanded abilities of structures.

Unions and Classes are Related

Just as structures and classes are related in C++, unions are also related to classes. A union is essentially a structure in which all elements are stored in the same location. A union can contain constructor and destructor functions as well as member and **friend** functions. For example, the following program uses a union to display the characters that make up the low- and high-order bytes of an integer (assuming 2-byte integers):

```
#include <iostream.h>

union u_type {
  u_type(int a);  // public by default
  void showchars(void);
  int i;
  char ch[2];
};

// constructor
u_type::u_type(int a)
{
  i = a;
}
```

```
// show the characters that comprise an int
void u_type::showchars(void)
{
  cout << ch[0] << " ";
  cout << ch[1] << "\n";
}

main(void)
{
  u_type u(1000);

  u.showchars();

  return 0;
}
```

As you can see, since a union resembles a structure, its members are **public** by default. However, a **union** may not be inherited by another class, nor may it inherit one.

One interesting feature of C++ unions not found in C is the *anonymous union*. An *anonymous union* is a union that has neither a tag name nor any objects specified in its declaration. The names of the members of the union are accessed directly without using any form of the dot or arrow operator. For example, here is a short example using an anonymous union.

```
#include <iostream.h>

main(void)
{
  // This declares an anonymous union.
  union {  // no tag name
    int i;
    char ch[2];
  } ;  // no variables specified

  /* Now reference i and ch without referencing
     a union name or dot or arrow operators.
  */
  i = 88;
  cout << i << " " << ch[0];

  return 0;
}
```

Anonymous unions have some restrictions. For obvious reasons, the names of the members of an anonymous union must be different from all other identifiers in the scope of the union. (That is, the member names must not conflict with other identifiers within the union's scope.) Also, global anonymous unions must be specified as **static**. Anonymous unions may not contain member functions. Finally, anonymous unions cannot include **private** or **protected** elements.

Remember, just because C++ gives unions greater power and flexibility does not mean that you have to use it. In cases where you simply need a C-style union you are free to use one in that manner. However, in cases where you can encapsulate a union along with the routines that manipulate it, you add considerable structure to your program.

In-Line Functions

While not pertaining specifically to object-oriented programming, C++ contains one very important feature not found in C. This feature is called *in-line functions*. An in-line function is a function that is expanded at the point at which it is called instead of actually being called. This is much like a parameterized function-like macro in C, but more flexible. There are two ways to create an in-line function. The first is to use the **inline** modifier. For example, to create an in-line function called **f** that returns an **int** and takes no parameters, you must declare it like this:

```
inline int f(void)
{
    .
    .
    .
}
```

The general form of **inline** is

inline *function_declaration*

The **inline** modifier precedes all other aspects of a function's declaration.

The reason for in-line functions is efficiency. Every time a function is called, a series of instructions must be executed to set up the function call, including pushing any arguments onto the stack, and returning from the function. In some cases, many CPU cycles are used to perform these procedures. However, when a function is expanded in line, no such overhead exists, and the overall speed of your program increases. However, in cases where the in-line function is large, the overall size of your program also increases. For this reason, the best in-line functions are those that are very small. Larger functions should be left as normal functions.

As an example, the following program uses **inline** to make this program more efficient:

```
#include <iostream.h>

class cl {
  int i; // private by default
public:
  int get_i(void);
  void put_i(int j);
} ;

inline int cl::get_i(void)
{
  return i;
}

inline void cl::put_i(int j)
{
  i = j;
}

main(void)
{
  cl s;

  s.put_i(10);
  cout << s.get_i();

  return 0;
}
```

When you compile this version of the program and compare it to a compiled version of the previous program, the in-line version is several bytes smaller.

It is important to understand that, technically, **inline** is a *request*, not a *command*, to the compiler to generate in-line code. There are various situations that can prevent the compiler from complying with the request. If a loop, a **switch**, or a **goto** exists, the compiler will not generate in-line code. For functions not returning values, if a **return** statement exists, in-line code will not be generated. You cannot have in-line recursive functions nor can you create in-line functions that contain **static** variables.

Creating In-Line Functions Inside a Class

There is another way, in C++, to create an in-line function—by defining the code to a function *inside* a **class** declaration. Any function that is defined inside a **class** declaration is automatically made into an in-line function. It is not necessary to precede its declaration with the keyword **inline**. For example, the previous program can be rewritten as shown here:

```
#include <iostream.h>

class cl {
  int i; // private by default
public:
  // automatic inline functions
  int get_i(void) { return i; }
  void put_i(int j) { i = j; }
} ;

main(void)
{
  cl s;

  s.put_i(10);
  cout << s.get_i();

  return 0;
}
```

Notice the way the function code is arranged. For very short functions, this arrangement reflects common C++ style. However, you could also write them as shown here:

```
class cl {
  int i; // private by default
public:
  // inline functions
  int get_i(void)
  {
    return i;
  }

  void put_i(int j)
  {
    i = j;
```

```
      }
} ;
```

In professionally written C++ code, short functions like those illustrated in the example, are commonly defined inside the **class** declaration. This convention is followed in most of the C++ examples in this book.

More About Inheritance

As you saw in the previous chapter, it is possible for one class to inherit the attributes of another class. This section examines some more details relating to inheritance.

Let's begin with the terminology. A class that is inherited by another class is called the *base class*. Sometimes it is also referred to as the *parent class*. The class that does the inheriting is called the *derived class,* or the *child class*. This book uses the terms *base* and *derived* because they are the traditional terms.

In C++, a class can categorize its elements into three classifications: **public**, **private**, or **protected**. As you know, a **public** element can be accessed by any other function in the program. A **private** or **protected** element can be accessed only by member or **friend** functions.

When one class inherits another class, all **private** elements of the base class are inaccessible to the derived class. For example, in the following program

```
class X {
  int i;
  int j;
public:
  void get_ij(void);
  void put_ij(void);
} ;

class Y : public X {
  int k;
public:
  int get_k(void);
  void make_k(void);
} ;
```

the elements of **Y** can access **X**'s **public** functions **get_ij( )** and **put_ij( )**, but cannot access **i** or **j** because they are **private** to **X**.

You can grant the derived class access to a class's **private** elements by making them **protected**. For example,

```
class X {
protected:
  int i;
  int j;
public:
  void get_ij(void);
  void put_ij(void);
} ;

class Y : public X {
  int k;
public:
  int get_k(void);
  void make_k(void);
} ;
```

gives **Y** access to **i** and **j** even though they are still inaccessible to the rest of the program. When you make an element **protected** you restrict its access to only the member functions of the class, but you allow this access to be inherited. When an element is **private**, access is not inherited.

The general form for inheriting a class is

> class *class-name*: *access class-name* {
>
> .
>
> .
>
> .
>
> };

Here, *access* must be either **private** or **public**. (It can also be omitted, in which case **public** is assumed if the base class is a structure; or **private** if the base class is a class.) If *access* is **public**, all **public** and **protected** elements of the base class become **public** and **protected** elements of the derived class, respectively. If *access* is **private**, all **public** and **protected** elements of the base class become **private** elements of the derived class. To understand the ramifications of these conversions, let's work through an example. Consider the following program:

```
#include <iostream.h>

class X {
protected:
  int i;
  int j;
public:
  void get_ij(void);
```

```
    void put_ij(void);
} ;

// In Y, i and j of X become protected members.
class Y : public X {
  int k;
public:
  int get_k(void);
  void make_k(void);
} ;

// Z has access to i and j of X, but not to
// k of Y, since it is private by default.
class Z : public Y {
public:
  void f(void);
} ;

void X::get_ij(void)
{
  cout << "Enter two numbers: ";
  cin >> i >> j;
}

void X::put_ij(void)
{
  cout << i << " " << j << "\n";
}

int Y::get_k(void)
{
  return k;
}

void Y::make_k(void)
{
  k = i*j;
}

void Z::f(void)
{
  i = 2;
  j = 3;
}
```

```
main(void)
{
  Y var;
  Z var2;

  var.get_ij();
  var.put_ij();

  var.make_k();
  cout << var.get_k();
  cout << "\n";

  var2.f();
  var2.put_ij();

  return 0;
}
```

Since **Y** declares **X** as **public**, the **protected** elements of **X** become **protected** elements of **Y**, which means that they can be inherited by **Z** and this program compiles and runs correctly. However, changing **X**'s status in **Y** to **private**, as shown in the following program, causes **Z** to be denied access to **i** and **j**, and the functions **get_ij( )** and **put_ij( )** that access them, because they have been made **private** in **Y**.

```
#include <iostream.h>

class X {
protected:
  int i;
  int j;
public:
  void get_ij(void);
  void put_ij(void);
} ;

// Now, i and j are converted to private members of Y.
class Y : private X {
  int k;
public:
  int get_k(void);
  void make_k(void);
} ;

// Because i and j are private in Y, they
```

```
// may not be inherited by Z.
class Z : public Y {
public:
  void f(void);
} ;

void X::get_ij(void)
{
  cout << "Enter two numbers: ";
  cin >> i >> j;
}

void X::put_ij(void)
{
  cout << i << " " << j << "\n";
}

int Y::get_k(void)
{
  return k;
}

void Y::make_k(void)
{
  k = i*j;
}

// This function no longer works.
void Z::f(void)
{
//  i = 2;  i and j are no longer accessible
//  j = 3;
}

main(void)
{
  Y var;
  Z var2;

//  var.get_ij();  no longer accessible
//  var.put_ij();  no longer accessible

  var.make_k();
  cout << var.get_k();
  cout << "\n";
```

```
   var2.f();
//   var2.put_ij();   no longer accessible

   return 0;
}
```

When **X** is made **private** in **Y**'s declaration, it causes **i**, **j**, **get_ij( )**, and **put_ij( )** to be treated as **private** in **Y**, which means they cannot be inherited by **Z**; thus, **Z**'s class can no longer access them.

One final point about **private**, **protected**, and **public**. These keywords can appear in any order and any number of times in the declaration of a **struct** or **class**. For example, this code is perfectly valid:

```
class my_class {
protected:
   int i;
   int j;
public:
   void f1(void);
   void f2(void);
protected:
   int a;
public:
   int b;
} ;
```

However, it is usually considered good form to have only one heading for each access specifier inside each **class** or **struct** declaration.

Multiple Inheritance

It is possible for one class to inherit the attributes of two or more classes. To accomplish this, use a comma-separated inheritance list in the derived class's base class list. The general form is

```
class derived-class-name: base-class list
{
  .
  .
  .
};
```

For example, in this program **Z** inherits both **X** and **Y**.

```
#include <iostream.h>

class X {
protected:
  int a;
public:
  void make_a(int i);
};

class Y {
protected:
  int b;
public:
  void make_b(int i);
} ;

// Z inherits both X and Y
class Z : public X, public Y {
public:
  int make_ab(void);
} ;

void X::make_a(int i)
{
  a = i;
}

void Y::make_b(int i)
{
  b = i;
}

int Z::make_ab(void)
{
  return a*b;
}

main(void)
{
  Z i;

  i.make_a(10);
```

```
  i.make_b(12);
  cout << i.make_ab();

  return 0;
}
```

In this example, **Z** has access to the **public** and **protected** portions of both **X** and **Y**.

In the preceding example, neither **X**, **Y**, nor **Z** contained constructor functions. However, the situation is more complex when a base **class** contains a constructor function. For example, let's change the preceding example so that the classes **X**, **Y**, and **Z** each have a constructor function:

```
#include <iostream.h>

class X {
protected:
  int a;
public:
  X(void);
};

class Y {
protected:
  int b;
public:
  Y(void);
} ;

// Z inherits both X and Y
class Z : public X, public Y {
public:
  Z(void);
  int make_ab(void);
} ;

X::X(void)
{
  a = 10;
  cout << "initializing X\n";
}

Y::Y(void)
{
  cout << "initializing Y\n";
```

```
   b = 20;
}

Z::Z(void)
{
  cout << "initializing Z\n";
}

int Z::make_ab(void)
{
  return a*b;
}

main(void)
{
  Z i;

  cout << i.make_ab();

  return 0;
}
```

When this program runs, it displays the following:

```
initializing X
initializing Y
initializing Z
200
```

Notice that the base classes are constructed in the order they appear from left to right in **Z**'s declaration. In C++ the constructor functions for any inherited base classes are called in the order in which they appear. Once the base class or classes have been initialized the derived class's constructor executes.

As long as no base class takes any arguments, the derived class need not have a constructor function even though one or more base classes do. However, when a base class contains a parameterized constructor function, any derived class must also contain a constructor function. This allows a means of passing arguments to the constructor functions of the base class or classes. To pass arguments to a base class, you specify them after the derived class's constructor function declaration, as shown in this general form:

derived-constructor(arg-list) : *base1(arg-list)*, base2(*arg-list*), . . ., *baseN(arg-list)*
```
{
```

```
      .

        .

          .

  }
```

Here, *base1* through *baseN* are the names of the base classes inherited by the derived class. Notice that the colon is used to separate the derived class's constructor function from the argument lists of the base classes. It is very important to understand that the argument lists associated with the base classes can consist of constants, global variables, or the parameters to the derived class's constructor function. Since an object's initialization occurs at run-time, you can use as an argument any identifier that is defined within the scope of the class.

The following program illustrates how to pass arguments to the base classes of a derived class by modifying the preceding program:

```
#include <iostream.h>

class X {
protected:
  int a;
public:
  X(int i);
};

class Y {
protected:
  int b;
public:
  Y(int i);
} ;

// Z inherits both X and Y
class Z : public X, public Y {
public:
  Z(int x, int y);
  int make_ab(void);
} ;

X::X(int i)
{
  a = i;
}


Y::Y(int i)
```

```
{
  b = i;
}

// Initialize X and Y via Z's constructor.
// Notice that Z does not actually use x or y
// itself, but it could, if it so chooses.
Z::Z(int x, int y) : X(x), Y(y)
{
  cout << "initializing\n";
}

int Z::make_ab(void)
{
  return a*b;
}

main(void)
{
  Z i(10, 20);

  cout << i.make_ab();

  return 0;
}
```

Notice how the constructor **Z** does not actually use its parameters directly. Instead, in this example, they are simply passed along to the constructor functions for **X** and **Y**. There is no reason, however, that **Z** could not use these or other arguments.

Passing Objects to Functions

An object can be passed to a function in the same way as any other data type. Objects are passed to functions using the normal C++ call-by-value parameter passing convention. This means that a copy of the object is passed to the function, not the actual object itself. Therefore, any changes made to the object inside the function do not affect the object used to call the function. The following program illustrates this point:

```
#include <iostream.h>

class OBJ {
```

```
  int i;
public:
  void set_i(int x) { i = x; }
  void out_i() { cout << i << " "; }
};

void f(OBJ x);

main(void)
{
  OBJ o;

  o.set_i(10);
  f(o);
  o.out_i();  // still outputs 10, value of i unchanged
  return 0;
}

void f(OBJ x)
{
  x.out_i();  // outputs 10
  x.set_i(100);  // this affects only local copy
  x.out_i();  // outputs 100
}
```

As you will see later it is also possible to pass only the address of an object to a function. When an address to an object is passed, alterations made to the object inside the function affect the object used in the call.

> *When passing an object to a function, it is possible that a side effect will actually affect the original object used as the argument even though only a copy of that object is passed. Here's how. When the function that receives an object returns, all local variables and parameters go out-of-scope and are destroyed. Thus, the copy of the object used as a parameter is destroyed and its destructor function (if it exists) is called. In some circumstances, it is possible for the destructor of the copy to destroy something needed by the original object. For example, if the destructor frees dynamically allocated memory, this memory will be freed when the copy of the original object is destroyed even though the original object used as an argument still requires it. When passing objects to functions, you must watch out for side effects such as this. (A better way to pass an object to a function is to pass it as a reference parameter. References are discussed in Chapter 27.)*

Arrays of Objects

You can create arrays of objects in the same way that you create arrays of any other data types. For example, the following program establishes a class called **display** that holds information about the various display monitors that can be attached to a PC. Specifically, it contains the number of colors that can be displayed and the type of video adapter. Inside **main( )** an array of three **display** objects is created, and the objects that make up the elements of the array are accessed using the normal indexing procedure.

```
// An example of arrays of objects

#include <iostream.h>

enum disp_type {mono, cga, ega, vga};

class display {
  int colors;  // number of colors
  enum disp_type dt; // display type
public:
  void set_colors(int num) {colors = num;}
  int get_colors() {return colors;}
  void set_type(enum disp_type t) {dt = t;}
  enum disp_type get_type() {return dt;}
} ;

char names[4][5] = {
  "mono",
  "cga",
  "ega",
  "vga"
} ;

main(void)
{
  display monitors[3];
  register int i;

  monitors[0].set_type(mono);
  monitors[0].set_colors(1);
```

```
monitors[1].set_type(cga);
monitors[1].set_colors(4);

monitors[2].set_type(vga);
monitors[2].set_colors(16);

for(i=0; i<3; i++) {
  cout << names[monitors[i].get_type()] << " ";
  cout << "has " << monitors[i].get_colors();
  cout << " colors" << "\n";
}

return 0;
}
```

This program produces the following output:

```
mono has 1 colors
cga has 4 colors
vga has 16 colors
```

Although not related to arrays of objects, notice how the two-dimensional character array **names** is used to convert between an enumerated value and its equivalent character string. In all enumerations that do not contain explicit initializations, the first constant has the value 0, the second 1, and so on. Therefore, the value returned by **get_type( )** can be used to index the **names** array, causing the appropriate name to be printed.

Multidimensional arrays of objects are indexed in precisely the same way as arrays of other types of data.

Pointers to Objects

In C you can access a structure directly, or through a pointer to that structure. Similarly, in C++ you can reference an object either directly (as has been the case in all preceding examples) or by using a pointer to that object. Pointers to objects are among C++'s most important features.

To access an element of an object when using the actual object itself, you use the dot (.) operator. To access a specific element of an object when using a pointer to the object, you must use the arrow operator (−>). The use of the dot and arrow operators for objects is the same as their use for structures and unions.

You declare an object pointer using the same declaration syntax as you do for any other type of data. The following program creates a simple class called **P_example**, and defines an object of that class called **ob** and a pointer for an object of type **P_example** called **p**. It then illustrates how to access **ob** directly and indirectly using a pointer.

```
// A simple example using an object pointer.

#include <iostream.h>

class P_example {
  int num;
public:
  void set_num(int val) {num = val;}
  void show_num();
};

void P_example::show_num()
{
  cout << num << "\n";
}

main(void)
{
  P_example ob, *p; // declare an object and pointer to it

  ob.set_num(1); // access ob directly

  ob.show_num();

  p = &ob; // assign p the address of ob
  p->show_num();  // access ob using pointer

  return 0;
}
```

Notice that the address of **ob** is obtained using the **&** (address of) operator in the same way the address is obtained for any type of variable.

When a pointer is incremented or decremented, it is increased or decreased in such a way that it will always point to the next element of its base type. The same thing occurs when a pointer to an object is incremented or decremented: the next object is pointed to. The following example modifies the preceding program so that **ob** is a two-element array of type **P_example**. Notice how **p** is incremented and decremented to access the two elements in the array.

```
// Incrementing an object pointer
#include <iostream.h>

class P_example {
  int num;
public:
  void set_num(int val) {num = val;}
  void show_num();
};

void P_example::show_num()
{
  cout << num << "\n";
}

main(void)
{
  P_example ob[2], *p;

  ob[0].set_num(10);  // access objects directly
  ob[1].set_num(20);

  p = &ob[0];  // obtain pointer to first element
  p->show_num(); // show value of ob[0] using pointer

  p++;  // advance to next object
  p->show_num(); // show value of ob[1] using pointer

  p--;  // retreat to previous object
  p->show_num(); // again show value of ob[0]

  return 0;
}
```

The output from this program is 10, 20, 10.

Chapter *27*

Function and Operator Overloading

Chapter 25 introduced two of C++'s most important features, function and operator overloading. This chapter examines these topics in detail. In the course of these discussions, other, related topics are also discussed.

Overloading Constructor Functions

Although performing a unique service, constructor functions are not much different from other types of functions; they too can be overloaded. To overload a class's constructor function, simply declare the various forms it will take and define each action relative to these forms. For example, the following program declares a class called **timer** that acts as a countdown timer (such as a darkroom timer). When an object of type **timer** is created, it is given an initial time value. When the **run( )** function is called, the timer counts down to 0 and then rings the bell. In this example, the constructor is overloaded to allow the time to be specified in seconds as either an integer or a string, or in minutes and seconds by specifying two integers.

This program makes use of the **clock( )** library function, which returns the number of system clock ticks since the program began running. Dividing this value by the macro **CLK_TCK** converts the return value of **clock( )** into seconds. Both the prototype for **clock( )** and the definition of **CLK_TCK** are found in the header file **time.h.**

```
#include <iostream.h>
#include <stdlib.h>
#include <time.h>

class timer{
  int seconds;
public:
  // seconds specified as a string
  timer(char *t) { seconds = atoi(t); }

  // seconds specified as integer
  timer(int t) { seconds = t; }

  // time specified in minutes and seconds
  timer(int min, int sec) { seconds = min*60 + sec; }

  void run(void);
} ;

void timer::run(void)
{
  clock_t t1, t2;

  t1 = t2 = clock()/CLK_TCK;
  while(seconds) {
    if(t1/CLK_TCK+1 <= (t2=clock())/CLK_TCK) {
      seconds--;
      t1 = t2;
    }
  }
  cout << "\a"; // ring the bell
}

main(void)
{
  timer a(10), b("20"), c(1, 10);

  a.run(); // count 10 seconds
  b.run(); // count 20 seconds
  c.run(); // count 1 minute, 10 seconds

  return 0;
}
```

As you can see, when **a**, **b**, and **c** are created inside **main( )** they are given initial values using the three different methods supported by the overloaded constructor functions. Each approach causes the appropriate constructor to be used and initializes all three variables properly.

In the program just shown, you may see little value in overloading a constructor function because you could simply decide on a single way to specify the time. However, if you were creating a library of classes for someone else to use, you might want to supply constructors for the most common forms of initialization, allowing the programmer to choose the most appropriate form for his or her application.

Local Variables in C++

Before continuing with the discussion of overloaded functions, the declaration of local variables must be discussed.

In C you must declare all local variables used within a block at the start of that block. You cannot declare a variable in a block after another statement has occurred. For example, in C, this fragment is incorrect:

```
/* incorrect in C */
f()
{
  int i;

  i = 10;

  int j;
  .
  .
  .
}
```

Because the statement **i=10** falls between the declaration of **i** and that of **j**, a C compiler will flag an error and refuse to compile this function. However, in C++ this fragment is perfectly acceptable and will compile without error. For example, the following is an acceptable C++ program:

```
#include <iostream.h>
#include <string.h>

main(void)
{
  int i;
```

```
i = 10;

int j = 100; // perfectly legal in C++

cout << i*j << "\n";

cout << "Enter a string: ";
char str[80];  // also legal in C++
cin >> str;

// display the string in reverse order
int k;  // in C++, declare k where it is needed
k = strlen(str);
k--;
while(k>=0) {
  cout << str[k];
  k--;
}

return 0;
}
```

As this program illustrates, in C++ you can declare local variables anywhere within a block of code. Since much of the philosophy behind C++ is the encapsulation of code and data, it makes sense that you can declare variables close to where they are used instead of only at the beginning of the block. In this example, the declarations of **i** and **j** are separated simply for illustration. However, you can see how the localization of **k** to its relevant code helps encapsulate that routine. Declaring variables close to the point where they are used helps you avoid accidental side effects.

Dynamic Initialization

In C++, both local and global variables can be initialized at run-time. This is sometimes referred to as *dynamic initialization*. Using dynamic initialization, a variable can be initialized at run-time using any C++ expression valid at the time the variable is declared. This means you can initialize a variable using other variables or function calls as long as the overall expression has meaning when the declaration is encountered. This differs from C, in which a global variable's initial value must be known at compile time, requiring a constant expression that cannot use variables or function calls. For example, these are perfectly valid global variable initializations in C++ (but not in C):

```
.
.
.
int n = atoi(gets(str));

long pos = ftell(fp);

double d = 1.02 * count / deltax;
```

Because of its capabilities, dynamic initialization has found widespread use in many C++ programs. For example, we can make use of dynamic initialization to improve the example program from the preceding section, as shown here:

```
#include <iostream.h>
#include <string.h>

main(void)
{
  int i;

  i = 10;

  int j = 100;

  cout << i*j << "\n";

  cout << "Enter a string: ";
  char str[80];
  cin >> str;

  // ***********************************
  // initialize k dynamically at runtime
  int k = strlen(str)-1;
  // ***********************************

  while(k>=0) {
    cout << str[k];
    k--;
  }

  return 0;
}
```

Here, **k** is dynamically initialized because the call to **strlen( )** is resolved at run-time. This further illustrates how declaring variables close to where they are used can be valuable.

Applying Dynamic Initialization to Constructors

Like simple variables, objects can be initialized dynamically when they are created. This means you can create exactly the type of object you need using information that is known only at run-time. To illustrate how dynamic initialization works, let's rework the **timer** program from earlier in this chapter.

In the first example of the **timer** program there is little to be gained by overloading the **timer( )** constructor because all objects of its type were initialized using constants. However, in cases when an object will be initialized at run-time, there may be significant advantages in allowing various initialization formats to be used. This allows the programmer the flexibility of using the constructor that most closely matches the format of the data available at the moment. For example, in this version of the **timer** program, two objects, **b** and **c**, are constructed at run-time using dynamic initialization:

```
#include <iostream.h>
#include <stdlib.h>
#include <time.h>

class timer{
  int seconds;
public:
  // seconds specified as a string
  timer(char *t) { seconds = atoi(t); }

  // seconds specified as integer
  timer(int t) { seconds = t; }

  // time specified in minutes and seconds
  timer(int min, int sec) { seconds = min*60 + sec; }

  void run(void);
} ;

void timer::run(void)
{
  clock_t t1, t2;
```

```
  t1 = t2 = clock()/CLK_TCK;
  while(seconds) {
    if(t1/CLK_TCK+1 <= (t2=clock())/CLK_TCK) {
        seconds--;
        t1 = t2;
    }
  }
  cout << "\a"; // ring the bell
}
main(void)
{
  timer a(10);

  a.run();

  cout << "Enter number of seconds: ";
  char str[80];
  cin >> str;
  timer b(str);  // initialize at runtime
  b.run();

  cout << "Enter minutes and seconds: ";
  int min, sec;
  cin >> min >> sec;
  timer c(min, sec);  // initialize at runtime
  c.run();

  return 0;
}
```

As you can see, object **a** is constructed using an integer constant. However, objects **b** and **c** are constructed using information entered by the user. Since the user enters a string for **b**, it makes sense for **timer( )** to be overloaded to accept the string. In similar fashion, object **c** is also constructed at run-time using information input by the user. In this case, since the time is entered as minutes and seconds, it is logical to use this form to construct object **c**. By allowing various initialization formats, the programmer need not perform any unnecessary conversions from one form to another when initializing an object.

Overloading constructor functions allows the programmer to handle greater complexity by allowing objects to be constructed in the most natural manner relative to their specific use. Since there are three common ways to pass timing values to an object, it makes sense that **timer( )** be overloaded to accept each way. However, overloading **timer( )** to accept days or nanoseconds is probably not a good idea—littering your code with constructors that handle seldom-used contingencies

destabilizes your program. You must decide what constitutes valid constructor overloading and what is frivolous.

The this Keyword

Before moving on to operator overloading, it is necessary for you to learn about
another of C++'s keywords, **this**, which is an essential ingredient for many overloaded
operators.

Each time a member function is invoked, it is automatically passed a pointer to
the object that invoked it. You can access this pointer using **this**. The **this** pointer is
an *implicit* parameter to all member functions. (**friend** functions do not have a **this**
pointer.)

As you know, a member function can access the **private** data of its class directly.
For example, given the following class:

```
class cl {
  int i;
.
.
.
};
```

a member function can assign **i** the value 10 using this statement:

```
i = 10;
```

Actually, this statement is shorthand for the statement

```
this->i = 10;
```

To see how the **this** pointer works, examine this short program:

```
#include <iostream.h>

class cl {
  int i;
public:
  void load_i(int val) { this->i = val; } // same as i = val
  int get_i(void) { return this->i; } // same as return i
} ;
```

```
main(void)
{
  cl o;

  o.load_i(100);
  cout << o.get_i();

  return 0;
}
```

This program displays the number 100.

While the preceding example is trivial—in fact, no one would actually use the **this** pointer in this way—the following section shows why the **this** pointer is so important.

Operator Overloading

A feature of C++ that is related to function overloading is *operator overloading*. With very few exceptions, most of C++'s operators can be given special meanings relative to specific classes. For example, a class that defines a linked list might use the + operator to add an object to the list. Another class might use the + operator in an entirely different way. When an operator is overloaded, none of its original meaning is lost. It simply means that a new operation relative to a specific **class** is defined. Therefore, overloading the + to handle a linked list does not cause its meaning relative to integers (that is, addition) to be changed.

To overload an operator you must define what that operation means relative to the **class** that it is applied to. To do this you create an **operator** function, which defines its action. The general form of an **operator** function is

type classname::operator#(*arg-list*)
{
  // operation defined relative to the class
}

Here, the operator that you are overloading is substituted for the # and *type* is the type of value returned by the specified operation. To facilitate their use in complex expressions, the return value of an operator often is of the same type as the class for which the operator is being overloaded. (Although it could be of any type you choose.) The specific nature of *arg-list* is determined by several factors, as you will soon see.

Operator functions must be either members or **friend**s of the class for which they are being used. Although very similar, there are some differences between the way a member operator function is overloaded and the way a **friend** operator function is overloaded. In this section, only member functions will be overloaded. Later in this chapter, you will see how to overload **friend** operator functions.

To see how operator overloading works, let's start with a simple example that creates a **class** called **three_d** that maintains the coordinates of an object in three-dimensional space. This program overloads the + and = operators relative to the **three_d class**:

```
#include <iostream.h>

class three_d {
  int x, y, z; // 3-d coordinates
public:
  three_d operator+(three_d t);
  three_d operator=(three_d t);

  void show(void) ;
  void assign(int mx, int my, int mz);
} ;

// Overload the +.
three_d three_d::operator+(three_d t)
{
  three_d temp;

  temp.x = x+t.x;
  temp.y = y+t.y;
  temp.z = z+t.z;
  return temp;
}

// Overload the =.
three_d three_d::operator=(three_d t)
{
  x = t.x;
  y = t.y;
  z = t.z;
  return *this;
}

// show X, Y, Z coordinates
void three_d::show(void)
{
  cout << x << ", ";
  cout << y << ", ";
```

```
    cout << z << "\n";
}

// Assign coordinates
void three_d::assign(int mx, int my, int mz)
{
  x = mx;
  y = my;
  z = mz;
}

main(void)
{
  three_d a, b, c;

  a.assign(1, 2, 3);
  b.assign(10, 10, 10);

  a.show();
  b.show();

  c = a+b;   // now add a and b together
  c.show();

  c = a+b+c; // add a, b and c together
  c.show();

  c = b = a;  // demonstrate multiple assignment
  c.show();
  b.show();

  return 0;
}
```

This program produces the following output:

```
1, 2, 3
10, 10, 10
11, 12, 13
22, 24, 26
1, 2, 3
1, 2, 3
```

As you examine this program, you may be surprised to see that both operator functions had only one parameter each, even though they overloaded binary operations. This is because when a binary operator is overloaded using a member function only one argument is explicitly passed to it. The other argument is implicitly passed using the **this** pointer. Thus, in the line

```
temp.x = x + t.x;
```

the **x** refers to **this –>x**, which is the **x** associated with the object that prompted the call to the operator function. In all cases, it is the object on the left side of an operation that causes the call to the operator function. The object on the right side is passed to the function.

In general, when using a member function, no parameters are needed when overloading a unary operator, and only one parameter is required when overloading a binary operator. (You cannot overload the **?** ternary operator.) In either case, the object that causes the activation of the operator function is implicitly passed through the **this** pointer.

To understand how operator overloading works, let's examine the preceding program carefully, beginning with the overloaded operator +. When two objects of type **three_d** are operated on by the + operator, the magnitudes of their respective coordinates are added together, as shown in the **operator+( )** function associated with this **class**. Notice, however, that this function does not modify the value of either operand. Instead, an object of type **three_d**, which contains the result of the operation, is returned by the function. To understand why the + operation does not change the contents of either object, think about the standard arithmetic + operation as applied like this: 10+12. The outcome of this operation is 22, but neither 10 nor 12 are changed by it. Although there is no rule that states that an overloaded operator cannot alter the value of one of its operands, it usually makes sense for the overloaded operator to stay consistent with its original meaning. Further, related to the **three_d class**, we don't want the + to alter the contents of an operand.

Another key point about how the + operator is overloaded is that it returns an object of type **three_d**. Although the function could have returned any valid C++ type, the fact that it returns a **three_d** object allows the + operator to be used in more complex expressions, such as **a+b+c**. Here, **a+b** generates a result that is of type **three_d**. This value can then be added to **c**. Had any other type of value been generated by **a+b**, it could not have been added to **c**.

Contrasting with the + operator, the assignment operator does, indeed, cause one of its arguments to be modified. (This is, after all, the very essence of assignment.) Since the **operator=( )** function is called by the object that occurs on the left side of the assignment, it is this object that is modified by the assignment operation. However, even the assignment operation must return a value because in C++ (as well as C), the assignment operation produces the value that occurs on the right side. Thus, to allow statements like

```
a = b = c = d;
```

it is necessary for **operator=( )** to return the object pointed to by **this**, which will be the object that occurs on the left side of the assignment statement, allowing a string of assignments to be made.

You can also overload unary operators, such as ++ or – –. As stated earlier, when overloading a unary operator using a member function, no object is explicitly passed to the operator function. Instead, the operation is performed on the object that generates the call to the function through the implicitly passed **this** pointer. For example, here is an expanded version of the previous example program that defines the increment operation for objects of type **three_d**.

```
#include <iostream.h>

class three_d {
  int x, y, z; // 3-d coordinates
public:
  three_d operator+(three_d op2);  // op1 is implied
  three_d operator=(three_d op2);  // op1 is implied
  three_d operator++(void); // op1 is also implied here

  void show(void) ;
  void assign(int mx, int my, int mz);
} ;
three_d three_d::operator+(three_d op2)
{
  three_d temp;

  temp.x = x+op2.x;  // these are integer additions
  temp.y = y+op2.y;  // and the + retains its original
  temp.z = z+op2.z;  // meaning relative to them
  return temp;
}

three_d three_d::operator=(three_d op2)
{
  x = op2.x; // these are integer assigments
  y = op2.y; // and the = retains its original
  z = op2.z; // meaning relative to them
  return *this;
}

// Overload a unary operator.
three_d three_d::operator++(void)
```

```
{
  x++;
  y++;
  z++;
  return *this;
}

// show X, Y, Z coordinates
void three_d::show(void)
{
  cout << x << ", ";
  cout << y << ", ";
  cout << z << "\n";
}

// Assign coordinates
void three_d::assign(int mx, int my, int mz)
{
  x = mx;
  y = my;
  z = mz;
}

main(void)
{
  three_d a, b, c;

  a.assign(1, 2, 3);
  b.assign(10, 10, 10);

  a.show();
  b.show();

  c = a+b;  // now add a and b together
  c.show();

  c = a+b+c; // add a, b and c together
  c.show();

  c = b = a;  // demonstrate multiple assignment
  c.show();
  b.show();

  c++;  // increment c
  c.show();
```

```
   return 0;
}
```

In early versions of Turbo/Borland C++ that implemented C++ version 2.0, it was not possible to determine whether an overloaded ++ or −− preceded or followed its operand. For example, assuming some object called **O**, these two statements were identical:

```
O++;
```

```
++O;
```

However, current versions of Turbo/Borland C++ that implement C++ version 2.1 provide a means of determining whether an increment or decrement that prefixes or postfixes its operand was created. To accomplish this, your program must define two versions of the **operator++()** function. One is defined as shown in the foregoing program. The other is declared like this:

```
loc operator++(int x);
```

If the **++** precedes its operand, then the **operator++()** function is called. If the **++** follows its operand, then the **operator++(int x)** is called and **x** has the value 0.

The action of an overloaded operator as applied to the class for which it is defined need not have any relationship to that operator's default use with C++'s built-in types. For example, the **<<** and **>>** as applied to **cout** and **cin** have little in common with the same operators applied to integer types. However, for the purpose of structure and readability of your code, an overloaded operator should reflect, when possible, the spirit of the operator's original use. For example, the + relative to **three_d** is conceptually similar to the + relative to integer types. There is little benefit, for example, in defining the + operator relative to a particular class in such a way that it acts more like you would expect the || operator to perform. While you can give an overloaded operator any meaning you like, it is best, for clarity, to relate its new meaning to its original meaning.

Some restrictions to overloading operators also apply. First, you cannot alter the precedence of any operator. Second, you cannot alter the number of operands required by the operator, although your **operator( )** function could choose to ignore an operand. Finally, except for the =, overloaded operators are inherited by any derived classes. Each class must define explicitly its own overloaded = operator if one is needed. (Of course, you can overload one or more operators relative to the derived class if necessary.)

The only operators you cannot overload are

```
. :: .* ?
```

Friend Operator Functions

It is possible for an operator function to be a **friend** of a **class** rather than a member. As you learned earlier in this chapter, since **friend** functions are *not* members of a class, they do not have the implied argument **this**. Therefore, when a **friend** is used to overload an operator, both operands are passed when overloading binary operators and a single operand is passed when overloading unary operators. The only operators that cannot use **friend** functions are =, ( ), [], and –>. The rest can use either member or **friend** functions to implement the specified operation relative to its **class**. For example, here is a modified version of the preceding program using a **friend** instead of a member function to overload the + operator:

```
#include <iostream.h>

class three_d {
  int x, y, z; // 3-d coordinates
public:
  friend three_d operator+(three_d op1, three_d op2);
  three_d operator=(three_d op2);  // op1 is implied
  three_d operator++(void); // op1 is implied here, too

  void show(void) ;
  void assign(int mx, int my, int mz);
} ;

// This is now a friend function.
three_d operator+(three_d op1, three_d op2)
{
  three_d temp;

  temp.x = op1.x + op2.x;  // these are integer additions
  temp.y = op1.y + op2.y;  // and the + retains its original
  temp.z = op1.z + op2.z;  // meaning relative to them
  return temp;
}

three_d three_d::operator=(three_d op2)
{
  x = op2.x; // these are integer assignments
  y = op2.y; // and the = retains its original
  z = op2.z; // meaning relative to them
  return *this;
}

// Overload a unary operator.
```

```
three_d three_d::operator++(void)
{
  x++;
  y++;
  z++;
  return *this;
}

// show X, Y, Z coordinates
void three_d::show(void)
{
  cout << x << ", ";
  cout << y << ", ";
  cout << z << "\n";
}

// Assign coordinates
void three_d::assign(int mx, int my, int mz)
{
  x = mx;
  y = my;
  z = mz;
}
main(void)
{
  three_d a, b, c;

  a.assign(1, 2, 3);
  b.assign(10, 10, 10);

  a.show();
  b.show();

  c = a+b;  // now add a and b together
  c.show();

  c = a+b+c; // add a, b and c together
  c.show();

  c = b = a;  // demonstrate multiple assignment
  c.show();
  b.show();

  c++;  // increment c
  c.show();
```

```
    return 0;
}
```

As you can see by looking at **operator+( )**, now both operands are passed to it. The left operand is passed in **op1** and the right operand in **op2**.

In many cases, there is no benefit to using a **friend** function instead of a member function when overloading an operator. However, there is one situation in which you must use a **friend** function. As you know, a pointer to an object that invokes a member operator function is passed in **this**. In the case of binary operators, the object on the left invokes the function. This works as long as the object on the left defines the specified operation. For example, assuming an object called **O**, which has assignment and addition defined for it, this is a valid statement:

```
O = O + 10; // will work
```

Since the object **O** is on the left of the + operator, it invokes its overloaded operator function, which (presumably) is capable of adding an integer value to some element of **O**. However, this statement doesn't work:

```
O = 10 + O; // won't work
```

The reason this statement does not work is that the object on the left of the + operator is an integer, which is a built-in type for which no operation involving an integer and an object of **O**'s type is defined.

You can use built-in types on the left side of an operation if the + is overloaded using two **friend** functions. In this case, the operator function is explicitly passed both arguments and it is invoked like any other overloaded function, based upon the types of its arguments. One version of the + operator function handles *object+integer* and the other handles *integer+object*. Overloading the + (or any other binary operator) using a **friend** allows a built-in type to occur on the left or right side of the operator. The following program illustrates how to accomplish this:

```
#include <iostream.h>

class CL {
public:
  int count;
  CL operator=(int i);
  friend CL operator+(CL ob, int i);
  friend CL operator+(int i, CL ob);
};

CL CL::operator=(int i)
```

```
{
  count = i;
  return *this;
}

// This handles ob + int.
CL operator+(CL ob, int i)
{
  CL temp;

  temp.count = ob.count + i;
  return temp;
}

// This handles int + ob.
CL operator+(int i, CL ob)
{
  CL temp;

  temp.count = ob.count + i;
  return temp;
}

main(void)
{
  CL obj;
  obj = 10;
  cout << obj.count << " "; // outputs 10

  obj = 10 + obj; // add object to integer
  cout << obj.count << " "; // outputs 20

  obj = obj + 12; // add integer to object
  cout << obj.count;        // outputs 32

  return 0;
}
```

As you can see, the **operator+( )** function is overloaded twice to accommodate the two ways in which an integer and an object of type **CL** can occur in the addition operation.

Although you can use a **friend** function to overload a unary operator, such as ++, you first need to know about another feature of C++, called the reference, which is the subject of the next section.

References

By default, C and C++ pass arguments to a function using call-by-value. Passing an argument using call-by-value causes a copy of that argument to be used by the function and prevents the argument used in the call from being modified by the function. In C (and optionally in C++), when a function needs to be able to alter the values of the variables used as arguments, the parameters must be explicitly declared as pointer types and the function must operate on the calling variables using the * pointer operator. For example, the following program implements a function called **swap( )**, which exchanges the values of its two integer arguments:

```
#include <iostream.h>

void swap(int *a, int *b);

main(void)
{
   int x, y;

   x = 99;
   y = 88;

   cout << x << " " << y << "\n";

   swap(&x, &y); // exchange their values

   cout << x << " " << y << "\n";

   return 0;
}

// C-like, explicit pointer version of swap().
void swap(int *a, int *b)
{
   int t;

   t = *a;
   *a = *b;
   *b = t;
}
```

When calling **swap( )**, the variables used in the call must be preceded by the **&** operator in order to produce a pointer to each argument. This is the way that a call-by-reference is generated in C. However, even though C++ still allows this syntax, it supports a cleaner, more transparent method of generating a call-by-reference using a *reference* parameter.

In C++, it is possible to tell the compiler to automatically generate a call-by-reference rather than a call-by-value for one or more parameters of a particular function. This is accomplished by preceding the parameter name in the function's declaration by the **&**. For example, here is a function called **f( )** that takes one reference parameter of type **int**.

```
void f(int &f)
{
  f = rand(); // this modifies calling argument
}
```

This declaration form is also used in the function's prototype. Notice that the statement **f = rand( )** does not use the * pointer operator. When you declare a reference parameter, the C++ compiler automatically knows that it is a pointer and dereferences it for you.

Once the compiler has seen this declaration, it automatically passes **f( )** the *address* of any variable it is called with. For example, given this fragment

```
int val;

f(val);  // get random value
printf("%d", val);
```

the address of **val**, not its value, is passed to **f( )**. Thus, **f( )** can modify the value of **val**.

To see reference parameters in actual use, the **swap( )** function is rewritten using references. Look carefully at how **swap( )** is declared and called:

```
#include <iostream.h>

void swap(int &a, int &b); // declare as reference parameters

main(void)
{
  int x, y;

  x = 99;
  y = 88;

  cout << x << " " << y << "\n";

  swap(x, y); // exchange their values
```

```
  cout << x << " " << y << "\n";

  return 0;
}


// Here, swap() is defined as using call-by-reference,
// not call-by-value.
void swap(int &a, int &b)
{
  int t;

  t = a;
  a = b;  // this swaps x
  b = t;  // this swaps y
}
```

Notice that by making **a** and **b** reference parameters, there is no need to use the **&** or the * operators. In fact, it would be an error to do so. Remember that the compiler automatically generates the addresses of the arguments used to call **swap( )** and automatically dereferences **a** and **b**.

There are several restrictions that apply to reference variables:

1. You cannot reference a reference variable. That is, you cannot take its address.

2. You cannot create arrays of references.

3. You cannot create a pointer to a reference.

4. References are not allowed on bit fields.

Nonparameter Reference Variables

Even though references are included in C++ primarily for supporting call-by-reference parameter passing, it is possible to declare a reference variable that is not a parameter to a function. However, nonparameter reference variables are seldom a good idea because they tend to confuse and destructure your program. With these reservations in mind, we will take a short look at them here.

Nonparameter reference variables are sometimes called *independent* or *standalone* references. Since a reference variable must point to some object, an independent reference must be initialized when it is declared. Generally, this means that it will be assigned the address of a previously declared variable. Once this is done, the

Some C++ programmers associate the **&** *with the type rather than the variable when declaring a reference variable. For example, here is another way to write the prototype to* **swap( )**:

```
void swap(int& a, int& b);
```

*Further, some C++ programmers also specify pointers by associating the * with the type rather than the variable, as shown here:*

```
float* p;
```

The trouble with associating the **&** *or * with the type rather than the variable is that, according to formal C++ syntax, neither the* **&** *nor the * is distibutive over a list of variables and can lead to confusing declarations. For example, the following declaration creates* one, not two, *integer pointers. Here,* **b** *is declared as an integer (not an integer pointer) because, as specified by the C++ syntax, when used in a declaration the * and* **&** *are linked to the individual variable that they precede, not to the type that they follow:*

```
int* a, b;
```

It is important to understand that as far as the C++ compiler is concerned it doesn't matter whether you write **int *p** *or* **int* p.** *Thus, if you prefer to associate the * or* **&** *with the type rather than the variable, feel free to do so. However, to avoid confusion, this book will continue to associate the * and the* **&** *with the variable that they modify rather than the type.*

reference variable can be used anywhere that the variable it references can. In fact, there is virtually no distinction between the two. For example, consider this program:

```
#include <iostream.h>

main(void)
{
  int j, k;
  int &i = j; // independent reference
```

```
    j = 10;

    cout << j << " " << i; // outputs 10 10

    k = 121;
    i = k; // copies k's value into j
           // not k's address

    cout << "\n" << j;  // outputs 121

    return 0;
}
```

This program displays the following output:

```
10 10
121
```

The address pointed to by the reference variable is fixed and cannot be changed. Thus, when the statement **i = k** is evaluated, it is **k**'s value that is copied into **j** (pointed to by **i**), not its address. For another example, **i++** does *not* cause **i** to point to a new address. Instead, **k** is increased by 1. Remember that references are not pointers.

You can also use an independent reference to point to a constant. For example, the following is valid.

```
int &i = 100;
```

In this case, **i** references the location in your program's constant table where the value 100 is stored.

A reference may also be returned by a function. You will see examples of this in Chapter 29.

As stated earlier, in general it is not a good idea to use independent references because they are not necessary and tend to confuse your code.

Using a Reference to Overload a Unary Operator

Now that you have learned about references, you will see how to use them to allow a **friend** function to overload a unary operator. To begin, think back to the original version of the overloaded **++** operator relative to the **three_d class**. It is shown here for your convenience:

```
// Overload a unary operator.
three_d three_d::operator++(void)
{
  x++;
  y++;
  z++;
  return *this;
}
```

As you know, each member function has as an implicit argument a pointer to itself that is referenced inside the member function using the keyword **this**. For this reason, when overloading a unary operator using a member function, no argument is explicitly declared. The only argument needed in this situation is the implicit pointer to the object that activated the call to the overloaded operator function. Since **this** is a pointer to the object, any changes made to the object's private data affect the object that generates the call to the operator function. Unlike member functions, a **friend** function does not receive a **this** pointer and therefore cannot reference the object that activated it. For this reason, trying to create a **friend operator++( )** function as shown here does not work:

```
// THIS WILL NOT WORK
three_d operator++(three_d op1)
{
 op1.x++;
 op1.y++;
 op1.z++;
 return op1;
}
```

The reason this function does not work is because only a *copy* of the object that activated the call to **operator++( )** is passed to the function in parameter **op1**. Thus, the changes inside **operator++( )** do not affect the called object.

You might at first think that the solution to the above program is to define the **friend** operator function as shown here, using a pointer to the object that activates the call:

```
// THIS WILL NOT WORK
three_d operator++(three_d *op1)
{
  op1->x++;
  op1->y++;
  op1->z++;
  return *op1;
}
```

While this function is correct syntactically, it still will not work. For example, assuming this version of the **operator++( )** function, this code fragment does not compile:

```
three_d ob(1, 2, 3);
&ob++;  // will not compile
```

The trouble is that the statement **&ob++** is inherently ambiguous.

The way to use a **friend** when overloading a unary **++** or **– –** is to use a reference parameter. In this way the compiler knows in advance that it must generate an address when it calls the function. This avoids the ambiguity introduced by the previous attempt. Here is the entire **three_d** program, using a **friend operator++( )** function:

```
// This version uses a friend operator++() function.
#include <iostream.h>

class three_d {
  int x, y, z; // 3-d coordinates
public:
  friend three_d operator+(three_d op1, three_d op2);
  three_d operator=(three_d op2);  // op1 is implied
  // use a reference to overload the ++
  friend three_d operator++(three_d &op1);

  void show(void) ;
  void assign(int mx, int my, int mz);
} ;

// This is now a friend function.
three_d operator+(three_d op1, three_d op2)
{
  three_d temp;

  temp.x = op1.x + op2.x;  // these are integer additions
  temp.y = op1.y + op2.y;  // and the + retains its original
  temp.z = op1.z + op2.z;  // meaning relative to them
  return temp;
}

three_d three_d::operator=(three_d op2)
{
  x = op2.x; // these are integer assigments
  y = op2.y; // and the = retains its original
  z = op2.z; // meaning relative to them
  return *this;
```

```
}

// Overload a unary operator using a friend function.
// This requires the use of a reference parameter.
three_d operator++(three_d &op1)
{
  op1.x++;
  op1.y++;
  op1.z++;
  return op1;
}

// show X, Y, Z coordinates
void three_d::show(void)
{
  cout << x << ", ";
  cout << y << ", ";
  cout << z << "\n";
 }

// Assign coordinates
void three_d::assign(int mx, int my, int mz)
{
  x = mx;
  y = my;
  z = mz;
}

main(void)
{
  three_d a, b, c;
  a.assign(1, 2, 3);
  b.assign(10, 10, 10);

  a.show();
  b.show();

  c = a+b;  // now add a and b together
  c.show();

  c = a+b+c; // add a, b and c together
  c.show();

  c = b = a;  // demonstrate multiple assignment
  c.show();
```

```
    b.show();

    c++;  // increment c
    c.show();

    return 0;
}
```

*In general, you should use member functions to implement overloaded operators. Remember that **friend** functions are allowed in C++ mostly to handle some special-case situations.*

Another Example of Operator Overloading

This section develops another example of operator overloading that implements a string type and defines several operations relative to that type. Even though C's approach of implementing strings as character arrays rather than as a type is both flexible and efficiently implemented, to beginners it can lack the conceptual clarity of the way strings are implemented in languages such as BASIC. However, using C++ it is possible to combine the best of both worlds by defining a string **class** and operations that are related to that class.

To begin, the following **class** declares the type **str_type**:

```
#include <iostream.h>
#include <string.h>

class str_type {
  char string[80];
public:
  str_type(char *str = "\0") { strcpy(string, str); }



  str_type operator+(str_type str); // concatenate
  str_type operator=(str_type str); // assign

  // output the string
  void show_str(void) { cout << string; }
} ;
```

As you can see, **str_type** declares one string in its private portion. For the sake of this example, no string can be longer than 80 bytes. The **class** has one constructor function that can be used to initialize the array **string** with a specific value or assign it a null string in the absence of any initializer. It also declares two overloaded operators that perform concatenation and assignment. Finally, it declares the function **show_str( )**, which outputs **string** to the screen. The overloaded operator functions are shown here:

```
// Concatenate two strings.
str_type str_type::operator+(str_type str) {
  str_type temp;

  strcpy(temp.string, string);
  strcat(temp.string, str.string);
  return temp;
}

// Assign one string to another.
str_type str_type::operator=(str_type str) {
  strcpy(string, str.string);
  return *this;
}
```

Given these definitions, the following **main( )** illustrates their use:

```
main(void)
{
  str_type a("Hello "), b("There"), c;

  c = a + b;

  c.show_str();

  return 0;
}
```

This program outputs "Hello There" on the screen. It first concatenates **a** with **b** and then assigns this value to **c**. Keep in mind that both the **=** and the **+** are defined only for objects of type **str_type**. For example, this statement is invalid because it tries to assign object **a** a normal C++ string:

```
a = "this is currently wrong";
```

However, the **str_type class** can be enhanced to allow such a statement. To expand the types of operations supported by the **str_type class** so that you can assign normal C++ strings to **str_type** objects or concatenate a C++ string with a **str_type** object, you need to overload the + and = operations a second time. First, the **class** declaration is changed, as shown here:

```
class str_type {
  char string[80];
public:
  str_type(char *str = "\0") { strcpy(string, str); }

  str_type operator+(str_type str); // concatenate objects
  str_type operator+(char *str);  // concatenate object with
                                  // a string

  str_type operator=(str_type str); // assign object to
                                     // object
  char *operator=(char *str); // assign string to object

  void show_str(void) { cout << string; }
} ;
```

Next, the overloaded **operator+( )** and **operator =( )** are implemented, as shown here:

```
// Assign a string to an object
str_type str_type::operator=(char *str)
{
  str_type temp;

  strcpy(string, str);
  strcpy(temp.string, string);
  return temp;
}

// Add a string to an object
str_type str_type::operator+(char *str)
{
  str_type temp;

  strcpy(temp.string, string);
  strcat(temp.string, str);
  return temp;
}
```

Look carefully at these functions. Notice that the right-side argument is not an object of type **str_type** but rather simply a pointer to a null-terminated character array—that is, a normal string in C++. However, notice that both functions return an object of type **str_type**. Although the functions could, in theory, have returned some other type, it makes the most sense to return an object since the targets of these operations are also objects. The advantage to defining string operations that accept normal C++ strings as the right-side operand is that it allows some statements to be written in a natural way. For example, these are now valid statements:

```
str_type a, b, c;

a = "hi there";  // assign an object a string

c = a + " George";  // concatenate an object with a string
```

The following program incorporates the additional meanings for the + and = operations and illustrates their use.

```
// Expanding the string type.
#include <iostream.h>
#include <string.h>

class str_type {
  char string[80];
public:
  str_type(char *str = "\0") { strcpy(string, str); }

  str_type operator+(str_type str);
  str_type operator+(char *str);

  str_type operator=(str_type str);
  str_type operator=(char *str);

  void show_str(void) { cout << string; }
} ;

str_type str_type::operator+(str_type str) {
  str_type temp;

  strcpy(temp.string, string);
  strcat(temp.string, str.string);
  return temp;
}

str_type str_type::operator=(str_type str) {
  strcpy(string, str.string);
  return *this;
```

```
}

str_type str_type::operator=(char *str)
{
  str_type temp;

  strcpy(string, str);
  strcpy(temp.string, string);
  return temp;
}

str_type str_type::operator+(char *str)
{
  str_type temp;

  strcpy(temp.string, string);
  strcat(temp.string, str);
  return temp;
}

main(void)
{
  str_type a("Hello "), b("There"), c;

  c = a + b;

  c.show_str();
  cout << "\n";

  a = "to program in because";
  a.show_str();
  cout << "\n";

  b = c = "C++ is fun";

  c = c+" "+a+" "+b;
  c.show_str();

  return 0;
}
```

This program displays the following on the screen:

```
Hello There
to program in because
C++ is fun to program in because C++ is fun
```

On your own, try creating other string operations. For example, you might try defining the – so that it performs a substring deletion. For example, if object **A**'s string is "This is a test" and object **B**'s string is "is", then **A–B** yields "th a test". In this case, all occurrences of the substring are removed from the original string.

Chapter **28**

Inheritance, Virtual Functions, and Polymorphism

Crucial to object-oriented programming is polymorphism. Polymorphism is sometimes characterized by the phrase "one interface, multiple methods." This means that a general class of operations can be accessed in the same fashion even though the specific actions associated with each operation may differ.

In C++, polymorphism is supported both at run-time and at compile time. Operator and function overloading are examples of compile-time polymorphism. However, as powerful as operator and function overloading are, they cannot perform all tasks required by a true, object-oriented language. Therefore, C++ also allows run-time polymorphism through the use of derived classes and virtual functions, which are discussed in this chapter.

This chapter begins with a short discussion of pointers to derived types because they are needed to support run-time polymorphism.

Pointers to Derived Types

Pointers to base types and derived types are related. In C++, a base class pointer may point to an object of a class derived from that base. For example, assume that you have a base type called **B_class** and a type called **D_class**, that is derived from **B_class**.

In C++, any pointer declared as a pointer to **B_class** can also be a pointer to **D_class**. For example, given

```
B_class *p; // pointer to object of type B_class
B_class B_ob; // object of type B_class
D_class D_ob; // object of type D_class
```

the following is perfectly valid:

```
p = &B_ob;  // p points to object of type B_class

p = &D_ob;  /* p points to object of type D_class,
               which is an object derived from B_class. */
```

Using **p**, all elements of **D_ob** inherited from **B_ob** can be accessed. However, elements specific to **D_ob** cannot be referenced using **p** (unless a type cast is employed).

For a concrete example, consider this short program, which defines a base class called **B_class** and a derived class called **D_class**. The derived class implements a simple automated telephone book.

```
// Using pointers on derived class objects.

#include <iostream.h>
#include <string.h>

class B_class {
  char name[80];
public:
  void put_name(char *s) {strcpy(name, s); }
  void show_name(void) {cout << name << " ";}
} ;

class D_class : public B_class {
  char phone_num[80];
public:
  void put_phone(char *num) {
    strcpy(phone_num, num);
  }
  void show_phone() {cout << phone_num << "\n";}
};

main(void)
{
```

```
B_class *p;
B_class B_ob;

D_class *dp;
D_class D_ob;

p = &B_ob;   // address of base

// Access B_class via pointer.
p->put_name("Thomas Edison");

// Access D_class via base pointer.
p = &D_ob;
p->put_name("Albert Einstein");

// Show that each name went into proper object.
B_ob.show_name();
D_ob.show_name();
cout << "\n";

/* Since put_phone and show_phone are not part of the
   base class, they are not accessible via the base
   pointer p and must be accessed either directly,
   or, as shown here, through a pointer to the
   derived type.
*/
dp = &D_ob;
dp->put_phone("555 555-1234");
p->show_name(); // either p or dp can be used in this line
dp->show_phone();
return 0;
}
```

In this example, the pointer **p** is defined as a pointer to **B_class**. However, it can point to an object of the derived class **D_class** and can be used to access those elements of the derived class that are defined by the base class. However, remember that a base pointer cannot access those elements specific to the derived class without the use of a type cast. This is why **show_phone( )** is accessed using the **dp** pointer, which is a pointer to the derived class.

If you want to access elements defined by a derived type using a base type pointer, you must cast it into a pointer of the derived type. For example, this line of code properly calls the **show_phone( )** function of **D_ob**:

```
((D_class *)p)->show_phone();
```

The outer set of parentheses are necessary to associate the cast with **p** and not with the return type of **show_phone( )**. While there is technically nothing wrong with casting a pointer in this manner, it is best avoided because it simply adds confusion to your code.

While a base pointer can be used to point to any type of derived object, the reverse is not true. That is, you cannot use a pointer to a derived class to access an object of the base type.

One final point: a pointer is incremented and decremented relative to its base type. Therefore, when a pointer to a base class is pointing to a derived class, incrementing or decrementing it does *not* make it point to the next object of the derived class. Therefore, you should consider it invalid to increment or decrement a pointer when it is pointing to a derived object.

The fact that a pointer to a base type can be used to point to an object derived from that base is extremely important and fundamental to C++. In fact, as you will soon learn, it is crucial to the way C++ implements run-time polymorphism.

Virtual Functions

Run-time polymorphism is achieved through the use of derived types and virtual functions. In short, a *virtual function* is a function that is declared as **virtual** in a base class and redefined in one or more derived classes. Virtual functions are special because when one is accessed using a pointer of the base class to an object of a derived class, C++ determines which function to call *at run-time* based on the type of object *pointed to.* Thus, when different objects are pointed to, different versions of the virtual function are executed.

A virtual function is declared as **virtual** inside the base class by preceding its declaration with the keyword **virtual**. However, when a virtual function is redefined by a derived class, the keyword **virtual** need not be repeated (although it is not an error to do so).

As a first example of virtual functions, examine this short program:

```
// A short example that uses virtual functions.
#include <iostream.h>

class Base {
public:
  virtual void who(void) { // specify a virtual function
    cout << "Base\n";
  }
};

class first_d : public Base {
```

```
public:
  void who(void) { // define who() relative to first_d
    cout << "First derivation\n";
  }
};

class second_d : public Base {
public:
  void who(void) { // define who() relative to second_d
    cout << "Second derivation\n";
  }
};

main(void)
{
  Base base_obj;
  Base *p;
  first_d first_obj;
  second_d second_obj;

  p = &base_obj;
  p->who();  // access Base's who

  p = &first_obj;
  p->who(); // access first_d's who

  p = &second_obj;
  p->who();  // access second_d's who

  return 0;
}
```

This program produces the following output:

```
Base
First derivation
Second derivation
```

Let's examine the program in detail to understand how it works.

As you can see, in **Base**, the function **who( )** is declared as **virtual**. This means that the function can be redefined by a derived class. Inside both **first_d** and **second_d**, **who( )** is redefined relative to each class. Inside **main( )**, four variables are declared. The first is **base_obj**, which is an object of type **Base**; **p**, which is a pointer to **Base** objects; and **first_obj** and **second_obj**, which are objects of the two derived classes.

Next, **p** is assigned the address of **base_obj**, and the **who( )** function is called. Since **who( )** is declared as **virtual**, C++ determines at run-time which version of **who( )** is referred to by the type of object pointed to by **p**. In this case, it is an object of type **Base**, so the version of **who( )** declared in **Base** is executed. Next, **p** is assigned the address of **first_obj**. (Remember that a base class pointer can be used to reference any derived class.) Now when **who( )** is called, C++ again examines what type of object is pointed to by **p** to determine what version of **who( )** to call. Since **p** points to an object of type **first_d**, that version of **who( )** is used. Likewise, when **p** is assigned the address of **second_obj**, the version of **who( )** declared inside **second_d** is executed.

The key point to using virtual functions to achieve run-time polymorphism is that you must access those functions through the use of a pointer declared as a pointer to the base class. Although you can call a virtual function explicitly using the object name as you would call any other member function, it is only when a virtual function is accessed through a pointer to the base class that run-time polymorphism is achieved.

The redefinition of a virtual function in a derived class is a special form of function overloading. However, the reason that this term is not used in the preceding discussion is that several restrictions apply. First, the prototypes for virtual functions must match. As you know, when overloading normal functions, the number and type of parameters must differ. However, when overloading a virtual function, these elements must be unchanged. If the prototypes of the functions differ, then the function is simply considered overloaded, and its virtual nature is lost. Also, if only the return types of the function differ, an error occurs. (Functions that differ only in their return types are inherently ambiguous.) Another restriction is that a virtual function must be a member, not a **friend**, of the class for which it is defined. However, a virtual function can be a **friend** of another class. Also, destructor functions can be virtual, but constructors cannot.

Because of the restrictions and differences between overloading normal functions and "overloading" virtual functions, the term *overriding* is used to describe the virtual function redefinition.

Once a function is declared as **virtual** it stays virtual no matter how many layers of derived classes it can pass through. For example, if **second_d** is derived from **first_d** instead of **Base**, as shown in the following example, **who( )** is still virtual, and the proper version is still correctly selected:

```
// Derive from first_d, not Base
class second_d : public first_d {
public:
  void who(void) { // define who() relative to second_d
    cout << "Second derivation\n";
  }
};
```

When a derived class does not override a virtual function, then the version of the function in the base class is used. For example, try this version of the preceding program:

```cpp
#include <iostream.h>

class Base {
public:
  virtual void who(void) {
    cout << "Base\n";
  }
};

class first_d : public Base {
public:
  void who(void) {
    cout << "First derivation\n";
  }
};

class second_d : public Base {
// who() not defined
};

main(void)
{
  Base base_obj;
  Base *p;
  first_d first_obj;
  second_d second_obj;

  p = &base_obj;
  p->who();  // access Base's who()

  p = &first_obj;
  p->who(); // access first_d's who()

  p = &second_obj;
  p->who();  /* access Base's who() because
               second_d does not redefine it */

  return 0;
}
```

This program now outputs the following:

```
Base
First derivation
Base
```

Keep in mind that inherited characteristics are hierarchical. To illustrate this point, imagine that in the preceding example **second_d** is derived from **first_d** instead of **Base**. When **who( )** is referenced relative to an object of type **second_d** (in which **who( )** is not defined) it is the version of **who( )** declared inside **first_d** that is called since it is the class closest to **second_d**. In general, when a class does not override a virtual function, C++ uses the first definition that it finds in reverse order of derivation.

Why Virtual Functions?

As stated at the start of this chapter, virtual functions in combination with derived types allow C++ to support run-time polymorphism. Polymorphism is essential to object-oriented programming because it allows a generalized class to specify those functions that will be common to any derivative of that class, while allowing a derived class to specify the exact implementation of some or all of those functions. In other words, the base class dictates the general *interface* that any object derived from that class will have, but lets the derived class define the actual *method*. This is why the phrase "one interface, multiple methods" is often used to describe polymorphism.

Part of the key to successfully applying polymorphism is understanding that base and derived classes form a hierarchy that moves from greater to lesser generalization (base to derived). Hence, when used correctly, the base class provides all elements that a derived class can use directly plus the basis for those functions that the derived class must implement on its own.

Having a consistent interface with multiple implementations is important because it helps the programmer handle increasingly complex programs. For example, when you develop a program, all objects you derive from a particular base class are accessed in the same general way, even if the specific actions vary from one derived class to the next. This means that you need to remember only one interface rather than several. Further, the separation of interface and implementation allows the creation of *class libraries,* which can be provided by a third party. If these libraries are implemented correctly, they provide a common interface that you can use to derive your own specific classes.

To get an idea of the power of the "one interface, multiple methods" concept, examine this short program. It creates a base class called **figure**. This class is used to store the dimensions of various two-dimensional objects and to compute their areas. The function **set_dim( )** is a standard member function because its operation is common to all derived classes. However, **show_area( )** is declared as **virtual** because the way the area of each object is computed varies. The program uses **figure** to derive two specific classes, called **square** and **triangle**.

```
#include <iostream.h>

class figure {
protected:
  double x, y;
public:
  void set_dim(double i, double j) {
    x = i;
    y = j;
  }
  virtual void show_area(void) {
    cout << "No area computation defined ";
    cout << "for this class.\n";
  }
} ;

class triangle : public figure {
  public:
    void show_area(void) {
      cout << "Triangle with height ";
      cout << x << " and base " << y;
      cout << " has an area of ";
      cout << x * 0.5 * y << ".\n";
    }
};

class square : public figure {
  public:
    void show_area(void) {
      cout << "Square with dimensions ";
      cout << x << "x" << y;
      cout << " has an area of ";
      cout << x *  y << ".\n";
    }
};

main(void)
{
  figure *p;  /* create a pointer to base type */
```

```
triangle t;   /* create objects of derived types */
square s;

p = &t;
p->set_dim(10.0, 5.0);
p->show_area();
p = &s;
p->set_dim(10.0, 5.0);
p->show_area();

return 0;
}
```

As you can see by examining this program, the interface to both **square** and **triangle** is the same even though both provide their own methods for computing the area of each of their objects.

Given the declaration for **figure**, it is possible to derive a class called **circle** that computes the area of a circle given its radius. To do so you must create a new derived type that computes the area of a circle. The power of virtual functions is based in the fact that you can easily derive a new type that shares the same common interface as other related objects. For example, here is one way to do it:

```
class circle : public figure {
  public:
    void show_area(void) {
      cout << "Circle with radius ";
      cout << x;
      cout << " has an area of ";
      cout <<  3.14 * x * x;
    }
} ;
```

Before trying to use **circle**, look closely at the definition of **show_area( )**. Notice that it uses only the value of **x**, which is assumed to hold the radius. (Remember that the area of a circle is computed using the formula πR^2.) However, the function **set_dim( )** as defined in **figure** assumes that it will be passed, not just one, but two values. Since **circle** does not require this second value, what is the best course of action?

There are two ways to resolve this problem. First, you can call **set_dim( )** using a dummy value as the second parameter when using a **circle** object. This has the disadvantage of being sloppy as well as requiring you to remember a special exception, which violates the "one interface, many methods" approach.

A better way to resolve this problem is to give the **y** parameter inside **set_dim( )** a default value. In this way, when calling **set_dim( )** for a circle, you need specify only the radius. When calling **set_dim( )** for a triangle or a square, you would specify both values. The expanded program is shown here:

```
#include <iostream.h>

class figure {
protected:
  double x, y;
public:
  void set_dim(double i, double j=0) {
    x = i;
    y = j;
  }
  virtual void show_area(void) {
    cout << "No area computation defined ";
    cout << "for this class.\n";
  }
} ;

class triangle : public figure {
  public:
    void show_area(void) {
      cout << "Triangle with height ";
      cout << x << " and base " << y;
      cout << " has an area of ";
      cout << x * 0.5 * y << ".\n";
    }
};

class square : public figure {
  public:
    void show_area(void) {
      cout << "Square with dimensions ";
      cout << x << "x" << y;
      cout << " has an area of ";
      cout << x *  y << ".\n";
    }
};

class circle : public figure {
  public:
    void show_area(void) {
      cout << "Circle with radius ";
      cout << x;
```

```
        cout << " has an area of ";
        cout << 3.14 * x * x;
    }
} ;

main(void)
{
  figure *p;  /* create a pointer to base type */
  triangle t;  /* create objects of derived types */
  square s;
  circle c;

  p = &t;
  p->set_dim(10.0, 5.0);
  p->show_area();

  p = &s;
  p->set_dim(10.0, 5.0);
  p->show_area();

  p = &c;
  p->set_dim(9.0);
  p->show_area();

  return 0;
}
```

This points out that when defining base classes it is important to be as flexible as possible. Don't give your program unnecessary restrictions.

Pure Virtual Functions and Abstract Types

When a virtual function that is not overridden in a derived class is called for an object of that derived class, the version of the function as defined in the base class is used. However, in many circumstances there is no meaningful definition of a virtual function inside the base class. For example, in the base class **figure**, used in the preceding example, the definition of **show_area( )** is simply a place holder. It does not compute and display the area of any type of object. There are two ways you can handle this situation. One way is to simply have it report a warning message, as shown in the example. While this approach can be useful in certain situations, it is not appropriate for all circumstances. There can be virtual functions that must be defined by the derived class in order for the derived class to have any meaning. For example, the **class triangle** has no meaning if **show_area( )** is not defined. In this sort of case, you want some method to ensure that a derived class does, indeed, define all necessary functions. C++'s solution to this problem is the pure virtual function.

A *pure* virtual function is a function declared in a base class that has no definition relative to the base. Since it has no definition relative to the base, any derived type must define its own version—it cannot simply use the version defined in the base. To declare a pure virtual function, use this general form:

virtual *type func_name*(*parameter list*) = 0;

where *type* is the return type of the function and *func_name* is the name of the function. For example, in the following version of **figure**, **show_area( )** is a pure virtual function:

```
class figure {
  double x, y;
public:
  void set_dim(double i, double j=0) {
    x = i;
    y = j;
  }
  virtual void show_area(void) = 0; // pure
} ;
```

By declaring a virtual function as pure, you force any derived class to define its own implementation. If a class fails to do so, a compile-time error results. For example, if you try to compile this modified version of the **figure** program, in which the definition for **show_area( )** has been removed from the **circle class**, you will see an error message:

```
/*
   This program will not compile because the class
   circle does not override show_area().
*/
#include <iostream.h>

class figure {
protected:
  double x, y;
public:
  void set_dim(double i, double j) {
    x = i;
    y = j;
  }
```

```
    virtual void show_area(void) = 0; // pure
} ;

class triangle : public figure {
  public:
    void show_area(void) {
      cout << "Triangle with height ";
      cout << x << " and base " << y;
      cout << " has an area of ";
      cout << x * 0.5 * y << ".\n";
    }
};

class square : public figure {
  public:
    void show_area(void) {
      cout << "Square with dimensions ";
      cout << x << "x" << y;
      cout << " has an area of ";
      cout << x *  y << ".\n";
    }
};

class circle : public figure {
// no definition of show_area() will cause an error
};

main(void)
{
  figure *p;  /* create a pointer to base type */

  triangle t;  /* create objects of derived types */
  square s;

  p = &t;
  p->set_dim(10.0, 5.0);
  p->show_area();

  p = &s;
  p->set_dim(10.0, 5.0);
  p->show_area();

  return 0;
}
```

If a class has at least one pure virtual function, that class is said to be *abstract*. Abstract classes have one important feature: There can be no objects of that class. Instead, an abstract class must be used only as a base that other classes will inherit. The reason that an abstract class cannot be used to declare an object is that one or more of its member functions have no definition. However, even if the base class is abstract, you still can use it to declare pointers, which are needed to support run-time polymorphism.

Early Versus Late Binding

There are two terms that are commonly used when discussing object-oriented programming languages: early binding and late binding. Relative to C++, these terms refer to events that occur at compile time and events that occur at run-time, respectively.

In object-oriented terms, *early binding* means that an object is bound to its function call at compile time. That is, all information necessary to determine which function will be called is known when the program is compiled. Examples of early binding include standard function calls, overloaded function calls, and overloaded operator function calls. The principal advantage to early binding is efficiency—it is both faster and often requires less memory than late binding. Its disadvantage is a lack of flexibility.

Late binding means that an object is bound to its function call only at run-time, not before. Late binding is achieved in C++ by using virtual functions and derived types. The advantage to late binding is that it allows greater flexibility. It can be used to support a common interface while allowing various objects that use that interface to define their own implementations. Further, it can be used to help you create class libraries, which can be reused and extended.

Whether your program uses early or late binding depends on what your program is designed to do. (Actually, most large programs use a combination of both.) Late binding is one of C++'s most powerful additions to the C language. However, the price you pay for this power is that your program will run slightly slower. Therefore, it is best to use late binding only when it adds to the structure and manageability of your program. Keep in mind that the loss of performance is very small, so when the situation calls for late binding, you should most definitely use it.

Constructors and Destructors in Derived Classes

When using derived classes, it is important to understand how and when constructor and destructor functions are executed in both the base and derived classes. Let's begin with constructors.

It is possible for a base class and a derived class to each have a constructor function. (In fact, in the case of multiple inheritance, it is possible for all involved classes to have constructors, but we will start with the simplest case.) When a base class contains a constructor, that constructor is executed before the constructor in the derived class. For example, consider this short program:

```
#include <iostream.h>

class Base {
public:
  Base(void) {cout << "\nBase created\n";}
};

class D_class1 : public Base {
public:
  D_class1(void) {cout << "D_class1 created\n";}
};

main(void)
{
  D_class1 d1;

  // do nothing but execute constructors
  return 0;
}
```

This program creates an object of type **D_class1**. It displays this output:

```
Base created
D_class1 created
```

Here, **d1** is an object of type **D_class1**, which is derived using **Base**. Thus, when **d1** is created, first **Base( )** is executed, then **D_class1( )** is called.

It makes sense for constructors to be called in the same order in which the derivation takes place. Because the base class has no knowledge of the derived class, any initialization it needs to perform is separate from and possibly prerequisite to any initialization performed by the derived class, so it must be executed first.

Opposite from constructors, a destructor function in a derived class is executed before the destructor in the base. The reason for this is also easy to understand. Since the destruction of the base class implies the destruction of the derived class, the derived destructor must be executed before it is destroyed. This program illustrates the order in which constructors and destructors are executed:

```
#include <iostream.h>

class Base {
public:
  Base(void) {cout << "\nBase created\n";}
  ~Base(void) {cout << "Base destroyed\n\n";}
};

class D_class1 : public Base {
public:
  D_class1(void) {cout << "D_class1 created\n";}
  ~D_class1(void) {cout << "D_class1 destroyed\n";}
};

main(void)
{
  D_class1 d1;

  cout << "\n";

  return 0;
}
```

This program produces the following output:

```
Base created
D_class1 created

D_class1 destroyed
Base destroyed
```

As you know, it is possible for a derived class to be used as a base class in the creation of another derived class. When this happens, constructors are executed in the order of their derivation and destructors in the reverse order. For example, consider this program, which uses **D_class1** to derive **D_class2**:

```
#include <iostream.h>

class Base {
public:
  Base(void) {cout << "\nBase created\n";}
  ~Base(void) {cout << "Base destroyed\n\n";}
};
```

```
class D_class1 : public Base {
public:
  D_class1(void) {cout << "D_class1 created\n";}
  ~D_class1(void) {cout << "D_class1 destroyed\n";}
};

class D_class2 : public D_class1 {
public:
  D_class2(void) {cout << "D_class2 created\n";}
  ~D_class2(void) {cout << "D_class2 destroyed\n";}
};

main(void)
{
  D_class1 d1;
  D_class2 d2;

  cout << "\n";

  return 0;
}
```

The program produces this output:

```
Base created
D_class1 created

Base created
D_class1 created
D_class2 created

D_class2 destroyed
D_class1 destroyed
Base destroyed

D_class1 destroyed
Base destroyed
```

Multiple Base Classes

It is possible to specify more than one base class when creating a derived type. To do so, use a comma-separated list of the classes that will be inherited. For example, consider this program:

```
#include <iostream.h>

class Base1 {
public:
  Base1(void) {cout << "\nBase1 created\n";}
  ~Base1(void) {cout << "Base1 destroyed\n\n";}
};

class Base2 {
public:
  Base2(void) {cout << "Base2 created\n";}
  ~Base2(void) {cout << "Base2 destroyed\n";}
};

// multiple base classes
class D_class1 : public Base1, public Base2 {
public:
  D_class1(void) {cout << "D_class1 created\n";}
  ~D_class1(void) {cout << "D_class1 destroyed\n";}
};

main(void)
{
  D_class1 d1;

  cout << "\n";

  return 0;
}
```

In this program, **D_class1** is derived from both **Base1** and **Base2**. The program produces this output:

```
Base1 created
Base2 created
D_class1 created

D_class1 destroyed
Base2 destroyed
Base1 destroyed
```

As you can see, when a list of base classes is used, the constructors are called in order from left to right. Destructors are called in order from right to left.

Chapter 29

Using C++'s I/O Class Library

Although C++ supports all of C's I/O functions, most C++ programs ignore them in favor of C++'s I/O operators. Using C++'s method of I/O helps you to think in an object-oriented manner and to see the value of the "one interface, multiple methods" philosophy.

This chapter presents an overview of Turbo/Borland C++'s I/O class library. It also discusses how to overload the << and >> operators so that you can input or output objects of classes that you design. C++'s I/O system is very large and it isn't possible to cover every function or feature here, but this chapter introduces you to the most important and commonly used functions and features.

Why C++ Has Its Own I/O System

If you have programmed in other languages, you know that C has one of the most flexible, yet powerful I/O systems. (In fact, it may be safe to say that among the world's structured languages, C's I/O system is unparalleled.) In spite of the power of C's I/O functions, the C I/O system provides no support for user-defined objects. This is why C++ defines its own I/O functions. For example, in C if you create this structure:

```
struct my_struct {
  int count;
  char s[80];
```

```
   double balance;
} cust;
```

there is no way to customize or extend C's I/O system so that it knows about and can perform I/O operations directly on a variable of type **my_struct**.

However, using C++'s approach to I/O it is possible to overload the **<<** and **>>** operators so that they know about classes that you create. This includes the console I/O operations you have been using throughout this part of the book as well as file I/O. (As you will see, console and file I/O are linked in C++ as they are in C.)

Although the C and C++ I/O systems contain virtually the same operations, the fact that C++'s system can be made aware of user-defined types greatly increases its flexibility. The C++ I/O system can also help prevent bugs. For example, in this call to **scanf( )**:

```
char str[80];
int i;

scanf("%d%s", str, &i);
```

the string and the integer are inverted in the argument list; the **%d** is matched with the string **str** and the **%s** with the integer **i**. However, while this produces peculiar results, a call such as this is not technically an error in C. (It is conceivable that in some highly unusual situation, you might *want* to use a call to **scanf( )** as shown.) However, it is more likely that this call to **scanf( )** is, indeed, an error. In short, when calling **scanf( )**, C has no means of providing strong type checking. In C++, however, I/O operations for all built-in types are defined relative to the **<<** and **>>** operators so that there is no way for such an inversion to take place. Instead, the correct operation is automatically determined by the type of the operand. This feature can also be extended to user-defined objects. (If needed, you can still cause something like the unusual **scanf( )** call to be generated in C++ by type casting.)

C++ Streams

The C and C++ I/O systems have one important thing in common: they both operate on streams, which are discussed in Part One of this book. (That discussion is not repeated here.) The fact that C and C++ streams are similar means that what you already know about streams is completely applicable to C++. Also, with a few small exceptions, you can mix C and C++ I/O operations in the same program. Therefore, you can begin to evolve existing C programs toward C++ without having to convert every I/O operation at the outset.

The C++ Predefined Streams

Like C, C++ contains several predefined streams that are opened automatically when your C++ program begins execution. They are **cin**, **cout**, **cerr**, and **clog**. As you know, **cin** is the stream associated with standard input and **cout** is the stream associated with standard output. The difference between **cerr** and **clog**, which are both linked to standard output, is that **cerr** is not buffered, so any data sent to it is immediately output. Alternatively, **clog** is buffered, and output is only written when a buffer is full.

By default, the C++ standard streams are linked to the console, but they can be redirected to other devices or files by your program. Also, they can be redirected by the operating system.

The C++ Stream Classes

The C++ I/O system is defined by a hierarchy of classes that relate to streams. These definitions are found in the header file **iostream.h**. The lowest level class is called **streambuf** and it provides the basic stream operations but no formatting support. The next class in the hierarchy is called **ios**, which provides the basic support for formatted I/O. It is also used to derive three classes that you can use to create streams: **istream**, **ostream**, and **iostream**. Using **istream**, you can create an input stream; using **ostream**, you can create an output stream; and using **iostream**, you can create a stream capable of both input and output.

Creating Your Own Inserters and Extractors

In the preceding four chapters, special member functions were created in order to output or input a class's data. While there is nothing wrong with this approach, C++ allows a much better way of performing I/O operations on classes by overloading the << and >> operators.

In the language of C++, the << operator is referred to as the *insertion* operator because it inserts characters into a stream. Likewise, the >> operator is called the *extraction* operator because it extracts characters from a stream. The operator functions that overload the insertion and extraction operators are generally called *inserters* and *extractors*, respectively.

The insertion and extraction operators are already overloaded (in **iostream.h**) to perform stream I/O on any of C++'s built-in types. This section explains how to define these operators relative to classes that you define.

Creating Inserters

C++ provides an easy way to create inserters for classes that you create. This simple example creates an inserter for the **three_d class** (first defined in Chapter 27):

```
class three_d {
public:
  int x, y, z; // 3-d coordinates
  three_d(int a, int b, int c) {x=a; y=b; z=c;}
} ;
```

To create an inserter function for an object of type **three_d**, you must define what an insertion operation means relative to the class **three_d**. To do this, you must overload the **<<** operator, as shown here:

```
// Display X, Y, Z coordinates (three_d's inserter).
ostream &operator<<(ostream &stream, three_d obj)
{
  stream << obj.x << ", ";
  stream << obj.y << ", ";
  stream << obj.z << "\n";
  return stream; // return the stream
}
```

Many of the features in this function are common to all inserter functions. First, notice that it is declared as returning a reference to an object of type **ostream**. This is necessary to allow several insertion operations to be performed in a single statement. Next, the function has two parameters. The first is the reference to the stream that occurs on the left side of the **<<** operator; the second parameter is the object that occurs on the right side. Inside the function, the three values contained in an object of type **three_d** are output, and **stream** is returned. Here is a short program that demonstrates the inserter:

```
#include <iostream.h>

class three_d {
public:
  int x, y, z; // 3-d coordinates
  three_d(int a, int b, int c) {x=a; y=b; z=c;}
} ;

// Display X, Y, Z coordinates - three_d inserter
ostream &operator<<(ostream &stream, three_d obj)
{
```

```
   stream << obj.x << ", ";
   stream << obj.y << ", ";
   stream << obj.z << "\n";
   return stream;  // return the stream
}

main(void)
{
  three_d a(1, 2, 3), b(3, 4, 5), c(5, 6, 7);

  cout << a << b << c;

  return 0;
}
```

If you eliminate the code that is specific to the **three_d** class you are left with the general form of an inserter function, as shown here:

> ostream &operator<<(ostream &*stream*, *class_type obj*)
> {
>   // *type specific code goes here*
>   return *stream*; // return the stream
> }

What an inserter function actually does is up to you. Just make sure that you return **stream**.

*The **obj** parameter may also be passed as a reference.*

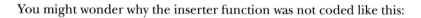

You might wonder why the inserter function was not coded like this:

```
// Limited version - don't use.
ostream &operator<<(ostream &stream, three_d obj)
{
  cout << obj.x << ", ";
  cout << obj.y << ", ";
  cout << obj.z << "\n";
  return stream;  // return the stream
}
```

In this version, the **cout** stream is hard-coded into the function. However, remember that the **<<** operator can be applied to *any stream*. Therefore, you must use the stream passed to the function if it is to work correctly in all cases.

In the **three_d** inserter program, the overloaded inserter function is not a member of **three_d**. In fact, neither inserter nor extractor functions can be members of a class. This is because when an **operator** function is a member of a class, the left operand (implicitly passed using the **this** pointer) is an object of the class that generated the call to the **operator** function. There is no way to change this. However, when overloading inserters, the left argument is a stream and the right argument is an object of the class. Therefore, overloaded inserters cannot be member functions.

The fact that inserters must not be members of the class they are defined to operate on raises a serious question: How can an overloaded inserter access the private elements of a class? In the previous program, the variables **x**, **y**, and **z** were made **public** so that the inserter could access them. But, hiding data is an important part of object-oriented programming, and forcing all data to be **public** is inconsistent with the object-oriented approach. However, there is a solution: An inserter can be a **friend** of a class. As a **friend** of the class it is defined for, it has access to private data. To see an example of this, the **three_d** class and sample program are reworked here, with the overloaded inserter declared as a **friend**.

```
#include <iostream.h>

class three_d {
  int x, y, z; // 3-d coordinates - - now private
public:
  three_d(int a, int b, int c) {x=a; y=b; z=c;}
  friend ostream &operator<<(ostream &stream, three_d obj);
} ;

// Display X, Y, Z coordinates - three_d inserter
ostream &operator<<(ostream &stream, three_d obj)
{
  stream << obj.x << ", ";
  stream << obj.y << ", ";
  stream << obj.z << "\n";
  return stream;  // return the stream
}

main(void)
{
  three_d a(1, 2, 3), b(3, 4, 5), c(5, 6, 7);

  cout << a << b << c;

  return 0;
}
```

Notice that the variables **x**, **y**, and **z** are now **private** to **three_d**, but can still be accessed directly by the inserter. Making inserters (and extractors) **friend**s of the classes they are defined for preserves the encapsulation principle of object-oriented programming.

Overloading Extractors

To overload an extractor, use the same general approach as when overloading an inserter. For example, this extractor inputs 3-D coordinates. Notice that it also prompts the user.

```
// Get three dimensional values - extractor.
istream &operator>>(istream &stream, three_d &obj)
{
  cout << "Enter X,Y,Z values: ";
  stream >> obj.x >> obj.y >> obj.z;
  return stream;
}
```

Extractors must return a reference to an object of type **istream**. Also, the first parameter must be a reference to an object of type **istream**. The second parameter is a reference to the variable that will be receiving input. Because it is a reference, the second argument can be modified when information is input.

The general form of an extractor is

```
istream &operator>>(istream &stream, object_type &obj)
{
  // put your extractor code here
  return stream;
}
```

Here is a program that demonstrates the extractor for objects of type **three_d**.

```
#include <iostream.h>

class three_d {
  int x, y, z; // 3-d coordinates
public:
  three_d(int a, int b, int c) {x=a; y=b; z=c;}
  friend ostream &operator<<(ostream &stream, three_d obj);
  friend istream &operator>>(istream &stream, three_d &obj);
} ;
```

```
// Display X, Y, Z coordinates - inserter.
ostream &operator<<(ostream &stream, three_d obj)
{
  stream << obj.x << ", ";
  stream << obj.y << ", ";
  stream << obj.z << "\n";
  return stream; // return the stream
}

// Get three dimensional values - extractor
istream &operator>>(istream &stream, three_d &obj)
{
  cout << "Enter X,Y,Z values: ";
  stream >> obj.x >> obj.y >> obj.z;
  return stream;
}

main(void)
{
  three_d a(1, 2, 3);

  cout << a;

  cin >> a;
  cout << a;

  return 0;
}
```

Like inserters, extractor functions cannot be members of the class they are designed to operate upon. As shown in the example, they can be **friend**s or simply independent functions.

Except for the fact that you must return a reference to an object of type **istream**, you can do anything you like inside an extractor function. However, for the sake of structure and clarity, it is best to limit the actions of an extractor to the input operation.

Formatting I/O

As you know, using **printf( )** you can control the format of information displayed on the screen. For example, you can specify field widths and left- or right-justification. You can also accomplish the same type of formatting using C++'s approach to I/O.

There are two ways to format output. The first uses member functions of the **ios** class. The second uses a special type of function called a *manipulator*. We will begin by looking at formatting using the member functions of **ios**.

Formatting Using the ios Member Functions

The following enumeration is defined in **iostream. h:**

```
// formatting flags
enum {
  skipws = 0x0001,
  left = 0x0002,
  right = 0x0004,
  internal = 0x0008,
  dec = 0x0010,
  oct = 0x0020,
  hex = 0x0040,
  showbase = 0x0080,
  showpoint = 0x0100,
  uppercase = 0x0200,
  showpos = 0x0400,
  scientific = 0x0800,
  fixed = 0x1000,
  unitbuf = 0x2000,
  stdio = 0x4000
};
```

The values defined by this enumeration are used to set or clear flags that control some of the ways information is formatted by a stream.

When the **skipws** flag is set, leading white-space characters (spaces, tabs, and newlines) are discarded when performing input on a stream. When **skipws** is cleared, white-space characters are not discarded.

When the **left** flag is set, output is left-justified. When **right** is set, output is right-justified. When the **internal** flag is set, a numeric value is padded to fill a field by inserting spaces between any sign or base character. (You will learn how to specify a field width shortly.)

By default, numeric values are output in decimal. However, you can override this default. For example, to output in decimal, set the **dec** flag. Setting the **oct** flag causes output to be displayed in octal. Setting the **hex** flag causes output to be displayed in hexadecimal.

Setting **showbase** causes the base of numeric values to be shown.

Setting **showpoint** causes a decimal point and trailing 0s to be displayed for all floating-point output—whether needed or not.

By default, when scientific notation is displayed, the 'e' is in lowercase. Also, when a hexadecimal value is displayed, the 'x' is in lowercase. When **uppercase** is set, these characters are displayed in uppercase.

Setting **showpos** causes a leading plus sign to be displayed before positive integer values.

If the **scientific** flag is set, floating-point numeric values are displayed using scientific notation. When **fixed** is set, floating-point values are displayed using normal notation. By default, when **fixed** is set, six decimal places are displayed. When neither flag is set, the compiler chooses an appropriate method.

When **unitbuf** is set, the C++ I/O system performance is improved because output is partially buffered. When set, the buffer is flushed after each insertion operation. This flag is on by default in Turbo/Borland C++.

When **stdio** is set, each stream is flushed after each output. Flushing a stream causes output to be written to the physical device linked to the stream.

The format flags are held in a **long** integer. To set a flag, use the **setf( )** function, whose most common form is shown here:

long setf(long *flags*);

This function returns the stream's previous settings of the format flags and turns on those flags specified by *flags*. For example, to turn on the **showbase** flag, you can use the following statement.

```
stream.setf(ios::showbase);
```

Here, **stream** can actually be any stream you wish to affect. For example, this program turns on both the **showpos** and **scientific** flags for **cout**:

```
#include <iostream.h>

main(void)
{
  cout.setf(ios::showpos);
  cout.setf(ios::scientific);
  cout << 123 << " " << 123.23 << " ";

  return 0;
}
```

The output produced by this program is

```
+123 +1.2323e+02
```

You can OR together as many flags as you like in a single call. For example, you can change the program so that only one call is made to **setf( )** by ORing together **scientific** and **showpos**, as shown here.

```
cout.setf(ios::scientific | ios::showpos);
```

To turn off a flag, use the **unsetf( )** function. Its prototype is shown here:

long unsetf(long *flags*);

The function returns the previous flag settings and turns off those flags specified by *flags*.

Sometimes it is useful to know the current flag settings. You can retrieve the current flag values using this form of the **flags( )** function:

long flags(void);

This function returns the current value of the flags relative to the associated stream.

The following form of **flags( )** sets the flag values to those specified by *flags* and returns the previous flag values:

long flags(long *flags*);

To see how **flags( )** and **unsetf( )** work, examine this program. It includes a function called **showflags( )** that displays the state of **cout**'s flags.

```
#include <iostream.h>

void showflags (long f);

main (void)
{
  long f;

  f = cout.flags();

  showflags(f);
  cout.setf(ios::showpos);
  cout.setf(ios::scientific);

  f = cout.flags();
  showflags(f);
```

```
    cout.unsetf(ios::scientific);

    f = cout.flags();
    showflags(f);

    return 0;
}

void showflags(long f)
{
    long i;

    for(i=0x4000; i; i = i >> 1)
      if(i & f) cout << "1 ";
      else cout << "0 ";

    cout << "\n";
}
```

When run, the program produces this output:

```
0 1 0 0 0 0 0 0 0 0 0 0 0 0 1
0 1 0 1 1 0 0 0 0 0 0 0 0 0 1
0 1 0 0 1 0 0 0 0 0 0 0 0 0 1
```

In addition to the formatting flags, you can also set a stream's field width, the fill character, and the number of digits displayed after a decimal point, using these functions:

> int width(int *len*);
> char fill(char *ch*);
> int precision(int *num*);

The **width( )** function returns the stream's current field width and sets the field width to *len*. By default the field width varies, depending upon the number of characters it takes to hold the data. The **fill( )** function returns the current fill character, which is a space by default, and makes the current fill character the same as *ch*. The fill character is the character used to pad output to fill a specified field width. The **precision( )** function returns the number of digits displayed after a decimal point and sets that value to *num*. Here is a program that demonstrates these three functions:

```
#include <iostream.h>

main(void)
```

```
{
  cout.setf(ios::showpos);
  cout.setf(ios::scientific);
  cout << 123 << " " << 123.23 << "\n";

  cout.precision(2); // two digits after decimal point
  cout.width(10);  // in a field of ten characters
  cout << 123 << " " << 123.23 << "\n";

  cout.fill('#');  // fill using #
  cout.width(10);  // in a field of ten characters
  cout << 123 << " " << 123.23;

  return 0;
}
```

The program displays this output:

```
+123 +1.2323e+02
      +123 +1.23e+02
######+123 +1.23e+02
```

Remember, each stream maintains its own set of format flags. Changing the flag settings of one stream does *not* affect another stream.

Using Manipulators

The C++ I/O system includes a second way to alter the format parameters of a stream. This way uses special functions called *manipulators,* which can be included in an I/O expression. The standard manipulators are shown in Table 29-1.

To access these manipulators, you must include **iomanip.h** in your program.

A manipulator can be used as part of an I/O expression. Here is an example program that uses manipulators to change the format of output:

```
#include <iostream.h>
#include <iomanip.h>

main(void)
{
  cout << setprecision(2) << 1000.243 << endl;
  cout << setw(20) << "Hello there.";
```

```
  return 0;
}
```

It produces this output:

```
1000.24
        Hello there.
```

Notice how the manipulators occur in the chain of I/O operations. Also, notice that when a manipulator does not take an argument, such as **endl** in the example, it is not followed by parentheses. This is because the address of the function is passed to the overloaded **<<** operator.

This program uses **setiosflags( )** to set **cout**'s **scientific** and **showpos** flags:

```
#include <iostream.h>
#include <iomanip.h>

main(void)
{
  cout << setiosflags(ios::showpos);
  cout << setiosflags(ios::scientific);
  cout << 123 << " " << 123.23;

  return 0;
}
```

The following program uses **ws** to skip any leading white space when inputting a string into **s**.

```
#include <iostream.h>

main(void)
{
  char s[80];

  cin >> ws >> s;
  cout << s;
}
```

Creating Your Own Manipulator Functions

You can create your own manipulator functions. There are two types of manipulator functions: those that take an argument (parameterized) and those that don't

Manipulator	Purpose	Input/Output
dec	Format numeric data in decimal	Input and output
endl	Output a newline character and flush the stream	Output
ends	Output a null	Output
flush	Flush a stream	Output
hex	Format numeric data in hexadecimal	Input and output
oct	Format numeric data in octal	Input and output
resetiosflags(long *f*)	Turn off the flags specified in *f*	Input and output
setbase(int base)	Set the number base to *base*	Output
setfill(int *ch*)	Set the fill character to *ch*	Input and output
setiosflags(long *f*)	Turn on the flags specified in *f*	Input and output
setprecision(int *p*)	Set the number of digits displayed after a decimal point	Input and output
setw(int w)	Set the field width to *w*	Input and output
ws	Skip leading white space	Input

Table 29-1. *The C++ Manipulators*

(parameterless). There are some differences between the way each is created. This section discusses how to create each type, starting with parameterless manipulators.

Creating Parameterless Manipulators

All parameterless manipulator output functions have this skeleton:

```
ostream &manip-name(ostream &stream)
{
  // your code here
  return stream;
}
```

Here, *manip-name* is the name of the manipulator. It is important to understand that even though the manipulator has as its single argument a pointer to the stream upon

which it is operating, no argument is used when the manipulator is inserted in an output operation.

The following program creates a manipulator called **setup( )** that turns on left-justification, sets the field width to 10, and specifies the dollar sign as the fill character.

```
#include <iostream.h>
#include <iomanip.h>

ostream &setup(ostream &stream)
{
  stream.setf(ios::left);
  stream << setw(10) << setfill('$');
  return stream;
}

main(void)
{
  cout << 10 << " " << setup << 10;

  return 0;
}
```

Custom manipulators are useful for two reasons. First, you might need to perform an I/O operation on a device for which none of the predefined manipulators apply—a plotter, for example. In this case, creating your own manipulators makes it more convenient when outputting to the device. Second, you may find that you are repeating the same sequence of operations many times. You can consolidate these operations into a single manipulator, as the preceding program illustrates.

All parameterless manipulator input functions have this general form:

> istream &*manip-name*(istream &*stream*)
> {
>   *// your code here*
>   return *stream*;
> }

For example, this program creates the **prompt( )** manipulator to display a prompting message and switches numeric input to hexadecimal:

```
#include <iostream.h>
#include <iomanip.h>

istream &prompt(istream &stream)
```

```
{
  cin >> hex;
  cout << "Enter number using hex format: ";

  return stream;
}

main(void)
{
  int i;

  cin >> prompt >> i;
  cout << i;

  return 0;
}
```

It is crucial that your manipulator return **stream**. If this is not done, then your manipulator cannot be used in a complex I/O statement.

Creating Parameterized Manipulators

Creating a manipulator function that takes an argument is more difficult than creating one that doesn't. Before discussing the theory, let's look at an example. The following program creates a parameterized version of **setup( )** from the previous section. In this version, you can specify the field width as an argument to **setup( )**.

```
#include <iostream.h>
#include <iomanip.h>

// Insertion (output) manipulator.
ostream &setup(ostream &stream, int length)
{
  stream.setf(ios::left);
  stream << setw(length) << setfill('$');
  return stream;
}

// Overload.
OMANIP (int) setup(int length) {
  return OMANIP (int) (setup, length);
}

main(void)
```

```
{
  cout << 10 << " ";
  cout << setup(7) << 10;

  return 0;
}
```

As you can see, **setup( )** is now overloaded. When **setup(7)** is encountered in the output expression, the second version of **setup( )** is executed, with the value 7 passed to the **length** parameter. This version then executes the first version with the value 7 again passed in **length** and is used by the **setw( )** manipulator to set the field width. The stream **cout** is passed to **stream** in the first version of **setup( )**.

The class **OMANIP** is defined in **iomanip.h**, and is used to create manipulators that take an argument. In general, whenever you want to create a manipulator that takes an argument, you need to create two overloaded manipulator functions. In one, you need to define two parameters: The first is a reference to the stream and the second is the parameter that will be passed to the function. The second version of the manipulator defines only one parameter, which is the one specified when the manipulator is used in an I/O expression. This second version of the manipulator is used to generate a call to the first version. You will use these general forms for creating parameterized output manipulators:

> ostream &*manip-name*(ostream &*stream, type param*)
> {
>   // your code here
>   return *stream*;
> }
> // Overload
> OMANIP (*type*) *manip-name*(*type param*) {
>   return OMANIP (*type*) (*manip-name, param*);
> }

Here, *type* specifies the type of parameter used by the manipulator. By default, you can only use types **int** and **long** for *type*. However, if you want to use a different type of parameter, you must first alert Turbo/Borland C++ by using the **IOMANIPdeclare** macro (defined in **iomanip.h**), as shown here:

> IOMANIPdeclare(*type*);

Here, *type* is the type of the parameter that you want your manipulator to have. For example, this program shows how to pass a **double** value to a manipulator function:

```
#include <iostream.h>
#include <iomanip.h>
```

```
IOMANIPdeclare(double);  // specify double parameters

ostream &out_d(ostream &stream, double length)
{
  stream << setprecision(2) << length;
  return stream;
}

OMANIP (double) out_d(double length) {
  return OMANIP (double) (out_d, length);
}

main(void)
{
  cout << out_d(123.123456);

  return 0;
}
```

You can use parameters of any valid type, including classes that you define. However, the parameter to **IOMANIPdeclare** must be a single identifier. Therefore, if you need to use a pointer or reference type, you need to define a new type name using **typedef**. For example, to tell the compiler about a character pointer parameter to a manipulator, you must use this statement sequence:

```
typedef char * charptr;

IOMANIPdeclare(charptr);
```

Input manipulators can also take a parameter, as illustrated by this program:

```
#include <iostream.h>
#include <iomanip.h>

// Extraction (input) manipulator.
istream &setup(istream &stream, int length)
{
  cout << "Enter a string ";
  cout << length << " characters long: ";
  return stream;
}

// Overloaded.
```

```
IMANIP(int) setup(int length) {
  return IMANIP(int)(setup, length);
}

main(void)
{
  char str[80];

  cin >> setup(22) >> str;
  cout << str;

  return 0;
}
```

Notice that the format is the same as for output manipulators with two exceptions: The input stream **istream** must be used and the class **IMANIP** is specified.

File I/O

You can use the C++ I/O system to perform file I/O. Although the end result is the same, C++'s approach to file I/O differs somewhat from the ANSI C I/O system discussed earlier. For this reason, you should pay special attention to this section.

In order to perform file I/O, you must include the header file **fstream.h** in your program. It defines several important classes and values.

Opening and Closing a File

In C++, a file is opened by linking it to a stream. There are three types of streams: input, output, and input/output. To open an input stream you must declare the stream to be of class **ifstream**. To open an output stream, it must be declared as class **ofstream**. Streams that will perform both input and output operations must be declared as class **fstream**. For example, this fragment creates one input stream, one output stream, and one stream capable of both input and output:

```
ifstream in;  // input

ofstream out; // output

fstream both; // input and output
```

Once you have created a stream, one way to associate it with a file is by using the **open( )** function. This function is a member of each of the three stream classes. Its prototype is

void open(char *filename, int mode, int access);

Here, *filename* is the name of the file and can include a path specifier. The value of *mode* determines how the file is opened. It must be one (or more) of these values (defined in **fstream.h**):

ios::app
ios::ate
ios::binary
ios::in
ios::nocreate
ios::noreplace
ios::out
ios::trunc

You can combine two or more of these values by ORing them together. Beginning with Turbo/Borland C++ 3.0, the additional mode called **ios::binary** was added. This mode is not available in earlier versions.

Including **ios::app** causes all the output to that file to be appended to the end. This value can only be used with files capable of output. Including **ios::ate** causes a seek to the end of the file to occur when the file is opened.

The **ios::in** specifies that the file is capable of input. The **ios::out** specifies that the file is capable of output. However, creating a stream using **ifstream** implies input and creating a stream using **ofstream** implies output, so in these cases it is unnecessary to supply these values.

Including **ios::nocreate** causes the **open( )** function to fail if the file does not already exist. The **ios::noreplace** value causes the **open( )** function to fail if the file already exists.

The **ios::trunc** value causes the contents of a preexisting file by the same name to be destroyed and the file is truncated to 0 length.

The **ios::binary** mode causes a file to be opened for binary operations. This means that no character translations will occur.

The value of *access* determines how the file can be accessed. In Turbo/Borland C++, these values correspond to DOS's file attribute codes. They are

Attribute	Meaning
0	Normal file, open access
1	Read-only file
2	Hidden file

Attribute	Meaning
4	System file
8	Archive bit set

You can OR two or more of these together.

The following fragment opens a normal output file:

```
ofstream out;
out.open("test", ios::out, 0);
```

However, you will seldom (if ever) see **open( )** called as shown because both the *mode* and *access* parameters have default values: For **ifstream**, *mode* defaults to **ios::in**, and for **ofstream** it defaults to **ios::out**. The *access* parameter has a default value of 0 (normal file). Therefore, the preceding statement will usually look like this:

```
out.open("test");  // defaults to output and normal file
```

To open a stream for both input and output, you must specify both the **ios::in** and the **ios::out** *mode* values, as shown in this example:

```
fstream mystream;
mystream.open("test", ios::in | ios::out);
```

If **open( )** fails, **mystream** will be 0.

Although opening a file using the **open( )** function is perfectly acceptable, most of the time you will not do so because the **ifstream**, **ofstream**, and **fstream** classes include constructor functions that automatically open the file. The constructor functions have the same parameters and defaults as the **open( )** function. Therefore, the most common way to open a file is shown here:

```
ifstream  mystream("myfile"); // open file for input
```

If, for some reason, the file cannot be opened, the value of the associated stream variable is 0. You can use the following code to confirm that the file has actually been opened:

```
ifstream  mystream("myfile"); // open file for input
if(!mystream) {
  cout << "cannot open file";
  //  process error
}
```

To close a file, use the member function **close( )**. For example, to close the file linked to a stream called **mystream**, use this statement:

```
mystream.close();
```

The **close( )** function takes no parameters and returns no value.

Reading and Writing Text Files

To read from or write to a text file you simply use the **<<** and **>>** operators with the stream you opened. For example, the following program writes an integer, a floating-point value, and a string to a file called TEST.

```
#include <iostream.h>
#include <fstream.h>

main(void)
{
  ofstream out("test");
  if(!out) {
    cout << "Cannot open file";
    return 1;
    }

  out << 10 << " " << 123.23 << "\n";
  out << "This is a short text file.";

  out.close();

  return 0;
}
```

The following program reads an integer, a **float**, a character, and a string from the file created by the preceding program:

```
#include <iostream.h>
#include <fstream.h>

main(void)
{
  char ch;
  int i;
  float f;
```

```
char str[80];

ifstream in("test");
if(!in) {
  cout << "Cannot open file";
  return 1;
}

in >> i;
in >> f;
in >> ch;
in >> str;

cout << i << " " << f << " " << ch << "\n";
cout << str;

in.close();
return 0;
}
```

When reading text files using the **>>** operator, keep in mind that certain character translations occur. For example, white-space characters are omitted. If you want to prevent any character translations, you must use C++'s binary I/O functions, discussed in the next section.

Binary I/O

There are two ways to write and read binary data to or from a file. First, you can write a byte using the member function **put( )** and read a byte using the member function **get( )**. The **get( )** function has many forms, but the most commonly used version is shown here along with **put( )**:

istream &get(char &*ch*);
ostream &put(char *ch*);

The **get( )** function reads a single character from the associated stream and puts that value in *ch*. It returns a reference to the stream. The **put( )** function writes *ch* to the stream and returns a reference to the stream.

This program displays the contents of any file on the screen. It uses the **get( )** function.

```
#include <iostream.h>
#include <fstream.h>

main(int argc, char *argv[])
{
  char ch;

  if(argc!=2) {
    cout << "Usage: PR <filename>\n";
    return 1;
  }

  ifstream in(argv[1]);
  if(!in) {
    cout << "Cannot open file";
    return 1;
  }

  while(in) { // in will be 0 when eof is reached
    in.get(ch);
    cout << ch;
  }

  return 0;
}
```

When **in** reaches the end of the file it will become 0, causing the **while** loop to stop.

There is a more compact way to code the loop that reads and displays a file, as shown here:

```
while(in.get(ch))
  cout << ch;
```

This works because **get( )** returns the stream **in** and **in** will be 0 when the end of the file is encountered.

This program uses **put( )** to write a string to a file.

```
#include <iostream.h>
#include <fstream.h>

main(void)
{
  char *p = "hello there";
```

```
ofstream out("test");
if(!out) {
  cout << "Cannot open file";
  return 1;
 }

while(*p) out.put(*p++);

out.close();

return 0;
}
```

The second way to read and write binary data uses C++'s **read( )** and **write( )** member functions. Their prototypes are

istream &read(unsigned char *buf, int num);
ostream &write(const unsigned char *buf, int num);

The **read( )** function reads num bytes from the associated stream and puts them in the buffer pointed to by buf. The **write( )** function writes num bytes to the associated stream from the buffer pointed to by buf.

The following program writes and then reads an array of integers:

```
#include <iostream.h>
#include <fstream.h>

main(void)
{
  int n[5] = {1, 2, 3, 4, 5};
  register int i;

  ofstream out("test");
  if(!out) {
    cout << "Cannot open file";
    return 1;
   }

  out.write((unsigned char *) &n, sizeof n);

  out.close();

  for(i=0; i<5; i++) // clear array
    n[i] = 0;
```

```
ifstream in("test");
in.read((unsigned char *) &n, sizeof n);

for(i=0; i<5; i++) // show values read from file
  cout << n[i] << " ";

in.close();

return 0;
}
```

Note that the type casts inside the calls to **read( )** and **write( )** are necessary when operating on a buffer that is not defined as a character array.

If the end of the file is reached before *num* characters have been read, **read( )** simply stops and the buffer contains as many characters as were available. You can find out how many characters have been read using another member function called **gcount( )**, which has this prototype:

    int gcount( );

It returns the number of characters read by the last binary input operation.

Detecting EOF

You can detect when the end of the file is reached using the member function **eof( )**, which has the prototype

    int eof( );

It returns non-0 when the end of the file has been reached; otherwise it returns 0.

Random Access

In C++'s I/O system you perform random access using the **seekg( )** and **seekp( )** functions. Their most common forms are

    istream &seekg(streamoff *offset*, seek_dir *origin*);
    ostream &seekp(streamoff *offset*, seek_dir *origin*);

Here, **streamoff** is a type defined in **iostream.h** that is capable of containing the largest valid value that *offset* can have.

The C++ I/O system manages two pointers associated with each file. One is the *get* pointer, which specifies where in the file the next input operation will occur. The other is the *put* pointer, which specifies where in the file the next output operation will occur. Each time an input or an output operation takes place, the appropriate pointer is automatically advanced. However, using the **seekg( )** and **seekp( )** functions, it is possible to access the file in a nonsequential fashion.

The **seekg( )** function moves the associated file's current get pointer *offset* number of bytes from the specified *origin*, which must be one of these three values:

Value	Meaning
ios::beg	Beginning of file
ios::cur	Current location
ios::end	End of file

The **seekp( )** function moves the associated file's current put pointer *offset* number of bytes from the specified *origin*, which must be one of the same three values.

This program demonstrates the **seekp( )** function. It allows you to specify a file name on the command line followed by the specific byte in the file you want to change. It then writes an "X" at the specified location. Notice that the file must be opened for read/write operations.

```
#include <iostream.h>
#include <fstream.h>
#include <stdlib.h>

main(int argc, char *argv[])
{
  if(argc!=3) {
    cout << "Usage: CHANGE <filename> <byte>\n";
    return 1;
  }

  fstream out(argv[1], ios::in|ios::out);
  if(!out) {
    cout << "Cannot open file";
    return 1;
  }

  out.seekp(atoi(argv[2]), ios::beg);

  out.put('X');
  out.close();
```

```
  return 0;
}
```

The next program uses **seekg( )** to display the contents of a file beginning with the location you specify on the command line:

```
#include <iostream.h>
#include <fstream.h>
#include <stdlib.h>

main(int argc, char *argv[])
{
  char ch;

  if(argc!=3) {
    cout << "Usage: NAME <filename> <starting location>\n";
    return 1;
  }

  ifstream in(argv[1]);
  if(!in) {
    cout << "Cannot open file";
    return 1;
  }

  in.seekg(atoi(argv[2]), ios::beg);

  while(in.get(ch))
    cout << ch;

  return 0;
}
```

You can determine the current position of each file pointer using these functions:

streampos tellg( );
streampos tellp( );

Here, **streampos** is a type defined in **iostream.h** that is capable of holding the largest value that either function can return.

As you have seen, C++'s I/O system is both powerful and flexible. Although this chapter discusses the most important and commonly used functions, C++ includes several other I/O functions. You should consult your Turbo/Borland C++ user guide.

A Short Note About the Old Stream Class Library

When C++ was first invented, a smaller and slightly different I/O class library was created. This library is defined in the file **stream.h**. However, when C++ Version 2.0 was released by AT&T, the I/O library was enhanced and was put in the file **iostream.h**. Although Turbo/Borland C++ implements the latest version of C++, you can still access the old **stream.h** class if you need to compile an older, existing C++ program. However, you should use the **iostream.h** library when writing new programs.

Chapter **30**

Array-based I/O

In addition to console and file I/O, C++'s stream-based I/O system allows array-based I/O. *Array-based I/O* uses RAM as either the input device, the output device, or both. Array-based I/O is performed through normal C++ streams. In fact, all the information presented in the preceding chapter is applicable to array-based I/O. The only thing that makes array-based I/O unique is that the device linked to the stream is memory.

In some C++ literature, array-based I/O is referred to as *in-RAM I/O*. Also, because the streams are, like all C++ streams, capable of handling formatted information, sometimes array-based I/O is called *in-RAM formatting*. (Sometimes the archaic term *incore formatting* is also used. But since core memory is largely a thing of the past, this book uses the terms "in-RAM" and "array-based.")

C++'s array-based I/O is similar in effect to C's **sprintf( )** and **sscanf( )** functions. Both approaches use memory as an input or output device.

To use array-based I/O in your programs, you must include **strstream.h**.

The Array-based Classes

The array-based I/O classes are **istrstream**, **ostrstream**, and **strstream**. You use these classes to create input, output, and input/output streams, respectively. All of these classes have **strstreambuf** as one of their base classes. This class defines several low-level details that are used by the derived classes. In addition to **strstreambuf**, the **istrstream** class also has **istream** as a base. The **ostrstream** class is also derived from **ostream** and the **strstream** class also contains the **iostream** classes. Therefore, all array-based classes also have access to the same member functions that the "normal" I/O classes do.

Creating an Array-based Output Stream

To link an output stream to an array, use this **ostrstream** constructor:

ostrstream *ostr*(char **buf*, int *size*, int *mode*=ios::out)

Here, *buf* is a pointer to the array that will be used to collect characters written to the stream *ostr*. The size of the array is passed in the *size* parameter. By default, the stream is opened for normal output, but you can OR various other options (discussed in Chapter 29) with it to create the mode you need. (For example, you might include the **ios::app** to cause output to be written at the end of any information already contained in the array.) For most purposes, *mode* will be allowed to default.

Once you have opened an array-based output stream, all output to that stream is put into the array. However, no output will be written outside the bounds of the array. An attempt to do so results in an error.

Here is a simple program that demonstrates an array-based output stream:

```
#include <strstream.h>
#include <iostream.h>

main()
{
  char str[80];
  int a = 10;

  ostrstream outs(str, sizeof(str));

  outs << "Hello there ";
  outs << a+44 << hex << " ";
  outs.setf(ios::showbase);
  outs << 100 << ends;

  cout << str;  // display string on console

  return 0;
}
```

This program displays "Hello there 54 0x64". Keep in mind that **outs** is a stream like any other stream and that it has the same capabilities as any of the other types of streams you saw earlier. The only difference is that the device it is linked to is memory. Because **outs** is a stream, manipulators like **hex** and **ends** are perfectly valid. Also, **ostream** member functions, such as **setf( )**, are also available for use.

   If you want the output array to be null terminated, you must explicitly write a null. In this program, the **ends** manipulator was used to null terminate the string, but you could also have used \0.

   If you're not quite sure what is really happening in the preceding program, compare it to the following C program. This program is functionally equivalent to the C++ version. However, it uses **sprintf( )** to construct an output array.

```
#include <stdio.h>

main()
{
  char str[80];
  int a = 10;

  sprintf(str, "Hello there %d %#x", a+44, 100);

  printf(str);

  return 0;
}
```

   You can determine how many characters are in the output array by calling the **pcount( )** member function. It has this prototype:

   int pcount( );

The number returned by **pcount( )** also includes the null terminator, if it exists.

   The next program illustrates **pcount( )**. It reports that 17 characters are in **outs**—16 characters plus the null terminator.

```
#include <strstream.h>
#include <iostream.h>

main()
{
  char str[80];

  ostrstream outs(str, sizeof(str));

  outs << "Hello ";
  outs << 34 << " " << 1234.23;
```

```
   outs << ends;   // null terminate

   cout << outs.pcount(); // display how many chars in outs

   cout << " " << str;

   return 0;
}
```

Using an Array as Input

To link an input stream to an array, use this **istrstream** constructor:

istrstream *istr*(const char **buf*);

Here, *buf* is a pointer to the array that will be used as a source of characters each time input is performed on the stream *istr*. The contents of the array pointed to by *buf* must be null terminated. However, the null terminator is never read from the array.

Here is an example that uses a string as input:

```
#include <iostream.h>
#include <strstream.h>

main()
{
  char s[] = "One 2 3.00";

  istrstream ins(s);

  int i;
  char str[80];
  float f;

  // reading: one 2
  ins >> str;
  ins >> i;
  cout << str << " " << i << endl;

  // reading 3.00
  ins >> f;
  cout << f << '\n';
```

```
   return 0;
}
```

If you wish only part of a string to be used for input, use this form of the **istrstream** constructor:

istrstream *istr*(const char **buf*, int *size*);

Here, only the first *size* elements of the array pointed to by *buf* will be used. This string need not be null terminated since it is the value of *size* that determines the size of the string.

Streams linked to memory behave just like those linked to other devices. For example, the following program illustrates the way that contents of any text array may be read. When the end of the array (same as end-of-file) is reached, **ins** will be zero.

```
/* This program shows how to read the contents of any
   array that contains text. */
#include <iostream.h>
#include <strstream.h>

main()
{
  char s[] = "C++ arrays are fun! 123.23 0x23\n";

  istrstream ins(s);

  char ch;

  // This will read and display the contents of any text array.
  ins.unsetf(ios::skipws); // don't skip spaces
  while (ins) {  // 0 when end of array is reached
    ins >> ch;
    cout << ch;
  }

  return 0;
}
```

Using Binary I/O

Arrays linked to array-based streams may also contain binary information. When reading binary information, you may need to use the **eof( )** function to determine when the end of the array has been reached. For example, this program shows how to read the contents of any array—binary or text—by using the binary input function **get( )**:

```
#include <iostream.h>
#include <strstream.h>

main()
{
  char s[] = "text and binary mixed\23\22\21\a\t\n";

  istrstream ins(s);

  char ch;

  // This will read the contents of any type of array.
  while (!ins.eof()) {
    ins.get(ch);
    cout << ch;
  }

  return 0;
}
```

In this example, the values formed by "\23\22\21" are the nontext control characters CTRL-W, CTRL-V, and CTRL-U. The "\a" is the bell character, and the "\t" is a tab. However, any type of binary data could have been read.

To output binary characters, use the **put( )** function. If you need to read buffers of binary data, you can use the **read( )** member function. To write buffers of binary data, use the **write( )** function.

Input/Output Array-based Streams

To create an array-based stream that can perform both input and output, use this **strstream** constructor function:

strstream *iostr*(char **buf*, int *size*, int *mode*);

Here, *buf* points to the string that will be used for I/O operations. The value of *size* specifies the size of the array. The value of *mode* determines how the stream operates. For normal input/output operations, *mode* will be **ios::in | ios::out**. For input, the array must be null terminated.

Here is a program that uses an array to perform both input and output:

```
// Perform both input and output.
#include <iostream.h>
#include <strstream.h>

main()
{
  char iostr[80];

  strstream ios(iostr, sizeof(iostr), ios::in | ios::out);

  int a, b;
  char str[80];

  ios << "1734 534abcdefghijklmnopqrstuvwxyz";
  ios >> a >> b >> str;
  cout << a << " " << b << " " << str << endl;

}
```

This program first writes two integers and the alphabet to the array and then reads it back.

Random Access Within Arrays

It is important to remember that all normal I/O operations apply to array-based I/O. This also includes random access using **seekg( )** and **seekp( )**. For example, the next program seeks to the eighth character inside **iostr** and displays what it is. (It outputs **h**.)

```
#include <iostream.h>
#include <strstream.h>

main()
{
  char iostr[80];

  strstream ios(iostr, sizeof(iostr), ios::in | ios::out);

  char ch;
```

```
ios << "abcdefghijklmnopqrstuvwxyz";
ios.seekg(7, ios::beg);
ios >> ch;
cout << "Character at 7: " << ch;

return 0;
}
```

You can seek anywhere *inside* the I/O array, but you are not allowed to seek past an array boundary.

You can also apply functions like **tellg( )** and **tellp( )** to array-based streams.

Using Dynamic Arrays

In the first part of this chapter, when you linked a stream to an output array, the array and its size were passed to the **ostrstream** constructor. This approach is fine as long as you know the maximum number of characters you will be outputting to that array. However, what if you don't know how large the output array needs to be? The solution to this problem is to use a second form of the **ostrstream** constructor, shown here:

    ostrstream( );

When this constructor is used, **ostrstream** creates and maintains a dynamically allocated array. This array is allowed to grow in length to accommodate the output it must store.

Notice that the **ostrstream** constructor does *not* return a pointer to the allocated array. Accessing the dynamically allocated array requires the use of a second function called **str( )**. This function "freezes" the array and returns a pointer to it. Once a dynamic array is frozen, it may not be used for output again. Therefore, you will not want to freeze the array until you are through outputting characters to it.

Here is a program that uses a dynamic output array:

```
#include <strstream.h>

#include <iostream.h>

main()
{
  char *p;

  ostrstream outs;  // dynamically allocate array
```

```
   outs << "I like C++ ";
   outs << -10 << hex << " ";
   outs.setf(ios::showbase);
   outs << 100 << ends;

   p = outs.str(); // Freeze dynamic buffer and return
                   // pointer to it.

   cout << p;

   delete p;  // Free dynamic buffer created by ostrstream().
   return 0;
}
```

As this program illustrates, once a dynamic array has been frozen, it is your responsibility to release its memory back to the system when you are through with it. However, if you never freeze the array, the memory is automatically freed when the stream is destroyed.

You can also use dynamic I/O arrays with the **strstream** class, which may perform both input and output on an array.

Manipulators and Array-based I/O

Since array-based streams are the same as any other stream, manipulators that you create for I/O in general can be used with array-based I/O with no changes whatsoever. For example, in Chapter 29, the output manipulator **setup( )** was created, which turned on left-justification and set the field width to 10 and the fill character to the dollar sign. This manipulator can be used unchanged when using an array as output, as shown here:

```
/* This program uses a custom manipulator with
   array-based I/O. */

#include <strstream.h>
#include <iostream.h>
#include <iomanip.h>

// Custom output manipulator.
ostream &setup(ostream &stream)
{
  stream.setf(ios::left);
  stream << setw(10) << setfill('$');
```

```
  return stream;
}


main()
{
  char str[80];

  ostrstream outs(str, sizeof(str));

  outs << setup << 99 << ends;

  cout << str << '\n';

  return 0;
}
```

Custom Extractors and Inserters

As has been said many times in this chapter, since array-based streams are just that—streams—you can create your own extractor and inserter functions in just the same way you do for other types of streams. For example, the following program creates a class called **plot** that maintains the X,Y coordinates of a point in two-dimensional space. The overloaded inserter for this class displays a small coordinate plane and plots the location of the point. For simplicity, the range of the X,Y coordinates is restricted to 0 through 5.

```
#include <iostream.h>
#include <strstream.h>

const int size=5;

class plot {
  int x, y;
public:
  plot(int i, int j) {
    // For simplicity, restrict x and y to 0 through size.
    if(i>size) i = size;  if (i<0) i=0;
    if(j>size) j = size;  if (j<0) j=0;
    x=i; y=j;
  }
  // An inserter for plot.
  friend ostream &operator<<(ostream &stream, plot o);
};
```

```
ostream &operator<<(ostream &stream, plot o)
{
  register int i, j;

  for(j=size; j>=0; j--) {
    stream << j;
    if(j == o.y) {
      for(i=0; i<o.x; i++) stream << "  ";
      stream << '*';
    }
    stream << "\n";
  }

  for(i=0; i<=size; i++) stream << " " << i;
  stream << "\n";

  return stream;
}

main()
{
  plot a(2, 3), b(1, 1);

  // output first using cout
  cout << "Output using cout:\n";
  cout << a << "\n" << b << "\n\n";

  char str[200];  // now use RAM-based I/O
  ostrstream outs(str, sizeof(str));

  // now output using outs and in-RAM formatting
  outs << a << b << ends;

  cout << "Output using in-RAM formatting:\n";
  cout << str;
}
```

This program produces the following output:

```
Output using cout:
5
4
3    *
```

```
2
1
0
 0  1  2  3  4  5


5
4
3
2
1   *
0
 0  1  2  3  4  5



Output using in-RAM formatting:
5
4
3     *
2
1
0
 0  1  2  3  4  5
5
4
3
2
1   *
0
 0  1  2  3  4  5
```

Uses for Array-based Formatting

In C, the in-RAM I/O functions **sprintf( )** and **sscanf( )** were particularly useful for preparing output or reading input from nonstandard devices. However, because of C++'s ability to overload inserters and extractors relative to a class and to create custom manipulators, you can handle many exotic devices easily by using these features, making the need for in-RAM formatting less important. Nevertheless, there are still many uses for array-based I/O.

One common use of array-based formatting is to construct a string that will be used as input by either a standard library or a third-party function. For example, you may need to construct a string that will be parsed by the **strtok( )** standard library function. (The **strtok( )** function *tokenizes*—that is, decomposes to its elements—a string.) Another place where you can use array-based I/O is in text editors that perform complex formatting operations. Often it is easier to use C++'s array-based formatted I/O to construct a complex string than it is to do so by "manual" means.

Perhaps the single most important use of RAM-based I/O as it relates to Windows programming is that it allows you to fully construct and maintain a complete screen image in memory. As you will see, all Windows applications must be able to restore their screens after they have been overwritten by another window. You might find array-based I/O the easiest way to accomplish this task.

Chapter *31*

Miscellaneous C++
Topics

This chapter discusses several aspects of C++ not covered in the previous chapters. It also looks at some differences between C and C++, as well as some design philosophy.

Dynamic Allocation Using new and delete

As you know, C uses the functions **malloc( )** and **free( )** (among others) to dynamically allocate memory and to free dynamically allocated memory. However, C++ contains two operators that perform the function of allocating and freeing memory in a more efficient and easier way. The operators are **new** and **delete**. Their general forms are

> *pointer_var* = new *var_type*;
> delete *pointer_var*;

Here, *pointer_var* is a pointer of type *var_type*. The **new** operator allocates sufficient memory to hold a value of type *var_type* and returns an address to it. Any valid data type can be allocated using **new**. The **delete** operator frees the memory pointed to by *pointer_var*.

Like **malloc( )**, **new** returns a null pointer if the allocation request fails. Therefore, you must always check the pointer produced by **new** before using it. Also, like **malloc( )**, **new** allocates memory from the heap.

Because of the way dynamic allocation is managed, you must use **delete** only with a pointer to memory that was allocated using **new**. Using **delete** with any other type of address will cause serious problems.

There are several advantages to using **new** over **malloc( )**. First, **new** automatically computes the size of the type being allocated. You don't have to make use of the **sizeof** operator, which saves you some effort. More important, it prevents the wrong amount of memory from being accidentally allocated. Second, it automatically returns the correct pointer type—you don't need to use a type cast. Third, as you will soon see, it is possible to initialize the object being allocated using **new**. Finally, it is possible to overload **new** (and **delete**) relative to a class.

Here is a simple example of **new** and **delete**:

```
#include <iostream.h>

main(void)
{
  int *p;

  p = new int; // allocate memory for int
  if(!p) {
    cout << "allocation failure\n";
    return 1;
  }

  *p = 20; // assign that memory the value 20
  cout << *p; // prove that it works by displaying value

  delete p; // free the memory

  return 0;
}
```

This program assigns to **p** an address in memory that is large enough to hold an integer. It then assigns that memory the value 20 and displays the contents of that memory on the screen. Finally, it frees the dynamically allocated memory.

As stated, you can initialize the memory using the **new** operator. To do this, specify the initial value inside parentheses after the type name. For example, this program uses initialization to give the memory pointed to by **p** the value 99:

```
#include <iostream.h>

main(void)
{
  int *p;
```

```
  p = new int (99);   // initialize with 99
  if(!p) {
    cout << "allocation failure\n";
    return 1;
  }

  cout << *p;

  delete p;

  return 0;
}
```

You can allocate arrays using **new**. The general form for a singly dimensioned array is

   pointer_var = new *var_type* [*size*];

Here, *size* specifies the number of elements in the array.

   This program allocates space for 10 **float**s, assigns the array the values 100 to 109, and displays the contents of the array on the screen:

```
#include <iostream.h>

main(void)
{
  float *p;
  int i;

  p = new float [10]; // get a 10-element array
  if(!p) {
    cout << "allocation failure\n";
    return 1;
  }

  // assign the values 100 through 109
  for(i=0; i<10; i++) p[i] = 100.00 + i;

  // display the contents of the array
  for(i=0; i<10; i++)  cout << p[i] << " ";

  delete p; // delete the entire array
```

```
  return 0;
}
```

It is important to remember that when allocating an array, you cannot initialize it.

Allocating Objects

As stated, you can allocate memory for any valid type. This includes objects. For example, in this program, **new** allocates memory for an object of type **three_d**:

```
#include <iostream.h>

class three_d {
public:
  int x, y, z; // 3-d coordinates
  three_d(int a, int b, int c);
  ~three_d() {cout << "destructing\n";}
} ;

three_d::three_d(int a, int b, int c)
{
  cout << "constructing\n";
  x = a;
  y = b;
  z = c;
}

// Display X, Y, Z coordinates - three_d inserter.
ostream &operator<<(ostream &stream, three_d &obj)
{
  stream << obj.x << ", ";
  stream << obj.y << ", ";
  stream << obj.z << "\n";
  return stream;  // return the stream
}

main(void)
{
  three_d *p;

  p = new three_d (5, 6, 7);
  if(!p) {
```

```
      cout << "allocation failure\n";
      return 1;
   }

   cout << *p;

   delete p;

   return 0;
}
```

Notice that this program makes use of the inserter function for the **three_d** class to output the coordinate values. When you run the program, you will see that **three_d**'s constructor function is called when **new** is encountered and that its destructor function is called when **delete** is reached. Also note that the initializers are automatically passed to the constructor by **new**.

You can allocate an array of user-defined objects using **new**. When you free a dynamically allocated array of objects that have destructor functions, you must use this form of **delete**:

delete [*size*] *pointer_var*,

Here, *size* specifies the number of elements in the array. The reason you must specify the size of the array is that when you free the memory of an array containing objects, the destructor function for each object must be executed.

Technically, the requirement to specify the size (as specified by size) *of the dynamically allocated array of objects that you are deleting has been dropped in the latest specification for Turbo/Borland C++. (You still need to use the square brackets.) However, if you want your code to be compatible with earlier versions or other compilers, continue to include the size specification.*

Here is an example that allocates an array of objects of type **three_d**.

```
#include <iostream.h>
class three_d {
public:
   int x, y, z; // 3-d coordinates
   three_d(int a, int b, int c) ;
   three_d(){cout << "constructing\n";} // needed for arrays
   ~three_d() {cout << "destructing\n";}
};
```

```
three_d::three_d(int a, int b, int c)
{
  cout << "constructing\n";
  x = a;
  y = b;
  z = c;
}

// Display X, Y, Z coordinates - three_d inserter.
ostream &operator<<(ostream &stream, three_d &obj)
{
  stream << obj.x << ", ";
  stream << obj.y << ", ";
  stream << obj.z << "\n";
  return stream;  // return the stream
}

main(void)
{
  three_d *p;
  int i;

  p = new three_d [10];
  if(!p) {
    cout << "allocation failure\n";
    return 1;
  }

  for(i=0; i<10; i++) {
    p[i].x = 1;
    p[i].y = 2;
    p[i].z = 3;
  }

  for(i=0; i<10; i++) cout << *p;

  delete [10] p;

  return 0;
}
```

Notice that a second constructor function has been added to the **three_d** class. Because allocated arrays cannot be initialized, a constructor function that does not have any parameters is needed. If you don't supply this constructor, a compile-time message will be displayed.

Overloading new and delete

It is possible to overload **new** and **delete**. You might want to do this when you want to use some special allocation method. For example, you may want allocation routines that automatically begin using a disk file as virtual memory when the heap has been exhausted. Whatever the reason, it is a very simple matter to overload these operators.

The skeletons for the functions that overload **new** and **delete** are

```
void *operator new(size_t size)
{
  // perform allocation
  return pointer_to_memory;
}

void operator delete(void *p)
{
  // free memory pointed to by p
}
```

The type **size_t** is defined by Turbo/Borland C++ as a type capable of containing the largest single piece of memory that can be allocated. **Size_t** is an integer type. The parameter *size* will contain the number of bytes needed to hold the object being allocated. This value is automatically obtained for you. The overloaded **new** function must return a pointer to the memory that it allocates or null if an allocation error occurs. Beyond these constraints, the overloaded **new** function can do anything else you require.

The **delete** function receives a pointer to the region of memory to free.

You can overload the **new** and **delete** operators globally so that all uses of these operators call your custom versions or just those relative to one or more classes. Let's begin with an example of overloading **new** and **delete** relative to the **three_d** type. For the purposes of illustration, no new allocation scheme will be used. Instead, the overloaded functions will simply invoke **malloc( )** and **free( )**. However, you are free to implement any alternative allocation scheme you like.

To overload the **new** and **delete** operators relative to a class, simply make the overloaded operator functions class members. For example, here the **new** and **delete** operators are overloaded relative to the **three_d** class:

```
#include <iostream.h>
#include <stdlib.h>
```

```
class three_d {
public:
  int x, y, z; // 3-d coordinates
  three_d(int a, int b, int c) ;
  ~three_d() {cout << "destructing\n";}
  void *operator new(size_t size);
  void operator delete(void *p);
} ;

three_d::three_d(int a, int b, int c)
{
  cout << "constructing\n";
  x = a;
  y = b;
  z = c;
}

// Overload new relative to three_d.
void * three_d::operator new(size_t size)
{
  cout << "in three_d new\n";
  return malloc(size);
}

// Overload delete relative to three_d.
void three_d::operator delete(void *p)
{
  cout << "in three_d delete\n";
  free(p);
}

// Display X, Y, Z coordinates - three_d inserter.
ostream &operator<<(ostream &stream, three_d &obj)
{
  stream << obj.x << ", ";
  stream << obj.y << ", ";
  stream << obj.z << "\n";
  return stream;  // return the stream
}

main(void)
{
  three_d *p, *p1;
```

```
p = new three_d (1, 2, 3);
p1 = new three_d (4, 5, 6);
if(!p || !p1) {
  cout << "allocation failure\n";
  return 1;
}

cout << *p << *p1;

delete p;
delete p1;

return 0;
}
```

It is important to understand that when **new** and **delete** are overloaded relative to a specific class, the use of these operators on any other type of data causes the original **new** or **delete** to be employed. The overloaded operators are applied only to the types for which they are defined. This means that if you add the following line to **main( )**, the global **new** is executed:

```
int *i = new int;
```

You can overload **new** and **delete** globally by overloading these operators outside any class declaration. When **new** and **delete** are overloaded globally, C++'s original **new** and **delete** are ignored and the new operators are used for all allocation requests. Of course, if you have defined any versions of **new** and **delete** relative to one or more classes, the class-specific versions are used when allocating objects of the class for which they are defined. In other words, when either **new** or **delete** is encountered, the compiler first checks to see whether they are defined relative to the class they are operating on. If so, those specific versions are used. If not, C++ uses the globally defined **new** and **delete**. However, if these have been overloaded, the overloaded versions are used.

To see an example of overloading **new** and **delete** globally, examine this program:

```
#include <iostream.h>
#include <stdlib.h>

class three_d {
public:
  int x, y, z; // 3-d coordinates
  three_d(int a, int b, int c) ;
  ~three_d() {cout << "destructing\n";}
```

```
} ;

three_d::three_d(int a, int b, int c)
{
  cout << "constructing\n";
  x = a;
  y = b;
  z = c;
}

// Overload new globally.
void * operator new(size_t size)
{
  cout << "in new new\n";
  return malloc(size);
}

// Overload delete globally.
void operator delete(void *p)
{
  cout << "in new delete\n";
  free(p);
}

// Display X, Y, Z coordinates - three_d inserter.
ostream &operator<<(ostream &stream, three_d &obj)
{
  stream << obj.x << ", ";
  stream << obj.y << ", ";
  stream << obj.z << "\n";
  return stream;  // return the stream
}

main(void)
{
  three_d *p, *p1;

  p = new three_d (1, 2, 3);
  p1 = new three_d (4, 5, 6);
  if(!p || !p1) {
    cout << "allocation failure\n";
    return 1;
  }
```

```
  cout << *p << *p1;

  delete p;
  delete p1;

  int *i = new int;
  if(!i) {
    cout << "allocation failure\n";
    return 1;
  }

  *i = 10;
  cout << *i << "\n";
  return 0;
}
```

If you run this program, you will see that the built-in **new** and **delete** operators have, indeed, been overloaded.

static Class Members

The keyword **static** can be applied to members of a class. Its meaning in this context is similar to its original C-like meaning. When you declare a member of a class as **static**, you are telling the compiler that no matter how many objects of the class are created, there is only one copy of the **static** member. A **static** member is *shared* by all objects of the class. All **static** data is initialized to 0 when the first object of its class is created and no other initialization is specified.

When you declare a **static** data member within a class, you are *not* defining it. Instead, you must provide a global definition for it elsewhere, outside the class. You do this by redeclaring the **static** variable, using the scope resolution operator to identify which class it belongs to. This is necessary for storage to be allocated for the **static** variable.

As an example, examine the following program and try to understand how it works:

```
#include <iostream.h>

class counter {
  static int count;
public:
  void setcount(int i) {count = i;};
```

```
   void showcount() {cout << count << " ";}
};

int counter::count; // define count

main(void)
{
  counter a, b;

  a.showcount(); // prints 0
  b.showcount(); // prints 0

  a.setcount(10); // set static count to 10

  a.showcount(); // prints 10
  b.showcount(); // also prints 10

  return 0;
}
```

Notice first that the static integer **count** is both declared inside the **counter** class and then defined as a global variable. Turbo/Borland C++ initializes **count** to 0 since no other initialization is given. This is why the first calls to **showcount( )** both display 0. Next, object **a** sets **count** to 10. Then, both **a** and **b** use **showcount( )** to display its value. Because there is only one copy of **count** shared by both **a** and **b**, both cause the value 10 to be displayed.

Remember, when you declare a member of a class as **static**, you are causing only one copy of that member to be created and then shared by all objects of that class.

You can also have **static** member functions. **static** member functions have access only to **static** data and other **static** functions declared in a class. They cannot access non-**static** data or call non-**static** functions. This is because a **static** member function does not have a **this** pointer; it has no way of knowing which object's non-**static** data to access. For example, if there are two objects of a class that contains a **static** function called **f( )** and if **f( )** attempts to access a non-**static** variable called **var**, defined in the class, which copy of **var** should the call be routed to? The compiler has no way of knowing. This is why **static** functions can access only other **static** functions or data.

The following short program illustrates one of the many ways you can use **static** functions. It is not uncommon for an object to require access to some scarce resource, such as a shared file in a network. As the program illustrates, the use of **static** data and functions provides a method by which an object can check on the status of the resource and access it if it is available.

```
#include <iostream.h>

enum access_t {shared, in_use, locked, unlocked};

// a scarce resource control class
class access {
  static enum access_t acs;
  // ...
public:
  static void set_access(enum access_t a) {acs = a;}
  static enum access_t get_access()
  {
    return acs;
  }
  // ...
};

enum access_t access::acs; // define acs

main(void)
{
  access  obj1, obj2;

  obj1.set_access(locked);

  // ... intervening code

  // see if obj2 can access resource
  if(obj2.get_access()==unlocked) {
    obj2.set_access(in_use);
    cout << "access resource\n";
  }
  else cout << "locked out\n";

  // ...

  return 0;
}
```

When you compile this skeleton, "locked out" is displayed. You might want to play with the program a little to make sure you understand the effect of **static** on both data and functions.

As stated, **static** functions can access only other **static** functions or **static** data within the same class. To prove this, try compiling this version of the program:

```
#include <iostream.h>

enum access_t {shared, in_use, locked, unlocked};

// a scarce resource control class
class access {
  static enum access_t acs;
  int i;  // non-static
  // ...
public:
  static void set_access(enum access_t a) {acs = a;}
  static enum access_t get_access()
  {
    i = 100; // this will not compile
    return acs;
  }
  // ...
};

enum access_t access::acs; // define acs

main(void)
{
  access  obj1, obj2;

  obj1.set_access(locked);

  // ... intervening code

  // see if obj2 can access resource
  if(obj2.get_access()==unlocked) {
    obj2.set_access(in_use);
    cout << "access resource\n";
  }
  else cout << "locked out\n";

  // ...
}
```

This program does not compile because **get_access( )** is attempting to access a non-**static** variable.

You may not see an immediate need for **static** members, but as you continue to write programs in C++, you will find them very useful in certain situations because they allow you to avoid the use of global variables.

Virtual Base Classes

As you know, in C++, the **virtual** keyword is used to declare **virtual** functions that will be overridden by a derived class. However, **virtual** also has another use that enables you to specify *virtual base classes*. To understand what a virtual base class is and why the keyword **virtual** has a second meaning, let's begin with the short, incorrect program shown here:

```
// This program contains an error and will not compile.
#include <iostream.h>

class base {
public:
  int i;
};

// d1 inherits base.
class d1 :  public base {
public:
  int j;
};

// d2 inherits base.
class d2 : public base {
public:
  int k;
};

// d3 inherits both d1 and d2. This means that there
// are two copies of base in d3!
class d3 : public d1, public d2 {
public:
  int m;
};

main(void)
{
  d3 d;

  d.i = 10;  // this is ambiguous, which i???
  d.j = 20;
  d.k = 30;
  d.m = 40;
```

```
  // also ambiguous, which i???
  cout << d.i << " ";
  cout << d.j << " " << d.k << " ";
  cout << d.m;

  return 0;
}
```

As the comments in the program indicate, both **d1** and **d2** inherit **base**. However, **d3** inherits both **d1** and **d2**. This means there are two copies of **base** present in an object of type **d3**. Therefore, in an expression like

```
d.i = 20;
```

which **i** is being referred to? The one in **d1** or the one in **d2**? Since there are two copies of **base** present in object **d**, there are two **d.i**'s. As you can see, the statement is inherently ambiguous.

There are two ways to remedy the preceding program. The first is to apply the scope resolution operator to **i** and manually select one **i**. For example, this version of the program does compile and run as expected:

```
#include <iostream.h>

class base {
public:
  int i;
};

// d1 inherits base.
class d1 : public base {
public:
  int j;
};

// d2 inherits base.
class d2 : public base {
public:
  int k;
};

/* d3 inherits both d1 and d2. This means that there
   are two copies of base in d3! */
class d3 : public d1, public d2 {
```

```
public:
  int m;
};

main(void)
{
  d3 d;

  d.d2::i = 10; // scope resolved, using d2's i
  d.j = 20;
  d.k = 30;
  d.m = 40;


  // scope resolved, using d2's i
  cout << d.d2::i << " ";
  cout << d.j << " " << d.k << " ";
  cout << d.m;

  return 0;
}
```

As you can see, by applying the **::**, the program has manually selected **d2**'s version of **base**. However, this solution raises a deeper issue: What if only one copy of **base** is actually required? Is there some way to prevent two copies from being included in **d3**? The answer, as you probably have guessed, is yes. And this solution is achieved by using virtual base classes.

   When two or more objects are derived from a common base class, you can prevent multiple copies of the base class from being present in an object derived from those objects by declaring the base class as **virtual** when it is inherited. For example, here is another version of the example program in which **d3** contains only one copy of **base**:

```
#include <iostream.h>

class base {
public:
  int i;
};

// d1 inherits base as virtual.
class d1 : virtual public base {
public:
  int j;
```

```
};

// d2 inherits base as virtual.
class d2 : virtual public base {
public:
  int k;
};

/* d3 inherits both d1 and d2. However, now there is
   only one copy of base in d3. */
class d3 : public d1, public d2 {
public:
  int m;
};

main(void)
{
  d3 d;

  d.i = 10; // no longer ambiguous
  d.j = 20;
  d.k = 30;
  d.m = 40;

  cout << d.i << " "; // no longer ambiguous
  cout << d.j << " " << d.k << " ";
  cout << d.m;

  return 0;
}
```

As you can see, the keyword **virtual** precedes the rest of the inherited class's specification. Now that both **d1** and **d2** have inherited **base** as **virtual**, any multiple inheritance involving them will cause only one copy of **base** to be present. Therefore, in **d3**, there is only one copy of **base**, so **d.i = 10** is perfectly valid and unambiguous.

One further point to keep in mind: Even though both **d1** and **d2** specify **base** as **virtual**, **base** is still present in any objects of either type. For example, the following sequence is perfectly valid:

```
// define a class of type d1
d1 myclass;

myclass.i = 100;
```

Virtual base classes and normal ones differ only when an object inherits the base more than once. If virtual base classes are used, only one base class is present in the object. Otherwise, multiple copies will be found.

Using the asm Keyword

In Turbo/Borland C++, you can embed assembly language directly into your program by using the **asm** keyword. The **asm** keyword has three slightly different general forms:

```
asm instruction ;
asm instruction newline
asm {
    instruction sequence
}
```

Here, *instruction* is any valid 80x86 assembly language instruction. Unlike any other Turbo/Borland C++ statement, an **asm** statement does not have to end with a semicolon; it can end with either a semicolon or a newline.

As a first simple example, this program uses **asm** to execute an **INT 5** instruction, which invokes the PC's print screen function:

```
// Print the screen.
#include <iostream.h>

main(void)
{
  asm int 5;
  return 0;
}
```

If you want to use a sequence of assembly language statements, surround them with braces, as shown in this do-nothing (but harmless) example.

```
#include <iostream.h>

main(void)
{
  // this effectively does nothing
  asm {
    push ds
```

```
    pop ds
  }

  return 0;
}
```

If you want to put a comment on the same line as an assembly language statement, use C-like, not TASM-like, comments. (In TASM, a comment begins with a semicolon, but this just won't work in C++.)

 A thorough working knowledge of assembly language programming is required to use the **asm** *statement. If you are not proficient at assembly language, it is best to avoid using it because nasty errors may result.*

Linkage Specification

In C++ you can specify how a function is linked. Specifically, you can tell Turbo/Borland C++ to link a function as a C function or as a C++ function. By default, functions are linked as C++ functions. However, by using a *linkage specification* you can cause a function to be linked as a different type of language function. The general form of a linkage specifier is

    extern "*language*" *function-prototype*

where *language* denotes the desired language. In Turbo/Borland C++, *language* must be either C or C++, but other implementations may allow other language types.

    This program causes **myCfunc( )** to be linked as a C function:

```
#include <iostream.h>

extern "C" void myCfunc(void);

main(void)
{
  myCfunc();

  return 0;
}

// This will link as a C function.
```

```
void myCfunc(void)
{
  cout << "This links as a C function.\n";
}
```

*The **extern** keyword is a necessary part of the linkage specification. Further, the linkage specification must be global; it cannot be used inside a function.*

You can specify more than one function at a time by using this form of the linkage specification:

extern *"language"* {
 prototypes
}

The use of a linkage specification is rare; you will probably not need to use one.

The .* and –>* Operators

The .* and –>* are called *pointer-to-member* operators. Their job is to allow you to access a member of a class given a pointer to that member. These two operators are needed because a pointer to a member does not fully define an address. Instead, it provides an offset into an object of the member's class at which that member can be found. Therefore, accessing a member of a class given a pointer to it requires the use of both the class and the member. Since the * operator cannot link a class with a pointer to a member, the .* and –> operators were created.

Let's begin with an example. The following program displays the summation of the number 7. It accesses the function **sum_it( )** and the variable **sum** using member pointers.

```
#include <iostream.h>

class myclass {
public:
  int sum;
  void myclass::sum_it(int x);
};

void myclass::sum_it(int x) {
  int i;
```

```
    sum = 0;
    for(i=x; i; i--) sum += i;
}

main(void)
{
    int myclass::*dp;  // pointer to an integer class member
    void (myclass::*fp)(int x); // pointer to member function
    myclass c;

    dp = &myclass::sum;  // get address of data
    fp = &myclass::sum_it; // get address of function

    (c.*fp)(7);  // compute summation of 7
    cout << "summation of 7 is " << c.*dp;

    return 0;
}
```

Inside **main( )**, this program creates two member pointers: **dp**, which points to the
variable **sum**, and **fp**, which points to the function **sum_it( )**. Note carefully the syntax
of each declaration. The scope resolution operator is used to specify which class is
being referred to. The program also creates an object of **myclass** called **c**.

   The program then obtains the addresses of **sum** and **sum_it( )**. As stated earlier, these
addresses are really just offsets into an object of **myclass** where **sum** and **sum_it( )** are
found. Next, the program uses a function pointer **fp** to call the **sum_it( )** function of
c. The extra parentheses are necessary in order to correctly associate the **.*** operator.
Finally, the summed value is displayed by accessing **c**'s **sum** through **dp**.

   When you are accessing a member of an object using an object or a reference,
you must use the **.*** operator. However, if you are using a pointer to the object, you
need to use the **–>*** operator, as illustrated in this version of the preceding program:

```
#include <iostream.h>

class myclass {
public:
    int sum;
    void myclass::sum_it(int x);
};

void myclass::sum_it(int x) {
    int i;
```

```
  sum = 0;
  for(i=x; i; i--) sum += i;
}

main(void)
{
  int myclass::*dp;  // pointer to an integer class member
  void (myclass::*fp)(int x); // pointer to member function
  myclass *c, d; // c is now a pointer to an object

  c = &d; // give c the address of an object

  dp = &myclass::sum;  // get address of data
  fp = &myclass::sum_it; // get address of function

  (c->*fp)(7);  // now, use ->* to call function
  cout << "summation of 7 is " << c->*dp; // use ->*

  return 0;
}
```

In this version **c** is now a pointer to an object of type **myclass**, and the **–>*** operator is used to access **sum** and **sum_it( )**.

Creating Conversion Functions

Sometimes you will create a class that you want to be able to freely mix in an expression with other types of data. While overloaded operator functions can provide a means of mixing types, sometimes a simple conversion is all that you want. In these cases, you can use a type conversion function to convert your class into a type compatible with that of the rest of the expression. The general form of a type conversion function is

>   operator (*type*)( ) {return *value*;}

Here, *type* is the target type that you are converting your class to and *value* is the value of the class after conversion. A conversion function must be a member of the class for which it is defined.

To illustrate how to create a conversion function, let's use the **three_d** class once again. Suppose you want to be able to convert an object of type **three_d** into an integer so it can be used in an integer expression. Further, the conversion will take place by using the product of the three dimensions. To accomplish this, you use a conversion function that looks like this:

```
operator int() { return x * y * z; }
```

Here is a program that illustrates how the conversion function works:

```
#include <iostream.h>

class three_d {
  int x, y, z; // 3-d coordinates
public:
  three_d(int a, int b, int c) {x=a; y=b, z=c;}

  three_d operator+(three_d op2) ;
  friend ostream &operator<<(ostream &stream, three_d &obj);

  operator int() {return x*y*z;}
} ;

// Display X, Y, Z coordinates - three_d inserter.
ostream &operator<<(ostream &stream, three_d &obj)
{
  stream << obj.x << ", ";
  stream << obj.y << ", ";
  stream << obj.z << "\n";
  return stream;  // return the stream
}

three_d three_d::operator+(three_d op2)
{
  three_d temp(0, 0, 0);

  temp.x = x+op2.x;  // these are integer additions
  temp.y = y+op2.y;  // and the + retains its original
  temp.z = z+op2.z;  // meaning relative to them
  return temp;
}

main(void)
{
  three_d a(1, 2, 3), b(2, 3, 4);

  cout << a << b;
```

```
   cout <<  b+100;  // displays 124 because of conversion to int
   cout << "\n";
   cout << a+b;  // displays 3, 5, 7 - no conversion

   return 0;
}
```

This program displays the output

```
1, 2, 3
2, 3, 4
124
3, 5, 7
```

As the program illustrates, when a **three_d** object is used in an integer expression, such as **cout << b+100**, the conversion function is applied to the object. In this specific case, the conversion function returns the value 24, which is then added to 100. However, when no conversion is needed, as in **cout << a+b**, the conversion function is not called.

Remember that you can create different conversion functions to meet different needs. You could define one that converts to **double** or **long**, for example. Each is applied automatically.

Copy Constructors

By default, when one object is used to initialize another, C++ performs a bitwise copy to make an exact copy of the object. While this is fine for many, and perhaps most, situations, there are times when a bitwise copy must be avoided, such as when an object allocates dynamic memory or opens files. For example, consider this class fragment:

```
class sample {
  int *p;
  int i;
public:
  sample() { p = new int;}
  .
  .
  .
};
```

```
sample o1;
.

.

.
sample o2 = o1; // initialize o2 using o1;
```

Here, a simple bitwise copy is insufficient because **o2.p** will be pointing to the same piece of memory as that used by **o1.p**. That is, **o1** allocates storage for an integer and puts that address into **p**. Later, when **o1** is initialized, it also allocates memory for an integer and stores that location in its version of **p**; however, this version is overwritten when the initialization is performed. This situation causes both copies of **p** to point to the same location.

To solve the type of problem just described, you must use a copy constructor. A *copy constructor* is a special type of constructor function that is called when one object is used to initialize another, bypassing the default bitwise copy. The general form of a copy constructor is

> *classname* (const *classname* &*obj*) {
>   // body of constructor
>   }

Here, *obj* is a reference to the object on the right side of the initialization, and *classname* is the name of the class for which the copy constructor is being created. In the body of the function, you must manually perform all initializations. For example, here is a copy constructor that corrects the problem described at the start of this section:

```
class sample {
   int *p;
   int i;
public:
   sample() { p = new int;}
   sample (const sample &o) { p = new int; i = o.i;);
.

.

.
};

sample o1;
.

.

.
sample o2 = o1; // initialize o2 using o1;
```

In this case, **o2.p** will point to its own piece of memory, but the value of **o1.i** is still assigned to **o2.i**.

Granting Access

When you declare a base class as **private** when inherited by a derived class, all elements (including **public** elements) of the base class become **private** elements of the derived class. However, in some instances you may wish to grant certain **public** elements of the base **public** status in the derived class. To accomplish this, you must use an *access declaration*. An access declaration has the general form

    base-class-name::element;

The access declaration is put in the **public** portion of the derived class.

    Here is a simple example that illustrates how to use an access declaration:

```
#include <iostream.h>

class B_class {
public:
  int i, j;
};

class D_class : private B_class {
public:
  // access declaration
  B_class::i;  // i from B_class is now public again

  int k;
} ;

main(void)
{
  D_class d;

  d.i = 10;  // legal because i is made public in D_class
  d.k = 20;
// d.j = 30; // illegal because j is private in D_class

  cout << d.i * d.k;
```

```
    return 0;
}
```

In this example, **B_class** is inherited by **D_class** as **private**. This means that both **i** and **j** become **private** elements of **D_class**. However, inside **D_class**, an access declaration specifies that **i** should become **public** again.

You can also use an access declaration to grant **protected** elements in the base class **protected** status in a derived class. Keep in mind, however, that you cannot raise or lower an element's access status. For example, a **private** element of the base cannot become a **public** element in a derived class.

Using Templates

Starting with version 3.0 of Turbo/Borland C++, a new feature called *templates* has been added. Using templates, it is possible to create generic functions and classes. In a generic function or class, the type of data is specified as a parameter. Thus, one function or class can be used with several different types of data. This section discusses how to create both generic functions and generic classes.

Generic Functions

A *generic function* defines a general set of operations that will be applied to various types of data. A generic function has the type of data that it will operate upon passed to it as a parameter. Thus, the same general procedure can be applied to a wide range of data. As you know, many algorithms are logically the same no matter what type of data is being operated upon. For example, the Quicksort algorithm is the same whether it is applied to an array of integers or an array of **float**s. It is just that the type of the data being sorted is different. By creating a generic function, you can define, independent of any data, the nature of the algorithm. Once this is done, the compiler automatically generates the correct code for the type of data that is actually used when you execute the function. In essence, when you create a generic function you are creating a function that can automatically overload itself.

Let's begin with an example. The following program creates a generic function that swaps the values of the two variables it is called with. Because the general process of exchanging two values is independent of the type of the variables, it is a good choice to be made into a generic function.

```
// Function template example.
#include <iostream.h>

template <class X> // template
```

```
void swap(X &a, X &b)
{
  X temp;

  temp = a;
  a = b;
  b = temp;
}

main()
{
  int i=10, j=20;
  float x=10.1, y=23.3;

  cout << "Original i, j: " << i << ' ' << j << endl;
  cout << "Original x, y: " << x << ' ' << y << endl;

  swap(i, j); // swap integers
  swap(x, y); // swap floats

  cout << "Original i, j: " << i << ' ' << j << endl;
  cout << "Original x, y: " << x << ' ' << y << endl;

  return 0;
}
```

The new keyword **template** is used to define a generic function. The line

```
template <class X>
```

tells the compiler two things. First it indicates that a template class is being created and that a generic definition is beginning. Here, **X** is a generic type that is used as a placeholder. After the **template** statement, the function **swap( )** is declared, using **X** as the data type of the values to be swapped. In **main( )**, the **swap( )** function is called using two different types of data: integers and **floats**. Because **swap( )** is a generic function, the compiler automatically creates two versions of **swap( )**—one that exchanges integer values and one that exchanges floating-point values.

The general form of a **template** function definition is

```
template <class type>
type func-name(parameter list)
{
  // body of function
}
```

It is important to understand that no other statements may occur between the
template statement and the start of the generic function definition. For example, this
fragment will not compile:

```
// This will not compile.
template <class X> // template
int i; // this is an error
void swap(X &a, X &b)
{
  X temp;

  temp = a;
  a = b;
  b = temp;
}
```

You can define more than one generic type with the **template** statement, using a
comma-separated list. For example, this program creates a generic function that has
two generic types:

```
#include <iostream.h>

template <class type1, class type2>
void myfunc(type1 x, type2 y)
{
  cout << x << ' ' << y << endl;
}

main()
{
  myfunc(10, "hi");

  myfunc(0.23, 10L);

  return 0;
}
```

*When you create a generic function, you are, in essence, allowing the compiler to generate
as many different versions of that function as are necessary to handle the various ways
your program calls that function.*

Generic functions are similar to overloaded functions except that they are more
restrictive. When functions are overloaded, you can have different actions performed

within the body of each function. A generic function must perform the same general action for all versions.

Generic Classes

In addition to generic functions, you can also define a *generic class*. When you do this, you create a class that defines all algorithms used by that class, but the actual type of the data being manipulated will be specified as a parameter when objects of that class are created.

Generic classes are useful when a class contains generalizable logic. For example, the same algorithm that maintains a queue of integers will also work for a queue of characters. Also, the same mechanism that maintains a linked list of mailing addresses will also maintain a linked list of auto parts information. By using a generic class, you can create a class that will maintain a queue, linked list, and so on, for any type of data. The compiler automatically generates the correct type of object based upon the type you specify when the object is created.

Here is an example of a generic class. This program creates a very simple generic singly linked list class. It then demonstrates the class by creating a linked list that stores characters.

```
// A simple generic linked list.
#include <iostream.h>

template <class data_t>
class list {
  data_t data;
  list *next;
public:
  list(data_t d);
  void add(list *node) {node->next = this; next = 0; }
  list *getnext() { return next; }
  data_t getdata() { return data; }
};

template <class data_t>
list<data_t>::list(data_t d)
{
  data = d;
  next = 0;
}

main()
{
  list<char> start('a');
```

```
list<char> *p, *last;
int i;

// build a list
last = &start;
for(i=0; i<26; i++) {
  p = new list<char> ('a' + i);
  p->add(last);
  last = p;
}

// follow the list
p = &start;
while(p) {
  cout << p->getdata();
  p = p->getnext();
}

return 0;
}
```

As you can see, the declaration of a generic class is similar to that of a generic function. Notice, however, how a function defined outside the class is handled. The actual type of data stored by the list is made generic in the class declaration. In **main( )**, objects and pointers are created that specify that the data type of the list will be **char**. Pay special attention to this declaration:

```
list<char> start('a');
```

Notice how the desired data type is passed inside the angle brackets.

If you enter and execute this program, you will see that it builds a linked list that contains the characters of the alphabet and then displays them. However, by simply changing the type of data specified when **list** objects are created, you can change the type of data stored by the list. For example, you could create another object that stores integers by using this declaration:

```
list<int> int_start(1);
```

You can also use **list** to store data types that you create. For example, suppose you want to store address information using this structure:

```
struct addr {
  char name[40];
  char street[40];
```

```
    char city[30];
    char state[3];
    char zip[12];
}
```

Then, to use **list** to generate objects that will store objects of type **addr**, use a declaration like this (assuming that **structvar** contains a valid **addr** structure):

```
list<addr> obj(structvar);
```

Generic functions and classes provide a powerful tool you can use to maximize your programming time because they allow you to define the general form of an algorithm that can be used with any type of data. You are saved from the tedium of creating separate implementations for each data type you want the algorithm to work with.

The overload Anachronism

In the first versions of C++ created by Bjarne Stroustrup, overloaded functions had to be explicitly declared as such using the **overload** keyword. For example, if **myfunc( )** was to be overloaded, you would need to put this line of code in your program:

```
overload myfunc;
```

However, beginning with the 2.0 specification for C++, the **overload** keyword is no longer needed. For compatibility with older C++ programs, it is still allowed in C++ programs, but its use is now considered anachronistic.

Differences Between C and C++

For the most part, C++ is a superset of ANSI-standard C, and virtually all C programs are also C++ programs. However, a few differences do exist, the most important of which are discussed here.

One of the most important yet subtle differences between C and C++ is the fact that in C, a function declared like this:

```
int f();
```

says *nothing* about any parameters to that function. That is, when there is nothing specified between the parentheses following the function's name, in C this means that nothing is being stated, one way or the other, about any parameters to that function. It might have parameters and it might not have parameters. However, in C++, a function declaration like this means that the function does *not* have parameters. That is, in C++, these two declarations are equivalent:

```
int f();
```

```
int f(void);
```

In C++, the **void** is optional. Many C++ programmers include the **void** as a means of making it completely clear to anyone reading the program that a function does not have any parameters, but this is technically unnecessary.

In C++, all functions must be prototyped. This is an option in C (although good programming practice suggests full prototyping be used in a C program).

A small, but potentially important, difference between C and C++ is that in C, a character constant is automatically elevated to an integer. In C++, it is not.

In C, it is not an error to declare a global variable several times, even though it is bad programming practice. In C++, this is an error.

As you learned earlier, in C, an identifier can be up to 31 characters long. In C++, no such limit exists. However, from a practical point of view, extremely long identifiers are unwieldy and are seldom needed.

The Complex and BCD Classes

In addition to the classes and overloaded operators defined by **iostream.h** and its derivatives, Turbo/Borland C++ includes two additional class libraries that perform complex and BCD arithmetic.

As you may know, a *complex* number has two parts: a real half and an imaginary half. The real half is an ordinary number; the imaginary part is a multiple of the square root of –1. To use complex numbers, you must include **complex.h** in your program.

To construct a complex number, use the **complex** constructor function. It has this prototype:

complex(double *real_part*, double *imaginary_part*);

The **<<** and **>>** operators are overloaded relative to complex numbers. For example, this program constructs an imaginary number and displays it on the screen:

```
#include <iostream.h>
#include <complex.h>

main(void)
{
  complex num(10, 1);

  cout << num;

  return 0;
}
```

The program outputs the following:

(10, 1)

This output also illustrates the general format used when displaying complex numbers.

You can mix complex numbers with any other type of number, including integers, **floats**, and **doubles**. The arithmetic operators **+, –, *,** and / are overloaded relative to complex numbers, as are the relational operators = = and !=. This program illustrates how complex and regular numbers can be mixed in an expression:

```
#include <iostream.h>
#include <complex.h>

main(void)
{
  complex num(10, 1);

  num = 123.23 + num / 3;

  cout << num;

  return 0;
}
```

Turbo/Borland C++ has overloaded many mathematical functions, such as **sin( )** (which returns the sine of its argument), relative to complex numbers. It also defines several functions that apply specifically to complex numbers. The complex functions are shown in Table 31-1.

Turbo/Borland C++ also defines the **bcd** class. As you may know, real numbers can be represented inside the computer a number of different ways. The most

Name	Purpose
complex abs(complex *n*)	Returns the absolute value of *n*
double acos(complex *n*)	Returns the arc cosine of *n*
double arg(complex *n*)	Returns the angle of *n* in the complex coordinate plane
complex asin(complex *n*)	Returns the arc sine of *n*
complex atan(complex *n*)	Returns the arc tangent of *n*
complex atan2(complex *n*)	Returns the arc tangent2 of *n*
double conj(complex *n*)	Returns the conjugate of *n*
complex cos(complex *n*)	Returns the cosine of *n*
complex cosh(complex *n*)	Returns the hyperbolic cosine of *n*
complex exp(complex *n*)	Returns e to the *n*th
double imag(complex *n*)	Returns the imaginary part of *n*
complex log(complex *n*)	Returns the natural log of *n*
complex log10(complex *n*)	Returns the log base 10 of *n*
double norm(complex *n*)	Returns the square of *n*
complex polar(double magnitude, double angle)	Returns the complex number given its polar coordinates
complex pow(complex *x*, complex *y*) complex pow(complex *x*, double *y*) complex pow(double *x*, complex *y*)	Returns *x* to the *y* power
double real(complex *n*)	Returns the real part of *n*
complex sin(complex *n*)	Returns the sine of *n*
complex sinh(complex *n*)	Returns the hyperbolic sine of *n*
complex sqrt(complex *n*)	Returns the square root of *n*
complex tan(complex *n*)	Returns the tangent of *n*
complex tanh(complex *n*)	Returns the hyperbolic tangent of *n*

Table 31-1.   *The Complex Functions*

common is as binary floating-point values. However, another way to represent a real number is to use *Binary Coded Decimal,* or *BCD.* In BCD, base 10 rather than base 2 is used to represent a number. The major advantage of the BCD representation is that no round-off errors occur. For example, using binary floating point, the number 100.23 cannot be accurately represented and is rounded to 100.230003. However, using BCD, no rounding occurs. For this reason, BCD numbers are often used in accounting programs and the like. The major disadvantage of BCD numbers is that

BCD calculations are slower than binary floating-point calculations. To use BCD numbers you must include **bcd.h** in your programs.

The **bcd** class has these constructor functions:

bcd(int *n*)
bcd(double *n*)
bcd(double *n*, int *digits*)

The first two are self-explanatory. The third creates a BCD number that uses *digits* number of digits after the decimal point.

In Turbo/Borland C++, BCD numbers have a range of 10^{-125} to 10^{125} with 17 digits of precision.

To convert a number from BCD format to normal binary floating-point format, use **real( )**. Its prototype is

long double real(bcd *n*)

The **bcd** class overloads the arithmetic and relational operators, as well as the functions shown in Table 31-2.

Name	Purpose
bcd abs(bcd *n*)	Returns the absolute value of *n*
bcd acos(bcd *n*)	Returns the arc cosine of *n*
bcd asin(bcd *n*)	Returns the arc sine of *n*
bcd atan(bcd *n*)	Returns the arc tangent of *n*
bcd cos(bcd *n*)	Returns the cosine of *n*
bcd cosh(bcd *n*)	Returns the hyperbolic cosine of *n*
bcd exp(bcd *n*)	Returns e to the *n*th
bcd log(bcd *n*)	Returns the natural log of *n*
bcd log10(bcd *n*)	Returns the log base 10 of *n*
bcd pow(bcd *x*, bcd *y*)	Returns *x* to the *y* power
bcd sin(bcd *n*)	Returns the sine of *n*
bcd sinh(bcd *n*)	Returns the hyperbolic sine of *n*
bcd sqrt(bcd *n*)	Returns the square root of *n*
bcd tan(bcd *n*)	Returns the tangent of *n*
bcd tanh(bcd *n*)	Returns the hyperbolic tangent of *n*

Table 31-2.   The BCD functions

Here is a sample program that illustrates the advantage of BCD numbers when the prevention of round-off errors is important:

```
#include <iostream.h>
#include <bcd.h>

main(void)
{
  float f = 100.23, f1 = 101.337;
  bcd b(100.23), b1(101.337);

  cout << f+f1 << " " << b+b1;

  return 0;
}
```

This program displays

201.567001 201.567

The Turbo/Borland Container Class Libraries

Beginning with Turbo/Borland C++ version 2.0, a container class library has been included. This class library defines several classes that maintain various storage mechanisms, such as linked lists, stacks, queues, and sorted arrays. This class library is too large to be included in this book, but it's a good idea to examine this library on your own.

The Message-based Philosophy

A few words are in order about a programming philosophy that fits very well with OOP in general and C++ in particular. This programming philosophy is based upon the concept of *messages*. In a message-based approach, all (or at least most) data is held privately inside a class. To retrieve or alter an item of data, you send the object a message to this effect. Code outside the class never operates directly on any data privately held by the class. Instead, the only things capable of altering data are the member (or **friend**) functions of the object that contains the data. This approach reduces the possibility of accidental side effects. It also lets you govern precisely what values the private data of an object may have because the member functions that access the data can filter out incorrect values.

In C++, sending an object a message means calling a member (or **friend**) function. To better understand this concept, think about a class that manages access to a database. In normal C code, to modify an entry in the database, you would simply write a line of code something like this (assume that **database** is an array of C-like structures):

```
database[record].balance = 100.75;
```

However, using a message-based approach and C++, you would call a member function with the record number and new value as arguments. For example, you would use a statement something like this (here, **database** is an object):

```
database.newbalance(record, 100.75);
```

In this case, no other code actually "touches" the data protected within the object.

To see how the message-based approach works in practice, here is a class that emulates a stopwatch along with a short **main( )** to illustrate its use:

```
#include <iostream.h>
#include <time.h>
#include <conio.h>

class stopwatch {
  clock_t time1, time2;
public:
  stopwatch() {time1 = time2 = 0;}
  void reset() {time1 = time2 = 0;}
  void start() {time1 = clock()/CLK_TCK;}
  void stop() {time2 = clock()/CLK_TCK;}
  clock_t elapsed() {return time2 - time1;}
} ;

main(void)
{
  stopwatch timer;

  cout << "wait a while, then press a key\n";
  timer.start();

  while(!kbhit()) ; // wait for keypress

  timer.stop();
  cout << (long) timer.elapsed();
  cout << " seconds have elapsed\n";
```

```
   return 0;
}
```

This program displays the number of seconds between the time it starts running and the time you press a key. It uses Turbo/Borland C++'s **clock( )** function. This function returns a value that, when divided by **CLK_TCK**, is the number of seconds since the program started running. The type **clock_t** is defined in the **time.h** header file required by the **clock( )** function. This type is essentially a **long** integer. The macro **CLK_TCK** is also defined in this file.

The **stopwatch** class declares the variables **time1** and **time2** as private members. The only access to them is by sending messages through the member functions. For example, to start the stopwatch, send the message "start the clock" by calling the **start( )** function. This function then sets the value of **time1**. To stop the clock, send the message "stop the clock" by calling **stop( )**. To obtain the elapsed time, call the **elapsed( )** function. The key point here is that at no time does any other part of the program access **time1** or **time2** directly.

Although the implementation of **stopwatch** is correct as far as it goes, it does not provide all the protection for **time1** and **time2** that it might. For example, there is nothing that prevents the **start( )** function from being called a second time before a call to **stop( )**. Also, there is nothing that prevents **stop( )** from being called before **start( )** has been called. However, using the message-based architecture, it is possible to not only closely regulate access to private data, but to prevent it from being misused. For example, here is an improved version of the program that prevents the accidental misuse of the stopwatch:

```
#include <iostream.h>
#include <time.h>
#include <conio.h>

class stopwatch {
  clock_t time1, time2;
  int ready;
public:
  stopwatch() {time1 = time2 = 0; ready = 1;}
  void reset() {time1 = time2 = 0; ready = 1;}
  void start();
  void stop();
  clock_t elapsed();
} ;

void stopwatch::start()
{
  if(!ready)
```

```
      cout << "timer has not been reset\n";
    else {
      time1 = clock()/CLK_TCK;
      ready = 0;
    }
}

void stopwatch::stop()
{
  if(ready)
    cout << "timer has not been started\n";
  else {
    time2 = clock()/CLK_TCK;
    ready = 1;
  }
}

clock_t stopwatch::elapsed()
{
  if(!ready) {
    cout << "timer has not been stopped\n";
    return -1;
  }
  else
    return time2 - time1;
}

main(void)
{
  stopwatch timer;

  cout << "wait a while, then press a key\n";
  timer.start();

  while(!kbhit()) ; // wait for keypress
  getch(); // read and dispose of keystroke

  timer.stop();
  cout << (long) timer.elapsed();
  cout << " seconds have elapsed\n";

  timer.stop(); // this will cause error message because
                // the timer is not currently running

  timer.start();
```

```
cout << "now running, wait a while, then press a key\n";

while(!kbhit()) ; // wait for keypress

timer.stop(); // now, this will work
cout << (long) timer.elapsed();
cout << " seconds have elapsed\n";

return 0;
}
```

In this version, it is not possible to accidentally misuse the stopwatch because the **ready** flag is turned on only when the stopwatch is not currently running.

Although you don't have to use a message-based approach to programming in C++, you will be ignoring much of C++'s power if you don't. If you master this method, you will write programs that are more bug free, extensible, and flexible.

Final Thoughts

If you are new to object-oriented programming but want to become proficient, the best approach is to write many object-oriented programs. Programming is best learned by doing. Also, look at examples of C++ programs written by other people. If possible, study the C++ code written by several different programmers, paying attention to how each program is designed and implemented. Look for shortcomings as well as strong points. This will broaden the way you think about programming. Finally, experiment. Push your limits. You will be surprised at how quickly you become an expert C++ programmer!

The Turbo/Borland C++ Environment

Part Five of this book covers the Turbo/Borland C++ programming environment. This includes both the integrated development environment (IDE) and the command-line compiler.

   If you have used the Turbo/Borland C environment, the C++ compiler will seem familiar to you. However, there are many differences between the two, so read carefully the chapters in this section.

Chapter **32**

The Integrated Development Environment

Turbo/Borland C++ has two separate modes of operation. The first is called its integrated development environment, or IDE. Using the IDE, editing, compilation, and execution are controlled by single keystrokes and easy-to-use menus. In fact, the IDE is so easy to use that its operation is almost intuitive. The other method of operation involves the traditional command-line approach where you first use an editor to create a program source file and then you compile it, link it, and run it. The command-line approach is covered in Chapter 34.

The IDE described here is based on the Turbo/Borland C++ version 3.0, which differs slightly from earlier versions. However, if you have an older version of Turbo/Borland C++, most of the information is still applicable. This chapter assumes that you have properly installed Turbo or Borland C++ according to the instructions given in the Borland manual.

Both Turbo C++ and Borland C++ use the same IDE, so the features discussed in this and the following chapters apply to both.

Executing the C++ IDE

To execute the integrated version of Turbo C++, simply type **TC** at the DOS prompt. To execute Borland C++, type **BC**. When the IDE begins execution you see the screen shown in Figure 32-1. It consists of these four parts, in order from top to bottom:

- The main menu
- The editor window
- The message window
- The status line

Each of these areas is examined briefly in this chapter.

Using the Mouse

You can operate the IDE using either the keyboard or the mouse. Although the mouse is not required, mouse support has been carefully integrated into the IDE and a mouse is certainly an excellent addition.

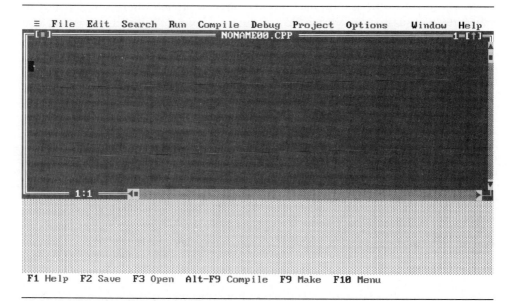

Figure 32-1.   *The IDE opening screen*

To make the discussion of the IDE that follows easier, a few mouse operations and terms are defined now. In general, to select an item, position the mouse pointer on that item and press the left mouse button. Doing this is called *clicking* on an item. Sometimes you need to *double click* in order to select something. Double clicking means that you press the left mouse button twice in rapid succession without moving the mouse between clicks. Some objects can be *dragged* around the screen. To drag an object using a mouse, position the mouse pointer at the appropriate part of the object, press and hold down the left mouse button, and then move the mouse. As you move the mouse, the object moves in the same direction. When the object reaches the desired part of the screen, stop moving the mouse and release the left button.

The Main Menu

By default, when you begin execution of the IDE, the editor window is active. To activate the main menu, press the F10 key. When you do this, one of the menu items becomes highlighted. To reactivate the editor window, press ESC.

The main menu is used either to tell the IDE to do something, such as load a file or compile a program, or to set an option. Once the main menu is activated, there are two ways to make a main menu selection using the keyboard. First, you can use the arrow keys to move the highlight to the item you want and then press ENTER. Second, you can simply type the first letter of the desired menu item. For example, to select **Edit** you would type an **E**. You may enter the letters in either upper- or lowercase. If you have a mouse, you can simply click on the main menu item that you want to activate. Table 32-1 summarizes what each menu selection does.

When you select a main menu item, a *pull-down menu* is displayed that contains a list of choices. This menu allows you to select an action that relates to the main menu item. To make a selection using the arrow keys, move the highlight to the item you want and press ENTER. Or you can simply type the letter of the option that is shown in a different color on a color monitor or as boldface on a monochrome monitor. (Most of the time, the different-color letter is the first letter, but not always.) If you have a mouse, simply click on the desired item. You can cancel any menu at any time by pressing the ESC key or by clicking on another part of the screen using the mouse.

Sometimes a menu entry will not be available in a given situation. When this occurs, no letter is shown in a different color, and if you move the highlight to this option (or click on it with the mouse) it is displayed as a black bar.

Some pull-down menus produce another pull-down menu that displays additional options relating to the first menu. Secondary pull-down menus operate just like primary pull-down menus. When one menu will generate another, it is shown with a dark arrow to its right.

Some menu entries are on/off selections. To change the state of an on/off entry, move the highlight to that entry and press ENTER. This reverses the state. You can also click on it using the mouse or type the letter that is in a different color.

Item	Purpose
≡	Clears or restores the screen and executes various utility programs
File	Loads and saves files, handles directories, invokes DOS, and exits the IDE
Edit	Performs various editing functions
Search	Performs various text searches and replacements
Run	Compiles, links, and runs the program currently loaded in the environment
Compile	Compiles the program currently in the environment
Debug	Sets various debugger options, including the setting of breakpoints
Project	Manages multifile projects
Options	Sets various compiler, linker, and environmental options
Window	Controls the way various windows are displayed
Help	Activates the context-sensitive help system

Table 32-1.   *Summary of the Main Menu Items*

Dialog Boxes

If a pull-down menu item is followed by three periods, it means that selecting this item will cause a *dialog box* to be displayed. Dialog boxes allow input that is not easily accomplished using a menu. Dialog boxes consist of one or more of the following items:

Action buttons
Check boxes
Input boxes
List boxes
Radio buttons

An *action button* is an option that affects your activity inside a dialog box. Most dialog boxes have at least three action buttons. They are **OK**, **Cancel**, and **Help**. To activate one of these using the keyboard, press the TAB key until the desired action is highlighted and then press ENTER. If you have a mouse, simply click on the appropriate button. There may be other action buttons in a dialog box that relate to the specific function of the dialog box.

A check box looks something like this:

[X] *option*

Here, *option* is some option that can be enabled or disabled. When the box has an "X" in it, that option is selected. If the box is empty, that option is not selected. To change the state of a check box, TAB to the box and then press the SPACEBAR. The SPACEBAR acts as a toggle: each time you press it, the state of the box changes. You can also change the state of a check box by clicking on it with the mouse.

An *input box* allows you to enter text, such as a file name. To activate the input box, either press TAB until the box is active or click on it using the mouse. Once the box is selected, enter text using the keyboard and press ENTER when done.

An input box may have a *history list* associated with it. If it does, you will see a down arrow to the right of the box. A history list contains the information entered previously into the box. To activate the history list, press the DOWN ARROW key. You can then reuse a previous entry by selecting it from the list.

A *list box* presents a list of items from which you can choose. To activate the list box, either press TAB until the box is active or click on it using the mouse. Once the box is activated, select the item you want by moving the highlight to the appropriate item and pressing ENTER or by double clicking on the item using the mouse.

Radio buttons make up a list of mutually exclusive options that takes this general form:

( ) *option 1*
(.) *option 2*
  .
  .
  .
( ) *option N*

Since the options are mutually exclusive, only one can be active at any one time. The one active option has a period between the parentheses. To activate radio buttons, TAB to them or click on them using the mouse. Use the arrow keys to change the location of the period or click on the desired selection using the mouse. An example of a dialog box is shown in Figure 32-2.

Now that you have been shown an overview of the IDE, let's take a closer look at some of its features.

Turning On Full Menus

Early versions of Turbo C++ (1.0 and 1.1) do not display all menu options by default. Instead, only the most commonly used options are presented. If you are using an old

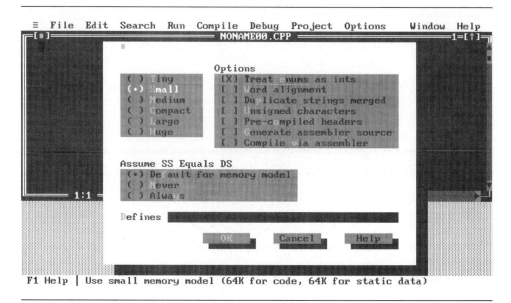

```
 ≡  File  Edit  Search  Run  Compile  Debug  Project  Options   Window  Help
┌─[■]────────────────────────── NONAME00.CPP ───────────────────────1═[↑]═┐
│   [■]                                                                    ▲
│              ┌────────────────── Options ──────────────────────┐         │
│              │             Options                             │         │
│              │  ( ) Tiny        [X] Treat enums as ints        │         │
│              │  (•) Small       [ ] Word alignment             │         │
│              │  ( ) Medium      [ ] Duplicate strings merged   │         │
│              │  ( ) Compact     [ ] Unsigned characters        │         │
│              │  ( ) Large       [ ] Pre-compiled headers       │         │
│              │  ( ) Huge        [ ] Generate assembler source  │         │
│              │                  [ ] Compile via assembler      │         │
│              │                                                 │         │
│              │  Assume SS Equals DS                            │         │
│              │  (•) Default for memory model                   │         │
│    ─ 1:1 ─   │  ( ) Never                                      │         ▼
│              │  ( ) Always                                     │         
│              │                                                 │         
│              │  Defines ─────────────────────────────────     │         
│              │                                                 │         
│              │      [   OK   ]    [  Cancel  ]   [  Help  ]    │         
│              └─────────────────────────────────────────────────┘         
├──────────────────────────────────────────────────────────────────────────┤
│ F1 Help │ Use small memory model (64K for code, 64K for static data)      │
└──────────────────────────────────────────────────────────────────────────┘
```

Figure 32-2.   *An example dialog box*

version of Turbo C++, you need to turn on full menu displays. To do this, activate the main menu (if you have not already done so) by pressing F10. Next, move the highlight on the main menu to the **Options** entry and press ENTER. If, by previous usage, **Full menus** is on, change nothing on this menu. Otherwise, move the highlight to the **Full menus** entry and press ENTER to turn it on.

Exploring the Main Menu

This section examines each entry of the main menu. To follow along, activate the main menu (by pressing F10), position the highlight on the System menu symbol, and press ENTER. As each option is discussed, move the highlight to that option.

The System Menu

The System menu lets you clear the work area and redisplay the screen. You might want to redisplay the screen if a program overwrites the video memory when it executes, causing the screen to become messy. Using the System menu, you can also execute some utility programs supplied by Turbo/Borland C++.

File

Highlighting the **File** option activates the **File** pull-down menu, as shown in Figure 32-3. Let's look at each of the **File** options.

New opens another editing window and lets you create a new file. The file is called NONAME*n*.CPP, where *n* is a value between 0 and 99. However, you can rename the file whatever you want when you save it. The **Open** option prompts you for a file name and then loads that file into the editor. If the file does not exist, it is created. The **Open** option also displays a list of files from which you can choose. Use the arrow keys to move the highlight until it is on the file you wish to load and press ENTER to load the file, or double click on the desired file name. The **Save** option saves the file in the active window. The **Save as** option lets you save a file using a different file name. The **Save all** option saves the files in all open windows. The **Change dir** option lets you change the default directory in which your files reside. The **Print** option prints the file in the active window. The **DOS shell** option loads the DOS command processor and lets you execute DOS commands. You must type **EXIT** to return to the IDE. Finally, **Quit** quits the IDE and returns to DOS.

Edit

The **Edit** option allows you to perform several editor operations. These commands and the operation of the editor are discussed at length in Chapter 33.

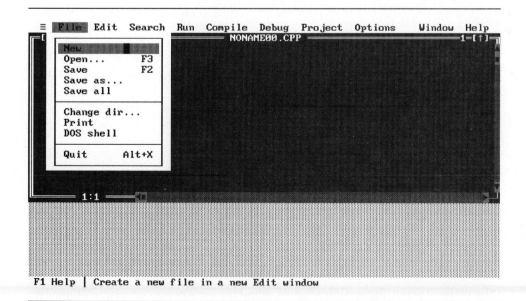

Figure 32-3. *The File pull-down menu*

Search

The **Search** main menu entry allows you to perform various types of searches and search-and-replace operations on the text in the active window. Since the **Search** options relate to the editor, they are discussed in Chapter 33.

Run

The **Run** option activates a submenu containing six selections:

Run
Program reset
Go to cursor
Trace into
Step over
Arguments...

The **Run** option executes the current program. If the program has not yet been compiled, **Run** compiles it for you.

The next four options relate to the execution of a program using the debugger. To use them you must compile your program with the debugging information option turned on, as it is by default. Although the operation of the debugger is deferred until later in this book, the following descriptions will give you an idea about what they do. The **Program reset** option terminates your program when it is being run in a debug mode. **Go to cursor** executes your program until it reaches the line of code where the cursor is positioned. The **Trace into** option executes your program one statement at a time. If the next statement includes a function call, the code of that function is also traced. The **Step over** option executes the next line of code but does not trace into any functions that may be called.

The **Arguments** entry is used to pass command-line arguments to a program that is run from the IDE.

Compile

When you highlight the **Compile** option, you see the screen shown in Figure 32-4. The first option allows you to compile the file currently in the editor to an .OBJ file. (An .OBJ file is a relocatable object file that is ready to be linked into an .EXE file that can be executed.) The **Make** option invokes the IDE's MAKE facility. This causes your project to be recompiled as necessary. The **Link** option lets you link your current program. The **Build all** option recompiles all the files related to your program. The **Information** option displays information about the file you are currently editing. The **Remove messages** option clears the message window.

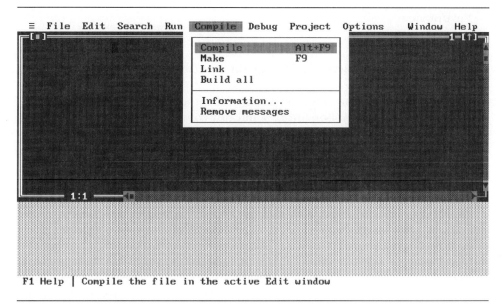

Figure 32-4.   *The Compile pull-down menu*

Debug

The **Debug** option lets you use and control the integrated debugger. The operation of the debugger and its options are discussed in Appendix A.

Project

The **Project** option is used to aid in the development and maintenance of large, multifile programs.

Options

When you select **Options**, you see these entries in its pull-down menu:

Application
Compiler
Transfer...
Make...
Linker...
Librarian
Debugger
Directories...

Environment
Save...

Each of these entries allows you to change the way Turbo/Borland C++ operates or generates code.

The **Application** option determines how your program is compiled and linked. (Older versions of Turbo/Borland C++ did not contain this option.) Depending upon what version of Turbo/Borland C++ you are using, it may also let you specify that your program is to be compiled as a DOS or a Windows application.

The **Compiler** option lets you change aspects about the way code is generated. The **Transfer** option lets you add programs to the System menu. Programs listed in the System menu can be executed from within the IDE.

The **Make** option changes how your program is compiled. The **Linker** option changes the way your program is linked. The **Librarian** option controls the operation of the IDE library features.

The **Debugger** option controls various debugging features. The **Directories** option lets you set the default directories used by the IDE compiler. The **Environment** option lets you change the way the IDE operates. The **Save** option lets you determine how various IDE options are saved for future use.

Window

The IDE interface is based upon the window. The **Window** option allows you to perform various operations on a window. The Window pull-down menu is shown in Figure 32-5.

The first entries let you perform various operations on the active window. The first option is **Size/Move**. If you select this option you are able to change the size of the active window and/or move it to a new location on the screen. The **Zoom** option increases the size of the active window so that it fills the entire screen. Once a window has been zoomed, selecting **Zoom** a second time returns the window to its normal size.

The IDE allows several windows to be open at the same time. There are two ways that multiple windows may be displayed: tiled or cascaded. By default, windows are cascaded; this means that each time a new one is created, it partially overlays one or more other windows. For example, Figure 32-6 shows an example of several cascaded windows. By contrast, if you select the **Tile** option, no window overlays another. Each is given a reduced part of the screen. Figure 32-7 shows the same windows as those in Figure 32-6, but in tiled format.

If you have several open windows, you can progressively jump from one to the next by selecting **Next**. You can remove a window from the screen by selecting **Close**. You can close all windows by selecting **Close all**.

The second part of the Window menu allows you to activate one of the IDE's built-in windows. The Message window is the one used to hold compiler error

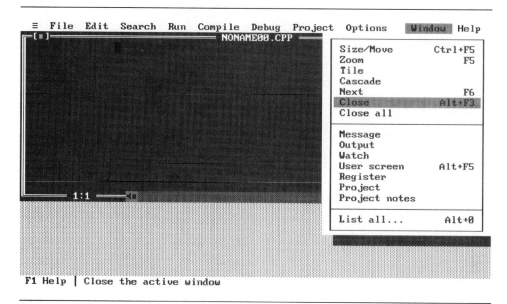

Figure 32-5.   *The Window pull-down menu*

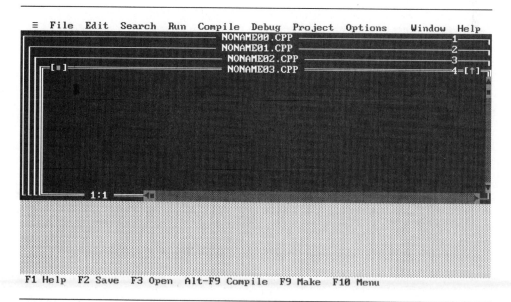

Figure 32-6.   *Cascaded windows*

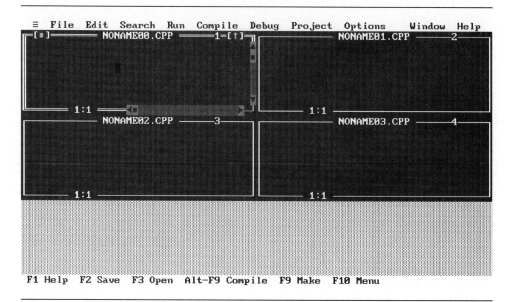

Figure 32-7. *Tiled windows*

messages. The Output window displays the output generated by your program. The Watch window is used in debugging. The User Screen window shows the full screen output of a program. If you select this option, to return to the IDE screen you must press F5. The Register window displays the contents of each register of the CPU. The Project and Project Notes windows relate to projects.

To list all open windows, select **List All**. You can activate a window by selecting it from the list.

Help

Activating the **Help** option displays the following menu selections:

Contents
Index
Topic search
Previous Topic
Help on help
About

The **Contents** option displays the table of contents to the help system. The **Index** option activates an index of topics covered by the help system. To make a selection, move the highlight to the topic you want and press ENTER. You will then see information relating to the topic you selected. To exit the help system, press ESC.

One very convenient feature of IDE's help system is that when you select the **Topic search** option, the keyword that the cursor is currently located on will have information displayed about it. To review the previous topic, select **Previous Topic**. You can receive help about the help system by selecting **Help on help**.

The **About** option displays the version of Turbo/Borland C++ you are using.

You may also have an entry called **Active File** in your Help menu. If you do, this option lets you control which help file will be used when **Help** is activated.

The Hot Keys

You can activate the IDE's most common operations directly, without going through the main menu, by using *hot keys,* which are various key combinations that are displayed to the right of various menu entries. (You probably remember seeing some of these keys when examining the main menu.) These keys are ready for use whenever you need them. The hot keys are summarized in Table 32-2.

Using Context-Sensitive Help

The IDE contains an on-line help system from which you can obtain information about any feature of Turbo/Borland C++ simply by pressing the F1 key. The help system works a little differently when you use the F1 hot key to activate it than it does when you use the main menu. The difference is that when activated by pressing F1, the help system is *context sensitive*. This means it displays help information that relates to what you are doing at the time. More specifically, it displays information that relates to the current focus of activity. For example, if the editor is currently active, activating the help system by pressing F1 displays information about the editor. If a menu item is highlighted, pressing F1 gives you information about the highlighted entry.

To see how this works, activate the main window and highlight the **Options** entry. Now, press F1. As you can see, information relating to the **Options** entry is displayed. When you are done with the help system, press ESC.

Before moving on, you might want to try the context-sensitive help feature on your own. As you will see, it is a powerful aid.

Hot key	Purpose
F1	Activates the on-line help system
F2	Saves the file currently being edited
F3	Loads a file
F4	Executes the program until the cursor is reached
F5	Zooms the active window
F6	Switches between windows
F7	Traces the program into function calls
F8	Traces the program, skipping function calls
F9	Compiles and links your program
F10	Activates the main menu
ALT-0	Lists open windows
ALT-n	Activates window n (n must be 1 through 9)
ALT-F1	Shows the previous help screen
ALT-F3	Deletes the active window
ALT-F4	Opens an Inspector window
ALT-F5	Toggles between the user screen and the IDE
ALT-F7	Previous error
ALT-F8	Next error
ALT-F9	Compiles file to .OBJ
ALT-SPACEBAR	Activates the main menu
ALT-C	Activates the Compile menu
ALT-D	Activates the Debug menu
ALT-E	Activates the editor
ALT-F	Activates the File menu
ALT-H	Activates the Help menu
ALT-O	Activates the Options menu
ALT-P	Activates the Project menu
ALT-R	Activates the Run menu
ALT-S	Activates the Search menu
ALT-W	Activates the Window menu
ALT-X	Quits the IDE and returns to DOS

Table 32-2.   *The Hot Keys*

Hot key	Purpose
CTRL-F1	Requests help about the item under the cursor
CTRL-F2	Resets the program
CTRL-F3	Shows the function call stack
CTRL-F4	Evaluates an expression
CTRL-F5	Changes the size or location of the active window
CTRL-F7	Sets a watch expression (debugging)
CTRL-F8	Sets or clears a break point
CTRL-F9	Executes the current program

Table 32-2. *The Hot Keys* (continued)

Understanding Windows

The IDE is based upon the *window*, which is a portion of the screen. All windows have similar characteristics. The features common to most windows are shown in Figure 32-8. All windows have a title that describes what the window is being used for, and most have a number that identifies that window. All windows also include a *zoom box*, which can enlarge or reduce the size of a window; a *close box*, with which you can remove a window; and a *resize corner*, which allows you to change the size of a window. You can access the zoom box, close box, and resize corner only by using a mouse. (If you don't have a mouse, you can perform the same operations by using special keyboard commands.)

Some, but not all, windows also have horizontal and vertical *scroll bars*. The scroll bars allow you to scroll text in the window. They work only with a mouse. When scrolling vertically, you can scroll one line at a time by clicking on the up or down arrow of the vertical scroll bar. The slider box moves along the scroll bar, indicating your relative position in the file. If you press and hold down the left mouse button while on an arrow, a continuous scroll is produced. You can click anywhere on the scroll bar, and the corresponding location in the file is displayed. Finally, you can drag the slider box along the bar, and the text scrolls accordingly. These operations are paralleled by the horizontal scroll bar except that text is moved from side to side.

When a window is on the screen, it is said to be open. Although there may be several open windows on the screen at the same time, only one can be active. When a window is active, it is the focus of any input you generate from the keyboard. There are several ways to make a window active. If you know the number of the window, you can simply hold down the ALT key and press the number of the window you want. The windows are numbered 1 through 9. Pressing ALT-0 causes a list of all windows

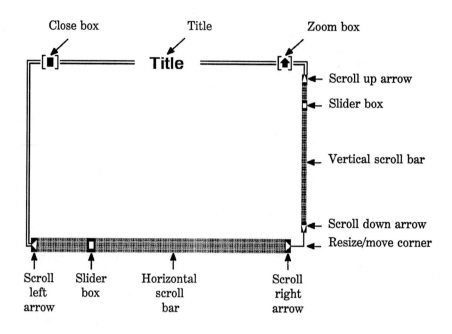

Figure 32-8.   *Common window features*

currently in use to be displayed. You can then activate a window by selecting it from that list. If you have a mouse, you can activate a window simply by clicking on it.

Sizing and Moving Windows

By far, the easiest way to resize or move a window is by using the mouse. To move a window, move the mouse pointer so it is on the top border of the window. Press and hold the left button and drag the window to its new location. To change the size of a window, move the mouse pointer to the resize corner of the window, press and hold the left mouse button, and move the mouse in the appropriate direction.

If you do not have a mouse, to resize and/or move a window you must first make that window active. Next, activate the **Window** main menu entry and select the **Size/Move** option. Now, using the arrow keys you can move the window around the screen. To change its size, hold down the SHIFT key while using the arrow keys. To stop moving or resizing, press any other key.

Keep in mind that dialog boxes and menus are not windows, and they cannot be resized or moved.

The Editor Window

The editor window is where you create the source code for your C++ programs. As you can see in Figure 32-1, the title of this window is NONAME00.CPP. The reason for this is that when you executed Turbo or Borland C++, you did not specify any file name; in this case the editor automatically gives the file a temporary name. (You can change it when you save a file.) Notice that the editor window is window number 1. Keep in mind that you can have several open editor windows at any one time.

You can move and/or resize the editor window. You might want to experiment now by changing its size or location.

We will look more closely at the editor window in Chapter 33.

The Message Window

The message window lies beneath the editor window and displays various compiler or linker messages. It is most commonly used to display any error messages generated by the compiler. You can move and/or resize the message window.

The Status Line

The line at the bottom of the screen is called the status line. It displays a short comment relating to whatever you are currently doing. For example, when the **Window** main menu option is selected, the status line displays the following:

```
F1 Help | Open, arrange, and list windows
```

The information displayed on the status line provides clues about the meaning of whatever is the current focus of the IDE.

Chapter **33**

Using the Editor

This chapter discusses the IDE editor. If you already know how to use the original Turbo C IDE editor then you will feel right at home because its operation is similar to the original. The main additions found in the Turbo/Borland C++ editor are that it supports the mouse, that several of the text manipulation and search commands can be executed using menus, and that multiple edit windows can be created to allow concurrent editing of two or more files.

Although the editor contains about 50 commands, you will not have to learn all of them at once. The most important deal with insertion, deletion, block moves, searching, and replacement. Once you have mastered these basic areas, you will easily be able to learn the rest of the editor commands and put them to use as you need them. Actually, learning to use the editor is surprisingly simple because you have the on-line context-sensitive help system at your disposal.

Much of this chapter parallels Chapter 13, which discusses the Turbo C editor. The material is repeated here for the convenience of those readers learning Turbo/Borland C++ who are not familar with Turbo C. Further, there are several subtle differences between the Turbo C editor and the Turbo/Borland C++ editor.

Editor Commands

With few exceptions, all editor commands begin with a control character. Many are then followed by another character. For example, the sequence CTRL-Q F is the command that tells the editor to find a string. To execute this command, hold down the CTRL key, and then press Q followed by F in either upper- or lowercase.

Although you can enter all editor commands from the keyboard, some are also available from the main menu and some can be executed using the mouse. When menu or mouse alternatives exist, they are pointed out.

Invoking the Editor and Entering Text

When the IDE begins executing, the editor window is active. When you activate the main menu to perform some operation, you can return to the editor window by pressing ESC.

The top line of the editor window displays the name of the file currently being edited, which is also the title of the editor window. The bottom left of the editor window displays the current line and column position of the cursor.

When the editor window is active and you are not in the middle of giving it a command, it is ready to accept input. This means that when you strike keys on the keyboard, they will appear in the editor at the current cursor location.

By default, the editor is in *insert mode*. This means that as you enter text, it is inserted in the middle of what (if anything) is already there. The opposite, *overwrite mode,* overwrites existing text with new text. You can toggle between these two modes by pressing the INS key. You can tell which mode is currently active by the shape of the cursor. When in insert mode, the cursor is represented as a blinking underscore. In overwrite mode, it is a blinking rectangle.

Make sure the editor window is active and type the following lines:

```
This is a
test of the
Turbo/Borland C++ IDE editor.
```

Press ENTER at the end of the last line. If you make a mistake, you can use the BACKSPACE key to correct it. Your screen now looks like the one in Figure 33-1. Notice the position of the cursor and the values associated with the line and column display at the lower left of the editor window. Also, notice that now an asterisk is displayed to the left of the line and column indicators. The asterisk is displayed only after a change has been made to the file.

Because the editor is a *screen editor,* you can use the arrow keys to move the cursor around the text at random. Also, when you click the mouse, the cursor moves to the position of the mouse pointer. At this time, use either the arrow keys or the mouse to position the cursor at the far left of the line "test of the". Now, type **very small** and press ENTER. As you do so, watch the way the existing line is moved to the right instead of being overwritten. This is what happens when the editor is in insert mode. Had you toggled the editor into overwrite mode, the original line would have been overwritten. Your screen now looks like the one in Figure 33-2.

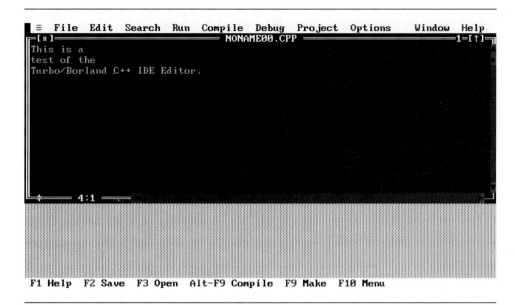

Figure 33-1. *Editor screen with text entered*

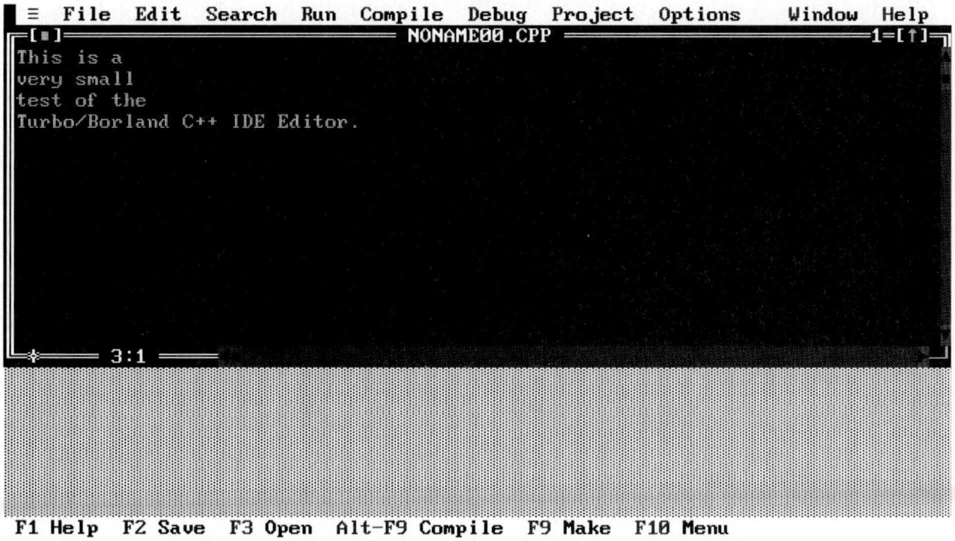

Figure 33-2. *Editor screen after inserting a line*

Deleting Characters, Words, and Lines

You can delete a single character two ways: with the BACKSPACE key or with the DEL key. The BACKSPACE key deletes the character immediately to the left of the cursor, while the DEL key deletes the character the cursor is under.

You can delete an entire word that is to the right of the cursor by pressing CTRL-T. A word is any set of characters delimited by one of the following characters:

space $ / − + * ' ^ [ ] ( ) . ; , < >
@ \ ' : % & ! ? | ~ = # "

You can remove an entire line by pressing CTRL-Y. It does not matter where the cursor is positioned in the line; the entire line is deleted. Try deleting a few lines and words now.

If you wish to delete from the current cursor position to the end of the line, press the sequence CTRL-Q Y.

Moving, Copying, and Deleting Blocks of Text

The IDE editor allows you to manipulate a block of text by moving or copying it to another location or deleting it altogether. In order to do any of these things, you must first define a block. A *block* can be as short as a single character or as large as your entire file. However, a block is typically somewhere between these two extremes. You can define a block two different ways: by using the keyboard or by using the mouse. To define a block by using the keyboard, move the cursor to the start of the block and press the sequence CTRL-K B. Next, move the cursor to the end of the block and press the sequence CTRL-K K. The block you have defined is highlighted. To define a block by using the mouse, first position the mouse pointer at the start of the block. Next, press and hold down the left mouse button and move the mouse pointer to the end of the block. Finally, release the button.

You can also define a block with the keyboard by holding down the SHIFT key and using the arrow keys and the PGUP, PGDN, HOME, and END keys. As you move the cursor with the SHIFT key down, the area the cursor moves over becomes highlighted. By pressing SHIFT-CTRL-END, you define a block that begins at the current cursor location and stops at the end of the file. By pressing SHIFT-CTRL-HOME, you define a block that begins at the current cursor location and stops at the start of the file.

To practice, move the cursor to the "t" at the start of the third line and press CTRL-K B. Next, move the cursor to the end of the last line and press CTRL-K K, or use the mouse to highlight the block. Your screen should look like the one in Figure 33-3.

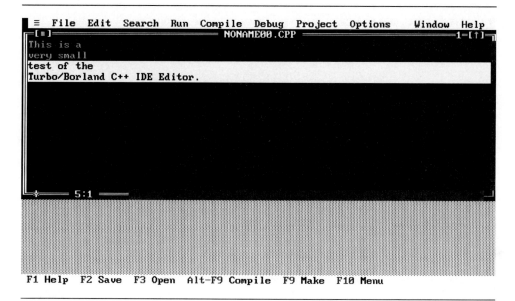

Figure 33-3.   *Editor screen after defining a block*

To move a block of text, place the cursor where you want the text to go and press the sequence CTRL-K V. This causes the previously defined block of text to be deleted from its current position and placed at the new location.

To copy a block, press the sequence CTRL-K C. For example, move the cursor to the top of the file and press CTRL-K C. Your screen should look like the one in Figure 33-4.

Once a block has been defined, you can also copy it by using the **Copy** option in the Edit menu. You can move a block with the Edit menu by first deleting the block by using **Cut** and then restoring it at the desired location by using **Paste**.

To delete the currently marked block, press CTRL-K Y. You can also execute this command by activating the **Edit** option in the main menu and then selecting the **Cut** entry. Either way you execute this command, the block you delete is also automatically put into a special editor window called the *clipboard*. You will see how to use the clipboard in the next section.

You can mark a single word by positioning the cursor under the first character in the word and pressing CTRL-K T.

To indent an entire block one character position, use the command CTRL-K I. To unindent a block one character position, use CTRL-K U.

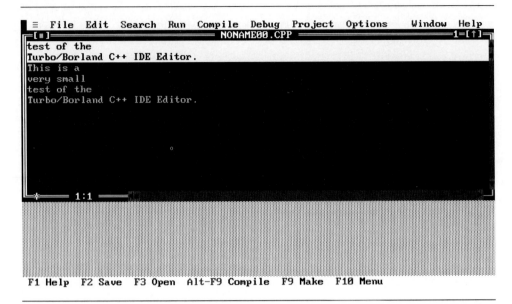

Figure 33-4. *Editor screen after block move*

Using the Clipboard

Using the Edit main menu options, you can make use of the clipboard to add greater flexibility when moving or copying text. Also, using the clipboard, you can easily move text between two editor windows.

In general, the clipboard is a temporary depository for fragments of text that have been copied from another file. To move text into the clipboard, you need to mark the region and then either delete that block or, using the Edit menu, select the **Copy** option. If you select **Copy**, the block is not deleted from the file, but it is still copied into the clipboard.

To retrieve a block of text from the clipboard, use the Edit menu's **Paste** command. This causes the most recently deleted or copied block of text in the clipboard to be copied into the current editor window at the current cursor location.

You can see the contents of the clipboard by selecting the **Show clipboard** option in the Edit menu. This also activates the clipboard window, and you can select any part of the contents of the clipboard.

If you wish to delete a block without having it copied into the clipboard, select the block and execute the **Clear** option in the Edit menu. This removes the block but does not copy it to the clipboard.

You can edit more than one file at a time simply by loading another file or selecting the **New** option in the File menu. This creates another editor window. To copy text from one window to another, define the block you want in the source window, copy it to the clipboard, and then paste it into the target window.

When you activate the help system and request information on a C++ feature, a programming example is frequently included. If this is the case, you can automatically move the example code into the clipboard by selecting the **Copy example** *option in the Edit menu.*

More on Cursor Movement

The IDE editor has a number of special cursor commands. These commands are summarized in Table 33-1. You might want to experiment with these commands now. Of course, you can also move the cursor by positioning the mouse pointer at the desired location and clicking.

Command	Action
CTRL-A	Moves to the start of the word to the left of the cursor
CTRL-S	Moves left one character
CTRL-D	Moves right one character
CTRL-F	Moves to the start of the word to the right of the cursor
CTRL-E	Moves the cursor up one line
CTRL-R	Moves the cursor up one full screen
CTRL-X	Moves the cursor down one line
CTRL-C	Moves the cursor down one full screen
CTRL-W	Scrolls the screen down
CTRL-Z	Scrolls the screen up
PGUP	Moves the cursor up one full screen
PGDN	Moves the cursor down one full screen
HOME	Moves the cursor to the start of the line
END	Moves the cursor to the end of the line
CTRL-Q E	Moves the cursor to the top of the screen
CTRL-Q X	Moves the cursor to the bottom of the screen
CTRL-Q R	Moves the cursor to the beginning of the file
CTRL-Q C	Moves the cursor to the end of the file
CTRL-PGUP	Moves the cursor to the beginning of the file
CTRL-PGDN	Moves the cursor to the end of the file
CTRL-HOME	Moves the cursor to the top of the screen
CTRL-END	Moves the cursor to the bottom of the screen

Table 33-1. *The Cursor Commands*

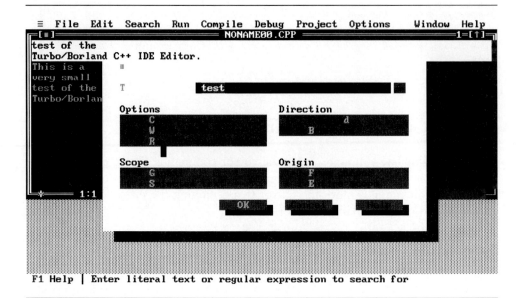

Figure 33-5.   *The Find dialog box*

Find and Replace

To find a specific sequence of characters, use the CTRL-Q F command. You are then prompted by the dialog box shown in Figure 33-5 for the string you wish to find. You can also specify various search options to alter the way the search is conducted.

By default, the search for the string you enter is conducted from the current cursor location forward in the file. To change this so the search proceeds in the opposite direction, select the **Backward** option. You can also have the search cover the entire file by selecting the **Entire scope** option.

The search is case sensitive by default. This means that upper- and lowercase characters, such as "A" and "a", are treated as different characters. However, you can choose to have the search treat these characters as though they are the same.

By default, if the string you enter is contained within another, larger string, this produces a match. (This is called a *substring match.*) For example, if you enter "is" for the search string, the editor will find a match in the word "this". You can cause the search to match only whole words by checking the **Whole words only** box.

You can confine the search to a block by selecting the **Selected text** option.

If you check the **Regular Expression** box, you can use the wildcard characters shown in Table 33-2 in your search string. Here are some examples of how the wildcard characters work:

Expression	Matches
h..lo	hello (and others)
^test	test (at start of line)
test$	test (at end of line)
[two]	t, w, or o
x*	x, xx, xxx, etc.

Remember, to use regular expressions, you must check the **Regular expression** box in the Find dialog box.

You can repeat a search simply by pressing CTRL-L. This is very convenient when you are looking for something specific in the file.

To activate the replace command, press CTRL-Q A. Its operation is identical to the find command except that it allows you to replace the string you are looking for with another. When you activate the command, you see the dialog box shown in Figure 33-6.

As you can see, the options available in the Replace dialog box are similar to those available with Find, with one addition. By default, the editor asks you before making a change. You can turn off this feature by deselecting **Prompt on replace**.

You can enter control characters into the search string by first pressing CTRL-P and then typing the control character you want.

Character	Purpose
^	Matches the start of a line
$	Matches the end of a line
.	Matches any character
*	Matches any number (including 0) of occurrences of the character it follows
+	Matches any number (except 0) of occurrences of the character it follows
[*string*]	Matches a single occurrence of any one character in *string*. You can specify a range by using the hyphen. If the first character in the string is a ^, the construct will match any characters except those in the string
\	Causes the character it precedes to be treated literally and not as a wildcard

Table 33-2. *The Regular Expression Wildcard Characters*

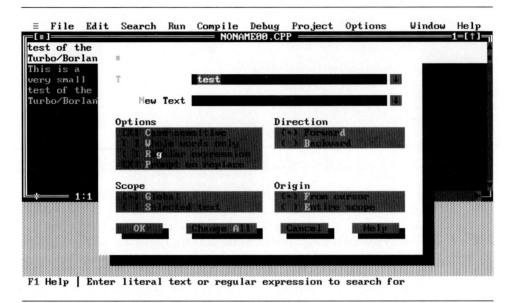

Figure 33-6.   The Replace dialog box

Setting and Finding Place Markers

You can set up to four place markers in your file by pressing CTRL-K *n*, where *n* is the number of the place marker (0 through 3). After a marker has been set, the command CTRL-Q *n*, where *n* is the marker number, causes the cursor to go to that marker. Place markers are especially convenient in large files.

Saving and Loading Your File

There are three ways to save your file. Two of them save it to a file that has the same name as that shown in title of the editor window. The third way allows you to save your file under a different name and then makes that the current name of your file. Let's look at how each works. First, exit the editor and return to the main menu by pressing F10, and then display the File menu.

In the File menu, selecting the **Save** option saves what is currently in the editor into a disk file with the name shown in the window title. If you have not specified a file to edit, invoking this option causes the file to be saved as NONAME00.CPP. Because you will probably want to use a different file name, you are prompted to do so. This prompt occurs only if NONAME*nn*.CPP is the name of the source file. Otherwise, the file is saved without further interaction.

If you wish to save the contents of the editor into a file with a name other than that shown on the editor status line, use the **Save as** option. This allows you to enter the name of the file to which you wish to write the current contents of the editor. It also makes this the default file name.

You can also save your file while inside the editor by pressing the F2 key. This is simply a shortcut for selecting the **Save** option in the File menu.

To load a file, you can either press F3 while inside the editor or select the **Open** option in the File menu. This displays a dialog box, and you are prompted for the name of the file you wish to load. There are two ways to specify the file name. First, you can type it. Second, you can TAB to the list of files shown in the dialog box and make a selection. By default, all files with the .CPP extension are displayed. If you have a mouse, you can also double click on the desired file to load it.

By default, when you save a file that already exists on disk, the old version of the file is not overwritten. Instead, it is kept as a backup file and its extension is changed to .BAK. (You can turn off automatic backup, as you will see later in this chapter.)

Understanding Autoindentation

As you most likely know, good programmers use indentation to help make the programs they write clearer and easier to understand. To assist in this practice, after you press ENTER, the editor automatically places the cursor at the same indentation level as the line that was previously entered. You toggle this feature on and off by pressing CTRL-O I. To see how autoindentation works, enter the following lines exactly as they are shown here:

```
This is an illustration
  of the autoindentation
  mechanism
    of the Turbo/Borland C++
    editor.
```

As you enter the text, notice that the editor automatically maintains the last indentation level. You will find this feature quite handy when entering C++ source code.

Moving Blocks of Text to and from Disk Files

It is possible to move a block of text into a disk file for later use. You do this by first defining a block and then pressing CTRL-K W. You are then prompted for the name of the file in which you wish to save the block. The original block of text is not removed from your program.

To read a block into a file, use the command CTRL-K R. You are prompted for the file name. The contents of that file will be read in at the current cursor location.

These two commands are most useful when you are moving text between two or more files, as is often the case during program development.

Pair Matching

There are several delimiters in C++ that work in pairs—for example, the { }, the [ ], and the ( ). In very long or complex programs, it is sometimes difficult to find the proper companion to a delimiter. It is possible to have the editor automatically find the companion delimiter for the following delimiter pairs:

```
{ }
[ ]
( )
< >
/* */
" "
' '
```

To find the matching delimiter, place the cursor on the delimiter you wish to match and press CTRL-Q [for a forward match or CTRL-Q] for a backward match. The editor moves the cursor to the matching delimiter.

Some delimiters are nestable and some are not. The nestable delimiters are { }, [ ], ( ), < >, and sometimes the comment symbols (when the nested comments option is enabled). The editor finds the proper matching delimiter in accordance with C++ syntax. If for some reason the editor cannot find a proper match, the cursor does not move.

Miscellaneous Commands

You can abort any command that requests input by pressing ESC at the prompt or by clicking the mouse on the **Cancel** button, if one exists. For example, if you execute the **Find** command and then change your mind, simply press ESC or click the mouse on **Cancel.**

If you wish to enter a control character into the file, first press CTRL-P and then type the control character you want. Control characters are displayed in either low intensity or reverse intensity, depending upon how your system is configured.

To undo an edit, select the **Undo** option in the Edit menu. To undo an undo, select **Redo** in the Edit menu.

If you wish to move the cursor to the start of a block, press CTRL-Q B. Pressing CTRL-Q K takes you to the end of a block.

You can print a block of text by using the CTRL-K P command. To print the entire file, select the **Print** command in the File menu.

One particularly useful command is CTRL-Q P, which puts the cursor back to its previous position. This is handy if you want to search for something and then return to where you were.

By default, when you press the TAB key, the tab character is entered into your file. However, using the command CTRL-O T causes an equivalent number of spaces to be inserted instead of the tab. The CTRL-O T command is actually a toggle that lets you change between the two ways that tabs are processed.

By default, when you press the BACKSPACE key at the start of a new line, the cursor automatically moves to the left one indentation level each time it is pressed. You can toggle this feature by using the CTRL-O U command. When it is off, the cursor backs up only one space each time the BACKSPACE key is pressed, no matter how deeply indented it is.

Changing the Editor Defaults

You can change some aspects of the way the editor operates by selecting **Options** from the main menu and then selecting the **Environment** entry. Next, select the **Editor** item. You will see the dialog box shown in Figure 33-7.

The **Create backup files**, **Insert mode**, and **Autoindent mode** options are self-explanatory. If you turn off the **Use tab character** option, the appropriate number of spaces is substituted for the tab character. The **Optimal fill** option controls what characters the editor uses when it autoindents. When on, it mixes spaces and tabs. When off, it uses spaces only. When **Backspace unindents** is on, each time you press BACKSPACE on a blank line, the cursor backs up one indentation level. If the option is off, the cursor backs up one character each time BACKSPACE is pressed. If **Cursor through tabs** is on, when you move the cursor through a tab, it does not jump to the next tab position. When the option is off, the cursor jumps to the next tab position.

In addition to the options just mentioned, you may have one or more of the following options available (depending upon the version of Turbo/Borland C++ you are using). If **Syntax highlighting** is on, all C++ keywords are shown in boldface. If **Group undo** is on, performing an undo causes the immediately preceding command and all commands similar to it to be undone. If **Persistent blocks** is off, a previously selected block of text is deselected if the cursor is moved out of that block. If **Overwrite blocks** is on, you can overwrite blocks of text that have been selected. You can also change the tab size and the default file name extension.

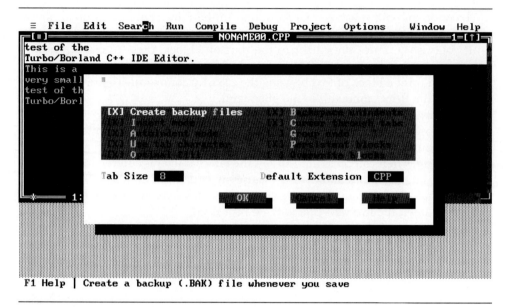

Figure 33-7.   *The Editor Options dialog box*

Invoking the IDE with a File Name

As mentioned earlier, you can specify the name of the file you want to edit when you invoke the IDE. To do this you simply specify the name of the file after the "TC" or the "BC" on the command line. For example, **TC MYFILE.CPP** executes Turbo C++ and loads MYFILE.CPP into the editor. If MYFILE.CPP does not exist, it will be created. If you don't supply an extension, Turbo/Borland C++ automatically appends .CPP. For example, **TC MYFILE** will execute Turbo/Borland C++ and cause MYFILE.CPP to be loaded into the editor. If you do not want to use an extension on the file name, place a period after the name. This causes Turbo/Borland C++ to not append the .CPP extension.

Command Summary

Table 33-3 shows all the Turbo/Borland C++ editor commands.

Cursor Commands

Command	Action
LEFT ARROW or CTRL-S	Moves left one character
RIGHT ARROW or CTRL-D	Moves right one character
CTRL-A	Moves left one word
CTRL-F	Moves right one word
UP ARROW or CTRL-E	Moves up one line
DOWN ARROW or CTRL-X	Moves down one line
CTRL-W	Scrolls up
CTRL-Z	Scrolls down
PGUP or CTRL-R	Moves up one page
PGDN or CTRL-C	Moves down one page
HOME or CTRL-Q S	Moves to start of line
END or CTRL-Q D	Moves to end of line
CTRL-Q E	Moves to top of screen
CTRL-Q X	Moves to bottom of screen
CTRL-Q R	Moves to beginning of file
CTRL-Q C	Moves to end of file
CTRL-Q B	Moves to start of block
CTRL-Q K	Moves to end of block
CTRL-Q P	Moves to last cursor position

Insert Commands

Command	Action
INS or CTRL-V	Toggles insert mode
ENTER or CTRL-N	Inserts a blank line

Delete Commands

Command	**Action**
CTRL-Y	Deletes entire line
CTRL-Q Y	Deletes to end of line
BACKSPACE	Deletes character on left

Table 33-3.   *Turbo/Borland C++ Editor Command Summary by Category*

Delete Commands

Command	Action
DEL or CTRL-G	Deletes character at cursor
CTRL-T	Deletes word to the right

Block Commands

Command	Action
CTRL-K B	Marks start of block
CTRL-K K	Marks end of block
CTRL-K T	Marks a word
CTRL-K C	Copies a block
CTRL-K Y	Deletes a block
CTRL-K H	Hides or displays a block
CTRL-K V	Moves a block
CTRL-K R	Writes a block to disk
CTRL-K W	Reads a block from disk
CTRL-K I	Indents a block
CTRL-K U	Exdents a block
CTRL-K P	Prints a block
CTRL-INS	Copies to clipboard
SHIFT-DEL	Cuts to clipboard

Find Commands

Command	Action
CTRL-Q F	Finds
CTRL-Q A	Finds and replaces
CTRL-Q n	Finds a place marker
CTRL-L	Repeats find

Pair Matching

Command	Action
CTRL-Q [	Matches pair forward
CTRL-Q]	Matches pair reverse

Table 33-3. *Turbo/Borland C++ Editor Command Summary by Category* (continued)

Miscellaneous Commands

Command	Action
CTRL-U	Aborts
CTRL-O I	Toggles autoindentation mode
CTRL-P	Control character prefix
F10	Exits editor
F3	Opens new file
CTRL-Q W	Restores overwritten error message
F2	Saves
CTRL-K *n*	Sets a place marker
CTRL-O T	Toggles tab mode
ALT-BACKSPACE	Performs an undo
SHIFT-ALT-BACKSPACE	Undoes an undo
CTRL-O U	Toggles backspace mode

Table 33-3.   *Turbo/Borland C++ Editor Command Summary by Category* (continued)

Chapter 34

Using the Command-Line Compiler, VROOMM, and Multiple-File Projects

This chapter examines three important features of Turbo/Borland C++: the command line compiler, managing multiple-file projects by using the IDE, and the VROOMM overlay capability.

Compiling Using the Command-Line Compiler

Unlike the IDE, which provides a complete development environment, Turbo/Borland C++'s command-line compiler performs only two tasks: it compiles and links your C++ program. This means that you will most likely use your own text editor to create a program and then use the command-line compiler to translate it into executable code. This procedure represents the traditional method of compilation and linking. The main reason you might want to use the command-line compiler instead of the IDE is if you have a favorite text editor you do not want to give up. Whatever the reason, if you choose to use the command-line version compiler, you will be happy to know that it compiles your programs in just the same way that the compiler inside the IDE does.

If you already know how to run the Turbo C command-line compiler, you know how to run the Turbo/Borland C++ command-line compiler; their operation is virtually identical. The only significant differences between them are in the options accepted by each.

For users of Turbo C++, the name of the command-line compiler is TCC.EXE. If you are using Borland C++, the command-line compiler is called BCC.EXE. The simplest way to compile a program from the command line is to use one of these general forms, depending on which compiler you have:

C>TCC *program-name*

or

C>BCC *program-name*

For example, if you want to compile a program called MYPROG.CPP using the Turbo C++ command-line compiler, use the command

C>TCC MYPROG.CPP

Assuming that there are no errors in the program, this causes MYPROG.CPP to be compiled and linked with the standard library files. (You may have to specify additional library files, depending on what functions your program uses, as explained later in this section.)

Like the IDE compiler, the command-line compiler allows you to control its exact operation by using command-line options. All compiler/linker options are put before the file that is to be compiled on the command line. Also, all options begin with a minus sign. Generally, following an option with a dash turns off that option. Table 34-1 shows many of the options available in the command-line version of Turbo C++. Keep in mind that the options are case sensitive. Also, since the exact nature of many of these options changes with different versions of Turbo/Borland C++, refer to your user manuals for their exact meanings.

In addition to options, you may also specify a list of other files you want compiled and/or linked into your program. In this way you can compile and link multiple-file programs using the command-line compiler. If a file ends in .C or .CPP, it is compiled and linked. If it ends in .OBJ, the file is linked with the rest of your program. If a file ends in .LIB, the file is treated as an additional library and its contents are searched, if necessary.

Including options and multiple files, the general form of the command line is

TCC/BCC [*option1 option2 ... optionN*] *fname1 fame2 ... fnameN*

Turbo/Borland C++'s Options

Option	Meaning
–A	Recognize ANSI keywords only
–AT	Use Turbo/Borland C++ keywords
–AK	Recognize only K&R keywords
–AU	Recognize only UNIX C keywords
–a	Use word alignment for data
–a–	Use byte alignment for data
–B	In-line assembly code in source file
–b	Treat enumerations as integers
–b–	Treat enumerations as characters
–C	Accept nested comments
–c	Compile to .OBJ only
–D*name*	Defines a macro name
–D*name=string*	Defines and gives a value to a macro name
–d	Merge duplicate strings
–E*fname*	Specifies name of assembler
–e*fname*	Specifies executable file name
–Fc	Create a common definition for noninitialized global variables
–Ff	Make global variables FAR
–Fm	Turn on options Fc, Ff, and Fs
–Fs	Compiler assumes DS == SS
–f	Use floating-point emulation
–f–	No floating point
–ff	Optimize for fast floating point
–f87	Use 8087
–f287	Use 80287
–G	Optimize code for speed
–g*N*	Stop after *N* warning errors
–H	Use precompiled header files—generate as needed
–Hu	Use precompiled header files, but do not generate
–H=*fname*	Specifies name of precompiled header

Table 34-1. *Turbo/Borland C++'s Command-Line Options*

Turbo/Borland C++'s Options

Option	Meaning
–I*path*	Specifies path to the include directory
–i*N*	Specifies identifier length as *N*
–Jg	Generate all necessary template definitions
–Jgd	Same as Jg except that duplicate definitions will cause errors if a template is multiply-defined in two or more modules
–Jgx	Assume external definition of templates
–j*N*	Stop after *N* fatal errors
–K	Char unsigned
–K–	Char signed
–k	Use standard stack frame
–L*path*	Specifies library directory
–l*x*	Passes an option to the linker
–M	Create map file
–mc	Use compact memory model
–mh	Use huge memory model
–ml	Use large memory model
–mm	Use medium memory model
–mm!	Use medium memory model, but DS != SS
–ms	Use small memory model
–ms!	Use small memory model, but DS != SS
–mt	Use tiny memory model
–mt!	Use tiny memory model, but DS != SS
–N	Check for stack overflows
–n*path*	Specifies output directory
–O	Optimize jumps
–o*name*	Specifies .OBJ file name
–P	Compile as a C++ program
–P*ext*	Compile as a C++ program and changes default C++ extension to *ext*
–p	Use Pascal calling conventions

Table 34-1. *Turbo/Borland C++'s Command-Line Options* (continued)

Turbo/Borland C++'s Options

Option	Meaning
–Qe	Use all EMS memory
–Qe–	Use no EMS memory
–Qx=*N*	Use *N* bytes extended memory
–r	Use register variables
–r–	Ignore register variables
–rd	Use only declared register variables
–S	Generate assembly code output
–T*opt*	Pass an option to the assembler
–TDe	Make .EXE file
–TDc	Make .COM file
–U*name*	Undefine a macro name
–u	Prefix identifiers with underscores in object file
–v	Enable source code debugging
–vi	Enable expansion of inline functions
–V*x*	Special compatibility options (see your compiler reference manual
–v	Include debug information
–w	Display warning errors (see Table 34-2)
–w–	Do not display warning errors
–X	Suppress autodependency output (generally used to generate a library file)
–Y	Must use when creating overlay modules
–Yo	Compile as an overlay
–y	Embed line numbers into object code
–Z	Register optimization on
–z	Specify segment names (see your compiler's reference manual)
–1	Generate 80186 instructions
–1–	Do not generate 80186/80286 instructions
–2	Generate 80286 protected mode instructions

Table 34-1. *Turbo/Borland C++'s Command-Line Options* (continued)

Borland C++ Only Options

Option	Meaning
–O1	Optimize for size
–O2	Optimize for speed
–Od	Turn off all optimizations
–O*x*	Additional optimizations (see your compiler manual)
–pr	Pass parameters in registers
–R	Generate code for Windows ObjectBrowser (Windows programs only
–tW	Make a Windows executable program
–W	Compile to Windows OBJ with all functions exported
–WD	Compile as Windows DLL with all functions exported
–Wde	Compile as Windows DLL with specific functions exported
–WE	Compile to Windows OBJ with specific functions exported
–WS	Compile to Windows OBJ using smart callbacks

Table 34-1.   *Turbo/Borland C++'s Command-Line Options* (continued)

where *option* refers to a compiler or linker option and *fname* is either a C or C++ source file, an .OBJ file, or a library file having the extension .LIB.

For example, to compile MYPROG.CPP so it is optimized for speed using Turbo C++, type the following on the command line:

TCC –G MYPROG.CPP

One of the most interesting options is –S. This option causes the compiler to generate a file that contains the assembly language code produced by the compiler. If your file is called MYPROG.CPP, the assembly language output will be in MYPROG.ASM. Not only is it interesting to see how Turbo/Borland C++ generates code, but it can also be useful. For example, by studying the code generated for various types of expressions and statements, you learn what type of code produces the most efficient executable code. Further, if you are an accomplished assembly language programmer, you can actually "hand optimize" the assembly language version of your program.

The **–w** option lets you control what type of warning messages are displayed when you compile your program. The available options are shown in Table 34-2. Keep in mind that the warning options have evolved over the lifetime of Turbo/Borland C++ and your compiler may not support all that are shown or may no longer support some that are. Also, some options relate only to C++ programs.

Option	Warning
–wamb	Ambiguous statement needs parentheses
–wamp	Unnecessary &
–wapt	Pointer assignment is nonportable
–wasm	Assembly instruction not recognized
–watt	Assignment to this is obsolete
–waus	Variable assigned a value that is never used
–wbbf	Bit-fields must be either signed or unsigned
–wbei	Wrong type used in initialization
–wbfs	Untyped bit-field defaulted to signed integer
–wbig	Hexadecimal constant is too large
–wccc	Boolean expression always true
–wcln	Constant is too long
–wcpt	Pointer comparison is nonportable
–wdcl	Declaration needs tag-name or variable
–wdef	Possible use of a variable before it is defined
–wdpu	Declare a function using a prototype
–wdsz	Unnecessary array size for delete operator
–wdup	Redefinition of a macro is not identical
–weas	Assigning an integer to an enumeration variable
–weff	Code has no effect
–wext	Identifier is declared as both **extern** and **static**
–wflo	Initialization may not occur
–whid	A function hides another virtual function
–wias	Array identifier is NEAR
–wibc	Base class not accessible
–will	Incorrectly formed **#pragma** directive
–winl	Function not expanded inline
–wlin	A temporary variable is used in initialization
–wlvc	A temporary variable is used in a function call
–wmpc	Invalid type conversion for members of virtual base class
–wmpd	Member pointer uses maximum precision
–wncf	Non-**const** function called a **const** object

Table 34-2.   *The –w Warning Message Options*

Option	Warning
−wnci	A **const** member is not initialized
−wnod	No declaration for function
−wnst	Nested type accessed via scope specifier
−wnvf	**volatile** object calls non-**volatile** function
−wobi	Base initialization with a class name is obsolete
−wofp	Old-style function declaration is obsolete
−womf	Syntax obsolete, use ::
−wovl	The overload keyword is obsolete
−wpar	A parameter is not used by a function
−wpia	Possibly incorrect assignment statement
−wpin	Initialization is incorrectly bracketed
−wpre	Overloaded prefix operator used as postfix
−wpro	Function must be prototyped
−wrch	Function has unreachable code
−wret	Function uses both return and return with a value
−wrng	Constant is out of range
−wrpt	Return type conversion is nonportable
−wrvl	Function should return a value
−wscp	Identifier cannot be used as both variable and tag name
−wsig	Significant digits may be lost in conversion
−wstr	Function may not be part of structure or union
−wstu	Undefined structure
−wstv	Structure passed by value
−wsus	Suspicious pointer conversion
−wucp	Mixing pointer types
−wuse	Variable declared but not used
−wvoi	A void function cannot have a return value
−wzdi	Division by zero
−wzst	Zero length structure detected

Table 34-2.   *The −w Warning Message Options* (continued)

Remember that not all "warning" messages actually pertain to errors. For example, enabling the **–wlin** warning message causes the compiler to tell you if it uses a temporary variable to perform an initialization. This is not an error in the normal sense of the word.

The command-line compiler automatically adds the .CPP extension to any file name if no extension is specified. For example, both of these command lines are functionally the same:

```
C>TCC MYPROG.CPP
C>TCC MYPROG
```

To cause Turbo/Borland C++ to compile a file as a C rather than a C++ file, you must specify the .C extension.

You can compile a file with an extension other than .C or .CPP by specifying its extension. For example, to compile MYPROG.TMP, the command line looks like this:

```
C>TCC MYPROG.TMP
```

Using a Response File

If your command line is quite long and tedious to type, you might want to use a response file. A *response file* is a text file that contains the information you would normally specify on the command line. Using a response file lets you avoid repeatedly typing the same long command line. To use the file, simply specify its full name, preceding it with an @ sign after the name of the compiler (either TCC or BCC). For example, assume you are using Borland C++ and you want to compile and link three files called PROG1.CPP, PROG2.CPP, and PROG3.CPP. Further, you want the compiler to warn you about any variables declared but not used. The response file for this scenario is shown here:

```
-wuse PROG1.CPP PROG2.CPP PROG3.CPP
```

Assuming this file is called MYRESP, you would use this command line to compile your program:

```
C>BCC  @MYRESP
```

You can use as many response files as you like. The contents of each is processed in the order in which it occurs.

Compiling Multiple-File Programs Using the IDE

Most real-world C++ programs are too large to easily fit into one file. Extremely large files are difficult to edit. Also, making a small change in the program requires that the entire program be recompiled. Although both Turbo and Borland C++ are very fast at compiling, at some point, no matter how fast the compiler, the time it takes to compile will become unacceptable.

The solution to these types of problems is to break the program into smaller pieces, compile these pieces, and then link them together. This process is known as *separate compilation and linking,* and it forms the backbone of most development efforts. You have already seen how to compile and link multiple-file programs using the command-line compiler. In this section, you see how to compile and link multiple-file programs using the IDE.

Projects and the Project Option

In the Turbo/Borland C++ integrated environment, multiple-file programs are called *projects.* Each project is associated with a *project file* that determines which files are part of the project. The **Project** main menu option lets you manage project files. All project files must end with a .PRJ extension.

If you are familiar with Turbo C, Turbo/Borland C++'s approach to multiple-file programs will be familar. However, be aware that there are differences, so read this section carefully.

When you select the **Project** option, you are presented with these choices:

Open project...
Close project
Add item...
Delete item
Local options...
Include files...

To create a project, you must first select **Open project**. You are then prompted for the name of the project, which must have the extension .PRJ. To clear a project, use **Close Project**. Once you have created a project file, use **Add item** to put into the project file the names of the files that form the project. For example, if you want to call your project MYPROJ.PRJ and your project contains the two files TEST1.CPP and TEST2.CPP, you would first open the project using the name MYPROJ.PRJ and then add the two files TEST1.CPP and TEST2.CPP to it. To remove an item, select **Delete item**. You specify various options using **Local options**. The **Include files** option lets you see what **#include** files are used by each file in your project.

As an example, assume you have a project file that contains the files TEST1.CPP and TEST2.CPP. Further assume that neither TEST1.CPP nor TEST2.CPP has yet been compiled. There are two ways to compile and link these files. First, you can select the **Run** main menu option. When there is a .PRJ file specified in the **Project** option, this file is used to guide the IDE in compiling your program. The contents of the .PRJ file are read, and each file that needs to be compiled is compiled to an .OBJ file. Next, those files are linked together and the program is executed.

The second way you can compile a project is to use the built-in **Make** facility. By pressing F9 or selecting the **Make** option under the **Compile** main menu option, you cause the IDE to compile and link all files specified in the project file. The difference between this and the **Run** option is that the program is not executed. In fact, you can think of the **Run** option as first performing a **Make** and then executing the .EXE file.

Whenever you **Make** a program, only those files that need to be compiled will actually be compiled. This is determined by checking the time and date associated with each source file and its .OBJ file. If the .CPP file is newer than the .OBJ file, **Make** knows that the .CPP file has been changed and it recompiles it. Otherwise, it simply uses the .OBJ file. In this situation, the *target* .OBJ file is said to be *dependent* upon the .CPP file. The same sort of thing is true of the .EXE file. As long as the .EXE file is newer than all of the .OBJ files in the project, nothing is recompiled. Otherwise, the necessary file or files are compiled and the project relinked.

In addition to checking the dates on .CPP, .OBJ, and .EXE files, **Make** checks to see if any header files used by your program have changed. If this is the case, any file that uses a changed header file is automatically recompiled.

Without a doubt, the project capabilities of the IDE are among its most important aspects because they let you manage multiple source file programs with little difficulty. Also, as you will see in the next section, they allow you to take advantage of VROOMM technology.

Using the VROOMM Overlay System

With the introduction of Turbo C++, Borland has made its VROOMM (Virtual Runtime Object-Oriented Memory Manager) technology available to all programmers. As you probably know, overlays are a time-honored method of dealing with a program that is too large to fit in available memory. When overlays are used, pieces of your program are stored on disk and swapped into memory only when needed. This reduces the amount of memory required by the program, but it does slow down execution speed because of the time it takes to load a module.

In general, to use overlays you need an overlay manager that will swap parts of your program into memory from disk. You also need to break your program into several smaller pieces suitable for overlays. What makes the VROOMM technology special is that it automatically handles the details of overlays for you. You don't need to calculate any sizes or determine any calling dependencies. In fact, to let your large programs take advantage of VROOMM, you simply change a few compiler options. Nothing else needs to change.

When compiling for overlays, you must use the medium, large, or huge memory model. If you forget to do this, the linker will not link your program.

Since you will only use VROOMM on a very large program, most likely that program will be split among several files.

To enable your program to use VROOMM, you will need to set some options in the IDE or specify an option if using the command-line compiler. For the IDE, make sure you have defined a project file for your program. (Projects are described in the previous section.) The rest of the instructions in this paragraph apply to users of Turbo/Borland C++ version 3.0. (If you are using 2.0, see the following note.) From the main menu, select **Options** followed by **Application**. Now, select **Overlay**. This tells the IDE that you will be compiling for overlays. Next, select **Project** from the main menu followed by **Local Options**. Now, specify those files that need to be made into an overlay.

If you are using Turbo/Borland C++ version 2.0, follow these instructions to prepare the IDE to use VROOMM. Select the **Options** *entry in the main menu. Next, select* **Compiler** *followed by* **Code generation**. *Turn on the* **Overlay support** *check box. Also, select the medium, large, or huge memory model. Return to the main menu. Now, activate the* **Options** *entry a second time and select* **Linker**. *Turn on the* **Overlay EXE** *check box. Finally, to specify which files in your project will be overlaid, in turn highlight each file in the project window and then from the main menu select the* **Project** *entry and select the* **Local options** *entry. You will then be able to specify each file for overlaying.*

If you are using the command-line version of Turbo/Borland C++, you must specify the **–Yo** option before the file or files that you want to be overlays. Also, if there is a part of your program that you want to stay resident, precede its file name with just **–Y**. Since you must compile any program using overlays for the medium, large, or huge memory model, you must also specify the **–mm**, **–ml**, or **–mh** option. For example, the following series of command lines compiles a program consisting of the files PROG.CPP, PROG1.CPP, and PROG2.CPP for overlays. Notice that PROG.CPP is resident all the time. The other two files will be overlaid.

```
tcc -ml -Yo prog1.cpp
tcc -ml -Yo prog2.cpp
tcc -ml -Y prog.cpp prog2.obj prog3.obj
```

Using the VROOMM overlay manager, when a piece of code is called that is not currently in memory, it is read from disk into a buffer set aside for overlays. If the buffer is already full, another module is discarded. By default, the size of the buffer is twice the size of the largest overlayable module. However, you can increase the size of the buffer (and thereby increase performance) by setting the built-in global variable **_ovrbuffer**. The size of the buffer is specified in paragraphs (16 bytes). Experimentation may prove the easiest way to determine what buffer size is best for your program. Remember, except for running out of memory, there is nothing wrong with making the buffer as large as you can because it reduces disk accesses.

When using overlays, keep in mind that you will almost certainly want to keep parts of your program resident and other parts as overlays. The best modules to make into overlays are those parts of your programs that are executed infrequently—for example, a help system or a sort. However, you should not make any module that depends upon timing into an overlay.

Part VI

Windows Programming Using Borland C++

Part Six of this book shows you how to use Borland C++ to create Windows applications. As you will see, writing a Windows application is not as easy as writing a DOS program. However, programming for Windows is also not as difficult as you may have been lead to believe. To create a successful Windows program, you simply follow a well-defined set of rules.

To do Windows programming you must have Borland C++. Turbo C++ does not support Windows.

While this section contains all information necessary for you to write the most common type of Windows application, it does not discuss all aspects of the Windows operating system. Windows is simply too large a system. (In fact, several large books are required to fully document the Windows programming environment.) The purpose of this section is to introduce the basics of Windows programming and explain how to use Borland C++ to accomplish it. If you will be writing extensively for Windows, you will absolutely need a Windows programming reference that details the over 600 Windows API (Application Program Interface) functions. One good source for this information is *Microsoft Windows Programming Reference* (Redmond, Wash.: Microsoft Press, 1990). Because Windows is a very large and complex environment, you will want to have available as much information as possible about how to use it.

This section teaches Windows programming using the traditional approach supported by Borland C++. However, Borland has released a Windows-based compiler called Turbo C++ for Windows *that runs under Windows and contains a special class library called* ObjectWindows *that can simplify Windows programming. Because of space limitations,*

971

this compiler is not discussed in this book. However, it is covered extensively in my book
Turbo C++ for Windows: Inside and Out *(Berkeley, Calif.: Osborne/McGraw-Hill, 1992).*

Chapter **35**

Windows Programming Overview

This chapter introduces Windows programming. First, it discusses in a general way what Windows is, how a program must interact with it, and what rules must be followed by every Windows application. Second, it develops an application skeleton that will be used as a basis for all other Windows programs. All Windows programs share a few common traits. It is these shared attributes that are contained in the application skeleton.

What Is Windows?

To an extent, what Windows is depends upon whether you are an end user or a programmer. From the user's point of view, Windows is a shell with which he or she interacts in order to run applications. However, from the programmer's point of view, Windows is a graphics-oriented, multitasking operating system, a collection of several hundred API functions that support a specific application-designed philosophy. From the programmer's point of view, Windows is one giant toolbox of interrelated services that, when used correctly, allow the creation of application programs that all share a common interface.

The goal of Windows is to enable a person who has basic familiarity with the system to sit down and run virtually any application without prior training. In theory, if you can run one Windows program, you can run them all. Of course, in actuality, most useful programs will still require some sort of training in order to be used effectively, but at least this instruction can be restricted to what the program does, not how the user must interact with it. In fact, much of the code in a Windows application is there just to support the user interface.

It is important to understand that not every program that runs under Windows will necessarily present the user with a Windows-style interface; only those programs written to take advantage of Windows will look and feel like Windows programs. While you can override the basic Windows design philosophy, you had better have a good reason to do so, because the users of your programs will, most often, be very disturbed. If you are writing application programs for Windows, it makes the most sense for them to conform to the accepted Windows programming philosophy.

As mentioned, Windows is graphics oriented, which means that it provides a Graphical User Interface (GUI). While graphics hardware and video modes are quite diverse, many of the differences are handled by Windows. This means that for the most part, your program does not need to worry about what type of graphics hardware or video mode is being used.

Even though Windows runs on top of DOS, your Windows programs will not generally interact directly with DOS. Windows provides a complete set of its own services. If your program calls a DOS function, it may not be able to run as a Windows application. Therefore, your program will usually interact with the Windows API.

Let's look at a few of the more important features of Windows.

The Desktop Model

With few exceptions, the point of a window-based user interface is to provide on the screen the equivalent of a desktop. On a desk may be found several different pieces of paper, one on top of another, often with fragments of different pages visible beneath the top page. The equivalent of the desktop in Windows is the screen. The equivalents of pieces of paper are windows on the screen. On a desk you can move pieces of paper around, maybe switching which piece of paper is on top or how much of another is exposed to view. Windows allows the same types of operations on its windows. By selecting a window you can make it *current,* which means putting it on top of all other windows. You can enlarge or shrink a window or move it around on the screen. In short, Windows lets you control the surface of the screen the way you control the surface of your desk.

The Mouse

Unlike DOS, Windows allows the use of the mouse for almost all control, selection, and drawing operations. Actually, to say that it *allows* the use of the mouse is an understatement. The Windows interface was *designed* for the mouse—it *allows* the use of the keyboard! Although it is certainly possible for an application program to ignore the mouse, it does so only in violation of a basic Windows design principle.

Icons and Graphics Images

Windows allows (but does not require) the use of icons and bit-mapped graphics images. The theory behind the use of icons and graphics images is found in the old adage: A picture is worth a thousand words.

An icon is a small symbol that represents some function or program you can activate by moving the mouse to the icon and double clicking on it. A graphics image is generally used to convey information quickly to the user.

Menus and Dialog Boxes

Aside from standard windows, Windows also provides special-purpose windows. The most common of these are the menus and dialog boxes. A *menu* is, as you would expect, a special window that contains only a list from which the user makes a selection. However, instead of having to provide the menu selection functions in your program, you simply create a standard menu window using Windows functions.

A *dialog box* is a special window that allows more complex interaction with the application than that allowed by a menu. For example, your application might use a dialog box to input a file name. With few exceptions, nonmenu input is accomplished in Windows via a dialog box.

How Windows and Your Program Interact

When you write a program for many operating systems, it is your program that initiates interaction with the operating system. For example, in a DOS program, it is the program that requests such things as input and output. Put differently, programs written in the traditional way call the operating system. The operating system does not call your program. However, in large measure, Windows works the opposite way. It is Windows that calls your program. The process works like this: A Windows program waits until it is sent a *message* by Windows. The message is passed to your program through a special function that is called by Windows. Once a message is received, your program is expected to take an appropriate action. While your program may call one or more Windows API functions when responding to a message, it is still Windows that initiates the activity. More than anything else, it is the message-based interaction with Windows that dictates the general form of all Windows programs.

There are many different types of messages Windows may send your program. For example, each time the mouse is clicked on a window belonging to your program, a mouse-clicked message is sent to your program. Another type of message is sent each time a window belonging to your program must be redrawn. Still another message is sent each time the user presses a key when your program is the focus of input. Keep one fact firmly in mind: As far as your program is concerned, messages arrive randomly. This is why Windows programs resemble interrupt-driven programs. You can't know what message will be next.

Windows Is Multitasking

Windows is a multitasking operating system. As a multitasking operating system it is somewhat unique in that it uses *nonpreemptive multitasking*. This means that each program executing in the system retains use of the processor until it relinquishes it. This differs radically from the type of multitasking done by other operating systems that employ preemptive task switches based upon time slices. When time slicing, the operating system simply stops executing one program and moves on to the next, in a round-robin fashion. Remember that this is not how Windows works. A Windows program must relinquish the CPU.

One of the most important rules a Windows program must follow is to return control to Windows when it is inactive. This allows Windows to grant the processor to another task. As you will see, returning control to Windows is generally quite easy. Keep in mind, however, that it is possible for a program to monopolize the processor, effectively halting all other tasks.

The API

The Windows environment is accessed through a call-based interface called the API (Application Program Interface). The approximately 600 API functions provide all the system services performed by Windows.

There is a subsystem to the API called the GDI (Graphics Device Interface). This is the part of Windows that provides device-independent graphics support. It is the GDI functions that make it possible for a Windows application to run on a variety of different hardware.

The I/O your program will perform that is not completely under the control of Windows is file I/O. Your program may use the standard C/C++ file I/O functions.

The Components of a Window

Before moving on to specific aspects of Windows programming, there are a few important terms to learn. Figure 35-1 shows a standard window with each of its elements pointed out.

All windows have a *border* that defines the limits of the window and is used to move or resize the window. At the top of the window are several items. On the far left is the *System menu icon* (or box, as it is commonly called). Clicking on this box causes the System menu to be displayed. To the right of the System menu box is the window's *title bar*. At the far right are the *minimize* and *maximize boxes*. The *client area* is the part of the window in which your program activity takes place. Most windows also have horizontal and vertical scroll bars that are used to move text through the window.

Preparing the Compiler for Windows Applications

Windows executable files differ from DOS executables. Therefore, you must set a number of options to cause a Windows executable file to be produced.

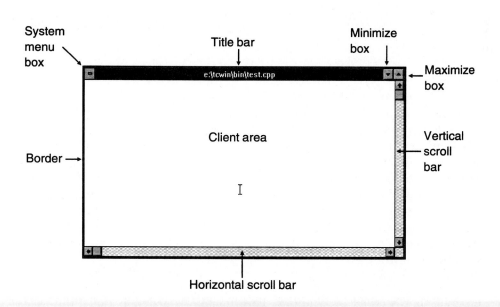

Figure 35-1.   The elements of a standard window

You can compile a Windows application using Borland C++ with either the command-line compiler or the IDE. If you are compiling with the command-line compiler, you must specify the **–W** option. For example, if your Windows program is called MYAPP.CPP, this command line will compile the program for use under Windows:

```
BCC -W MYAPP
```

Using the **–W** option causes Borland C++ to set a number of switches so that a Windows executable file is produced.

If you want to compile a Windows program using the IDE, you must set several options. First, all Windows applications, no matter how small, must be made into projects. To accomplish this, select the **Project** main menu entry and then select **Open project**. Next, add the name of the source file you want to compile to the project. (Since your first program is a simple skeleton, use SKEL.CPP.)

Next, once again select the main menu **Options** entry and then select **Application**. To develop Windows applications, select **Windows App** at this time.

However you compile your program, to test it, first execute Windows and then run your program.

Some Windows Application Basics

Before developing the Windows application skeleton, here is some basic information you need to know.

WinMain( )

All Windows programs begin execution with a call to **WinMain( )**. (Windows programs do not have a **main( )** function.) **WinMain( )** has some special properties that differentiate it from other functions in your application. First, it must be compiled as a Pascal function. As you may know, how functions are called varies among computer languages. The two most common calling conventions are those used by C and those used by Pascal. For various technical reasons, Windows begins executing your program by using the Pascal calling convention to call **WinMain( )**.

The Window Function

All Windows programs must contain a special function that is *not* called by your program, but is called by Windows. This function is generally called the *window function*. The window function is called by Windows when it needs to pass a message to your program. It is through this function that Windows communicates with your program. The window function receives the message in its parameters. All window functions must be declared as **far pascal**.

In addition to receiving the messages sent by Windows, the window function must initiate any actions indicated by a message. Typically, a window function's body consists of a **switch** statement that links a specific response to each message the program will respond to. Your program need not respond to every message that Windows sends. For messages your program doesn't care about, you can let Windows provide default proccessing of them. Since there are over 100 different messages Windows can generate, it is common for most messages to simply be processed by Windows and not your program.

All messages are 16-bit integer values. Further, all messages are linked with any additional information the messages require.

Window Classes

When your Windows program first begins execution, it needs to define and register a *window class*. (Here, the word "class" is not being used in its C++ sense. In this usage, it means "style" or "type.") When you register the window class, you are telling Windows about the form and function of the window. However, registering the window class does not cause a window to come into existence. To actually create a window requires additional steps.

The Message Loop

As explained earlier, Windows communicates with your program by sending it messages. All Windows applications must establish a *message loop* inside the **WinMain( )** function. This loop reads any pending message from the application's message queue and dispatches that message back to Windows, which then calls your program's window function with that message as a parameter. This may seem to be an overly complex way of passing messages, but it is, nevertheless, the way all Windows programs must function. (Part of the reason for this scheme is to force your application to return control to Windows from time to time, thus supporting Windows' nonpreemptive approach to multitasking.)

Windows Data Types

Windows does not use standard C/C++ data types such as **int** and **char** *. Instead, all data types used by Windows have been **typdef**ed within the **windows.h** file. This file is supplied by Borland C++ and is included in all Windows programs. Some of the most common types are **HANDLE**, **HWND**, **BYTE**, **WORD**, **DWORD**, **LONG**, **BOOL**, and **LPSTR**. **HANDLE** is a 16-bit integer that is used as a handle. A *handle* is simply a value that identifies some resource. **HWND** is a 16-bit integer that is used as a window handle. **BYTE** is an unsigned character. **WORD** is a 16-bit integer and is simply another name for **int**. **DWORD** is an unsigned 32-bit integer. **LONG** is another name for **long**, which is a 32-bit integer. **BOOL** is an integer. This type is used to indicate values that are either true or false. **LPSTR** is a pointer to a string.

In addition to these basic types, Windows defines several structures. The two that are needed by the first skeleton program are **MSG** and **WNDCLASS**. The **MSG** structure holds a Windows message, and **WNDCLASS** is a structure that defines a window class. These structures are discussed later in this chapter.

A Windows Skeleton

Now that the necessary background information has been covered, it is time to develop a minimal Windows application. As stated, all Windows programs have certain things in common. In this section a Windows skeleton is developed that provides these necessary features. In the world of Windows programming, application skeletons are commonly used because there is a substantial "price of admission" when creating a Windows program. Unlike DOS programs you may have written, in which a minimal program is about 5 lines long, a minimal Windows program is approximately 50 lines long.

A minimal Windows program contains two functions: **WinMain( )** and the window function. The **WinMain( )** function must perform the following general steps:

1. Define a window class.

2. Register that class with Windows.

3. Create a window of that class.

4. Display the window.

5. Begin running the message loop.

The window function must respond to all relevant messages. Since the skeleton program does nothing but display its window, the only message it must respond to is the one that tells the application that the user has terminated the program.

Before a discussion of the specifics, examine the following program, which is a minimal Windows skeleton. It creates a standard window. The window contains the system menu and is, therefore, capable of being minimized, maximized, moved, resized, and closed. It also contains the standard minimize and maximize icons. Before continuing, enter this program and compile it. (Ignore any warning message about a definition file. Definition files are discussed in the section "Using a Definition File" later in this chapter.)

```
// A minimal Windows Skeleton.
#include <windows.h>
```

```
LONG FAR PASCAL _export WindowFunc(HWND hwnd, unsigned message,
                                   WORD wParam, LONG lParam);


char szWinName[] = "MyWin"; // name of window class


int PASCAL WinMain(HANDLE hThisInst, HANDLE hPrevInst,
                   LPSTR lpszArgs, int nWinMode)
{
  HWND hwnd;
  MSG msg;
  WNDCLASS wcl;

  /* If this is the first instance of the program, then
     the window class must be registered.
  */
  if(!hPrevInst) { // if no previous instance
    wcl.hInstance = hThisInst; // handle to this instance
    wcl.lpszClassName = szWinName; // window class name
    wcl.lpfnWndProc = WindowFunc; // window function
    wcl.style = NULL; // no style

    wcl.hIcon = LoadIcon(NULL, IDI_APPLICATION); // icon style
    wcl.hCursor = LoadCursor(NULL, IDC_CROSS); // cursor style
    wcl.lpszMenuName = NULL; // no menu

    wcl.cbClsExtra = 0; // no extra
    wcl.cbWndExtra = 0; // information needed

    // Make the window light gray.
    wcl.hbrBackground = GetStockObject(LTGRAY_BRUSH);

    // Register the window.
    if(!RegisterClass (&wcl)) return 0;
  }

  /* Now that a window class has been registered, a window
     can be created. */
  hwnd = CreateWindow(
    szWinName, // name of window class
    "My Window", // title
    WS_OVERLAPPEDWINDOW, // window style - normal
    CW_USEDEFAULT, // X coordinate - let Windows decide
    CW_USEDEFAULT, // Y coordinate - let Windows decide
    CW_USEDEFAULT, // width - let Windows decide
```

```
     CW_USEDEFAULT, // height - let Windows decide
     NULL, // handle of parent window - there isn't one
     NULL, // no menu
     hThisInst, // handle of this instance of the program
     NULL // no additional arguments
  );

  // Display the window.
  ShowWindow(hwnd, nWinMode);

  // Create the message loop.
  while(GetMessage(&msg, NULL, 0, 0))
  {
    TranslateMessage(&msg); // allow use of keyboard
    DispatchMessage(&msg); // return control to Windows
  }
  return msg.wParam;
}

/* This function is called by Windows and is passed messages
   from the message queue.
*/
long FAR PASCAL WindowFunc(HWND hwnd, WORD message, WORD wParam,
                 LONG lParam)
{
  HDC hdc;
  RECT rect;

  switch(message) {
    case WM_DESTROY: // terminate the program
      PostQuitMessage(0);
      break;
  }

  /* Let Windows process any messages not specified in
     the preceding switch statement. */
  return DefWindowProc(hwnd, message, wParam, lParam);
}
```

Let's go through this program step by step. First, all Windows programs must include the header **windows.h**. This file contains the API function prototypes and various types and definitions used by Windows. For example, the data types **HWND** and **WNDCLASS** are defined in **windows.h**.

The window function used by the program is called **WindowFunc( )**, and its prototype includes the Borland-specific keyword **_export**. In general, any function that will be called by Windows must be exported. The traditional way to do this is to include the name of a function to be exported in the **EXPORTS** section of the .DEF (definition) file associated with the program. However, Borland C++ also allows you to export a function by simply including the **_export** keyword in the function's prototype, and this approach is used in the programs in this book.

As stated, program execution begins with **WinMain( )**. **WinMain( )** is passed four parameters. **hThisInst** and **hPrevInst** are handles that refer to the current instance and any previous instance of the application. Remember, Windows is a multitasking system, so it is possible for more than one instance of your program to be running at the same time. **hPrevInst** will be zero if there are no previous instances. The **lpszArgs** parameter is a pointer to a string that holds any command-line arguments specified when the application was begun. The **nWinMode** parameter contains a value that determines if the window will be displayed when your program begins execution or shown only in its iconic form.

Inside the function, three variables are created. The **hwnd** variable will hold a value that identifies the program's window. The **msg** structure variable will hold Window messages, and the **wcl** structure variable will be used to define the window class.

Defining the Window Class

The first two actions that **WinMain( )** takes are to define a window class and then register it. However, in Windows, each window class must be registered only once. Therefore, if another instance of the program is running, the current instance must not define and register the window class. To avoid this possibility, the value of **hPrevInst** is tested. If it is nonzero, then the window class has already been registered by a previous instance. If not, then the window class is defined and registered.

A window class is defined by filling in the fields defined by the **WNDCLASS** structure. Its definition is shown here:

```
typedef struct tagWNDCLASS
  {
    WORD      style; // type of window

    // address of window function
    LONG      (FAR PASCAL *lpfnWndProc)( HWND, WORD, WORD, LONG );
    int       cbClsExtra; // extra info
    int       cbWndExtra; // extra info
    HANDLE    hInstance; // handle of this instance
    HICON     hIcon; // handle of minimized icon
    HCURSOR   hCursor; // handle of mouse cursor
    HBRUSH    hbrBackground; // background color
    LPSTR     lpszMenuName; // name of main menu
```

```
    LPSTR        lpszClassName; // name of this window class
} WNDCLASS;
```

As you can see by looking at the program, the **hInstance** field is assigned the current instance handle as specified by **hThisInst**. The name of the window class is pointed to by **lpszClassName**, which points to the string "MyWin" in this case. The address of the window function is assigned to **lpfnWndProc**. No default style is specified. No extra information is needed.

All Windows applications need to define a default shape for the mouse cursor and for the minimized icon. An application can define its own custom version of these resources or it can use one of the built-in styles, as the skeleton does. The style of the minimized icon is loaded by the API function **LoadIcon( )**, whose prototype is

HICON LoadIcon(HANDLE *hInst*, LPSTR *lpszName*)

This function returns a handle to an icon. Here, *hInst* specifies the handle of the module that contains the icon, and its name is specified in *lpszName*. However, to use one of the built-in icons, you must use null for the first parameter and specify one of the following macros for the second:

Icon Macro	Shape
IDI_APPLICATION	Default icon
IDI_ASTERISK	Information icon
IDI_EXCLAMATION	Exclamation point icon
IDI_HAND	Stop sign
IDI_QUESTION	Question mark icon

To load the mouse cursor, use the API **LoadCursor( )** function. Its prototype is

HCURSOR LoadCursor(HANDLE *hInst*, LPSTR, *lpszName*);

This function returns a handle to a cursor resource. Here, **hInst** specifies the handle of the module that contains the mouse cursor, and its name is specified in **lpszName**. However, to use one of the built-in cursors, you must use null for the first parameter and specify one of the built-in cursors, using its macro, for the second parameter. Some of the most common built-in cursors are shown here:

Cursor Macro	Shape
IDC_ARROW	Default arrow pointer
IDC_CROSS	Cross hairs

Cursor Macro	Shape
IDC_IBEAM	Vertical I-beam
IDC_WAIT	Hourglass

The background color of the window created by the skeleton is specified as light gray, and a handle to this brush is obtained using the API function **GetStockObject()**. A *brush* is a resource that paints the screen using a predetermined size, color, and pattern. The function **GetStockObject()** is used to obtain a handle to a number of standard display objects, including brushes, pens (which draw lines), and character fonts. The following built-in brushes are available to your program:

Macro Name	Background Type
BLACK_BRUSH	Black
DKGRAY_BRUSH	Dark gray
HOLLOW_BRUSH	See-through window
LTGRAY_BRUSH	Light gray
WHITE_BRUSH	White

Once the window class has been fully specified, it is registered with Windows using the API function **RegisterClass( )**, whose prototype is

BOOL RegisterClass(LPWNDCLASS *lpWClass*);

If the window class pointed to by *lpWClass* has already been registered, the function returns false. Otherwise, the function returns true.

Creating a Window

Once a window class has been defined and registered, your application can actually create a window of that class using the API function **CreateWindow()**, whose prototype is

```
HWND CreateWindow(
  LPSTR lpszClassName, // name of window class
  LPSTR lpszWinName, // title of window
  DWORD dwStyle, // type of window
  int X, Y, // upper-left coordinates
  int Width, Height, // dimensions of window
  HWND hParent, // handle of parent window
```

```
HMENU hMenu, // handle of main menu
HANDLE hThisInst, // handle of creator
LPSTR lpszAdditional); // additional information
```

As you can see by looking at the skeleton program, many of the parameters to **CreateWindow( )** may be defaulted or specified as null. In fact, most often the **X, Y, Width**, and **Height** parameters will simply use the macro **CW_USEDEFAULT**, which tells Windows to select an appropriate size and location for the window. If the window has no parent, which is the case in the skeleton, **hParent** must be specified as null. If the window does not contain a main menu, **hMenu** must be null. Also, if no additional information is required, as is most often the case, **lpszAdditional** is null.

The remaining four parameters must be explicitly set by your program. First, **lpszClassName** must point to the name of the window class. (This is the name you gave it when it was registered.) The title of the window is a string pointed to by **lpszWinName**. This can be a null string, but usually a window is given a title. The style (or type) of window actually created is determined by the value of **dwStyle**. The macro **WS_OVERLAPPEDWINDOW** specifies a standard window that has a system menu, a border, and minimize and maximize boxes. While this style of window is the most common, you can construct one to your own specifications. To accomplish this, simply OR together the various style macros you want. Here are some of the most common styles:

Style Macro	Window Feature
WS_OVERLAPPED	Overlapped window with border
WS_MAXIMIZEBOX	Maximize box
WS_MINIMIZEBOX	Minimize box
WS_SYSMENU	System menu
WS_HSCROLL	Horizontal scroll bar
WS_VSCROLL	Vertical scroll bar

The **hThisInst** parameter must contain the current instance handle of the application.

Once the window has been created, it is still not displayed on the screen. To cause the window to be displayed, call the **ShowWindow( )** API function. This function has the prototype

BOOL ShowWindow(HWND *hwnd*, int *nHow*)

The handle of the window to display is specified in *hwnd*. The display mode is specified in *nHow*. The first time the window is displayed, you will want to pass **WinMain( )**'s **nWinMode** to *nHow*. Remember, the value of **nWinMode** determines whether the window will be displayed as an icon or as an active window when the program begins execution. Subsequent calls can display (or remove) the window as necessary. Some common values for *nHow* are

Display Macro	Effect
SW_HIDE	Removes the window
SW_MINIMIZE	Minimizes the window into an icon
SW_MAXIMIZE	Maximizes the window
SW_RESTORE	Returns a window to normal size

The **ShowWindow( )** function returns the previous display status of the window. If the window was displayed, non-0 is returned. If the window was not displayed, 0 is returned.

The Message Loop

The final part of the skeletal **WinMain( )** is the message loop. The message loop is a part of all Windows applications. Its purpose is to receive and process messages sent by Windows. When a Windows application is running, it is continually being sent messages. These messages are stored in the application's message queue until they can be read and processed. Each time your application is ready to read another message, it must call the API function **GetMessage( )**, which has the prototype

BOOL GetMessage(LPMSG *msg*, HWND *hwnd*, WORD *min*, WORD *max*)

The message will be received by the structure pointed to by *msg*. All Windows messages are of structure type **MSG**, shown here:

```
/* Message structure */
typedef struct tagMSG
  {
    HWND hwnd; // window that message is for
    WORD message; // message
    WORD wParam; // message-dependent info
    LONG lParam; // more message-dependent info
    DWORD time; // time message received
    POINT pt; // X,Y location of mouse
  } MSG;
```

The handle of the window for which the message is intended is contained in **hwnd**. All Windows messages are 16-bit integers, and the message is contained in **message**. Additional information relating to each message is passed in **wParam** and **lParam**.

The time is specified in milliseconds since the application began execution. The structure POINT is defined like this:

```
typedef struct tagPOINT {
  int x, y;
} POINT;
```

If there are no messages in the application's message queue, a call to **GetMessage( )** will pass control back to Windows. In this way, nonpreemptive multitasking is accomplished. (We will explore messages in greater detail in Chapter 36.)

The *hwnd* parameter to **GetMessage( )** specifies which window messages will be obtained for. It is possible (and even likely) that an application will contain several windows and you may want to receive messages only for a specific window. If you want to receive all messages directed at your application, this parameter must be null.

The remaining two parameters to **GetMessage( )** specify a range of messages that will be received. Generally, you want your application to receive all messages. To accomplish this, specify both *min* and *max* as 0, as the skeleton does.

The **GetMessage( )** function returns 0 when the user terminates the program, causing the message loop to terminate. Otherwise it returns non-0.

Inside the message loop, two functions are called. The first is the API function **TranslateMessage( )**. This function translates virtual key codes generated by Windows into actual characters. (Virtual keys are discussed in Chapter 37.) Although not necessary for all applications, most call **TranslateMessage( )** because it is needed to allow full integration of the keyboard.

Once the message has been read and translated, it is dispatched back to Windows using the **DisplatchMessage( )** API function. Windows then holds this message until it can pass it to the program's window function.

The **WinMain( )** function terminates by returning the value of **msg.wParam** to Windows. This value contains the return code generated when your program terminates.

The Window Function

The second function in the application skeleton is its window function. In this case the function is called **WindowFunc( )**, but it could have any name. The window function is passed the first four members of the **MSG** structure as parameters. For the skeleton, the only parameter that is used is the message itself. However, in Chapter 36 you will learn more about the parameters to this function.

The skeleton's window function responds to only one message explicitly: **WM_DESTROY**. This message is sent when the user terminates the program. When this message is received, your program must execute a call to the API function

PostQuitMessage( ). The argument to this function is an exit code that is returned in **msg.wParam** inside **WinMain( )**. Calling **PostQuitMessage( )** causes a **WM_QUIT** message to be sent to your application, which causes the message loop to stop iterating, thus stopping your program.

Any other messages received by **WindowFunc( )** are passed along to Windows, via a call to **DefWindowProc( )**, for default processing. This step is necessary because all messages must be dealt with in one fashion or another.

Using a Definition File

When you compiled the skeleton, you probably received a warning message indicating that no definition file for the program was found. A *definition file* is simply a text file that specifies certain information and settings needed by your Windows program. However, Borland C++ automatically supplies default settings, so you don't actually need to have a definition file.

If you want to prevent the warning message, you can provide a definition file. All definition files use the extension .DEF. For example, the definition file for the skeleton program could be called SKEL.DEF. Here is a definition file that you can use. Unless otherwise stated, this file is sufficient for the programs in this book:

```
NAME WinSkel
DESCRIPTION 'Skeleton Program'
EXETYPE WINDOWS
CODE PRELOAD MOVEABLE DISCARDABLE
DATA PRELOAD MOVEABLE MULTIPLE
HEAPSIZE 8192
STACKSIZE 8192
```

This file specifies the name of the program and its description, both of which are optional. It also states that the executable file will be compatible with Windows. The **CODE** statement tells Windows to load all of the program at startup (**PRELOAD**). It also tells Windows that the code may be moved in memory (**MOVEABLE**) and that the code may be removed from memory and reloaded if (and when) necessary (**DISCARDABLE**). The **DATA** statement tells Windows that your program's data must be loaded upon execution and may be moved around in memory. It also specifies that each instance of the program has its own data (**MULTIPLE**). Finally, the sizes of the heap and stack are specified.

Once you have created the definition file, remember to add its name to your project.

Prefix	Data Type
b	Boolean (one byte)
c	Character (one byte)
dw	Long unsigned integer
f	16-bit bitfield
h	Handle
l	Long integer
lp	Long pointer
n	Short integer
p	Short pointer
pt	Long integer holding screen coordinates
w	Short unsigned integer
sz	Pointer to null-terminated string
lpsz	Long pointer to null-terminated string
rgb	Long integer holding RGB color values

Table 35-1.   *Variable Type Prefix Characters*

Naming Conventions

If you are new to Windows programming, several of the variable and parameter names in the skeleton program and its description probably seemed rather unusual. This is because they follow a set of naming conventions that was invented by Microsoft for Windows programming. For functions, the name consists of a verb followed by a noun. The first character of both the verb and the noun are capitalized. The Windows program developed in this book uses this method.

For variable names, Microsoft chose to use a rather complex system of embedding the data type into a variable's name. To accomplish this, a lowercase type prefix is added to the start of the variable's name. The name itself is begun with a capital letter. The type prefixes are shown in Table 35-1. The use of type prefixes is controversial and is not universally supported. Many Windows programmers use this method, but many do not. This method is used by the Windows programs in this book. However, you are free to use any naming convention you like.

Chapter 36

Processing Messages

As explained in Chapter 35, Windows communicates with your application by sending it messages. For this reason, the processing of these messages is at the core of all Windows applications. In the previous chapter, you learned how to create a skeletal Windows application. In this chapter, that skeleton is expanded to receive and process several common Windows messages.

What Are Windows Messages?

There are over 100 Windows messages. Each message is represented by a unique 16-bit integer value. In the header file **windows.h** there are standard names for these messages. Generally, you use the macro name, not the actual integer value, when referring to a message. Here are some common Windows message macros:

    WM_CHAR
    WM_PAINT
    WM_MOVE
    WM_LBUTTONUP
    WM_LBUTTONDOWN

Two other values accompany each message and contain information related to the specific message. One of these values is an integer; the other is a long integer. These values are called **wParam** and **lParam**, respectively. They typically hold things like cursor or mouse coordinates; the value of a keypress; or a system-related value, such as character size. As each message is discussed, the meaning of the values contained in **wParam** and **lParam** are described.

As mentioned in Chapter 35, the function that actually processes Windows messages is your program's window function. This function is passed four parameters: the handle of the window that the message is for, the message itself, an integer parameter, and a long integer parameter. The last two parameters are **wParam** and **lParam**.

Sometimes two pieces of information are encoded into the two words that make up the long integer **lParam**. To provide easy access to each half of **lParam**, the **windows.h** header file defines two macros called **LOWORD** and **HIWORD**. They return the low-order and high-order words that make up a long integer. Relative to **lParam**, they are used like this:

```
LOWORD(lParam);

HIWORD(lParam);
```

You will see these macros in use later in this chapter.

Responding to a Keypress

One of the most common Windows messages is generated when a key is pressed. This message is called **WM_CHAR**. This section extends the skeletal application developed in Chapter 35 so that it processes keystroke messages.

Each time a **WM_CHAR** is sent, the value of **wParam** contains the ASCII value of the key pressed. **LOWORD(lParam)** contains the number of times the key has been repeated as a result of the key being held down. The bits of **HIWORD(lParam)** are encoded as shown here:

15	Set if the key is being pressed; cleared if the key has been released
14	Set if the key was pressed before the message was sent; cleared if it was not pressed
13	Set if the ALT key is also being pressed; cleared if ALT is not pressed
12	Used by Windows
11	Used by Windows
10	Not used
9	Not used
8	Set if the key pressed is a function key or an extended key; cleared otherwise
7-0	Manufacturer-dependent key code

For our purposes, the only value that is important at this time is **wParam**, since it holds the key that was pressed. However, notice how much information Windows supplies about the state of the system. In general, Windows gives you more information than does DOS. Of course, you are free to use as much or as little of this information as you like.

To process a **WM_CHAR** message, you must add it to the **switch** statement inside your program's window function. For example, here is a window function that processes a keystroke by displaying it on the screen:

```
char str[80] = "Windows Are Fun"; // holds output string

long FAR PASCAL WindowFunc(HWND hwnd, WORD message, WORD wParam,
                LONG lParam)
{
  HDC hdc;

  switch(message) {
    case WM_CHAR: // process keystroke
      ostrstream ostr(str, sizeof(str)); // make string stream

      hdc = GetDC(hwnd); // get device context
      TextOut(hdc, 1, 1, "  ", 2); // erase old character
      ostr << (char) wParam << ends; // stringize new character
      TextOut(hdc, 1, 1, str, strlen(str)); // output new char
      ReleaseDC(hwnd, hdc); // release device context
      break;
    case WM_DESTROY: // terminate the program
      PostQuitMessage(0);
      break;
  }

  /* Let Windows process any messages not specified in
     the preceding switch statement. */
  return DefWindowProc(hwnd, message, wParam, lParam);
}
```

The purpose of the code inside the **WM_CHAR** case is very simple: It simply echoes the key to the screen. You are probably surprised that it takes so many lines of code to accomplish this seemingly trivial feat. There are two reasons for this. First, Windows is multitasking and you cannot output a character if your program is not the focus of output—for example, if another task has overlaid your window. The second reason is that another part of your program may have overlaid your window. In either situation, before performing output, your program must acquire permission. This is done by calling **GetDC( )**, which obtains a device context. (For now, don't worry about what this means. It is discussed in the next section.) Once you obtain a device context, you may write to the screen. At the end of the function, the device context is released using **ReleaseDC( )**. Your program *must* release the device context when it is done with it. If it doesn't, the device context cannot be granted to another program or to your own program when requested again. Both **GetDC( )** and **ReleaseDC( )** are API functions. Their prototypes are

> HDC GetDC(HWND *hWnd*);
> int ReleaseDC(HWND *hWnd*, HDC *hDC*);

The type **HDC** specifies a handle to a device context. **ReleaseDC( )** returns true if the device context was released and false otherwise.

The function that actually outputs the character is the API function **TextOut( )**. Its prototype is

> BOOL TextOut(HDC DC, int *x*, int *y*, LPSTR *lpstr*,
>   int *ncount*);

The type **BOOL** is a 16-bit integer that holds true/false values. The **TextOut( )** function outputs the string pointed to by *lpstr* at the screen coordinates specified by *x, y*. The length of the string is specified in *ncount*. The **TextOut( )** function returns non-0 if successful and 0 otherwise.

In the window function, each time a **WM_CHAR** message is received, the character typed by the user is converted, using array-based I/O, into a string one character long and then displayed using **TextOut( )** at location 1, 1. (The string **str** is global because it will need to keep its value between function calls in later examples.) In a window, the upper left corner of the client area is location 1, 1. Window coordinates are always relative to the window, not the screen. Therefore, as characters are entered, they are displayed in the upper left corner no matter where the window is physically located on the screen.

The reason for the first call to **TextOut( )** is to erase whatever previous character was just displayed. Because Windows is a graphics-based system, characters are of different sizes and the overwriting of one character by another does not necessarily cause all of the previous character to be erased. For example, if you typed a "w" followed by an "i," part of the "w" would still be displayed if it wasn't manually erased. (Try commenting out the first call to **TextOut( )** and observe what happens.)

It is important to understand that no Windows function allows output beyond the borders. Output is automatically clipped to prevent the window's boundaries from being crossed.

At first you might think that using **TextOut( )** to output a character is not an efficient application of the function. The fact is that Windows does not contain a function that simply outputs a character. As you will see, Windows performs much of its user interaction through dialog and menu boxes. For this reason, it contains only a few functions that output text to the client area.

Here is the entire skeleton that processes keystrokes:

```
// A minimal Windows skeleton that processes a WM_CHAR message.
#include <windows.h>
#include <string.h>
#include <strstrea.h>
LONG FAR PASCAL _export WindowFunc(HWND hwnd, unsigned message,
                                   WORD wParam, LONG lParam);


char szWinName[] = "MyWin"; // name of window class

char str[80] = ""; // holds output string

int PASCAL WinMain(HANDLE hThisInst, HANDLE hPrevInst,
                   LPSTR lpszArgs, int nWinMode)
{
  HWND hwnd;
  MSG msg;
  WNDCLASS wcl;

  /* If this is the first instance of the program, then
     the window class must be registered.
  */
  if(!hPrevInst) { // if no previous instance
    wcl.hInstance = hThisInst; // handle to this instance
    wcl.lpszClassName = szWinName; // window class name
    wcl.lpfnWndProc = WindowFunc; // window function
    wcl.style = NULL; // no style

    wcl.hIcon = LoadIcon(NULL, IDI_APPLICATION); // icon style
    wcl.hCursor = LoadCursor(NULL, IDC_CROSS); // cursor style
    wcl.lpszMenuName = NULL; // no menu

    wcl.cbClsExtra = 0; // no extra
    wcl.cbWndExtra = 0; // information needed

    // Make the window light gray.
    wcl.hbrBackground = GetStockObject(LTGRAY_BRUSH);

    // Register the window.
    if(!RegisterClass (&wcl)) return 0;
  }

  /* Now that a window class has been registered, a window
```

```
      can be created. */
  hwnd = CreateWindow(
    szWinName, // name of window class
    "My Window", // title
    WS_OVERLAPPEDWINDOW, // window style - normal
    CW_USEDEFAULT, // X coordinate - let Windows decide
    CW_USEDEFAULT, // Y coordinate - let Windows decide
    CW_USEDEFAULT, // width - let Windows decide
    CW_USEDEFAULT, // height - let Windows decide
    NULL, // handle of parent window - there isn't one
    NULL, // no menu
    hThisInst, // handle of this instance of the program
    NULL // no additional arguments
  );

  // Display the window.
  ShowWindow(hwnd, nWinMode);

  // Create the message loop.
  while(GetMessage(&msg, NULL, 0, 0))
  {
    TranslateMessage(&msg); // allow use of keyboard
    DispatchMessage(&msg); // return control to Windows
  }
  return msg.wParam;
}

/* This function is called by Windows and is passed messages
   from the message queue.
*/
long FAR PASCAL WindowFunc(HWND hwnd, WORD message, WORD wParam,
                            LONG lParam)
{
  HDC hdc;

  switch(message) {
    case WM_CHAR: // process keystroke
      ostrstream ostr(str, sizeof(str)); // make string stream

      hdc = GetDC(hwnd); // get device context
      TextOut(hdc, 1, 1, "  ", 2); // erase old character
      ostr << (char) wParam << ends; // stringize new character
      TextOut(hdc, 1, 1, str, strlen(str)); // output new char
      ReleaseDC(hwnd, hdc); // release device context
      break;
```

```
   case WM_DESTROY: // terminate the program
     PostQuitMessage(0);
     break;
 }

 /* Let Windows process any messages not specified in
    the preceding switch statement. */
 return DefWindowProc(hwnd, message, wParam, lParam);
}
```

Device Contexts

The program in the previous section had to obtain a device context prior to outputting to the window. Also, that device context had to be released prior to the termination of that function. A *device context* is an output path from your Windows application, through the appropriate device driver, to the client area of your window. The device context also fully defines the state of the device driver.

Before your application can output information to the client area of the window, a device context must be obtained. Until this is done, there is no linkage between your program and the window relative to output. As mentioned earlier, several things can occur that temporarily prevent a device context from being obtained. For example, if another application has obscured your window, it must be brought to the forefront again. In any event, remember that it is necessary to obtain a device context prior to performing any output to a window. Since **TextOut( )** and other output functions require a handle to a device context, this is a self-enforcing rule.

Processing the WM_PAINT Message

Before continuing, run the second skeleton program and enter a few characters. Next, minimize and then restore the window. As you will see, the last character typed is not displayed after the window is restored. Also, if the window is overwritten by another window and then redisplayed, the character is not redisplayed. The reason for this is simple: In general, Windows does not keep a record of what a window contains. Instead, it is your program's job to maintain the contents of a window. To help your program accomplish this, each time the contents of a window must be redisplayed, your program is sent a **WM_PAINT** message. (This message is also sent when your window is first displayed.) Each time your program receives this message, it must redisplay the contents of the window. In this section, you add a message response function that processes the **WM_PAINT** message.

For various technical reasons, when the window is moved or resized, its contents are redisplayed. However, this will not occur when the window is minimized or overwritten and then redisplayed.

Before an explanation of how to respond to a **WM_PAINT** message, it might be useful to explain why Windows does not automatically rewrite your window. The answer is short and to the point. In many situations, it is easier for your program, which has intimate knowledge of the contents of the window, to rewrite it than it would be for Windows to do so. While the merits of this approach have been much debated by programmers, it is a good idea to accept it because it is unlikely to change.

The first step in processing a **WM_PAINT** message is to add its **case** to the **switch** statement inside the window function:

```
PAINTSTRUCT paintstruct;

case WM_PAINT: // process a paint request
  hdc = BeginPaint(hwnd, &paintstruct); // get DC
  TextOut(hdc, 1, 1, str, strlen(str)); // output message
  EndPaint(hwnd, &paintstruct); // release DC
  break;
```

Let's look at this closely. First, notice that a device context is obtained using a call to **BeginPaint( )** instead of **GetDC( )**. For various reasons, when you process a **WM_PAINT** message, you must obtain a device context using **BeginPaint( )**, which has this prototype:

HDC BeginPaint(HWND *hwnd*, LPPAINTSTRUCT *lpPS*);

The second parameter is a pointer to a structure of type **PAINTSTRUCT**, which is defined like this:

```
typedef struct tagPAINTSTRUCT {
  HDC hdc; // handle to device context
  BOOL fErase; // true if background has been redrawn
  RECT rcPaint; // coordinates of region to redraw
  BOOL fRestore;  // reserved
  BOOL fIncUpdate; // reserved
  BYTE rgbReserved[16]; // reserved
} PAINTSTRUCT;
```

The type **RECT** is a structure that specifies the upper left and lower right coordinates of a rectangular region. This structure is shown here:

```
typedef tagRECT {
  int left, top; // upper left
  int right, bottom; // lower right
} RECT;
```

In **PAINTSTRUCT**, the **rcPaint** element contains the coordinates of the region of the window that needs to be repainted. For now, you will not need to use the contents of this structure because you can assume that the entire window must be redisplayed.

Here is the full program that now processes **WM_PAINT** messages:

```
// A minimal Windows skeleton that adds a WM_PAINT message.
#include <windows.h>
#include <string.h>
#include <strstrea.h>
LONG FAR PASCAL _export WindowFunc(HWND hwnd, unsigned message,
                                   WORD wParam, LONG lParam);

char szWinName[] = "MyWin"; // name of window class

char str[80] = "Windows Are Fun"; // holds output string

int PASCAL WinMain(HANDLE hThisInst, HANDLE hPrevInst,
                   LPSTR lpszArgs, int nWinMode)
{
  HWND hwnd;
  MSG msg;
  WNDCLASS wcl;

  /* If this is the first instance of the program, then
     the window class must be registered.
  */
  if(!hPrevInst) { // if no previous instance
    wcl.hInstance = hThisInst; // handle to this instance
    wcl.lpszClassName = szWinName; // window class name
    wcl.lpfnWndProc = WindowFunc; // window function
    wcl.style = NULL; // no style

    wcl.hIcon = LoadIcon(NULL, IDI_APPLICATION); // icon style
    wcl.hCursor = LoadCursor(NULL, IDC_CROSS); // cursor style
    wcl.lpszMenuName = NULL; // no menu

    wcl.cbClsExtra = 0; // no extra
    wcl.cbWndExtra = 0; // information needed
```

```
    // Make the window light gray.
    wcl.hbrBackground = GetStockObject(LTGRAY_BRUSH);

    // Register the window.
    if(!RegisterClass (&wcl)) return 0;
  }

  /* Now that a window class has been registered, a window
     can be created. */
  hwnd = CreateWindow(
    szWinName, // name of window class
    "My Window", // title
    WS_OVERLAPPEDWINDOW, // window style - normal
    CW_USEDEFAULT, // X coordinate - let Windows decide
    CW_USEDEFAULT, // Y coordinate - let Windows decide
    CW_USEDEFAULT, // width - let Windows decide
    CW_USEDEFAULT, // height - let Windows decide
    NULL, // handle of parent window - there isn't one
    NULL, // no menu
    hThisInst, // handle of this instance of the program
    NULL // no additional arguments
  );

  // Display the window.
  ShowWindow(hwnd, nWinMode);

  // Create the message loop.
  while(GetMessage(&msg, NULL, 0, 0))
  {
    TranslateMessage(&msg); // allow use of keyboard
    DispatchMessage(&msg); // return control to Windows
  }
  return msg.wParam;
}

/* This function is called by Windows and is passed messages
   from the message queue.
*/
long FAR PASCAL WindowFunc(HWND hwnd, WORD message, WORD wParam,
                           LONG lParam)
{
  HDC hdc;
  PAINTSTRUCT paintstruct;

  switch(message) {
```

```
    case WM_PAINT: // process a paint request
      hdc = BeginPaint(hwnd, &paintstruct); // get DC
      TextOut(hdc, 1, 1, str, strlen(str)); // output message
      EndPaint(hwnd, &paintstruct); // release DC
      break;
    case WM_CHAR: // process a keystroke
      ostrstream ostr(str, sizeof(str)); // create string stream

      hdc = GetDC(hwnd); // get DC
      TextOut(hdc, 1, 1, "  ", 2); // erase old character
      ostr << (char) wParam << ends; // stringize new character
      TextOut(hdc, 1, 1, str, strlen(str)); // output new char
      ReleaseDC(hwnd, hdc); // release DC
      break;
    case WM_DESTROY: // terminate the program
      PostQuitMessage(0);
      break;
  }

  /* Let Windows process any messages not specified in
     the preceding switch statement. */
  return DefWindowProc(hwnd, message, wParam, lParam);
}
```

Before continuing, enter, compile, and run this program. Try typing a few characters and then minimizing and restoring the window. As you will see, each time the window is redisplayed, the last character you typed is automatically redrawn. Notice that the global array **str** is initialized to **Windows are Fun** and that this is displayed when the program begins execution. The reason for this is that when a window is created, a **WM_PAINT** message is automatically generated.

While the handling of the **WM_PAINT** message in the skeleton is quite simple, it must be emphasized that most real-world versions of this will be more complex because most windows contain considerably more output.

Since it is your program's responsibility to restore the window if it is resized or overwritten, you must always provide some mechanism to accomplish this. In real-world programs, this is usually accomplished in one of three ways. First, your program can simply regenerate the output by computational means. This is most feasible when no user input is used. Second, your program can maintain a virtual screen that you simply copy to the window each time it must be redrawn. Finally, in some instances, you can keep a record of events and replay the events when the window needs to be redrawn. Which approach is best depends completely upon the application. Most of the examples in this book won't bother to redraw the window because doing so typically involves substantial additional code that often just muddies the point of an example. However, your programs will need to restore their windows in order to be conforming Windows applications.

Responding to Mouse Messages

Since Windows is, to a great extent, a mouse-based operating system, all Windows programs should respond to mouse input. Because the mouse is so important, there are several different types of mouse messages. This section examines the two most common. These are **WM_LBUTTONDOWN** and **WM_RBUTTONDOWN**, which are generated when the left button and right button are pressed, respectively.

To begin, you must add the responses to the two mouse messages to the **switch** statement in the window function:

```
case WM_RBUTTONDOWN: // process right button
   hdc = GetDC(hwnd);
   ostr << "Right Button is down." << ends;
   TextOut(hdc, LOWORD(lParam), HIWORD(lParam),
           str, strlen(str));
   ReleaseDC(hwnd, hdc);
   break;
case WM_LBUTTONDOWN: // process left button
   hdc = GetDC(hwnd);
   ostr << "Left Button is down." << ends;
   TextOut(hdc, LOWORD(lParam), HIWORD(lParam),
           str, strlen(str));
   ReleaseDC(hwnd, hdc);
   break;
```

When either button is pressed, the mouse's current X, Y location is specified in **LOWORD(lParam)** and **HIWORD(lParam)**, respectively. The mouse message response routines use these coordinates as the location to display their output. That is, each time you press a mouse button, a message is displayed at the location of the mouse pointer.

Following is the complete skeleton that responds to the mouse messages. Figure 36-1 shows sample output from this program.

```
// A minimal Windows skeleton that processes mouse messages.
#include <windows.h>
#include <string.h>
#include <strstrea.h>
LONG FAR PASCAL _export WindowFunc(HWND hwnd, unsigned message,
                                   WORD wParam, LONG lParam);

char szWinName[] = "MyWin"; // name of window class

char str[80] = "Windows Are Fun"; // holds output string
```

Figure 36-1.   *Sample output from the application skeleton*

```
int PASCAL WinMain(HANDLE hThisInst, HANDLE hPrevInst,
                   LPSTR lpszArgs, int nWinMode)
{
  HWND hwnd;
  MSG msg;
  WNDCLASS wcl;

  /* If this is the first instance of the program, then
     the window class must be registered.
  */
  if(!hPrevInst) { // if no previous instance
    wcl.hInstance = hThisInst; // handle to this instance
    wcl.lpszClassName = szWinName; // window class name
    wcl.lpfnWndProc = WindowFunc; // window function
    wcl.style = NULL; // no style

    wcl.hIcon = LoadIcon(NULL, IDI_APPLICATION); // icon style
    wcl.hCursor = LoadCursor(NULL, IDC_CROSS); // cursor style
    wcl.lpszMenuName = NULL; // no menu

    wcl.cbClsExtra = 0; // no extra
    wcl.cbWndExtra = 0; // information needed

    // Make the window light gray.
    wcl.hbrBackground = GetStockObject(LTGRAY_BRUSH);
```

```
      // Register the window.
      if(!RegisterClass (&wcl)) return 0;
    }

    /* Now that a window class has been registered, a window
       can be created. */
    hwnd = CreateWindow(
      szWinName, // name of window class
      "My Window", // title
      WS_OVERLAPPEDWINDOW, // window style - normal
      CW_USEDEFAULT, // X coordinate - let Windows decide
      CW_USEDEFAULT, // Y coordinate - let Windows decide
      CW_USEDEFAULT, // width - let Windows decide
      CW_USEDEFAULT, // height - let Windows decide
      NULL, // handle of parent window - there isn't one
      NULL, // no menu
      hThisInst, // handle of this instance of the program
      NULL // no additional arguments
    );

    // Display the window.
    ShowWindow(hwnd, nWinMode);

    // Create the message loop.
    while(GetMessage(&msg, NULL, 0, 0))
    {
      TranslateMessage(&msg); // allow use of keyboard
      DispatchMessage(&msg); // return control to Windows
    }
    return msg.wParam;
  }

  /* This function is called by Windows and is passed messages
     from the message queue.
  */
  long FAR PASCAL WindowFunc(HWND hwnd, WORD message, WORD wParam,
                             LONG lParam)
  {
    HDC hdc;
    PAINTSTRUCT paintstruct;
    ostrstream ostr(str, sizeof(str));

    switch(message) {
      case WM_PAINT: // process a paint request
        hdc = BeginPaint(hwnd, &paintstruct); // get DC
```

```
      TextOut(hdc, 1, 1, str, strlen(str)); // output message
      EndPaint(hwnd, &paintstruct); // release DC
      break;
    case WM_CHAR: // process a keystroke
      hdc = GetDC(hwnd); // get DC
      TextOut(hdc, 1, 1, "  ", 2); // erase old character
      ostr << (char) wParam << ends; // stringize new character
      TextOut(hdc, 1, 1, str, strlen(str)); // output new char
      ReleaseDC(hwnd, hdc); // release DC
      break;
    case WM_RBUTTONDOWN: // process right button
      hdc = GetDC(hwnd);
      ostr << "Right Button is down." << ends;
      TextOut(hdc, LOWORD(lParam), HIWORD(lParam),
              str, strlen(str));
      ReleaseDC(hwnd, hdc);
      break;
    case WM_LBUTTONDOWN: // process left button
      hdc = GetDC(hwnd);
      ostr << "Left Button is down." << ends;
      TextOut(hdc, LOWORD(lParam), HIWORD(lParam),
              str, strlen(str));
      ReleaseDC(hwnd, hdc);
      break;
    case WM_DESTROY: // terminate the program
      PostQuitMessage(0);
      break;
  }

  /* Let Windows process any messages not specified in
     the preceding switch statement. */
  return DefWindowProc(hwnd, message, wParam, lParam);
}
```

A Closer Look at the Mouse Messages

Each time a **WM_LBUTTONDOWN** or **WM_RBUTTONDOWN** message is generated, several pieces of information are also supplied in the **wParam** parameter. It may contain any combination of the following values:

MK_CONTROL
MK_SHIFT
MK_LBUTTON
MK_RBUTTON

If the CTRL key is pressed when a mouse button is pressed, **wParam** will contain **MK_CONTROL.** If the SHIFT key is pressed when a mouse button is pressed, **WParam** will contain **MK_SHIFT.** If the right button is down when the left button is pressed, **wParam** will contain **MK_RBUTTON.** If the left button is down when the right button is pressed, **wParam** will contain **MK_LBUTTON.** Before moving on, you might want to try experimenting with these messages.

Generating a WM_PAINT Message

Your program can cause a **WM_PAINT** message to be generated. You might wonder why your program would need to generate a **WM_PAINT** message since, it seems, it can repaint its window whenever it wants. However, this is a false assumption. Because Windows is a nonpreemptive multitasking system, it is best that your program return control to Windows as soon as possible, letting Windows decide when it is best to perform output to your window by sending a **WM_PAINT** message. This allows Windows to better manage the system. If you use this approach, your program holds all output until this message is received and then updates the window.

In the previous skeleton applications, the **WM_PAINT** message was received only when the window was resized or uncovered. However, if all output is held until a **WM_PAINT** message is received, then to acheive interactive I/O, there must be some way to tell Windows that it needs to send a **WM_PAINT** message to your window whenever output is pending. As expected, Windows includes such a feature. Thus, when your program has information to output, it simply requests that a **WM_PAINT** message be sent when Windows is ready to do so.

To cause Windows to send a **WM_PAINT** message, your program will call the **InvalidateRect()** API function. Its prototype is

```
void InvalidateRect(HWND hwnd, LPRECT lpRect, BOOL bErase);
```

Here, *hwnd* is the handle of the window that you want to send the **WM_PAINT** message to. The type **LPRECT** is a pointer to a **RECT** structure. This structure specifies the coordinates within the window that must be redrawn. If this value is null, the entire window is specified. If *bErase* is true, the background is erased. If it is false, the background is left unchanged.

When **InvalidateRect( )** is called, it tells Windows that the window is invalid and must be redrawn. This, in turn, causes Windows to send a **WM_PAINT** message to the window.

Here is a reworked version of the previous application skeleton that performs all output by generating a **WM_PAINT** message. The other message response routines simply prepare the information to be displayed and then call **InvalidateRect( ).**

```
/* A minimal Windows skeleton that routes all output
   through the WM_PAINT message. */
#include <windows.h>
#include <string.h>
#include <strstrea.h>
LONG FAR PASCAL _export WindowFunc(HWND hwnd, unsigned message,
                                   WORD wParam, LONG lParam);

char szWinName[] = "MyWin"; // name of window class

char str[80] = "Windows Are Fun"; // holds output string

int X = 1, Y=1; // screen location

int PASCAL WinMain(HANDLE hThisInst, HANDLE hPrevInst,
                   LPSTR lpszArgs, int nWinMode)
{
  HWND hwnd;
  MSG msg;
  WNDCLASS wcl;

  /* If this is the first instance of the program, then
     the window class must be registered.
  */
  if(!hPrevInst) { // if no previous instance
    wcl.hInstance = hThisInst; // handle to this instance
    wcl.lpszClassName = szWinName; // window class name
    wcl.lpfnWndProc = WindowFunc; // window function
    wcl.style = NULL; // no style

    wcl.hIcon = LoadIcon(NULL, IDI_APPLICATION); // icon style
    wcl.hCursor = LoadCursor(NULL, IDC_CROSS); // cursor style
    wcl.lpszMenuName = NULL; // no menu

    wcl.cbClsExtra = 0; // no extra
    wcl.cbWndExtra = 0; // information needed

    // Make the window light gray.
    wcl.hbrBackground = GetStockObject(LTGRAY_BRUSH);

    // Register the window.
    if(!RegisterClass (&wcl)) return 0;
  }

  /* Now that a window class has been registered, a window
```

```
      can be created. */
  hwnd = CreateWindow(
    szWinName, // name of window class
    "My Window", // title
    WS_OVERLAPPEDWINDOW, // window style - normal
    CW_USEDEFAULT, // X coordinate - let Windows decide
    CW_USEDEFAULT, // Y coordinate - let Windows decide
    CW_USEDEFAULT, // width - let Windows decide
    CW_USEDEFAULT, // height - let Windows decide
    NULL, // handle of parent window - there isn't one
    NULL, // no menu
    hThisInst, // handle of this instance of the program
    NULL // no additional arguments
  );

  // Display the window.
  ShowWindow(hwnd, nWinMode);

  // Create the message loop.
  while(GetMessage(&msg, NULL, 0, 0))
  {
    TranslateMessage(&msg); // allow use of keyboard
    DispatchMessage(&msg); // return control to Windows
  }
  return msg.wParam;
}

/* This function is called by Windows and is passed messages
   from the message queue.
*/
long FAR PASCAL WindowFunc(HWND hwnd, WORD message, WORD wParam,
                           LONG lParam)
{
  HDC hdc;
  PAINTSTRUCT paintstruct;
  ostrstream ostr(str, sizeof(str));

  switch(message) {
    case WM_PAINT:
      hdc = BeginPaint(hwnd, &paintstruct);
      TextOut(hdc, X, Y, "  ", 2);
      TextOut(hdc, X, Y, str, strlen(str));
      EndPaint(hwnd, &paintstruct);
      break;
    case WM_CHAR:
```

```
      X = Y = 1; // display characters in upper-left corner
      ostr << (char) wParam << ends;
      InvalidateRect(hwnd, NULL, 1); // Generate WM_PAINT
      break;
    case WM_RBUTTONDOWN:
      ostr << "Right Button is down." << ends;
      X = LOWORD(lParam); // set X,Y to current
      Y = HIWORD(lParam); // mouse location
      InvalidateRect(hwnd, NULL, 1); // Generate WM_PAINT
      break;
    case WM_LBUTTONDOWN:
      ostr << "Left Button is down." << ends;
      X = LOWORD(lParam); // set X, Y to current
      Y = HIWORD(lParam); // mouse location
      InvalidateRect(hwnd, NULL, 1); // Generate WM_PAINT
      break;
    case WM_DESTROY: // terminate the program
      PostQuitMessage(0);
      break;
  }

  /* Let Windows process any messages not specified in
     the preceding switch statement. */
  return DefWindowProc(hwnd, message, wParam, lParam);
}
```

Notice that the program adds two new global variables called **X** and **Y** that hold the location at which the text will be displayed when a **WM_PAINT** message is received.

As you can see, by channeling all output through **WM_PAINT**, the program has actually become smaller and, in some ways, easier to understand. Also, as stated at the start of this section, the program allows Windows to decide when it is most appropriate to update the window.

Many Windows applications route all (or most) output through **WM_PAINT***, for the reasons already stated. However, the previous programs are not technically wrong by outputting text within their message response functions. It is just that this approach is not the best for all purposes.*

Generating Timer Messages

Using Windows, it is possible to establish a timer that will interrupt your program at periodic intervals. Each time the timer goes off, it sends a **WM_TIMER** message to your window function. Using a timer is a good way to "wake up" your program every so often. This is particularly useful when your program is running as a background task.

To start a timer, use the **SetTimer( )** API function, whose prototype is

WORD SetTimer(HWND *hwnd*, int *nID*, WORD *wLength*,
        FARPROC *lpTFunc*);

Here, *hwnd* is the handle of the window that uses the timer. The value of *nID* specifies a value that will be associated with this timer. (More than one timer can be active.) The value of *wLength* specifies the length of the period, in milliseconds. That is, *wLength* specifies how long a time there is between interrupts. The function pointed to by *lpTFunc* is the timer function that will be called when the timer goes off. This must be a function that uses the same prototype (except for its name) as a window function. (That is, it must return **FAR PASCAL** and take the same type of parameters as the window function.) However, if *lpTFunc* is null, as it commonly is, your program's window function will be used for this purpose. In this case, each time the timer goes off, a **WM_TIMER** message is put into the message queue for your program, and your program's window function processes it like any other message. This is the approach used by the example that follows. The function returns *nID* if successful. If the timer cannot be allocated, 0 is returned.

Once a timer has been started, it continues to interrupt your program until either you terminate the application or your program executes a call to the **KillTimer( )** API function, whose prototype is

BOOL KillTimer(HWND *hwnd*, int *nID*);

Here, *hwnd* is the window that contains the timer, and *nID* is the value that identifies that particular timer.

Each time a **WM_TIMER** message is generated, the value of **wParam** contains the ID of the timer, and **lParam** contains the time the event occurred.

The following program uses a timer to create a clock. It uses the ANSI C standard time functions to obtain and display the current system time and date. Each time the timer goes off, which is approximately once each second, the time is updated. Thus, the time displayed is accurate to within 1 second. Sample output from this program is shown in Figure 36-2.

Figure 36-2.   *The Clock window*

```
/* A clock program. */
#include <windows.h>
#include <string.h>
#include <strstrea.h>
#include <time.h>

LONG FAR PASCAL _export WindowFunc(HWND hwnd, unsigned message,
                                   WORD wParam, LONG lParam);

char szWinName[] = "Clock"; // name of window class

char str[80] = ""; // holds output string

int PASCAL WinMain(HANDLE hThisInst, HANDLE hPrevInst,
                   LPSTR lpszArgs, int nWinMode)
{
  HWND hwnd;
  MSG msg;
  WNDCLASS wcl;

  /* If this is the first instance of the program, then
     the window class must be registered.
  */
  if(!hPrevInst) { // if no previous instance
    wcl.hInstance = hThisInst; // handle to this instance
    wcl.lpszClassName = szWinName; // window class name
    wcl.lpfnWndProc = WindowFunc; // window function
    wcl.style = NULL; // no style

    wcl.hIcon = LoadIcon(NULL, IDI_APPLICATION); // icon style
    wcl.hCursor = LoadCursor(NULL, IDC_ARROW); // normal style
    wcl.lpszMenuName = NULL; // no menu

    wcl.cbClsExtra = 0; // no extra
    wcl.cbWndExtra = 0; // information needed

    // Make the window light gray.
    wcl.hbrBackground = GetStockObject(LTGRAY_BRUSH);

    // Register the window.
    if(!RegisterClass (&wcl)) return 0;
  }

  /* Now that a window class has been registered, a window
     can be created. */
```

```
    hwnd = CreateWindow(
      szWinName, // name of window class
      "Clock", // title
      WS_OVERLAPPEDWINDOW, // window style - normal
      CW_USEDEFAULT, // X coordinate - let Windows decide
      CW_USEDEFAULT, // Y coordinate - let Windows decide
      CW_USEDEFAULT, // width - let Windows decide
      CW_USEDEFAULT, // height - let Windows decide
      NULL, // handle of parent window - there isn't one
      NULL, // no menu
      hThisInst, // handle of this instance of the program
      NULL // no additional arguments
    );

    // Display the window.
    ShowWindow(hwnd, nWinMode);

    // Start a timer - interrupts once every second.
    SetTimer(hwnd, 1, 1000, NULL);

    // Create the message loop.
    while(GetMessage(&msg, NULL, 0, 0))
    {
      TranslateMessage(&msg); // allow use of keyboard
      DispatchMessage(&msg); // return control to Windows
    }
    return msg.wParam;
}

/* This function is called by Windows and is passed messages
   from the message queue.
*/
long FAR PASCAL WindowFunc(HWND hwnd, WORD message, WORD wParam,
                          LONG lParam)
{
  HDC hdc;
  PAINTSTRUCT paintstruct;
  ostrstream ostr(str, sizeof(str));

  switch(message) {
    case WM_PAINT:
      hdc = BeginPaint(hwnd, &paintstruct);
      TextOut(hdc, 1, 1, str, strlen(str));
      EndPaint(hwnd, &paintstruct);
      break;
```

```
   case WM_TIMER: // timer went off
     struct tm *newtime;
     time_t t;

     // get the new time
     t = time(NULL);
     newtime = localtime(&t);

     // display the time
     ostr << asctime(newtime) << ends;
     InvalidateRect(hwnd, NULL, 0);
     break;
   case WM_DESTROY: // terminate the program
     PostQuitMessage(0);
     break;
 }

 /* Let Windows process any messages not specified in
    the preceding switch statement. */
 return DefWindowProc(hwnd, message, wParam, lParam);
}
```

Now that you have learned how a Windows program processes messages, you can move on to message boxes and menus, which are the subject of the next chapter.

Chapter 37

Message Boxes and Menus

Now that you know how to construct a basic Windows skeleton and receive and process messages, it is time to begin exploration of Windows' user interface components. Although you can write a Windows application that appears just like a DOS application, doing so is not in the spirit of Windows programming. In order for your Windows applications to conform to Windows' general design principles, you need to communicate with the user by using several different types of special windows. There are three basic types of user interface windows: message boxes, menus, and dialog boxes. This chapter discusses message boxes and menus. (The next chapter examines dialog boxes.) As you will see, the basic style of each of these windows is predefined by Windows. You need only supply the specific information that relates to your application.

Keep in mind that message boxes and menus are *child windows* of your original application windows. This means they are owned by your application and are dependent upon it. They cannot exist by themselves. Your application must always create a main window.

Message Boxes

By far, the simplest interface window is the message box. A message box simply displays a message to the user and waits for an acknowledgment. It is possible to construct message boxes that allow the user to select among a few basic alternatives, but in general, the purpose of a message box is simply to inform the user that some event has taken place.

To create a message box, use the **MessageBox( )** API function. Its prototype is

int MessageBox(HWND *hwnd*, LPSTR *lpText*, LPSTR *lpCaption*,
        WORD *wMBType*);

Here, *hwnd* is the handle to the parent window. The *lpText* parameter is a pointer to a string that will appear inside the message box. The string pointed to by *lpCaption* is used as the caption for the box. The value of *wMBType* determines the exact nature of the message box, including what type of buttons will be present. Some of its most common values are shown here:

Value	Effect
MB_ABORTRETRYIGNORE	Displays Abort, Retry, and Ignore push buttons
MB_ICONEXCLAMATION	Displays an exclamation-point icon
MB_ICONHAND	Displays a stop sign icon
MB_ICONINFORMATION	Displays an information icon
MB_ICONQUESTION	Displays a question mark icon
MB_ICONSTOP	Same as MB_ICONHAND
MB_OKCANCEL	Displays OK and Cancel push buttons
MB_RETRYCANCEL	Displays Retry and Cancel push buttons
MB_YESNO	Displays Yes and No push buttons
MB_YESNOCANCEL	Displays Yes, No, and Cancel push buttons

These macros are defined in **windows.h,** and you can OR together two or more of these macros as long as they are not mutually exclusive.

MessageBox( ) returns the user's response to the box. The possible return values are shown here:

Button Pressed	Return Value
Abort	IDABORT
Retry	IDRETRY
Ignore	IDIGNORE
Cancel	IDCANCEL
No	IDNO
Yes	IDYES
OK	IDOK

These macros are defined in **windows.h**. Remember, depending upon the value of *wMBType*, only certain buttons will be present.

To display a message box, simply call the **MessageBox( )** function. Windows will display it at its first opportunity. You do not need to obtain a device context or generate a **WM_PAINT** message. **MessageBox( )** handles all of these details for you.

Here is a simple example that displays a message box when you press a mouse button:

```
// A minimal Windows skeleton that demonstrates message boxes.
#include <windows.h>
#include <string.h>
#include <strstrea.h>
LONG FAR PASCAL _export WindowFunc(HWND hwnd, unsigned message,
                                   WORD wParam, LONG lParam);

char szWinName[] = "MyWin"; // name of window class

char str[80] = "Windows Are Fun"; // holds output string

int X = 1, Y=1; // screen location

int PASCAL WinMain(HANDLE hThisInst, HANDLE hPrevInst,
                   LPSTR lpszArgs, int nWinMode)
{
  HWND hwnd;
  MSG msg;
  WNDCLASS wcl;

  /* If this is the first instance of the program, then
     the window class must be registered.
  */
  if(!hPrevInst) { // if no previous instance
    wcl.hInstance = hThisInst; // handle to this instance
    wcl.lpszClassName = szWinName; // window class name
    wcl.lpfnWndProc = WindowFunc; // window function
    wcl.style = NULL; // no style

    wcl.hIcon = LoadIcon(NULL, IDI_APPLICATION); // icon style
    wcl.hCursor = LoadCursor(NULL, IDC_CROSS); // cursor style
    wcl.lpszMenuName = NULL; // no menu

    wcl.cbClsExtra = 0; // no extra
    wcl.cbWndExtra = 0; // information needed
```

```
    // Make the window light gray.
    wcl.hbrBackground = GetStockObject(LTGRAY_BRUSH);

    // Register the window.
    if(!RegisterClass (&wcl)) return 0;
  }

  /* Now that a window class has been registered, a window
     can be created. */
  hwnd = CreateWindow(
    szWinName, // name of window class
    "Demonstrate Message Boxes", // title
    WS_OVERLAPPEDWINDOW, // window style - normal
    CW_USEDEFAULT, // X coordinate - let Windows decide
    CW_USEDEFAULT, // Y coordinate - let Windows decide
    CW_USEDEFAULT, // width - let Windows decide
    CW_USEDEFAULT, // height - let Windows decide
    NULL, // handle of parent window - there isn't one
    NULL, // no menu
    hThisInst, // handle of this instance of the program
    NULL // no additional arguments
  );

  // Display the window.
  ShowWindow(hwnd, nWinMode);

  // Create the message loop.
  while(GetMessage(&msg, NULL, 0, 0))
  {
    TranslateMessage(&msg); // allow use of keyboard
    DispatchMessage(&msg); // return control to Windows
  }
  return msg.wParam;
}

/* This function is called by Windows and is passed messages
   from the message queue.
*/
long FAR PASCAL WindowFunc(HWND hwnd, WORD message, WORD wParam,
                           LONG lParam)
{
  HDC hdc;
  PAINTSTRUCT paintstruct;
  ostrstream ostr(str, sizeof(str));
```

```
int response;

switch(message) {
  case WM_PAINT:
    hdc = BeginPaint(hwnd, &paintstruct);
    TextOut(hdc, X, Y, "  ", 2);
    TextOut(hdc, X, Y, str, strlen(str));
    EndPaint(hwnd, &paintstruct);
    break;
  case WM_CHAR:
    X = Y = 1; // display characters in upper-left corner
    ostr << (char) wParam << ends;
    InvalidateRect(hwnd, NULL, 1); // Generate WM_PAINT
    break;
  case WM_RBUTTONDOWN:
    response = MessageBox(hwnd, "Press One:", "Right Button",
              MB_ABORTRETRYIGNORE);

    switch(response) {
      case IDABORT:
        MessageBox(hwnd, "", "Abort", MB_OK);
        break;
      case IDRETRY:
        MessageBox(hwnd, "", "Retry", MB_OK);
        break;
      case IDIGNORE:
        MessageBox(hwnd, "", "Ignore", MB_OK);
        break;
    }
    break;
  case WM_LBUTTONDOWN:
    response = MessageBox(hwnd, "Continue?", "Left Button",
              MB_ICONHAND | MB_YESNO);

    switch(response) {
      case IDYES:
        MessageBox(hwnd, "", "Yes Selected", MB_OK);
        break;
      case IDNO:
        MessageBox(hwnd, "", "No Selected", MB_OK);
        break;
    }
    break;
  case WM_DESTROY: // terminate the program
    PostQuitMessage(0);
```

```
        break;
   }

   /* Let Windows process any messages not specified in
      the preceding switch statement. */
   return DefWindowProc(hwnd, message, wParam, lParam);
}
```

Each time a button is pressed, a message box is displayed. For example, pressing the right button displays the message box shown in Figure 37-1.

When you press the right button, a message box displays the buttons Abort, Retry, and Ignore. Depending upon your response, a second message box will be displayed that indicates which button you pressed. Pressing the left mouse button causes a message box to be displayed that contains a stop sign. This box allows a Yes or a No response.

Before continuing, experiment with message boxes, trying different types.

Introducing Menus

As you know, in Windows the most common element of control is the menu. Virtually all main windows have some type of menu associated with them. Because menus are so common and important in Windows applications, Windows provides substantial built-in support for them. Adding a menu to a window involves these relatively few steps:

1. Define the form of the menu in a resource file.

2. Load the menu when your program creates its main window.

3. Process menu selections.

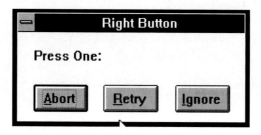

Figure 37-1.   A sample message box

In Windows, the top level of a menu is displayed across the top of the window. Submenus are displayed as popup menus. (You should be accustomed to this approach because it is used by virtually all Windows programs.)

Before beginning, it is necessary to explain what Windows resources and resource files are.

Using Resources

Windows defines several common types of objects as *resources*. Resources include items such as menus, icons, dialog boxes, and bitmapped graphics. Since a menu is a resource, you need to understand resources before you can add a menu to your program.

A resource is created separately from your program but is added to the .EXE file when your program is linked. Resources are contained in *resource files,* which have the extension .RC. In general, the file name should be the same as that of your program's .EXE file. For example, if your program is called PROG.EXE, then its resource file should be called PROG.RC.

Depending upon what the resource files contain, some are text files that you create using a standard text editor. Others, such as icons, are most easily generated using Borland C++'s resource workshop (called WORKSHOP.EXE), but they still must be referred to in the .RC file that is associated with your application. The example resource files in this chapter are simply text files.

Resource files are not Borland C++ files. Instead, you must compile them using a *resource compiler.* The resource compiler converts an .RC file into a .RES file, which may be linked with your program.

Compiling .RC files

Once you have created an .RC file, you can compile it into a .RES file by using the resource compiler, which has the name RC.EXE. You then link the .RES file with your program. If you are using the command-line compiler, the process works like this. First, compile your Windows program. Next, invoke the resource compiler as shown here:

```
RC filename
```

Don't specify any extension. This will cause the resource compiler to compile the resource file and automatically link it to your program (assuming that the name of the resource file is the same as the name of the executable file).

To compile a resource file if you are using the IDE, simply add the name of the .RC file to your program's project file. This causes Borland C++ to execute the resource compiler automatically.

Creating a Simple Menu

Before a menu can be included, you must define its content in a resource file. All menu definitions have this general form:

MenuName MENU [*options*]
{
 menu items
}

Here, *MenuName* is the name of the menu. (It may also be an integer value identifying the menu, but all examples in this book will use the name when referring to the menu.) The keyword **MENU** tells the resource compiler that a menu is being created. There are several options you can specify when creating the menu. They are shown in the following table:

Option	Meaning
DISCARDABLE	Menu may be removed from memory when no longer needed
FIXED	Menu is fixed in memory
LOADONCALL	Menu is loaded when used (default)
MOVEABLE	Menu may be moved in memory (default)
PRELOAD	Menu is loaded when your program begins execution

(Again, these macros are defined in **windows.h**.) You may use any nonconflicting combination. The examples in this book simply use the default settings.

There are two types of items you can use to define the menu: **MENUITEM**s and **POPUP**s. A **MENUITEM** specifies a final selection. A **POPUP** specifies a popup submenu, which may, in itself, contain other **MENUITEM**s or **POPUP**s. The general form of these two statements is

MENUITEM "*ItemName*", *MenuID* [*,Options*]

POPUP "*PopupName*" [*,Options*]

Here, *ItemName* is the name of the menu selection, such as Help or File. *MenuID* is a unique integer associated with a menu item that will be sent to your Windows application when a selection is made. Typically, these values are defined as macros inside a header file that is included in both your application code and the .RC resource file. *PopupName* is the name of the popup menu. For both cases, the values for *Options* (defined in **windows.h**) are shown here:

Option	Meaning
CHECKED	A check mark is displayed next to the name (not applicable to top-level menus)
GRAYED	The name is shown in gray and may not be selected
HELP	The name, usually Help, is displayed at the far right of the menu bar
INACTIVE	The option may not be selected
MENUBARBREAK	For menu bars, this causes a vertical bar to separate this item from the previous one. For popup menus, it causes the item to be put in a different column. In any case, the item is separated using a bar
MENUBREAK	Same as MENUBARBREAK except that no separator bar is used

Here is an example of a simple menu. Enter it into your computer now. Call the file MENU.RC.

```
; Sample menu resource file.
#include "menu.h"

MYMENU MENU
{
  POPUP "&One"
  {
    MENUITEM "&Alpha", IDM_ALPHA
    MENUITEM "&Beta", IDM_BETA
  }
  POPUP "&Two"
  {
    MENUITEM "&Gamma", IDM_GAMMA
    POPUP "&Delta"
    {
      MENUITEM "&Epsilon", IDM_EPSILON
      MENUITEM "&Zeta", IDM_ZETA
    }
```

```
   MENUITEM "&Eta", IDM_ETA
   MENUITEM "&Theta", IDM_THETA
  }
 MENUITEM "&Help", IDM_HELP
}
```

This menu, called MYMENU, contains three top-level menu bar options: One, Two, and Help. The One and Two options contain popup submenus. The Delta option activates a popup submenu of its own. Notice that options that activate submenus do not have menu ID values associated with them. Only actual menu items have ID numbers. In this menu, all menu ID values are specified as macros beginning with **IDM**. (These macros are defined in the header file **menu.h**.) The names you give these values are arbitrary.

The **&** causes the key it precedes to become the shortcut key associated with that option. That is, once that menu is active, pressing that key causes that menu item to be selected. It doesn't have to be the first key in the name, but it should be unless a conflict with another name exists.

 You can embed comments into a resource file on a line-by-line basis by beginning them with a semicolon, as the first line of the resource file shows. You cannot use C- or C++-like comments.

The **menu.h** header file contains the macro definitions of the menu ID values. It is shown here. Enter it now.

```
#define IDM_ALPHA     100
#define IDM_BETA      101
#define IDM_GAMMA     102
#define IDM_DELTA     103
#define IDM_EPSILON   104
#define IDM_ZETA      105
#define IDM_ETA,      106
#define IDM_THETA     107
#define IDM_HELP      108
```

This file defines the menu ID values that will be returned when the various menu items are selected. This file will also be included in the program that uses the menu. Remember, the actual names and values you give the menu items are arbitrary, but each value must be unique.

Including a Menu in Your Program

Once you have created a menu, you include that menu in a Windows program by specifying its name when you create the window's class. Specifically, you assign the **lpszMenuName** field a pointer to a string that contains the name of the menu. For example, to load the menu **MYMENU**, you would use this line when defining the window's class:

```
wcl.lpszMenuName = "MYMENU"; // main menu
```

Responding to Menu Selections

Each time the user makes a menu selection, your program's window function is sent a **WM_COMMAND** message. When that message is received, the value of **wParam** corresponds to the menu item's ID constant. (That is, **wParam** contains the value you associated with the item when you defined the menu in its .RC file.) Since **WM_COMMAND** is sent whenever a menu item is selected and the value associated with that item is contained in **wParam**, you need to use a nested **switch** statement to determine which item was selected. For example, this fragment responds to a selection made from MYMENU:

```
switch(message) {
  case WM_COMMAND:
    switch(wParam) {
      case IDM_ALPHA: MessageBox(hwnd, "Alpha", "", MB_OK);
        break;
      case IDM_BETA: MessageBox(hwnd, "Beta", "", MB_OK);
        break;
      case IDM_GAMMA: MessageBox(hwnd, "Gamma", "", MB_OK);
        break;
      case IDM_EPSILON: MessageBox(hwnd, "Epsilon", "", MB_OK);
        break;
      case IDM_ZETA: MessageBox(hwnd, "Zeta", "", MB_OK);
        break;
      case IDM_ETA:
        X = Y = 1;
        ostr << "ETA ETA ETA" << ends;
        InvalidateRect(hwnd, NULL, 1);
```

```
     break;
  case IDM_THETA: MessageBox(hwnd, "Theta", "", MB_OK);
     break;
  case IDM_HELP: MessageBox(hwnd, "No Help", "Help", MB_OK);
     break;
}
```

For the sake of illustration, the response to each selection simply displays an acknowledgment of that selection on the screen. However, in real applications, the response to menu selections will generally be more complex.

A Sample Menu Program

Here is a program that demonstrates the menu created in the previous section. Enter it now, calling it MENU.CPP.

```
// A Windows skeleton that demonstrates menus.
#include <windows.h>
#include <string.h>
#include <strstrea.h>
#include "menu.h"

LONG FAR PASCAL _export WindowFunc(HWND hwnd, unsigned message,
                                   WORD wParam, LONG lParam);

char szWinName[] = "MyWin"; // name of window class

char str[80] = "Windows Are Fun"; // holds output string

int X = 1, Y=1; // screen location

int PASCAL WinMain(HANDLE hThisInst, HANDLE hPrevInst,
                   LPSTR lpszArgs, int nWinMode)
{
  HWND hwnd;
  MSG msg;
  WNDCLASS wcl;

  /* If this is the first instance of the program, then
     the window class must be registered.
  */
  if(!hPrevInst) { // if no previous instance
```

```
  wcl.hInstance = hThisInst; // handle to this instance
  wcl.lpszClassName = szWinName; // window class name
  wcl.lpfnWndProc = WindowFunc; // window function
  wcl.style = NULL; // no style

  wcl.hIcon = LoadIcon(NULL, IDI_APPLICATION); // icon style
  wcl.hCursor = LoadCursor(NULL, IDC_CROSS); // cursor style
  wcl.lpszMenuName = "MYMENU"; // main menu

  wcl.cbClsExtra = 0; // no extra
  wcl.cbWndExtra = 0; // information needed

  // Make the window light gray.
  wcl.hbrBackground = GetStockObject(LTGRAY_BRUSH);

  // Register the window.
  if(!RegisterClass (&wcl)) return 0;
}

/* Now that a window class has been registered, a window
   can be created. */
hwnd = CreateWindow(
  szWinName, // name of window class
  "Demonstrate Menus", // title
  WS_OVERLAPPEDWINDOW, // window style - normal
  CW_USEDEFAULT, // X coordinate - let Windows decide
  CW_USEDEFAULT, // Y coordinate - let Windows decide
  CW_USEDEFAULT, // width - let Windows decide
  CW_USEDEFAULT, // height - let Windows decide
  NULL, // handle of parent window - there isn't one
  NULL, // no menu
  hThisInst, // handle of this instance of the program
  NULL // no additional arguments
);

// Display the window.
ShowWindow(hwnd, nWinMode);

// Create the message loop.
while(GetMessage(&msg, NULL, 0, 0))
{
  TranslateMessage(&msg); // allow use of keyboard
  DispatchMessage(&msg); // return control to Windows
}
return msg.wParam;
```

```
}

/* This function is called by Windows and is passed messages
   from the message queue.
*/
long FAR PASCAL WindowFunc(HWND hwnd, WORD message, WORD wParam,
                           LONG lParam)
{
  HDC hdc;
  PAINTSTRUCT paintstruct;
  ostrstream ostr(str, sizeof(str));

  int response;

  switch(message) {
    case WM_COMMAND:
      switch(wParam) {
        case IDM_ALPHA: MessageBox(hwnd, "Alpha", "", MB_OK);
          break;
        case IDM_BETA: MessageBox(hwnd, "Beta", "", MB_OK);
          break;
        case IDM_GAMMA: MessageBox(hwnd, "Gamma", "", MB_OK);
          break;
        case IDM_EPSILON: MessageBox(hwnd, "Epsilon", "", MB_OK);
          break;
        case IDM_ZETA: MessageBox(hwnd, "Zeta", "", MB_OK);
          break;
        case IDM_ETA:
          X = Y = 1;
          ostr << "ETA ETA ETA" << ends;
          InvalidateRect(hwnd, NULL, 1);
          break;
        case IDM_THETA: MessageBox(hwnd, "Theta", "", MB_OK);
          break;
        case IDM_HELP: MessageBox(hwnd, "No Help", "Help", MB_OK);
          break;
      }
    case WM_PAINT:
      hdc = BeginPaint(hwnd, &paintstruct);
      TextOut(hdc, X, Y, "   ", 2);
      TextOut(hdc, X, Y, str, strlen(str));
      EndPaint(hwnd, &paintstruct);
      break;
```

```
    case WM_CHAR:
      X = Y = 1; // display characters in upper-left corner
      ostr << (char) wParam << ends;
      InvalidateRect(hwnd, NULL, 1); // Generate WM_PAINT
      break;
    case WM_RBUTTONDOWN:
      response = MessageBox(hwnd, "Press One:", "Right Button",
               MB_ABORTRETRYIGNORE);

      switch(response) {
        case IDABORT:
          MessageBox(hwnd, "", "Abort", MB_OK);
          break;
        case IDRETRY:
          MessageBox(hwnd, "", "Retry", MB_OK);
          break;
        case IDIGNORE:
          MessageBox(hwnd, "", "Ignore", MB_OK);
          break;
      }
      break;
    case WM_LBUTTONDOWN:
      response = MessageBox(hwnd, "Continue?", "Left Button",
               MB_ICONHAND | MB_YESNO);

      switch(response) {
        case IDYES:
          MessageBox(hwnd, "", "Yes Selected", MB_OK);
          break;
        case IDNO:
          MessageBox(hwnd, "", "No Selected", MB_OK);
          break;
      }
      break;
    case WM_DESTROY: // terminate the program
      PostQuitMessage(0);
      break;
  }

  /* Let Windows process any messages not specified in
     the preceding switch statement. */
  return DefWindowProc(hwnd, message, wParam, lParam);
}
```

Adding Menu Accelerator Keys

This section discusses one more feature relating to menus: the accelerator key. *Accelerator keys* are special keystrokes you define that, when pressed, automatically select a menu option even though the menu in which that option resides is not displayed. Put differently, you can select an item directly by pressing an accelerator key, bypassing the menu entirely. The term "accelerator key" is an accurate description because pressing one is generally a faster way to select a menu item than first activating its menu and then selecting the item.

To define accelerator keys relative to a menu, you must add an accelerator key table to your resource file. All accelerator table definitions have this general form:

```
MenuName ACCELERATORS
{
Key1, MenuID1 [,type] [option]
Key2, MenuID2 [,type] [option]
Key3, MenuID3 [,type] [option]
  .
  .
  .
Keyn, MenuIDn [,type] [option]
}
```

Here, *MenuName* is the name of the menu the accelerators will be applied to and is also the name of the accelerator table. *Key* is the keystroke that selects the item, and *MenuID* is the ID value associated with the desired item. The *type* specifies whether the key is a standard key (the default) or a virtual key (discussed shortly). The options may be one of the following macros: **NOINVERT**, **ALT**, **SHIFT**, or **CONTROL**. **NOINVERT** causes no top-level menu to be displayed when an item is selected. With one exception, the other three macros apply only to virtual keys.

The value of *Key* will be a quoted character, an ASCII integer value corresponding to a key, or a virtual key code. If a quoted character is used, it is assumed to be an ASCII character. If it is an integer value, you must tell the resource compiler explicitly that this is an ASCII character by specifying *type* as **ASCII**. If it is a virtual key, *type* must be **VIRTKEY**.

If the key is an uppercase quoted character, its corresponding menu item will be selected if it is pressed while holding down the SHIFT key. If it is a lowercase character, its menu item will be selected if the key is pressed by itself. If the key is specified as a lowercase character and **ALT** is specified as an option, pressing ALT and the character will select the item. Finally, if you want the user to press CTRL and the key to select an item, specify the key in uppercase and precede it with a ^.

A *virtual key* is a system-independent code for a variety of keys. Virtual keys include the function keys F1 through F12, the arrow keys, and various non-ASCII keys. They are defined by macros in the header file **windows.h**. All virtual key macros begin with

VK_. The function keys are **VK_F1** through **VK_F12**, for example. Refer to **windows.h** for the other virtual key code macros. To use a virtual key as an accelerator, simply specify its macro for the *key* and specify **VIRTKEY** for its *type*. You may also specify **ALT**, **SHIFT**, or **CONTROL** to achieve the desired key combination.

Here are some examples:

```
"A", IDM_x            ; select by pressing SHIFT-A
"a", IDM_x            ; select by pressing a
"^A", IDM_x           ; select by pressing CTRL-A
"a", IDM_x, ALT       ; select by pressing ALT-A
VK_F2, IDM_x          ; select by pressing F2
VK_F2, IDM_x, SHIFT   ; select by pressing SHIFT-F2
```

Here is the MENU.RC resource file that now contains accelerator key definitions for the menu specified in the previous section:

```
; Sample menu resource file
#include "menu.h"
#include <windows.h>

MYMENU MENU
{
  POPUP "&One"
  {
    MENUITEM "&Alpha\tF2", IDM_ALPHA
    MENUITEM "&Beta\tF3", IDM_BETA
  }
  POPUP "&Two"
  {
    MENUITEM "&Gamma\tSHIFT-G", IDM_GAMMA
    POPUP "&Delta"
    {
      MENUITEM "&Epsilon\tCntl-E", IDM_EPSILON
      MENUITEM "&Zeta\tCntl-Z", IDM_ZETA
    }
    MENUITEM "&Eta\tCntl-F4", IDM_ETA
    MENUITEM "&Theta\tF5", IDM_THETA
  }
  MENUITEM "&Help", IDM_HELP
}

; Define menu accelerators
MYMENU ACCELERATORS
{
```

```
    VK_F2, IDM_ALPHA, VIRTKEY
    VK_F3, IDM_BETA, VIRTKEY
    "G", IDM_GAMMA
    "^E", IDM_EPSILON
    "^Z", IDM_ZETA
    VK_F4, IDM_ETA, VIRTKEY, CONTROL
    VK_F5, IDM_THETA, VIRTKEY
    VK_F1, IDM_HELP, VIRTKEY
}
```

Notice that the menu definition has been enhanced to display the accelerator key that selects each option. Each item is separated from its accelerator key using a tab.

Loading the Accelerator Table

Even though the accelerators are contained in the same resource file as the menu, they must be loaded separately by using another API function called **LoadAccelerators( )**, whose prototype is

> HANDLE LoadAccelerators(HANDLE *ThisInst*, LPSTR *Name*);

where *ThisInst* is the handle of the application and *Name* is the name of the accelerator table. The function returns a handle to the accelerator table.

You must call **LoadAccelerators( )** soon after the window is created. For example, this shows how to load the **MYMENU** accelerator table:

```
HANDLE hAccel;

hAccel = LoadAccelerators(hThisInst, "MYMENU");
```

The value of **hAccel** will be used later to help process accelerator keys.

Although the **LoadAccelerators( )** function loads the accelerator table, your program still cannot process the accelerator keys until you add another API function to the message loop. This function is called **TranslateAccelerator( )** and its prototype is

> int TranslateAccelerator(HWND *hwnd*, HANDLE *hAccel*, LPMSG *lpMess*);

Here, *hwnd* is the handle of the window for which accelerator keys will be translated. *hAccel* is the handle to the accelerator table that will be used. This is the handle returned by **LoadAccelerators( )**. Finally, *lpMess* is a pointer to the message. The **TranslateAccelerator( )** function returns true if an accelerator key was pressed and false otherwise. This function translates your keystrokes into the proper menu ID values.

When you use **TranslateAccelerator( )**, your message loop should look like this:

```
while(GetMessage(&msg, NULL, 0, 0))
{
  if(!TranslateAccelerator(hwnd, hAccel, &msg)) {
    TranslateMessage(&msg); // allow use of keyboard
    DispatchMessage(&msg); // return control to Windows
  }
}
```

To try using accelerators, substitute the following version of **WinMain( )** into the preceding application and add the accelerator table to your resource file:

```
int PASCAL WinMain(HANDLE hThisInst, HANDLE hPrevInst,
                   LPSTR lpszArgs, int nWinMode)
{
  HWND hwnd;
  MSG msg;
  WNDCLASS wcl;
  HANDLE hAccel; // handle to accelerator table

  /* If this is the first instance of the program, then
     the window class must be registered.
  */
  if(!hPrevInst) { // if no previous instance
    wcl.hInstance = hThisInst; // handle to this instance
    wcl.lpszClassName = szWinName; // window class name
    wcl.lpfnWndProc = WindowFunc; // window function
    wcl.style = NULL; // no style

    wcl.hIcon = LoadIcon(NULL, IDI_APPLICATION); // icon style
    wcl.hCursor = LoadCursor(NULL, IDC_CROSS); // cursor style
    wcl.lpszMenuName = "MYMENU"; // main menu

    wcl.cbClsExtra = 0; // no extra
    wcl.cbWndExtra = 0; // information needed

    // Make the window light gray.
    wcl.hbrBackground = GetStockObject(LTGRAY_BRUSH);

    // Register the window.
    if(!RegisterClass (&wcl)) return 0;
```

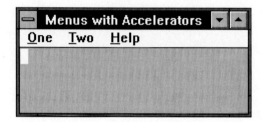

Figure 37-2.   *Sample output from the menu example that includes accelerators*

```
}

/* Now that a window class has been registered, a window
   can be created. */
hwnd = CreateWindow(
  szWinName, // name of window class
  "Menus with Accelerators", // title
  WS_OVERLAPPEDWINDOW, // window style - normal
  CW_USEDEFAULT, // X coordinate - let Windows decide
  CW_USEDEFAULT, // Y coordinate - let Windows decide
  CW_USEDEFAULT, // width - let Windows decide
  CW_USEDEFAULT, // height - let Windows decide
  NULL, // handle of parent window - there isn't one
  NULL, // no menu
  hThisInst, // handle of this instance of the program
  NULL // no additional arguments
);

hAccel = LoadAccelerators(hThisInst, "MYMENU");

// Display the window.
ShowWindow(hwnd, nWinMode);

// Create the message loop.
while(GetMessage(&msg, NULL, 0, 0))
{
  if(!TranslateAccelerator(hwnd, hAccel, &msg)) {
    TranslateMessage(&msg); // allow use of keyboard
    DispatchMessage(&msg); // return control to Windows
  }
}
```

```
    return msg.wParam;
}
```

Sample output is shown in Figure 37-2. Before moving on to the next chapter, experiment on your own using message boxes, menus, and accelerators. Try the various options and see what they do.

Chapter *38*

Using Dialog Boxes

After menus, there is no more important Windows interface element than the dialog box. A *dialog box* is a type of window that provides a more flexible means by which the user can interact with your Windows application. In general, dialog boxes allow the user to select or enter information that would be difficult or impossible to select or enter using a menu.

How Dialog Boxes Interact with the User

A dialog box interacts with the user through one or more controls. A *control* is a specific type of input or output window. A control is owned by its parent window, which, for the examples presented in this chapter, is the dialog box. Windows supports the following controls: push buttons, check boxes, radio buttons, list boxes, edit boxes, combination boxes, scroll bars, and static controls.

A *push button* is a control that the user "pushes" (by clicking the mouse or by tabbing to it and then pressing ENTER) to activate some response. You have already been using push buttons in message boxes. For example, the OK button you have been using in most message boxes is a push button. There can be one or more push buttons in a dialog box.

A *check box* contains one or more items that are either checked or not checked. If the item is checked, it means it is selected. In a check box, more than one item may be selected.

A *radio button* is essentially a check box in which one and only one item may be selected at any given time.

A *list box* displays a list of items from which the user selects one or more. List boxes are commonly used to display things such as file names.

An *edit box* allows the user to enter a string. Edit boxes provide all necessary text editing features required by the user. Therefore, to input a string, your program simply displays an edit box and waits until the user has finished typing the string.

A *combination box* is a combination of a list box and an edit box.

As you know, a *scroll bar* is used to scroll text in a window.

A *static control* is used to output text (or graphics) that provides information to the user but accepts no input.

In the course of explaining how to use dialog boxes with Windows, the examples in this chapter illustrate three of these controls: push buttons, the list box, and the edit box.

It is important to understand that controls both generate messages (when accessed by the user) and receive messages (from your application). A message generated by a control indicates what type of interaction the user has had with the control. A message sent to the control is essentially an instruction to which the control must respond. You will see examples of this type of message-passing later in this chapter.

Modal Versus Modeless Dialog Boxes

There are two types of dialog boxes: modal and modeless. The most common dialog boxes are modal. A *modal dialog box* demands a response before the parent program will continue. That is, a modal dialog box will not allow you to refocus input to another part of the parent application without first responding to the dialog box.

A *modeless dialog box* does not prevent the parent program from running. That is, it does not demand a response before input can be focused to another part of the parent program.

Since the modal dialog box is the most common, it is the type of dialog box examined in this chapter.

Receiving Dialog Box Messages

A dialog box is a window (albeit, a special kind of window). Events that occur within it are sent to your program using the same message-passing mechanism the main window uses. However, dialog box messages are not sent to your program's main window function. Instead, each dialog box you define will need its own window function. This function must have the following prototype. (Of course, the name of the function can be anything you like.)

```
BOOL FAR PASCAL _export DFunc(HWND hdwnd, unsigned message,
                              WORD wParam, LONG lParam);
```

As you can see, this function receives the same parameters as the main window function. However, it differs from the main window function in that it returns a true or false result. Like your program's main window function, the dialog box window function will receive many messages. If it processes a message, it must return true. If it does not respond to a message, it must return false.

Because the dialog function is called by Windows, it must be exported using the **_export** keyword.

In general, each control within a dialog box is given its own resource ID. Each time that control is accessed by the user, a message is sent to the dialog box's window function, indicating the ID of the control and the type of action the user has taken. That function then decodes the message and takes appropriate actions. This process parallels the way messages are decoded by your program's main window function.

Activating a Dialog Box

To activate a dialog box you must call the **DialogBox( )** API function, whose prototype is

> int DialogBox(HANDLE *hThisInst*, LPSTR *lpName*,
> HWND *hwnd*, FARPROC *lpDFunc*)

Here, *hThisInst* is a handle to the current application that is passed to your program in the instance parameter to **WinMain( )**. The name of the dialog box as defined in the resource file is pointed to by *lpName*. The handle to the window that activates the dialog box is passed in *hwnd*. The *lpDFunc* parameter contains a pointer to the procedure-instance address of the dialog box. A *procedure-instance* is a short piece of code that links a function with the data segment that the program is currently using. A procedure-instance is obtained using the **MakeProcInstance( )** API function. Its prototype is

> FARPROC MakeProcInstance(FARPROC *lpFunc*, HANDLE *hThisInst*);

This function returns the procedure-instance of the function pointed to by *lpFunc*. The current instance handle is passed in *hThisInst*.

After a dialog box terminates, you must release the procedure-instance by calling the API function **FreeProcInstance( )**. It has this prototype:

> void FreeProcInstance(FARPROC *lpProcAddr*)

Here, *lpProcAddr* is a pointer to the procedure-instance returned by **MakeProcInstance( )**.

The following code fragment illustrates how to activate a dialog box:

```
FARPROC lpDlg; // pointer to dialog function

lpDlg = MakeProcInstance((FARPROC) DialogFunc, hInst);
DialogBox(hInst, "MYDB", hwnd, lpDlg);
FreeProcInstance(lpDlg);
```

Here, **hInst** is the current instance handle of the program, and **hwnd** is the handle of the parent window.

Creating a Simple Dialog Box

For a first dialog box, a simple example will be created. This dialog box will contain three push buttons called Red, Green, and Cancel. When either the Red or Green button is selected, it will activate a message box indicating the choice selected. The box will be removed from the screen when the Cancel button is selected.

The program will have a top-level menu containing three options: Dialog 1, Dialog 2, and Help. Only Dialog 1 will have a dialog box associated with it. The Dialog 2 entry is a placeholder so you can define your own dialog box as you work through the examples.

While this and other examples in this chapter don't do much with the information provided by the dialog box, they illustrate the central features you will use in your own applications.

The Dialog Box Example Resource File

A dialog box is another resource that is contained in your program's resource file. Before developing a program that uses a dialog box, you need a resource file that specifies one. Although it is possible to specify the contents of a dialog box using a text editor and enter its specifications as you do when creating a menu, this is seldom done. Instead, most programmers use Borland C++'s resource workshop, called WORKSHOP. The main reasons for this are that dialog box definitions involve relatively complex specifications and that the placement of the various items inside the dialog box is best done interactively. For these reasons, the resource files in this chapter were created using the resource workshop. However, since the complete .RC files for the examples in this chapter are supplied in their text form in this book, you should simply enter them as text. Just remember that when creating your own dialog boxes, you will want to use the resource workshop.

Since most dialog boxes are created using the resource workshop, no explanation of the dialog box definition in the resource file is given in this chapter. However, a Windows programming reference will include such a description if you are interested.

The following file includes a menu that is used to activate the dialog box; accelerator keys; and then the dialog box itself. Enter it into your computer at this time, calling it MYDIALOG.RC.

```
; Sample dialog box and menu resource file.
#include "mydialog.h"
#include <windows.h>

MYMENU MENU
{
  MENUITEM "Dialog &1", IDM_DIALOG1
  MENUITEM "Dialog &2", IDM_DIALOG2
  MENUITEM "&Help", IDM_HELP
}


MYMENU ACCELERATORS
{
  VK_F2, IDM_DIALOG1, VIRTKEY
  VK_F3, IDM_DIALOG2, VIRTKEY
  VK_F1, IDM_HELP, VIRTKEY
}

MYDB DIALOG 18, 18, 142, 92
CAPTION "Test Dialog Box"
STYLE DS_MODALFRAME | WS_POPUP | WS_CAPTION | WS_SYSMENU
{
  DEFPUSHBUTTON "Red", IDD_RED, 32, 36, 28, 13,
             WS_CHILD | WS_VISIBLE | WS_TABSTOP
  PUSHBUTTON "Green", IDD_GREEN, 74, 36, 30, 13,
             WS_CHILD | WS_VISIBLE | WS_TABSTOP
  PUSHBUTTON "Cancel", IDCANCEL, 52, 65, 37, 14,
             WS_CHILD | WS_VISIBLE | WS_TABSTOP
}
```

The header file **mydialog.h**, which is also used by the example program, is shown here:

```
#define IDM_DIALOG1   100
#define IDM_DIALOG2   101
```

```
#define IDM_HELP     102

#define IDD_RED      103
#define IDD_GREEN    104
```

Enter this file now.

The Dialog Box Window Function

The following dialog window function responds to the events that can occur within the MYDIALOG dialog box:

```
BOOL FAR PASCAL DialogFunc(HWND hdwnd, unsigned message,
                           WORD wParam, LONG lParam)
{
  switch(message) {
    case WM_COMMAND:
      switch(wParam) {
        case IDCANCEL:
          EndDialog(hdwnd, NULL);
          return 1;
        case IDD_RED:
          MessageBox(hdwnd, "You Picked Red", "RED", MB_OK);
          return 1;
        case IDD_GREEN:
          MessageBox(hdwnd, "You Picked Green", "GREEN", MB_OK);
          return 1;
      }
  }
  return 0;
}
```

Each time a control within the dialog box is accessed, a **WM_COMMAND** message is sent to **DialogFunc( )** and **wParam** contains the ID of the control affected.

DialogFunc( ) processes the three messages that can be generated by the box. First, if the user selects **Cancel**, **IDCANCEL** is sent, causing the dialog box to be closed using a call to the API function **EndDialog( )**. (**IDCANCEL** is a standard ID defined in **windows.h**.) **EndDialog( )** has this prototype:

   void EndDialog(HWND *hdwnd*, int *nStatus*)

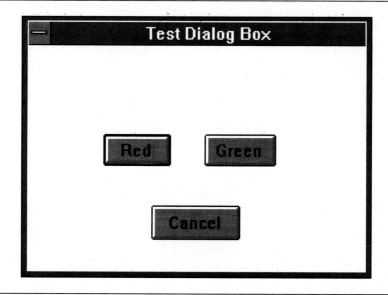

Figure 38-1.   *Sample output from the first dialog box program*

Here, *hdwnd* is the handle to the dialog box, and *nStatus* is a status code returned by the **DialogBox( )** function. (You can ignore the value of *nStatus* if it is not relevant to your program.)

Selecting either of the other two buttons causes a message box to be displayed that confirms the selection.

The First Dialog Box Sample Program

Following is the entire dialog box example. When the program begins execution, only the top-level menu is displayed on the menu bar. By selecting **Dialog 1**, the user causes the dialog box to be displayed. Once the dialog box is displayed, selecting a push button causes the appropriate response. A sample screen is shown in Figure 38-1.

```
// A Windows skeleton that demonstrates dialog boxes.
#include <windows.h>
#include <string.h>
#include <strstrea.h>
#include "mydialog.h"

LONG FAR PASCAL _export WindowFunc(HWND hwnd, unsigned message,
```

```
                                  WORD wParam, LONG lParam);
BOOL FAR PASCAL _export DialogFunc(HWND hdwnd, unsigned message,
                                  WORD wParam, LONG lParam);

char szWinName[] = "MyWin"; // name of window class

HANDLE hInst; // holds a copy of current instance handle

int PASCAL WinMain(HANDLE hThisInst, HANDLE hPrevInst,
                   LPSTR lpszArgs, int nWinMode)
{
  HWND hwnd;
  MSG msg;
  WNDCLASS wcl;
  HANDLE hAccel;

  /* If this is the first instance of the program, then
     the window class must be registered.
  */
  if(!hPrevInst) { // if no previous instance
    wcl.hInstance = hThisInst; // handle to this instance
    wcl.lpszClassName = szWinName; // window class name
    wcl.lpfnWndProc = WindowFunc; // window function
    wcl.style = NULL; // no style

    wcl.hIcon = LoadIcon(NULL, IDI_APPLICATION); // icon style
    wcl.hCursor = LoadCursor(NULL, IDC_ARROW); // cursor style
    wcl.lpszMenuName = "MYMENU"; // main menu

    wcl.cbClsExtra = 0; // no extra
    wcl.cbWndExtra = 0; // information needed

    // Make the window light gray.
    wcl.hbrBackground = GetStockObject(LTGRAY_BRUSH);

    // Register the window.
    if(!RegisterClass (&wcl)) return 0;
  }

  /* Now that a window class has been registered, a window
     can be created. */
  hwnd = CreateWindow(
    szWinName, // name of window class
    "Dialog Boxes", // title
    WS_OVERLAPPEDWINDOW, // window style - normal
```

```
        CW_USEDEFAULT, // X coordinate - let Windows decide
        CW_USEDEFAULT, // Y coordinate - let Windows decide
        CW_USEDEFAULT, // width - let Windows decide
        CW_USEDEFAULT, // height - let Windows decide
        NULL, // handle of parent window - there isn't one
        NULL, // no menu
        hThisInst, // handle of this instance of the program
        NULL // no additional arguments
    );
    hAccel = LoadAccelerators(hThisInst, "MYMENU");
    hInst = hThisInst; // save the current instance handle

    // Display the window.
    ShowWindow(hwnd, nWinMode);

    // Create the message loop.
    while(GetMessage(&msg, NULL, 0, 0))
    {
      if(!TranslateAccelerator(hwnd, hAccel, &msg)) {
        TranslateMessage(&msg); // allow use of keyboard
        DispatchMessage(&msg); // return control to Windows
      }
    }
    return msg.wParam;
}

/* This function is called by Windows and is passed messages
   from the message queue.
*/
long FAR PASCAL WindowFunc(HWND hwnd, WORD message, WORD wParam,
                           LONG lParam)
{
  FARPROC lpDlg; // pointer to dialog function

  int response;

  switch(message) {
    case WM_COMMAND:
      switch(wParam) {
        case IDM_DIALOG1:
          lpDlg = MakeProcInstance((FARPROC) DialogFunc, hInst);
          DialogBox(hInst, "MYDB", hwnd, lpDlg);
          FreeProcInstance(lpDlg);
          break;
        case IDM_DIALOG2:
```

```
        MessageBox(hwnd, "Not Implemented", "", MB_OK);
        break;
      case IDM_HELP:
        MessageBox(hwnd, "Not Implemented", "HELP", MB_OK);
        break;
    }
    break;
  case WM_DESTROY: // terminate the program
    PostQuitMessage(0);
    break;
  }

  /* Let Windows process any messages not specified in
     the preceding switch statement. */
  return DefWindowProc(hwnd, message, wParam, lParam);
}


BOOL FAR PASCAL DialogFunc(HWND hdwnd, unsigned message,
                           WORD wParam, LONG lParam)
{
  switch(message) {
    case WM_COMMAND:
      switch(wParam) {
        case IDCANCEL:
          EndDialog(hdwnd, NULL);
          return 1;
        case IDD_RED:
          MessageBox(hdwnd, "You Picked Red", "RED", MB_OK);
          return 1;
        case IDD_GREEN:
          MessageBox(hdwnd, "You Picked Green", "GREEN", MB_OK);
          return 1;
      }
  }
  return 0;
}
```

Notice the global variable **hInst**. This variable is assigned a copy of the current instance handle passed to **WinMain( )**. The reason for this variable is that the dialog box needs access to the current instance handle. However, the dialog box is not created in **WinMain( )**. Instead, it is created in **WindowFunc( )**. Therefore, a copy of the instance parameter must be made so it can be accessible outside of **WinMain( )**.

Adding a List Box

To continue exploring dialog boxes, let's add another control to the dialog box defined in the previous program. One of the most common controls after the push button is the list box. This section adds a list box to the skeleton.

First, add this list box description to the dialog definition in the **mydialog.rc** resource file:

```
CONTROL "Listbox Tester", ID_LB1,
        "LISTBOX", LBS_NOTIFY | WS_CHILD | WS_VISIBLE |
        WS_BORDER | WS_VSCROLL, 2, 10, 47, 28
```

Your dialog box definition should now look like this:

```
MYDB DIALOG 18, 18, 142, 92
CAPTION "Test Dialog Box"
STYLE DS_MODALFRAME | WS_POPUP | WS_CAPTION | WS_SYSMENU
{
  DEFPUSHBUTTON "Red", IDD_RED, 32, 36, 28, 13,
            WS_CHILD | WS_VISIBLE | WS_TABSTOP
  PUSHBUTTON "Green", IDD_GREEN, 74, 36, 30, 13,
            WS_CHILD | WS_VISIBLE | WS_TABSTOP
  PUSHBUTTON "Cancel", IDCANCEL, 52, 65, 37, 14,
            WS_CHILD | WS_VISIBLE | WS_TABSTOP
  CONTROL "Listbox Tester", ID_LB1,
            "LISTBOX", LBS_NOTIFY | WS_CHILD | WS_VISIBLE |
            WS_BORDER | WS_VSCROLL, 2, 10, 47, 28
}
```

You also need to add this macro to **mydialog.h**:

```
#define ID_LB1          105
```

ID_LB1 identifies the list box specified in the dialog box definition in the resource file.

Responding to a List Box

Responding to list box events requires a simple addition to the preceding program. When using a list box, you must perform two basic operations. First, you must initialize the list box when the dialog box is first displayed. This consists of sending the list box the list it will display. (By default, the list box is empty.) Second, once the list box has been initialized, your program will need to respond to the user selecting an item from the list.

List boxes generate various types of messages. The only one used here is **LBN_DBLCLK**. This message is sent when the user has double clicked on an entry in the list or selected it using the keyboard. This message is contained in **HIWORD(lParam)**. Once a selection has been made, you will need to query the list box to find out which item has been selected.

Unlike a push button, a list box is a control that receives messages as well as generating them. You can send a list box any of 26 different messages. However, the example sends only these two:

Macro	Purpose
LB_ADDSTRING	Adds a string (selection) to the list box
LB_GETCURSEL	Requests the index of the item selected

LB_ADDSTRING is a message that tells the list box to add a specified string to the list. That is, the specified string becomes another selection within the box. You will see how to use this message shortly. **LB_GETCURSEL** causes the list box to return the index of the item within the list box that the user selects. All list box indexes begin with 0.

To send a message to the list box (or any other control), use the **SendDlgItemMessage( )** API function. Its prototype is

```
DWORD SendDlgItemMessage(HWND hdwnd, int ID,
                         WORD ID_Msg, WORD wParam,
                         DWORD lParam);
```

SendDlgItemMessage( ) sends to the control (within the dialog box) whose ID is specified by *ID* the message specified by *ID_Msg*. The handle of the dialog box is specified in *hdwnd*. Any additional information required by the message is specified in *wParam* and *lParam*. The additional information, if any, varies from message to message. If there is no additional information to pass to a control, the *wParam* and the *lParam* arguments should be 0.

Initializing the List Box

Since a list box is empty by default, you need to initialize it when the dialog box that contains it is first displayed. This proves to be quite simple because each time a dialog box is activated, its window function is sent a **WM_INITDIALOG** message. Therefore, you need to add this case to the outer **switch** statement:

```
case WM_INITDIALOG: // initialize list box
  SendDlgItemMessage(hdwnd, ID_LB1,
                     LB_ADDSTRING, 0, (LONG)"Apple");
  SendDlgItemMessage(hdwnd, ID_LB1,
                     LB_ADDSTRING, 0, (LONG)"Orange");
  SendDlgItemMessage(hdwnd, ID_LB1,
                     LB_ADDSTRING, 0, (LONG)"Pear");
  SendDlgItemMessage(hdwnd, ID_LB1,
                     LB_ADDSTRING, 0, (LONG)"Grape");
  return 1;
}
```

Each string is added to the list box by calling **SendDlgItemMessage()** with the **LB_ADDSTRING** message. The string to add is pointed to by the *lParam* parameter. (The type cast to **LONG** is necessary.) In this case, each string is added to the list box in the order in which it is sent. (However, depending upon how you construct the list box, it is possible to have the items displayed in alphabetical order.) If the number of items you send to a list box exceeds what it can display in its window, vertical scroll bars are added automatically.

Processing a Selection

After the list box has been initialized, it is ready for use. Each time the user selects an item in the list box by either double clicking or positioning the highlight using the arrow keys and then pressing ENTER, a **WM_COMMAND** message is passed to the dialog box's window function and the **LBN_DBLCLK** message is contained in **wParam**. Therefore, you must add **LBN_DBLCLK** to the inner **switch** statement of the dialog box's window function.

Once a selection has been made, you determine which item was chosen by sending the **LB_GETCURSEL** message to the list box. The list box then returns the index of the item.

To demonstrate how to process a list box selection, add the following case to the the inner switch inside **DialogFunc()**. Each time a selection is made, a message box will display the index of the item selected.

```
case ID_LB1:
  // see if user made a selection
  if(HIWORD(lParam)==LBN_DBLCLK) {
    i = SendDlgItemMessage(hdwnd, ID_LB1,
           LB_GETCURSEL, 0, 0L);  // get index

    ostr << "Index in list is: " << i << ends;
    MessageBox(hdwnd, str, "Selection Made", MB_OK);
```

```
    }
    return 0;
```

The Entire List Box Example

For your convenience, the entire expanded dialog box program is shown here. (Be sure to update **mydialog.h** and **mydialog.rc** before compiling this program.) Sample output from this program is shown in Figure 38-2.

```
// A Windows skeleton that demonstrates dialog boxes.
#include <windows.h>
#include <string.h>
#include <strstrea.h>
#include "mydialog.h"

LONG FAR PASCAL _export WindowFunc(HWND hwnd, unsigned message,
                                   WORD wParam, LONG lParam);
BOOL FAR PASCAL _export DialogFunc(HWND hdwnd, unsigned message,
                                   WORD wParam, LONG lParam);

char szWinName[] = "MyWin"; // name of window class


HANDLE hInst; // holds a copy of current instance handle

int PASCAL WinMain(HANDLE hThisInst, HANDLE hPrevInst,
                   LPSTR lpszArgs, int nWinMode)
{
  HWND hwnd;
  MSG msg;
  WNDCLASS wcl;
  HANDLE hAccel;

  /* If this is the first instance of the program, then
     the window class must be registered.
  */
  if(!hPrevInst) { // if no previous instance
    wcl.hInstance = hThisInst; // handle to this instance
    wcl.lpszClassName = szWinName; // window class name
    wcl.lpfnWndProc = WindowFunc; // window function
    wcl.style = NULL; // no style

    wcl.hIcon = LoadIcon(NULL, IDI_APPLICATION); // icon style
    wcl.hCursor = LoadCursor(NULL, IDC_ARROW); // cursor style
    wcl.lpszMenuName = "MYMENU"; // main menu
```

```
  wcl.cbClsExtra = 0; // no extra
  wcl.cbWndExtra = 0; // information needed

  // Make the window light gray.
  wcl.hbrBackground = GetStockObject(LTGRAY_BRUSH);

  // Register the window.
  if(!RegisterClass (&wcl)) return 0;
}

/* Now that a window class has been registered, a window
   can be created. */
hwnd = CreateWindow(
  szWinName, // name of window class
  "Dialog Boxes", // title
  WS_OVERLAPPEDWINDOW, // window style - normal
  CW_USEDEFAULT, // X coordinate - let Windows decide
  CW_USEDEFAULT, // Y coordinate - let Windows decide
  CW_USEDEFAULT, // width - let Windows decide
  CW_USEDEFAULT, // height - let Windows decide
  NULL, // handle of parent window - there isn't one
  NULL, // no menu
  hThisInst, // handle of this instance of the program
  NULL // no additional arguments
);

hAccel = LoadAccelerators(hThisInst, "MYMENU");
hInst = hThisInst; // save current instance handle

// Display the window.
ShowWindow(hwnd, nWinMode);

// Create the message loop.
while(GetMessage(&msg, NULL, 0, 0))
{
  if(!TranslateAccelerator(hwnd, hAccel, &msg)) {
    TranslateMessage(&msg); // allow use of keyboard
    DispatchMessage(&msg); // return control to Windows
  }
}
return msg.wParam;
}

/* This function is called by Windows and is passed messages
```

```
     from the message queue.
*/
long FAR PASCAL WindowFunc(HWND hwnd, WORD message, WORD wParam,
                           LONG lParam)
{
  FARPROC lpDlg;

  int response;

  switch(message) {
    case WM_COMMAND:
      switch(wParam) {
        case IDM_DIALOG1:
          lpDlg = MakeProcInstance((FARPROC) DialogFunc, hInst);
          DialogBox(hInst, "MYDB", hwnd, lpDlg);
          FreeProcInstance(lpDlg);
          break;
        case IDM_DIALOG2:
          MessageBox(hwnd, "Not Implemented", "", MB_OK);
          break;
        case IDM_HELP:
          MessageBox(hwnd, "Not Implemented", "HELP", MB_OK);
          break;
      }
      break;
    case WM_DESTROY: // terminate the program
      PostQuitMessage(0);
      break;
  }

  /* Let Windows process any messages not specified in
     the preceding switch statement. */
  return DefWindowProc(hwnd, message, wParam, lParam);
}


BOOL FAR PASCAL DialogFunc(HWND hdwnd, unsigned message,
                           WORD wParam, LONG lParam)
{
  LONG i;
  char str[80];
  ostrstream ostr(str, sizeof(str));

  switch(message) {
    case WM_COMMAND:
```

```
     switch(wParam) {
       case IDCANCEL:
         EndDialog(hdwnd, NULL);
         return 1;
       case IDD_RED:
         MessageBox(hdwnd, "You Picked Red", "RED", MB_OK);
         return 1;
       case IDD_GREEN:
         MessageBox(hdwnd, "You Picked Green", "GREEN", MB_OK);
         return 1;
       case ID_LB1:
          // see  if user made a selection
         if(HIWORD(lParam)==LBN_DBLCLK) {
           i = SendDlgItemMessage(hdwnd, ID_LB1,
                   LB_GETCURSEL, 0, 0L);   // get index

           ostr << "Index in list is: " << i << ends;
           MessageBox(hdwnd, str, "Selection Made", MB_OK);
         }
         return 1;
     }
   case WM_INITDIALOG: // initialize list box
     SendDlgItemMessage(hdwnd, ID_LB1,
                     LB_ADDSTRING, 0, (LONG)"Apple");
     SendDlgItemMessage(hdwnd, ID_LB1,
```

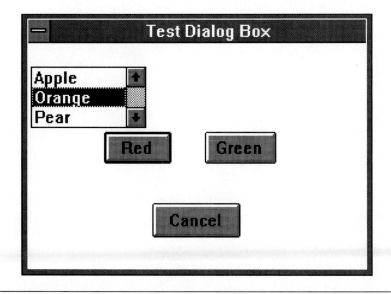

Figure 38-2.   *Sample output that includes a list box*

```
                              LB_ADDSTRING, 0, (LONG)"Orange");
      SendDlgItemMessage(hdwnd, ID_LB1,
                              LB_ADDSTRING, 0, (LONG)"Pear");
      SendDlgItemMessage(hdwnd, ID_LB1,
                              LB_ADDSTRING, 0, (LONG)"Grape");
      return 1;
    }
    return 0;
}
```

Adding an Edit Box

The last control you will add to the sample dialog box is the edit box. Edit boxes are particularly useful because they allow users to enter a string of their own choosing. Before you can use an edit box, you must define one in your resource file. For this example, change MYDIALOG.RC so it looks like this:

```
MYDB DIALOG 18, 18, 142, 92
CAPTION "Test Dialog Box"
STYLE DS_MODALFRAME | WS_POPUP | WS_CAPTION | WS_SYSMENU
{
  DEFPUSHBUTTON "Red", IDD_RED, 16, 44, 30, 13,
                WS_CHILD | WS_VISIBLE | WS_TABSTOP
  PUSHBUTTON "Green", IDD_GREEN, 16, 70, 30, 13,
            WS_CHILD | WS_VISIBLE | WS_TABSTOP
  PUSHBUTTON "Cancel", IDCANCEL, 78, 54, 37, 18,
              WS_CHILD | WS_VISIBLE | WS_TABSTOP
  PUSHBUTTON "Edit OK", IDOK, 82, 22, 30, 14,
            WS_CHILD | WS_VISIBLE | WS_TABSTOP
  CONTROL "Listbox Tester", ID_LB1, "LISTBOX",
          LBS_NOTIFY | WS_CHILD | WS_VISIBLE |
          WS_BORDER | WS_VSCROLL, 6, 10, 47, 28
  CONTROL "Default", ID_EB1, "EDIT",
          ES_LEFT | ES_AUTOHSCROLL | WS_CHILD | WS_VISIBLE |
          WS_BORDER | WS_TABSTOP, 61, 8, 72, 12
}
```

This version adds a push button called Edit OK that will be used to tell the program you are done editing text in the edit box. It also adds the edit box itself. The ID for the edit box is **ID_EB1**. This definition causes a standard edit box to be created that contains the default text "Default".

Next, add this macro definition to **mydialog.h**:

```
#define ID_EB1          106
```

Edit boxes recognize many messages and generate several of their own. However, for the purposes of this example, there is no need for the program to respond to any messages. As you will see, edit boxes perform the editing function on their own. There is no need for program interaction when text is edited. Your program simply decides when it wants to obtain the current contents of the edit box.

In order to obtain the current contents of the edit box, use the API function **GetDlgItemText( )**. It has this prototype:

WORD GetDlgItemText(HWND *hdwnd*, int *nID*, LPSTR *lpstr*, int *nMax*)

This function causes the edit box to copy the current contents of the box to the string pointed to by *lpstr*. The handle of the dialog box is specified by *hdwnd*. The ID of the edit box is specified by *nID*. The maximum number of characters to copy is specified by *nMax*. The function returns the length of the string.

To add an edit box to the sample program, add the following **case** statement to the inner **switch** of the **DialogFunc()** function. Each time the Edit OK push button is selected, a message window is displayed that contains the current text that is inside the edit box.

```
case IDOK:
  // Display contents of the edit box.
  GetDlgItemText(hdwnd, ID_EB1, str, 80);
  MessageBox(hdwnd, str, "Edit Box Contains", MB_OK);
  return 1;
```

The macro **IDOK** is a built-in value defined in **windows.h**.

A Note About Using WORKSHOP

WORKSHOP is the Windows-based program Borland supplies that helps you easily create resource files. Although the resource workshop WORKSHOP is easy to use and virtually intuitive, there are a few points about it that you must understand. First, by default, WORKSHOP does not save the compiled version of your .RC file (which is what you need to link to your Windows application). To cause WORKSHOP to save the compiled version of your resource file, you need to set two options. First, select the **File** menu and then select **Preferences**. Next, in the **Multi-save** box, check the **.RES** and **Executable** options. By selecting these options, when you save your resource project, you can also create the .RES file that will be linked to your program. Also, if your program already exists in an .EXE form, the updated resources will automatically be added to it. Remember, neither of these options is on by default.

Second, in order to create or update the .RES or .EXE file, you must explicitly save your project before leaving the resource workshop. To do so, select **File** and then **Save project**. If you don't do this, no changes will be made to the .RES or .EXE files on disk. (Remember, you must have already turned on the options described in the preceding paragraph.)

Third, once you have compiled the .RC file, if you have not yet compiled your program, return to DOS and compile and link your application. Next, use RC.EXE to bind your .RES file created by WORKSHOP to your application.

Concluding Thoughts

While the chapters in this section introduce you to Windows programming using Borland C++ and provide a quick start to Windows' essential principles, they only scratch the surface of Windows programming. If you want to become an excellent Windows programmer, you will need to acquire several books on the topic and write a number of programs. A period of one year to become familiar with all aspects of Windows programming is not uncommon. However, be persistent; your efforts will be rewarded.

Part VII

Appendixes

Appendix *A*

Using Turbo/Borland C++'s Debugger

Turbo/Borland C++ includes a built-in source-level debugger in its integrated development environment. This appendix introduces the debugger and explores some of its most important features.

Preparing Your Programs for Debugging

Although Turbo/Borland C++'s debugger is available for use at the press of a key, you must make sure that your programs are compiled for a debugging session, and you must include debugging information in your program's executable file. By default, the proper debugging information is automatically included in your program. The option that controls the inclusion of debugging information is found under the **Debugger** entry in the **Options** menu. Make sure that **Source debugging** is on. The debugging information contained in the compiled version of your program helps link your source code to its object code.

What Is a Source-Level Debugger?

To understand what a source-level debugger is and why it is so valuable, it is necessary to understand how a traditional debugger works. A traditional debugger is designed to provide object-code debugging, in which you monitor the contents of the CPU's registers or memory. To use a traditional debugger, the linker generates a symbol table that shows the memory address of each function and variable in memory. To debug a program, you use this symbol table and begin executing your program, monitoring the contents of various registers and memory locations. Most debuggers allow you to step through your program one instruction at a time, and to set breakpoints in the object code. However, the biggest drawback to a traditional debugger is that the object code of your program bears little resemblance to the source code. This makes it difficult, even with the use of a symbol table, to know exactly what is happening.

A source-level debugger offers a vast improvement over the older, traditional form in that it allows you to debug your program using the original source code. The debugger automatically links the compiled object code associated with each line in your program with its corresponding source code. You no longer need to use a symbol table. You can control the execution of your program by setting breakpoints in the source code. You can watch the values of various variables using the variables' names. You can step through your program one statement at a time and watch the contents of the program's call stack. Also, communication with Turbo/Borland C++'s debugger is accomplished using C-like expressions, so there is nothing new to learn.

Debugger Basics

This section introduces the most common debugging commands. To get started, enter the following demonstration program at this time:

```
#include <iostream.h>

void sqr_it(int n);

main(void) {
  int i;

  for(i=0; i<10; i++) {
    cout << i << " ";
    sqr_it(i);
  }
  return 0;
}

void sqr_it(int n)
{
```

```
    cout << n*n << " ";
}
```

After you have entered the program, compile and run it to make sure that you entered it correctly. It prints the values 0 through 9 along with their squares.

Single-Stepping

Single-stepping is the process by which you execute your program one statement at a time. To accomplish this, press the F7 key (called the **Trace into** key). Notice that the line containing the **main( )** function declaration is highlighted. This is where your program begins execution. Note also that the line **#include <iostream.h>** and **sqr_it( )**'s prototype are skipped over. Statements that do not generate code, such as the preprocessor directives, obviously cannot be executed, so the debugger automatically skips them. Variable declaration statements without initializers are also skipped when single-stepping as they are not action statements that can be traced.

Pressing F7 *is the same as selecting the* **Trace into** *option in the* **Run** *menu.*

Press F7 several times. Notice how the highlight moves from line to line. Also notice that when the function **sqr_it( )** is called, the highlight moves into the function and then returns from it. The F7 key causes the execution of your program to be traced into function calls.

There can be times when you only want to watch the performance of the code within one function. To accomplish this, use the F8 (step-over) key. Each time this key is pressed, another statement is executed, but calls to functions are not traced. The F8 key is very useful when you want to watch what is happening inside of only one function. Pressing F8 is the same as selecting the **Step over** entry in the **Run** menu.

Experiment with the F8 key at this time. Notice that the highlight never enters the **sqr_it( )** function.

Setting Breakpoints

As useful as single-stepping is, it can be very tedious in a large program—especially if the piece of code that you want to debug is deep in the program. Instead of pressing F7 or F8 repeatedly to get to the section you want to debug, it is easier to set a breakpoint at the beginning of the critical section. A *breakpoint* is, as the name implies, a break in the execution of your program. When execution reaches the breakpoint, your program stops running and control returns to the debugger, allowing you to check the value of certain variables or to begin single-stepping the routine.

To set a breakpoint, move the cursor to the appropriate line in your program, invoke the **Debug** menu, and select the **Toggle breakpoint** option. (You can also use the hot key CTRL-F8.) The line of code at which the breakpoint is set is shown in either high-intensity video or in another color, depending on your video adapter and monitor. You can have several active breakpoints in a program.

Once you have defined one or more breakpoints, execute your program using the **Run/Run** option. Your program runs until it encounters the first breakpoint. As an example, set a breakpoint at the line

```
cout << n*n << " ";
```

inside **sqr_it( )**, and then run the program. As you can see, execution stops at that line.

To remove a breakpoint, position the cursor on the line containing the breakpoint you want to remove and select the **Debug/Toggle breakpoint** option. Or press the CTRL-F8 hot key. You can toggle breakpoints on and off as needed.

Watching Variables

While debugging, you commonly need to see the value of one or more variables as your program executes. This is very easy to do using the debugger. To define a variable to watch, select the **Debug/Watches** option and select **Add watch**, or press the CTRL-F7 hot key. In the pop-up window, enter the name of the variable you want to watch. The debugger automatically displays the value of the variable in the watch window as the program executes. If the variable is global, its value is always available. However, if the variable is local, its value is reported only when the function containing that variable is being executed. When execution moves to a different function, the variable's value is unknown. Keep in mind that if two functions both use the same name for a variable, the value displayed relates to the function currently executing.

As an example, activate the **Watches** entry. To watch the value of **i** in the example program, enter **i**. If you are not currently running the program or if execution has been stopped inside the **sqr_it( )** function, you will first see the message

```
Undefined symbol 'i'
```

However, when execution is inside the **main( )** function, the value of **i** is displayed.

You are not limited to watching only the contents of variables. You can watch any valid C/C++ expression involving variables, with two restrictions: The expression cannot call a function, and it cannot use any **#define** values.

Watched-Expression Format Codes

Turbo/Borland C++'s debugger allows you to format the output of a watched expression by using format codes. To specify a format code, use this general form:

expression,format-code;

The format codes are shown in Table A-1. If you don't specify a format code, the debugger automatically provides a default format.

You can display integers in either decimal or hexadecimal. The debugger automatically knows the difference between **long** and **short** integers because it has access to the source code.

When specifying a floating-point format, you can tell the debugger to show a certain number of significant digits after the decimal point by adding a number to the **F** format. For example, if **average** is a **float** then this tells the debugger to show five significant digits:

```
average,F5
```

Pointers are displayed using segment/offset notation. However, a **near** pointer does not display a value for the segment. Instead, DS is substituted because all **near** pointers reside in the data segment. On the other hand, **far** pointers are shown using the full segment/offset address. You can display the value pointed to by using the * operator in front of the pointer in the watched expression.

Character arrays are displayed as strings. By default, the debugger translates non-ASCII characters into codes. For example, a CTRL-D is displayed as "\4." However,

Format Code	Meaning
C	Display as a character with no translation
D	Display in decimal
F	Display in floating point
H	Display in hexadecimal
M	Show memory
P	Display as a pointer
R	Display class, structure, or union element names and values
S	Display as a character with appropriate character translations
X	Display in hexadecimal (same as H)

Table A-1.   Debugger Format Codes

if you specify the **C** format code, all characters are displayed as is, using the PC's extended character set.

   When a structure or a union is displayed, the values associated with each field are shown using an appropriate format. By including the **R** format command, the name of each field is also shown. To see an example, enter the following program. Try watching both **sample** and **sample,R**.

```
#include <string.h>

struct inventory {
  char item[10];
  int   count;
  float cost;
} sample;

main(void)
{
  strcpy(sample.item, "hammer");
  sample.count = 100;
  sample.cost = 3.95;

  return 0;
}
```

After the three assignments have taken place, the output shown in the **Watch** window looks like this:

```
sample: {"hammer", 100, 3.95}
sample,R: {item: "hammer", count: 100, cost: 3.95}
```

   As you might expect, you can also watch an object of a class. When you watch an object, you are shown the current value of any data that is contained within the object. As with structures and unions, if you use the **R** format specifier, the names of each data item are also displayed. When watching an object of a class, all **private**, **protected**, and **public** data is displayed. For example, if the previous program is changed as shown here:

```
#include <string.h>

class inventory {
  int i;  // private data
public:
  inventory() {i=100;}
  char item[10];
```

```
  int  count;
  float cost;
} sample;

main(void)
{
  strcpy(sample.item, "hammer");
  sample.count = 100;
  sample.cost = 3.95;

  return 0;
}
```

the following output is obtained when watching **sample,R**:

```
sample,R: {i: 100, item: "hammer", count: 100, cost: 3.95}
```

As you can see, even though **i** is **private** to **inventory**, for the purposes of debugging, it is accessible to the debugger.

Using the **Debug/Watches** menu, it is possible to delete a watched expression, modify a watched expression, or remove all watched expressions. By default, when modifying an expression, the one modified is the last one entered. To specify another watched expression to modify, first switch to the watch window, and then move the highlight to the expression you want to modify. Finally, invoke the **Edit watch** option in the **Watches** menu.

Qualifying a Variable's Name

You can watch the value of a local variable no matter what function is currently executing by qualifying its name using this format:

filename.function-name.variable-name;

The *filename* is optional in single-file programs, and the *function-name* is optional when there is only one variable by the specified name.

As an example, assume that you want to watch both the **count** in **f1( )** and the **count** in **f2( )**, given this fragment:

```
f1(void)
{
  int count;
    .
    .
    .
```

```
        .
}

f2(void)
{
   int count;
        .
        .
        .
}
```

To specify these variables, use

```
f1.count
f2.count
```

To watch variables in other files you must specify the file name at the beginning. For example, if **f1( )** were in a file called MYFILE, refer to **f1( )**'s **count**, using this expression:

```
MYFILE.f1.count
```

Watching the Stack

During the execution of your program, you can display the contents of the call stack using the **Call stack** option under the **Debug** menu (or by pressing CTRL-F3). This option displays the order in which the various functions in your program are called. It also displays the value of any function parameters at the time of the call. To see how this feature works, enter this program:

```
#include <iostream.h>
void f1(void), f2(int i);

main(void)
{
   f1();
   return 0;
}

void f1(void)
{
   int i;
```

```
    for(i=0; i<10; i++) f2(i);
}

void f2(int i)
{
  cout << "in f2, value is " << i << " ";
}
```

Set a breakpoint at the line containing the **cout** statement in **f2( )**, and then inspect the call stack. The first time the breakpoint is reached, the call stack looks like this:

```
f2(0)
f1()
main()
```

Only functions written by you show up on the call stack. Calls to library functions are not recorded.

Evaluating an Expression

You can evaluate any legal C/C++ expression by selecting the **Evaluate/modify** option in the **Debug** menu (or by pressing CTRL-F4). To evaluate an expression, enter it in the **Expression** field. You will see its value in the **Result** field. Expressions can contain constants and variables defined in the program you are debugging. However, you cannot call any function or use any **#define** value.

A special feature of the **Evaluate/modify** option is that it automatically copies the identifier that is at the current cursor location into the **Expression** field. By repeatedly pressing the right arrow key, you can cause characters following that identifier to also be entered into the **Expression** field.

Modifying a Variable

Using the **Evaluate/modify** option in the **Debug** menu, you can set the value of any variable. To do this, specify the name of the variable you want to change in the **Expression** field. Next, TAB to the **New value** field and enter the value you want the variable to have. By changing a variable's value using the debugger, you can quickly get past a simple bug so that you can continue your debugging session. Also, in some situations you may have a loop that iterates a great number of times. To get past it, change the loop-control variable so that the loop exits. Remember, of course, that changing a variable's value using the debugger is only a temporary fix.

Inspecting a Variable

Although watching a variable using the **Watches** option is generally sufficient, in the most demanding of circumstances, you may need to monitor more closely what happens to a variable. To do this, use the **Inspect** option in the **Debug** menu. This option displays the contents and address of a variable. Knowing a variable's address can be of value when bugs involving things like wild pointers occur. Keep in mind that you can inspect any type of variable, including structures, unions, and objects. In the case of these types of variables, the names of the fields are displayed along with each value.

Use the Register Window

One final debugging tool at your disposal is the register window. If you select the **Window** main menu option and then select the **Register** entry, a small window pops up that displays the contents of each register in the CPU, as well as the state of each flag. When single-stepping, or each time a breakpoint is encountered, the contents of the register window change to reflect the values contained in the CPU registers.

Appendix B

Interfacing to Assembly Language Routines

Although the subject of assembly language interfacing is covered in significant detail in the Turbo/Borland C/C++ user manuals, it is such a difficult and confusing subject that it is examined here from a different perspective.

As efficient and powerful as Turbo/Borland C/C++ is, there are times when you must write a routine using assembler. There are three reasons for this:

- To increase speed and efficiency of the routine

- To perform some machine-specific function unavailable in Turbo C/C++

- To use third-party routines

Let's take a closer look at these reasons.

Although Turbo/Borland C/C++ produces extremely fast, compact object code, no compiler will consistently create code that is as fast or compact as that written by an excellent programmer using assembler. Most of the time the small difference does not matter, nor does it warrant the extra time needed to write in assembler. However, there are special cases where a specific function is coded in assembler to decrease its execution time. For example, a floating-point math package might be coded in assembler because it is used frequently and has a great effect on the execution speed of a program that uses it. Also, there can be situations when special hardware devices need exact timing, which means you must code in assembler to meet this strict timing requirement. Stated another way, even though Turbo/Borland C/C++ produces very fast, efficient code, in run-time-sensitive tasks, you will want to hand optimize various critical sections. Remember that you, as the programmer, know what the code is actually doing, so you can often perform optimizations that the compiler cannot.

There are certain instructions that cannot be executed by a Turbo/Borland C/C++ program. For example, there is no built-in bitwise rotate operation in C or C++. To efficiently perform a rotation, assembly language must be used.

It is very common in professional programming environments to purchase subroutine libraries for graphics, floating-point math, and the like. Sometimes it is necessary to take these in object format because the developer will not sell the source code. Occasionally it is possible to simply link these routines with code compiled by your compiler; at other times you must write an interface module to correct any differences in the interface used by Turbo/Borland C/C++ and the routines you purchased.

The interfacing of Turbo/Borland C/C++ code with assembly code is an advanced topic. This appendix is intended for those readers who have some familiarity with assembly language programming. (This chapter does not teach you how to program in assembler; it assumes you know how.) If you do not fall into this category, you will still find the material interesting, but please do not try the examples. It is very, very easy to do something slightly wrong and create a disaster, such as erasing your hard disk.

Each processor has a different assembly language. In this chapter the examples use the 8086 family of processors, assuming a DOS environment.

Trying the examples in this chapter requires that you have an assembler. Generally, this will be TASM (Turbo Assembler), supplied by Borland. You need an assembler to assemble the assembly language programs.

There are two ways of combining assembly code routines with Turbo/Borland C/C++. The first way involves the creation, assembly, and linkage of a separate assembly language routine with C functions. The second method uses **asm** to embed in-line assembly code instructions directly into C/C++ functions. Both ways are discussed here. However, before we begin, you need to know something about the way Turbo/Borland C/C++ calls functions.

The information contained in this chapter is applicable to Turbo C/C++ and Borland C/C++. However, all the examples are C programs so that they will work with either environment.

Calling Conventions

A *calling convention* is the method the implementers of a C compiler choose to pass information into functions and to return values. The usual solutions use either the internal register of the CPU or the system stack to pass information between functions. Generally, C compilers use the stack to pass arguments to functions and registers to hold function return values. If an argument is one of the basic data types, the actual value is placed on the stack. If the argument is an array, its address is placed on the stack. When a C function begins execution, it retrieves its argument's values from the stack. Upon termination, it passes back to the calling routine a return value in the register of the CPU.

In addition to defining the way parameters and return values are handled, the calling convention determines exactly what registers must be preserved and which ones you can use freely. Often a compiler will produce object code that needs only a portion of the registers available in the processor. You must preserve the contents of the register used by your compiler, generally by pushing them on the stack prior to using them. Any other registers are generally free for your use.

When you write an assembly language module that must interface to code compiled by Turbo/Borland C/C++, you must follow all the conventions that are defined by and used by Turbo/Borland C/C++. Only by doing this can you hope to have assembly language routines correctly interfaced to your C/C++ code.

The Calling Conventions of Turbo/Borland C/C++

In this section you learn how Turbo/Borland C/C++ passes arguments to and returns values from a function. Only the default C parameter-passing method is examined (the optional **pascal** is not) since it is by far the most common. Like most C compilers, Turbo C/C++ passes arguments to functions on the stack. The arguments are pushed onto the stack right to left. That is, given the call

```
func(a, b, c);
```

c is pushed first, followed by **b**, and then **a**.

The number of bytes occupied on the stack by each type is shown in Table C-1.

Upon entry into an assembly code procedure, the contents of the BP register must be saved on the stack, and the current value of the stack pointer (SP) must be placed into BP. You must preserve the CS, DS, and SS registers. You must also preserve SI and DI if your routine uses them.

If your assembly language function returns a value, it is placed into the AX register if it is a 16-bit value. Otherwise it is returned according to Table C-2. Contrary to what the table says, structures that are 1 or 2 bytes long are returned in AX and structures 4 bytes long are returned in AX and DX. All other structures are returned as indicated in the table.

Type	Number of Bytes
char	2
short	2
signed char	2
signed short	2
unsigned char	2
unsigned short	2
int	2
signed int	2
unsigned int	2
long	4
unsigned long	4
float	4
double	8
long double	10
(near) pointer	2 (offset only)
(far) pointer	4 (segment and offset)

Table B-1.   *The Number of Bytes on the Stack Required for Each Data Type When Passed to a Function*

Creating an Assembly Code Function

Without a doubt, the easiest way to learn to create assembly language functions is to see how Turbo/Borland C/C++ generates code by using the **–S** compiler option with the command-line version of Turbo/Borland C/C++. This option causes an assembly language listing of the code that it generates to be output. (It is not possible to produce an assembly language listing from the integrated development environ-

Type	Register and Meaning
char	AX
unsigned char	AX
short	AX
unsigned short	AX
int	AX
unsigned int	AX
long	Low-order word in AX
	High-order word in DX
unsigned long	Low-order word in AX
	High-order word in DX
float	Return on 8087 stack or at TOS in emulator
double	Return on 8087 stack or at TOS in emulator
long double	Return on 8087 stack or at TOS in emulator
struct & union	Address to value in AX:DX
class	Address to value in AX:DX
(near) pointer	AX
(far) pointer	Offset in AX, segment in DX

Table B-2. *Register Usage for Return Values for Turbo/Borland C/C++*

ment.) By examining this file you can learn a great deal not only about how to interface to the compiler, but also how Turbo/Borland C/C++ actually works.

Let's begin with the following short program:

```
int add(int a, int b);

int sum;
main(void)
```

```
{
  sum = add(10, 20);
  return 0;
}

add(int a, int b)
{
  int t;

  t = a+b;
  return t;
}
```

The variable **sum** is intentionally declared as global so you can see examples of both local and global data. If this program is called TEST.C, this command line will cause TEST.ASM to be created:

```
C>bcc -S test.c
```

The contents of TEST.ASM are shown here:

```
          ifndef    ??version
?debug    macro
          endm
publicdll macro     name
          public    name
          endm
$comm     macro     name,dist,size,count
          comm      dist name:BYTE:count*size
          endm
          else
$comm     macro     name,dist,size,count
          comm      dist name[size]:BYTE:count
          endm
          endif
          ?debug    V 300h
          ?debug    S "test.c"
          ?debug    C E95452D71803792E63
_TEXT     segment byte public 'CODE'
_TEXT     ends
DGROUP    group     _DATA,_BSS
          assume    cs:_TEXT,ds:DGROUP
_DATA     segment   word public 'DATA'
d@        label     byte
```

```
d@w label    word
_DATA        ends
_BSS         segment word public 'BSS'
b@           label    byte
b@w          label    word
_BSS         ends
_TEXT        segment byte public 'CODE'
   ;
   ;         main()
   ;
             assume    cs:_TEXT
_main        proc      near
             push      bp
             mov       bp,sp
   ;
   ;         {
   ;         sum = add(10, 20);
   ;
             mov       ax,20
             push      ax
             mov       ax,10
             push      ax
             call      near ptr _add
             pop       cx
             pop       cx
             mov       word ptr DGROUP:_sum,ax
   ;
   ;         return 0;
   ;
             xor       ax,ax
             jmp       short @1@58
@1@58:
   ;
   ;         }
   ;
             pop       bp
             ret
_main        endp
   ;
   ;         add(int a, int b)
   ;
             assume    cs:_TEXT
_add         proc      near
             push      bp
             mov       bp,sp
```

```
                sub         sp,2
        ;
        ;   {
        ;           int t;
        ;
        ;           t = a+b;
        ;
                mov         ax,word ptr [bp+4]
                add         ax,word ptr [bp+6]
                mov         word ptr [bp-2],ax
        ;
        ;           return t;
        ;
                mov         ax,word ptr [bp-2]
                jmp         short @2@58
@2@58:
        ;
        ;       }
        ;
                mov         sp,bp
                pop         bp
                ret
_add            endp
_TEXT           ends
_BSS            segment word public 'BSS'
_sum            label       word
                db          2 dup (?)
                ?debug      C E9
                ?debug      C FA00000000
_BSS            ends
_DATA           segment word public 'DATA'
s@              label       byte
_DATA           ends
_TEXT           segment byte public 'CODE'
_TEXT           ends
                public      _main
                public      _sum
                public      _add
_s@             equ         s@
end
```

The examples of assembly code created by the compiler were generated using Borland C++ version 3. If you are using a different compiler or version, you may see slightly different results, but the overall approach will be the same.

The program begins by establishing the various segments required by a program produced by Turbo/Borland C/C++. These will vary among the different memory models. (This file was produced by the small model compiler. All the other examples in this chapter also use the small model.) Notice that 2 bytes are allocated in the **_BSS** segment for the global variable **sum** near the end of the listing. The underscores in front of **main( )**, **add**, and **sum** are added by the compiler to avoid confusion with any internal compiler names. The underscore is added to the front of all function and global variable names. All code is contained in the **_TEXT** segment.

The first thing that happens inside the **_main** procedure is that BP is saved and the value of SP is copied to BP. The two arguments to **_add** are pushed on the stack and **_add** is called. Upon return from the **_add** function, the two **pop cx** instructions restore the stack to its original state. The next line moves the return value from **_add** into **_sum**. Finally, **_main** returns.

The function **_add** begins by saving BP on the stack and then placing the value of SP into BP. Next, the stack pointer is decremented by 2. This makes room on the stack for the local variable **t**. At this point the stack looks like this:

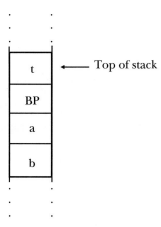

The next two lines of code add the numbers together. The result is put into the local variable **t**, which is at BP–2 on the stack. Finally, the answer is placed into AX, SP is restored, BP is popped, and **_add** returns.

You can literally assemble this assembly language file using TASM, link it using TLINK (Turbo Linker), and run it. If you want to try this, use the following link line, assuming that the file is called TEST. (You may need to change the name of the directory.)

```
TLINK \tc\lib\c0s test, test.exe,,\tc\lib\cs
```

The file **C0s.obj** contains startup and DOS-specific header information. The library **Cs.lib** is Turbo/Borland C/C++'s standard small model library. (Refer to the Turbo/Borland C/C++ manual for more information on these files.)

Once you have the assembly language version of your program you can modify it to make it run more quickly. For example, you could remove the instruction inside **_add** that loads AX with its return value because it already contains it. You could also eliminate the **jmp** instruction because it is useless. These are examples of *hand optimization*.

Locating Arguments and Local Variables

The arguments passed to a function are located on the stack. The first begins at BP+4. The size and number of any other arguments determine their positions further down on the stack. In the case of the two integers passed to **add( )** in the previous example, the second argument is at BP+6 because integers are 2 bytes long. If **add( )** had added **float**s, the first argument would still have been at BP+4, but the second would have been at BP+8 because **float**s are 4 bytes long.

If you are using a current version of Turbo/Borland C/C++, there is an easy way to locate the arguments to a function. This method employs the **ARG** directive, which computes the offset into the stack for each argument used by the function. Here is one form of **ARG**:

> ARG *arg1:size1:size2, arg2:size1:size2,...argN:size*

Here, *arg1* through *argN* are the names of the arguments. *size1* is the size of the argument, which must be one of these values:

Value	Size in Bytes
byte	1
word	2
dword	4
qword	8
tbyte	10

size2 is optional. When present, it specifies the number of items of *size1* that make up the argument. When not specified, a default of 1 is assumed. After the arguments have been defined, their names may be used instead of indexing BP. For example, using **ARG**, the **add( )** function looks like this:

```
_add    proc near
   ARG a:WORD, b:WORD
   push bp
   mov  bp,sp
```

```
  sub   sp,2
;
;         {
;         int t;
;
;         t = a+b;
;
  mov   ax,word ptr [a] ; use a instead of BP+4
  add   ax,word ptr [b] ; use b instead of BP+6
  mov   word ptr [bp-2],ax
;
;           return t;
;
  mov   ax,word ptr [bp-2]
  jmp   short @2@58
```

While using **ARG** is easier than manually indexing BP, it is not supported by earlier versions of TASM, so the examples that follow do not use it. However, feel free to use it if it is supported by your version.

Local variables are stored on the stack. You can make room for them by decrementing SP by the appropriate number of bytes. The **add( )** function shows an example of this when it makes room for **t**.

Creating Your Own Assembly Language Functions

Now that you have seen how Turbo/Borland C/C++ compiles functions, it is just a short step to writing your own assembly language functions. One of the easiest ways to do this is to let the compiler generate an assembly language skeleton for you. Once you have the skeleton, all you have to do is fill in the details. For example, let's say it is necessary to create an assembly routine that multiplies two integers together. To have the compiler generate a skeleton for this function, first create a file containing only this function:

```
mul(int a, int b)
{
}
```

Next, compile it with the **–S** option so an assembly language file is produced. The file will look like this:

```
    ifndef    ??version
?debug   macro
```

```
        endm
publicdll macro    name
    public    name
    endm
$comm    macro      name,dist,size,count
    comm dist name:BYTE:count*size
    endm
    else
$comm    macro      name,dist,size,count
    comm dist name[size]:BYTE:count
    endm
    endif
    ?debug    V 300h
    ?debug    S "mul.c"
    ?debug    C E9B781D7180479312E63
_TEXT    segment byte public 'CODE'
_TEXT    ends
DGROUP    group    _DATA,_BSS
    assume    cs:_TEXT,ds:DGROUP
_DATA    segment word public 'DATA'
d@  label    byte
d@w label    word
_DATA    ends
_BSS    segment word public 'BSS'
b@  label    byte
b@w label    word
_BSS    ends
_TEXT    segment byte public 'CODE'
    ;
    ;    mul(int a, int b)
    ;
    assume    cs:_TEXT
_mul    proc near
    push bp
    mov  bp,sp
    ;
    ;    {
    ;    }
    ;
    pop  bp
    ret
_mul    endp
    ?debug    C E9
    ?debug    C FA00000000
_TEXT    ends
```

```
_DATA    segment word public 'DATA'
s@ label      byte
_DATA    ends
_TEXT    segment byte public 'CODE'
_TEXT    ends
   public      _mul
_s@ equ   s@
   end
```

In this skeleton, the compiler has done all the work of defining the proper segments and setting up the stack and registers. All you have to do is fill in the details. The finished **mul( )** function is shown here:

```
   ifndef      ??version
?debug    macro
   endm
publicdll macro      name
   public      name
   endm
$comm     macro      name,dist,size,count
   comm dist name:BYTE:count*size
   endm
   else
$comm     macro      name,dist,size,count
   comm dist name[size]:BYTE:count
   endm
   endif
   ?debug      V 300h
   ?debug      S "mul.c"
   ?debug      C E9B781D7180479312E63
_TEXT    segment byte public 'CODE'
_TEXT    ends
DGROUP   group      _DATA,_BSS
   assume      cs:_TEXT,ds:DGROUP
_DATA    segment word public 'DATA'
d@ label      byte
d@w label      word
_DATA    ends
_BSS     segment word public 'BSS'
b@ label      byte
b@w label      word
_BSS     ends
_TEXT    segment byte public 'CODE'
   ;
```

```
;       mul(int a, int b)
;
   assume   cs:_TEXT
; **********************************
     PUBLIC _mul  ; make _mul public
; **********************************
_mul     proc near
   push bp
   mov  bp,sp
;
;        {
; **********************************
; actually perform the multiplication
;
   mov ax,[bp+4]  ; get a
   imul word ptr [bp+6]  ; multiply by b
;
; **********************************
;        }
;
   pop  bp
   ret
_mul     endp
   ?debug    C E9
   ?debug    C FA00000000
_TEXT     ends
_DATA     segment word public 'DATA'
s@ label       byte
_DATA     ends
_TEXT     segment byte public 'CODE'
_TEXT     ends
   public    _mul
_s@ equ   s@
   end
```

Once this file is assembled, it can be linked to any C program that requires it. For example, the following program prints the number 10 on the screen. (Remember to link in **mul( )**).

```c
#include <stdio.h>

int mul(int a, int b);

main(void)
```

```
{
  printf("%d ", mul(2, 5));

  return 0;
}
```

The easiest way to compile and link this program is to use a command line like this (assuming the C file is called MULTEST.C and the assembly file is MUL.ASM):

C>bcc multest.c mul.asm

Turbo/Borland C/C++ will automatically compile the C file, assemble the assembly file, and link them together.

Notice that a line of code has been added directly before the first code of the procedure **_mul**. It is the line **PUBLIC _mul**. This statement tells the assembler that the identifier **_mul** should be made available to any routine that needs it. This enables the C program to call **_mul**. You will have to do this with any function you want to be able to call from a C program. Also, if there is data that the C program must know about, it should be made public too. The rule for using **PUBLIC** is very simple: Place the names of functions you want public in the CODE segment and the names of variables in the DATA segment.

The opposite of this occurs when you want to call a C function or access a variable defined in a C program from an assembly language function. In this case you must declare the objects your assembly language routine needs to be external, using the **extrn** assembler command. The general form of the **extrn** statement is

extrn *object* : *attribute*

If the *object* is a function, *attribute* can be either **near** or **far**. If you are using a small code model, use **near**; otherwise use **far**. For variables, *attribute* may be one of the following values:

Value	Size in Bytes
byte	1
word	2
dword	4
qword	8
tbyte	10

For example, if your assembler routine needed to access the global integer variable **count** and the function **search()**, you would place these statements at the start of the assembly language file:

```
extrn _count : word
extrn _search : near
```

Name Mangling and C++

As stated, when you link an assembly file with a C program, all public identifiers need to be preceded with an underscore in the assembly language file. This is because Turbo/Borland C/C++ automatically prefixes an underscore when it compiles a C program. However, a different and more complex situation arises when you want to link an assembly language file with a C++ program. When a C++ program is compiled, all function names are *mangled*. The reason for this is that type information is embedded in a name that will be used to ensure that the proper version of a function is called depending upon the type and number of its arguments. (This is necessary because C++ supports function overloading.) However, mangled names generally look very strange. To avoid using mangled names in your assembly files, you can have your assembly file treated as if it were a C file by using the C linkage specifier in your C++ program. For example, to tell a C++ program that a function called **mul()** uses the C underscore convention, use this linkage specification:

```
extern "C" { mul(int a, int b); }
```

Using Pointers and References in Assembly Files

A more challenging situation occurs when linking assembly language functions that take pointers or references as parameters. In this case, accessing and altering the value of the argument requires the use of indirect addressing methods. For example, assume you need to create an assembly language function that negates the integer pointed to by the argument to the function. Assuming that this function is called **neg()**, the following fragment will print the number –10 on the screen.

```
x = 10;

neg(&x);

printf("%d", neg);  /* prints -10 */
```

In C, this function would look like

```
neg(int *a)
{
  *a = -*a;
}
```

The **neg( )** function coded in assembler would look like the following. (Remember, this assumes that the small data model is used.)

```
    ifndef     ??version
?debug    macro
    endm
publicdll macro     name
    public     name
    endm
$comm     macro      name,dist,size,count
    comm dist name:BYTE:count*size
    endm
    else
$comm     macro      name,dist,size,count
    comm dist name[size]:BYTE:count
    endm
    endif
    ?debug     V 300h
    ?debug     S "test.c"
    ?debug     C E99D85D7180479332E63
_TEXT     segment byte public 'CODE'
_TEXT     ends
DGROUP    group      _DATA,_BSS
    assume     cs:_TEXT,ds:DGROUP
_DATA     segment word public 'DATA'
d@ label      byte
d@w label      word
_DATA     ends
_BSS      segment word public 'BSS'
b@ label      byte
b@w label      word
_BSS      ends
_TEXT     segment byte public 'CODE'
    ;
    ;      neg(int *a)
    ;
    assume     cs:_TEXT
_neg      proc near
    push bp
    mov  bp,sp
    push si
    mov  si,word ptr [bp+4]
    ;
    ;      {
```

```
;          *a = -*a;
;
  mov  ax,word ptr [si]
  neg  ax
  mov  word ptr [si],ax
;
;          }
;
  pop  si
  pop  bp
  ret
_neg     endp
     ?debug    C E9
     ?debug    C FA00000000
_TEXT    ends
_DATA    segment word public 'DATA'
s@ label      byte
_DATA    ends
_TEXT    segment byte public 'CODE'
_TEXT    ends
     public    _neg
_s@ equ  s@
     end
```

The key lines of code are

```
mov  si,word ptr [bp+4]
mov  ax,word ptr [si]
neg  ax
mov  word ptr [si],ax
```

First, the address of the argument is loaded from the stack into the SI index register. Next, the relative addressing mode of the 8086 is used to load the integer to be negated. The **neg** instruction reverses the sign, and the last instruction places the value back at the location pointed to by SI.

You might be surprised to learn that if **neg( )** used a reference parameter instead of a pointer, the resulting assembly code would not be changed. That is, if **neg( )** were coded like this:

```
void neg(int &a)
{
  a = -a;
}
```

the assembly code produced would be the same as the pointer version. This result can be generalized. An assembly language function that uses a reference parameter is coded exactly the same as one that uses a pointer parameter. This is because a reference parameter simply tells the compiler to call the function using the address of its argument instead of the value of the argument. This means that as far as the function is concerned, it is receiving a pointer to the argument. Therefore, code inside the function is the same whether the argument is a pointer or a reference.

Learning More About Assembly Language Interfacing

The best way to learn more about interfacing assembly language code with your C/C++ programs is to write short functions in C/C++ that do something similar to what you want the assembly language version to do and, using the assembly language compiler option, create an assembly language file. Most of the time all you will have to do is hand optimize this code instead of actually creating an assembly language routine from the ground up.

As you have seen, it is really quite easy to use assembly language functions along with your Turbo C/C++ code if you follow the rules precisely.

Using asm

Turbo/Borland C/C++ contains the keyword **asm**, which allows in-line assembly code to be made part of a program without using a completely separate assembly language module. The advantage of this is twofold. First, you are not required to write and maintain all the interface code. Second, all the code is in "one place," making support a little easier.

The **asm** *keyword is formally part of the C++ language. However, for Turbo/Borland C, it is a nonstandard extension. The use of* **asm** *as described here is valid for both Turbo/Borland C and C++. However, in C++* **asm** *is more flexible; refer to Chapter 31 for details of its usage in C++.*

To put in-line assembly code in a function, you simply place the keyword **asm** at the beginning of each line of assembly code and then enter the assembly language statement. All code that follows the **asm** must be correct assembly code for the computer you are using. By default, in-line assembly code is assembled by using the assembler built in to Turbo/Borland C/C++. However, this is a "bare-bones" assembler. You can cause TASM to be invoked to generate assembly in-line code by specifying the **–B** option for the command-line compiler, turning on the IDE in-line option, or specifying the **#pragma inline** preprocessor directive. The use of TASM is recommended because it is a full-featured assembler.

For Turbo C, in-line assembly code may only be compiled using the command-line compiler—not the IDE version.

A very simple example of in-line assembly code is shown here. It is used to output information to a port, presumably for initialization purposes.

```
void init_port1(void)
{
  printf("Initializing Port\n");
  asm    out 26,255
  asm    out 26,0
}
```

Here, the compiler automatically provides the code to save registers and to return from the function. Notice that **asm** statements do not require a semicolon to terminate; instead, an assembly language statement is terminated by the end of the line.

You could use in-line assembly code to create **mul( )**, from the previous section, without actually creating a separate assembly language file. Using this approach, the code for **mul( )** is

```
mul(int a, int b)
{
  asm    mov ax,word ptr [bp+4]
  asm    imul word ptr [bp+6]
}
```

Remember that Turbo/Borland C/C++ provides all customary support for setting up and returning from a function call. All you have to do is provide the body of the function and follow the calling conventions to access the arguments.

If you wish to place comments in **asm** statements, you *must* use the standard C /* and */ method. Do not use the semicolon convention used by most assemblers.

Assembly code statements that are found inside a function are placed in the code segment. Those found outside any function are placed in the data segment.

Keep in mind that whatever method you use, you are creating machine dependencies that will make your program difficult to port to a new machine. However, for the demanding situations that require assembly code, it is usually worth the effort.

Appendix C

Turbo/Borland C/C++ Global Variables

Turbo/Borland C/C++ defines several built-in global variables that your program can use. Most of these variables contain information that reflects the state of various options or errors or determines the default behavior of certain functions.

The global variables covered in this appendix are those supported by Turbo/Borland C++ version 3. If you have an older compiler or are using Turbo C, some of the variables may not be applicable to your compiler.

char _ctype[]

The **_ctype** array contains information about each character. To obtain information about a character, index the array by using that character plus 1. To use this array, you must include **ctype.h** in your program.

int daylight

daylight will be set to 1 if daylight saving time is in effect. Otherwise it will be 0. It is set by various time functions, including **localtime( )**. You must include **time.h** to use this variable.

int directvideo

By default, **directvideo** has the value 1. This causes all screen output to be written directly to the video RAM when displaying text, which results in the fastest output. If you set this variable to 0, output is performed using BIOS routines, which is a slower method. You must include **conio.h** to use this variable.

char *environ[]

The **environ** array points to DOS environmental information. You must include **dos.h** to use this array.

int _doserrno

If a DOS function results in an error, **_doserrno** is set to the DOS error code associated with that error. You must include **dos.h** to use this variable.

int errno

errno contains an error code that is set by many standard library functions when an error occurs. For a list of the possible error codes this variable may contain, refer to the file **errno.h**. Also, you must include **errno.h** to use **errno**.

int _fmode

By default, files are opened in text mode if not explicitly opened as binary files. However, setting **_fmode** to **O_BINARY** causes files to be opened in binary mode by default. To return **_fmode** to its original default value, assign it the value **O_TEXT**. These macros are defined in **fnctl.h**, and you must include this file when using **_fmode**.

unsigned _heaplen

The **_heaplen** variable contains the size of the heap, in bytes. This variable is applicable only to programs compiled for the tiny, small, and medium memory models. You must include **dos.h** to use this variable.

_new_handler

_new_handler is a pointer to a function that is called if a **new** allocation request fails. To change which function is called, set **_new_handler** to the address of the new function. A better way to alter the operation of the function called when an allocation request fails, is to overload **new**. **_new_handler** is included for compatibility with older versions of C++. To access **_new_handler** you must include **new.h**.

unsigned char _osmajor, _osminor

_osmajor and **_osminor** contain the major and minor revision numbers for the version of DOS that is executing the program. You must include **dos.h** to use these variables.

unsigned _ovrbuffer

_ovrbuffer specifies the size, in paragraphs, of the overlay buffer. Generally, you will simply use the default size provided by Turbo/Borland C/C++, which is twice the size of the largest overlay module. You must include **dos.h** to access this variable.

unsigned _psp

_psp contains the segment of the *program segment prefix* (PSP), which is used by DOS as a process identifier. You must include **dos.h** to use this variable.

unsigned _stklen

The value of **_stklen** determines the size, in bytes, of the stack. Generally, you will simply use the default stack size provided by the compiler. However, in special situations, you may wish to expand or contract the stack. To use this variable you must include **dos.h**.

char *sys_errlist[]

sys_errlist is an array of pointers to the error messages. By indexing this array with **errno**, you will obtain its corresponding error message. You must include **errno.h** to access this array.

int sys_nerr

sys_nerr contains the number of error messages provided by Turbo/Borland C/C++. You must include **errno.h** to use this variable.

long timezone

timezone holds the difference between the local time of the system and Greenwich Mean Time (GMT). The difference is specified in seconds. You must include **time.h** to access this variable.

char *tzname[2]

The **tzname** array contains pointers to time zone name abbreviations. **tzname[0]** contains the normal time zone abbreviation and **tzname[1]** holds its daylight saving time abbreviation. You must include **time.h** to use this array.

unsigned _version

_version contains the DOS version number. The low-order byte contains the major revision number and the high-order byte contains the minor revision number. You can also access the DOS version numbers by using the global variables **_osmajor** and **_osminor**. To use **_version**, include **dos.h**.

int _wscroll

The value of **_wscroll** determines if the screen will be scrolled when output extends past the edge of the screen. If its value is non-0, scrolling will occur. If its value is 0, the screen will not be scrolled. You must include **conio.h** to use this variable.

Index

Using Turbo C++
by Herbert Schildt

Borland's Turbo C++ with object-oriented programming is thoroughly covered in Herb Schildt's introductory guide for all C programmers. Since Turbo C++ can be used with or without its C++ object-oriented extensions, Schildt has carefully structured the book to cover both environments. Schildt has perfected the way to build programming fundamentals into more sophisticated skills.
$24.95, ISBN: 0-07-881610-6, 755 pp., 7 3/8 x 9 1/4

C++: The Complete Reference
by Herbert Schildt

C++: The Complete Reference covers C++ in full detail starting with aspects common to the C and C++ languages. This example-filled book thoroughly discusses those features specific to C++ and includes several chapters on effective C++ software development.
$29.95, ISBN: 0-07-881654-8, 784 pp., 7 3/8 x 9 1/4

C++ Inside & Out
by Bruce Eckel

C++ Inside & Out provides a comprehensive, fast-paced guide for all C programmers who want to develop their skills and write full-fledged C++ programs complete with bells and whistles. Eckel covers the latest advancements in C++ and new information on major C++ compilers from Borland and Microsoft.
$27.95, ISBN: 0-07-881809-5, 640 pages, 7 3/8 x 9 1/4

Teach Yourself C++
by Herbert Schildt

Teach Yourself C++ instructs programmers in the use of the popular C++ programming language through clear descriptions, short chapters, and plenty of exercises and skill checks. This book will prepare you to work with UNIX or DOS programs written in C++, including Borland's Turbo C++.
$24.95, ISBN: 0-07-881760-9, 515 pp., 7 3/8 X 9 1/4

▶ ──────── Osborne **McGraw-Hill** ■ **Available at local book and computer stores**

C: The Complete Reference, Second Edition
by Herbert Schildt
This renowned reference guide, revised to comply with the new ANSI C standard, is the best and most complete reference on ANSI C. C programmers at every level can take advantage of Schildt's expanded sections on the C language and the ANSI libraries. Comprehensive reference sections are conveniently organized by topic for quick fact-finding.
$29.95, ISBN: 0-07-881538-X, 823 pp., 7 3/8 x 9 1/4

The Art of C: Elegant Programming Solutions
(Includes One 5.25-Inch Disk)
by Herbert Schildt
Ace C programmer Herb Schildt has written a book for all programmers who truly appreciate the art of C programming. This sophisticated book provides elegant programming solutions that enable you to write world-class C programs that stand apart from all the rest. A disk of programming examples is included.
$39.95, ISBN: 0-07-881691-2, 459 pp., 7 3/8 x 9 1/4

C DiskTutor
(Includes One 3.5-Inch Disk)
by L. John Ribar
This DiskTutor provides all would-be C programmers with an easy, hassle-free way to learn C programming. A comprehensive yet simple-to-follow book guides you step-by-step along with a disk containing a special version of the Watcom C compiler. With all the examples and screen illustrations, you'll be writing effective ANSI C programs in no time.
$39.95, ISBN: 0-07-881798-6, 464 pages, 7 3/8 x 9 1/4

Teach Yourself C
by Herbert Schildt
Herb Schildt, the widely recognized C expert, is back with another clear, concise volume on the programming language of the 1990s. *Teach Yourself C* uses numerous exercises and skill checks to make sure your programming abilities grow lesson by lesson. By the final chapter, you will possess a solid command of C programming principles.
$24.95, ISBN: 0-07-881596-7, 681 pp., 7 3/8 x 9 1/4

ANSI C Made Easy
by Herbert Schildt
ANSI standards establish new criteria for programming and anyone working in C will want to ensure compliance. This volume is ideal for anyone in the fast-growing C programming field, including students, beginning systems programmers, and career C programmers who need to stay abreast. This "Made Easy" book includes step-by-step exercises that facilitate both quick and lasting comprehension.
$19.95, ISBN: 0-07-881500-2, 450 pp., 7 3/8 x 9 1/4

C: The Pocket Reference, Second Edition
by Herbert Schildt
The first edition of this bestseller helped tens of thousands of programmers find valuable C information fast. The second edition has now been revised to cover the ANSI C standard. With this quick reference, you'll find vital C commands, functions, and libraries, arranged alphabetically for easy use along with a state-of-the-art lay-flat binding.
$9.95, ISBN: 0-07-881783-8, 208 pages, 4 1/4 x 8

Visual Basic for Windows Inside & Out
by Gary Cornell
Here's the best all-round guide for Basic programmers, Windows developers and anyone else who's interested in programming with Visual Basic. Cornell provides comprehensive coverage of structured Basic programming while teaching you how to take full advantage of Visual Basic.
$27.95, ISBN: 0-07-881764-1, 450 pages, 7 3/8 x 9 1/4

Windows 3.1 Programming
(Includes One 3.5-Inch)
by William H. Murray and Chris H. Pappas
With this outstanding guide, you'll have the opportunity to learn the powerful programming secrets of Windows 3.1. Murray and Pappas take C programmers into the next generation of Microsoft Windows Release 3.1 with the aid of numerous programming examples that are written in C/C++.
$39.95, ISBN: 0-07-881855-9, 752 pages, 7 3/8 x 9 1/4
Available Fall 1992

▶ ———— Osborne **McGraw-Hill**   ■   **Available at local book and computer stores**

Object-Oriented Programming: An Introduction
by Greg Voss

This significant programming advancement and its methodologies are clearly presented as Greg Voss compares and contrasts OOP with traditional structured programming techniques. Object-oriented design is stressed. You'll learn how OOP is used in the real world through examples and exercises that are written in C++ as well as object-oriented Turbo Pascal and Quick PASCAL
$24.95, ISBN: 0-07-881682-3, 584 pp.,7 3/8 x 9 1/4

Turbo Pascal 6: The Complete Reference
by Stephen K. O'Brien

The most complete single resource ever published for all Turbo Pascal programmers is now available in a special edition that covers all the features of Borland's version 6. The revolutionary Turbo Vision application framework is also covered so you can use this tool to write professional-quality applications.
$29.95, ISBN: 0-07-881703-X, 690 pp., 7 3/8 x 9 1/4

Turbo Pascal 6 DiskTutor, Second Edition
(Includes One 5.25-Inch Disk)
by Werner Feibel

A must for beginning and experienced programmers who want to learn Pascal or switch to the leading-edge technology of Turbo Pascal 6.0 with object-oriented programming. This book/disk package features an easy-to-understand text that takes you step-by-step through the practical example programs on disk.
$39.95, ISBN: 0-07-881738-2, 896 pp., 7 3/8 x 9 1/4

DOS Programming: The Complete Reference
by Kris Jamsa

In this new Complete Reference, Jamsa provides in-depth DOS programming information. All function calls and programming services necessary to take full advantage of DOS are discussed and numerous examples are included, enabling DOS programmers to expand their skills.
$29.95, ISBN: 0-07-881782-X, 896 pages, 7 3/8 x 9 1/4

Jamsa's 1001 DOS & PC Tips
(Includes One 3.5-Inch Disk)
by Kris Jamsa

Jamsa's one-of-a-kind book is bursting at the seams, filled with secrets, tips, and powerful techniques you can instantly use to get more from your computer. The companion disk contains powerful batch files, DEBUG script files, and utilities used for each tip.

$39.95, ISBN: 0-07-881821-4, 1000 pages, 7 3/8 x 9 1/4

Dvorak's Guide to PC Telecommunications, Second Edition
(Includes One 3.5-Inch Disk)
by John C. Dvorak and Nick Anis

With rave reviews from around the world, this outstanding bestseller established itself as THE bible for everyone who wants to understand telecommunications. Packaged with this comprehensive guide is a 3.5-inch disk jam-packed with quality software and special discounts from the major on-line services.

$39.95, ISBN: 0-07-881787-0, 912 pages, 7 3/8 x 9 1/4

Network Know-How: Concepts, Cards, & Cables
by Dan Derrick

If you've been thinking about setting up a network but don't know the first thing about it, look no further -- this is the book for you. Bestselling author Dan Derrick has written an unintimidating, straight forward guide to networks.

$19.95, ISBN: 0-07-881833-8, 300 pages, 7 3/8 x 9 1/4

Prodigy Made Easy, Second Edition
by Pamela Kane

Take full advantage of this popular telecommunications service with Pamela Kane's updated version of her bestselling book that teaches users the basics and covers many new services for more experienced Prodigy users. It's jam-packed with illustrations, hands-on examples, and much more.

$19.95, ISBN: 0-07-881840-0, 512 pages, 7 3/8 x 9 1/4